Data Refinement:
Model-Oriented Proof Methods and their Comparison

The goal of this book is to provide a comprehensive and systematic
introduction to the important and highly applicable method of data refinement and the simulation methods used for proving its correctness. The
authors concentrate in the first part on the general principles needed to prove
data refinement correct. They begin with an explanation of the fundamental
notions, showing that data refinement proofs reduce to proving simulation.
The topics of Hoare Logic and the Refinement Calculus are introduced and a
general theory of simulations is developed and related to them. Accessibility
and comprehension are emphasised in order to guide newcomers to the area.
The book's second part contains a detailed survey of important methods in
this field, such as VDM, and the methods due to Abadi & Lamport, Hehner,
Lynch and Reynolds, Back's refinement calculus and Z. All these methods
are carefully analysed, and shown to be either incomplete, with counter-
examples to their application, or to be always applicable whenever data
refinement holds. This is shown by proving, for the first time, that all these
methods can be described and analysed in terms of two simple notions:
forward and backward simulation.
The book is self-contained, going from advanced undergraduate level and
taking the reader to the state of the art in methods for proving simulation.

Willem-Paul de Roever is Professor of Software Technology at the Institute
for Computer Science and Applied Mathematics, Christian Albrechts
University in Kiel.

Kai Engelhardt is Postdoctoral Research Fellow at the School of Computing
Science, University of Technology, Sydney.

Cambridge Tracts in Theoretical Computer Science

Titles in the series

Data Refinement

Model-Oriented Proof Methods and their Comparison

Willem-Paul de Roever

Kai Engelhardt

with the assistance of

Karl-Heinz Buth

Jos Coenen

Paul Gardiner

Yassine Lakhnech

Frank Stomp

CAMBRIDGE
UNIVERSITY PRESS

CAMBRIDGE UNIVERSITY PRESS
Cambridge, New York, Melbourne, Madrid, Cape Town, Singapore, São Paulo

Cambridge University Press
The Edinburgh Building, Cambridge CB2 8RU, UK

Published in the United States of America by Cambridge University Press, New York

www.cambridge.org
Information on this title: www.cambridge.org/9780521641708

First published 1998

A catalogue record for this publication is available from the British Library

ISBN 978-0-521-64170-8 hardback

Transferred to digital printing 2008

Contents

Preface

The goal of this monograph is the introduction of, and comparison between, various methods for proving implementations of programs correct. Although these methods are illustrated mainly by applying them to correctness proofs of implementations of abstract data structures, the techniques developed apply equally well to proving correctness of implementations in general. For we shall prove that all these methods are only variations on one central theme: that of proof by simulation, of which we analyze at least 13 different formulations.

As the central result we prove that these methods either imply or are equivalent to L-simulation (also called forward or downward simulation in the literature) or a combination of L- with L^{-1}-simulation (the latter is also called backward or upward simulation). Since, as shown by Hoare, He, and Sanders, only the combination of these forms of simulation is complete, this immediately establishes when these methods are complete, namely, when they are equivalent to this combination.

Our motivation for writing this monograph is that we believe that in this area of computer science (as well as in various other areas) the duty of universities is not to train students in particular methods, but rather to give students insight in both similarities and differences between methods such as VDM, Z, the methods advocated by Reynolds and Hehner, and methods more directly based on Hoare Logic or predicate transformers. The reason for this conviction is that computer science develops far too quickly for us to believe that any of these methods will survive in its present form. Therefore, it makes more sense to emphasize the general principles behind these methods, since these are more likely to maintain their value when the students of today have become the specialists of tomorrow.

This monograph consists of two parts. In Part I we develop the general theory required for comparing model-oriented data refinement methods. Part II concerns applications, such as Reynolds' method, VDM, Z, Hehner's condition for data refinement, Back's refinement calculus, Abadi and Lamport's theory of refinement mappings, and Lynch's theory of possibilities mappings.

In the first part of this monograph we develop the relational theory of simulation and a general version of Hoare logic, show how data refinement can be expressed in this logic, extend these results to total correctness, and show how all this theory can be uniformly expressed inside the refinement calculus of Ralph Back, Paul Gardiner, Carroll Morgan, and Joakim von Wright.

Chapter Dependencies

The chapter dependencies are depicted in the figure below.

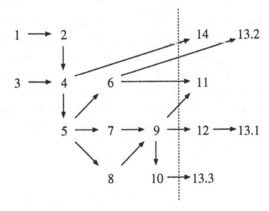

In this diagram, $X \to Y$ means that X is a prerequisite for Y.

Using this Book as a Classroom Text

We use this book as a classroom text for a one-semester course on techniques for proving data refinement, given to advanced undergraduate and beginning graduate students. In general we move the material on applications forward, e.g., by discussing Chapter 11 on Reynolds' method after going through Chapter 7 which constitutes the technical heart of the book, and summarize the results of Section 9.2 briefly in order to discuss Sections 11.3.2 and 11.3.3 (concerning situations where Reynolds' method only works for total correctness).

Depending on the teacher's preference, when focusing on applications we have skipped Chapter 10 on the refinement calculus, and when focusing on the refinement calculus skipped Chapters 13 (with the exception of Section 13.3) and 14.

In both cases it is necessary that students have a minimal knowledge of

Hoare logic in order to be able to understand the main applications of our theory, namely Chapters 11 and 12 on Reynolds' method and VDM. Such minimal knowledge is provided by, e.g., the first three sections of Appendix A. Appendix B collects an equally minimal body of knowledge about ordinals, which is needed in Section 8.1 on semantic models for total correctness in order to understand the characterization of the least fixed point of a monotone function on a cpo by means of the least upper bound of its, in general transfinite, approximations.

Section 3.5 can be skipped upon first reading.

Proof Format

This monograph contains many proofs. Their degree of formality varies between rather informal, as found in mathematical textbooks, and formal, mostly for demonstration purposes. Most proofs are presented semi-formally, line by line. Usually we provide a short justification for each of these steps, e.g., by giving the name or number of the lemma or theorem applied in this step. Some of the more tedious proofs have been checked using the Prototype Verfication System. (See [ORS92] for an overview or browse SRI's web site for all things PVS at http://www.csl.sri.com/pvs.html.)

Feedback

We would love to receive feedback from you, our dear readers. Please email your comments to bkmail1@informatik.uni-kiel.de. As soon as it makes sense, we will compile a list of errata and make it available on the World Wide Web at http://www.informatik.uni-kiel.de/deRoever/bkerr1.html.

Acknowledgments

Travel involved in this work has been partially supported by ESPRIT-BRA projects SPEC (no. 3096) and REACT (no. 6021), and the Förderverein Technische Fakultät.

This monograph contains photographs of many of the researchers whose work is discussed. We thank them for their permission to publish these. In particular, we thank Mrs Sophie Bekić and her children for their kind permission to publish a dear picture of their late husband and father Hans Bekić, and for providing it. Also we thank Mrs Joanna Park for her kind permission to publish a picture of her late husband David Park, and Mike Patterson for providing that picture. Finally our gratitude goes to Peter van Emde Boas, photographer par excellence of computer scientists, for generously putting his collection at our disposal.

We would like to thank those people who contributed parts to this monograph, at various stages of its development. These are:

- Karl-Heinz Buth, who has written Section 13.1 on Z.
- Jos Coenen, who has been involved in its early stages, and who contributed especially to its planning by helping to write first versions of many sections. We were shocked last year when we heard of his untimely death, realizing how unevenly happiness has been bestowed upon people.
- Paul Gardiner, who has made essential contributions to Chapter 10 on the refinement calculus, helped us by writing a first version which appeared as [Gar95], and advised us on later versions.
- Yassine Lakhnech, who has contributed to the formulation of Section 3.4 on the relational semantics of recursion, to initial versions of Chapter 9 on simulation and total correctness, and to Chapter 14 on refinement methods due to Abadi and Lamport and to Lynch.
- Frank Stomp, who wrote Section 14.2 on possibility mappings together with Yassine Lakhnech and contributed at an early stage to Appendix A on an introduction to Hoare logic.

David Tranah and the helpful staff at CUP deserve our gratitude for helping us improve and, finally, publish this book. We would also like to thank: Ralph Back, Rudolf Berghammer, Marcello Bonsangue, Pierre Collette, Marja de Vroome, Loe Feijs, Martin Fränzle, John Guttag, Barry Jay, Bengt Jonsson, Jens Knappmann, Lars Kühne, Justus Kurth, Ben Lukoschus, Nancy Lynch, Helge Marquardt, Oliver Matz, Kees Middelburg, Ulf Milanese, Carroll Morgan, Markus Müller-Olm, Sascha Ott, Amir Pnueli, Bodo Rosenhahn, Markus Schneider, Jan-Hendrik Schöler, Carsten Scholz, Michael Siegel, Karsten Stahl, Martin Steffen, Änne Straßner, Markus Tiedt, Frank Tonn, Ron van der Meyden, Jan Vitt, Jörg Wiechert, and Job Zwiers for their help, without which writing this book would have been impossible.

More important is that life would have been impossible without the support of our wives, Corinne and Claudia. We dedicate this book to them.

Christian-Albrechts-Universität zu Kiel	W.-P. de Roever
University of Technology, Sydney	K. Engelhardt

Part I
Theory

1

Introduction to Data Refinement

1.1 Goal and Motivation

During the process of stepwise, hierarchical program development, a step represents a transformation of a so-called abstract higher level result into a more concrete lower level one. In general, this development process corresponds to increasing the amount of detail required for the eventual implementation of the original specification on a given machine.

In the first part of this book we develop the relational theory of simulation and a general version of Hoare logic, show how data refinement can be expressed within this logic, extend these results to total correctness, and show how all this theory can be uniformly expressed inside the refinement calculus of Ralph Back, Paul Gardiner, Carroll Morgan and Joakim von Wright. We develop this theory as a reference point for comparing various existing data refinement methods in the second part, some of which are syntax-based methods. This is one of the main reasons why we are forced to clearly separate syntax from semantics.

The second part of this monograph focuses on the introduction of, and comparison between, various methods for proving correctness of such transformation steps. Although these methods are illustrated mainly by applying them to correctness proofs of implementations of data types, the techniques developed apply equally well to proving correctness of such steps in general, because all these methods are only variations on one central theme: that of proof by simulation, of which we analyze at least 13 different formulations.

We study in particular the similarities and the differences between such widely known methods as the methods advocated by John Reynolds [Ger78, Rey81] and Rick Hehner [Heh93], VDM [J90], Z [Spi92b], and methods more directly based on Hoare logic [Hoa72] or predicate transformers [B78, B88b, Mor89a, Mor90, GM93, MV94, Gar95]. Moreover, we consider methods that,

2

although primarily developed for proving correctness of parallel programs, have as their main ingredient a nucleus which essentially concerns sequential (albeit nondeterministic) program refinement, such as the method of Martín Abadi and Leslie Lamport [AL91], and the possibilities mappings of Nancy Lynch [LT87, Lyn90].

This study makes sense because in the final analysis a surprisingly uniform picture emerges when comparing these proof methods — notwithstanding their wide differences in formulation. Either they are special cases of the method based on L-simulation (also called *forward* or *downward* simulation), and therefore incomplete as shown in Section 2.2.2, or they are equivalent to the combination of L- and L^{-1}-simulation (also called *backward* or *upward* simulation), and then complete by a theorem of He, Hoare, and Sanders [HHS87]. This strengthens our conviction that it makes more sense to emphasize the general principles behind these methods, since we believe these will preserve their value when the students of today have become the specialists of tomorrow, even if present day methods are superseded by more modern ones.

This first chapter presents intuitive explanations and some definitions of key notions in the field of data refinement, such as (abstract/concrete) data type, observability, operation, (data) refinement. The second chapter then introduces the notions of abstraction relation, representation invariant, and simulation, which are used throughout this monograph. In this way the reader is guided to the main questions answered in this part, viz.:

- What is refinement? What is data refinement? What is a correct refinement step, and how can such correctness be proven?

- What is simulation? When one faces a correct case of data refinement, can one always prove its correctness given a particular simulation method? That is, which methods for proving data refinement are complete? Are these methods always sound?

- What is the weakest (i.e., most general) concrete specification simulating a given abstract specification with respect to a given abstraction relation?

- How can one guarantee that termination is preserved during simulation?

The first two chapters serve as motivation and set the scene for the remainder of this monograph, starting with our first technical chapter, Chapter 3. We try to lead gently into the topic and therefore sometimes sacrifice rigor and mathematical precision for intuition.

1.2 Introduction to Data Refinement

1.2.1 Basic Issues

Designing a large and complex program usually involves application of some refinement method providing a way to *gradually transform* an *abstract* program, possibly a *specification*, into a *concrete* implementation. The main principle of such a method is that if the initial abstract program is correct and the *transformation steps* preserve correctness, then the resulting implementation will be correct by construction. Because an abstract program is, in general, easier to prove correct than a concrete one, this simplifies the structuring of the verification process.

This monograph focuses on methods for proving the correctness of such transformation steps. So we ask ourselves what it means to say that the result of applying a transformation step is regarded as a correct implementation of the construct to which that step is applied. In the context of data refinement, this amounts to the question of when an abstract program $P(\mathcal{A})$ using a data type $\mathcal{A}$ is implemented correctly by the more concrete program $P(C)$ obtained from $P(\mathcal{A})$ by replacing operations A_j from $\mathcal{A}$ by corresponding operations C_j which belong to a more concrete data type C. This question becomes more interesting if we abstract from the particular pair of programs $P(\mathcal{A})$ and $P(C)$ to which this data type transformation is applied. This narrows our subject down to that of *data refinement*, i.e., formulating when the family of operations $(C_j)_{j \in J}$ belonging to a more concrete data type C correctly implements the family of operations $(A_j)_{j \in J}$ of the more abstract data type $\mathcal{A}$. The solution of this problem depends on realizing that A_j and C_j in general constitute programs themselves, which are used as modules inside other, for the moment arbitrary, programs P. Now, intuitively, a concrete program *module* is a correct implementation of an abstract program module, if no program using the concrete module can *observe* that it is not using the first. That is, "implementation correctness" means that using the concrete program module does not lead to an *observation* which is not also an observation of the corresponding abstract program module. Note that this does not imply that the concrete and the abstract program display the same observations. There may be observations of the abstract program which are not observations of the corresponding concrete program. Hence, this definition only implies that the observations of the concrete program are contained in those of the corresponding abstract program. This is called *refinement*.

Example 1.1 (Data refinement step) Consider, for instance, the following two sketches of program fragments in a pseudo-Pascal notation, where S_1 and S_2

are dummies for program fragments not involving program variables U, l, and x, and $\langle\,\rangle$ denotes the empty sequence.

begin	**begin**
var U : *set of* $\mathbb{N}$; $U := \emptyset$;	**var** l : *sequence of* $\mathbb{N}$; $l := \langle\,\rangle$;
S_1;	S_1;
$U := U \cup \{x\}$;	$l := append(x, l)$;
S_2;	S_2;
$y := a\ member\ of\ U$	$y := first(l)$
end	**end**

At this point nothing more than an intuitive understanding of the operational meaning of these program sketches is required. Any observable behavior in terms of values of the common program variables x and y exposed by the RHS[1] program should also be a possible behavior of the LHS program. This refinement step comprises of replacing the variable U (ranging over finite subsets of the natural numbers) and operations on it by the sequence-valued variable l and corresponding operations.   ♡

Which particular set of observations, i.e., semantics, should characterize a program depends on the particular notion of correctness which a transformation step is intended to preserve. For instance, in the context of relational semantics of programs, this meaning is given by pairs of initial and corresponding final states of its computations. In the case of partial correctness, only terminating computations are represented by such pairs, and then refinement is expressed by inclusion between the corresponding relations. In the case of total correctness nonterminating computations are also made observable through pairs. As explained in Chapter 8, there are then various possibilities for characterizing the meaning of a program relationally, and, consequently, different ways to express refinement.

The above account, suggestive as it may be, introduces a number of terms, those in italics, which need further explanation.

What is an *abstract* or a *concrete* program? The notion of abstractness used here is relative. Program refinement distinguishes an upper level, called abstract, from a lower level, called concrete, in order to indicate the direction in which the process of refinement is taking place.

Then, what does "gradually transform" mean in this context? Calling the level at which the transformation starts level 0, this level is transformed into level 1, which may be subsequently transformed into level 2, and so on. Thus,

---

[1] We use RHS and LHS as acronyms for **R**ight (respectively, **L**eft) **H**and **S**ide.

a series of successive transformations or *transformation steps* takes effect, until a sufficiently concrete level of implementation has been reached (by some external criterion). As already indicated, we consider this process of transformation to consist of several individual transformation steps, each of which is considered to transform an abstract level (say, level n) into a more concrete one (level $n + 1$).

In what sense should the terms *data type* and *abstract data type* be understood? Abstract data types are usually defined by a set of operators and a set of axioms, typically given in the form of equations; see e.g. [GH78, LG86, Cle86, BHK89, Par90, Wir90]. As an example of this style we present the equations for an abstract data type $stack(Z)$, where Bool refers to the abstract data type of Boolean values (with the usual propositional operators such as $\neg$, $\Rightarrow$, $\vee$, $\wedge$) and Z to the abstract data type of the elements to be stacked (regarded as primitive at this level of specification).

Example 1.2 (Characterization of stacks through equations)

> **Name:** $stack(Z)$
>
> **Operators:**
>
> $$\begin{array}{llll} emptystack: & & \longrightarrow & stack(Z) \\ push & : Z \times stack(Z) & \longrightarrow & stack(Z) \\ pop & : stack(Z) & \longrightarrow & stack(Z) \\ top & : stack(Z) & \longrightarrow & Z \\ empty? & : stack(Z) & \longrightarrow & \text{Bool} \end{array}$$
>
> **Axioms:**
>
> 1. $pop(push(z,s)) \quad = s$
> 2. $top(push(z,s)) \quad = z$
> 3. $empty?(emptystack) = \text{true}$
> 4. $empty?(push(z,s)) \quad = \text{false}$ ♡

This algebraic characterization of data types is attractive in that it is both program and implementation independent. It merely describes which properties one expects from a data type, not how it is implemented.

In contrast, the, as we call it, model-oriented notion of data types turns out to be less elegant, more implementation dependent, and certainly less abstract.

However, there exist some arguments in favor of the model-oriented approach, which we consider convincing.

First of all there is the essential point whether a method scales up to industrial applications. The methods whose study gave rise to this book, e.g., Reynolds' method, VDM, and the method by Abadi and Lamport, scale up to such applications. These methods can be adapted to concurrency[AL91, MP95, He 89], which is another important point.

Another strong point of model-oriented methods is the characterization of pointer manipulation; it can be easily embedded in the model-oriented style, see, for instance, [AdB94, Mor82].

This does not imply that this algebraic style using equations for defining abstract data types should not be used whenever elegantly applicable. Ole-Johan Dahl's beautiful monograph [Dah92] is full of examples of data types for cases in which we too consider the algebraic style to be superior. He argues convincingly that for programs using simple data structures whose implementation requires no considerations of efficient memory management, and no carefully defined balance between control flow and data encoding techniques, representation by algebraic terms is preferable because of its simplicity and elegance. This elegance is lost whenever any notion of centralized memory enters the picture, as is, e.g., the case with algorithms for efficient list manipulation or graph traversal. Then other techniques are called for, for instance Reynolds' method as applied in [LdRG79, vDdR86] for proving correctness of efficient list copying techniques. These techniques do not characterize a data type anymore in the abstract sense using axioms as above. As we shall see, a considerably more application-oriented characterization is used in the context of state-based program verification. This is the reason we reserve the term *data type* for the latter, and use the terms *abstract* and *concrete data type* in the context of refinement steps to indicate the data type on the higher, respectively, lower level of that step [HH90].

Yet even in simple cases the algebraic style requires some elaboration. Assume, for instance, that the stack in Example 1.2 is implemented as an array and a pointer to array cells. This implementation (further investigated in Example 2.6) cannot be proven correct with respect to the above characterization because it does not satisfy axiom 1, as shown in Example 1.3. Although the algebraic method can be extended to solve such problems too, their solution requires an amount of technical machinery which we are not prepared to pay for when facing such a simple, yet fundamental, problem.

But the main reason for adhering to the model-oriented style is that the algebraic approach does not extend very well to concurrency. On the other hand, several of the methods compared here have been exclusively developed with concurrent or distributed systems in mind. These are the methods of Abadi and Lamport and of Lynch presented in Chapter 14. After all, the verification problem is urgent for all but the most trivial concurrent and distributed algorithms. This view is shared by Nancy Lynch in her monograph on distributed algorithms [Lyn96].

Example 1.3 Consider an array $a[1..max]$ and an integer variable p. Let stack s be represented by the pair (a, p) such that $0 \leq p \leq max$, where the contents of s are stored in $a[1..p]$, and p points to the top of the stack. Then $push(z, s)$ can essentially be represented by $p := p + 1 ; a[p] := z$, and $pop(s)$ by $p := p - 1$, disregarding for the moment the size of the stack. Consider the case that $p = 2$ and $a[p + 1] = 66$. Execution of $pop(push(77, s))$ then results in a representation (a', p) of s different from the representation (a, p) before, since $a'[3] = 77$, whereas $a[3] = 66$ (see Figure 1.1).

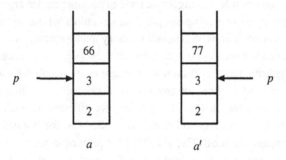

Fig. 1.1. Two different stack representations which cannot be distinguished by using the stack operations.

Hence, this representation of stacks does not satisfy axiom 1. Yet this representation is a common one inside a computer. Verifying correctness of this implementation apparently requires taking more aspects into account than the rather idealized ones listed in Example 1.2.

Notice that the difference between (a, p) and (a', p) cannot be determined by using any of our stack operations (i.e., *emptystack, pop, push, top*, and *empty?*). Observe that, therefore, such distinctions cannot be expressed in this simple axiomatic style (by its very definition).   ♡

Implementations like the one in the example above are called *biased*. The characteristic property of biased data types is that different representations exist which cannot be distinguished using the data type operations.

We can summarize the above discussion regarding styles by the remark that, in the context of program verification, implementation bias occurs far too often to be ignored. Indeed, our theory deals seamlessly with this concept.

Instead, we shall define data types by means of their models, and so obtain a hierarchy of models when implementing these data types; as stated above, the model at level n is considered to be more abstract than the one at level $n + 1$, which is considered to be more concrete.

From now onwards we shall resort to an *imperative* style using state transformations involving the updating of program variables. All the methods studied in this book adhere to the imperative style. This style is called *model-oriented*. The main difference between this style and the axiomatic approaches is the way operations of data types are specified.

As an example of this style we consider a variant of Example 1.1 in more detail.

Example 1.4 (Representation of sets by lists) Consider the data type of finite sets over some nonempty base type Z. We introduce the following operations on a finite-set-valued variable U:

- $U := \emptyset$, i.e., assign the empty set to U,
- $U := U \cup \{x\}$, provided $x \notin U$ and $x \in Z$, i.e., enlarge the set by the element x from Z,
- $x := pick(U)$, provided $U \neq \emptyset$, i.e., choose a random element from the nonvoid set U, delete it from U, and assign it to x,
- $x \in U$, test whether x belongs to U,
- $U = \emptyset$, test whether U denotes the empty set.

Similarly, we introduce the data type LL of linear lists over base type Z. We identify linear lists and finite sequences. In general, the set of linear lists LL over a given nonempty set Z is defined as the smallest set LL such that

- the empty linear list $\langle \, \rangle \in LL$,
- whenever $x \in Z$ and $l \in LL$ then $append(x, l) \in LL$.

We abbreviate $append(z_1, append(z_2, \ldots, append(z_k, \langle \, \rangle)))$ to $\langle z_1, \ldots, z_k \rangle$. The following additional operations upon linear lists are needed:

$$first(append(z, l)) \stackrel{\text{def}}{=} z \text{ and}$$

$$rest(append(z, l)) \stackrel{\text{def}}{=} l \, ,$$

where $first(\langle \, \rangle)$ and $rest(\langle \, \rangle)$ are undefined. Furthermore we need the function *elts* recursively defined by $elts(\langle \, \rangle) \stackrel{\text{def}}{=} \emptyset$ and $elts(append(z, l)) \stackrel{\text{def}}{=} \{z\} \cup elts(l)$.

Having defined the set LL of linear lists over a nonempty base set Z of atoms, we proceed with representing the above operations upon a set-valued variable U by operations upon an LL-valued variable l. Linear list l corresponds to set U if U equals the set of elements contained in l, i.e., $U = elts(l)$. Notice that, in general, this representation is not unique as an element can occur in a linear list more than once, and elements may occur in different order. However, in this particular example insertion of an element x into U only occurs when

$x \notin U$. Since set U is represented by list l such that $U = elts(l)$, this implies that adding x to l only occurs when $x \notin elts(l)$. Now we also want to represent the operation of deleting an element from a set. When deleting an element from the corresponding linear list, in general all the occurrences of this element within that list must also be deleted. This is an expensive operation because it requires scanning the whole list. Since efficiency of the implemented operations is an important factor in choosing an implementation, we restrict ourselves to representing sets by linear lists without such repetitions.

operation on U	operation on l
$U := \emptyset$	$l := \langle \rangle$
$U := U \cup \{x\}$ for $x \in Z, x \notin U$	$l := append(x, l)$ for $x \in Z, x \notin elts(l)$
$x := pick(U)$ for $U \neq \emptyset$	$x := first(l) ; l := rest(l)$ for $l \neq \langle \rangle$
$x \in U$	$x \in elts(l)$
$U = \emptyset$	$l = \langle \rangle$

Notice that for a given list l representing the set U, the nondeterministic operation $pick(U)$ is implemented by a deterministic operation, which therefore restricts the nondeterminism inherent in $pick(U)$, and is therefore a typical example of refinement.   ♡

Notice that the example above introduces the notion of *representing* a data type by another one; we shall soon return to this important concept.

1.2.2 Observability and Refinement

What do the notions *observable, observable values, observer* mean? The criterion introduced above for the notion of a correct implementation is based on the initial/final state behavior of programs. In our sequential framework the behavior of a program (here, we also consider operations as above to be programs) is supposed to be completely characterized by this behavior, i.e., its relational semantics. Such semantics are defined in Chapter 5 for characterizing terminating computations, and in Chapter 8 in which nonterminating computations are also characterized. Hence one may test a sequential program by providing it with an initial state, and then observing whether a final state is produced, and if so, which one. In such a set-up the program is considered as a black box whose structure (or program text) is hidden from the observer, who has access only to the (initial) values consumed and (final) values produced by that black box, if any. These (pairs of) values are called its observables. As observers programs will again be used. As already remarked above, the latter viewpoint implies that the black box program to be tested is viewed as a *program module*, and such a module is contained inside a larger program observing it, which makes use of that module by providing it with an initial state and consuming its corresponding final state in case of termination. For a nonterminating computation, obviously some abstraction of the notion "requiring an infinite amount of time" is needed to characterize the corresponding observation.

When defining implementation correctness, what do we mean by stipulating that the behavior of the implementing program is "in some sense contained" in that of the original program?

Reconsider Example 1.4, where finite sets plus a number of operations upon them are represented by finite lists, plus operations upon these lists, using state transformations. Let U be the set variable in question occurring in the state of some program P, as indicated by writing $P(U)$, and let $P(l)$ denote the same program in which all occurrences of U and operations upon U are replaced by a list variable l and its corresponding operations. Assume furthermore that U occurs as part of P's final state, i.e., both (the value of) U in $P(U)$ and (the value of) l in $P(l)$ are observable on this level. Since the meaning of a program is its initial/final state behavior, it is impossible that the meaning of $P(U)$ is contained in the meaning of $P(l)$, because the values of U are different from those of l. So viewed in this way data refinement cannot be straightforwardly characterized by relational containment, as stated previously. In this example the abstract data type is represented within P's state vector, and consequently, when comparing $P(U)$ and $P(l)$, we compare two programs whose sets of observables have different types. In general, when observable components of a program are implemented, we speak of *interface refinement*. To be able to define this notion, one needs a relation between P's state vectors at the concrete and abstract level. Such a relation is called an *abstraction relation*. For instance, in Example 1.4 above $U = elts(l)$ expresses such an abstraction relation, under the assumption that the values of variable x on both levels are the same. Such relations play a fundamental rôle when formulating proof methods for all forms of refinement involving replacement of data types and the variables on which they operate.

1.2.3 Data Types and Data Refinement

To reconcile the view that abstract data types are represented by other more concrete data types with the concept of data refinement as containment between sets of observations, we will further analyze the notions of data type and data refinement semantically, and provide a link with proof methods for data refinement. Before doing so, we repeat the intuitive notion of what implementation correctness semantically means, and introduce some technical concepts needed for the formal definition of data types and data refinement and for formulating *simulation*, a proof technique for data refinement, in Chapter 2.

Definition 1.5 (Semantic implementation correctness [GM93]) Given two programs, one called concrete and the other called abstract, the concrete program *implements* (or *refines*) the abstract program correctly whenever the use of the concrete program does not lead to an observation which is not also an observation of the abstract program.   ♣

Definition 1.6 Let A, B, and C denote sets. For binary relations $R \subseteq A \times B$ and $S \subseteq B \times C$ we define

- R is *total* on A iff $\forall a \in A \, (\exists b \in B \, ((a,b) \in R))$. We simply say that R is total if A is clear from the context.
- R is *functional* iff $\forall a \in A, b_1, b_2 \in B \, (\{(a,b_1),(a,b_2)\} \subseteq R \Rightarrow b_1 = b_2)$.
- The *sequential composition* of R and S:

$$R \, ; S \overset{\text{def}}{=} \{ (a,c) \mid \exists b \, ((a,b) \in R \wedge (b,c) \in S) \}$$

- The *inverse* of R:

$$R^{-1} \overset{\text{def}}{=} \{ (b,a) \mid (a,b) \in R \}$$ ♣

The most basic semantic notion for the following is the notion of states. As usual, a state σ is a total function from a set *Pvar* of program variable names into a set $\mathbb{V}$ of values. The state space Σ is $[Pvar \longrightarrow \mathbb{V}]$, the set of all such functions from *Pvar* to $\mathbb{V}$. In the following, statements are considered as syntactic representations of binary relations on states, where the pairs contained in such a binary relation consist of an initial and a final state in the case of termination, and, in the case of nontermination, of an initial state and some formal representation of nontermination, depending on which convention is used.

As stated before, data refinement concerns the question: "When does replacement of the program modules A_j belonging to some data type $\mathcal{A}$ by their corresponding more concrete program modules C_j from some concrete data type C result in a correct implementation?"

Now given an arbitrary program P operating upon $\mathcal{A}$ — this is abbreviated to $P(\mathcal{A})$ — we may assume that its operations operate on variables from two finite disjoint sets: $\vec{x}$ and $\vec{a}$. The original specification which P is intended to solve is assumed to be formulated in terms of (a transformation of states involving) $\vec{x}$ only; for instance, P is to compute the average of a number of real values which are provided as input. This has the following reason: the original specification of P should abstract from certain implementation dependent details such as the use of a particular data type in a particular context (see, e.g., Examples 1.4 and 2.5) in order to implement this specification; from this viewpoint the variables from $\vec{a}$ are used for an auxiliary purpose, namely to store these details, for instance, variable U in Examples 1.1 and 1.4. The variables in $\vec{x}$ will be called the *normal variables* of this refinement step, whereas the variables from $\vec{a}$ will be called the *representation variables* on $\mathcal{A}$'s abstraction level. Now, because we want to compare the (observable) behaviors of $P(\mathcal{A})$ and $P(C)$ in a way which reflects Def. 1.5, we need versions of $P(\mathcal{A})$ and $P(C)$ in which the representation variables $\vec{a}$, resp., $\vec{c}$ (indicating the representation variables at level C) are not observable anymore. In order to obtain such a version, we define for every data type $\mathcal{A}$ an initialization operator AI, essentially adding these variables to the state and initializing them properly, and a finalization operator AF which essentially projects these variables away from the current state. Thus AI operates on an initial state which assigns values only to the normal variables $\vec{x}$ of this refinement step, and results in a final state which extends this initial state to one also assigning appropriate initial values to the representation variables $\vec{a}$. Similarly, AF operates on an initial state assigning values to both $\vec{x}$ and $\vec{a}$ and results in a final state assigning values to $\vec{x}$ only.[2]

Using the notation introduced above, $AI;P(\mathcal{A});AF$ yields a version of $P(\mathcal{A})$ whose initial and final states do not involve $\vec{a}$ anymore. Now data refinement in our sense can be characterized in this relational setting by requiring that, for all pairs of programs $P(\mathcal{A})$ and $P(C)$, the following inclusion holds:

$$CI;P(C);CF \subseteq AI;P(\mathcal{A});AF \tag{1.1}$$

This is illustrated in Figure 1.2. If this diagram weakly commutes, (1.1) holds, where weak commutativity combines containment with commutativity of a diagram.

The meaning of data types and data refinement can now be given precisely, based on [HHS87].

Definition 1.7 (Data type) Given a finite list of variables $\vec{x}$, called *normal variables*, with values in some set $\mathbb{V}$, and another disjoint finite list of variables $\vec{a}$, called *representation variables*, with values in some set $\mathbb{V}^A$, state spaces Σ^N, Σ_A, and Σ^A are defined by $\Sigma^N \stackrel{\text{def}}{=} [\vec{x} \longrightarrow \mathbb{V}]$, $\Sigma_A \stackrel{\text{def}}{=} [\vec{a} \longrightarrow \mathbb{V}^A]$,

---

[2] Notice that here operations AI, A_j, and AF (and other terms) are identified with their meaning. This is done for the sake of readability. Usually, a term and its semantics will be distinguished, since in our set-up the distinction between syntactic operations and semantic operations is crucial for the application of our results to different formalisms.

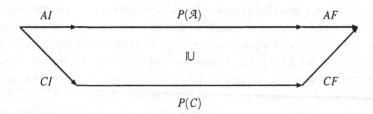

Fig. 1.2. Data refinement.

and $\Sigma^A \stackrel{\text{def}}{=} \Sigma^N \times \Sigma_A$. Let $(A_j)_{j \in J}$ denote a family of operations on variables $\vec{x} \cup \vec{a}$, i.e., $A_j \subseteq \Sigma^A \times \Sigma^A$ for $j \in J$. Furthermore assume that the initialization operation AI satisfies $AI \subseteq \Sigma^N \times \Sigma^A$, and the finalization operation AF satisfies $AF \subseteq \Sigma^A \times \Sigma^N$. Then we call

$$\mathcal{A} \stackrel{\text{def}}{=} \left(\vec{x}, \vec{a}, \mathbb{V}, \mathbb{V}^A, AI, (A_j)_{j \in J}, AF\right)$$

a *data type*. In case $\vec{x}$, $\vec{a}$, $\mathbb{V}$, and $\mathbb{V}^A$ are clear from the context, we simplify this characterization by just defining a data type by

$$\mathcal{A} \stackrel{\text{def}}{=} \left(AI, (A_j)_{j \in J}, AF\right) \ .$$

Two data types are *compatible* iff they share the set of normal states Σ^N as well as the set of operation indices J and have disjoint sets of representation variables. ♣

Before formally stating our definition of data refinement, we need to specify the class of programs considered, since in this definition we need to quantify over all programs from this class (or rather, over all meanings of programs belonging to this class).

For the moment, given a data type $\mathcal{A} = \left(AI, (A_j)_{j \in J}, AF\right)$, let us assume this class $\mathcal{P}(\mathcal{A})$ consists of all while-programs, guarded commands, and recursive programs which are built up from the tests and basic operations collected in $(A_j)_{j \in J}$. Such a class will be formally defined in Chapter 3. Notice that this immediately raises the question how tests and other value-returning operations are modelled as operations in the sense of the definition above. In Chapter 5 tests will be modelled as subsets of the identity relation, therefore acting like filters when used as a left argument with respect to sequential composition. Other value-returning operations will be considered within the context of assignments in Section 2.4.

Having fixed the notion of programs, we are now in a position to formally define data refinement.

Definition 1.8 (Data refinement) Let $\mathcal{A}$ and C be compatible data types defined by, respectively,

$$\mathcal{A} \stackrel{\text{def}}{=} (AI, (A_j)_{j \in J}, AF) \quad \text{and} \quad C \stackrel{\text{def}}{=} (CI, (C_j)_{j \in J}, CF) \ ,$$

and let $\mathcal{P}(\mathcal{A})$ and $\mathcal{P}(C)$ be defined as above. Then C is called a *data refinement* of $\mathcal{A}$ whenever for all pairs of programs $(P(\mathcal{A}), P(C)) \in \mathcal{P}(\mathcal{A}) \times \mathcal{P}(C)$, with $P(C)$ obtained from $P(\mathcal{A})$ by replacing operations A_j by C_j for $j \in J$, the following inclusion holds:

$$CI ; P(C) ; CF \subseteq AI ; P(\mathcal{A}) ; AF \qquad \clubsuit$$

Data representation is the inverse process of data abstraction. E.g., a list is abstracted (i.e., related by some abstraction relation) to a set consisting of the elements contained in that list; and, vice versa, a set is represented by any list containing the elements in that set as its elements.

A program uses one data type

Although the building blocks of a program $P(\mathcal{A})$ are members[3] of $(A_j)_{j \in J}$, not all operations occurring in $P(\mathcal{A})$ necessarily change the representation variables $\vec{a}$ of $\mathcal{A}$. This is illustrated in Figure 1.3.

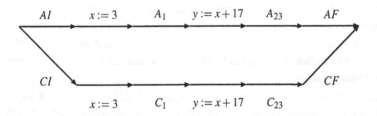

Fig. 1.3. Operations $x := 3$ and $y := x + 17$ on normal variables x and y.

Here $P(\mathcal{A}) \stackrel{\text{def}}{=} x := 3 ; A_1 ; y := x + 17 ; A_{23}$, $P(C) \stackrel{\text{def}}{=} x := 3 ; C_1 ; y := x + 17 ; C_{23}$, and $\vec{x} = \{x, y\}$. In case data type $\mathcal{A}$ is data refined by data type C, this implies that $CI ; P(C) ; CF \subseteq AI ; P(\mathcal{A}) ; AF$, and therefore that Figure 1.3 weakly commutes.

The key observation here is that the operations $x := 3$ and $y := x + 17$ belong to both $\mathcal{A}$ and C: on the higher level these operations are interpreted as transformations of Σ^A, whereas on the lower level they transform Σ^C. This immediately explains why we have included these operations in $\mathcal{A}$ and C. For their

---

[3] In the sequel we tend to forget about the mathematical difference between indexed families and sets. For instance, when speaking about *members* of a family $(A_j)_{j \in J}$ we mean the elements of set $\{ A_j \mid j \in J \}$.

meanings as state transformations on the higher and lower level of this data refinement step differ because Σ^A and Σ^C are different, whereas their syntactic representation remains the same. Therefore we are unable to define a data type semantically without these operations, which only influence the normal variables, as reflected in their name, *normal operations*. One might have expected (as the authors did for a long time) that a data type only concerns operations which transform state components depending on representation variables. As we have argued above, in the context of Def. 1.8 this leads to type inconsistency. The reason for this is, following [HHS87], that data refinement is a semantic notion and consequently a semantic notion of data type is required. If we were going to give just a syntactic characterization of data types, as in [J90], normal operations would not need to be included. (This is discussed in Section 2.3.2.)

This remark is summarized by stating that in this set-up a program always operates on one monolithic data type.

How data refinement is modelled when intuitively more than one data type is involved

Consider now the following case. Suppose we have a program operating on, say, a normal variable x and two set-valued representation variables a and b. For reasons of efficiency, a is implemented by bit-vector c, and b by array d without duplicates. Now it is our intention to separate the correct implementation of a from that of b. This can be achieved within our framework by splitting the refinement step into two.

First we implement a w.r.t. the set of normal variables $\{x,b\}$ of this step, and then we implement b w.r.t. the set of normal variables $\{x,c\}$. Therefore, we start by considering the program as belonging to $\mathcal{P}(\mathcal{A})$, with $\mathcal{A}$ defined by

$$\mathcal{A} \stackrel{\text{def}}{=} (\{x,b\},\{a\},\mathbb{V}\cup\mathbb{V}_b,\mathbb{V}_a,AI,(A_l)_{l\in L},AF) \ .$$

Here AI only initializes a. Furthermore we collect the operations involving a and b. W.l.o.g. we assume these to be indexed by disjoint sets. Now $(A_l)_{l\in L}$ is the union of the operations not involving a and b with the operations involving a and those involving b.

A second data type C is similarly defined, but now w.r.t. representation variable c. The implementation of a can now be described by a data refinement of $\mathcal{A}$ by C.

Next we repeat this procedure for a data type $\mathcal{B}$ w.r.t. normal variables $\{x,c\}$ and representation variable b which is refined by a data type $\mathcal{D}$ with representation variable d.

What justifies the setting of binary relations?

Observe that the inclusion

$$CI\,;P(C)\,;CF \subseteq AI\,;P(\mathcal{A})\,;AF$$

is parameterized by the program variables $\vec{x}$, $\vec{a}$, and $\vec{c}$. Correspondingly, when defining data refinement, we quantify over all programs P whose normal variables belong to the variable set $\vec{x}$. This restriction implies that our notion of data refinement is rather limited. That is, we do not consider *all* programs using, e.g., stacks and we refuse to define a general data type called stack, for in our set-up one additionally needs to specify $\vec{x}$ and $\vec{a}$ and their corresponding domains of values.

Our only reason for adhering to these rather specialized notions of data type and data refinement is the elegance and simplicity they provide to the resulting soundness and completeness proofs of our proof methods for data refinement.[4] As we shall see, the rather specialized set-up adopted here suffices for the purpose of comparing the various model-oriented approaches mentioned at the beginning of this chapter.

1.3 Historical Background

The main sources for our definitions of data type and data refinement are Nipkow's [Nip86] and Hoare, He, and Sanders' [HHS87]; of these we could trace the following precursors: a preprint of [Nip86] dated March 1985, and a preprint of [HHS86] dated May 1985.

The characterization of data types by means of a set of axioms has already been discussed in the thesis of John Guttag [Gut75], in which he also proved correctness of some refinement steps between such data types.

Nipkow refers to an already rich tradition in characterizing data types and reasoning about them before 1985 ([BS82, BW82]) and describes his concepts as slight abstractions of ideas contained in [J80] and [J81]. Nipkow writes:

> However, ... , only Schoett explicitly connects data types with programming. [Sch81] contains an informal proof, modelled closely after that in [Hoa72], that his implementation criterion guarantees that the behaviour of a program is independent of whether it uses some data type $\mathcal{A}$ or its implementation C. [Nip86, p. 630]

For a description of the development of the field of data types in the context of proofs of implementation correctness in the period 1960–1986 consult Jones' [J92].

---

[4] Tobias Nipkow achieved a comparable completeness result for data types in a more general model-oriented approach, using so-called multi-algebras, allowing for a smoother integration of parameters and results [Nip86].

The notions of observable values and observer were already implicitly used in Plotkin's full abstraction proof of a denotational semantics for an LCF-based programming language with respect to an operational semantics for that language [Plo74], and in Jones' notion of implementation bias [J80]. Later early references to these notions are contained in [Sch81, dNH83, BR83, ST85].

For early references to abstraction functions and relations see [Mil69, J70, Mil70, Hoa72].

Lynch and Fischer use in [LF80] a special kind of abstraction function to prove a shared memory mutual exclusion algorithm correct. Later work on abstraction functions is discussed in Chapters 12 and 14, where they are called, respectively, retrieve functions and refinement mappings.

2

Simulation as a Proof Method for Data Refinement

The definition of data refinement given in the previous chapter requires that an infinite number of inclusions should hold, namely one for every choice of program involved. Consequently it does not yield an effective proof method. In this chapter we define such a method, called *simulation*, and investigate its soundness and completeness w.r.t. the criterion of proving data refinement. In order to define simulation one needs the concept of abstraction relation, relating concrete data values to abstract ones. We briefly discuss why abstraction relations rather than abstraction functions are used, and how data invariants (characterizing the reachable values in a data type) solve one of the problems associated with converting abstraction relations into abstraction functions. Since ultimately proofs are carried out in predicate logic, this raises the question how to express abstraction relations within that logic. As we shall see, this forces us to distinguish between those variables within a program that are unaffected by the data refinement step in question (these are called *normal variables*) and those that are affected by that step (called *representation variables*). This raises a number of technical issues which are discussed and for which we present a solution. Next, two methods presently in use for proving data refinement, namely Reynolds' method and VDM, are briefly introduced by way of an example. Finally, we discuss both the distinction between, and the relative values of, syntax-based methods for proving data refinement and semantically oriented ones.

2.1 Introducing Simulation

The definition of data refinement given in the previous chapter is a global criterion, in the sense that $CI;P(C);CF \subseteq AI;P(\mathcal{A});AF$ should hold for all pairs of programs $P(\mathcal{A})$ and $P(C)$ using compatible data types $\mathcal{A}$ and C, respectively. This inclusion should be verified for infinitely many programs, i.e., an infinite number of inclusions should hold. Consequently, the definition of data refinement does not embody an effective method for proving data refinement. What we are after is a local criterion resulting in a finite number of verification conditions, and hence providing an effective proof method. Such a criterion can be obtained by introducing

(i) abstraction relations α to relate concrete data values (e.g., lists) to abstract ones (e.g., the set of elements in those lists), and

(ii) a notion of weak commutativity of the diagrams in Figure 2.1 (this is indicated by $\star$) for all $j \in J$, such that this notion implies the inclusion $CI; P(C); CF \subseteq AI; P(\mathcal{A}); AF$ for all pairs of programs $P(\mathcal{A})$ and $P(C)$ (see Figure 2.2). Here index set J is assumed to be finite.

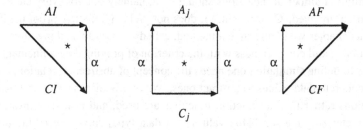

Fig. 2.1. Weak commutativity of single operations constituting a data type.

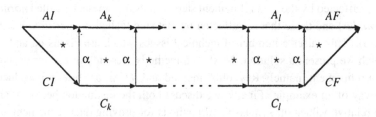

Fig. 2.2. Data refinement reduced to weak commutativity of single diagrams.

The resulting criterion is called *simulation*. There are essentially four ways to define simulation, each corresponding to a different way in which weak commutativity of the diagram in the middle of Figure 2.1, and hence a proof method, can be defined. This is because there exist four combinations of C_j, A_j and the two occurrences of α (for linking the concrete with the abstract level before and after execution of C_j and A_j) for defining $\ldots C_j \ldots \subseteq \ldots A_j \ldots$, namely

$$\alpha^{-1};C_j \subseteq A_j;\alpha^{-1}$$
$$\alpha^{-1};C_j;\alpha \subseteq A_j$$
$$C_j;\alpha \subseteq \alpha;A_j$$
$$C_j \subseteq \alpha;A_j;\alpha^{-1}$$

The corresponding possibilities for defining weak commutativity for the pairs (AI, CI) and (AF, CF) follow by observing that one of these occurrences of α is reduced to the identity relation, after which the above schema applies. This results in the following definitions of simulation, each formulating a proof method in which the verification conditions have the form of inclusions between relations.

Definition 2.1 (Simulation) Let $\mathcal{A}$ and C be defined as above, and $\alpha \subseteq \Sigma^C \times \Sigma^A$. C *L-simulates* $\mathcal{A}$ w.r.t. α (denoted $C \sqsubseteq_\alpha^L \mathcal{A}$) iff

$$CI \subseteq AI;\alpha^{-1} \qquad \qquad (\text{init}^L)$$
$$\text{for all } j \in J: \quad \alpha^{-1};C_j \subseteq A_j;\alpha^{-1} \qquad \qquad (\text{op}_j^L)$$
$$\alpha^{-1};CF \subseteq AF \qquad \qquad (\text{final}^L)$$

C L^{-1}-*simulates* $\mathcal{A}$ w.r.t. α (denoted $C \sqsubseteq_\alpha^{L^{-1}} \mathcal{A}$) iff

$$CI;\alpha \subseteq AI \qquad \qquad (\text{init}^{L^{-1}})$$
$$\text{for all } j \in J: \quad C_j;\alpha \subseteq \alpha;A_j \qquad \qquad (\text{op}_j^{L^{-1}})$$
$$CF \subseteq \alpha;AF \qquad \qquad (\text{final}^{L^{-1}})$$

C *U-simulates* $\mathcal{A}$ w.r.t. α (denoted $C \sqsubseteq_\alpha^U \mathcal{A}$) iff

$$CI;\alpha \subseteq AI \qquad \qquad (\text{init}^U)$$
$$\text{for all } j \in J: \quad \alpha^{-1};C_j;\alpha \subseteq A_j \qquad \qquad (\text{op}_j^U)$$
$$\alpha^{-1};CF \subseteq AF \qquad \qquad (\text{final}^U)$$

C U^{-1}-*simulates* $\mathcal{A}$ w.r.t α (denoted $C \sqsubseteq_\alpha^{U^{-1}} \mathcal{A}$) iff

$$CI \subseteq AI;\alpha^{-1} \qquad \qquad (\text{init}^{U^{-1}})$$
$$\text{for all } j \in J: \quad C_j \subseteq \alpha;A_j;\alpha^{-1} \qquad \qquad (\text{op}_j^{U^{-1}})$$
$$CF \subseteq \alpha;AF \qquad \qquad (\text{final}^{U^{-1}})$$

L-simulation is also called *forward* or *downward* simulation. L^{-1}-simulation is also called *backward* or *upward* simulation [Jon91, HHS87].   ♣

Remark For those who are informed about the formalization of concurrency, it is important to realize that the operations interpreted above need not correspond to atomic, indivisible operations in some programming language. Within our framework, this marks the distinction between sequential and concurrent programming.   ◊

All four notions in the above definition are essentially different, i.e., for every notion of simulation there exist interpretations of A_j, C_j and α satisfying only that particular one. This is because in general α (like A_j and C_j) is a relation, and therefore not necessarily total or functional (see Def. 1.6). When α is both total and functional, these four notions coincide. Such results are studied in Chapter 4.

Def. 2.1 raises the following two questions.

(i) When do these notions of simulation imply the global criterion of data refinement? This question concerns the *soundness* of these methods.

(ii) Assuming that C is a data refinement of $\mathcal{A}$, can this fact always be proven using one or more of these notions of simulation? This question concerns the *completeness* of these methods.

These topics are discussed next.

2.2 Soundness and (In)completeness of Simulation

When facing new proof methods, the question of soundness and (relative) completeness of these methods rises. That is, are these methods sound? And do they cover all foreseeable cases?

First we prove soundness of the method of L-simulation w.r.t. proving data refinement. A full formal proof of this requires a formalization of our notion of programs, because data refinement is defined in terms of this notion. We present such a proof as well as soundness proofs for the other notions of simulation in Chapter 4. However, it is also the intention of this chapter to give a taste of the main issues discussed in this monograph. Therefore, in order to highlight the characteristic features of such proofs, by way of example an alternative soundness proof of L-simulation is given below (i.e., a proof that L-simulation implies data refinement) which is phrased in terms of the computation sequences these programs give rise to.

2.2.1 Soundness

Below we present a proof which is independent of the structure of programs, and which is based on induction on the length of sequences of pairs of corresponding operations considered when defining data refinement.

Lemma 2.2 (L-simulation implies data refinement) Let $\mathcal{A}$ and C be compatible data types and let α be an abstraction relation such that $C \sqsubseteq_\alpha^L \mathcal{A}$. Then C is a data refinement of $\mathcal{A}$.

Proof: Let $C \stackrel{\text{def}}{=} (CI, (C_j)_{j \in J}, CF)$ and $\mathcal{A} \stackrel{\text{def}}{=} (AI, (A_j)_{j \in J}, AF)$ be compatible data types such that C L-simulates $\mathcal{A}$ w.r.t. abstraction relation $\alpha \subseteq \Sigma^C \times \Sigma^A$. We have to show that for all pairs of programs $P(\mathcal{A}) \in \mathcal{P}(\mathcal{A})$ and $P(C) \in \mathcal{P}(C)$, with $P(C)$ obtained from $P(\mathcal{A})$ by replacing operations A_j by C_j for $j \in J$, the following inclusion holds:

$$CI\,; P(C)\,; CF \subseteq AI\,; P(\mathcal{A})\,; AF$$

Now let $P(\mathcal{A})$ and $P(C)$ be such a pair and consider an execution of $CI\,; P(C)\,;$ CF starting in $\sigma \in \Sigma^N$ and terminating in $\tau \in \Sigma^N$. Then there exist $\sigma^C, \tau^C \in \Sigma^C$ such that $(\sigma, \sigma^C) \in CI$, $(\sigma^C, \tau^C) \in P(C)$, and $(\tau^C, \tau) \in CF$.

Furthermore there exists an $n \geq 0$ and indices $j_1, \ldots, j_n \in J$ of operations such that $C_{j_1}\,; \ldots\,; C_{j_n}$ is a possible sequence of operations executed by $P(C)$ starting in initial state σ^C and terminating in final state τ^C. Hence there exist states $\sigma_0^C, \ldots, \sigma_n^C \in \Sigma^C$ such that $\sigma_0^C = \sigma^C$, $\sigma_n^C = \tau^C$, and $(\sigma_{i-1}^C, \sigma_i^C) \in C_{j_i}$ for $0 < i \leq n$.

Next we prove by induction on the length n of this sequence of operations that there exists a sequence $\sigma_0^A, \ldots, \sigma_n^A \in \Sigma^A$ such that $(\sigma, \sigma_0^A) \in AI$, $(\sigma_{i-1}^A, \sigma_i^A) \in A_{j_i}$ for $0 < i \leq n$, and $(\sigma_i^C, \sigma_i^A) \in \alpha$ for $0 \leq i \leq n$. Finally we prove that $(\sigma_n^A, \tau) \in AF$, thus also establishing that $(\sigma, \tau) \in AI\,; A_{j_1}\,; \ldots\,; A_{j_n}\,; AF$.

Induction base: Since (init^L) holds, there exists $\sigma_0^A \in \Sigma^A$ such that $(\sigma, \sigma_0^A) \in AI$ and $(\sigma_0^C, \sigma_0^A) \in \alpha$.

This provides us with $\sigma_0^A \in \Sigma^A$ such that $(\sigma_0^C, \sigma_0^A) \in \alpha$.

Induction step: Next, assuming that we already constructed $\sigma_0^A, \ldots, \sigma_k^A \in \Sigma^A$ such that $(\sigma, \sigma_k^A) \in AI\,; A_{j_1}\,; \ldots\,; A_{j_k}$ and $(\sigma_k^C, \sigma_k^A) \in \alpha$ for some $0 \leq k < n$, we can derive from condition $(\text{op}_{j_{k+1}}^L)$ that there exists $\sigma_{k+1}^A \in \Sigma^A$ such that $(\sigma_k^A, \sigma_{k+1}^A) \in A_{j_{k+1}}$ and $(\sigma_{k+1}^C, \sigma_{k+1}^A) \in \alpha$.

This provides us with $\sigma_{k+1}^A \in \Sigma^A$ such that $(\sigma, \sigma_{k+1}^A) \in AI\,; A_{j_1}\,; \ldots\,;$ $A_{j_{k+1}}$ and $(\sigma_{k+1}^C, \sigma_{k+1}^A) \in \alpha$.

Finally, the sequence $\sigma_0^C, \ldots, \sigma_n^C$ at the concrete level corresponds under α to the computation sequence $\sigma_0^A, \ldots, \sigma_n^A$ at the abstract level which we deter-

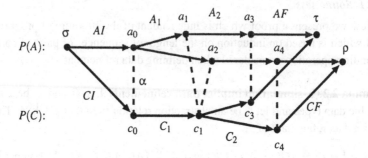

Fig. 2.3. Data refinement but not L-simulation.

mined above. We know already that $\sigma_n^C = \tau^C$ and $(\tau^C, \tau) \in CF$. Then, condition (final^L) ensures that $(\sigma_n^A, \tau) \in AF$. Hence, $(\sigma, \tau) \in AI; A_{j_1}; \ldots; A_{j_n}; AF$.

We conclude that $CI; P(C); CF \subseteq AI; P(\mathcal{A}); AF$.   □

2.2.2 Incompleteness of L-simulation

Is L-simulation complete? I.e., given that a data type is a data refinement of another one, as defined in Def. 1.8, can that result always be proven using L-simulation in the sense of Def. 2.1? The following example, inspired by Robin Milner, demonstrates that this is not always the case.

Example 2.3 Consider the following two compatible data types $\mathcal{A}$ and C with only two operations (index set $J = \{1, 2\}$).

$\mathcal{A} = (AI, (A_i)_{i \in \{1,2\}}, AF)$	$C = (CI, (C_i)_{i \in \{1,2\}}, CF)$
$AI = \{(\sigma, a_0)\}$	$CI = \{(\sigma, c_0)\}$
$A_1 = \{(a_0, a_1), (a_0, a_2)\}$	$C_1 = \{(c_0, c_1)\}$
$A_2 = \{(a_1, a_3), (a_2, a_4)\}$	$C_2 = \{(c_1, c_3), (c_1, c_4)\}$
$AF = \{(a_3, \tau), (a_4, \rho)\}$	$CF = \{(c_3, \tau), (c_4, \rho)\}$

The maximal — and most reasonable — program using C is, when enclosed in initialization and finalization, $CI; C_1; C_2; CF$. This denotes the relation $\{(\sigma, \tau), (\sigma, \rho)\}$ (see Figure 2.3). Also $AI; A_1; A_2; AF$ denotes $\{(\sigma, \tau), (\sigma, \rho)\}$; thus C refines $\mathcal{A}$ according to Def. 1.8. (A formal proof of this refinement can be given by an induction argument.)

There does not exist an L-simulation relation α between C and $\mathcal{A}$, however. Condition (init^L) implies that $(c_0, a_0) \in \alpha$; this together with (op$_1^L$) implies that

$(c_1, a_1) \in \alpha$ or $(c_1, a_2) \in \alpha$. Assume w.l.o.g. $(c_1, a_1) \in \alpha$; then, for (op$_2^L$) to hold, $(c_4, a_3) \in \alpha$. This leads to violation of condition (final^L) since it would imply $(a_3, \rho) \in \alpha^{-1}$; CF whereas $(a_3, \rho) \notin AF$. Hence L-simulation does not hold. ♡

So L-simulation is incomplete; it is possible, however, to make it complete by additionally taking L^{-1}-simulation into account. In the previous example L^{-1}-simulation suffices to prove the data refinement correct. That L^{-1}-simulation is also incomplete is worked out in Exercise 2.5.

As we shall see in Chapter 4.6, by the theorem of [HHS87] the fact that C is a data refinement of $\mathcal{A}$ implies that there exists an intermediate data type $\mathcal{B}$ and abstraction relations ρ and α such that $C \subseteq_\rho^L \mathcal{B}$ and $\mathcal{B} \subseteq_\alpha^{L^{-1}} \mathcal{A}$, as indicated in Figure 2.4. Abadi and Lamport obtained a similar result but in a different

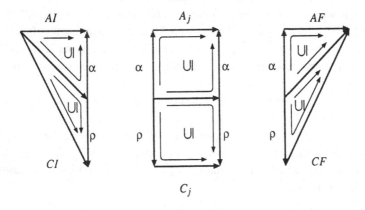

Fig. 2.4. Sketch of the completeness result using L- and L^{-1}-simulation.

setting using history variables, prophecy variables and functional abstraction relations [AL91] (see Section 14.1).

2.3 Data Invariants, Abstraction Relations, and Normal Variables

We show in Section 2.3.1 that situations in which the abstraction relation is neither total nor functional arise quite naturally.

Then we investigate in Section 2.3.2 the most commonly used notion of simulation, namely L-simulation, in more detail, slightly changing its characterization from the previous section in order to reduce the number of verification conditions required for checking that two data types L-simulate each other w.r.t. α, while preserving soundness of the method; this is done by formulating a condition which, if satisfied by the abstraction relation, renders checks for normal operations redundant.

After that we investigate in Section 2.4 what consequences this has for syntax-based proof methods (rather than semantics-based ones), and formulate within predicate logic an extra verification condition for value-returning operations (e.g., Boolean expressions used as tests) which are subject to data refinement. We illustrate that without this extra condition our method is unsound.

2.3.1 Relations vs. Functions

As remarked above, since α may be neither total nor functional, i.e., both partial and inherently nondeterministic, there are essentially four different ways to define weak commutativity of diagrams. Had α been functional and/or total then fewer differences would have resulted, the corresponding proof methods would have been simpler to apply, and, as we shall see for example in Part II of this monograph, fewer methods for establishing (data) refinement would have resulted.

To demonstrate that such restrictions on α are not always natural, we show in this section why general relations (i.e., relations which are neither total nor functional) are sometimes indispensable.[1] We also introduce the concept of *data (type) invariant* which allows us in principle to characterize the set of reachable states of a data type, and can therefore be used to identify a subspace on which α is total.

Example 2.4 (Total and functional abstraction relation) Let us reconsider representing sets by linear lists, but this time without the restriction from Example 1.4 concerning the absence of duplicates in such lists.

Recall that, given a nonempty set A of atoms, the set LL of linear lists over A is defined as the smallest set LL such that

- $\langle \, \rangle \in LL$, denoting the empty linear list,
- if $a \in A$ and $l \in LL$ then $append(a,l) \in LL$.

As before, we employ a sequence notation for linear lists to increase readability. The set $\{a,b\}$ can be represented by the linear list $\langle a,b \rangle$, but also by the linear list $\langle b,a \rangle$ or $\langle a,a,b \rangle$ and so on. Note that in this example the abstraction relation *elts* (introduced in Example 1.4) is both total and functional. $\heartsuit$

---

[1] In Part II a technique is presented due to Abadi and Lamport to "functionalize" relations by using so-called prophecy and history variables.

Non-functionality of abstraction relations arises easily. Example 2.5 below illustrates two ways of computing the average of a number of elements.

Example 2.5 (Non-functional abstraction relation) Nowadays, most scientific pocket calculators provide a function that computes the average of a nonempty bag (i.e., a multiset) of real numbers. To compute the average of a bag of numbers, one first enters these numbers one by one and then presses the button that starts the computation.

Before discussing how such a function is specified at an abstract level and implemented at a more concrete level, we define the abstract data type *bag*. Given a nonempty set of elements A, the set of bags over A is defined as the smallest set B such that

- $\emptyset_b \in B$, i.e. the empty bag $\emptyset_b$ belongs to B,
- if $b \in B$ and $a \in A$ then $b \oplus a \in B$,
- $b \oplus a \oplus a' = b \oplus a' \oplus a$ for $b \in B$ and $a, a' \in A$.

Moreover, since we do not identify $b \oplus a \oplus a$ and $b \oplus a$, elements may occur more than once inside a bag; they have a *multiplicity*. Consequently, bags are modelled by sets with multiple occurrences of (the same) elements, i.e., multisets. We let $\{a_1, \dots, a_k\}_b$ denote the bag containing the *occurrences* $a_1, \dots, a_k$ of its elements, that is, $\{a_1, \dots, a_k\}_b$ is a model for $\emptyset_b \oplus a_1 \oplus \dots \oplus a_k$. For later use we introduce the cardinality of, and the sum over, a bag: the value of $\#b$ is the number of occurrences of elements contained in b, e.g., $\#(\{a, a\}_b) = 2$, and the value of $\Sigma_b b$ is the sum of bag elements in b, e.g., $\Sigma_b\{5, 4, 3, 5\}_b = 17$. (Of course, the sum makes sense only in case the bag elements are from a type for which addition is defined.) We define these two functions inductively.

- $\#\emptyset_b \overset{\text{def}}{=} 0$ and $\#(b \oplus x) \overset{\text{def}}{=} \#b + 1$, and
- $\Sigma_b\emptyset_b \overset{\text{def}}{=} 0$ and $\Sigma_b(b \oplus x) \overset{\text{def}}{=} \Sigma_b b + x$.

Returning to our example, in pseudo-Pascal an algorithm for computing the average of a nonempty bag of real numbers might look like

```
begin
    var b : bag of Real;
    b := ∅_b;
    while input(x) do b := b ⊕ x od;
    if b ≠ ∅_b then av := mean(b) fi
end
```

where $input(x)$ is an operation which upon each invocation reads the next element from an external file, assigns its value to x, and returns true. If the end of this file is reached, the value *eof* is assigned to x and the value false is returned. The expression $mean(b)$ denotes the average of the occurrences of real numbers contained in the bag b if this bag is nonempty, and x and av are global variables of type Real. Thus, b is the only representation variable used in this algorithm, and x and av are its only normal variables, used for its specification. Note that b is properly initialized.

This abstract algorithm can be implemented as follows. At every entry of a number a variable called *sum* is increased by the value of this number and another variable, say *num*, is increased by 1. Initially these variables have value 0. Computing the average of a nonempty bag of numbers is now done by dividing *sum* by *num*. This results in the following refinement.

> **begin**
>   **var** *sum* : Real ; *num* : Integer;
>   *sum* := 0 ; *num* := 0;
>   **while** *input*(x) **do** *sum* := *sum* + x ; *num* := *num* + 1 **od**;
>   **if** *num* $\neq$ 0 **then** *av* := *sum*/*num* **fi**
> **end**

In this program, *sum* and *num* are the representation variables; x and av keep their rôles as normal variables. Note that also *sum* and *num* are properly initialized.

The following table lists the abstract bag operations against the concrete operations.

Abstract	Concrete
$b := \emptyset_b$	*sum* := 0 ; *num* := 0
$b := b \oplus x$	*sum* := *sum* + x ; *num* := *num* + 1
$b = \emptyset_b$	*num* = 0
$av := mean(b)$ (for $b \neq \emptyset_b$)	$av := sum/num$ (for $num \neq 0$)

Note that in the case of an empty bag, the implementation of the operation *mean* is not defined since *sum*/*num* is regarded as nonterminating (and hence produces no observable value). It is easy to see that the abstraction relation is not functional: take for example the abstract states ζ and ξ, such that $\zeta(b) = \{1,1\}_b$ and $\xi(b) = \{0,2\}_b$. Both abstract states have the same representation at the concrete level, viz., σ where $\sigma(sum) = 2$ and $\sigma(num) = 2$.

The corresponding abstraction relation α is defined by $(\sigma, \tau) \in \alpha$ iff

$$\sigma(av) = \tau(av) \wedge \sigma(x) = \tau(x) \wedge \Sigma_b(\tau(b)) = \sigma(sum) \wedge \#(\tau(b)) = \sigma(num) \ .$$

$\heartsuit$

The relation between abstract and concrete states can be non-functional in both directions. This happens especially when both levels feature implementation bias. Recall that a data type featuring implementation bias of its underlying model contains information which cannot be extracted using the operations of that data type. If two such data types refine each other, their abstraction relation is in general non-functional in both directions, as illustrated in Example 2.6.

Example 2.6 Suppose we represent a stack of integers with depth at most *max* by an array $St : \textbf{array}[1 .. max]$ **of** Integer and an integer p such that the segment $St[1 .. p]$ contains the current contents of the stack and $St(p)$ is the top of the stack at any moment.

Now suppose that, for reasons of efficiency, we also want to keep track of the number of pushes and the number of pops and therefore decide to use instead another stack St' and two integers m for the number of pushes and n for the number of pops.

Now, there does not exist a functional abstraction relation from (St', m, n) to (St, p) or, in the other direction, from (St, p) to (St', m, n). The reason for this is that on the one hand we cannot retrieve the number of pushes and pops from p or the contents of St, but only their difference $m - n$. On the other hand, it is not possible to reconstruct the contents of the segment $St[p + 1 .. max]$ from the number of pushes and pops. Both these implementations feature implementation bias.   ♡

On a given level of abstraction nondeterminism also arises easily. Example: sorting pairs of numbers by their first component with no ordering imposed on their second component in case the two first components are equal. Then a concrete operation can be less nondeterministic than the corresponding abstract operation, e.g., by sorting pairs with equal first component according to their second component (a case of refinement).

Another complication arises when some states of the abstract and concrete state spaces are not reachable. This is especially relevant for VDM, which deals with preserving total correctness. VDM is discussed below in Section 2.4.2 and in Chapter 12. One of VDM's verification conditions, called *adequacy*, requires that for every state at the abstract level there exists a corresponding representation at the concrete level. Here, reachable states are defined relative to a particular precondition imposed on the initial state of a program and a given finite set of operations under consideration; sometimes these are left implicit, as illustrated in Example 2.7. Obviously, imposing adequacy upon unreachable states is not required for obtaining a sound proof method.

To characterize the subspace of reachable states, the concept of data type invariant is introduced. Since an abstraction relation only needs to be defined on this subspace, such a characterization eliminates one possible cause preventing abstraction relations from being total. A typical way of using a data invariant is described in Example 2.7 below, which is taken from [J90]. Technically, this discussion is resumed in Section 4.3.

Example 2.7 (Data invariant) Consider the abstract type *Datec* which is used to represent dates in our calendar:

$$Datec = Day \times Year$$
$$Day = [1..366]$$
$$Year = [1583..2599]$$

Although the field *Day* is restricted so that, for instance, 399 cannot be a value, it is still possible that (366, 1989) is a date. To rule out such impossible dates we add a data invariant *DI*:

$$DI(d,y) \stackrel{\text{def}}{=} \textit{leap-year}(y) \vee d \leq 365$$

Assuming that *leap-year* is defined, this gives the set of dates

$$\{ (d,y) \mid d \in [1..366] \wedge y \in [1583..2599] \wedge DI(d,y) \} \ . \qquad \heartsuit$$

The relation between concrete and abstract states is in general determined by a *representation invariant*. A representation invariant consists of two parts: a data invariant of the concrete data type and an abstraction relation between concrete and abstract data, cf. [Hoa72]. In VDM the distinction between data invariant and abstraction relation is essential because, as observed above, one of its verification conditions requires mapping reachable states on the abstract level to reachable states on the concrete level. Reynolds' method is based on the (less discriminating) notion of representation invariant. Reynolds' method is the topic of Section 2.4.1 below and Chapter 11.

2.3.2 Abstraction Relations and Normal Variables

Next, how shall we prove data refinement in these examples?

Recall that for reasons of type consistency when defining data refinement, a data type $\mathcal{A}$ is monolithic in that it is not restricted to operations involving its representation variables $\vec{a}$ — called *represented* operations — but also involves *normal* operations which purely concern its normal variables $\vec{x}$. Although this is a necessary consequence of the relational theory developed by Hoare, He and their colleagues [HHS87, HH90] which is presented here, at least there should be no need to check verification conditions for these normal operations when proving data refinement, i.e., weak commutativity of diagrams for normal operations should hold immediately, without the need to impose additional verification conditions.

Now in a purely semantic set-up, the distinction between normal and represented operations cannot be made, for the simple reason that the only distinction that can be made here is between operations that possibly change the value of a variable and those that do not, and this distinction is unrelated to whether particular variables occur in those operations. E.g., $x := x$ and $a := a$ may both denote $id_{\Sigma A}$. Consequently it is impossible to deduce from their meaning whether x or a was involved. Therefore, the former distinction can only be based upon the syntactic representation of an operation by examining its free variables. This encourages us to emphasize in this monograph a style of presentation in which syntax and semantics of terms and operations are separated. Thus, we assume below that such a distinction between normal and represented operations has already been given.

Incorporating this distinction into our notion of data refinement requires a further analysis of our notion of abstraction relation. This analysis is consistent with the way abstraction relations are formulated in, e.g., Reynolds' method, VDM, or Z (which will be discussed in Section 13.1). In these methods, abstraction relations merely describe a relation between the representation variables $\vec{c}$ at the concrete level and $\vec{a}$ at the abstract level, and do not involve normal variables. This is because these formalisms are geared towards practice, and are, therefore, syntax-based. Primarily, their aim is to formalize data refinement, and this is a concept which is independent of the particular program under consideration.

We mention that VDM and Reynolds' method are slightly different in this respect, in that in VDM only represented operations are considered, thus disregarding normal operations, whereas Reynolds introduces data refinement in the setting of a single program in which, therefore, normal operations may occur. This may be due to the fact that he does not consider the concept of data refinement formally, and therefore leaves it to us to guess exactly what he has in mind. Yet he does define his representation invariants with only representation variables as free variables, and this allows us to deduce that data refinement is indeed intended.

Anyhow, the assumption seems to be correct that these methods do not address normal operations explicitly in the part of their theory that deals with data refinement. However, soundness of these methods is self-evidently based on their semantics, and that is where normal operations do come in. For data refinement is a semantic concept which is formulated in terms of all possible programs using a given pair of data types, and such programs use normal operations — indeed, our very notion of data type includes them.

As we shall see, it takes some effort to reconcile these two points of view — the syntactic, predicate-logic-based, methods for data refinement of Reynolds and VDM, and the semantics-based ones of Hoare, He, and their colleagues. In fact, reconciling their differences calls for the introduction of a new verification condition (or, alternatively, a reformulation of previously introduced verification conditions) for which it is not immediately evident that it implies soundness of these syntax-based methods. Therefore a soundness proof is called for, and this is given for each of these methods in Part II of this monograph.

To throw some light on the common nature of such syntax-based methods, we investigate what syntactic proof obligations are sufficient to ensure that the semantics of a pair of corresponding (concrete and abstract) operations and an abstraction relation fulfill the requirement for L-simulation. Now, the gist of both Reynolds' method and VDM's verification conditions for data refinement is, as we shall see, a formula which expresses syntactically that these corresponding operations preserve the abstraction relation. Therefore we consider the case of proving invariance under α of a normal operation whose semantic representation consists of a pair of operations (op_C, op_A), where α is formulated syntactically by means of a term of first order predicate logic containing only representation variables as its free variables. Notice that this marks another difference from Hoare's notion of data refinement. Whereas the latter is formulated in a relational setting, Reynolds' method and VDM are based on predicate calculus.

So, given that α has been established (initially), and given that the next operation at both levels is a normal operation, say $x := x + 1$ with x a normal variable, it seems obvious that such an α is preserved under this pair, because α only involves the representation variables. Thus, for such α, only represented operations generate proof obligations. Of course, this observation needs to be substantiated by proof. Therefore we state below which properties must be satisfied by α and the interpretations of normal operations in order for L-simulation to be satisfied, and then prove this statement.

In the relational set-up, the semantics α of an abstraction relation is contained in $\Sigma^C \times \Sigma^A$, i.e., in principle the values of the normal variables at the different levels may have an impact on whether α holds or not. As explained above, this is not our intention.

Therefore, we define α semantically relative to a given relation $\tilde{\alpha} \subseteq \Sigma_C \times \Sigma_A$ between representation variables only, by

$$\alpha \stackrel{\text{def}}{=} \left\{ \, ((\sigma, \sigma_C), (\sigma, \sigma_A)) \in \Sigma^C \times \Sigma^A \mid (\sigma_C, \sigma_A) \in \tilde{\alpha} \, \right\} . \qquad (2.1)$$

For abstraction relations α which satisfy this restriction, the following property holds, for arbitrary $\sigma, \tau, \in \Sigma^N$, $\sigma_C \in \Sigma_C$, and $\sigma_A \in \Sigma_A$:

$$((\sigma, \sigma_C), (\sigma, \sigma_A)) \in \alpha \Rightarrow ((\tau, \sigma_C), (\tau, \sigma_A)) \in \alpha \ . \tag{2.2}$$

This means that whether a pair consisting of a concrete and an abstract state is contained in α does not depend on the values of normal variables at the two levels, as long as these values are the same.

Since normal operations change at most normal variables, this restriction implies that whether α holds after a normal operation depends only on whether α holds prior to that operation and not on its impact on normal variables.

Formally, such a pair (op_C, op_A) defining the semantics of a normal operation at the concrete and the abstract level is always based on a given relation $op \subseteq \Sigma^N \times \Sigma^N$ between states of normal variables:

$$
\begin{aligned}
op_C &\overset{\text{def}}{=} \left\{ ((\sigma, \sigma_C), (\tau, \sigma_C)) \in \Sigma^C \times \Sigma^C \mid (\sigma, \tau) \in op \right\} \\
op_A &\overset{\text{def}}{=} \left\{ ((\sigma, \sigma_A), (\tau, \sigma_A)) \in \Sigma^A \times \Sigma^A \mid (\sigma, \tau) \in op \right\}
\end{aligned}
\tag{2.3}
$$

This implies that op_C and op_A have the same impact on normal variables and neither of them influences representation variables.

For pairs (op_C, op_A) which satisfy this restriction, the following property holds, for arbitrary $\sigma, \tau, \in \Sigma^N$, $\sigma_C \in \Sigma_C$, and $\sigma_A \in \Sigma_A$:

$$((\sigma, \sigma_C), (\tau, \sigma_C)) \in op_C \Rightarrow ((\sigma, \sigma_A), (\tau, \sigma_A)) \in op_A \ . \tag{2.4}$$

We now show that under the above conditions the verification condition for L-simulation is satisfied.

Lemma 2.8 The L-simulation condition for pairs of corresponding normal operations (op_C, op_A) is satisfied if (2.1) and (2.3) are satisfied:

$$\alpha^{-1} ; op_C \subseteq op_A ; \alpha^{-1} \tag{2.5}$$

Proof: Let $\sigma, \tau \in \Sigma^N$, $\sigma_A \in \Sigma_A$, and $\sigma_C \in \Sigma_C$. Then

$$
\begin{aligned}
&((\sigma, \sigma_A), (\tau, \sigma_C)) \in \alpha^{-1} ; op_C \\
\Rightarrow &((\sigma, \sigma_C), (\sigma, \sigma_A)) \in \alpha \wedge ((\sigma, \sigma_C), (\tau, \sigma_C)) \in op_C && \text{Def. 1.7, (2.1), (2.3)} \\
\Rightarrow &((\tau, \sigma_C), (\tau, \sigma_A)) \in \alpha \wedge ((\sigma, \sigma_A), (\tau, \sigma_A)) \in op_A && \text{(2.2) and (2.4)} \\
\Rightarrow &((\sigma, \sigma_A), (\tau, \sigma_C)) \in op_A ; \alpha^{-1} && \text{Def. 1.7} \qquad \square
\end{aligned}
$$

The same holds for the other forms of simulation; this is left as an exercise.

2.4 Towards a Syntactic Characterization of Simulation using Predicate Logic

In this section we investigate what consequences restriction (2.1) on the semantics of abstraction relations has for the formulation of verification conditions for syntax-based methods. Having thus determined which verification conditions to impose, we can give a syntax-based data refinement proof for Example 2.5 which is based on predicate logic.

In the following example we further investigate the rôle of normal variables when characterizing abstraction relations using predicate logic.

Example 2.9 Reconsider Example 1.4, in which sets are represented by linear lists. The representation variable on the concrete level is l, on the abstract level U, and the normal variable is x. The abstraction relation α is induced by the predicate $elts(l) = U$, and defined by

$$\tilde{\alpha} \stackrel{\text{def}}{=} \{ (\sigma_C, \sigma_A) \in \Sigma_C \times \Sigma_A \mid elts(\sigma_C(l)) = \sigma_A(U) \} \text{ , hence}$$

$$\alpha \stackrel{\text{def}}{=} \{ (\sigma^C, \sigma^A) \in \Sigma^C \times \Sigma^A \mid elts(\sigma^C(l)) = \sigma^A(U) \wedge \sigma^C(x) = \sigma^A(x) \} .$$

Now $AI \stackrel{\text{def}}{=} \textbf{var } U : Set ; U := \emptyset$ and $CI \stackrel{\text{def}}{=} \textbf{var } l : LL ; l := \langle \rangle$ in Pascal-like notation.

Since $elts(\langle \rangle) = \emptyset$, α is established after executing CI and AI.

Consider as the next pair of operations $(l := append(x,l), U := U \cup \{x\})$. Does this pair preserve α, and why?

Semantically, we have to check that, provided

$$elts(\sigma^C(l)) = \sigma^A(U) \wedge \sigma^C(x) = \sigma^A(x)$$

holds before executing this pair, after its execution

$$elts(append(\sigma^C(x), \sigma^C(l))) = (\sigma^A(U) \cup \{\sigma^A(x)\}) \wedge \sigma^C(x) = \sigma^A(x) ,$$

i.e., $\{\sigma^C(x)\} \cup elts(\sigma^C(l)) = \sigma^A(U) \cup \{\sigma^A(x)\}$ holds, which follows from the definition[2] of $elts$ and the assumption. Note that we did indeed have to use that $\sigma^C(x) = \sigma^A(x)$.

The latter is not necessary in a syntactic set-up (provided one is sufficiently careful, as will be explained in the next example). For then one only has to check that the following predicate holds:

$$elts(l) = U \Rightarrow elts(append(x,l)) = U \cup \{x\}.$$

---

[2] By overloading the notation, we use $elts$ both for expressing this operation syntactically and semantically, whenever the context determines which usage is meant.

Observe that now no distinction is made between x occurring on the concrete and on the abstract level — it is just the same variable, with the same value, in this setting. ♡

Conclusion of Example 2.9 This example illustrates the difference between the rôle of normal variables in the semantic and syntactic versions of an abstraction relation. In its semantic version their interpretation at both levels of abstraction should be mentioned explicitly, whereas in its syntactic version one wishes to suppress this distinction.

As we shall see below, the latter leads to problems when dealing with value-returning operations within our formalism. The logically inclined reader will object that these problems are a pure artifact of our approach and that they can be easily done away with by introducing for each normal variable x two versions, x^A and x^C, and replacing α by $\alpha \wedge \forall x \in \vec{x} \left(x^A = x^C \right)$, where x^A is evaluated in a state pair (σ^C, σ^A) by $\sigma^A(x)$, x^C by $\sigma^C(x)$, and the $\forall$-quantifier ranges over (the finite set of) normal variables $\vec{x}$ used in the data type in question.

However, since in our monograph we compare amongst others the refinement methods due to Jones and to Reynolds, we have to stick to their conventions when discussing these methods. And, as said before, one of these is that in their set-up normal variables do not occur freely within the expressions they use for abstraction relations, because of their aim of characterizing data refinement in a way which is independent of the particular program under consideration.

Example 2.10 (Value-returning operations) Consider the following pathological example. Represent a linear-list-valued variable l_1 at the abstract level by another such variable l_2 at the concrete level. The predicate characterizing the abstraction relation α is (syntactically expressed by) $l_1 = l_2$. The operation $x := first(l_1)$ at the abstract level is refined by $x := last(l_2)$ at the concrete level, where x is a normal variable. Assume that $l_1 = \langle 1, 2 \rangle$ and that $l_1 = l_2$ holds. Then, since both operations preserve the representation variables at their respective levels, $l_1 = l_2$ still holds after execution of these operations, yet the values of x on these levels are different. Executing $l_1 := append(x, l_1)$ and $l_2 := cons(x, l_2)$ as the next operation at, respectively, the abstract and concrete level, results in $l_1 = \langle 1, 1, 2 \rangle \neq \langle 2, 1, 2 \rangle = l_2$, i.e., $l_1 = l_2$ does not hold anymore. However, keep in mind that this difference is caused by execution of the first pair of operations, and that the restriction that normal variable x should not occur freely in our abstraction relation does not allow us to measure this difference immediately after execution of the first pair by checking that $l_1 = l_2$ is preserved.

Now the problem with a (hypothetical) simple-minded syntax-oriented set-up based on predicate logic might be that this inequality is not discovered when checking locally whether our two pairs of operations preserve $l_1 = l_2$. In order to check that the first pair of operations $(x := first(l_1), x := last(l_2))$ preserves $l_1 = l_2$, one might generate the verification condition

$$\models l_1 = l_2 \Rightarrow l_1[^{first(l_1)}/_x] = l_2[^{last(l_2)}/_x]$$

where $e_1[^{e_2}/_x]$ denotes the result of substituting expression e_2 for the free occurrences of x inside expression e_1. Since x does not occur in l_1 or l_2 this results in verifying

$$\models l_1 = l_2 \Rightarrow l_1 = l_2$$

which obviously holds. Analogously, checking that the second pair of operations $(l_1 := append(x, l_1), l_2 := append(x, l_2))$ preserves $l_1 = l_2$ generates the verification condition

$$\models l_1 = l_2 \Rightarrow append(x, l_1) = append(x, l_2) \ ,$$

which, again, obviously holds. This is because, by the very definition of validity of a predicate logic formula (this is what $\models$ means), occurrences of normal variables on the higher level, e.g., the one in $append(x, l_1)$, are given the same interpretation as such occurrences on the lower level, e.g., the one in $append(x, l_2)$, since we did not express the distinction between these occurrences. States such as σ above do not model our situation, in which there may be a possible distinction between the values of a variable x on the higher and lower level, since we did not introduce different symbols, such as, e.g., x^A and x^C, for them. Consequently, such a simple-minded set-up is unsound.

Yet, when we check for L-simulation, this distinction is discovered. In Chapter 5 we will introduce semantics functions $\mathcal{A}[\![.]\!]$ and $\mathcal{P}[\![.]\!]$ which assign meanings in terms of binary relations on states to syntactic representations of abstraction relations (e.g., $l_1 = l_2$) and operations (e.g., $x := first(l_1)$), respectively. In this example $\Sigma = [\{x\} \longrightarrow \mathbb{V}]$, $\Sigma_A = [\{l_1\} \longrightarrow LL]$, and $\Sigma_C = [\{l_2\} \longrightarrow LL]$, hence $\mathcal{A}[\![l_1 = l_2]\!] \subseteq \Sigma^C \times \Sigma^A$, $\mathcal{P}[\![x := first(l_1)]\!] \subseteq \Sigma^A \times \Sigma^A$, and $\mathcal{P}[\![x := last(l_2)]\!] \subseteq \Sigma^C \times \Sigma^C$. In Chapter 5 these semantics functions are defined in detail such that the following holds.

$$\mathcal{A}[\![l_1 = l_2]\!] = \left\{ (\sigma^C, \sigma^A) \in \Sigma^C \times \Sigma^A \ \middle| \ \begin{array}{l} \sigma^C(l_2) = \sigma^A(l_1) \\ \wedge \sigma^C(x) = \sigma^A(x) \end{array} \right\}$$

$$\mathcal{P}[\![x := first(l_1)]\!] = \left\{ (\sigma^A, \tau^A) \in \Sigma^A \times \Sigma^A \;\middle|\; \begin{array}{l} \sigma^A(l_1) = \tau^A(l_1) \\ \wedge\, \tau^A(x) = first(\sigma^A(l_1)) \end{array} \right\}$$

$$\mathcal{P}[\![x := last(l_2)]\!] = \left\{ (\sigma^C, \tau^C) \in \Sigma^C \times \Sigma^C \;\middle|\; \begin{array}{l} \sigma^C(l_2) = \tau^C(l_2) \\ \wedge\, \tau^C(x) = last(\sigma^C(l_2)) \end{array} \right\}$$

With these definitions we can now check whether, e.g., L-simulation holds, i.e., whether the following inclusion is valid:

$$\mathcal{A}[\![l_1 = l_2]\!]^{-1} \,;\, \mathcal{P}[\![x := last(l_2)]\!] \subseteq \mathcal{P}[\![x := first(l_1)]\!] \,;\, \mathcal{A}[\![l_1 = l_2]\!]^{-1}$$

This is equivalent to

$$\forall \sigma^A \in \Sigma^A, \tau^C \in \Sigma^C \left(\begin{array}{l} (\sigma^A, \tau^C) \in \mathcal{A}[\![l_1 = l_2]\!]^{-1} \,;\, \mathcal{P}[\![x := last(l_2)]\!] \\ \Rightarrow (\sigma^A, \tau^C) \in \mathcal{P}[\![x := first(l_1)]\!] \,;\, \mathcal{A}[\![l_1 = l_2]\!]^{-1} \end{array} \right)$$

This can be reformulated by using Def. 1.6 to the condition: For all σ^A and τ^C the implication

$$\exists \sigma^C \in \Sigma^C \left((\sigma^C, \sigma^A) \in \mathcal{A}[\![l_1 = l_2]\!] \wedge (\sigma^C, \tau^C) \in \mathcal{P}[\![x := last(l_2)]\!] \right)$$
$$\Rightarrow \exists \tau^A \in \Sigma^A \left((\tau^C, \tau^A) \in \mathcal{A}[\![l_1 = l_2]\!] \wedge (\sigma^A, \tau^A) \in \mathcal{P}[\![x := first(l_1)]\!] \right)$$

holds. Let us check whether this implication holds for $\sigma^A(l_1) = \sigma^C(l_2) = \tau^C(l_2) = \langle 1, 2 \rangle$ and $\sigma^A(x) = \sigma^C(x) = \tau^C(x) = 2$.

The LHS of the implication is fulfilled but the RHS is not, since the first conjunct of the RHS implies $\tau^A(x) = 2$ whereas the second implies $\tau^A(x) = 1$; consequently, there does not exist such a τ^A. We conclude that L-simulation does not hold for this pair of operations w.r.t. abstraction relation $\mathcal{A}[\![l_1 = l_2]\!]$. Nor should it, for by Lemma 2.2 L-simulation is sound. Similarly, none of the other three simulations holds in this case.

When reasoning about data refinement one does not want to go back each time to the semantics of operations and abstraction relations to preclude such inconsistencies and check for L-simulation. Therefore, one has to strengthen one's syntactic proof obligations such that they are consistent with their semantic counterparts, even for value-returning operations. That is, we face the question how to formulate a proof method for data refinement which is based on predicate logic and which is sound. In VDM as well as in Reynolds' method this is done by introducing additional verification conditions for value-returning operations, resulting in a method which can be proven to imply L-simulation (the proofs are given in Part II) and which is therefore sound by Lemma 2.2.

The literature suggests at least two different, yet equivalent, solutions to this problem:

(i) In Reynolds' method one adds an extra verification condition in the spirit of:

$$\left.\begin{array}{l}\text{Any value-returned at the lower level can also be returned}\\ \text{at the higher level, assuming that the abstraction relation}\\ \text{holds before computing these values.}\end{array}\right\} \quad (2.6)$$

In our example above, this amounts to proving

$$\models (l_1 = l_2) \Rightarrow (l_1 = l_2 \wedge last(l_2) = first(l_1)) \ ,$$

which obviously fails.

(ii) Alternatively, and this corresponds to the solution to similar problems in VDM, one adds an extra (normal) variable to record and compare the two return values, and then checks them for consistency, as expressed by the extra verification condition in Reynolds' method. In our example, this would result in

$$\models (l_1 = l_2 \wedge r = last(l_2)) \Rightarrow (l_1 = l_2 \wedge r = first(l_1)) \ ,$$

which is also false.   ♡

Conclusion of Example 2.10 When value-returning operations occur within represented operations in assignments to normal variables, the restriction that α should not contain normal variables freely has the consequence that the verification conditions for checking preservation of α must be strengthened in order to be sound.

Tests are also value-returning operations. They are Boolean expressions, and if they involve representation variables they are subject to data refinement, such as the pairs $(U = \emptyset, l = \langle \rangle)$ and $(b = \emptyset_b, num = 0)$ in the previous examples. Consequently, when proving simulation they are also subject to the extra verification condition (2.6).

Observe that we have applied the way VDM models value-returning operations already in Example 1.4 to $x := pick(U)$ and in Example 2.5 to $av := mean(b)$. Indeed, adding an extra normal variable to record the result of a value-returning operation is a general scheme for modelling such operations within a context of binary relations. Observe that the formulation of the extra verification condition added above to Reynolds' method (and to VDM) also takes care of the case of a nondeterministic value-returning operation on the abstract level, such as $pick(U)$, which is simulated by a less nondeterministic value-returning operation on the concrete level, such as $first(l) ; l := rest(l)$ (see Exercise 2.10).

We now return to the question posed before, how to prove data refinement using predicate logic in Examples 2.5 and 2.6. A proof of the former is given below, whereas a proof of the latter constitutes an exercise.

Example 2.11 (Proving data refinement in Example 2.5) Recall Example 2.5. Data refinement is proved using the syntax-based method discussed above, based on proving invariance of the representation invariant. In this example the representation invariant immediately corresponds to the abstraction relation because the data invariant at the concrete level, $num = 0 \Rightarrow sum = 0$, follows from the abstraction relation. On the other hand we do not care about data invariants during data refinement proofs; data invariants should be proven invariant under all operations beforehand. We therefore prove only preservation of the (characterization in predicate logic of the) abstraction relation.

The required abstraction relation is expressed syntactically by

$$\alpha((sum, num), b) \stackrel{\text{def}}{=} \Sigma_b b = sum \land \#b = num$$

Since this example contains several value-returning operations involving the data types, namely the pairs $(mean(b), sum/num)$ and $(b = \emptyset_b, num = 0)$, we have to check verification condition (2.6) for them.

Syntactically, the proof runs as follows. First we check that *CI* and *AI* establish α. This follows from taking as *CI* the operation **var** sum : Real ; num : Integer ; $sum := 0$; $num := 0$, as *AI* the operation **var** b : **bag of** Real ; $b := \emptyset_b$, and checking that $\alpha((0,0), \emptyset_b)$ holds, which is trivial.

Secondly, we check invariance of α under operation $b := b \oplus x$ at the abstract level, and operation $sum := sum + x$; $num := num + 1$ at the concrete level, which amounts to proving the implication

$$\alpha((sum, num), b) \Rightarrow \alpha((sum + x, num + 1), b \oplus x)$$

This follows from

$$\Sigma_b b = sum \land \#b = num$$
$$\Rightarrow \Sigma_b b + x = sum + x \land \#b + 1 = num + 1$$
$$\Rightarrow \Sigma_b (b \oplus x) = sum + x \land \#(b \oplus x) = num + 1$$

Thirdly, we check for the value-returning pair of operations $(num = 0, b = \emptyset_b)$ that it satisfies the extra verification condition (2.6):

$$\alpha((sum, num), b) \Rightarrow (b = \emptyset_b \Leftrightarrow num = 0) \ .$$

Finally, we check verification condition (2.6) for the pair of operations $(av := sum/num, av := mean(b))$, provided $num \neq 0$ and $b \neq \emptyset_b$ (which are equivalent under α, as observed above). By defining $mean(b) \stackrel{\text{def}}{=} \Sigma_b b/\#b$, one obtains validity of $(num \neq 0 \wedge b \neq \emptyset_b) \Rightarrow (\alpha((sum, num), b) \Rightarrow sum/num = mean(b))$. Notice that in case $num = 0 \wedge b = \emptyset_b$ both value-returning operations are undefined. $\heartsuit$

2.4.1 A First Encounter with Reynolds' Method

Based on this first analysis of the verification conditions required for establishing refinement of nondeterministic operations, the following informal method is suggested, which is taken from Reynolds [Rey81, p. 311].

R1 One or more concrete variables are introduced to store the representation of one or more abstract variables.

R2 A general invariant called the *representation invariant* is introduced, which describes the relationship between the abstract and concrete variables.

R3 Each assignment to an abstract variable (or more generally, each assignment that affects the representation invariant) is augmented with assignments to the concrete variables that reestablish the representation invariant (or achieve it, in case of an initialization).

R4 Each expression that contains an abstract variable but occurs outside of an assignment to an abstract variable is replaced by an expression that does not contain abstract variables but is guaranteed by the representation invariant to have the same value.

The last step will render the abstract variables auxiliary, so that their declarations and assignments can be eliminated.

Note Observe that there is no verification condition for the finalization operation since, syntactically, this can only be a block ending command (**end**) and the verification conditions for the initialization and other represented operations ensure that normal variables have the same values at both levels when reaching a block ending. $\Diamond$

Example 2.12 Recall Example 1.1. We started out with the following program using a representation variable U ranging over finite sets of natural numbers.

> **begin**
>   **var** $U : set\ of\ \mathbb{N}; U := \emptyset;$
> $S_1;$
> $U := U \cup \{x\};$
> $S_2;$

  $y := a\ member\ of\ U$
  end

In step R1 of Reynolds' method we introduce the concrete level representation variable l ranging over linear lists of natural numbers.

  begin
  var U : *set of* $\mathbb{N}$; l : *sequence of* $\mathbb{N}$;
  $U := \emptyset$;
  S_1;
  $U := U \cup \{x\}$;
  S_2;
  $y := a\ member\ of\ U$
  end

Next we introduce a representation invariant according to step R2.

  begin
  var U : *set of* $\mathbb{N}$; l : *sequence of* $\mathbb{N}$;
  $\{\textbf{geninv}\ I :\ U = elts(l)\}$
  $U := \emptyset$;
  S_1;
  $U := U \cup \{x\}$;
  S_2;
  $y := a\ member\ of\ U$
  end

In this example step R3 amounts to adding two assignments.

  begin
  var U : *set of* $\mathbb{N}$; l : *sequence of* $\mathbb{N}$;
  $\{\textbf{geninv}\ I :\ U = elts(l)\}$
  $U := \emptyset$; $l := \langle\ \rangle$;
  S_1;
  $U := U \cup \{x\}$; $l := append(x, l)$;
  S_2;
  $y := a\ member\ of\ U$
  end

Moreover, we have to prove that the representation invariant is established by the first pair and preserved by the second. In Chapter 5 we introduce all the machinery for proving such obligations formally. In this case these proof obligations are not too hard. The first, $elts(\langle\ \rangle) = \emptyset$, and the second,

$U = elts(l) \Rightarrow U \cup \{x\} = elts(append(x,l))$, follow immediately from the two clauses of the inductive definition of *elts* given in Example 1.4.

In step R4 of Reynolds' method the expression *a member of U* will be replaced by an expression not referring to U but having the same value whenever the representation invariant holds. This is problematic, because how should we prophesy which of the elements of U is returned by a call of this presumably nondeterministic operation? The solution here is to interpret step R4 more liberally so that we are satisfied with, for instance, both *first*(l) and *last*(l) as replacement for *a member of U*. For both return a value that is a member of U if the representation invariant holds.

Thus step R4 leads to the following transformation of our original program:

> **begin**
>   **var** U : *set of* $\mathbb{N}$; l : *sequence of* $\mathbb{N}$;
> $\{$**geninv** l : $U = elts(l)\}$
> $U := \emptyset; l := \langle\,\rangle;$
> $S_1;$
> $U := U \cup \{x\}; l := append(x,l);$
> $S_2;$
> $y := first(l)$
> **end**

Now U no longer has any influence on the normal variables (and l); hence we can safely remove it from the program. We arrive at the RHS of Example 1.1.

> **begin**
>   **var** l : *sequence of* $\mathbb{N}$;
> $l := \langle\,\rangle;$
> $S_1;$
> $l := append(x,l);$
> $S_2;$
> $y := first(l)$
> **end**

$\heartsuit$

Once we have developed our technical machinery, we shall argue in Chapter 11 that all applications of Reynolds' method are cases of L-simulation, though we sometimes have to resort to a total correctness interpretation to support this claim.

2.4.2 A First Encounter with VDM

We treat the sets-and-lists example from above in another syntax-based method, called VDM [J90, BFL$^+$94], to illustrate the different flavor of these methods. This acronym stands for the *Vienna Development Method* which emerged from research that started out at the IBM laboratory in Vienna (for instance by Hans Bekić, Dines Bjørner, Cliff B. Jones and Peter Lucas). Chapter 12 treats VDM in more detail.

Example 2.13 We formalize our example using VDM. First the state variables are declared for the abstract and concrete versions of our example. As with the other components yet to come, we place the abstract and concrete versions side by side, the former on the LHS and the latter on the RHS.

$$U : \text{set of } \mathbb{N} \qquad\qquad l : \mathbb{N}^*$$

Then their initial values are fixed.

$$U_0 = \emptyset \qquad\qquad l_0 = []$$

The operations for the two levels are specified next, beginning with the operations assigning to representation variables.

$$ADDa\ (x : \mathbb{N}) \qquad\qquad ADDc\ (x : \mathbb{N})$$
$$\text{ext wr } U : \text{set of } \mathbb{N} \qquad\qquad \text{ext wr } l : \mathbb{N}^*$$
$$\text{post } U = \overleftarrow{U} \cup \{x\} \qquad\qquad \text{post } l = \overleftarrow{l} \frown [x]$$

The keyword ext announces that an external variable is assumed to occur in the context of the operation. External variables are called external because they are the variables an operation has access to, that are not local to the operation concerned; they may be normal or, as in our example, representation variables. In the two cases above, the value of this external variable can be changed inside the operation; this is indicated by the keyword wr. The keyword post introduces the postcondition of an operation. Within such a postcondition the value of a read–write accessible external variable (like the ones above) before invoking the operation is referred to by placing a hook $\overleftarrow{}$ over the variable's name. The unhooked occurrences refer to the state after invocation of the operation. Returning to the example, we finally introduce the value-returning operations at both levels:

$$GETa\ ()y : \mathbb{N} \qquad\qquad GETc\ ()y : \mathbb{N}$$
$$\text{ext rd } U : \text{set of } \mathbb{N} \qquad\qquad \text{ext rd } l : \mathbb{N}^*$$

pre $U \neq \emptyset$ pre $\text{len}(l) > 0$

post $y \in U$ post $y = \text{first}(l)$

These operations have only read access to their respective external variables, as indicated by the keyword rd. The keyword pre precedes a predicate characterizing the intended initial states of an operation.

Look for instance at *GETc*. It has read-only access to an external variable (in this case the VDM equivalent of a representation variable) l of type finite sequence over natural numbers. It assigns the first element of l to its named result y when invoked in a state in which l has positive length, i.e., is not the empty list.

How is the relationship between the LHS and the RHS operations listed above expressed and proven in VDM?

The connection between the state spaces of the two levels under consideration is provided by the *retrieve function* elems : $\mathbb{N}^* \longrightarrow$ **set of** $\mathbb{N}$. The function elems is the VDM equivalent of our function *elts* defined in Example 1.4.

The concrete data model ($\mathbb{N}^*$) is required to be *adequate* in VDM terminology, i.e., every abstract value (a finite set of natural numbers) has a corresponding concrete value (a finite sequence of natural numbers); in VDM notation this is expressed as

$$U : \textbf{set of } \mathbb{N} \vdash \exists l : \mathbb{N}^* \, (\text{elems } (l) = U)$$

All images of concrete initial states must be abstract initial states.

$$\vdash \text{elems } ([\,]) = \emptyset$$

The precondition of the concrete operation must hold whenever the corresponding abstract precondition does. This proof obligation is called the *domain rule* in VDM terminology, and stated here for *GETa* and *GETc*.[3]

$$l : \mathbb{N}^*, \text{elems } (l) \neq \emptyset \quad \vdash \quad \text{len}(l) > 0$$

The concrete operation should not break the abstract postcondition (*result rule* for *ADDa* and *ADDc*)

$$\overleftarrow{l}, l : \mathbb{N}^*, l = \overleftarrow{l} \frown [x] \quad \vdash \quad \text{elems } (l) = \text{elems } (\overleftarrow{l} \frown [x])$$

The reason for using the entailment sign ($\vdash$) rather than ordinary implication ($\Rightarrow$) will be clarified in Chapter 12. As we shall see there, VDM uses a three-valued logic rather than a two-valued one; using $\vdash$ yields a more general yet sound proof method.

---

[3] In general the proof obligations have a more complicated form than those given here, unless, as it is the case in this particular example, the relationship between concrete and abstract values is described by a total function. Consult Chapter 12 for the general case.

We shall prove in Chapters 11 and 12 that correctness of a data refinement step according to Reynolds [Rey81] on the one hand or according to VDM [J90] on the other hand both can be reduced to proving L-simulation, although the way of proving a refinement step correct is really different for these methods. One difference is that Reynolds deals with partial correctness in the first place and establishes termination in a separate argument, whereas Jones is always concerned with total correctness.

2.4.3 Syntax vs. Semantics: No Value Judgment Implied

The distinction between syntax-based methods and semantically oriented ones refers here to the following.

In a syntax-based method terms and formulae are generated using fixed machine checkable patterns, laid down by their syntax, and subsequently given semantic justification using particular universes and operations upon these universes through interpretation functions, as illustrated in Chapters 5 and 8. On this semantic basis a notion of truth is developed for these formulae, resulting in the definition of validity of a formula. This leads to the development of logics to characterize the set of valid formulae for such a method using deductive means, i.e., again using fixed syntactic patterns.

In a semantically oriented method only these universes and operations upon them are given, for which ad-hoc mathematical notation is used. In principle, the whole language of mathematics can be used to reason about these entities. Of course, in practice this distinction is less strict. Even in the case of semantically oriented methods fixed patterns of reasoning can often be distinguished. This may eventually lead to the development of syntactic characterizations of such methods (if at all possible).

Since we compare in Part II different existing, mostly syntax-based, methods for proving data refinement, we can only proceed by relating their semantics. Consequently, throughout this monograph the development of semantic techniques is emphasized.

This does not imply that syntax-based methods have no right to exist. On the contrary, within an industrial environment such methods are still regarded as the main ones, due to their fixed format (which makes them easier to learn and to communicate, and allows their format to be checked using syntax analysis), the possibility they offer for checking proofs by machine, but, first and foremost, their practical usability. Consequently a flexible method which can be easily applied, but which is incomplete, may be preferable within an industrial environment to a more complex complete one. This provides the justification for such, as we shall see, incomplete methods as Reynolds' method and VDM: their proof obligations are simpler than those of (most) other methods.

Thus, our emphasis on the development of semantically oriented methods (couched in the language of mathematics) should be regarded as a consequence of our efforts to reach our goal, the comparison of existing methods for proving data refinement, rather than as a value judgment about these methods.

On the other hand, the methods discussed in this monograph originate mostly in the late 1970s and 1980s, while presently, in the second half of the 1990s, it has become possible to machine-check complex semantic arguments as well. Indeed, some of the most complex proofs involving intricate semantical reasoning in this book have been machine-checked using PVS.

Also it is nowadays realized that specifying complex tasks reliably is at least as difficult as programming them, and certainly impossible without the support of a wide range of tools such as model checkers, theorem provers, static analyzers, and the like. In the end all specifications and problems to be checked for consistency have to be reformulated within special-purpose formalisms destined for use by particular tools.

The efforts involved in such a reformulation need not always be excessive. For instance, the effort to formulate and check the most intricate argument in this monograph, the proof of Theorem 9.9, with PVS required no more than 40 man-hours. It seems therefore that at the time of writing this monograph the main emphasis in specification methodology is shifting more and more towards convenience and tool-use, and that whether semantic arguments are involved or a more rigid syntactic characterization is adhered to is a past station. For it has become clear that there is at present no single formalism which is optimal w.r.t. all desiderata listed above.

2.5 Historical Background

The earliest references to simulation are, in connection with deterministic programming, Milner's [Mil71], and in connection with nondeterministic automata, Park's [Par81a]. Park points out a related notion of weak homomorphism in [Gin68].

Soundness and completeness issues in the context of data refinement were first considered in [Nip86]. Our particular approach is based on [HHS87], in which also the terms *upward* and *downward* simulation are defined. Data invariants occur already in [Hoa72]. The historical origins of what we call Reynolds' method are described in Section 11.4, and of VDM in Section 3.3 "Development Methods" of [J92] by Jones, in which [BJ78], by Bjørner and Jones, and [J80] are cited as early references.

Exercises

2.1 The Gregorian calendar was introduced in 1582. It is marked by the fact that a centennial year not divisible by 400 cannot be a leap-year. Define a data invariant for the Gregorian calendar.

2.2 Give a representation invariant for Example 2.4 such that the representation is minimal in the number of elements.

2.3 Prove that L^{-1}-simulation is a sound proof method for data refinement.

2.4 In Section 2.2.2 it is proven that L-simulation on its own is incomplete. The example given concerns a nondeterministic choice on the higher level which is postponed on the lower level. Prove that these data types L^{-1}-simulate each other.

2.5 Similarly as in Section 2.2.2 one can find a counterexample to completeness of L^{-1}-simulation on its own. Find such an example.

2.6 Prove that pairs (op_C, op_A) of semantics of a normal operation which satisfy condition (2.3) fulfill the verification conditions for L^{-1}-, U-, and U^{-1}-simulation, when α fulfills condition (2.1).

2.7 Given an abstraction relation $\alpha : \Sigma^N \times \Sigma_C \longrightarrow \Sigma^N \times \Sigma_A$, define $\alpha|_{\Sigma^N \times \Sigma^N}$ by

$$(\nu, \sigma) \in \alpha|_{\Sigma^N \times \Sigma^N} \stackrel{\text{def}}{=} \exists \rho, \tau (((\nu, \rho), (\sigma, \tau)) \in \alpha) \ .$$

In Section 2.3 we define a restriction on α which implies that normal operations simulate themselves under α without requiring extra verification conditions. Abstraction relations α satisfying this restriction satisfy the property $\alpha|_{\Sigma^N \times \Sigma^N} = id_{\Sigma^N}$.

Prove that this property on its own is not strong enough to imply that normal operations simulate themselves.

Hint: It suffices to consider Σ^N, Σ_A and Σ_C having only two elements.

2.8 Given the problem and the notation stated in the exercise above, let $\alpha|_{\Sigma^N \times \Sigma^N} = \Sigma^N \times \Sigma^N$. Does L-simulation w.r.t. such an α still hold for normal operations? And what is the situation for L^{-1}-simulation?

2.9 Consider the following program, which uses the integer-valued normal variables x and hd.

```
begin
  var l : LL;
  l := ⟨ ⟩;
  while input(x) do l := append(x, l) od;
```

if $l \neq \langle \rangle$ **then** $hd := first(l)$; $l := rest(l)$ **fi**
end

The linear-list-valued representation variable l is to be replaced by a pair (a, p) of variables. The values of a are (unbounded) arrays of integers, and p holds an array index. Define syntactically an abstraction relation between (a, p) on the lower level and l on the higher level. Prove your development step correct.

2.10   This exercise concerns nondeterministic value-returning operations which are implemented by less nondeterministic operations, such as $pick(U)$ in Example 1.4 concerning the representation of sets by lists. Prove semantically that the operations on l which are listed in that example L-simulate the corresponding operations on U w.r.t. the abstraction relation $elts(l) = U$. Does the inverse also hold, i.e., do these operations on U L-simulate those on l?

2.11   Formulate the proof requested in Exercise 2.10 syntactically in first order predicate logic, using the extra verification condition (2.6).

2.12   Redo Exercise 2.10, this time for a different notion of simulation.

2.13   Prove that the (sum, num) data type is L-simulated by the $_b$ data type, given in Example 2.5.

2.14   Prove that the data types given in Example 2.6 L-simulate each other.

2.15   Suppose we optimize the storage requirements of the concrete level program given in Example 2.5 by dropping the sum component and using the normal variable av instead. This is possible because av is used at most once and sum is not needed anymore afterwards.

> **begin**
>   **var** num : Integer;
> $av := 0$; $num := 0$;
>   **while** $input(x)$ **do** $av := av + x$; $num := num + 1$ **od**;
>   **if** $num \neq 0$ **then** $av := av/num$ **fi**
> **end**.

What can be said about this implementation w.r.t. the abstract level of Example 2.5? Is it a (data) refinement, and if so, how does one prove such an implementation correct?

3
Relations and Recursion

The investigations undertaken in later chapters require some technical machinery necessary to deal with binary relations. This chapter provides the necessary technical background. Since we deal with recursion, in particular the principles behind the so-called μ-calculus of Scott and de Bakker and of Park are explained.

3.1 Partial Orders and Monotonicity

In order to express and prove how our four notions of simulation behave under horizontal and vertical composition we introduce partial orders and monotonicity of functions between partial orders.

Definition 3.1 (Partial order) Let L be a set and $\leq \subseteq L \times L$ a binary relation on L. We call $\leq$ a *partial order* on L and $(L, \leq)$ a *partially ordered set* (or poset) iff $\leq$ is

- *reflexive*: $\forall a \in L (a \leq a)$,
- *transitive*: $\forall a, b, c \in L (a \leq b \wedge b \leq c \Rightarrow a \leq c)$, and
- *antisymmetric*: $\forall a, b \in L (a \leq b \wedge b \leq a \Rightarrow a = b)$. ♣

Example 3.2 We list a few simple examples of posets.

- Let L be a set; then the subset relation ($\subseteq$) is a partial order on the powerset ($\mathfrak{P}(L)$) of L. In particular, the set of binary relations $\mathfrak{P}(\Sigma^C \times \Sigma^C)$ on some level C is partially ordered by $\subseteq$.
- If $(L, \leq)$ is a poset then so is $(L, \geq)$, where $\geq \overset{\text{def}}{=} \leq^{-1}$. These posets are said to be *dual*.
- If $(L, \leq)$ and $(M, \preceq)$ are posets then so is $(L \times M, \leq \otimes \preceq)$ with $\leq \otimes \preceq$ defined by $((l, m), (l', m')) \in \leq \otimes \preceq \Leftrightarrow l \leq l' \wedge m \preceq m'$, for all $l, l' \in L$ and $m, m' \in M$.

- If S is a set and $(L, \leq)$ is a poset then so is the set of all total functions from S to L, denoted by $[S \longrightarrow L]$, ordered by the *pointwise extension* of $\leq$: we use the same symbol and write $f \leq f'$ iff $\forall s \in S (f(s) \leq f'(s))$.   ♡

Definition 3.3 (Bounds) Let $(L, \leq)$ be a poset, $b \in L$, and $A \subseteq L$.

- b is an *upper bound* of A if $\forall a \in A (a \leq b)$. The set of all upper bounds of A is denoted by $\downarrow(A)$.
- b is a *lower bound* of A if $\forall a \in A (b \leq a)$. The set of all lower bounds of A is denoted by $\uparrow(A)$.
- b is the *least upper bound* (or *lub*) of A if $b \in \downarrow(A)$ and $\forall a \in \downarrow(A) (b \leq a)$.
- b is the *greatest lower bound* (or *glb*) of A if $b \in \uparrow(A)$ and $\forall a \in \uparrow(A) (a \leq b)$.

♣

Example 3.4 Observe that bounds need not exist. Take for instance the left open interval $(0, 1]$ of real numbers. It is (partially) ordered by $\leq$ but there is no lower bound for it (in it): $\uparrow((0, 1]) = \emptyset$.

On the other hand, let L be a set and consider the subset relation on the powerset, $(\mathfrak{P}(L), \subseteq)$. This partial order has lub's and glb's for all subsets $A \subseteq L$, namely union $\bigcup A$ and intersection $\bigcap A$ of the elements of A.   ♡

Definition 3.5 Let $(L, \leq)$ and $(M, \preceq)$ be posets. A function $f : L \longrightarrow M$ is

- *monotone* (or *order-preserving*) iff $\forall a, b \in L (a \leq b \Rightarrow f(a) \preceq f(b))$, and
- *antitone* (or *order-reversing*) iff $\forall a, b \in L (a \leq b \Rightarrow f(b) \preceq f(a))$.

$a \in L$ is a *fixed point* of the function $g : L \longrightarrow L$ if $g(a) = a$. If, in addition, a is the glb of the set of all fixed points of g, then we call a the *least fixed point* μ_g of g.   ♣

3.2 Binary Relations

Defining data refinement and associated concepts required the introduction of some operations involving binary relations. Below we give a more complete list of such concepts and prove some elementary facts about them, as a preparation for Section 3.3 on characterizing recursion in a relational setting by means of least fixed points.

Definition 3.6 By $\{ x \mid p \}$ we denote the set of all objects x such that p holds. Let A, B, and C be sets. Define the *identity relation* on A by $id_A \overset{\text{def}}{=} \{ (a, a) \mid a \in A \}$, and define the *powerset* of A by $\mathfrak{P}(A) \overset{\text{def}}{=} \{ p \mid p \subseteq A \}$. For binary relations $R \subseteq A \times B$ and $S \subseteq B \times C$ we define

- R is *total* on A iff $\forall a \in A\,(\exists b \in B\,((a,b) \in R))$. We simply say that R is total if A is clear from the context.
- R is *functional* iff $\forall a \in A, b_1, b_2 \in B\,(\{(a,b_1),(a,b_2)\} \subseteq R \Rightarrow b_1 = b_2)$.
- The *sequential composition* of R and S:

$$R\,;S \overset{\text{def}}{=} \{\,(a,c) \mid \exists b\,((a,b) \in R \wedge (b,c) \in S)\,\}$$

- The *inverse* of R:

$$R^{-1} \overset{\text{def}}{=} \{\,(b,a) \mid (a,b) \in R\,\}$$

- The *complement* of R:

$$\overline{R} \overset{\text{def}}{=} \{\,(a,b) \in A \times B \mid (a,b) \notin R\,\}$$

- The *relational image* of set $A' \subseteq A$ through R:

$$R(A') \overset{\text{def}}{=} \{\,b \mid \exists a \in A'\,((a,b) \in R)\,\}$$

Let I be a set of indices and $(R_i)_{i \in I} : I \longrightarrow \mathfrak{P}(A \times B)$ an I-indexed family of relations. Define *union* and *intersection* of this family respectively by

$$\bigcup_{i \in I} R_i \overset{\text{def}}{=} \{\,(a,b) \in A \times B \mid \exists i \in I\,((a,b) \in R_i)\,\}\ \ , \text{and}$$

$$\bigcap_{i \in I} R_i \overset{\text{def}}{=} \{\,(a,b) \in A \times B \mid \forall i \in I\,((a,b) \in R_i)\,\}\ \ . \qquad \clubsuit$$

Next we present a little lemma relating some of the concepts introduced in the last definition.

Lemma 3.7 Let $R \subseteq A \times B$.

(i) R is total if, and only if, $id_A \subseteq R\,;R^{-1}$.
(ii) R is functional if, and only if, $R^{-1}\,;R \subseteq id_B$.
(iii) Sequential composition distributes over union.

Proof: We start by proving (i).

R is total on A

$\Leftrightarrow \forall a \in A\,(\exists b \in B\,((a,b) \in R))$

$\Leftrightarrow \forall a \in A\,\left(\exists b \in B\,((a,b) \in R \wedge (b,a) \in R^{-1})\right)$

$\Leftrightarrow \forall a \in A\,\left((a,a) \in R\,;R^{-1}\right)$

$\Leftrightarrow id_A \subseteq R\,;R^{-1}$

Next comes (ii):

R is functional

$$\Leftrightarrow \forall a \in A \left(\forall b_1, b_2 \in B \left((a,b_1) \in R \wedge (a,b_2) \in R \Rightarrow b_1 = b_2 \right) \right)$$

$$\Leftrightarrow \forall a \in A \left(\forall b_1, b_2 \in B \left((b_1,a) \in R^{-1} \wedge (a,b_2) \in R \Rightarrow b_1 = b_2 \right) \right)$$

$$\Leftrightarrow \forall b_1, b_2 \in B \left((b_1,b_2) \in R^{-1}; R \Rightarrow b_1 = b_2 \right)$$

$$\Leftrightarrow R^{-1}; R \subseteq id_B$$

Finally, for (iii) let $(R_i)_{i \in I} : I \longrightarrow \mathfrak{P}(A \times B)$ be an I-indexed family of relations and $S \subseteq B \times C$.

$$\left(\bigcup_{i \in I} R_i \right) ; S$$

$$= \left\{ (a,c) \in A \times C \;\middle|\; \exists b \in B \left((a,b) \in \bigcup_{i \in I} R_i \wedge (b,c) \in S \right) \right\}$$

$$= \left\{ (a,c) \in A \times C \mid \exists b \in B (\exists i \in I ((a,b) \in R_i) \wedge (b,c) \in S) \right\}$$

$$= \left\{ (a,c) \in A \times C \mid \exists b \in B (\exists i \in I ((a,b) \in R_i \wedge (b,c) \in S)) \right\}$$

$$= \left\{ (a,c) \in A \times C \mid \exists i \in I (\exists b \in B ((a,b) \in R_i \wedge (b,c) \in S)) \right\}$$

$$= \left\{ (a,c) \in A \times C \mid \exists i \in I ((a,c) \in R_i ; S) \right\}$$

$$= \bigcup_{i \in I} (R_i ; S)$$

The proof of $T ; \bigcup_{i \in I} R_i = \bigcup_{i \in I} (T ; R_i)$ for $T \subseteq C \times A$ has a similar structure. $\square$

The following property turns out to be crucial in subsequent sections, e.g., for establishing implications between our four kinds of simulation.

Lemma 3.8 Our relational operators ";" and "$\cup$" are monotone in both their arguments.

Proof: We prove this only for ";". Let X_1, X_2, Y_1, Y_2 be binary relations such that $X_i \subseteq Y_i$, for $i = 1, 2$.

$$(\sigma, \tau) \in X_1 ; X_2$$

$$\Leftrightarrow \exists \rho ((\sigma, \rho) \in X_1 \wedge (\rho, \tau) \in X_2) \qquad \text{Def. 3.6}$$

$$\Rightarrow \exists \rho ((\sigma, \rho) \in Y_1 \wedge (\rho, \tau) \in Y_2) \qquad \text{premises}$$

$$\Leftrightarrow (\sigma, \tau) \in Y_1 ; Y_2 \qquad \text{Def. 3.6}$$

For "$\cup$" this is even more obvious. $\square$

For later reference we also list a few basic properties of relational operators.

Lemma 3.9 Let A, B, C, and D be sets. Let $r, r' \subseteq A \times B$, $s, s' \subseteq B \times C$, and $t \subseteq C \times D$ be binary relations.

(i) ";" is associative: $((r;s);t) = (r;(s;t))$.

(ii) "$^{-1}$" reverses the order of arguments of ";": $(r;s)^{-1} = s^{-1};r^{-1}$.

(iii) The complement function is antitone: $r \subseteq r' \Leftrightarrow \overline{r'} \subseteq \overline{r}$.

Proof: An easy exercise. □

To be able to express certain relations concisely we introduce three relational operators, each of them mapping two binary relations to another binary relation.

Two of these operators enable us to express maximal solutions for each of the relations on the LHS of

$$r;t \subseteq s \qquad (3.1)$$

in terms of the remaining two relations (see Figure 3.1), which will become important in subsequent sections and chapters. The third operator is the dual[1] of one of the other two.

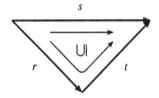

Fig. 3.1. Motivation for the additional relational operators.

Obviously we do not need a new expression for the minimal solution of (3.1) in s; it is already expressed by $r;t$. For reasons that will only become clear in later chapters we refer to the maximal solution of (3.1) in t by r *leads to* s, denoted $r \rightsquigarrow s$. This operator is closely connected with a particular kind of correctness formulae called Hoare triples. This connection will be worked out in Section 5.4. We call the maximal solution of (3.1) in r the *weakest prespecification* of t w.r.t. s, denoted by $[t]s$. This operator will turn out to be crucial in our completeness proof of simulation techniques in Section 4.6. Finally we introduce the dual of the weakest prespecification operator, denoted by $\langle t \rangle s$. Formally we define these operators as follows.

---

[1] The dual of a function f from one complemented lattice to another is $\lambda l.\overline{f(\bar{l})}$. Complemented lattices are defined in Def. 10.1.

Definition 3.10 Let A, B, and C be sets. Let $r \subseteq A \times B$, $s \subseteq A \times C$, and $t \subseteq B \times C$ be binary relations.

$$r \rightsquigarrow s \stackrel{\text{def}}{=} \{ (b,c) \in B \times C \mid \forall a \in A ((a,b) \in r \Rightarrow (a,c) \in s) \} \qquad (3.2)$$

$$[t]s \stackrel{\text{def}}{=} \{ (a,b) \in A \times B \mid \forall c \in C ((b,c) \in t \Rightarrow (a,c) \in s) \} \qquad (3.3)$$

$$\langle t \rangle s \stackrel{\text{def}}{=} \{ (a,b) \in A \times B \mid \exists c \in C ((b,c) \in t \wedge (a,c) \in s) \} \qquad (3.4)$$

♣

In the following three lemmas, let A, B, C, r, s, and t be as in Def. 3.10. Point (i) of Lemma 3.11 and Lemma 3.12.(i) are known as the *Schröder equivalences* and go back to de Morgan's work in 1860 [Sch95, SS93, GB96].

Lemma 3.11

  (i) $t \subseteq r \rightsquigarrow s$ iff $r;t \subseteq s$, and hence

  (ii) $r \rightsquigarrow s = \bigcup \{ t \mid r;t \subseteq s \}$

  (iii) $r;(r \rightsquigarrow s) \subseteq s$

  (iv) $s = id_A \rightsquigarrow s$

  (v) $(r \rightsquigarrow s)^{-1} = \bar{s} \rightsquigarrow \bar{r}$

  (vi) $(r;t) \rightsquigarrow s = t \rightsquigarrow (r \rightsquigarrow s)$

Proof: We only prove parts (i) and (v). Ad point (i):

$$r;t \subseteq s$$

$$\Leftrightarrow \forall \sigma, \tau (\exists \rho ((\sigma,\rho) \in r \wedge (\rho,\tau) \in t) \Rightarrow (\sigma,\tau) \in s) \qquad \text{Def. 3.6}$$

$$\Leftrightarrow \forall \rho, \tau ((\rho,\tau) \in t) \Rightarrow \forall \sigma ((\sigma,\rho) \in r \Rightarrow (\sigma,\tau) \in s) \qquad \text{pred. calc.}$$

$$\Leftrightarrow t \subseteq r \rightsquigarrow s \qquad (3.2)$$

Ad point (v):

$$(r \rightsquigarrow s)^{-1}$$

$$= \{ (\tau,\sigma) \mid \forall \zeta ((\zeta,\sigma) \in r \Rightarrow (\zeta,\tau) \in s) \} \qquad (3.2)$$

$$= \{ (\tau,\sigma) \mid \forall \zeta ((\zeta,\tau) \notin s \Rightarrow (\zeta,\sigma) \notin r) \} \qquad \text{pred. calc.}$$

$$= \{ (\tau,\sigma) \mid \forall \zeta ((\zeta,\tau) \in \bar{s} \Rightarrow (\zeta,\sigma) \in \bar{r}) \} \qquad \text{Def. 3.6}$$

$$= \bar{s} \rightsquigarrow \bar{r} \qquad (3.2) \qquad \square$$

Lemma 3.12

  (i) $r \subseteq [t]s$ iff $r;t \subseteq s$

  (ii) $[t]s = \bigcup \{ r \mid r;t \subseteq s \}$

(iii) $[r]([t]s) = [r;t]s$

(iv) $[t](r \rightsquigarrow s) = r \rightsquigarrow [t]s$

Proof: Exercise. □

Lemma 3.13

(i) (duality) $\overline{\langle t \rangle \bar{s}} = [t]s$

(ii) $\langle r \rangle (\langle t \rangle s) = \langle r;t \rangle s$

(iii) $\langle t^{-1} \rangle r = r;t$

Proof: Exercise. □

Lemma 3.14

- If t is functional then $\langle t \rangle s \subseteq [t]s$.
- If t is total then $[t]s \subseteq \langle t \rangle s$.

Proof: Exercise. □

3.3 Recursion and Termination — the μ-Calculus

So far we have restricted ourselves mostly to ";" and "∪" as operators for combining relations to form new relations. They correspond to sequential composition and nondeterministic choice for sequential programs, as we shall formalize in Chapter 5. For now, it suffices to realize that these two concepts alone are not yet powerful enough to express the meaning of a loop or a recursive procedure as a finite term. For how would we describe the meaning of a loop **while** $x > 0$ **do** $x := x - 1$ **od** given two binary relations b and S on natural numbers representing the guard $x > 0$ and the loop body $x := x - 1$, respectively? Let us abstract from the name of variable x and talk about binary relations over the natural numbers $\mathbb{N} = \{0, 1, 2, \ldots\}$. The guard is then represented by the identity relation $id_\mathbb{N}$ without the pair $(0,0)$. This implies that one can pass this guard whenever x is greater than 0. Otherwise, the computation is *blocked*. In our simplified model the loop body denotes the predecessor relation $S \stackrel{\text{def}}{=} \{(n+1,n) \mid n \in \mathbb{N}\}$. Observe that this relation is partial because 0 has no predecessor; however, it is total on the range $b(\mathbb{N}) = \mathbb{N}_{>0}$ of b. Recall the operational meaning of a loop: as long as the entry guard holds, repeat the loop body, and exit as soon as the guard becomes false. The latter means that the computation passes the guard $x \not> 0$, i.e., $x = 0$, which we represent relationally by $b' \stackrel{\text{def}}{=} \{(0,0)\} (= id_\mathbb{N} \setminus b)$. Thus, at the begin of each iteration, a computation has a choice between two paths: either it passes through $b;S$ or through b', and if it chooses the first alternative it has to start all over again. Consequently, a relation X capturing the semantics of our loop satisfies the following equation:

$$X = b;S;X \cup b' \qquad\qquad (3.5)$$

(Here we use the convention that ";" binds tighter than "$\cup$".) In other words, we are looking for a fixed point of the function

$$f(X) \stackrel{\text{def}}{=} b;S;X \cup b'$$

The unique solution is $\mathbb{N} \times \{0\}$. It reflects exactly our operational understanding of the loop since we expect x to be 0 after execution of the loop, regardless of its initial value. In fact, this solution is the least fixed point of f in the partial order $(\mathfrak{P}(\mathbb{N}^2), \subseteq)$. In general there is more than one solution to such an equation. A deeper analysis of the connection between recursion (a more general case than loops) and least fixed points is presented in Section 3.4. Section 3.5 then presents an analysis of termination. In the case of our loop one guesses that it will always terminate, that is, there is no possibility of the computation 'getting lost', be it in an infinite loop or because of being stuck in front of a partial relation. This is different for two simple variations of our loop:

(i) Take for S the successor instead of the predecessor relation. In this case, termination is impossible because the loop goes on forever, unless computation starts with $x = 0$ already. Such an endless computation is called *diverging*.

(ii) Take $S;S$ for S, i.e., $S \stackrel{\text{def}}{=} \{(n+2,n) \mid n \in \mathbb{N}\}$. Suppose computation starts with x having an odd value $n \in 2\mathbb{N}+1$. After $\frac{n-1}{2}$ iterations, $x = 1$ holds, guard b is passed, but S does not provide a successor state. Since $x \neq 0$ the other guard b' cannot be passed either. Such a computation is called *blocking*; the situation is called *deadlock*.

In the next two sections, we present two versions of the μ-calculus: the continuous μ-calculus and the monotone one.

3.4 Relational Semantics of Recursion — the Continuous μ-Calculus

Definition 3.15 (Terms and programs over a data type) We assume an I-indexed family $A = (A_i)_{i \in I}$ of names of operations of some data type $\mathcal{A}$ and a set *Rvar* of recursion variables, with typical element X ranging over $\mathfrak{P}(\Sigma^A \times \Sigma^A)$.
    The set of *terms* over A is the smallest set $T(A)$ containing

(i) name id^A for the identity relation id_{Σ^A}

   (ii) name $\emptyset$ for the empty relation
   (iii) for $i \in I$, name A_i of an atomic operation,
   (iv) recursion variables $X \in Rvar$ ranging over $\mathfrak{P}(\Sigma^A \times \Sigma^A)$
   (v) $P\,;Q$ with $P,Q \in T(A)$
   (vi) $P \cup Q$ with $P,Q \in T(A)$
   (vii) least fixed point terms $\mu X.P(X)$ with $P(X) \in T(A)$

The least fixed point term $\mu X.P(X)$ expresses application of the least fixed
point operator μ to the transformation $\lambda X.P(X)$ between relations in our language. μ serves as a binding operator for recursion variables just as $\forall$ does for
ordinary variables.

   Next we define the set $\mathcal{P}(A)$ of *programs over A* as those terms in $T(A)$ that
do not contain free occurrences of recursion variables.   ♣

As we shall see in Cor. 3.23, $\mu X.P(X)$ expresses the initial/final state behavior
of a recursive procedure S with body $S(P)$.

   We face here a distinction between syntax and semantics, since recursion
variable X is necessarily a term.[2] Consequently as the next step one should
define a semantics function $\mathcal{P}[\![P]\!]$ for programs $P \in \mathcal{P}(A)$. Since this significantly reduces readability of the soundness and completeness proofs presented
below, we postpone such a definition to Chapter 5, and within this chapter
identify syntax with semantics following [SdB69]. Terms id^A, $\emptyset$, A_i, and X
stand within the remainder of this chapter for the relations they are intended to
denote (unless stated otherwise) and, e.g., $\mu X.P(X)$ for the least fixed point of
the transformation that maps the relation denoted by X to the relation denoted
by $P(X)$.

   The basis of our account is that all three operators of our relational language are monotone w.r.t. relational containment. For sequential composition
("$;$") and nondeterministic choice ("$\cup$") we proved this already in Lemma 3.8
above. Monotonicity of least fixed point terms $\mu X.P(X,Y)$ in Y is proven in
Lemma 3.17 below. Any monotone function has a unique least fixed point (this
is later proven in Theorem 8.10), and this justifies choosing $\bigcap\{\,X \mid P(X) = X\,\}$
as the meaning for $\mu X.P(X)$. However, to facilitate formulating proof rules for
least fixed points (e.g., Park's least fixed point rule below) characterizing the
meaning of $\mu X.P(X)$ by $\bigcap\{\,X \mid P(X) \subseteq X\,\}$ is more convenient. The latter is
called the *least prefixed point* of P. By Lemma 3.18.(i) below this then leads
to Def. 3.16.

   For the set-up of binary relations in this section we prove that all three operators of our relational language are even ω-continuous (see Def. 3.19), leading

---

[2] That the usual semantic definition of $T(A)$ leads to inconsistency, is worked out in Exercise 4.5.

to a particularly simple existence proof and characterization of such a least
fixed point as the union of its finite approximations (see Theorem 3.22).

Definition 3.16 (Least fixed point operator)

$$\mu X.P(X) \stackrel{\text{def}}{=} \bigcap \{\, X \mid P(X) \subseteq X \,\} \qquad\qquad \clubsuit$$

Lemma 3.17 (Monotonicity of $\mu X.P(X,Y)$ in Y)

$$Y_1 \subseteq Y_2 \Rightarrow \mu X.P(X,Y_1) \subseteq \mu X.P(X,Y_2)$$

Proof: By induction on the depth of nesting of μ-operators in P. Assume
$Y_1 \subseteq Y_2$.

 (i) P contains no μ-operators. Then $P(X,Y_1) \subseteq P(X,Y_2)$ follows immedi-
    ately from Lemma 3.8 by induction on the complexity of P. Hence

$$\{\, X \mid P(X,Y_2) \subseteq X \,\} \subseteq \{\, X \mid P(X,Y_1) \subseteq X \,\} \;, \qquad (3.6)$$

   and therefore

$$\mu X.P(X,Y_1)$$
$$= \bigcap \{\, X \mid P(X,Y_1) \subseteq X \,\} \qquad \text{Def. 3.16}$$
$$\subseteq \bigcap \{\, X \mid P(X,Y_2) \subseteq X \,\} \qquad (3.6)$$
$$= \mu X.P(X,Y_2) \qquad \text{Def. 3.16}$$

(ii) The proof of the induction step has a similar structure; the only differ-
    ence is that the induction hypothesis is needed to establish (3.6). □

Lemma 3.18 (Properties of the μ-operator)

 (i) $\mu X.P(X) = \bigcap \{\, X \mid P(X) = X \,\}$
(ii) $\mu X.P(X) = P(\mu X.P(X))$

Proof:

 (i) "$\subseteq$" is obvious, since $P(X) = X$ implies $P(X) \subseteq X$.
    "$\supseteq$": By Lemma 3.17 and monotonicity of $P(X)$ in X we have that

$$P(\bigcap \{\, X \mid P(X) \subseteq X \,\}) \subseteq \bigcap \{\, P(X) \mid P(X) \subseteq X \,\} \;.$$

   Also

$$\bigcap \{\, P(X) \mid P(X) \subseteq X \,\} \subseteq \bigcap \{\, X \mid P(X) \subseteq X \,\} \;.$$

Hence $Y \stackrel{\text{def}}{=} \bigcap \{ X \mid P(X) \subseteq X \}$ satisfies

$$P(Y) \subseteq Y \tag{3.7}$$

and therefore Y is the minimal such Y, i.e., $Y \subseteq \bigcap \{ X \mid P(X) \subseteq X \}$. Now $P(Y) \subseteq Y$ implies $P^2(Y) \subseteq P(Y)$ by monotonicity.

Therefore $P(Y) \in \{ X \mid P(X) \subseteq X \}$, and hence

$$Y \subseteq P(Y) . \tag{3.8}$$

Points (3.7) and (3.8) imply

$$Y = P(Y) , \tag{3.9}$$

and a fortiori $\bigcap \{ X \mid P(X) = X \} \subseteq Y \subseteq \bigcap \{ X \mid P(X) \subseteq X \}$.
   (ii) By point (3.9). □

By Lemma 3.18 $\mu X.P(X)$ is a fixed point of P and also its least fixed point. Since $\emptyset \subseteq \mu X.P(X)$, P is monotone, and $\mu X.P(X)$ is a fixed point, $P(\emptyset) \subseteq \mu X.P(X)$.

Define $P^i(\emptyset)$ inductively by $P^0(\emptyset) \stackrel{\text{def}}{=} \emptyset$ and $P^{i+1}(\emptyset) \stackrel{\text{def}}{=} P(P^i(\emptyset))$. Then one has in general that $P^i(\emptyset) \subseteq \mu X.P(X)$ and thus

$$\bigcup_{i \in \mathbb{N}} P^i(\emptyset) \subseteq \mu X.P(X) \tag{3.10}$$

We deduce below that the inverse inclusion also holds.

Definition 3.19 (ω-continuity) Function f over binary relations is called *ω-continuous* iff $f(\bigcup_{i \in \mathbb{N}} X_i) \subseteq \bigcup_{i \in \mathbb{N}} f(X_i)$ for all sequences $(X_i)_{i \in \mathbb{N}}$ satisfying $X_i \subseteq X_{i+1}$. Such a sequence is also called an *ω-chain*. ♣

Lemma 3.20 If $P(X)$ is ω-continuous in X, then $\mu X.P(X) = \bigcup_{i \in \mathbb{N}} P^i(\emptyset)$.

Proof: "$\supseteq$" by point (3.10), "$\subseteq$":

$$P(\bigcup_{i \in \mathbb{N}} P^i(\emptyset))$$

$$\subseteq \bigcup_{i \in \mathbb{N}} P^{i+1}(\emptyset) \qquad \text{premise}$$

$$\subseteq \bigcup_{i \in \mathbb{N}} P^i(\emptyset) \qquad \text{set theory}$$

Hence $\mu X.P(X) \subseteq \bigcup_{i \in \mathbb{N}} P^i(\emptyset)$. □

Lemma 3.21 (ω-continuity of relational terms) All terms $P(X)$ of our relational language are ω-continuous in X.

Proof: Structural induction, immediate for all base cases and induction steps ";" and "∪". The only interesting case is that of $\mu X.P(X,Y)$ with $P(X,Y)$ ω-continuous in X and Y. Let $(Y_i)_{i \in \mathbb{N}}$ satisfy $Y_i \subseteq Y_{i+1}$. Then

$$\mu X.P(X, \bigcup_i Y_i)$$

$$= \bigcup_j P^j(\emptyset, \bigcup_i Y_i) \qquad \text{Lemma 3.20}$$

$$\subseteq \bigcup_j \bigcup_i P^j(\emptyset, Y_i) \qquad \text{premise}$$

$$= \bigcup_i \bigcup_j P^j(\emptyset, Y_i) \qquad \text{set theory}$$

$$= \bigcup_i \mu X.P(X, Y_i) \qquad \text{Lemma 3.20} \qquad \qquad \Box$$

Theorem 3.22

$\mu X.P(X) = \bigcup_{i \in \mathbb{N}} P^i(\emptyset)$ for all relational terms $P(X)$.

Proof: By Lemmas 3.20 and 3.21. $\Box$

Corollary 3.23 (Least fixed point characterization of recursion) Relational term $\mu X.P(X)$ expresses the initial/final state behavior of recursive procedure S with body $P(S)$.

Proof: Consider a recursive procedure S with body $P(S)$. Calls of S with recursion depth 0, i.e., where execution does not involve any invocation of an inner call of S, are described by $P(\emptyset)$. Calls with recursion depth at most 1 are described by $P^2(\emptyset)$, and so on. In general, calls with recursion depth at most i are described by $P^{i+1}(\emptyset)$, for $i \in \mathbb{N}$. Since only terminating calls of S display any initial/final state behavior, and every terminating call has a finite maximal recursion depth, the initial/final state behavior of S is expressed by $\bigcup_{i \in \mathbb{N}} P^{i+1}(\emptyset)$, which is the same as $\bigcup_{i \in \mathbb{N}} P^i(\emptyset)$, since $P^0(\emptyset) = \emptyset$. Since by Lemma 3.21 term $P(X)$ of our relational language is ω-continuous in X, Lemma 3.20 implies that $\mu X.P(X) = \bigcup_{i \in \mathbb{N}} P^i(\emptyset)$. Therefore, in case body $P(S)$ of recursive procedure S corresponds to a term $P(X)$ in our relational language, the least fixed point $\mu X.P(X)$ expresses the initial/final state behavior of S. $\Box$

This characterization of least fixed point terms leads to a simple calculus for reasoning about such ω-continuous μ-terms, called the *continuous μ-calculus*, of which we state only the most salient features (see [dB80, Chapter 7] for a full treatment):

- The fixed point axiom:

$$\vdash \mu X.P(X) = P(\mu X.P(X))$$

- Park's least fixed point rule:

$$\frac{P(Q) \subseteq Q}{\mu X.P(X) \subseteq Q}$$

- Scott's induction rule:

$$\frac{\Phi \vdash \Psi(\emptyset) \qquad \Phi, \Psi(X) \vdash \Psi(P(X))}{\Phi \vdash \Psi(\mu X.P(X))} \quad ,$$

where Φ and Ψ are finite lists of inclusions[3] between relational terms, and recursion variable X does not occur freely in Φ.

Park's least fixed point rule occurred first in [Par69], and Scott's induction rule appears in [SdB69], which is considered one of the most famous unpublished manuscripts in computer science.

Soundness of the fixed point axiom follows from Lemma 3.18.(ii) and of Park's least fixed point rule from Def. 3.16. As to soundness of Scott's induction rule: by an induction argument on $i \in \mathbb{N}$ one obtains that $\Phi \vdash \Psi(P^i(\emptyset))$ for all $i \in \mathbb{N}$. By ω-continuity of our terms and Theorem 3.22 this implies that $\Psi(\mu X.P(X))$ is entailed by Φ.

Example 3.24 How to prove $\mu X.(B;X \cup C) = \mu Y.(B;Y \cup id);C$, where B and C express operations of a data type?

We prove mutual implication, beginning with "$\subseteq$". To prove this using Park's least fixed point rule, we need to prove

$$B;(\mu Y.(B;Y \cup id);C) \cup C \subseteq \mu Y.(B;Y \cup id);C \ ,$$

which follows from

$$\begin{aligned}
&B;(\mu Y.(B;Y \cup id);C) \cup C \\
&= (B;\mu Y.(B;Y \cup id) \cup id);C \qquad \text{Lemma 3.7.(iii)} \\
&= \mu Y.(B;Y \cup id);C \qquad\qquad \text{fixed point axiom}
\end{aligned}$$

To prove the "$\supseteq$" part we use Scott's induction rule and therefore need to prove:

- $\emptyset;C \subseteq \mu X.(B;X \cup C)$, which follows immediately from $\emptyset$ being both the zero of ";" and the least element w.r.t. partial order "$\subseteq$".

---

[3] This is a special case of Scott's induction rule. The general version of this rule applies to continuous (also called *admissible*) predicates Φ and Ψ.

- $Y;C \subseteq \mu X.(B;X \cup C) \vdash (B;Y \cup id);C \subseteq \mu X.(B;X \cup C)$. Assuming the LHS we prove the RHS as follows:

$$
\begin{array}{ll}
(B;Y \cup id);C & \text{LHS} \\
= B;Y;C \cup C & \text{Lemma 3.7.(iii)} \\
\subseteq B;\mu X.(B;X \cup C) \cup C & \text{assumption, Lemma 3.8} \\
= \mu X.(B;X \cup C) & \text{fixed point axiom} \qquad \heartsuit
\end{array}
$$

Later, Hitchcock and Park formulated an extension of Scott's induction rule to monotone terms [HP72]. It allows a proof of Park's least fixed point rule within this calculus, which is called the *monotone μ-calculus* (in contrast to the continuous μ-calculus of the present section). This calculus is the subject of the next section. We shall encounter an elegant reformulation of Park's least fixed point rule within the setting of Hoare logic in Chapter 6.

In general, recursion appears in the form of a system of so-called mutually recursive procedures, for instance, procedure S with body $P(S,T)$ and procedure T with body $Q(S,T)$. The semantics of S can now be expressed by

$$\mu X.P(X,\mu Y.Q(X,Y))$$

and, similarly, T is characterized by $\mu Y.Q(\mu X.P(X,Y),Y)$, a result of [Bek69, SdB69, Par69]. Consequently our relational language, simple as it may seem, also describes the semantics of mutually recursive (parameterless) procedures by nesting terms for fixed points.

In Chapter 8 we develop a similar theory of relations representing a particular total correctness semantics of programs. In Chapter 10 this is done for an interpretation of programs as transformers of predicates. In both cases we shall see that some of the simplicity of the framework in the present section is lost because the transformations to which the least fixed point operator is applied are in general no longer continuous, but merely monotone.

3.5 Reasoning about Termination — the Monotone μ-Calculus[4]

In one of the most impressive contributions to the theory of verification of programs and their equivalence written in the 1970s, David Park and Peter Hitchcock put forward in [HP72, Hit74] the so-called *monotone μ-calculus* as a formalism for reasoning about properties of recursive programs, in particular about termination and absence of blocking (deadlock).

---

[4] This is a technical section which can be skipped upon first reading. It sketches a formalism for reasoning about recursive procedures, in particular about termination, which is in certain aspects an alternative to that of Chapter 8 and may be consulted thereafter.

3.5.1 The monotone μ-calculus

This calculus is obtained in three stages.

The starting point is the usual algebra of binary relations with $\cup$, $\cap$, ;, $^{-1}$, and $^-$ (for complementation) as operations, and as constants $\emptyset$, *id*, and U for denoting the empty, identity, and universal relation, respectively. In [Tar41] Tarski made an effort to axiomatize this algebra but failed to obtain a complete characterization, as proved in Lyndon's [Lyn50, Lyn61]. The argument is as follows. Define *concrete* binary relations as subsets of $V \times V$, for some nonempty set V (as opposed to *abstract* binary relations which by definition model Tarski's axiomatization). That Tarski's axiomatization is not complete is demonstrated in the following example.

Example 3.25 (Lyndon [Lyn61]) Lyndon exhibits a model for Tarski's axiomatization (a finite projective plane) in which the following inclusion, which is shown below to be valid for all interpretations by concrete binary relations, does not hold (here "$^{-1}$" binds more strongly than ";" which binds more strongly than "$\cap$"):

$$X_1 ; X_2 \cap Y_1 ; Y_2 \cap Z_1 ; Z_2$$

$$\subseteq X_1 ; \begin{pmatrix} X_1^{-1} ; Y_1 \cap X_2 ; Y_2^{-1} \\ \cap (X_1^{-1} ; Z_1 \cap X_2 ; Z_2^{-1}) ; (Z_1^{-1} ; Y_1 \cap Z_2 ; Y_2^{-1}) \end{pmatrix} ; Y_2$$

The validity of the above inclusion for concrete binary relations can be seen as follows. Let $(\sigma, \rho) \in X_1 ; X_2 \cap Y_1 ; Y_2 \cap Z_1 ; Z_2$. Then there exist intermediate elements τ_1, τ_2, and τ_3 to which σ is related by, respectively, X_1, Y_1, and Z_1. These elements are in turn related to ρ by X_2, Y_2, and Z_2, respectively. (This situation is suggested in Figure 3.2.)

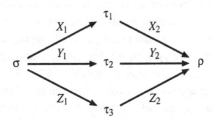

Fig. 3.2.

Now it is easy to see that (σ, ρ) is also contained in the RHS of the above inclusion, as suggested in Figure 3.3.

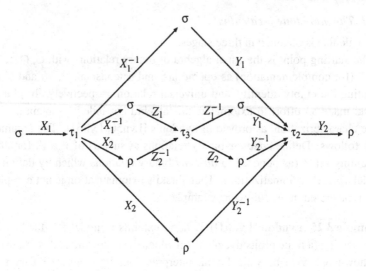

Fig. 3.3.

The generalization of this undecidable inclusion to the intersection of more terms than the three above is now straightforward and results in an infinite number of undecidable inclusions. Only for the intersection of (at most) two terms

$$X_1 ; X_2 \cap Y_1 ; Y_2 \subseteq X_1 ; (X_1^{-1} ; Y_1 \cap X_2 ; Y_2^{-1}) ; Y_2$$

can such inclusions be proven in Tarski's axiomatization [dBdR72].   ♡

In the next stage this relation algebra is extended to binary relations over Cartesian products of zero or more sets in order to capture some notion of program variables by introducing projection functions to access state components. This requires the introduction of a simple typing scheme for relation terms. A relation term of type (n,m), for natural numbers n and m, is interpreted as subset of some Cartesian product $V^n \times V^m$. The case $m = 0$ is used to express predicates and $n = 0$ to express the creation of (auxiliary) variables. Then the relation operators and constants are extended to this typing scheme so that these typed relations become closed under the corresponding partial operations (e.g., only terms of type (m,n) and (n,p) are composed by ;). Surprisingly enough, a complete axiomatization (of binary relations over Cartesian products with projection functions) can now be obtained. Such an axiomatization is provided in [dR76], and has recently been proven complete by Frias and Maddux in [FM97]. Intuitively, completeness follows from the fact that auxiliary variable components can be added to the state for remembering old state components.

In a third stage (typed versions of) least fixed point operators μ are added for expressing recursively defined terms. Least fixed point terms are axiomatized within the monotone μ-calculus by

(i) the *fixed point axiom*, stipulating that their application results in fixed points as in the continuous μ-calculus, and

(ii) their *minimality*, by means of an induction rule, which is an appropriate extension of Scott's induction rule to *monotone terms* [SdB69, HP72].

Now relation terms may contain complementation, which is antitone (i.e., $S_1 \subseteq S_2$ implies $\overline{S_1} \supseteq \overline{S_2}$). Since least fixed points of non-monotone functionals need not exist, care must be taken that $S(X)$ in $\mu X.S(X)$ is monotone in X. This is done by requiring $S(X)$ to be *syntactically monotone*, i.e., the recursion variable X occurs only under an even number of occurrences of complementation operators within $S(X)$. This guarantees monotonicity of $S(X)$ in X in every interpretation. Now completeness is lost. For in, e.g., [KP75] it is proven that the set of valid inclusions between the resulting relation terms is not recursively enumerable.

(Actually least fixed point operators μ_i are added for expressing the i-th component of the least fixed point of a set of fixed point equations used for expressing mutual recursion; but these can be eliminated using μ operators as above [SdB69, Bek69].) This finishes our description of the monotone μ-calculus.

3.5.2 Hitchcock and Park's analysis of the termination properties of μ-terms

The fundamental contribution of [HP72] is that it shows that the monotone μ-calculus can be used for giving a full analysis of the termination properties of recursive program schemes (over recursively defined data structures); for proving partial correctness properties, Park had already given such an analysis in [Par69].

This analysis of termination properties consists of two stages. First the so-called domain of wellfoundedness of a binary relation is expressed, and secondly for each μ-term $\mu X.S(X)$ another term is derived whose domain of wellfoundedness is equal to the domain of termination of $\mu X.S(X)$. The laws of the μ-calculus are then used to provide proofs of termination.

For any relation S its domain of wellfoundedness $\iota(S)$ is defined as the set of states σ_0 for which there does not exist an infinite computation sequence $(\sigma_i)_{i\in\mathbb{N}}$ such that $(\sigma_i, \sigma_{i+1}) \in S$ for $i \in \mathbb{N}$. Hitchcock and Park prove

$$\iota(S) = \mu X. [S] X , \qquad\qquad (3.11)$$

with variable X ranging over predicates, i.e., of sort $(m, 0)$, and the *box operator*[5] $[.]$ defined by $[S]X \stackrel{\text{def}}{=} \overline{S; \overline{X}}$. By Def. 3.6 of sequential composition and complementation $\sigma \in [S]X \Leftrightarrow \forall \tau((\sigma, \tau) \in S \Rightarrow \tau \in X)$. Note that application of μX to $[S]X$ is justified because X occurs within $\overline{S; \overline{X}}$ under an even number of complementation signs only. Next we prove (3.11). Thinking of X as a set of states and S as a successor relation, $[S]X$ is the set of states all of whose S-successors (if any) are in X. Clearly, $\iota(S)$ is a fixed point of this function since $\iota(S)$ is closed under S, and since if every S-predecessor of a state σ is in $\iota(S)$ then so is σ. Conversely, if $\sigma_0 \notin \mu X. [S]X$, then σ_0 has an S-successor $\sigma_1 \notin \mu X. [S]X$; consequently one then obtains an infinite sequence of states not contained in $\mu X. [S]X$. Hence (3.11) holds.

In the second stage of their analysis, Hitchcock and Park derive a term $\ulcorner S \urcorner \sqcup \llcorner S \lrcorner$ from S whose domain of wellfoundedness expresses the domain of termination of $\mu X. S(X)$. The intuition behind this characterization is explained by appealing to an operational evaluation mechanism for recursive procedures. Let $P \Leftarrow S(P)$ express a recursive procedure declaration. The nondeterministic possibility that P is undefined in state σ_0 arises just in case there exists a computation of P starting in σ_0 which computes

(i)   either an infinite number of inner recursive calls of P,

(ii) or a finite number (possibly none) of inner recursive calls of P, leading to an intermediate state σ and a still-to-be-executed part of S starting with some statement T which is undefined in σ and which contains no calls of P. (For example, a state σ such that $\sigma(x) = 0$ and T starting with $y := y/x$.)

First observe that $\mu X. S(X)$ expresses the initial/final state behavior of P. Then situation (i) above implies that there exists an infinite sequence $(\sigma_i)_{i\in\mathbb{N}}$ such that computation of P in σ_i requires computation of P in σ_{i+1}. One may envisage this sequence as representing the potentially infinite stack of intermediate values which is required to implement computation of P in σ_0 on some iterative machine. Now the relation between consecutive values σ_i and σ_{i+1} can be expressed more precisely by introducing the state transformation $\ulcorner S \urcorner$, the *derivative* of S (w.r.t. X), in between a call of P and the constituent inner calls of $S(P)$. Derivative $\ulcorner S \urcorner$ can be syntactically defined by, for instance,

---

[5] The box operator will be further analyzed in Section 3.2 and plays an important rôle in later chapters.

- $\ulcorner X \urcorner \overset{\text{def}}{=} id$, and if S has no free occurrences of X then $\ulcorner S \urcorner \overset{\text{def}}{=} 0$,
- $\ulcorner S_1 ; S_2 \urcorner \overset{\text{def}}{=} \ulcorner S_1 \urcorner \cup S_1 ; \ulcorner S_2 \urcorner$, and $\ulcorner S_1 \cup S_2 \urcorner \overset{\text{def}}{=} \ulcorner S_1 \urcorner \cup \ulcorner S_2 \urcorner$, etc.

Situation (ii) above implies the existence of a finite sequence $(\sigma_i)_{0 \le i \le N}$ such that computation of P in σ_i requires computation of P in σ_{i+1} for $0 \le i < N$, i.e., $(\sigma_i, \sigma_{i+1}) \in \ulcorner S \urcorner$, and such that P is undefined in σ_N because some constituent statement T of S containing no call of P is undefined. To characterize the latter more precisely $\llcorner S \lrcorner$, the *co-derivative* of S — a subset of the identity relation — is introduced for which $(\sigma_N, \sigma_N) \in \llcorner S \lrcorner$. Also $\llcorner S \lrcorner$ can be defined syntactically, for instance:

- $\llcorner X \lrcorner \overset{\text{def}}{=} 0$, and if S has no free occurrences of X then $\llcorner S \lrcorner = \overline{S ; U} \cap id$,
- $\llcorner S_1 ; S_2 \lrcorner = \llcorner S_1 \lrcorner \cup (S_1 ; \llcorner S_2 \lrcorner ; U \cap id)$ and $\llcorner S_1 \cup S_2 \lrcorner = \llcorner S_1 \lrcorner \cap \llcorner S_2 \lrcorner$, etc.

Now situation (ii) can be reduced to situation (i) by observing that, since $\llcorner S \lrcorner$ denotes a subset of the identity relation, repetition of $\llcorner S \lrcorner$ transforms σ_N into itself ad infinitum.

Consequently, there is the nondeterministically arising possibility that P is undefined in σ_0 just in case there exists an infinite sequence $(\sigma_i)_{i \in \mathbb{N}}$ such that $(\sigma_i, \sigma_{i+1}) \in \ulcorner S \urcorner \cup \llcorner S \lrcorner$, i.e., $\ulcorner S \urcorner \cup \llcorner S \lrcorner$ is not wellfounded in σ_0. Using (3.11), termination of P when starting in σ_0 is therefore characterized by the absence of such a possibility, i.e., by $\sigma_0 \in \mu X . [\ulcorner S \urcorner \cup \llcorner S \lrcorner] X$.

Let us consider what $\sigma_0 \in \mu X . [\ulcorner S \urcorner \cup \llcorner S \lrcorner] X$ implies in practice.

(i) σ_0 cannot serve as the starting point of any nondeterministically arising infinite computation for P:

For $\ulcorner S \urcorner$ expresses the transformation between a call of P and any inner recursive call of P. And this follows from the definition of $\ulcorner S \urcorner$. E.g., $\ulcorner S_1 \cup S_2 \urcorner = \ulcorner S_1 \urcorner \cup \ulcorner S_2 \urcorner$, expresses that all nondeterministically arising possibilities for inner recursive calls are taken into account.

(ii) σ_0 cannot serve as the starting point of any nondeterministically arising finite computation for P leading to a state with no S-successor:

For $\sigma_0 \in \mu X . [\ulcorner S \urcorner \cup \llcorner S \lrcorner] X$ implies that there does not exist a finite sequence $(\sigma_{i+1})_{i \in \mathbb{N}_{<N}}$ such that $\forall i \in \mathbb{N}_{<N} ((\sigma_i, \sigma_{i+1}) \in \ulcorner S \urcorner)$ and $(\sigma_N, \sigma_N) \in \llcorner S \lrcorner$, because such a sequence could be prolonged to a sequence $(\sigma_i)_{i \in \mathbb{N}}$ by appending infinitely many states σ_N. This would imply that $(\sigma_i, \sigma_{i+1}) \in \ulcorner S \urcorner \cup \llcorner S \lrcorner$ for $i \in \mathbb{N}_{<N}$, which contradicts $\sigma_0 \in \iota(\ulcorner S \urcorner \cup \llcorner S \lrcorner)$. That all nondeterministically arising possibilities for undefined results or blocking are indeed detected follows from the definition of $\llcorner S \lrcorner$. E.g., $\llcorner S_1 \cup S_2 \lrcorner = \llcorner S_1 \lrcorner \cap \llcorner S_2 \lrcorner$ implies that $\llcorner S_1 \cup S_2 \lrcorner$ expresses those states in which both S_1 and S_2 lead to undefined results or blocking, as explained in the example below, and $\llcorner S_1 ; S_2 \lrcorner =$

$\llcorner S_1 \lrcorner \cup (S_1 ; \llcorner S_2 \lrcorner ; U \cap id)$ implies that every possibility resulting in un-definedness or blocking within a sequential computation is expressed.

Example 3.26 Let us reconsider the example discussed at the beginning of Section 3.3, and construct the derivative and co-derivative of the RHS of (3.5), that is, $\ulcorner b ; S ; X \cup b' \urcorner$ and $\llcorner b ; S ; X \cup b' \lrcorner$ for $b = id_{N_{>0}}, S = \{ (n+1,n) \mid n \in N \}$, and $b' = \{(0,0)\}$.

We start with the derivative:

$$\ulcorner b ; S ; X \cup b' \urcorner$$
$$= \ulcorner b \urcorner \cup b ; \ulcorner S \urcorner \cup b ; S ; \ulcorner X \urcorner \cup \ulcorner b' \urcorner$$
$$= \emptyset \cup b ; \emptyset \cup b ; S ; id_N \cup \emptyset$$
$$= S$$

Next comes the co-derivative:

$$\llcorner b ; S ; X \cup b' \lrcorner$$
$$= (\llcorner b \lrcorner \cup (b ; \llcorner S \lrcorner ; U) \cap id_N \cup (b ; S ; \llcorner X \lrcorner ; U) \cap id_N) \cap \llcorner b' \lrcorner$$
$$= ((\overline{b ; U} \cap id_N) \cup (b ; (\overline{S ; U} \cap id_N) ; U) \cap id_N) \cap (\overline{b' ; U} \cap id_N)$$
$$= ((\overline{id_{N_{>0}} ; U} \cap id_N) \cup (id_{N_{>0}} ; (\overline{\{ (n+1,n) \mid n \in N \} ; U} \cap id_N) ; U) \cap id_N)$$
$$\quad \cap (\overline{\{(0,0)\} ; U} \cap id_N)$$
$$= (\{(0,0)\} \cup (id_{N_{>0}} ; \{(0,0)\} ; U) \cap id_N) \cap id_{N_{>0}}$$
$$= \emptyset$$

Hence the domain of termination of the loop **while** $x > 0$ **do** $x := x - 1$ **od** is given by the least fixed point of the function $\lambda X . [S] X$ where X ranges over relational terms of type $(1,0)$, i.e., predicates over the single variable x. We shall prove that this fixed point is the universal relation of type $(1,0)$. Consequently, the loop is guaranteed to terminate.

We identify the predicate X with its domain set of natural numbers (since the range is $N^0 = \{\emptyset\}$ whenever $X \neq \emptyset$).

$$n \in \overline{S ; \overline{X}} \Leftrightarrow \neg \exists m \in N((n,m) \in S \wedge m \notin X)$$
$$\Leftrightarrow \forall m \in N(n = m + 1 \Rightarrow m \in X)$$
$$\Leftrightarrow n = 0 \vee n - 1 \in X$$

By induction this is true for all $n \in N$.

Recall that we also presented two variations of this loop, each of which exposed a different reason for being undefined in particular initial states:

(i) **while** $x > 0$ **do** $x := x + 1$ **od** diverges for initial values of x other than 0.

(ii) **while** $x > 0$ **do** $x := x - 2$ **od** blocks for odd initial values of x.

By $T_1 \stackrel{\text{def}}{=} \{ (n, n+1) \mid n \in \mathbb{N} \}$ and $T_2 \stackrel{\text{def}}{=} \{ (n+2, n) \mid n \in \mathbb{N} \}$ we express (in our simplified model) the meaning of the assignments $x := x + 1$ and $x := x - 2$, respectively. Then $\ulcorner b ; T_1 ; X \cup b' \urcorner = b ; T_1 = T_1 \setminus \{(0,1)\}$ and $\ulcorner b ; T_2 ; X \cup b' \urcorner = T_2$, in analogy to the calculation of the derivative of the original loop body above. Similarly, $\llcorner b ; T_1 ; X \cup b' \lrcorner = \emptyset$ and $\llcorner b ; T_2 ; X \cup b' \lrcorner = \{(1,1)\}$. We guess that the domain of termination of the first variation is just $\{0\}$. Indeed, it is the case that $\overline{b ; T_1 ; \overline{\{0\}}} = \{0\} \; (= \overline{b ; T_1 ; \overline{0}})$. Thus $\{0\}$ is the least fixed point of $\lambda X . [b ; T_1] X$.

The situation for the second variation is slightly more complicated.

$$n \in [T_2 \cup \{(1,1)\}] X \Leftrightarrow n \in \overline{\{ (n, m) \mid n = m + 2 \vee n = m = 1 \} ; \overline{X}}$$
$$\Leftrightarrow \forall m \, (n = m + 2 \vee n = m = 1 \Rightarrow m \in X)$$

This is true for $n = 0$, and, by induction, for all even n. Furthermore, the set of even natural numbers $2\mathbb{N}$ is a fixed point of $\lambda X . [T_2 \cup \{(1,1)\}] X$. Thus, $2\mathbb{N}$ is the domain of termination of the second variation of our loop example. ♡

Returning to the general case, we may conclude that $\sigma_0 \in \mu X . [\ulcorner S \urcorner \cup \llcorner S \lrcorner] X$ expresses the absence of any nondeterministically arising possibility of

(i) an infinite computation of P,

(ii) blocking when executing P, and

(iii) execution of an undefined operation within P.

In fact, this characterization of $\mu X . [\ulcorner S \urcorner \cup \llcorner S \lrcorner] X$ can be proven. This is done by de Bakker in [dB80] by giving an independent semantic analysis of the behavior of recursive procedures that takes all three points above into account — all in the presence of (bounded) nondeterminism. This is the subject of Section 3.5.3.

In a number of fundamental contributions Park also proves that finiteness cannot be expressed in the monotone μ-calculus [Par76], and that this calculus is an appropriate vehicle for reasoning about notions of fairness [Par80, Par81a, Par81b]. These results, together with Park's already mentioned full analysis of partial correctness properties, establish the monotone μ-calculus as one of the few satisfactory formalisms for reasoning about the correctness of programs, covering partial correctness, termination, and fairness arguments.

From the altogether different perspective of model checking (a term associated with automatic verification procedures for finite state programs) Allen

Emerson reaches in [Eme90] a similar conclusion, although he considers the so-called propositional μ-calculus, which is geared towards extending temporal logic and expressing fairness arguments. The propositional μ-calculus has been put forward and axiomatized by Dexter Kozen [Koz83], proved complete in a famous paper by Walukiewicz [Wal93, Wal95, Wal96], and advocated in the works of, e.g., Colin Stirling [Sti92].

3.5.3 The Hitchcock–Park–de Bakker theorem

In [dB80] Hitchcock and Park's analysis of the termination properties of recursion is proven to correspond to a semantic analysis based on the so-called Egli–Milner interpretation of relations [Egl75, Plo76], which expresses *erratic* nondeterminism. This notion captures that a nondeterministic union of relations is correct if it generates at least one computation leading to a desired result (even in the presence of a nonterminating computation). That this is a satisfactory notion for analyzing termination can be understood as follows.

Add as an artifact the element $\perp$, pronounced "bottom", to the state space Σ to express any undesirable computation, i.e., nontermination, blocking, or the result of an undefined operation. Next characterize the meaning of a statement S as a function f_S mapping each initial state σ to some nonempty set of states, possibly containing $\perp$, such that f_S is *strict* in the sense that $f_S(\perp) = \{\perp\}$. The nondeterministic choice between statements S_1 and S_2 is described by the function mapping each initial state σ to the union of the individual results $f_{S_1}(\sigma) \cup f_{S_2}(\sigma)$. Thus, whenever S_1 or S_2 has the nondeterministic possibility of producing an undesirable result, then so does their nondeterministic choice. As the resulting sets of final states one obtains in this analysis the so-called Egli–Milner powerset of states:

$$\mathfrak{P}_{\text{E–M}}(\Sigma) \stackrel{\text{def}}{=} \{\, s \subseteq \Sigma \cup \{\perp\} \mid s \text{ is finite and nonempty, or contains } \perp \,\}$$

Why are infinite subsets of Σ not considered possible sets of final states in this model? Under the assumption that all basic building blocks of relational terms produce only finite, nonempty sets of possible final states, an infinite set of possible final states can only be generated when an infinite computation is possible. This can be seen as follows. Structure the set of all possible computations starting in a given state σ_0 as a tree with root σ_0 and states as nodes. The set of leaves is then exactly the set of possible final states reachable from σ_0, except for $\perp$, which might be missing among the leaves but is represented in the set of final states by the fact that there is an infinite path in the tree. By the assumption above, and since only finite nondeterministic choice is available, this tree is finitely branching. Thus, there is only a finite number of leaves at any given finite depth. Consequently an infinite number of possible final states can only be generated in the presence of an infinite computation (an application of König's lemma [Kön32]).

$(\mathfrak{P}_{E-M}(\Sigma), \sqsubseteq_{E-M})$ is a poset for $\sqsubseteq_{E-M}$ defined by: for $s, t \in \mathfrak{P}_{E-M}(\Sigma)$,

$$s \sqsubseteq_{E-M} t \stackrel{\text{def}}{=} (\bot \in s \wedge s \setminus \{\bot\} \subseteq t) \vee (\bot \notin s \wedge s = t) .$$

Here, $\bot$ can be seen as a placeholder through which $\sqsubseteq_{E-M}$-greater sets can be generated by inserting more states in lieu of $\bot$. Therefore, $\{\bot\}$ is the least element of $(\mathfrak{P}_{E-M}(\Sigma), \sqsubseteq_{E-M})$. As worked out in the exercises to Chapter 8, the poset $(\mathfrak{P}_{E-M}(\Sigma), \sqsubseteq_{E-M})$ possesses lub's for ω-chains. Similarly, the strict functions from $\Sigma \cup \{\bot\}$ to $\mathfrak{P}_{E-M}(\Sigma)$ are partially ordered by the pointwise extension of $\sqsubseteq_{E-M}$. Moreover, the least such function is $\lambda\sigma.\{\bot\}$ and lub's of ω-chains of such functions exist, too. These observations allow the development of a μ-calculus for our relational language similar to that in Section 3.4 above, but based on the Egli–Milner powerset instead of the ordinary powerset. However, this does not lead to a model of, for instance, VDM or Hoare logic for total correctness, because these require a model of nondeterminism in which all possible computations lead to a correct result; such a model is discussed below. This is the reason why we do not pursue this direction further.

Erratic nondeterminism should be contrasted with *demonic* nondeterminism, as used in Chapter 8, which stipulates that all possible computations (whose initial state satisfies some predicate) lead to a correct result. As we shall see, this leads to a semantics in which the nondeterministic possibility of blocking is not expressed. Roger Maddux [Mad96] discusses all these issues in the context of a comprehensive fundamental study on relation-algebraic semantics.

3.6 Historical Background

For early references to the theory of relations, and its applications to computer science, consult the scholarly handbook [SS93].

The least fixed point theory of recursion originates from [Bek69, Par69, SdB69, Maz71]. This theory is based on [Tar55], and has been developed into a rich mathematical theory by Scott, Plotkin, and others (consult, e.g., [Plo83]).

Park's contributions to the μ-calculus are pioneering and impressive — he perceived the full significance of the subject and extended it in a number of fundamental publications to the monotone μ-calculus (together with Hitchcock [HP72, Hit74]) and fairness [Par80, Par81a, Par81b], and discovered that finiteness is not expressible in the μ-calculus [Par76]. The full formulation of the Hitchcock–Park theorem stating semantic correctness of Hitchcock and

Park's 1972 characterization of nontermination first appeared in [dB76], using the so-called Egli–Milner order [Egl75].

The axiomatization of binary relations started out with [Tar41], was subsequently extended in [CT51], led to some confusion in [Lyn50, Lyn56] in which a complete axiomatization was falsely claimed (why Tarski's 1941 axiomatization is incomplete is neatly explained in [Lyn61]), and was finally resolved in a number of papers: in Wadge's [Wad76] (which he never published for fear that it might make the algebra of relations seem more attractive than the *Lucid* formalism which he was then promoting), in [dR76, FM97] and in [FHV96] on fork algebras; see [Mad96] for an overview.

One of the first connections between the relational theory of programming and predicate transformers was made in [dBdR72, dBM75].

Exercises

3.1   Prove Lemma 3.9.

3.2   Formulate the RHS for an inclusion in the style of that given in Example 3.25 for three terms (six variables), but with intersecting four terms, i.e., for the LHS $U_1 ; U_2 \cap X_1 ; X_2 \cap Y_1 ; Y_2 \cap Z_1 ; Z_2$. Give an inductive definition of such inclusions for k terms.

3.3   Prove parts (ii)–(iv) and (vi) of Lemma 3.11.

3.4   Prove Lemma 3.12.

3.5   Prove Lemma 3.13.

3.6   Prove Lemma 3.14.

4

Properties of Simulation

In Chapter 2 it was already mentioned that correctness of an implementation essentially means that the corresponding diagrams commute weakly. Recall that there are four possible ways in which this can be defined, each implying a notion of simulation. This is depicted in Figures 4.1–4.4 for a single operation (note the direction of the inner arrows).

In this chapter the subtle differences between these notions of simulation are studied. Such differences must be taken into account, e.g., when concatenating simulation diagrams. Also we investigate how these notions behave under vertical stacking and how they are related to each other. The outcome has serious consequences for the value of U- and U^{-1}-simulation.

With the necessary technical machinery at hand, we are finally able to show how data invariants can be used to convert partial abstraction relations into total ones.

Then we analyze soundness and completeness of simulation as a method for proving data refinement.

We undertake most of our investigations in a purely semantic set-up, suppressing the distinction between syntax and semantics as much as possible.

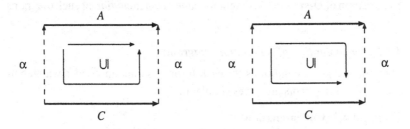

Fig. 4.1. U-simulation. Fig. 4.2. L-simulation.

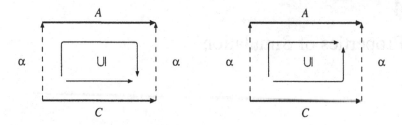

Fig. 4.3. U^{-1}-simulation.   Fig. 4.4. L^{-1}-simulation.

Figure 4.1 represents U-simulation, and Figure 4.2 represents L-simulation. The diagrams in Figures 4.3 and 4.4 represent U^{-1}-simulation and L^{-1}-simulation, respectively.[1] Because a concrete operation can be less nondeterministic than the corresponding abstract operation, we say that the diagrams commute *weakly*. This weak form of commutativity is expressed by "⊆" in the following definitions. (Strong commutativity would be expressed by "=".)

Definition 4.1 (Simulation, cf. Def. 2.1) Let $\alpha \subseteq \Sigma^C \times \Sigma^A$, $A \subseteq \Sigma^A \times \Sigma^A$ and $C \subseteq \Sigma^C \times \Sigma^C$. We say that

- C *U-simulates* A w.r.t. α (denoted $C \subseteq_\alpha^U A$) iff $\alpha^{-1} ; C ; \alpha \subseteq A$.
- C *L-simulates* A w.r.t. α (denoted $C \subseteq_\alpha^L A$) iff $\alpha^{-1} ; C \subseteq A ; \alpha^{-1}$.
- C *U^{-1}-simulates* A w.r.t. α (denoted $C \subseteq_\alpha^{U^{-1}} A$) iff $C \subseteq \alpha ; A ; \alpha^{-1}$.
- C *L^{-1}-simulates* A w.r.t. α (denoted $C \subseteq_\alpha^{L^{-1}} A$) iff $C ; \alpha \subseteq \alpha ; A$. ♣

4.1 Composing Simulation Diagrams

To obtain a compositional theory of simulation, it would be interesting to have a sufficiently strong condition under which these kinds of simulation hold for composed diagrams. Figure 4.5 illustrates this requirement for the horizontal composition of U-simulation diagrams, called *concatenation* of such diagrams.

4.1.1 Concatenation of Simulation Diagrams

Theorem 4.2 gives conditions for each form of simulation under which concatenation of diagrams preserves simulation.

Theorem 4.2 (Concatenation)
Let $A_1, A_2 \subseteq \Sigma^A \times \Sigma^A$, $C_1, C_2 \subseteq \Sigma^C \times \Sigma^C$ and $\alpha \subseteq \Sigma^C \times \Sigma^A$.

---

[1] In the literature, L-simulation is often called *forward simulation* or *downward simulation*, and L^{-1}-simulation *backward simulation* or *upward simulation*.

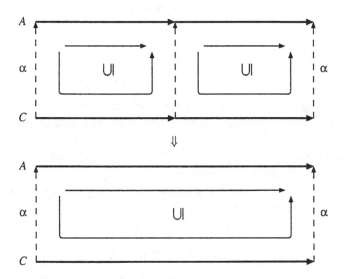

Fig. 4.5. Concatenation requirement for U-simulation.

(i) Concatenated U-diagrams U-simulate if the abstraction relation is total, i.e., if $C_i \subseteq^U_\alpha A_i$, for $i = 1, 2$, and $id_{\Sigma C} \subseteq \alpha ; \alpha^{-1}$ then $C_1 ; C_2 \subseteq^U_\alpha A_1 ; A_2$.

(ii) Concatenated U^{-1}-diagrams U^{-1}-simulate if the abstraction relation is functional, i.e., if $C_i \subseteq^{U^{-1}}_\alpha A_i$, for $i = 1, 2$, and $\alpha^{-1} ; \alpha \subseteq id_{\Sigma A}$ then $C_1 ; C_2 \subseteq^{U^{-1}}_\alpha A_1 ; A_2$.

(iii) Concatenated L-diagrams L-simulate, i.e., if $C_i \subseteq^L_\alpha A_i$, for $i = 1, 2$, then $C_1 ; C_2 \subseteq^L_\alpha A_1 ; A_2$.

(iv) Concatenated L^{-1}-diagrams L^{-1}-simulate, i.e., if $C_i \subseteq^{L^{-1}}_\alpha A_i$, for $i = 1, 2$, then $C_1 ; C_2 \subseteq^{L^{-1}}_\alpha A_1 ; A_2$.

Proof: We only prove parts (i) and (iii). For the proof of (i), assume that α is total, $C_1 \subseteq^U_\alpha A_1$, and $C_2 \subseteq^U_\alpha A_2$.

$$\alpha^{-1} ; C_1 ; C_2 ; \alpha$$
$$= \alpha^{-1} ; C_1 ; id_{\Sigma C} ; C_2 ; \alpha \qquad \text{\textit{id} is the unit of ``;''}$$
$$\subseteq \alpha^{-1} ; C_1 ; \alpha ; \alpha^{-1} ; C_2 ; \alpha \qquad \text{Lemma 3.7, } \alpha \text{ is total}$$
$$\subseteq A_1 ; A_2 \qquad \text{Lemma 3.8, } C_1 \subseteq^U_\alpha A_1, \text{ and } C_2 \subseteq^U_\alpha A_2$$

For the proof of (iii), assume that $C_1 \subseteq_\alpha^L A_1$ and $C_2 \subseteq_\alpha^L A_2$.

$$\alpha^{-1} ; C_1 ; C_2$$
$$\subseteq A_1 ; \alpha^{-1} ; C_2 \qquad\qquad \text{Lemma 3.8, } C_1 \subseteq_\alpha^L A_1$$
$$\subseteq A_1 ; A_2 ; \alpha^{-1} \qquad\qquad \text{Lemma 3.8, } C_2 \subseteq_\alpha^L A_2 \qquad\qquad \square$$

The following example clarifies why the abstraction relation in general has to be total to obtain U-simulation for the concatenation of U-simulations.

Example 4.3 Let $\Sigma^A = \{\zeta, \xi, \eta, \eta'\}$ and $\Sigma^C = \{\sigma, \tau, \tau', \rho, \rho'\}$ such that all these states are pairwise distinct. Furthermore, let $A_1 = \{(\zeta, \xi)\}, A_2 = \{(\xi, \eta)\}, C_1 = \{(\sigma, \tau), (\sigma, \tau')\}, C_2 = \{(\tau, \rho), (\tau', \rho')\}$, and $\alpha = \{(\sigma, \zeta), (\tau, \xi), (\rho, \eta), (\rho', \eta')\}$. Then we have that $C_1 \subseteq_\alpha^U A_1$ and $C_2 \subseteq_\alpha^U A_2$:

$$\alpha^{-1} ; C_1 ; \alpha = \{(\zeta, \xi)\} \subseteq A_1$$
$$\alpha^{-1} ; C_2 ; \alpha = \{(\xi, \eta)\} \subseteq A_2$$

α is not total on $\{\sigma, \tau, \tau', \rho, \rho'\}$ since $\alpha(\{\tau'\}) = \emptyset$, and $C_1 ; C_2 \not\subseteq_\alpha^U A_1 ; A_2$ (see Figure 4.6):

$$\alpha^{-1} ; C_1 ; C_2 ; \alpha = \{(\zeta, \eta), (\zeta, \eta')\} \not\subseteq \{(\zeta, \eta)\} = A_1 ; A_2 . \qquad \heartsuit$$

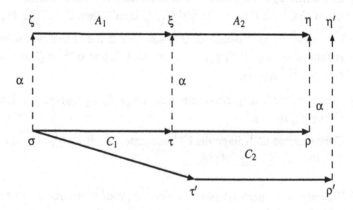

Fig. 4.6. U-simulation concatenation problem for non-total α.

U-simulation might intuitively be more appealing than the other three notions — it is like looking through different pairs of spectacles: with one pair you see the abstract level, with the other pair you see the concrete level. Changing glasses enables you to compare the operations on different levels. Yet it has the disadvantage that the abstraction relation must be total in order for it to be preserved under concatenation. In fact, for soundness of U-simulation one only needs totality on the set of states reachable from proper initial states of the data type.

4.1.2 Vertical Composition of Simulation Diagrams

As a corollary of Lemma 3.8 we achieve that vertically composed simulation diagrams commute, too. This also holds for initializations and finalizations. Altogether this is not surprising since we already know that the semantic criterion for data refinement is transitive.

Corollary 4.4 (Vertical composition of simulation diagrams) Let $A \subseteq \Sigma^A \times \Sigma^A$, $I \subseteq \Sigma^I \times \Sigma^I$, $C \subseteq \Sigma^C \times \Sigma^C$, and let $\alpha \subseteq \Sigma^I \times \Sigma^A$, $\beta \subseteq \Sigma^C \times \Sigma^I$.

Vertically composed simulation diagrams of the same kind commute weakly, i.e., if C X-simulates I w.r.t. β and I X-simulates A w.r.t. α, then C X-simulates A w.r.t. β ; α, where X is U, L, U^{-1}, or L^{-1}.

Proof: All four proofs are simple, as is demonstrated for L-simulation:

$$
\begin{aligned}
(\beta ; \alpha)^{-1} ; C &= \alpha^{-1} ; \beta^{-1} ; C && \text{Lemma 3.9} \\
&\subseteq \alpha^{-1} ; I ; \beta^{-1} && \text{Lemma 3.8, } C \subseteq_\beta^L I \\
&\subseteq A ; \alpha^{-1} ; \beta^{-1} && \text{Lemma 3.8, } I \subseteq_\alpha^L A \\
&= A ; (\beta ; \alpha)^{-1} && \text{Lemma 3.9} \qquad \square
\end{aligned}
$$

4.2 Implications between Simulations

Let us see whether there is a relationship between the different kinds of simulation.

Theorem 4.5
If abstraction relation α is functional, then (with respect to α)

(i) U^{-1}-simulation implies L-simulation.

(ii) U^{-1}-simulation implies L^{-1}-simulation.

(iii) L-simulation implies U-simulation.

(iv) L^{-1}-simulation implies U-simulation.

Proof: We only prove part (iii). Let $\alpha \subseteq \Sigma^C \times \Sigma^A$, $A \subseteq \Sigma^A \times \Sigma^A$ and $C \subseteq \Sigma^C \times \Sigma^C$. Suppose α is functional.

$$\alpha^{-1};C \subseteq A;\alpha^{-1} \qquad \text{L-simulation}$$
$$\Rightarrow \alpha^{-1};C;\alpha \subseteq A;\alpha^{-1};\alpha \qquad \text{Lemma 3.8}$$
$$\Rightarrow \alpha^{-1};C;\alpha \subseteq A \qquad \text{Lemma 3.7.(ii), } \alpha \text{ functional} \qquad \square$$

The following is a case of L-simulation and a non-functional abstraction relation where U-simulation does not hold. Take $(\zeta,\xi) \in A$, $(\sigma,\tau) \in C$ and (σ,ζ), (τ,ξ), $(\tau,\eta) \in \alpha$. In case $(\zeta,\eta) \notin A$, L-simulation holds, but not U-simulation (see Figure 4.7).

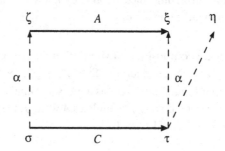

Fig. 4.7. L- but not U-simulation with a non-functional abstraction relation.

Corollary 4.6 U^{-1}-simulation implies U-simulation if the abstraction relation is functional.   ♠

The implications of Theorem 4.5 can be reversed by taking a total abstraction relation rather than a functional one.

Theorem 4.7
If the abstraction relation is total, then (with respect to α)

    (i) U-simulation implies L-simulation.
   (ii) U-simulation implies L^{-1}-simulation.
  (iii) L-simulation implies U^{-1}-simulation.
  (iv) L^{-1}-simulation implies U^{-1}-simulation.

Proof: We only prove part (i). Let $\alpha \subseteq \Sigma^C \times \Sigma^A$, $A \subseteq \Sigma^A \times \Sigma^A$ and $C \subseteq \Sigma^C \times \Sigma^C$. Suppose α is total.

$$\alpha^{-1};C;\alpha \subseteq A \qquad \text{U-simulation}$$

$$\Rightarrow \alpha^{-1};C;\alpha;\alpha^{-1} \subseteq A;\alpha^{-1} \qquad \text{Lemma 3.8}$$

$$\Rightarrow \alpha^{-1};C \subseteq A;\alpha^{-1} \qquad \text{Lemma 3.7.(i), } \alpha \text{ total} \qquad \square$$

To illustrate the fact that implication (i) of Theorem 4.7 is generally not valid if α is not total take $(\zeta,\xi) \in A$, $(\sigma,\tau) \in C$ and $(\sigma,\zeta) \in \alpha$, but $(\xi,\xi) \notin \alpha$ (see Figure 4.8).

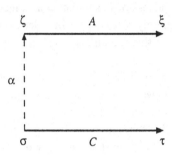

Fig. 4.8. U- but not L-simulation with a partial abstraction relation.

Corollary 4.8 U-simulation implies U^{-1}-simulation if the abstraction relation is total. ♠

The diagrams in Figure 4.9 and Figure 4.10 summarize the results of Theorems 4.5 and 4.7, respectively.

$$U^{-1} \Rightarrow L \qquad\qquad U \Rightarrow L$$

$$\Downarrow \qquad \Downarrow \qquad\qquad \Downarrow \qquad \Downarrow$$

$$L^{-1} \Rightarrow U \qquad\qquad L^{-1} \Rightarrow U^{-1}$$

Fig. 4.9. Implications between simulations if α is functional.

Fig. 4.10. Implications between simulations if α is total.

Notice that the above theorems neglect any relation between L- and L^{-1}-simulation. This is because, in general, these two kinds of simulation are not comparable, except if the abstraction relation is both total and functional, in which case all these four notions of simulation are equivalent.

4.3 Data Invariants and Totality of Abstraction Relations

Observe that by choosing for α the empty relation, one can always prove that a single operation C simulates A w.r.t. α (except for U^{-1}). For data types such anomalies are usually ruled out by the conditions for initialization (in the case of L-simulation) or finalization (in the case of L^{-1}-simulation). This is not true of U-simulation, i.e., any two compatible data types U-simulate one another w.r.t. $\emptyset$. In general, soundness of U-simulation as a method for proving data refinement is guaranteed only if α is total. In order to explain to what extent totality of α, as needed in this soundness proof, can be obtained, we have to discuss the rôle of data invariants.

As we have already seen in Example 2.7 on page 30, introducing a data invariant on the concrete level may restrict the concrete state space to a proper subset of Σ^C such that a previously partial abstraction relation becomes total on that subset. Observe that this does not solve our problem with U-simulation w.r.t. $\emptyset$ as the abstraction relation. This can only be solved by requiring that every reachable abstract state is related to at least one reachable state on the concrete level. This is indeed a reasonable obligation for data refinement steps, but we will not stress it any further at this point since it is rather orthogonal to the concept of partial correctness.

The equally reasonable converse obligation, namely, that every reachable concrete state is related to at least one reachable abstract state, only matters for U-simulation — a technique we shall soon see to be less important than L- and L^{-1}-simulation — whereas this obligation follows from the verification conditions for each of the remaining three notions of simulation.

In the above we informally used the notion of reachable states of a data type. Mathematically speaking, for a given data type $\mathcal{A} = (AI, (A_j)_{j \in J}, AF)$ the set of *reachable states*, denoted by $reach(\mathcal{A})$, forms the smallest subset of Σ^A that is closed under the operations A_j and contains $AI(\Sigma^N)$:

$$reach(\mathcal{A}) \stackrel{\text{def}}{=} \bigcap \{ S \subseteq \Sigma^A \mid AI(\Sigma^N) \subseteq S \wedge \forall j \in J (A_j(S) \subseteq S) \}$$

Example 4.9 (cf. Example 2.11) The reachable states on the concrete level of the bag example are those which can be reached from the initial state $sum = num = 0$ by performing any finite sequence of operations like adding an element x to sum while increasing num by 1, testing whether $num = 0$, or assigning sum/num to av. Obviously, all reachable states satisfy $num = 0 \Rightarrow sum = 0$, which is, indeed, a reasonable data invariant since any combination of $sum \neq 0$ with $num = 0$ does not represent a bag in this model. Consequently, when restricting the concrete state space to those states satisfying this data invariant, the suggested abstraction relation $\Sigma_b b = sum \wedge \#b = num$ becomes total. $\heartsuit$

4.4 Soundness of Simulation

In Def. 2.1 we defined four notions of simulation between data types. In retrospect, this definition is based on the four notions of simulation between single operations defined in Def. 4.1. Using Theorem 4.2 and the monotonicity results from Lemma 3.8 we can now prove soundness of simulation between data types formally, that is, simulation between data types implies data refinement.

Theorem 4.10 (Soundness of simulation)
L- and L^{-1}-simulation are sound. U-simulation is sound if the abstraction relation is total. U^{-1}-simulation is sound if the abstraction relation is functional.

Proof: We prove this only for L-simulation. Only minor changes are necessary to adapt this proof to L^{-1}-simulation. The results for U- and U^{-1}-simulation then follow from Theorems 4.7 and 4.5, respectively.

Let $\mathcal{A} \stackrel{\text{def}}{=} (AI,A,AF)$, and $C \stackrel{\text{def}}{=} (CI,C,CF)$ be compatible data types, i.e., the state spaces involved fit together, and $A = (A_j)_{j \in J}$ and $C = (C_j)_{j \in J}$ for the same index set J. Furthermore, let $\alpha \subseteq \Sigma^C \times \Sigma^A$ be an abstraction relation such that $C \subseteq_\alpha^L \mathcal{A}$.

Let $P(A) \in \mathcal{P}(A)$ and let $P(C) \in \mathcal{P}(C)$ be obtained from $P(A)$ by replacing each occurrence of an abstract operation A_j by the corresponding concrete operation C_j. Observe that this already requires the syntactic structure of $P(A)$ to be known. We show by induction over the structure of $P(A)$ that $P(C) \subseteq_\alpha^L P(A)$.

The basic cases are either trivial (id_{Σ^A}, $\emptyset$) or assumed above (A_j). We consider three induction steps, namely ";", "$\cup$", and "μX":

- $P(A)$ is the sequential composition $P_1(A) ; P_2(A)$ of two smaller programs $P_1(A)$, $P_2(A) \in \mathcal{P}(A)$. From the induction hypothesis (for $i = 1, 2$: $P_i(C) \subseteq_\alpha^L P_i(A)$) and Theorem 4.2.(iii) it follows that $P(C) \subseteq_\alpha^L P(A)$.
- $P(A)$ is the nondeterministic choice $P_1(A) \cup P_2(A)$ of two smaller programs $P_1(A)$, $P_2(A) \in \mathcal{P}(A)$. The induction hypothesis in this case is $P_i(C) \subseteq_\alpha^L P_i(A)$, for $i = 1, 2$.

$$\alpha^{-1} ; (P_1(C) \cup P_2(C))$$
$$= (\alpha^{-1} ; P_1(C)) \cup (\alpha^{-1} ; P_2(C)) \qquad \text{Lemma 3.7}$$
$$\subseteq (P_1(A) ; \alpha^{-1}) \cup (P_2(A) ; \alpha^{-1}) \qquad \text{ind. hyp.}$$
$$= (P_1(A) \cup P_2(A)) ; \alpha^{-1} \qquad \text{Lemma 3.7}$$

- $P(A)$ is $\mu X.Q(A)(X)$. The induction hypothesis in this case is $(Q(C))^i(\emptyset) \subseteq_\alpha^L (Q(A))^i(\emptyset)$, for all $i \in \mathbb{N}$.

$$\alpha^{-1} ; \mu X.Q(C)(X)$$

$$= \alpha^{-1} ; \bigcup ((Q(C))^i(\emptyset))_{i \in \mathbb{N}} \qquad \text{Th. 3.22}$$

$$= \bigcup (\alpha^{-1} ; (Q(C))^i(\emptyset))_{i \in \mathbb{N}} \qquad \text{Lemma 3.7}$$

$$\subseteq \bigcup ((Q(A))^i(\emptyset) ; \alpha^{-1})_{i \in \mathbb{N}} \qquad \text{ind. hyp.}$$

$$= \bigcup ((Q(A))^i(\emptyset))_{i \in \mathbb{N}} ; \alpha^{-1} \qquad \text{Lemma 3.7}$$

$$= \mu X.Q(A)(X) ; \alpha^{-1} \qquad \text{Th. 3.22}$$

Using that $P(C) \subseteq^{\mathsf{L}}_\alpha P(A)$ we can conclude

$$CI ; P(C) ; CF$$

$$\subseteq AI ; \alpha^{-1} ; P(C) ; CF \qquad (\text{init}^{\mathsf{L}})$$

$$\subseteq AI ; P(A) ; \alpha^{-1} ; CF \qquad \text{proved above}$$

$$\subseteq AI ; P(A) ; AF \qquad (\text{final}^{\mathsf{L}}) \qquad\qquad \square$$

The implications depicted in Figure 4.9 and 4.10 summarize the implications between our four notions of simulation when the abstraction relation α is functional, or when it is total. These are interesting when placed in the context of the soundness theorem Theorem 4.10: in general, neither U- nor U^{-1}-simulation allows one to prove data refinements not already provable by both L- and L^{-1}-simulation. Therefore we shall concentrate on L- and L^{-1}-simulation, treating U- and U^{-1}-simulation less thoroughly in the sequel.

4.5 Maximal Data Types

Given an abstract data type $\mathcal{A}$ and an abstraction relation α, we define the maximal (concrete) data type that L-, respectively, L^{-1}-simulates $\mathcal{A}$ w.r.t. α.

Here, maximality of a solution data type means that none of its operations, initialization, or finalization can be extended without losing the property of simulation stated above.

In Chapter 7 we solve this problem for a single abstract level operation, but there we are more ambitious, for we express the solution syntactically. Here we neglect this syntactic layer on top of the semantic world of binary relations. This trivializes the task for a single abstract operation A_i.

For L-simulation, one has to solve $X \subseteq^{\mathsf{L}}_\alpha A_i$ for the maximal relation X satisfying it.

$$X \subseteq^{\mathsf{L}}_\alpha A_i$$

$$\Leftrightarrow \alpha^{-1} ; X \subseteq A_i ; \alpha^{-1} \qquad \text{Def. 4.1}$$

$$\Leftrightarrow X \subseteq \alpha^{-1} \rightsquigarrow (A_i ; \alpha^{-1}) \qquad \text{Lemma 3.11.(i)}$$

For L^{-1}-simulation, one has to solve $X \subseteq_\alpha^{L^{-1}} A_i$ for maximal X.

$$X \subseteq_\alpha^{L^{-1}} A_i$$
$$\Leftrightarrow X; \alpha \subseteq \alpha; A_i \qquad \text{Def. 4.1}$$
$$\Leftrightarrow X \subseteq [\alpha](\alpha; A_i) \qquad \text{Lemma 3.12.(i)}$$

This motivates the following two notions.

Definition 4.11 (Relation transformers) Let $A \subseteq \Sigma^A \times \Sigma^A$ and $\alpha \subseteq \Sigma^C \times \Sigma^A$.

$$L_\alpha^{-1}(A_i) \stackrel{\text{def}}{=} [\alpha](\alpha; A_i)$$
$$L_\alpha(A_i) \stackrel{\text{def}}{=} \alpha^{-1} \rightsquigarrow (A_i; \alpha^{-1})$$

Moreover, for data type $\mathcal{A} = (AI, (A_i)_{i \in I}, AF)$ define data types $I_\alpha^{-1}(\mathcal{A})$ and $L_\alpha(\mathcal{A})$ by

$$L_\alpha^{-1}(\mathcal{A}) \stackrel{\text{def}}{=} ([\alpha]AI, (L_\alpha^{-1}(A_i))_{i \in I}, (\alpha; AF))$$
$$L_\alpha(\mathcal{A}) \stackrel{\text{def}}{=} ((AI; \alpha^{-1}), (L(\alpha^{-1})(A_i))_{i \in I}, (\alpha^{-1} \rightsquigarrow AF)) \qquad \clubsuit$$

With this definition the following corollary is immediate.

Corollary 4.12 $L_\alpha^{-1}(\mathcal{A})$ is the maximal data type L^{-1}-simulating data type $\mathcal{A}$ w.r.t. α. $L_\alpha(\mathcal{A})$ is the maximal data type L-simulating $\mathcal{A}$ w.r.t. α. $\spadesuit$

4.6 Completeness

4.6.1 Overview

In this section we prove that the combination of L- and L^{-1}-simulation is complete, i.e., whenever a data type C refines a data type $\mathcal{A}$, this can be proven using these two notions of simulation by defining appropriate abstraction relations.

Our completeness proof is based on that of Hoare, He, and Sanders [HHS87].

Hoare, He, and Sanders (HHS) present their result using a total correctness relational semantics based on Smyth [Smy78], in which the mere nondeterministic possibility of diverging already has the same characterization as sure divergence (this corresponds to Dijkstra's requirement in [Dij76] that in case a program has a nondeterministic possibility of diverging or of violating the postcondition after its execution when starting in a certain state, the weakest precondition in this state is false; this is discussed in Chapter 8).

We present this result in two stages. First, in the present section, a closely related completeness proof is given, but for the relational semantics of programs used in the previous and present chapter, which is adequate for describing partial correctness. Then, in Chapter 9, the completeness result of HHS is presented for their relational total correctness semantics of programs. This strategy has the advantage that it leads to a better exposition of the main idea of their proof, since its gist turns out to be independent of the particular notion of relational semantics used and is simpler to present for the usual (partial correctness) interpretation used in the present chapter.

4.6.2 The Completeness Theorem of HHS — the Theorem and Proof Proper

In Section 2.2.2 we already saw an example of a data refinement which is not an L-simulation. Similarly one can find an example of a data refinement which is not an L^{-1}-simulation (this is Exercise 2.5). By juxtaposing these two examples (by a disjoint union) one obtains a data refinement which is neither an L- nor an L^{-1}-simulation.

This demonstrates that in general more than one simulation step is needed to prove data refinement. To this end, HHS introduce an intermediate level, which essentially applies the powerset construction of Rabin and Scott [RS59] to convert a nondeterministic automaton into an equivalent deterministic one [HU79]. (This construction is attributed by Büchi in [Sie89] to Myhill [Myh57] and Copi *et al.* [CEW58], and also appears in Rabin and Scott's [RS59].)

Given a relation $X \subseteq A \times B$ with domain set A and range set B, its *powerset construction* is the total function mapping each subset of A to its relational image through X (as defined in Def. 3.6 on page 50). This definition poses a minor problem. The powerset construction of operation A_i, for instance, does not qualify as an operation of a data type since we would rather work with its graph than this total function itself. This is reflected in the following definition.

Definition 4.13 (Powerset construction) The inverse $\ni$ of membership $\in$ is defined in the usual manner. We say that $S \ni x$ iff $x \in S$ holds.

When adapted to data types, the powerset constructions for initialization $AI \subseteq \Sigma^N \times \Sigma^A$ and finalization $AF \subseteq \Sigma^A \times \Sigma^N$ of a data type $\mathcal{A}$ are defined such that data refinement between $\mathcal{A}$ and $PC(\mathcal{A})$ does not already fail for typing reasons.

$$PC(AI) \stackrel{\text{def}}{=} \left\{ (\sigma, AI(\{\sigma\})) \mid \sigma \in \Sigma^N \right\}$$

$$PC(A_i) \stackrel{\text{def}}{=} \left\{ (V, A_i(V)) \mid V \subseteq \Sigma^A \right\}$$

$$PC(AF) \stackrel{\text{def}}{=} \left\{ (V, \tau) \mid V \subseteq \Sigma^A \wedge \tau \in AF(V) \right\}$$

$$PC(\mathcal{A}) \stackrel{\text{def}}{=} (PC(AI),(PC(A_i))_{i\in I},PC(AF)) \qquad \clubsuit$$

The remainder of the proof consists of two parts. Remember that we want to prove now that if C refines $\mathcal{A}$ then this can be proven using L^{-1}- and L-simulation for appropriate abstraction relations, introducing $PC(\mathcal{A})$ as an intermediate stage of refinement.

Given a data type $\mathcal{A}$, one proves that the data types $PC(\mathcal{A})$ and $\mathcal{A}$ are *bisimilar* ([Mil71, Mil80]), i.e., $PC(\mathcal{A})$ and $\mathcal{A}$ mutually simulate each other. Consequently one obtains that if C is a data refinement of $\mathcal{A}$ then C is also a data refinement of $PC(\mathcal{A})$ by transitivity of data refinement.

Theorem 4.14

$\mathcal{A}$ and $PC(\mathcal{A})$ are mutual data refinements.

Proof: We prove that $PC(\mathcal{A})$ refines $\mathcal{A}$ by $PC(\mathcal{A}) \subseteq_{\ni}^{L^{-1}} \mathcal{A}$ and the inverse refinement by $\mathcal{A} \subseteq_{\ni-1}^{L} PC(\mathcal{A})$. Since the parts of the proofs for initialization and finalization are simplifications of the proof for a single operation A_i we restrict ourselves to proving points $(op_i^{L^{-1}})$ and (op_i^{L}) of Def. 2.1 simultaneously, by establishing $PC(A_i)\,;\ni\, =\, \ni\,;A_i$.

$$(X,y) \in (\ni\,;A_i)$$
$$\Leftrightarrow \exists z \in X\,((z,y) \in A_i) \qquad \text{Def. 4.13}$$
$$\Leftrightarrow y \in A_i(X) \qquad \text{Def. 3.6}$$
$$\Leftrightarrow (X,y) \in (PC(A_i)\,;\ni) \qquad \text{Def. 4.13} \qquad \square$$

HHS observe that $PC(\mathcal{A})$ satisfies an important property: its initialization $PC(AI)$ and its operations $PC(A_i)$ are total and functional by definition. Together with the following lemma this enables HHS to prove that if C refines $\mathcal{A}$ then C does indeed L-simulate $PC(\mathcal{A})$.

Lemma 4.15

  (i) If X is total and functional then $X\,;([Y]Z) = [Y]\,(X\,;Z)$
  (ii) If X is functional and index set I is nonempty then $X\,;\bigcap_{i\in I}Y_i = \bigcap_{i\in I}(X\,;Y_i)$

Proof: Exercise. $\qquad \square$

The crux of their proof is the construction of the corresponding abstraction relation α.

Theorem 4.16 (Existence of an L-simulation relation)

If C refines $\mathcal{A}$ and initialization and operations of $\mathcal{A}$ are both total and functional then there exists a relation α such that $C \subseteq_{\alpha}^{L} \mathcal{A}$.

Proof: Assume that C refines $\mathcal{A}$ and that AI and A_i ($i \in I$) of $\mathcal{A}$ are both total and functional. Define $\alpha_P \overset{\text{def}}{=} ([(P(C);CF)](P(A);AF))^{-1}$ for $P(A) \in \mathcal{P}(A)$. Then α is defined by $\alpha \overset{\text{def}}{=} \bigcap_{P(A)\in\mathcal{P}(A)} \alpha_P$. Next we prove each of the conditions listed in Def. 2.1 for L-simulation. First we check (init^L), i.e., we have to show that $CI \subseteq AI;\alpha^{-1}$.

$$\forall P(A) \in \mathcal{P}(A)\,(CI\,;P(C)\,;CF \subseteq AI\,;P(A)\,;AF) \qquad \text{assumption}$$

$$\Leftrightarrow \forall P(A) \in \mathcal{P}(A)\,(CI \subseteq [P(C)\,;CF]\,(AI\,;P(A)\,;AF)) \qquad \text{Lemma 3.12.(i)}$$

$$\Leftrightarrow \forall P(A) \in \mathcal{P}(A)\,(CI \subseteq AI\,;[P(C)\,;CF]\,(P(A)\,;AF)) \qquad \text{Lemma 4.15}$$

$$\Leftrightarrow CI \subseteq \bigcap_{P(A)\in\mathcal{P}(A)} (AI\,;[P(C)\,;CF]\,(P(A)\,;AF)) \qquad \text{set theory}$$

$$\Leftrightarrow CI \subseteq AI\,;\bigcap_{P(A)\in\mathcal{P}(A)} ([P(C)\,;CF]\,(P(A)\,;AF)) \qquad \text{Lemma 4.15}$$

$$\Leftrightarrow CI \subseteq AI\,;\alpha^{-1} \qquad \text{def. of } \alpha$$

Observe that validity of the initialization condition is proven to be equivalent to the assumption that C refines $\mathcal{A}$. As we shall see next, the conditions for operations and finalizations only depend on the construction of α, not on the refinement.

Second comes condition (op$_i^L$), i.e., $\alpha^{-1}\,;C_i \subseteq A_i\,;\alpha^{-1}$. Let $i \in I$ and $P(A) \in \mathcal{P}(A)$. Then $P'(A) \overset{\text{def}}{=} A_i\,;P(A) \in \mathcal{P}(A)$ and $P'(C) = (C_i\,;P(C))$ is the corresponding concrete level program.

$$\alpha^{-1}\,;C_i \subseteq [C_i\,;P(C)\,;CF]\,(A_i\,;P(A)\,;AF)\,;C_i \qquad \text{def. of } \alpha$$

$$\Leftrightarrow \alpha^{-1}\,;C_i \subseteq [C_i]\,([P(C)\,;CF]\,(A_i\,;P(A)\,;AF))\,;C_i \qquad \text{Lemma 3.12.(iii)}$$

$$\Rightarrow \alpha^{-1}\,;C_i \subseteq [P(C)\,;CF]\,(A_i\,;P(A)\,;AF) \qquad \text{Lemma 3.12.(i)}$$

Similarly to the proof of (init^L) it follows that $\alpha^{-1}\,;C_i \subseteq A_i\,;\alpha^{-1}$. Finally we prove (final^L), i.e., $\alpha^{-1}\,;CF \subseteq AF$. We use that $id_{\Sigma A} \in \mathcal{P}(A)$ and that the corresponding concrete level program is $id_{\Sigma C}$. (Observe that, regardless of α, $id_{\Sigma C}$ L- and L^{-1}-simulates $id_{\Sigma A}$.)

$$\alpha^{-1} \subseteq [id_{\Sigma C}\,;CF]\,(id_{\Sigma A}\,;AF) \qquad \text{def. of } \alpha$$

$$\Leftrightarrow \alpha^{-1} \subseteq [CF]\,AF \qquad id \text{ is the unit of ``;''}$$

$$\Leftrightarrow \alpha^{-1}\,;CF \subseteq AF \qquad \text{Lemma 3.12} \qquad \square$$

Theorem 4.17 (Completeness)
L- and L^{-1}-simulation are sufficient to prove that C refines $\mathcal{A}$ whenever this is the case.

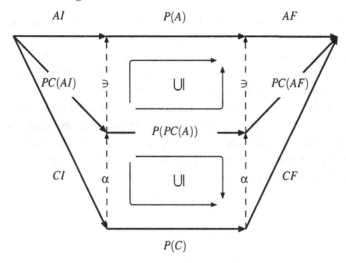

Fig. 4.11. Structure of the completeness proof.

Proof: Let C and $\mathcal{A}$ be compatible data types such that C refines $\mathcal{A}$. By Theorem 4.14, $PC(\mathcal{A})$ and $\mathcal{A}$ are bisimilar, and $PC(\mathcal{A})$ L^{-1}-simulates $\mathcal{A}$. It follows that C refines $PC(\mathcal{A})$. The initialization and the operations of $PC(\mathcal{A})$ are total and functional by Def. 4.13. Thus, by Theorem 4.16, the fact that C refines $PC(\mathcal{A})$ can be proven using L-simulation. $\square$

The proof of the completeness theorem is illustrated in Figure 4.11.

4.7 Historical Background

The first reference to soundness and completeness proofs for data refinement is the 1985 preprint of [Nip86]. Our proofs are based on [HHS87].

Given an abstract data type $\mathcal{A}$ and an abstraction relation α, we solved in Section 4.5 the problem of finding the maximal concrete data type C, which L-simulates $\mathcal{A}$ w.r.t. α. The converse of this problem, namely of finding the minimal $\mathcal{A}$ provided C and α are given, is interesting too. In the relational setting, however, a unique solution to that problem exists in general only for the less interesting case of U-simulation. For as soon as α is non-functional, it need not be the case that just because C L-simulates two candidate abstract operations, also the intersection of the two satisfies the L-simulation requirement (see Exercise 4.10):

$$C \subseteq^L_\alpha A_1 \wedge C \subseteq^L_\alpha A_2 \not\Rightarrow C \subseteq^L_\alpha A_1 \cap A_2$$

We owe this observation to Markus Müller-Olm who circumvented this difficulty in his work on compiler verification [Mül97] by moving to the richer semantic space of predicate transformers (see Chapter 10). The underlying general technique for designing approximative semantics of programs, which solves the problem posed above, is due to Patrick and Radhia Cousot [CC77, Cou81, CC92a, CC92b, Cou96] and is called *abstract interpretation*. This technique has found many applications, for instance, in the design of automatic program analyzers that complement or enhance compilers by extracting interesting program properties to provide conservative answers[2] to questions about the to-be-expected run-time behavior of programs.

Exercises

4.1   Prove parts (ii) and (iv) of Theorem 4.2.

4.2   (cf. Example 4.3) Construct an example showing that the abstraction relation in general has to be functional for U^{-1}-simulation to propagate from diagrams to concatenations of diagrams.

4.3   Prove parts (i), (ii), and (iv) of Theorem 4.5.

4.4   Prove parts (ii)–(iv) of Theorem 4.7.

4.5   What effects would there be, for instance, on the soundness proof for simulation if we had taken "$\bigcup_{i \in \mathbb{N}} P_i$ for $\subseteq$-chains $(P_i)_{i \in \mathbb{N}}$ in $T(A)$" instead of "$\mu X.P(X)$ with $P(X) \in T(A)$" as the last clause in Def. 3.15?

4.6   In Example 2.3 we presented a data refinement which is not provable using only L-simulation. Now give examples of data refinements that are provable using a single notion of simulation but not provable using respectively

        (a) L^{-1}-simulation only,

        (b) U^{-1}-simulation only,

        (c) U-simulation only.

4.7   Adapt the proof of Theorem 4.10 to L^{-1}-simulation.

4.8   Prove Lemma 4.15.

---

[2] In this context a "conservative answer" is one that does not lead to overly optimistic expectations about the program behavior. A conservative approximation of the answer "yes" to the question "Does the program terminate?" may be "no", but not vice versa, provided the goal of the programmer is to write a terminating program.

4.9 Consider the two compatible data types $\mathcal{A}$ and C defined by

$\mathcal{A} = (AI, (A_j)_{j \in \{1,2\}}, AF)$	$C = (CI, (C_j)_{j \in \{1,2\}}, CF)$
$AI = \{(\sigma_0, a_{00}), (\sigma_1, a_{01})\}$	$CI = \{(\sigma_0, c_0), (\sigma_1, c_0)\}$
$A_1 = \{(a_{00}, a_1), (a_{01}, a_1)\}$	$C_1 = \{(c_0, c_1)\}$
$A_2 = \{(a_1, a_{20}), (a_1, a_{21})\}$	$C_2 = \{(c_1, c_2)\}$
$AF = \{(a_{20}, \tau_0), (a_{21}, \tau_1)\}$	$CF = \{(c_2, \tau_0), (c_2, \tau_1)\}$

C is a data refinement of $\mathcal{A}$. Show that this fact is unprovable using either L- or L^{-1}-simulation alone. Prove it using a combination of these two simulation techniques.

4.10 Consider the converse of the problem of finding the least refined concrete operation L-simulating an abstract one. Construct a concrete relation C and an abstraction relation α such that the smallest abstract relation A for which $C \subseteq_\alpha^L A$ is not uniquely determined. Try to find a minimal such example.

5

Notation and Semantics

In the previous chapter, our proof techniques for data refinement, namely the notions of simulation introduced in Def. 2.1, have been proven adequate in Theorem 4.17 and sound in Theorem 4.10. This establishes proving simulation as an appropriate technique for verifying data refinement.

In Chapters 9 and 10 we shall encounter other notions of data refinement and simulation defined for frameworks different from that of the binary relations considered until now, for which similar soundness and completeness results will be proven.

In Part II of this monograph a number of established methods for proving data refinement will be similarly analyzed. (These methods are: VDM, Z, and those of Reynolds, Hehner, Back, Abadi and Lamport, and Lynch.) This is done by showing to what extent they are special cases of, or are equivalent to, the previously investigated notions of simulation referred to above, which are the subject of Part I of this monograph.

This justifies considering simulation as a generic term for all these techniques, where the connection with data refinement is made through appropriate soundness and completeness theorems.

Now an immediate consequence of our goal of comparing these simulation methods for proving data refinement is that we must be able to compare semantically expressed methods such as L-simulation and the methods of Abadi and Lamport and of Lynch (see Chapter 14) with syntactically formulated ones such as VDM, Z, and Reynolds' method. This implies immediately that we have to distinguish between syntax and semantics. We bridge this gap by introducing interpretation functions for several classes of expressions, such as arithmetic expressions and predicates built on them (see Section 5.2), programs (see Section 5.3), and relations (see Section 5.4).

Some of these simulation methods are formulated using relations, others using predicates only, and several of them are based on the interaction between the two (see Section 5.5). Thus, another consequence of our goal is the need to switch between representations of relations and predicates on both the semantic and the syntactic level in order to be able to give proofs about their interaction (see, e.g., Lemmas 5.17 and 5.19, Theorems 7.2 and 9.9, or Section 13.2). By way of example, consider the expression $x < z$; within our mixed setting of predicates and binary relations it is desirable to be able to interpret this expression both as a set of states $\{ \sigma \in [\{x,z\} \longrightarrow \mathbb{V}] \mid \sigma(x) < \sigma(z) \}$ and as a binary relation, such as $\{ (\sigma,\tau) \in [\{x\} \longrightarrow \mathbb{V}] \times [\{z\} \longrightarrow \mathbb{V}] \mid \sigma(x) < \tau(z) \}$, depending on the context in which this expression occurs. This has a number of compelling technical consequences. The usual view that predicates are interpreted by truth-valued functions needs to be complemented by interpreting them as sets and even relations. And when interpreting predicates as relations, one has to identify which of their free variables are used as input and which as output variables since that choice is still open. This modest amount of typing information in our interpretation functions for predicates eventually permeates our whole set-up.

So much for explaining the technical consequences of our goal in this monograph, consequences which represent the distinguishing feature of our approach and which are worked out in detail within this chapter.

Next follows a more systematic account of its technical contents.

5.1 Introduction

This chapter provides a formal basis for characterizing and reasoning about data refinement as introduced in Chapter 1.

In later chapters we reduce the task of proving data refinement to proving validity of *Hoare-style partial correctness formulae*. An example of the structure of such formulae is depicted in Figure 5.1.

Such a formula, also called a *Hoare triple*, consists of a *program* enclosed by two *assertions* called respectively *pre-* and *postcondition*. Curly brackets enclose each of the assertions.

The validity of the Hoare triple $\{\pi_1\}\, S\, \{\pi_2\}$ informally means:

If precondition π_1 holds, and if program S terminates, then postcondition π_2 holds after termination of S.

Observe that this does not impose that termination of S is implied by π_1.

Assertions (formally introduced in Section 5.2.2) are first order predicate logic expressions ranging over two different categories of variables: *program variables* whose values are subject to change during program execution, and *logical variables* whose appearance is restricted to Hoare-style assertions and

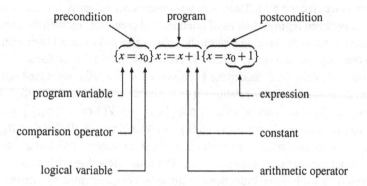

Fig. 5.1. Structure of a Hoare-style partial correctness formula.

whose values are not accessible to, and therefore not changed by, programs. The sole use of logical variables is to increase the expressiveness of assertions. Without such variables, a statement as simple as $x := x + 1$ cannot be characterized by a single Hoare triple; this is proven in Section 5.5.

In the process of data refinement, abstract level operations are refined to concrete level operations. But what are operations supposed to be syntactically?

Operations at the most concrete level are pieces of program text in some sequential, imperative programming language, for instance, Pascal or Guarded Commands. For this purpose we introduce a toy programming language with recursion in Section 5.3.

This restriction to a programming language makes no sense on higher specification levels since there the specification of initial/final state behavior is not necessarily tied to one particular implementation. Instead one has to decouple specifications from implementations and work with pure specifications.

To provide a common ground for reasoning about operations on all levels we add *specification statements* to our toy programming language. Remember that the meaning of Hoare triple $\{\pi_1\} S \{\pi_2\}$ depends on the actual initial/final state behavior of S. However, π_1 and π_2 together characterize the maximal initial/final state behavior which S is allowed to expose. Specification statement $\pi_1 \rightsquigarrow \pi_2$ denotes this maximal behavior; it is pronounced "π_1 leads to π_2".

Our formal justification for reducing the task of proving data refinement to proving validity of Hoare-style partial correctness formulae is carried out within a calculus of binary relations. Our relations are sets of state pairs. On the syntactic level they are expressed by assertions, abstraction relations, toy language programs (including specification statements): in general, relational terms.

In Chapter 1 we have explained that inclusion between initial/final state behavior coincides with refinement. Hence, the obvious choice for correctness formulae on top of relational terms is inclusions between relational terms. Hoare triples are shown to be just a different notation for certain inclusions.

In this chapter we subsequently define syntax and semantics of assertions, abstraction relations, toy language programs, relational terms, and correctness formulae. Proof obligations for data refinement are correctness formulae. The most important ones are those for pairs of operations (A_i, C_i). That these can be reduced to Hoare triples is the subject of Chapter 7 and provides sufficient motivation for the presentation of a sound and relatively complete proof system for Hoare triples for our programming language in Chapter 6.

These concepts are a prerequisite for our development of a simple theory of data refinement culminating in the formal characterization of data refinement in Hoare-style and VDM-style frameworks in later chapters, and in the comparison between these characterizations.

5.2 Predicates

We first briefly repeat the routine definitions of arithmetic expressions and predicates from first order logic with equality over the integers. Therefore, we introduce the following syntactic categories:

- constants *Const*, with typical meta-variable c, abbreviated to *Const* $\ni c$ in syntax definitions,
- variables *Var* $\ni x$,
- arithmetic operators *Op* $\ni op$,
- comparison operators *Cop* $\ni cop$,
- arithmetic expressions *Exp* $\ni e, e_1, e_2$, and
- first order predicates *Pred* $\ni p, p_1, p_2$.

The structure of objects of these syntactic categories is defined in BNF notation by

$$c ::= 1$$
$$op ::= + \mid - \mid *$$
$$cop ::= < \mid =$$
$$e ::= c \mid x \mid e_1 \; op \; e_2$$
$$p ::= \text{false} \mid e_1 \; cop \; e_2 \mid p_1 \Rightarrow p_2 \mid \forall x(p_1)$$

We employ parentheses to indicate aggregation and assign priorities to operators to save parentheses. (See Appendix D for tables of precedence.) Officially we restrict ourselves to the constants and operators mentioned above to economize on the number of lines in semantics definitions. However, the traditional operators not mentioned above can be easily expressed by them. Hence, we freely use, e.g., the following abbreviations, just to name the more common ones.

$$0 \stackrel{\text{def}}{=} 1 - 1$$
$$-e_1 \stackrel{\text{def}}{=} 0 - e_1$$
$$\neg p_1 \stackrel{\text{def}}{=} p_1 \Rightarrow \text{false}$$
$$\text{true} \stackrel{\text{def}}{=} \neg\text{false}$$
$$p_1 \vee p_2 \stackrel{\text{def}}{=} \neg p_1 \Rightarrow p_2$$
$$e_1 \leq e_2 \stackrel{\text{def}}{=} e_1 = e_2 \vee e_1 < e_2$$
$$p_1 \wedge p_2 \stackrel{\text{def}}{=} \neg(\neg p_1 \vee \neg p_2)$$
$$p_1 \Leftarrow p_2 \stackrel{\text{def}}{=} p_2 \Rightarrow p_1$$
$$p_1 \Leftrightarrow p_2 \stackrel{\text{def}}{=} (p_1 \Rightarrow p_2) \wedge (p_2 \Rightarrow p_1)$$
$$\exists x(p_1) \stackrel{\text{def}}{=} \neg\forall x(\neg p_1)$$

The *interpretation* $\Im = (\mathfrak{S}, \sigma)$ of first order languages as defined in standard textbooks on mathematical logic (e.g., [Sho67, Men87]) depends on two components:

- a *structure* $\mathfrak{S} = (\mathbb{V}, s)$, where $\mathbb{V}$ is a nonempty set of values, the *carrier* of $\mathfrak{S}$. Function s maps each
  - constant $c \in Const$ to a value $c^s \in \mathbb{V}$,
  - n-ary arithmetic operator[1] $op \in Op$ to an n-ary function $op^s : \mathbb{V}^n \longrightarrow \mathbb{V}$, and
  - n-ary comparison operator $cop \in Cop$ to an n-ary relation $cop^s \subseteq \mathfrak{P}(\mathbb{V}^n)$.
- a *state* $\sigma : Var \longrightarrow \mathbb{V}$ assigning values to all variables.

The meaning assigned to operators (elements of Op and Cop) and constants in $Const$ is the standard one from integer arithmetic. For instance, 1^s is the mathematical object $1 \in \mathbb{Z}$ and $+^s$ is the usual integer addition $+ : \mathbb{Z} \times \mathbb{Z} \longrightarrow \mathbb{Z}$ mapping, e.g., the pair $(-2, 3)$ to 1.

For now, we restrict ourselves to the language given above and to the integers $\mathbb{Z}$ as the carrier $\mathbb{V}$. Later on we will work in a more general set-up, in which new operators are introduced and $\mathbb{Z}$ is replaced by $\mathbb{V}$, a set whose contents depend on which data types are to be interpreted in the context at hand.

---

[1] $+, -$, etc. are all binary arithmetic operators

The classical notation for the — yet to be defined — fact that predicate p holds in interpretation $\mathfrak{I}$ is $\mathfrak{I} \models p$ (or $\models_{\mathfrak{I}} p$), also pronounced "$\mathfrak{I}$ is a model of p" or "p is valid in $\mathfrak{I}$". Relation $\models$ is called the *satisfaction* or *entailment* relation. If p holds regardless of the interpretation we say that p is *valid*, denoted by $\models p$.

Regardless of interpretation $\mathfrak{I}$, Boolean constants and operators have a fixed meaning in first order languages. In our language, (officially) false and $\Rightarrow$ are the only such objects. Predicate false never holds, formally denoted by $\mathfrak{I} \not\models$ false for all interpretations $\mathfrak{I}$. Given two predicates p_1 and p_2, predicate $p_1 \Rightarrow p_2$ holds in interpretation $\mathfrak{I}$ if, and only if, whenever p_1 is valid in $\mathfrak{I}$ then so is p_2.

Instead of taking the satisfaction-based view we prefer to speak about *evaluating* predicates in interpretations to obtain a truth value in $\mathbb{B} = \{ff, tt\}$, where tt stands for true and ff for false. In this view, $(\mathfrak{S}, \sigma) \models p$ can be written as $T[\![p]\!]_{(\mathfrak{S},\sigma)} = tt$ or, stressing the rôle of σ, as $\sigma \in C[\![p]\!]_{\mathfrak{S}}$.

Since the structure $\mathfrak{S}$ is not subject to change in this section, only states σ are mentioned explicitly in the semantics definitions below. However, in later chapters we deliberately extend structure $\mathfrak{S}$, e.g., to cover operations on sets, lists, and bags. As long as no confusion arises we drop parentheses, subscripts, and superscripts.

Definition 5.1 State space Σ consists of all total functions $\sigma : Var \longrightarrow \mathbb{V}$; we write this $\Sigma \stackrel{\text{def}}{=} [Var \longrightarrow \mathbb{V}]$ for short. Thus Σ is parameterized by Var and $\mathbb{V}$.

The *variant state* $(\sigma : x \mapsto v)$ denotes a state similar to σ except for its value at variable x, which is v. Formally,

$$(\sigma : x \mapsto v) : Var \longrightarrow \mathbb{V}$$

$$(\sigma : x \mapsto v)(y) \stackrel{\text{def}}{=} \begin{cases} v & \text{if } y \text{ is } x \\ \sigma(y) & \text{otherwise} \end{cases}$$

This notation extends straightforwardly to lists of values and lists of variables.[2] Sometimes the notation for state variant $(\sigma : x \mapsto v)$ is too heavy. Then we use the more concise σ_x^v. ♣

Next, we define the semantics of arithmetic expressions.

Definition 5.2 (Semantics of arithmetic expressions)

$$\mathcal{E}[\![.]\!] : Exp \longrightarrow (\Sigma \longrightarrow \mathbb{V})$$

---

[2] Simple facts about variant states are used in the sequel, for instance, if x and y are different elements of Var then $((\sigma : x \mapsto v_1) : y \mapsto v_2) = ((\sigma : y \mapsto v_2) : x \mapsto v_1)$. We do not intend to axiomatize variant states, instead we use just mathematical reasoning over functions.

Let $\sigma \in \Sigma$ and define

$$\mathcal{E}[\![c]\!]\sigma \stackrel{\text{def}}{=} c^s$$

$$\mathcal{E}[\![x]\!]\sigma \stackrel{\text{def}}{=} \sigma(x)$$

$$\mathcal{E}[\![e_1 \; op \; e_2]\!]\sigma \stackrel{\text{def}}{=} op^s(\mathcal{E}[\![e_1]\!]\sigma, \mathcal{E}[\![e_2]\!]\sigma) \qquad \clubsuit$$

The semantics of first order logic predicates is defined similarly.

Definition 5.3 (Semantics of first order logic predicates) Define

$$C[\![.]\!] : Pred \longrightarrow \mathfrak{P}(\Sigma)$$

by

$$C[\![\text{false}]\!] \stackrel{\text{def}}{=} \emptyset$$

$$C[\![e_1 \; cop \; e_2]\!] \stackrel{\text{def}}{=} \{ \sigma \in \Sigma \mid (\mathcal{E}[\![e_1]\!]\sigma, \mathcal{E}[\![e_2]\!]\sigma) \in cop^s \}$$

$$C[\![p_1 \Rightarrow p_2]\!] \stackrel{\text{def}}{=} \{ \sigma \in \Sigma \mid \sigma \in C[\![p_1]\!] \Rightarrow \sigma \in C[\![p_2]\!] \}$$

$$C[\![\forall x(p_1)]\!] \stackrel{\text{def}}{=} \bigcap_{v \in V} \{ \sigma \in \Sigma \mid \sigma_x^v \in C[\![p_1]\!] \}$$

Observe that symbol $\Rightarrow$ on the LHS belongs to our syntax whereas the operator on the RHS belongs to the mathematical meta-language where it should be read as "implies". The latter is defined by the following standard truth table, stating that $p \Rightarrow q$ is *tt* unless p is *tt* and q is *ff*, in which case $p \Rightarrow q$ is *ff*:

$\Rightarrow$	*ff*	*tt*
ff	*tt*	*tt*
tt	*ff*	*tt*

$\clubsuit$

Sometimes we prefer to use a semantics of predicates with a slightly different signature, that is, $T[\![.]\!] : Pred \longrightarrow (\Sigma \longrightarrow \mathbb{B})$. The function $T[\![.]\!]$ is called a *truth-valued* semantics for this very reason. The value of $T[\![p]\!]\sigma$ is *tt* iff $\sigma \in C[\![p]\!]$, or equivalently $C[\![p]\!] = \{ \sigma \mid T[\![p]\!] = tt \}$.

As an immediate consequence of this definition we have the following corollary.

Corollary 5.4 Let $\sigma \in \Sigma$.

$$T[\![\text{false}]\!]\sigma = ff$$

$$T[\![e_1 \; cop \; e_2]\!]\sigma = (\mathcal{E}[\![e_1]\!]\sigma, \mathcal{E}[\![e_2]\!]\sigma) \in cop^s$$

$$\mathcal{T}[\![p_1 \Rightarrow p_2]\!]\sigma = \mathcal{T}[\![p_1]\!]\sigma \Rightarrow \mathcal{T}[\![p_2]\!]\sigma$$
$$\mathcal{T}[\![\forall x(p_1)]\!]\sigma = \forall v \in \mathbb{V}\,(\mathcal{T}[\![p_1]\!]\sigma_x^v) \qquad \spadesuit$$

In the sequel the standard notions of *free* and *bound* variables in terms and *substitution* of expressions for free occurrences of a variable in a term become important. We refer the reader to textbooks on mathematical logic, e.g., [Sho67, Men87], for the details and treat these topics only rudimentarily.

An occurrence of a variable x in a predicate is *bound* if it lies within the scope of a quantifier for x, e.g., $\forall x$, where the scope of a quantifier is simply the predicate in parentheses following the quantifier. Otherwise this occurrence of x is *free*. If such a free occurrence of x exists within a predicate p, x is called a free variable of p. This is formalized below.

The set of free variables in term t (i.e., an expression or predicate) is denoted by $fvar(t)$. We write $t_1[^e/_x]$ for the term obtained from t_1 by substituting all free occurrences of variable x by expression e, if necessary renaming bound variables in t_1 such that free occurrences of variables in e are not bound by quantifiers in t_1. To formalize this notion we inductively define the function *fvar* mapping expressions and predicates to the set of variables occurring freely in them.

$$fvar(c) \overset{\text{def}}{=} \emptyset$$
$$fvar(x) \overset{\text{def}}{=} \{x\}$$
$$fvar(e_1 \; op \; e_2) \overset{\text{def}}{=} fvar(e_1) \cup fvar(e_2)$$
$$fvar(\text{false}) \overset{\text{def}}{=} \emptyset$$
$$fvar(e_1 \; cop \; e_2) \overset{\text{def}}{=} fvar(e_1) \cup fvar(e_2)$$
$$fvar(p_1 \Rightarrow p_2) \overset{\text{def}}{=} fvar(p_1) \cup fvar(p_2)$$
$$fvar(\forall x(p_1)) \overset{\text{def}}{=} fvar(p_1) \setminus \{x\}$$

States coincide on a set of variables if they agree on the values of those variables.

Definition 5.5 (Coincidence of states) $\sigma \in \Sigma$ and $\tau \in \Sigma$ *coincide* on $V \subseteq Var$ (denoted by $\sigma \equiv_V \tau$) iff $\sigma(x) = \tau(x)$, for all $x \in V$. $\qquad \clubsuit$

The following lemma formalizes the intuitively trivial fact that the value of an expression in a state depends only on the values of its free variables in this state.

Lemma 5.6 (Coincidence) Let $e \in Exp$, $p \in Pred$, and $\sigma, \tau \in \Sigma$.

(i) If $\sigma \equiv_{fvar(e)} \tau$ then $\mathcal{E}[\![e]\!]\sigma = \mathcal{E}[\![e]\!]\tau$.

(ii) If $\sigma \equiv_{fvar(p)} \tau$ then $\sigma \in C[\![p]\!]$ iff $\tau \in C[\![p]\!]$.

Proof: By induction on the structure of e and p, respectively. Let $\sigma, \tau \in \Sigma$, $e \in Exp$, and $p \in Pred$.

(i) Assume $\sigma \equiv_{fvar(e)} \tau$. We have to show $\mathcal{E}[\![e]\!]\sigma = \mathcal{E}[\![e]\!]\tau$. To do so we consider the cases of e:

- e is c for some $c \in Const$: $\mathcal{E}[\![c]\!]\sigma = c^s = \mathcal{E}[\![c]\!]\tau$.

- e is x for some $x \in Var$: Since $x \in \{x\}$ and $fvar(e) = \{x\}$ it follows from the assumption about the coincidence between σ and τ that $\mathcal{E}[\![x]\!]\sigma = \sigma(x) = \tau(x) = \mathcal{E}[\![x]\!]\tau$.

- e is e_1 op e_2 for some $e_1, e_2 \in Exp$ and $op \in Op$: $fvar(e) = fvar(e_1) \cup fvar(e_2)$ implies that $\sigma \equiv_{fvar(e_i)} \tau$ follows from $\sigma \equiv_{fvar(e)} \tau$, for $i = 1, 2$. The induction hypothesis applied to e_i then implies $\mathcal{E}[\![e_i]\!]\sigma = \mathcal{E}[\![e_i]\!]\tau$, for $i = 1, 2$.

$$\mathcal{E}[\![e_1 \ op \ e_2]\!]\sigma$$
$$= op^s(\mathcal{E}[\![e_1]\!]\sigma, \mathcal{E}[\![e_2]\!]\sigma) \qquad \text{Def. 5.2}$$
$$= op^s(\mathcal{E}[\![e_1]\!]\tau, \mathcal{E}[\![e_2]\!]\tau) \qquad \text{induction hypothesis}$$
$$= \mathcal{E}[\![e_1 \ op \ e_2]\!]\tau \qquad \text{Def. 5.2}$$

(ii) Assume $\sigma \equiv_{fvar(p)} \tau$. We show that $\sigma \in C[\![p]\!]$ holds iff $\tau \in C[\![p]\!]$ does.

- p is false: Then $C[\![p]\!] = \emptyset$ and $\sigma, \tau \notin \emptyset$.

- p is e_1 cop e_2 for some $e_1, e_2 \in Exp$ and $cop \in Cop$: $fvar(p) = fvar(e_1) \cup fvar(e_2)$ implies that $\sigma \equiv_{fvar(e_i)} \tau$ follows from $\sigma \equiv_{fvar(p)} \tau$, for $i = 1, 2$.

$$\sigma \in C[\![e_1 \ cop \ e_2]\!]$$
$$\Leftrightarrow (\mathcal{E}[\![e_1]\!]\sigma, \mathcal{E}[\![e_2]\!]\sigma) \in cop^s \qquad \text{Def. 5.3}$$
$$\Leftrightarrow (\mathcal{E}[\![e_1]\!]\tau, \mathcal{E}[\![e_2]\!]\tau) \in cop^s \qquad \text{Lemma 5.6.(i)}$$
$$\Leftrightarrow \tau \in C[\![e_1 \ cop \ e_2]\!] \qquad \text{Def. 5.3}$$

- p is $p_1 \Rightarrow p_2$: In this case the induction hypothesis is $\sigma \in C[\![p_i]\!] \Leftrightarrow \tau \in C[\![p_i]\!]$ for $i = 1, 2$.

$$\sigma \in C[\![p_1 \Rightarrow p_2]\!]$$
$$\Leftrightarrow (\sigma \in C[\![p_1]\!] \Rightarrow \sigma \in C[\![p_2]\!]) \qquad \text{Def. 5.3}$$
$$\Leftrightarrow (\tau \in C[\![p_1]\!] \Rightarrow \tau \in C[\![p_2]\!]) \qquad \text{induction hypothesis}$$
$$\Leftrightarrow \tau \in C[\![p_1 \Rightarrow p_2]\!] \qquad \text{Def. 5.3}$$

- p is $\forall x(p_1)$: Observe that $fvar(p_1) \subseteq fvar(p) \cup \{x\}$. Hence $\sigma \equiv_{fvar(p)}$ implies that $\sigma_x^v \equiv_{fvar(p_1)} \tau_x^v$, for all $v \in \mathbb{V}$. In this case the induction hypothesis is: for all $v \in \mathbb{V}$, $\sigma_x^v \in C[\![p_1]\!]$ iff $\tau_x^v \in C[\![p_1]\!]$.

$$\sigma \in C[\![\forall x(p_1)]\!]$$
$$\Leftrightarrow \sigma_x^v \in C[\![p_1]\!] \ , \text{ for all } v \in \mathbb{V} \quad \text{Def. 5.3}$$
$$\Leftrightarrow \tau_x^v \in C[\![p_1]\!] \ , \text{ for all } v \in \mathbb{V} \quad \text{induction hypothesis}$$
$$\Leftrightarrow \tau \in C[\![\forall x(p_1)]\!] \quad \text{Def. 5.3} \qquad \Box$$

Definition 5.7 (Substitution) Let $e \in Exp$ and $x \in Var$. Define the *substitution* of all free occurrences of x (denoted by $[^e/_x]$) in an expression or predicate inductively by

$$c[^e/_x] \stackrel{\text{def}}{=} c$$

$$y[^e/_x] \stackrel{\text{def}}{=} \begin{cases} e & \text{if } y \text{ is } x \\ y & \text{otherwise} \end{cases}$$

$$(e_1 \ op \ e_2)[^e/_x] \stackrel{\text{def}}{=} e_1[^e/_x] \ op \ e_2[^e/_x]$$

$$\text{false}[^e/_x] \stackrel{\text{def}}{=} \text{false}$$

$$(e_1 \ cop \ e_2)[^e/_x] \stackrel{\text{def}}{=} e_1[^e/_x] \ cop \ e_2[^e/_x]$$

$$(p_1 \Rightarrow p_2)[^e/_x] \stackrel{\text{def}}{=} p_1[^e/_x] \Rightarrow p_2[^e/_x]$$

$$\forall y(p) \, [^e/_x] \stackrel{\text{def}}{=} \begin{cases} \forall y(p) & \text{if } y \text{ is } x \\ \forall z(p[^z/_y][^e/_x]) & \text{if } y \text{ is not } x \text{ and } y \in fvar(e) \\ \forall y(p[^e/_x]) & \text{otherwise} \end{cases}$$

In the second clause of the last definition z is a fresh variable, i.e., $z \notin fvar(p) \cup fvar(e) \cup \{x\}$. Here a *fresh* variable in a given context is a variable not yet used in that context.

From a formal point of view, this is not a proper definition because the term resulting from substituting e for x in $\forall y(p)$ is not necessarily unique in case y is not x and $y \in fvar(e)$ since z is not uniquely determined. To circumvent this flaw one could impose a total order on *Var* and require that z is, for instance, the next fresh variable that is greater than y in this total order. ♣

The substitution lemma explains how to trade state variants for syntactical substitutions.

Lemma 5.8 (Substitution) Let $e, e_1 \in Exp$, $p \in Pred$, $x \in Var$, and $\sigma \in \Sigma$. Then

- $\mathcal{E}[\![e_1]\!](\sigma : x \mapsto \mathcal{E}[\![e]\!]\sigma) = \mathcal{E}[\![e_1[^e/_x]]\!]\sigma$, and
- $(\sigma : x \mapsto \mathcal{E}[\![e]\!]\sigma) \in C[\![p]\!]$ iff $\sigma \in C[\![p[^e/_x]]\!]$.

Proof: By induction on the structure of e and p, respectively.   □

Most predicates in this monograph will be used to characterize binary relations over states rather than sets of states. How shall we do that, given the semantics defined above?

In the presentation above all variables are similar, for they all belong to *Var* and there is one uniform state space whose elements provide values for all variables in *Var*. Such states are rather inconvenient when dealing with several levels of abstraction. However, it is indeed possible to develop a theory similar to ours working solely with elements of Σ.

In Chapter 1 we already distinguished normal variables from representation variables on various levels of abstraction. Later on in this chapter the distinction between logical and program variables becomes clear. These distinctions lead to specialized sets of variables, e.g., one for the program variables on each particular level of abstraction.

These separations between designated subsets of variables lead to semantics of predicates relative to *two* nonvoid subsets of *Var*. We develop this relational semantics of predicates via an intermediate step of predicates and semantics relative to *one* set of variables $V \subseteq Var$.

Definition 5.9 Let $V \subseteq Var$, and define

- state space Σ^V (parameterized by its domain V) by $\Sigma^V \overset{\text{def}}{=} [V \longrightarrow \mathbb{V}]$, its elements being called V-states or simply states,
- *projection* $\sigma|_V \in \Sigma^V$ of state $\sigma \in \Sigma$ onto variables V by $\sigma|_V \equiv_V \sigma$,
- variants[3] $(\tau : x \mapsto v)$ of V-states $\tau \in \Sigma^V$ by

$$(\tau : x \mapsto v) : V \cup \{x\} \longrightarrow \mathbb{V}$$

$$(\tau : x \mapsto v)(y) \overset{\text{def}}{=} \begin{cases} v & \text{if } y \text{ is } x \\ \tau(y) & \text{otherwise,} \end{cases}$$

- syntactic category $Exp^V \overset{\text{def}}{=} \{ e \in Exp \mid fvar(e) \subseteq V \}$ of *expressions over* V,
- semantic function $\mathcal{E}[\![.]\!]^V : Exp^V \longrightarrow (\Sigma^V \longrightarrow \mathbb{V})$ by

$$\mathcal{E}[\![e]\!]^V \sigma \overset{\text{def}}{=} \mathcal{E}[\![e]\!]\delta ,$$

for some $\delta \in \Sigma$ satisfying $\delta|_V = \sigma$,

---

[3] Notice that variants of V-states can also be introduced as projections of variants of states in Σ.

- syntactic category $Pred^V \overset{\text{def}}{=} \{ p \in Pred \mid fvar(p) \subseteq V \}$ of *predicates over* V,
- semantic function $C[\![.]\!]^V : Pred^V \longrightarrow \mathfrak{P}(\Sigma^V)$ by

$$C[\![p]\!]^V \overset{\text{def}}{=} \{ (\delta|_V) \mid \delta \in C[\![p]\!] \} \ .$$

As above we accompany the set-valued semantics of predicates with a truth-valued semantics $T[\![.]\!]^V : Pred^V \longrightarrow (\Sigma^V \longrightarrow \mathbb{B})$ by stating that

$$T[\![p]\!]^V \sigma = tt \quad \text{iff} \quad \sigma \in C[\![p]\!]^V \ . \qquad \clubsuit$$

Notice that any V-state τ is a projection onto V of some state $\sigma \in \Sigma$, i.e., one has $\Sigma^V = \{ (\sigma|_V) \mid \sigma \in \Sigma \}$. Consequently it does not matter whether one defines Σ^V as above or through projections of Σ onto V. This justifies our definition of $\mathcal{E}[\![.]\!]^V$ and $C[\![.]\!]^V$.

Remark The degenerate case of $V = \emptyset$ is meaningful. $\Sigma^\emptyset$ has exactly one element, namely the nowhere defined function (i.e., the function with graph $\emptyset$) denoted by $\mathord{\text{\r{m}}}$ and pronounced "undefined". $Pred^\emptyset$ consists of all those predicates which have no free variables.

Next observe that $\mathfrak{P}(\Sigma^\emptyset) = \{\emptyset, \Sigma^\emptyset\}$, which corresponds in a natural way to $\mathbb{B}$. Consequently the meaning of such predicates from first order logic with integer arithmetic is either $\emptyset$ or $\Sigma^\emptyset$, corresponding to *ff* and *tt*, respectively.

$\Diamond$

Next we consider two (not necessarily disjoint) sets $V, W \subseteq Var$ of variables instead of a single set V. A notion of combining two states from different state spaces to form a bigger state ranging over the union of the two corresponding domains is helpful for defining the new relational semantics in terms of the one given in the previous definition.

Definition 5.10 Let $V, W \subseteq Var$.

- The *composition* of $\sigma \in \Sigma^V$ with $\tau \in \Sigma^W$ is denoted by $\sigma \dagger \tau \in \Sigma^{V \cup W}$, with "$\dagger$" pronounced "overwrite with".

$$(\sigma \dagger \tau)(x) \overset{\text{def}}{=} \begin{cases} \tau(x) & \text{if } x \in W \\ \sigma(x) & \text{if } x \in V \setminus W \end{cases}$$

- The syntactic category of *expressions over V and W* is defined by $Exp^{V,W} \overset{\text{def}}{=} Exp^{V \cup W}$. Its semantics is derived from the one for expressions over $V \cup W$ in a straightforward manner: its signature is $\mathcal{E}[\![.]\!]^{V,W} : Exp^{V,W} \longrightarrow (\Sigma^V \times \Sigma^W \longrightarrow \mathbb{V})$ and it is defined by $\mathcal{E}[\![e]\!]^{V,W}(\sigma,\tau) \overset{\text{def}}{=} \mathcal{E}[\![e]\!]^{V \cup W} \sigma \dagger \tau$, for all $e \in Exp^{V,W}$, $\sigma \in \Sigma^V$, and $\tau \in \Sigma^W$.

- The syntactic category of *predicates over V and W* is given by

$$Pred^{V,W} \stackrel{\text{def}}{=} Pred^{V \cup W} .$$

- Its semantics is derived straightforwardly from Def. 5.9.

$$C[\![.]\!]^{V,W} : Pred^{V,W} \longrightarrow \mathfrak{P}(\Sigma^V \times \Sigma^W)$$

$$C[\![p]\!]^{V,W} \stackrel{\text{def}}{=} \left\{ (\sigma,\tau) \in \Sigma^V \times \Sigma^W \ \middle| \ (\sigma \dagger \tau) \in C[\![p]\!]^{V \cup W} \right\}$$

Again a truth-valued version $T[\![.]\!]^V : Pred^V \longrightarrow (\Sigma^V \longrightarrow \mathbb{B})$ of $C[\![.]\!]^{V,W}$ is defined by $T[\![p]\!]^{V,W}(\sigma,\tau) = tt$ iff $(\sigma,\tau) \in C[\![p]\!]^{V,W}$.   ♣

Note that the $\dagger$ operator is not commutative in case V and W are not disjoint.

Corollary 5.11 Let $x \in Var$, $V,W,U \subseteq Var$, $\sigma \in \Sigma^V$, $\tau \in \Sigma^W$, $\delta \in \Sigma^U$ and $v \in \mathbb{V}$.

- $(\sigma \dagger \tau) \equiv_W \tau$
- $(\sigma \dagger \tau)|_W = \tau$
- $\sigma \equiv_{V \cap W} \tau$ iff $\sigma|_{V \cap W} = \tau|_{V \cap W}$
- $\sigma \dagger (\tau : x \mapsto v) = (\sigma \dagger \tau : x \mapsto v) = (\sigma : x \mapsto v) \dagger (\tau|_{W \setminus \{x\}})$
- $\dagger$ is associative: $(\sigma \dagger \tau) \dagger \delta = \sigma \dagger (\tau \dagger \delta)$. (Hence we shall write $\sigma \dagger \tau \dagger \delta$ for either side.)

If in addition $V \cap W = \emptyset$, then the following properties hold.

- $\sigma \dagger \tau = \tau \dagger \sigma$
- $(\sigma \dagger \tau) \equiv_V \sigma$
- $(\sigma \dagger \tau)|_V = \sigma$ ♠

The following two lemmas are of a rather technical nature and are only applied in the proof of Lemma 5.17. They can be skipped upon first reading. Next we provide a version of the coincidence lemma for our relational semantics of predicates.

Lemma 5.12 (Substitution) Let $V,W \subseteq Var$, $\sigma \in \Sigma^V$, $\tau \in \Sigma^W$, $x \in Var$, $e \in Exp^{V,W}$, $e_1 \in Exp^{V,W \cup \{x\}}$, and $p \in Pred^{V,W \cup \{x\}}$. Then

(i) the following three values are equal:

    (a) $\mathcal{E}[\![e_1[^e/_x]]\!]^{V,W}(\sigma,\tau)$

    (b) $\mathcal{E}[\![e_1]\!]^{V,W \cup \{x\}}(\sigma,(\tau : x \mapsto \mathcal{E}[\![e]\!]^{V,W}(\sigma,\tau)))$

    (c) $\mathcal{E}[\![e_1]\!]^{V \cup \{x\},W \setminus \{x\}}((\sigma : x \mapsto \mathcal{E}[\![e]\!]^{V,W}(\sigma,\tau)),\tau|_{W \setminus \{x\}})$

(ii) the following three properties are equivalent:

    (a) $(\sigma,\tau) \in C[\![p[^e/_x]]\!]^{V,W}$

(b) $(\sigma, (\tau : x \mapsto \mathcal{E}[\![e]\!]^{V,W}(\sigma, \tau))) \in C[\![p]\!]^{V,W \cup \{x\}}$

(c) $((\sigma : x \mapsto \mathcal{E}[\![e]\!]^{V,W}(\sigma, \tau)), \tau|_{W \setminus \{x\}}) \in C[\![p]\!]^{V \cup \{x\}, W \setminus \{x\}}$

Proof: Let $\delta \in \Sigma$, $\sigma \in \Sigma^V$, and $\tau \in \Sigma^W$. We prove the whole of (i) at once.

$\mathcal{E}[\![e_1[^e/_x]]\!]^{V,W}(\sigma, \tau)$

$= \mathcal{E}[\![e_1[^e/_x]]\!](\delta \dagger \sigma \dagger \tau)$ $\qquad$ Defs 5.10 and 5.9

$= \mathcal{E}[\![e_1]\!]((\delta \dagger \sigma \dagger \tau) : x \mapsto \mathcal{E}[\![e]\!](\delta \dagger \sigma \dagger \tau))$ $\qquad$ Lemma 5.8

$= \mathcal{E}[\![e_1]\!]((\delta \dagger \sigma \dagger \tau) : x \mapsto \mathcal{E}[\![e]\!]^{V,W}(\sigma, \tau))$ $\qquad$ Defs 5.9 and 5.10

$= \mathcal{E}[\![e_1]\!](\delta \dagger \sigma \dagger (\tau : x \mapsto \mathcal{E}[\![e]\!]^{V,W}(\sigma, \tau)))$ $\qquad$ Cor. 5.11

$= \mathcal{E}[\![e_1]\!]^{V,W \cup \{x\}}(\sigma, (\tau : x \mapsto \mathcal{E}[\![e]\!]^{V,W}(\sigma, \tau)))$ $\qquad$ Defs 5.9 and 5.10

$= \mathcal{E}[\![e_1]\!]^{V \cup \{x\}, W \setminus \{x\}}((\sigma : x \mapsto \mathcal{E}[\![e]\!]^{V,W}(\sigma, \tau)), \tau|_{W \setminus \{x\}})$ $\qquad$ Cor. 5.11

The proof of (ii) is similar. $\qquad\qquad\qquad\qquad\qquad\qquad\qquad\qquad\qquad\qquad$ □

Lemma 5.13 (Coincidence) Let $p \in Pred^{V,W}$, $\sigma \in \Sigma^V$, and $\tau \in \Sigma^W$. Consider two sets of variables $V', W' \subseteq Var$ such that V' and W' cover $fvar(p)$, formally $fvar(p) \subseteq V' \cup W'$, and let $\sigma' \in \Sigma^{V'}$ and $\tau' \in \Sigma^{W'}$ such that $\sigma \dagger \tau \equiv_{fvar(p)} \sigma' \dagger \tau'$. Then $(\sigma, \tau) \in C[\![p]\!]^{V,W}$ iff $(\sigma', \tau') \in C[\![p]\!]^{V',W'}$.

Proof: Let $\delta \in \Sigma$. Then, by definition of $\dagger$, $\delta \dagger \sigma \dagger \tau \equiv_{fvar(p)} \delta \dagger \sigma' \dagger \tau'$.

$(\sigma, \tau) \in C[\![p]\!]^{V,W}$

$\Leftrightarrow \delta \dagger \sigma \dagger \tau \in C[\![p]\!]$ $\qquad$ Defs 5.10 and 5.9

$\Leftrightarrow \delta \dagger \sigma' \dagger \tau' \in C[\![p]\!]$ $\qquad$ $\delta \dagger \sigma \dagger \tau \equiv_{fvar(p)} \delta \dagger \sigma' \dagger \tau'$ and Lemma 5.6

$\Leftrightarrow (\sigma', \tau') \in C[\![p]\!]^{V',W'}$ $\qquad$ Defs 5.9 and 5.10 $\qquad\qquad\qquad\qquad$ □

Since we prefer to work with state pairs rather than use the $\dagger$ operator we formulate the following lemma.

Lemma 5.14 Let $V, W \subseteq Var$, $\sigma \in \Sigma^V$, $\tau \in \Sigma^W$, $e_1, e_2 \in Exp^{V,W}$, $p \in Pred^{V,W \cup \{x\}}$, and $p_1, p_2 \in Pred^{V,W}$. Then the following holds.

$(\sigma, \tau) \notin C[\![false]\!]^{V,W}$

$(\sigma, \tau) \in C[\![e_1 = e_2]\!]^{V,W} \Leftrightarrow \mathcal{E}[\![e_1]\!]^{V \cup W}(\sigma \dagger \tau) =^s \mathcal{E}[\![e_2]\!]^{V \cup W}(\sigma \dagger \tau)$

$(\sigma, \tau) \in C[\![e_1 < e_2]\!]^{V,W} \Leftrightarrow \mathcal{E}[\![e_1]\!]^{V \cup W}(\sigma \dagger \tau) <^s \mathcal{E}[\![e_2]\!]^{V \cup W}(\sigma \dagger \tau)$

$(\sigma, \tau) \in C[\![p_1 \Rightarrow p_2]\!]^{V,W} \Leftrightarrow \left((\sigma, \tau) \in C[\![p_1]\!]^{V,W} \Rightarrow (\sigma, \tau) \in C[\![p_2]\!]^{V,W} \right)$

$(\sigma, \tau) \in C[\![\forall x(p)]\!]^{V,W} \Leftrightarrow \forall v \in \mathbb{V} \left((\sigma, \tau_x^v) \in C[\![p]\!]^{V,W \cup \{x\}} \right)$

$$\Leftrightarrow \forall v \in \mathbb{V}\left((\sigma_x^v, \tau|_{W\setminus\{x\}}) \in C[\![p]\!]^{V\cup\{x\}, W\setminus\{x\}}\right)$$

And, analogously, for some of the abbreviated constructs:

$$(\sigma, \tau) \in C[\![\text{true}]\!]^{V,W}$$

$$(\sigma, \tau) \in C[\![\neg p_1]\!]^{V,W} \Leftrightarrow (\sigma, \tau) \notin C[\![p_1]\!]^{V,W}$$

$$(\sigma, \tau) \in C[\![p_1 \vee p_2]\!]^{V,W} \Leftrightarrow (\sigma, \tau) \in C[\![p_1]\!]^{V,W} \vee (\sigma, \tau) \in C[\![p_2]\!]^{V,W}$$

$$(\sigma, \tau) \in C[\![p_1 \wedge p_2]\!]^{V,W} \Leftrightarrow (\sigma, \tau) \in C[\![p_1]\!]^{V,W} \wedge (\sigma, \tau) \in C[\![p_2]\!]^{V,W}$$

$$(\sigma, \tau) \in C[\![p_1 \Leftrightarrow p_2]\!]^{V,W} \Leftrightarrow \left((\sigma, \tau) \in C[\![p_1]\!]^{V,W} \Leftrightarrow (\sigma, \tau) \in C[\![p_2]\!]^{V,W}\right)$$

$$(\sigma, \tau) \in C[\![\exists x(p)]\!]^{V,W} \Leftrightarrow \exists v \in \mathbb{V}\left((\sigma, \tau_x^v) \in C[\![p]\!]^{V, W\cup\{x\}}\right)$$

$$\Leftrightarrow \exists v \in \mathbb{V}\left((\sigma_x^v, \tau|_{W\setminus\{x\}}) \in C[\![p]\!]^{V\cup\{x\}, W\setminus\{x\}}\right)$$

Proof: We demonstrate only the first equivalence for universal quantification.

$$(\sigma, \tau) \in C[\![\forall x(p)]\!]^{V,W}$$

$$\Leftrightarrow \sigma\dagger\tau \in C[\![\forall x(p)]\!]^{V\cup W} \qquad\qquad \text{Def. 5.10}$$

$$\Leftrightarrow \delta\dagger\sigma\dagger\tau \in C[\![\forall x(p)]\!] \qquad\qquad \text{Def. 5.9}$$

$$\Leftrightarrow \forall v \in \mathbb{V}((\delta\dagger\sigma\dagger\tau : x \mapsto v) \in C[\![p]\!]) \qquad \text{Def. 5.3}$$

$$\Leftrightarrow \forall v \in \mathbb{V}(\delta\dagger\sigma\dagger(\tau : x \mapsto v) \in C[\![p]\!]) \qquad \text{Cor. 5.11}$$

$$\Leftrightarrow \forall v \in \mathbb{V}\left(\sigma\dagger(\tau : x \mapsto v) \in C[\![p]\!]^{V\cup W\cup\{x\}}\right) \qquad \text{Def. 5.9}$$

$$\Leftrightarrow \forall v \in \mathbb{V}\left((\sigma, (\tau : x \mapsto v)) \in C[\![p]\!]^{V, W\cup\{x\}}\right) \qquad \text{Def. 5.10} \qquad \square$$

A similar lemma — which we omit for the sake of brevity — holds for $C[\![.]\!]^V$. Whenever this omitted lemma is called for in a proof we will refer to the one above for $C[\![.]\!]^{V,W}$ instead.

These lemmas will be used to show how the semantic operations introduced in Chapter 3 can be expressed in predicate logic and play an essential part in the proofs of our simulation theorems.

5.2.1 Abstraction Relations

To formalize reasoning about programs on different levels of abstraction we shall introduce separate instances of the above-defined syntactic and semantic categories as well as separate instances of semantic functions.

On abstraction level A objects are decorated with superscript A, e.g., Var^A expresses the collection of program variables on that level, whenever confusion is likely to occur. Σ^A abbreviates Σ^{Var^A}.

Now consider two abstraction levels, say, A and C, for the abstract and concrete level, respectively. Recall from Chapter 1 the distinction between normal variables, i.e., those variables which both levels have in common, and representation variables, which are specific to one of the levels. We assume w.l.o.g. that the normal variables are collected in some list $(x_1, \ldots, x_n)$, abbreviated to $\vec{x}$, whose elements constitute $Var^C \cap Var^A$. Usually we are somewhat sloppy about the distinction between lists and sets of variables, as we shall see in the declaration of $\vec{a}$ for instance. We assume that names of representation variables on different levels are disjoint; those on the abstract level are $\vec{a} = (a_1, \ldots, a_{n_A}) = Var^A \setminus Var^C$ and those on the concrete level are $\vec{c} = (c_1, \ldots, c_{n_C}) = Var^C \setminus Var^A$. We juxtapose such lists to express concatenation; for instance, $\vec{x}\vec{a}$ is a list containing exactly the program variables Var^A on level A.

An abstraction relation α expresses a relation between two abstraction levels C and A: more precisely, between the values of representation variables on level C and those on level A. This motivates that the basic elements of the new syntactic category Abs^{CA} of abstraction relations are first order predicates with free occurrences of representation variables from levels C and A only, i.e., $fvar(\alpha) \subseteq \vec{a}\vec{c}$. This explicitly excludes occurrences of normal variables in abstraction relations. The interpretation function $\mathcal{A}[\![.]\!]^{CA}$ is defined independently of the actual values of normal variables $x \in Var^C \cap Var^A$ as long as these values coincide on the two levels under consideration, which is consistent with our dicussion of abstraction relation semantics in Section 2.3.2, especially (2.1) on page 32.

Definition 5.15 (Semantics of abstraction relations)

$$\mathcal{A}[\![.]\!]^{CA} : Abs^{CA} \longrightarrow \mathfrak{P}(\Sigma^C \times \Sigma^A)$$

is defined by

$$\mathcal{A}[\![\alpha]\!]^{CA} \stackrel{\text{def}}{=} \left\{ ((\sigma \dagger \sigma^C), (\sigma \dagger \sigma^A)) \mid (\sigma^C, \sigma^A) \in C[\![\alpha]\!]^{\vec{c},\vec{a}} \wedge \sigma \in \Sigma^{\vec{x}} \right\} \quad \clubsuit$$

Observe that there is a fundamental difference between the abstraction relation semantics $\mathcal{A}[\![.]\!]^{CA}$ and the predicate semantics $C[\![.]\!]^{Var^C, Var^A}$: while $(\sigma, \zeta) \in \mathcal{A}[\![\alpha]\!]^{CA}$ implies that $\sigma \equiv_{\vec{x}} \zeta$ no such restriction on the $\vec{x}$-part can be made for $C[\![\alpha]\!]^{Var^C, Var^A}$. Both semantics are independent of the actual value of $\vec{x}$. For arbitrary lists of values $\vec{v}$ and $\vec{v'}$ having the same length as $\vec{x}$ we have the following implications.

$$(\sigma, \zeta) \in \mathcal{A}[\![\alpha]\!]^{CA} \Rightarrow (\sigma_{\vec{x}}^{\vec{v}}, \zeta_{\vec{x}}^{\vec{v}}) \in \mathcal{A}[\![\alpha]\!]^{CA} \tag{5.1}$$

$$(\sigma, \zeta) \in C[\![\alpha]\!]^{Var^C, Var^A} \Rightarrow (\sigma_{\vec{x}}^{\vec{v}}, \zeta_{\vec{x}}^{\vec{v'}}) \in C[\![\alpha]\!]^{Var^C, Var^A} \tag{5.2}$$

Restriction (5.1) reflects (2.2) on page 32. Implication (5.2) exposes the defect of $C[\![\alpha]\!]^{Var^C, Var^A}$ as the semantics of a predicate that serves as an abstraction relation: σ and ζ need not agree on the value of $\bar{x}$. If we add this requirement then we achieve another characterization of $\mathcal{A}[\![.]\!]^{CA}$.

Corollary 5.16 Let $\alpha \in Abs^{CA}$.

$$\mathcal{A}[\![\alpha]\!]^{CA} = \left\{ (\sigma, \zeta) \mid (\sigma, \zeta) \in C[\![\alpha]\!]^{Var^C, Var^A} \wedge \sigma \equiv_{Var^A \cap Var^C} \zeta \right\}$$

Furthermore, since elements of $Pred^{Var^A \cup Var^C \setminus Var^A \cap Var^C}$ can be interpreted as abstraction relations from level A to C as well as from C to A, we have that $\mathcal{A}[\![\alpha]\!]^{CA} = (\mathcal{A}[\![\alpha]\!]^{AC})^{-1}$.   ♠

5.2.2 Hoare-style Assertions

On each abstraction level A, Hoare-style assertions $\pi^A \in Pred^A$ are just first order logic predicates over two disjoint sets of variables: logical variables $Lvar^A$ and program variables Var^A. Recall that logical variables only occur in predicates and not in programs; consequently their values are not accessible to, and therefore not changed in, programs. (Note also that according to the definitions abstraction relations do not contain free occurrences of logical variables.)

$$Pred^A \stackrel{\text{def}}{=} Pred^{Lvar^A, Var^A}$$

Similarly we denote semantics function $C[\![.]\!]^{Lvar^A, Var^A}$ by $C[\![.]\!]^A$. Because of the different rôle logical variables play in our calculus we name their state space differently: $\Gamma^A \stackrel{\text{def}}{=} \Sigma^{Lvar^A}$.

We define some abbreviations for special assertions. In our theory of data refinement it so happens that the need arises to express an assertion on abstraction level C in terms of an abstraction relation α^{CA} and an assertion π^A on abstraction level A. There are essentially two ways to abstract from the actual values of abstract level representation variables $\bar{a}$ in such an assertion, namely by using existential and universal quantification. We introduce the following two operators respectively called *diamond* and *box* as abbreviations.

$$\langle \alpha^{CA} \rangle \pi^A \stackrel{\text{def}}{=} \exists \bar{a} \left(\alpha^{CA} \wedge \pi^A \right) \tag{5.3}$$

$$[\alpha^{CA}] \pi^A \stackrel{\text{def}}{=} \forall \bar{a} \left(\alpha^{CA} \Rightarrow \pi^A \right) \tag{5.4}$$

These operators, traditionally used in modal logic, were introduced into the calculus of binary relations by, among others [dBdR72, Pra76, Har79]. Box occurs in the literature as the weakest liberal precondition [Dij76, DS90].

This name stems from the original application of this operator to binary relations representing programs instead of abstraction relations and postconditions instead of assertions. Analogously, the *strongest postcondition* operator can be introduced. It is the syntactic counterpart of our relational image from Def. 3.6 and corresponds to the diamond of the inverse of a relation.

The correspondence between syntactic and semantic versions of box and diamond is the subject of the next lemma.

Lemma 5.17 Let $Lvar^A = Lvar^C$, $\pi \in Pred^A$, and $\alpha \in Abs^{CA}$.

(i) $C[\![[\alpha] \pi]\!]^C = \left[\mathcal{A}[\![\alpha]\!]^{CA} \right] C[\![\pi]\!]^A$

(ii) $C[\![\langle\alpha\rangle \pi]\!]^C = \left\langle \mathcal{A}[\![\alpha]\!]^{CA} \right\rangle C[\![\pi]\!]^A$

Proof: We only prove part (ii). Let

- $\vec{x}$ abbreviate $Var^A \cap Var^C$, i.e., the normal variables,
- $\vec{a}$ abbreviate $Var^A \setminus Var^C$, i.e., the representation variables on level A,
- $\vec{c}$ abbreviate $Var^C \setminus Var^A$, i.e., the representation variables on level C, and
- $\vec{x}_0$ abbreviate $Lvar^A$, i.e., the logical variables (here, they are common to both levels of abstraction),

and assume that $\vec{x}_0$ is disjoint from $\vec{x}$, $\vec{a}$, and $\vec{c}$. Then we know that $fvar(\alpha) \subseteq \vec{a}\vec{c}$ and $fvar(\pi) \subseteq \vec{x}_0\vec{x}\vec{a}$. Let $\sigma \in \Sigma^C$ and $\gamma \in \Gamma^A (= \Gamma^C)$.

$$(\gamma, \sigma) \in C[\![\langle\alpha\rangle \pi]\!]^C$$

$\Leftrightarrow$ (by (5.3))

$$(\gamma, \sigma) \in C[\![\exists\vec{a}(\alpha \wedge \pi)]\!]^C$$

$\Leftrightarrow$ (Lemma 5.14)

$$\exists\vec{v}\left((\gamma^{\vec{v}}_{\vec{a}}, \sigma) \in C[\![\alpha \wedge \pi]\!]^{\vec{x}_0\vec{a},\vec{x}\vec{c}} \right)$$

$\Leftrightarrow$ (Lemma 5.14)

$$\exists\vec{v}\left((\gamma^{\vec{v}}_{\vec{a}}, \sigma) \in C[\![\alpha]\!]^{\vec{x}_0\vec{a},\vec{x}\vec{c}} \wedge (\gamma^{\vec{v}}_{\vec{a}}, \sigma) \in C[\![\pi]\!]^{\vec{x}_0\vec{a},\vec{x}\vec{c}} \right)$$

$\Leftrightarrow$ (Lemma 5.13)

$$\exists\vec{v}\left((\gamma^{\vec{v}}_{\vec{a}}|_{\vec{a}}, \sigma) \in C[\![\alpha]\!]^{\vec{a},\vec{x}\vec{c}} \wedge (\gamma, (\sigma|_{\vec{x}} : \vec{a} \mapsto \vec{v})) \in C[\![\pi]\!]^{\vec{x}_0,\vec{x}\vec{a}} \right)$$

$\Leftrightarrow$ (Lemma 5.13, pred. calc.)

$$\exists\zeta \in \Sigma^A\left((\sigma, \zeta) \in C[\![\alpha]\!]^{\vec{x}\vec{c},\vec{x}\vec{a}} \wedge \sigma \equiv_{\vec{x}} \zeta \wedge (\gamma, \zeta) \in C[\![\pi]\!]^{\vec{x}_0,Var^A} \right)$$

$\Leftrightarrow$ (Cor. 5.16)

$$\exists \zeta \left((\sigma, \zeta) \in \mathcal{A}[\![\alpha]\!]^{\mathrm{CA}} \wedge (\gamma, \zeta) \in C[\![\pi]\!]^{\mathrm{A}} \right)$$

$$\Leftrightarrow \quad \text{(Def. 3.10)}$$

$$(\gamma, \sigma) \in \left\langle \mathcal{A}[\![\alpha]\!]^{\mathrm{CA}} \right\rangle C[\![\pi]\!]^{\mathrm{A}} \qquad\qquad\qquad \square$$

5.3 Programs

What are the basic operations needed to express programs and data structures on different levels of abstraction within our Hoare-style pre/post framework?

On the lower, implementation-oriented levels these are: assignments, sequential composition, conditional constructs, loops, and recursion; and on the higher, specification-oriented levels we also need nondeterministic choice and a means to construct basic building blocks from their specifications in terms of the pre/post formalism. We restrict ourselves to recursion w.r.t. one recursion variable, i.e., we do not consider mutual recursion, because the latter is expressible using the former [Bek69, SdB69] (see also the discussion at the end of Section 3.4).

In order to economize upon our constructs, conditional choice is modelled using nondeterministic choice and predicates over program variables in the form of filters (see below); similarly loops are expressed using recursion (see Section 5.3.1). Let us for now concentrate on one particular level of abstraction, say C.

Boolean expressions over program variables in Var^{C}, which filter out program states not satisfying them, are collected in the syntactic category $Bexp^{\mathrm{C}} \ni be$ which consists of the quantifier-free expressions of $Pred^{Var^{\mathrm{C}}}$; the notation for such filters is $b \rightarrow$. Recall that logical variables (elements of $Lvar^{\mathrm{C}}$) do not occur in such predicates since Var^{C} and $Lvar^{\mathrm{C}}$ are disjoint.

As remarked above, the most general program S satisfying a Hoare triple $\{\pi_1\} S \{\pi_2\}$ is denoted by $\pi_1 \rightsquigarrow \pi_2$. Its semantics is defined in this section although it can only be justified formally after giving semantics to Hoare triples in Section 5.5. Strictly speaking, none of the other basic programs (**abort**, **skip**, assignments, and filters) is primitive since all of them can be expressed using the $\rightsquigarrow$-operator. This is worked out in the exercises.

Nondeterministic choice is expressed by the infix operator $[\!]$, and recursion is expressed using a least fixed point operator μ applied to the transformation S, resulting in the expression $\mu X.S$.

The μ operator takes two arguments, a recursion variable X (drawn from a set $Rvar$ of recursion variables) and a program in which this recursion variable may occur freely as a program term.

As in Chapter 3, the semantics of recursion is introduced as the limit of a countable sequence of approximations of its operational behavior w.r.t. increasing recursion depth. In order to express these approximations we need the **abort** construct for denoting the program that never terminates.

Define the syntactic category $Prog^C \ni S$ of *programs*, where $x \in Var^C$, $e \in Exp^{Var^C}$, $b \in Bexp^C$, $\pi_1, \pi_2 \in Pred^C$, and $X \in Rvar$, by

$$S ::= \textbf{abort} \mid \textbf{skip} \mid x := e \mid b \rightarrow \mid \pi_1 \rightsquigarrow \pi_2 \mid X \mid S_1 ; S_2 \mid S_1 \; \square \; S_2 \mid \mu X . S_1$$

Recall that we employ parentheses to indicate aggregation. Operator μX serves as binding quantifier for X in *Prog* in a similar way to $\forall x$ for x in *Pred*. Well-formed programs do not contain free occurrences of recursion variables. In the sequel we will consider only well-formed programs to avoid difficulties arising from free occurrences of recursion variables. This restriction allows us to define the semantics of programs without giving an explicit meaning to program X. (See the remark below for an alternative.)

Definition 5.18 (Semantics of programs) Define $\mathcal{P}[\![.]\!]^C : Prog^C \longrightarrow \mathfrak{P}(\Sigma^C \times \Sigma^C)$ by

$$\mathcal{P}[\![\textbf{abort}]\!]^C \stackrel{\text{def}}{=} \emptyset$$

$$\mathcal{P}[\![\textbf{skip}]\!]^C \stackrel{\text{def}}{=} id_{\Sigma^C}$$

$$\mathcal{P}[\![x := e]\!]^C \stackrel{\text{def}}{=} \left\{ (\sigma, \tau) \in (\Sigma^C)^2 \; \middle| \; \tau = (\sigma : x \mapsto \mathcal{E}[\![e]\!]^{Var^C} \sigma) \right\}$$

$$\mathcal{P}[\![b \rightarrow]\!]^C \stackrel{\text{def}}{=} \left\{ (\sigma, \sigma) \; \middle| \; \sigma \in C[\![b]\!]^{Var^C} \right\}$$

$$\mathcal{P}[\![\pi_1 \rightsquigarrow \pi_2]\!]^C \stackrel{\text{def}}{=} \bigcap_{\gamma \in \Gamma^C} \left\{ (\sigma, \tau) \in (\Sigma^C)^2 \; \middle| \; \begin{array}{l} (\gamma, \sigma) \in C[\![\pi_1]\!]^C \\ \Rightarrow (\gamma, \tau) \in C[\![\pi_2]\!]^C \end{array} \right\}$$

$$\mathcal{P}[\![S_1 ; S_2]\!]^C \stackrel{\text{def}}{=} \mathcal{P}[\![S_1]\!]^C ; \mathcal{P}[\![S_2]\!]^C$$

$$\mathcal{P}[\![S_1 \; \square \; S_2]\!]^C \stackrel{\text{def}}{=} \mathcal{P}[\![S_1]\!]^C \cup \mathcal{P}[\![S_2]\!]^C$$

$$\mathcal{P}[\![\mu X . S_1]\!]^C \stackrel{\text{def}}{=} \bigcup_{i \in \mathbb{N}} \mathcal{P}[\![S_1^i(\textbf{abort})]\!]^C$$

where $S_1^0(S_2) \stackrel{\text{def}}{=} S_2$ and $S_1^{i+1}(S_2) \stackrel{\text{def}}{=} S_1(S_1^i(S_2))$ for $i \in \mathbb{N}$. In general the substitution of a program S_2 for a recursion variable X inside another program S_1 is defined similarly to substitution for predicates and expressions. For convenience, we employ the rather sloppy notation $S_1(S_2)$ for the resulting program whenever the recursion variable X substituted by S_2 is known from the context. ♣

Remark Alternatively, one can introduce an extra parameter $\rho : Rvar \longrightarrow$

$\mathfrak{P}((\Sigma^C)^2)$ for mappings from recursion variables to binary relations on Σ^C and define $\mathcal{P}[\![X]\!]^C(\rho)$ by $\rho(X)$ and $\mathcal{P}[\![\mu X.S_1]\!]^C(\rho)$ by $\mu(\lambda r.\mathcal{P}[\![S_1]\!]^C(\rho:X\mapsto r))$ where μ denotes a least fixed point operator for relation-to-relation transformers and r varies over $\mathfrak{P}((\Sigma^C)^2)$.[4] Consult [dB80, Chapter 5] for details and for the generalization to mutual recursion. $\Diamond$

The meaning of a specification statement can also be captured in a predicate. The implicit universal quantification of logical variables in a given specification statement has to be made explicit in that predicate. To model that program variables in the pre- and postcondition of a specification statement are evaluated in different states one has to replace, for instance, all program variables in the precondition by fresh variables in the predicate expression for that specification statement.

Lemma 5.19 Let $\vec{x}$ and $\vec{x}_0$ consist of the elements of Var^C and $Lvar^C$, respectively. Let assertions $\pi_1, \pi_2 \in Pred^C$. Let $\vec{y}$ denote a list of fresh variables that has the same length as $\vec{x}$. For all $\sigma, \tau \in \Sigma^C$ the following equivalences hold:

$$(\sigma, \tau) \in \mathcal{P}[\![\pi_1 \rightsquigarrow \pi_2]\!]^C \Leftrightarrow ((\mathrlap{\text{⋔}}:\vec{y}\mapsto\sigma(\vec{x})),\tau) \in C\left[\!\left[\forall\vec{x}_0\left(\pi_1[\vec{y}/\vec{x}] \Rightarrow \pi_2\right)\right]\!\right]^{\vec{y},\vec{x}}$$

$$\Leftrightarrow (\sigma, (\mathrlap{\text{⋔}}:\vec{y}\mapsto\tau(\vec{x}))) \in C\left[\!\left[\forall\vec{x}_0\left(\pi_1 \Rightarrow \pi_2[\vec{y}/\vec{x}]\right)\right]\!\right]^{\vec{x},\vec{y}}$$

Proof: We only prove the first equivalence since the second follows analogously. Let $\sigma, \tau \in \Sigma^C$ and let $\sigma' \stackrel{\text{def}}{=} (\text{⋔}:\vec{y}\mapsto\sigma(\vec{x}))$. (Recall that ⋔ is the nowhere defined function; see the remark after Def. 5.9 on page 101.)

$(\sigma,\tau) \in \mathcal{P}[\![\pi_1 \rightsquigarrow \pi_2]\!]^C$

$\Leftrightarrow$ (Def. 5.18)

$\forall\gamma\in\Gamma^C\left((\gamma,\sigma)\in C[\![\pi_1]\!]^C \Rightarrow (\gamma,\tau)\in C[\![\pi_2]\!]^C\right)$

$\Leftrightarrow$ (Def. 5.7)

$\forall\gamma\in\Gamma^C\left((\gamma,\sigma)\in C[\![\pi_1[\vec{y}/\vec{x}][\vec{x}/\vec{y}]]\!]^C \Rightarrow (\gamma,\tau)\in C[\![\pi_2]\!]^C\right)$

$\Leftrightarrow$ (Lemma 5.12)

$\forall\gamma\in\Gamma^C\left(\begin{array}{l}(\gamma,(\sigma:\vec{y}\mapsto\mathcal{E}[\![\vec{x}]\!]^{\vec{x}_0,\vec{x}}(\gamma,\sigma)))\in C[\![\pi_1[\vec{y}/\vec{x}]]\!]^{\vec{x}_0,\vec{x}\vec{y}}\\ \Rightarrow (\gamma,\tau)\in C[\![\pi_2]\!]^C\end{array}\right)$

$\Leftrightarrow$ (Defs 5.10, 5.9, and 5.3)

$\forall\gamma\in\Gamma^C\left((\gamma,(\sigma:\vec{y}\mapsto\sigma(\vec{x})))\in C[\![\pi_1[\vec{y}/\vec{x}]]\!]^{\vec{x}_0,\vec{x}\vec{y}} \Rightarrow (\gamma,\tau)\in C[\![\pi_2]\!]^C\right)$

---

[4] Such an approach is followed in Chapter 8, where *Prog* is given a demonic semantics that caters for expressing the nondeterministic possibility of nontermination.

$\Leftrightarrow$ (Def. Γ^C)

$$\forall \vec{v} \left(\begin{array}{l} ((\pitchfork : \vec{x}_0 \mapsto \vec{v}), (\sigma : \vec{y} \mapsto \sigma(\vec{x}))) \in C[\![\pi_1[\vec{y}/\vec{x}]]\!]^{\vec{x}_0, \vec{x}\vec{y}} \\ \Rightarrow ((\pitchfork : \vec{x}_0 \mapsto \vec{v}), \tau) \in C[\![\pi_2]\!]^C \end{array} \right)$$

$\Leftrightarrow$ (Lemma 5.13)

$$\forall \vec{v} \left(\begin{array}{l} (\sigma', (\tau : \vec{x}_0 \mapsto \vec{v})) \in C[\![\pi_1[\vec{y}/\vec{x}]]\!]^{\vec{y}, \vec{x}\vec{x}_0} \\ \Rightarrow (\sigma', (\tau : \vec{x}_0 \mapsto \vec{v})) \in C[\![\pi_2]\!]^{\vec{y}, \vec{x}\vec{x}_0} \end{array} \right)$$

$\Leftrightarrow$ (Lemma 5.14)

$$\forall \vec{v} \left((\sigma', (\tau : \vec{x}_0 \mapsto \vec{v})) \in C[\![\pi_1[\vec{y}/\vec{x}] \Rightarrow \pi_2]\!]^{\vec{y}, \vec{x}\vec{x}_0} \right)$$

$\Leftrightarrow$ (Lemma 5.14)

$$(\sigma', \tau) \in C \left[\!\!\left[\forall \vec{x}_0 \left(\pi_1[\vec{y}/\vec{x}] \Rightarrow \pi_2 \right) \right]\!\!\right]^{\vec{y}, \vec{x}} \qquad\qquad \square$$

5.3.1 Programming Language

The program constructors introduced so far look rather like inventions of ivory tower botanists. We do not dispute their power, but sometimes it is more convenient to use traditional while-loops and conditionals instead of recursion and nondeterministic choice. This is the reason why we introduce a few of the traditional constructs from imperative programming languages as abbreviations.

$$b \to S \stackrel{\text{def}}{=} b \to ; S$$
$$\textbf{if } b \textbf{ then } S_1 \textbf{ else } S_2 \textbf{ fi} \stackrel{\text{def}}{=} (b \to S_1) \,[\!]\, (\neg b \to S_2)$$
$$\textbf{if } b \textbf{ then } S_1 \textbf{ fi} \stackrel{\text{def}}{=} \textbf{if } b \textbf{ then } S_1 \textbf{ else skip fi}$$
$$\textbf{while } b \textbf{ do } S \textbf{ od} \stackrel{\text{def}}{=} \mu X.(\neg b \to [\!](b \to S; X))$$

Together with assignment statements these are known as the class of while-programs.

We conclude this section with a collection of equalities between programs. Here equality between programs means that they are semantically indistinguishable.

Lemma 5.20

- **abort** is a zero element of *Prog* w.r.t. sequential composition.

$$(\textbf{abort}; S) = \textbf{abort} = (S; \textbf{abort})$$

- **skip** is a unit element of *Prog* w.r.t. sequential composition.

$$(\textbf{skip}\,;S) = S = (S\,;\textbf{skip})$$

- Choice is commutative and associative.

$$(S_1 \,\square\, S_2) = (S_2 \,\square\, S_1) \quad (S_1 \,\square\, (S_2 \,\square\, S_3)) = ((S_1 \,\square\, S_2) \,\square\, S_3)$$

- **abort** is a unit element of *Prog* w.r.t. choice.

$$(\textbf{abort} \,\square\, S) = S$$

- Sequential composition distributes over choice.

$$S\,;(S_1 \,\square\, S_2) = (S\,;S_1) \,\square\, (S\,;S_2)$$
$$(S_1 \,\square\, S_2)\,;S = (S_1\,;S) \,\square\, (S_2\,;S)$$

- $(\mu X.\textbf{if}\ b\ \textbf{then}\ S_1\,;X\ \textbf{else}\ S_2\ \textbf{fi}) = \textbf{while}\ b\ \textbf{do}\ S_1\ \textbf{od}\,;S_2$
- **if** b **then** S **else** S **fi** $= S$.   ♠

Lemma 5.21 $\mathcal{P}[\![\textbf{while}\ b\ \textbf{do}\ S\ \textbf{od}]\!] = \bigcup_{i\in\mathbb{N}} \mathcal{P}[\![(b \to S)^{(i)}\,;\neg b \to]\!]$, where in general $S_1^{(0)} \stackrel{\text{def}}{=} \textbf{skip}$ and $S_1^{(i+1)} \stackrel{\text{def}}{=} S_1\,;S_1^{(i)}$, for $i \in \mathbb{N}$.

Proof: Exercise.   □

5.4 Relational Terms

Syntactic objects denoting binary relations have occurred so far in the shape of predicates, abstraction relations, and programs. These objects constitute the basic building blocks of the new syntactic category *Rel* of *relational terms*. To tap the full power of the calculus of binary relations, operators like ⤳, ⟨⟩, ;, and ¬ which we introduced semantically in Chapter 3, and syntactically for certain objects in this chapter, are generalized to *Rel*.

These generalized operators enable us to express maximal solutions for each of the relations on the LHS of $r_1\,;r_2 \subseteq r$ in terms of the remaining two relations (see Figure 5.2); this will become important in subsequent chapters.

As for abstraction relations it is necessary to express both domain and range of relations to prevent undesired applications of our generalized operators — in other words, we take care that the operators are not over-generalized. For every pair (D,R) of nonempty sets of variables we introduce a syntactic category $Rel^{D,R} \ni r^{D,R}$ of relational terms with domain D and range R defined in BNF by

$$r^{D,R} ::= br^{D,R} \mid \neg r^{D,R} \mid (r^{R,D})^{-1} \mid r^{D,M}\,;r^{M,R}$$

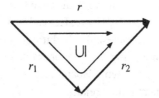

Fig. 5.2. Motivation for the relation transformers.

$$\mid r^{M,D} \rightsquigarrow r^{M,R} \mid \langle r^{R,M} \rangle r^{D,M} \mid [r^{R,M}] r^{D,M}$$

where M is some nonempty set of variables and $br^{D,R}$ some basic building block, for instance, a predicate $br^{Lvar^A, Var^A} \in Pred^A$ on some level A, an abstraction relation $br^{Var^C, Var^A} \in Abs^{CA}$ from level C to level A, or a program $br^{Var^A, Var^A} \in Prog^A$ at level A.

Definition 5.22 (Semantics of relational terms) For domain D and range R the semantics of relational terms is defined by semantic function $\mathcal{R}[\![.]\!]^{D,R} :$ $Rel^{D,R} \longrightarrow \mathfrak{P}(\Sigma^D \times \Sigma^R)$.

$$\mathcal{R}[\![\alpha^{CA}]\!]^{Var^C, Var^A} \overset{\text{def}}{=} \mathcal{A}[\![\alpha^{CA}]\!]^{CA}$$

$$\mathcal{R}[\![\pi^A]\!]^{Lvar^A, Var^A} \overset{\text{def}}{=} \mathcal{C}[\![\pi^A]\!]^A$$

$$\mathcal{R}[\![S^A]\!]^{Var^A, Var^A} \overset{\text{def}}{=} \mathcal{P}[\![S]\!]^A$$

$$\mathcal{R}[\![\neg r^{D,R}]\!]^{D,R} \overset{\text{def}}{=} \overline{\mathcal{R}[\![r^{D,R}]\!]^{D,R}}$$

$$\mathcal{R}[\![(r^{R,D})^{-1}]\!]^{D,R} \overset{\text{def}}{=} (\mathcal{R}[\![r^{R,D}]\!]^{R,D})^{-1}$$

$$\mathcal{R}[\![r^{D,M} ; r^{M,R}]\!]^{D,R} \overset{\text{def}}{=} \mathcal{R}[\![r^{D,M}]\!]^{D,M} ; \mathcal{R}[\![r^{M,R}]\!]^{M,R}$$

$$\mathcal{R}[\![r^{M,D} \rightsquigarrow r^{M,R}]\!]^{D,R} \overset{\text{def}}{=} \mathcal{R}[\![r^{M,D}]\!]^{M,D} \rightsquigarrow \mathcal{R}[\![r^{M,R}]\!]^{M,R}$$

$$\mathcal{R}[\![\langle r^{R,M} \rangle r^{D,M}]\!]^{D,R} \overset{\text{def}}{=} \langle \mathcal{R}[\![r^{R,M}]\!]^{R,M} \rangle \mathcal{R}[\![r^{D,M}]\!]^{D,M}$$

$$\mathcal{R}[\![[r^{R,M}] r^{D,M}]\!]^{D,R} \overset{\text{def}}{=} [\mathcal{R}[\![r^{R,M}]\!]^{R,M}] \mathcal{R}[\![r^{D,M}]\!]^{D,M}$$

Observe that on the LHS operators $(.)^{-1}$, $;$, $\rightsquigarrow$, $[.].$, and $\langle.\rangle.$ are the syntactic ones introduced in this section while their RHS counterparts are the semantic versions introduced in Chapter 3. ♣

Recall Figure 5.2. In case r_2 is to be specified the solution is easily expressed using the leads-to operator $\rightsquigarrow$. As we shall see in Lemma 5.24 the maximal solution of r_2 in $r_1 ; r_2 \subseteq r$ is $r_1 \rightsquigarrow r$. Hoare, He, and Sanders [HHS87] introduced this operator to computer science and called it *weakest postspecification*.

Similarly, but this time using the box operator [.] as suggested below by Lemma 5.25, one can express what Hoare, He, and Sanders call *weakest prespecification*, namely the maximal relation r_1 satisfying $r_1 ; r_2 \subseteq r$. It is $[r_2] r$.

Lastly, what about $\langle r_1 \rangle r_2$? Since $\langle r^{-1} \rangle \pi$ expresses the strongest postcondition operator of r w.r.t. π, $\langle r^{-1} \rangle r_1$ generalizes this operator to our relational setting. However, since it can be proven (see Lemma 5.26) that $\langle r_1^{-1} \rangle r_2 = r_2 ; r_1$, this operator does not give us more insight into calculating with relations than we had before. It is therefore only mentioned on systematic grounds.

Besides justifying the two solutions asked for in Figure 5.2, the following lemmas collect a few of the rich variety of properties valid for relational terms. The proofs are all omitted since these properties follow immediately from the semantic versions of these lemmas, i.e., Lemmas 3.9, 3.11, 3.12, and 3.13.

Lemma 5.23 Let $r_1, r_2, r_3 \in Rel$.

   (i) $((r_1 ; r_2) ; r_3) = (r_1 ; (r_2 ; r_3))$
   (ii) $(r_1 ; r_2)^{-1} = r_2^{-1} ; r_1^{-1}$ ♠

Lemma 5.24 Let $r, r_1, r_2 \in Rel$.

   (i) $r_2 \subseteq r_1 \rightsquigarrow r$ iff $r_1 ; r_2 \subseteq r$, and hence
   (ii) $r_1 \rightsquigarrow r = \bigcup \{ r_2 \mid r_1 ; r_2 \subseteq r \}$, suggesting an analogy with the specification statement, i.e., the leads-to operator between predicates.
   (iii) $r ; (r \rightsquigarrow r_1) \subseteq r_1$
   (iv) $r = \textbf{skip} \rightsquigarrow r$
   (v) $(r_1 \rightsquigarrow r_2)^{-1} = \neg r_2 \rightsquigarrow \neg r_1$
   (vi) $(r_1 ; r_2) \rightsquigarrow r = r_2 \rightsquigarrow (r_1 \rightsquigarrow r)$ ♠

Lemma 5.25 Let $r, r_1, r_2 \in Rel$.

   (i) $r_1 \subseteq [r_2] r$ iff $r_1 ; r_2 \subseteq r$, and hence
   (ii) $[r_2] r = \bigcup \{ r_1 \mid r_1 ; r_2 \subseteq r \}$, suggesting an analogy with the box operator over abstraction relations and predicates.
   (iii) $[r_1]([r_2] r) = [r_1 ; r_2] r$
   (iv) $[r](r_1 \rightsquigarrow r_2) = r_1 \rightsquigarrow [r] r_2$ ♠

Lemma 5.26 Let $r, r_1, r_2 \in Rel$.

   (i) $\neg \langle r_1 \rangle (\neg r_2) = [r_1] r_2$

(ii) $\langle r_1 \rangle (\langle r_2 \rangle r) = \langle r_1 ; r_2 \rangle r$

(iii) $\langle r_1^{-1} \rangle r_2 = r_2 ; r_1$

♠

Remark Def. 5.22, while generalizing the box, diamond, and leads-to operators, does not introduce inconsistencies. In particular, it makes no difference whether one regards relational terms

(i) $\langle \alpha \rangle \pi$ directly as a predicate as defined in (5.3),

(ii) $\pi_1 \rightsquigarrow \pi_2$ directly as a program as defined in Def. 5.18,

or as relational terms constructed from two relational subterms, as defined in Def. 5.22. ◇

5.5 Correctness Formulae

Recall the intended meaning of Hoare triples $\{\phi\} S \{\psi\}$: "If precondition ϕ holds, and if program S terminates, then postcondition ψ holds after termination of S. (However, termination is not guaranteed by ϕ.)" This intention is formulated without referring to logical variables. Are they therefore superfluous? No, they serve as glue between pre- and postconditions. Without logical variables, something as simple as "program S increments program variable x by 1" cannot be expressed by means of a single Hoare triple, as demonstrated in this section.

Hoare triples are examples of *correctness formulae*. This new syntactic category, denoted by *Cform* with typical element *cf*, is defined by

$$cf ::= r_1 \subseteq r_2 ,$$

where $r_1, r_2 \in Rel^{D,R}$ for some sets of variables D and R. Symbol $\subseteq$ is pronounced "refines" and interpreted as set-theoretical inclusion between binary relations.

Definition 5.27 (Semantics of correctness formulae) The semantics of correctness formulae is defined by semantic function $\mathcal{F}[\![.]\!] : Cform \longrightarrow \mathbb{B}$.

$$\mathcal{F}[\![r_1 \subseteq r_2]\!] \stackrel{\text{def}}{=} \mathcal{R}[\![r_1]\!]^{D,R} \subseteq \mathcal{R}[\![r_2]\!]^{D,R}$$

A different notation for $\mathcal{F}[\![cf]\!] = tt$ is $\models cf$ which we pronounce "*cf* is valid". Observe that evaluation of correctness formulae depends only on our globally fixed structure $\mathfrak{S}$, not on a state.

Hoare-style partial correctness formulae are just abbreviations for some particular correctness formulae. For $\phi, \psi \in Pred^A$ and $S \in Prog^A$ on some abstraction level A we define

$$\{\phi\} S \{\psi\} \stackrel{\text{def}}{=} \phi ; S \subseteq \psi \ . \qquad \qquad \clubsuit$$

Why does this definition capture the intended meaning of Hoare triples?

$$\mathcal{F}[\![\phi ; S \subseteq \psi]\!]$$

$$\Leftrightarrow \forall \gamma, \tau \left((\gamma, \tau) \in C[\![\phi]\!]^A ; \mathcal{P}[\![S]\!]^A \Rightarrow (\gamma, \tau) \in C[\![\psi]\!]^A \right)$$

$$\Leftrightarrow \forall \gamma, \tau \left(\exists \sigma \left((\gamma, \sigma) \in C[\![\phi]\!]^A \wedge (\sigma, \tau) \in \mathcal{P}[\![S]\!]^A \right) \Rightarrow (\gamma, \tau) \in C[\![\psi]\!]^A \right)$$

$$\Leftrightarrow \forall \gamma, \sigma, \tau \left((\gamma, \sigma) \in C[\![\phi]\!]^A \wedge (\sigma, \tau) \in \mathcal{P}[\![S]\!]^A \Rightarrow (\gamma, \tau) \in C[\![\psi]\!]^A \right) \qquad (5.5)$$

The three subformulae of this universally quantified term may be understood as follows.

- $(\gamma, \sigma) \in C[\![\phi]\!]^A$ means that precondition ϕ holds in initial state σ, in case its logical variables are evaluated in logical state γ.
- $(\sigma, \tau) \in \mathcal{P}[\![S]\!]^A$ means that program S started in initial state σ may terminate in final state τ. This expression precludes neither nontermination nor termination in different states; it merely expresses the existence of a terminating execution of S starting in σ and ending in τ.
- $(\gamma, \tau) \in C[\![\psi]\!]^A$ means that postcondition ψ holds in final state τ, in case its logical variables are evaluated in logical state γ.

Consequently (5.5) expresses the intended meaning of $\{\phi\} S \{\psi\}$.

Note that both precondition ϕ and postcondition ψ are evaluated using the same logical state γ. This mechanism provides an opportunity to refer in postconditions indirectly to initial states of program variables.

Universal quantification over logical states gets rid of the dependence on values of logical variables. The intended behavior was informally described without mentioning logical variables; hence the value of a Hoare triple is defined in such a way that all possible values of logical variables are covered.

The justification of the semantics given to $\phi \rightsquigarrow \psi$ is that $\models \{\phi\} S \{\psi\}$ iff $\models S \subseteq \phi \rightsquigarrow \psi$. This is an immediate consequence of Def. 5.27 and Lemma 5.24.(i), as explained in the introduction to this chapter.

Corollary 5.28 *The most general program S satisfying Hoare triple $\{\phi\} S \{\psi\}$ is denoted by $\phi \rightsquigarrow \psi$.* $\qquad \qquad \spadesuit$

A similar argument can be given to justify the name weakest liberal precondition for $[S] \psi$.

Corollary 5.29 The following three correctness formulae are equivalent:

$$S \subseteq \phi \rightsquigarrow \psi \qquad \phi ; S \subseteq \psi \qquad \phi \subseteq [S] \psi \qquad \spadesuit$$

Next, we define a *freeze predicate* as a predicate of the form $\vec{x} = \vec{x}_0$ with $\vec{x}$ and $\vec{x}_0$ lists of program and logical variables respectively, of equal length. Within preconditions freeze predicates serve to record the values of program variables in logical variables for later reference in postconditions.

The next lemma states that a program can be exactly specified if its strongest postcondition with respect to a particular freeze predicate as precondition can be expressed as an assertion.

Lemma 5.30 Let $S \in Prog^A$, $\psi \in Pred^A$, let $\vec{x}$ be a list representation of Var^A, and let $\vec{x}_0$ be an equally long list of logical variables without duplicates. If ψ expresses $(\vec{x} = \vec{x}_0) ; S$ then $(\vec{x} = \vec{x}_0 \rightsquigarrow \psi) = S$.

Proof: We give a direct, semantic proof of the equality although $S \subseteq \vec{x} = \vec{x}_0 \rightsquigarrow \psi$ follows already by Cor. 5.29.

$$(\sigma, \tau) \in \mathcal{R}[\![(\vec{x} = \vec{x}_0) \rightsquigarrow ((\vec{x} = \vec{x}_0) ; S)]\!]^{Var^A, Var^A}$$

$$\Leftrightarrow (\sigma, \tau) \in C[\![\vec{x} = \vec{x}_0]\!]^A \rightsquigarrow (C[\![\vec{x} = \vec{x}_0]\!]^A ; \mathcal{P}[\![S]\!]^A) \qquad \text{Def. 5.22}$$

$$\Leftrightarrow \forall \gamma \Big((\gamma, \sigma) \in C[\![\vec{x} = \vec{x}_0]\!]^A \Rightarrow (\gamma, \tau) \in C[\![\vec{x} = \vec{x}_0]\!]^A ; \mathcal{P}[\![S]\!]^A \Big) \qquad \text{Def. 3.10}$$

$$\Leftrightarrow \forall \gamma \Big(\gamma(\vec{x}_0) = \sigma(\vec{x}) \Rightarrow (\gamma, \tau) \in C[\![\vec{x} = \vec{x}_0]\!]^A ; \mathcal{P}[\![S]\!]^A \Big) \qquad \text{Def. 5.10}$$

$$\Leftrightarrow \forall \gamma \begin{pmatrix} \gamma(\vec{x}_0) = \sigma(\vec{x}) \\ \Rightarrow \exists \sigma' \left(\gamma(\vec{x}_0) = \sigma'(\vec{x}) \wedge (\sigma', \tau) \in \mathcal{P}[\![S]\!]^A \right) \end{pmatrix} \qquad \begin{array}{l} \text{Defs 5.10} \\ \text{and 3.6} \end{array}$$

$$\Leftrightarrow (\sigma, \tau) \in \mathcal{P}[\![S]\!] \qquad \text{pred. calc.}$$

$$\square$$

Example 5.31 All Hoare triples having a precondition equivalent to false or a postcondition equivalent to true are valid. $\heartsuit$

Example 5.32 (The need for logical variables) We claimed that without logical variables it is impossible to state by means of a single partial correctness Hoare triple $\{\phi\} S \{\psi\}$ as simple a fact as "program S increments variable x by 1". This can be seen as follows. Assume we managed to find assertions ϕ and ψ in $Pred^A$ not containing free occurrences of logical variables such that "program $\phi \rightsquigarrow \psi$ increments variable x by 1". For $i \in \mathbb{Z}$ and $\sigma \in \Sigma^A$ let $\sigma^{(i)}$ be an abbreviation for state $(\sigma : x \mapsto i)$. Then we obviously require that at least $(\sigma^{(i)}, \sigma^{(i+1)}) \in \mathcal{P}[\![\phi \rightsquigarrow \psi]\!]^A$ for all $i \in \mathbb{Z}$ and $\sigma \in \Sigma^A$. Clearly $(\sigma^{(i)}, \sigma^{(i+2)})$

should not be contained in $\mathcal{P}[\![\phi \leadsto \psi]\!]^A$. We can derive the following property of $\mathcal{P}[\![\phi \leadsto \psi]\!]^A$ from the absence of free logical variable occurrences in ϕ and ψ:

$$\mathcal{P}[\![\phi \leadsto \psi]\!]^A$$

$$= \left\{ (\sigma, \tau) \,\middle|\, \forall \gamma \big((\gamma, \sigma) \in C[\![\phi]\!]^A \Rightarrow (\gamma, \tau) \in C[\![\psi]\!]^A \big) \right\} \qquad \text{Def. 5.18}$$

$$= \left\{ (\sigma, \tau) \,\middle|\, \sigma \in C[\![\phi]\!]^{Var^A} \Rightarrow \tau \in C[\![\psi]\!]^{Var^A} \right\} \qquad \text{Lemma 5.13}$$

$$= (C[\![\phi]\!]^{Var^A} \times C[\![\psi]\!]^{Var^A}) \cup (\overline{C[\![\phi]\!]^{Var^A}} \times \Sigma^A) \qquad \text{set theory}$$

$$= (C[\![\phi]\!]^{Var^A} \times C[\![\psi]\!]^{Var^A}) \cup (C[\![\neg\phi]\!]^{Var^A} \times \Sigma^A) \qquad \text{Lemma 5.14}$$

The right half of this union contains $(\sigma^{(i)}, \sigma^{(i+2)})$ for any $\sigma^{(i)}$ for which ϕ as a Boolean expression does not hold. Hence, there is no such $\sigma^{(i)}$. This implies that $\sigma^{(i)} \in C[\![\phi]\!]^{Var^A}$ for any $i \in \mathbb{Z}$ and $\sigma \in \Sigma^A$. In other words, $C[\![\phi]\!]^{Var^A} = \Sigma^A$. Thus, with $(\sigma^{(i)}, \sigma^{(i+1)}) \in \mathcal{P}[\![\phi \leadsto \psi]\!]^A$ for $i = 0, 1$, we obtain the undesired $(\sigma^{(0)}, \sigma^{(2)}) \in \mathcal{P}[\![\phi \leadsto \psi]\!]^A$ which clearly means that x is incremented by 2. Contradiction! Hence, our assumption about the absence of logical variables in ϕ and ψ does not hold.

On the other hand, specification statement

$$x = x_0 \leadsto x = x_0 + 1 \tag{5.6}$$

has the desired property: x is incremented by 1. Note that in case x is not the only program variable, this specification is still more general than assignment statement $x := x + 1$ in that it allows program variables other than x to change their values arbitrarily. To prevent this, so-called *freeze predicates* may have to be added to the specification statement, for instance $x = x_0 \wedge y = y_0 \leadsto x = x_0 + 1 \wedge y = y_0$ states in addition that y remains unchanged.   ♡

Unproblematic as the introduction of logical variables may seem at first sight, this impression changes when one tries to interpret arbitrary specifications containing them. E.g., which operations are specified by the following specification statements?

$$x = x_0^2 \leadsto x = x_0 \tag{5.7}$$

$$\text{true} \leadsto x = x_0 \tag{5.8}$$

At first sight, the problem with specification (5.7) seems to be that, since it is not clear from the precondition whether the value of x_0 is positive or negative, the final value of x may be positive or negative depending on the value of x_0.

Similarly, the problem with specification (5.8) seems to be that the final value of x is specified as whatever value x_0 happens to have.

At second glance something seems to be seriously wrong. Since we have stated above explicitly that x_0 can only be used for expressing assertions, x_0 cannot occur inside any program implementing one of these specification statements, and hence any functional dependence of x's final value upon x_0 in any such program is absurd.

Our conclusion must be that any variation of the final value of x depending on the value of x_0 cannot be implemented. In Hoare's pre/postcondition calculus for partial correctness this implies that for any such final value of x which displays in the specification a choice depending on the value of x_0, the specified operation does not terminate.

This argument can be made formal by calculating, e.g., (5.8):

$$\mathcal{P}[\![\text{true} \rightsquigarrow x = x_0]\!]$$

$$= \bigcap_{\gamma} \{ (\sigma, \tau) \mid (\gamma, \sigma) \in C[\![\text{true}]\!] \Rightarrow (\gamma, \tau) \in C[\![x = x_0]\!] \} \qquad \text{Def. 5.18}$$

$$= \bigcap_{\gamma} \{ (\sigma, \tau) \mid \tau(x) = \gamma(x_0) \} \qquad \text{Lemma 5.14}$$

$$= \bigcap_{z \in \mathbb{Z}} \{ (\sigma, \tau) \mid \tau(x) = z \}$$

$$= \emptyset \qquad \text{set theory}$$

$$= \mathcal{P}[\![\text{abort}]\!] \qquad \text{Def. 5.18}$$

Later on, in Chapter 8, we shall introduce a notation for Hoare triples for total correctness, $\{\pi_1\} S \{\pi_2\}_\perp$, which stipulates, in addition to partial correctness, that whenever π_1 holds S terminates. Then, e.g., $\{\text{true}\} S \{x = x_0\}_\perp$ is unsatisfiable, cf. [ALW89]. For, on the one hand, $\{\text{true}\} S \{x = x_0\}_\perp$ implies $\{\text{true}\} S \{x = x_0\}$, and we have just derived that the latter is only satisfied by **abort**, which terminates nowhere, whereas, on the other hand, S should terminate whenever its precondition true holds, i.e., always. Contradiction!

5.6 Historical Background

The particular style of defining a so-called denotational semantics using semantic interpretation functions goes back to [SS71].

Hoare-style assertions and correctness formulae are constituents of Hoare logic, introduced by Hoare in his pioneering paper [Hoa69]. The leads-to operator $\rightsquigarrow$ originates from [Sch77]. The need for freezing values in fresh variables, for which we use logical variables, has already been introduced in [dBM75, Gor75, HPS76].

Exercises

5.1   Prove Lemma 5.8.
5.2   Show associativity of the † operator, i.e., $((\sigma \dagger \tau) \dagger \rho) = (\sigma \dagger (\tau \dagger \rho))$.
5.3   Prove Cor. 5.11.
5.4   Prove part (ii) of Lemma 5.12.
5.5   Prove Lemma 5.14.
5.6   Prove part (i) of Lemma 5.17.
5.7   Show that **abort, skip**, assignments, and filters can be expressed as specification statements.
5.8   Formulate and prove a claim for sequential compositions similar to the one for leads-to in Lemma 5.19.
5.9   Calculate the semantics of

        (a) **if** $x < 0$ **then** $x := -x$ **fi**,
        (b) **while** true **do skip od**, and
        (c) **while** $x > 0$ **do** $x := x - 1$ **od**.

5.10   Prove Lemma 5.20.
5.11   Prove Lemma 5.21.
5.12   Prove the claim contained in the remark following Lemma 5.26.
5.13   Express r^{-1}, $[r_1] \, r_2$, $\langle r_1 \rangle \, r_2$, and $r_1 ; r_2$ in *Rel* using operators $\neg$ and $\rightsquigarrow$ only.
5.14   (cf. Example 5.32) Can you show the need for logical variables by reformulating Example 5.32 with statement **skip** instead of $x := x + 1$?
5.15   Let $\phi, \psi \in Pred^A$ and $\psi' \in Pred^{Lvar^A}$. Prove that $\phi \rightsquigarrow (\psi' \Rightarrow \psi) = (\phi \wedge \psi') \rightsquigarrow \psi$.
5.16   Calculate $\mathcal{P}[\![x = x_0^2 \rightsquigarrow x = x_0]\!]$ and explain informally why the Hoare-style total correctness formula $\{x = x_0^2\} \, S \, \{x = x_0\}_{\perp}$ is not satisfiable.

6

A Hoare Logic

The correctness formulae we are most interested in proving are proof obligations for data refinement. In the next chapter we shall see that each data refinement proof obligation for a pair of operations can be reduced effectively to a single Hoare triple. This motivates the presentation of a proof system for Hoare triples instead of for general correctness formulae. The reader unfamiliar with Hoare logic is referred to Appendix A, which contains a gentle introduction to this topic. Hoare logic originates from C. A. R. Hoare's landmark paper [Hoa69].

In this chapter we present a pure, sound, and complete (in the sense of Cook) Hoare logic for our programming language, using Peano arithmetic over the natural numbers as the structure underlying the interpretation. This logic has been designed to have a minimal number of axioms and rules to simplify its soundness and completeness proofs.[1]

In the presentation we restrict ourselves to specification statements as atomic statements since the other constructs, i.e., **abort, skip**, assignments, and guards, can be easily expressed in terms of the specification statement. To ease the exposition below, we assume that vector $\vec{z}$ denotes the list of program variables at the level under consideration and that $\vec{z_0}$ is a logical variable vector of the same length without duplicates.

Lemma 6.1 Assignment $x := e$ of an arithmetic expression e to a program variable $x \in Var$ is expressed by $(\vec{z} = \vec{z_0})[^e/_x] \rightsquigarrow \vec{z} = \vec{z_0}$, and guard $b \rightarrow$ for a Boolean expression b over Var is expressed by $\vec{z} = \vec{z_0} \rightsquigarrow b \land \vec{z} = \vec{z_0}$. Using the

---

[1] Consequently this logic has not been designed for maximal ease of use. The latter issue, that of pragmatics, is of paramount importance to industrial users. A Hoare logic serving the latters' interest may be obtained from the one presented here by adding more derivable axioms and rules and formulating effective heuristics for their manipulation (which is still a research topic).

definition of guards, **skip** is expressed by true $\rightarrow$ and the never terminating program **abort** is expressed by false $\rightarrow$.

Proof: Exercise.   □

Next we formulate a *proof system* for the deduction of Hoare triples. A proof system T for a class $\mathcal{F}$ of formulae consists of *inference rules* $\Delta \vdash F$, where $\Delta \subseteq \mathcal{F}$ is a set of *premises* or *antecedent* formulae and $F \in \mathcal{F}$ is the *conclusion* or *succedent* formula. An *axiom* $\vdash F$ is a rule with an empty set of premises. Usually axioms and rules are given in terms of *schemes*, i.e., each of them represents a set of *instances* by leaving constituents of the formulae open to interpretation. For instance, the standard axiom scheme of Hoare logic for assignment statements $\vdash \{\pi[^e/_x]\}\,x := e\,\{\pi\}$ has variable parts π, x, and e, which may be instantiated by any assertion, variable, and expression, respectively. Thus $\vdash \{17 + 5 > 7\}\,y := 17\,\{y + 5 > 7\}$ is an instance of that axiom scheme (by Def. 5.7 of substitution). A *formal proof* of a formula $F_0 \in \mathcal{F}$ in T is a tree with formulae as nodes such that F_0 is the tree's root and for every node F there exists an instance of a rule such that F is the conclusion and the set of its immediate descendants in the tree is the set of premises of that rule instance. Thus, in case F is a leaf, $\vdash F$ must be an instance of an axiom. If there exists a formal proof of F in T we say that F is *deducible* in T (or $\vdash_T F$). To judge a proof system one compares deducibility with validity, that is, given a (semantic) notion of validity of formulae, two essential questions arise:

Soundness: Is every deducible formula valid?
Completeness: Is every valid formula deducible?

Validity of Hoare triples has been defined in the previous chapter. In Section 6.1 we present an axiom and five rules for Hoare triples. After that, in Section 6.2, we address the two questions asked above.

6.1 Proof System

Specification statements are the only basic statements left according to the restriction made at the beginning of this chapter (see Lemma 6.1). Therefore, the only axiom of our proof system $\mathfrak{H}$ for Hoare triples is one for specification statements.

Let $\vec{x}$ express the vector of free program variables inside assertions ϕ, ψ, and π, let $\vec{x}_0$ express the vector of free logical variables inside ϕ and ψ, and let $\vec{y}_0$ express a vector of fresh logical variables of the same length as $\vec{x}$.

$$\text{adaptation axiom} \quad \vdash \{\pi\}\,\phi \rightsquigarrow \psi\left\{\exists \vec{y}_0 \left(\pi[^{\vec{y}_0}/_{\vec{x}}] \wedge \forall \vec{x}_0 \left(\phi[^{\vec{y}_0}/_{\vec{x}}] \Rightarrow \psi\right)\right)\right\}$$

The word "adaptation" in the name of this axiom refers to the situation that Hoare triples for $\phi \rightsquigarrow \psi$ are derived for preconditions different from ϕ.

Example 6.2 By the definition of substitution, the Hoare triple

$$\{x < 17\}\, x + 3 = x_0 \rightsquigarrow x < x_0\, \{\exists \vec{y_0}\, (y_0 < 17 \wedge \forall \vec{x_0}\, (y_0 + 3 = x_0 \Rightarrow x < x_0))\}$$

is an instance of the adaptation axiom. The postcondition is easily simplified to $x < 20$, which was to be expected, given the precondition $x < 17$ and the specification statement $x + 3 = x_0 \rightsquigarrow x < x_0$. $\heartsuit$

The next two rules allow us to prove properties of sequential composition and nondeterministic choice from properties of their subcomponents. We present rules in the traditional vertical style; $\frac{\Delta}{F}$ is another notation for $\Delta \vdash F$.

$$\text{composition rule} \quad \frac{\{\pi\}\, S_1\, \{\phi\},\ \{\phi\}\, S_2\, \{\rho\}}{\{\pi\}\, S_1\, ;S_2\, \{\rho\}}$$

$$\text{choice rule} \quad \frac{\{\pi\}\, S_1\, \{\rho\},\ \{\pi\}\, S_2\, \{\rho\}}{\{\pi\}\, S_1\, [\,]\, S_2\, \{\rho\}}$$

The consequence rule allows us to strengthen the precondition and weaken the postcondition.

$$\text{consequence rule} \quad \frac{\pi \Rightarrow \phi,\ \{\phi\}\, S\, \{\psi\},\ \psi \Rightarrow \rho}{\{\pi\}\, S\, \{\rho\}}$$

Observe that two of the premises of the consequence rule are assertions, and not Hoare triples. We postpone the discussion of this topic until we address completeness of our Hoare logic.

The following rule states the desirable monotonicity of refinement: Subcomponent refinement preserves correctness.

$$\rightsquigarrow\text{-substitution rule} \quad \frac{\{\phi\}\, S_1\, \{\psi\},\ \{\pi\}\, S_2(\phi \rightsquigarrow \psi)\, \{\rho\}}{\{\pi\}\, S_2(S_1)\, \{\rho\}}$$

Our Hoare-style rule for recursion resembles Park's least fixed point rule (see page 61). The striking difference between Park's and our rule on the one hand and Scott's induction rule on the other hand (see page 61) is that we can do without deduction in the antecedent, i.e., we do not need premises of the form $\{.\}\,.\,\{.\} \vdash \{.\}\,.\,\{.\}$. This is considered simpler and more natural. It reflects the intuition of programmers concerning recursive procedures: a procedure is correct (w.r.t. a specification) if its body can be proven correct under the assumption that inner calls of the procedure behave correctly.

$$\text{recursion rule} \quad \frac{\{\pi\}\, S(\pi \rightsquigarrow \rho)\, \{\rho\}}{\{\pi\}\, \mu X.S\, \{\rho\}}$$

As indicated above, we let $\mathfrak{H}$ denote the set of instances of the above axiom scheme and five rules.

To simplify the presentation of our next example, we present a few useful derived rules and an example of a proof in $\mathfrak{H}$.

The standard axioms and rules for loops, conditionals, assignments, guarded commands, etc. can be derived from our rules. We demonstrate this only for a few axioms and rules. The rest is worked out in the exercises. Three more axioms turn out to be helpful in the example below.

$$\text{guard axiom} \quad \vdash \{\phi\}\, b \to \{\phi \wedge b\}$$

$$\text{assignment axiom} \quad \vdash \{\phi[^e/_x]\}\, x := e\, \{\phi\}$$

wlp-adaptation axiom

$$\vdash \left\{ \forall \vec{y_0} \left(\forall \vec{x_0} \left(\phi \Rightarrow \psi[^{\vec{v}_0}/_{\vec{x}}] \right) \Rightarrow \rho[^{\vec{v}_0}/_{\vec{x}}] \right) \right\} \phi \rightsquigarrow \psi \{\rho\}$$

Let us explain the intuition behind this last axiom. It is related to the second equivalence of Lemma 5.19 as the adaptation axiom relates to the first. The complicated assertion in the precondition of this Hoare triple expresses the weakest precondition such that after execution of $\phi \rightsquigarrow \psi$ postcondition ρ holds. Since Dijkstra introduced the term "weakest precondition" in a framework for total correctness, he uses a different name for such an assertion in the context of partial correctness, namely *weakest liberal precondition* (*wlp*). This explains the name of this axiom. That our precondition does indeed express the weakest such assertion follows from the second equivalence in Lemma 5.19, Lemma 5.25, and the remark following Lemma 5.26.

Lemma 6.3 The guard axiom, the assignment axiom, and the *wlp*-adaptation axiom are derivable in $\mathfrak{H}$.

Proof: For the guard axiom we start with the tautology

$$\vdash \phi \wedge b \Rightarrow \phi \wedge b$$

$\Rightarrow$ (predicate calculus)

$$\exists \vec{y_0} \left(\phi[^{\vec{v}_0}/_{\vec{z}}] \wedge \vec{z} = \vec{y_0} \wedge b \right) \Rightarrow \phi \wedge b$$

$\Rightarrow$ (predicate calculus, Def. 5.7)

$$\exists \vec{y_0} \left(\phi[^{\vec{v}_0}/_{\vec{z}}] \wedge \forall \vec{z_0} \left((\vec{z} = \vec{z_0})[^{\vec{v}_0}/_{\vec{z}}] \Rightarrow \vec{z} = \vec{y_0} \wedge b \right) \right) \Rightarrow \phi \wedge b$$

$\Rightarrow$ (consequence rule and adaptation axiom)

$$\vdash \{\phi\}\, \vec{z} = \vec{z_0} \rightsquigarrow b \wedge \vec{z} = \vec{z_0}\, \{\phi \wedge b\}$$

$\Leftrightarrow$ (Lemma 6.1)

$\vdash \{\phi\}\, b \to \{\phi \wedge b\}$

That the assignment axiom is also derivable in $\mathfrak{H}$ follows analogously. That the *wlp*-adaptation axiom is derivable follows by the consequence rule and the adaptation axiom from the validity of the assertion

$$\exists \vec{y_0}\left(\forall \vec{y_0}\left(\forall \vec{x_0}\left(\phi \Rightarrow \psi[\vec{y_0}/\vec{x}]\right) \Rightarrow \rho[\vec{y_0}/\vec{x}]\right)[\vec{y_0}/\vec{x}] \wedge \forall \vec{x_0}\left(\phi[\vec{y_0}/\vec{x}] \Rightarrow \psi\right)\right) \Rightarrow \rho \ ,$$

which is a straightforward exercise in predicate logic reasoning. $\square$

Many adaptation rules have been suggested in the literature [Old83]. The sound ones we are aware of are all derivable within $\mathfrak{H}$. For instance, the rule

$$\frac{\{\phi\}\, S\, \{\psi\}}{\left\{\forall \vec{y_0}\left(\forall \vec{x_0}\left(\phi \Rightarrow \psi[\vec{y_0}/\vec{x}]\right) \Rightarrow \rho[\vec{y_0}/\vec{x}]\right)\right\} S\, \{\rho\}}$$

suggested by Olderog in [Old83] can be derived easily using the *wlp*-adaptation axiom and the $\rightsquigarrow$-substitution rule.

Example 6.4 An operation that computes the factorial function on the natural numbers, which is defined recursively by

$$n! \stackrel{\text{def}}{=} \begin{cases} 1 & \text{if } n = 0 \\ n \cdot (n-1)! & \text{otherwise} \end{cases}$$

is specified in our set-up, for instance, by $n = n_0 \rightsquigarrow n = n_0!$, stating that the value of variable n after the operation is the factorial of its value before the operation. The point of this example is to demonstrate the usability of the rules of our system rather than to provide yet another correctness proof of a factorial function implementation. First we refine our specification to

$$m := 1\, ;\, (n, m = n_0, m_0 \rightsquigarrow n, m = n_0, m_0 \cdot n_0!)\, ;\, n := m \ .$$

Observe that we introduce an extra program variable m to store the result and that we let n maintain its value in the specification statement. If we manage to prove

$$\{n = n_0\}\, m := 1\, ;\, n, m = n_0, m_0 \rightsquigarrow n, m = n_0, m_0 \cdot n_0!\, ;\, n := m\, \{n = n_0!\}$$
$$(6.1)$$

then this first refinement step is justified. The assignment axiom provides the premise

$$\{1 \cdot n! = n_0!\}\, m := 1\, \{m \cdot n! = n_0!\}$$

to an instance of the consequence rule. The other two premises are

$$n = n_0 \Rightarrow 1 \cdot n! = n_0!$$

and

$$m \cdot n! = n_0!$$
$$\Rightarrow \forall a, b \left(\begin{array}{l} \forall n_0, m_0 \left(n, m = n_0, m_0 \Rightarrow (n, m = n_0, m_0 \cdot n_0!)[^{a,b}/_{n,m}] \right) \\ \Rightarrow (m = n_0!)[^{a,b}/_{n,m}] \end{array} \right)$$

which are both valid implications. An instance of the *wlp*-adaptation axiom, here presented vertically for reasons of space, is

$$\left\{ \forall a, b \left(\begin{array}{l} \forall n_0, m_0 \left(n, m = n_0, m_0 \Rightarrow (n, m = n_0, m_0 \cdot n_0!)[^{a,b}/_{n,m}] \right) \\ \Rightarrow (m = n_0!)[^{a,b}/_{n,m}] \end{array} \right) \right\}$$
$$n, m = n_0, m_0 \rightsquigarrow n, m = n_0, m_0 \cdot n_0!$$
$$\{m = n_0!\}$$

This serves as the second premise of an instance of the sequential composition rule. Its conclusion is

$$\{1 \cdot n! = n_0!\} \, m := 1 \, ; (n, m = n_0, m_0 \rightsquigarrow n, m = n_0, m_0 \cdot n_0!) \, \{m = n_0!\} \quad,$$

one of the premises of a second instance of the sequential composition rule. The second premise is another instance of the assignment axiom:

$$\{m = n_0!\} \, n := m \, \{n = n_0!\}$$

The conclusion is (6.1). Thus, our first refinement step is proven correct within $\mathfrak{H}$.

Next we shall see that the program

$$U(X) \stackrel{\text{def}}{=}$$
$$S \stackrel{\text{def}}{=} \mu X.\big(\underbrace{(n > 0 \to n := n - 1 \, ; X \, ; n := n + 1 \, ; m := m \cdot n)}_{T(X) \stackrel{\text{def}}{=}} \, [] \, n = 0 \to \big)$$

implements the specification $n, m = n_0, m_0 \rightsquigarrow n, m = n_0, m_0 \cdot n_0!$, i.e.,

$$\{n, m = n_0, m_0\} \, S \, \{n, m = n_0, m_0 \cdot n_0!\} \tag{6.2}$$

is a valid Hoare triple. According to the recursion rule it suffices to prove that

$$\{n, m = n_0, m_0\} \, T(n, m = n_0, m_0 \rightsquigarrow n, m = n_0, m_0 \cdot n_0!) \, \{n, m = n_0, m_0 \cdot n_0!\}$$

is valid. By the choice rule this follows from the validity of two Hoare triples, (6.3) and (6.4):

$$\{n, m = n_0, m_0\} \, n = 0 \to \{n, m = n_0, m_0 \cdot n_0!\} \tag{6.3}$$

This follows from the consequence rule and the guard axiom because $n,m = n_0,m_0 \land n = 0 \Rightarrow n,m = n_0,m_0 \cdot 0!$ is valid since, by definition of the factorial function, $0! = 1$.

$$\{n,m = n_0,m_0\} \, U \, (n,m = n_0,m_0 \rightsquigarrow n,m = n_0,m_0 \cdot n_0!) \, \{n,m = n_0,m_0 \cdot n_0!\} \tag{6.4}$$

By the sequential composition rule this follows from five simpler correctness formulae, (6.5)–(6.9). The first is an instance of the guard axiom:

$$\{n,m = n_0,m_0\} \, n > 0 \to \{n,m = n_0,m_0 \land n > 0\} \tag{6.5}$$

The second,

$$\{n,m = n_0,m_0 \land n > 0\} \, n := n - 1 \, \{n,m = n_0 - 1,m_0\} \ , \tag{6.6}$$

follows by the consequence rule and the assignment axiom from the validity of $n,m = n_0,m_0 \land n > 0 \Rightarrow n - 1 = n_0 - 1$, which is immediate.

By the consequence rule and the adaptation axiom the third

$$\left\{n,m = n_0 - 1,m_0\right\} \begin{array}{c} n,m = n_0,m_0 \\ \rightsquigarrow n,m = n_0,m_0 \cdot n_0! \end{array} \left\{n,m = n_0 - 1,m_0 \cdot (n_0 - 1)!\right\} \tag{6.7}$$

can be reduced to the following implication:

$$\exists a,b \left(\begin{array}{c} (n,m = n_0 - 1,m_0)[^{a,b}/_{n,m}] \\ \land \forall n_0,m_0 \, ((n,m = n_0,m_0)[^{a,b}/_{n,m}] \Rightarrow n,m = n_0,m_0 \cdot n_0!) \end{array} \right)$$
$$\Rightarrow n,m = n_0 - 1,m_0 \cdot (n_0 - 1)!$$

By the definition of substitution and two applications of the one-point rule[2], the LHS of this implication can be reduced to the RHS.

The fourth

$$\{n,m = n_0 - 1,m_0 \cdot (n_0 - 1)!\} \, n := n + 1 \, \{n,m = n_0,m_0 \cdot (n_0 - 1)!\} \tag{6.8}$$

is again an instance of the assignment axiom. The fifth correctness formula

$$\{n,m = n_0,m_0 \cdot (n_0 - 1)!\} \, m := m \cdot n \, \{n,m = n_0,m_0 \cdot n_0!\} \tag{6.9}$$

follows by the consequence rule from a last instance of the assignment axiom,

$$\{n,m \cdot n = n_0,m_0 \cdot n_0!\} \, m := m \cdot n \, \{n,m = n_0,m_0 \cdot n_0!\} \ ,$$

and the validity of $n,m = n_0,m_0 \cdot (n_0 - 1)! \Rightarrow n,m \cdot n = n_0,m_0 \cdot n_0!$, which holds by definition of the factorial function.

---

[2] By *one-point rule* we refer to proof steps involving the equivalence of either of $\forall a \, (a = b \Rightarrow p(a))$ or $\exists a \, (a = b \land p(a))$ with $p(b)$.

Finally, by the $\rightsquigarrow$-substitution rule, it follows from (6.1) and (6.2) that the program

$$m := 1;$$
$$\mu X. \left((n > 0 \to n := n - 1\,;X\,;n := n + 1\,;m := m \cdot n)\,[\!]\,n = 0 \to\right);$$
$$n := m$$

implements the specification $n = n_0 \rightsquigarrow n = n_0!$. $\heartsuit$

6.2 Soundness and (Relative) Completeness

Lemma 6.5 (Soundness) $\mathfrak{H}$ is sound.

Proof: We demonstrate soundness only of the less standard rules, i.e., the adaptation axiom, the $\rightsquigarrow$-substitution rule, and the recursion rule. The proof of the adaptation axiom is analogous to the proof of Lemma 5.30. We show

$$\pi\,;(\phi \rightsquigarrow \psi) \subseteq \exists \vec{y}_0 \left(\pi[^{\vec{y}_0}/_{\vec{x}}] \wedge \forall \vec{x}_0 \left(\phi[^{\vec{y}_0}/_{\vec{x}}] \Rightarrow \psi \right) \right)$$

beginning with the RHS.

$$(\gamma,\tau) \in C[\![\exists \vec{y}_0 \left(\pi[^{\vec{y}_0}/_{\vec{x}}] \wedge \forall \vec{x}_0 \left(\phi[^{\vec{y}_0}/_{\vec{x}}] \Rightarrow \psi \right) \right)]\!]^A$$

$$\Leftrightarrow \exists \sigma \left((\gamma,\sigma) \in C[\![\pi]\!]^A \wedge \forall \delta \left((\delta,\sigma) \in C[\![\phi]\!]^A \Rightarrow (\delta,\tau) \in C[\![\psi]\!]^A \right) \right)$$

$$\Leftrightarrow (\gamma,\tau) \in C[\![\pi]\!]^A\,;(C[\![\phi]\!]^A \rightsquigarrow C[\![\psi]\!]^A)$$

Soundness of the $\rightsquigarrow$-substitution rule follows from monotonicity of the constructs in *Prog*.

Next, turning to the recursion rule, since $\mathcal{P}[\![\mathbf{abort}]\!] = \emptyset \subseteq \mathcal{P}[\![\pi \rightsquigarrow \rho]\!]$ and the constructs in *Prog* are monotone one can show by induction that

$$\forall i \in \mathbb{N}\,(\,\mathcal{P}[\![S^i(\mathbf{abort})]\!] \subseteq \mathcal{P}[\![\pi \rightsquigarrow \rho]\!]\,) \quad.$$

Hence, by definition of $\mathcal{P}[\![\mu X.S]\!]$,

$$\mathcal{P}[\![\mu X.S]\!] = \bigcup_{i \in \mathbb{N}} \mathcal{P}[\![S^i(\mathbf{abort})]\!] \subseteq \mathcal{P}[\![\pi \rightsquigarrow \rho]\!] \quad.$$

Thus the recursion rule is sound. $\square$

Now we return to the topic of assertions as premises in the consequence rule. No formal proof in the above sense can be given using this rule without extending our proof system with axioms and rules for assertions. However, once we add such rules, the question of completeness can be answered negatively by Gödel's famous incompleteness result, which states that no sound and complete proof system for first order predicate logic over Peano arithmetic exists.

Consequently we need to develop a notion of proof system for Hoare formulae which separates the issue of proving Hoare triples from that of proving assertions. To investigate completeness of $\mathfrak{H}$ independently of the difficulties arising from assertions, we assume that all valid assertions (in the underlying structure) have the same status as axioms, i.e., we need not bother about proving them formally. The resulting notion of completeness is discussed extensively in [Apt81] and called *(relative) completeness in the sense of Cook* [Coo78]. Since the following statements depend on the underlying interpretation we subscript semantic brackets $[\![.]\!]$ with the current interpretation.

Definition 6.6 (Expressiveness) An interpretation I is *expressive* iff, for all $\pi \in Pred^A$ and $S \in Prog^A$, the strongest postcondition of S w.r.t. precondition π, that is, $C[\![\pi]\!]_I^A ; \mathcal{P}[\![S]\!]_I^A$, can be expressed within $Pred^A$.

$$\forall \pi \in Pred^A, S \in Prog^A \left(\exists \rho \in Pred^A \left(C[\![\rho]\!]_I^A = C[\![\pi]\!]_I^A ; \mathcal{P}[\![S]\!]_I^A \right) \right) \qquad \clubsuit$$

Let $\mathfrak{I}$ denote the standard interpretation of Peano arithmetic over the natural numbers $\mathbb{N}$.

Theorem 6.7 (Expressiveness)
$\mathfrak{I}$ is expressive.

Proof: By induction on the structure of the program. The strongest postcondition of specification statement $\phi \rightsquigarrow \psi$ w.r.t. precondition π is expressed by

$$\exists \vec{y_0} \left(\pi[\vec{y_0}/\vec{x}] \wedge \forall \vec{x_0} \left(\phi[\vec{y_0}/\vec{x}] \Rightarrow \psi \right) \right) ,$$

whence its appearance as postcondition in the adaptation axiom. The induction steps are standard, involving Gödel encoding in the case of recursion; we refer to [dB80] for more details. $\qquad \square$

Definition 6.8 (Relative completeness) A proof system $\mathcal{H}$ is *complete relative to an interpretation I* iff I is expressive and

$$\mathcal{F}[\![\{\pi\} S \{\rho\}]\!]_I \quad \Rightarrow \quad \vdash_{\mathcal{H} \cup \mathcal{T}_I} \{\pi\} S \{\rho\}$$

holds for all assertions $\pi, \rho \in Pred$ and programs $S \in Prog$, where the theory

$$\mathcal{T}_I \stackrel{\text{def}}{=} \{ \pi \in Pred \mid C[\![\pi]\!]_I = \Gamma \times \Sigma \}$$

of valid assertions under I is assumed as a set of additional axioms. $\qquad \clubsuit$

We refer to [Apt81] for a brilliant exposition of program verification using Hoare logic. It also explains why this particular notion of completeness is appropriate here.

Theorem 6.9 (Relative completeness)

$\mathfrak{H}$ is complete relative to $\mathfrak{J}$.

Proof: Let $\pi, \rho \in Pred^A$ and $S \in Prog^A$ such that $\mathcal{F}[\![\{\pi\} S \{\rho\}]\!]_{\mathfrak{J}}$. Let $\rho' \in Pred^A$ express $C[\![\pi]\!]_{\mathfrak{J}}^A$; $\mathcal{P}[\![S]\!]_{\mathfrak{J}}^A$; then $\rho' \Rightarrow \rho \in \mathcal{T}_{\mathfrak{J}}$. We show by induction on the structure of S how to prove $\{\pi\} S \{\rho'\}$. An instance of the consequence rule then finishes the proof. Consider the cases of S:

$S = \pi \leadsto \rho$: $\{\pi\} S \{\rho'\}$ is an instance of the adaptation axiom.

$S = S_1; S_2$: Let $\phi \in Pred^A$ express $C[\![\pi]\!]_{\mathfrak{J}}^A$; $\mathcal{P}[\![S_1]\!]_{\mathfrak{J}}^A$. The induction hypotheses are $\vdash_{\mathcal{H} \cup \mathcal{T}_{\mathfrak{J}}} \{\pi\} S_1 \{\phi\}$ and $\vdash_{\mathcal{H} \cup \mathcal{T}_{\mathfrak{J}}} \{\phi\} S_2 \{\rho'\}$. An instance of the composition rule with these two premises shows $\{\pi\} S \{\rho'\}$.

$S = S_1 \,[\!]\, S_2$: In this case the induction hypotheses are $\vdash_{\mathcal{H} \cup \mathcal{T}_{\mathfrak{J}}} \{\pi\} S_i \{\rho'\}$ for $i = 1, 2$. An application of the choice rule then proves $\{\pi\} S \{\rho'\}$.

$S = \mu X.T$: Let $\phi \equiv \vec{z} = \vec{z}_0$ and ψ express $C[\![\phi]\!]_{\mathfrak{J}}^A$; $\mathcal{P}[\![\mu X.T]\!]_{\mathfrak{J}}^A$. Then $\phi \leadsto \psi = \mu X.T$ holds semantically by Lemma 5.30. Thus, ρ' as the strongest postcondition of $\phi \leadsto \psi$ w.r.t. π must be equivalent to

$$\exists \vec{y}_0 \left(\pi[\vec{y}_0/\vec{x}] \wedge \forall \vec{x}_0 \left(\phi[\vec{y}_0/\vec{x}] \Rightarrow \psi \right) \right) ,$$

where $\vec{y}_0$, $\vec{x}_0$, and $\vec{x}$ are as in the adaptation axiom. To apply the $\leadsto$-substitution rule where S_2 is just X, two premises remain to be shown: firstly $\{\pi\} \phi \leadsto \psi \{\rho'\}$, which is an instance of the adaptation axiom, and secondly $\{\phi\} \mu X.T \{\psi\}$. By the induction hypothesis, the latter is provable using the recursion rule since its premise, $\{\phi\} T (\phi \leadsto \psi) \{\psi\}$, is valid. This validity can be seen as follows. By the fixed point property $\mu X.T = T(\mu X.T)$ and thus, by Lemma 5.30, $\phi \leadsto \psi = T(\phi \leadsto \psi)$. Hence $\mathcal{F}[\![\{\phi\} T (\phi \leadsto \psi) \{\psi\}]\!]_{\mathfrak{J}}$. $\square$

6.3 Historical Background

Hoare logic originates from [Hoa69]. The leads-to operator $\leadsto$ was first axiomatized in Hoare logic by Schwarz in [Sch77]. In the same paper a Hoare-style rule for recursion was given which does not use formal deduction in the antecedent; he also proved soundness and a form of completeness.

Relative completeness, the by now classical notion of completeness for Hoare logic, originates from [Coo78], in which Cook proves soundness and completeness of an axiom system for Hoare logic. In order to do so, he uses the standard interpretation of Peano arithmetic over the natural numbers for encoding finite computation sequences and operations on them. This technique is called Gödel encoding and goes back to [Göd31].

The historical origins of Hoare logic are extensively discussed in [Apt81]; see also Appendix A of this monograph.

Exercises

6.1   Derive the assignment axiom within our proof system for Hoare logic.

6.2   Derive the rule

$$\frac{\{\pi \wedge b\} S_1 \{\rho\}, \{\pi \wedge \neg b\} S_2 \{\rho\}}{\{\pi\} \text{ if } b \text{ then } S_1 \text{ else } S_2 \text{ fi} \{\rho\}}$$

for conditionals within our proof system for Hoare logic.

6.3   Derive the rule

$$\frac{\{b \wedge \pi\} S \{\pi\}}{\{\pi\} \text{ while } b \text{ do } S \text{ od} \{\pi \wedge \neg b\}}$$

for while-loops within our proof system for Hoare logic.

6.4*   Prove that expressiveness of an interpretation for strongest postconditions is equivalent to that for weakest liberal preconditions.

7

Simulation and Hoare Logic

In this chapter we solve a fundamental problem of data refinement. We show that, given an abstract level specification statement $\pi_1 \rightsquigarrow \pi_2 \in Prog^A$ and an abstraction relation $\alpha \in Abs^{CA}$, the least refined concrete level program $S \in Prog^C$ simulating the abstract level specification statement can be expressed as a specification statement on the concrete level. (See Figure 7.1, in which $\star$ denotes one of our four forms of weak commutativity.) In other words, the verification conditions for simulation can be expressed by Hoare triples whenever the abstract operation is just a specification statement (which should be the standard case).

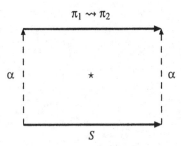

Fig. 7.1. The main question of this chapter: How to express S?

Answers are sought for all of our four kinds of simulation. The solution for U-simulation will be rather simple, whereas the complexity of expressions for L-, L^{-1}-, and U^{-1}-simulation solutions increases (in the order given) remarkably. However, in case the precondition π_1 is just a freeze predicate for all program variables or abstraction relation α is total and functional, these solutions may be substantially simplified. Fortunately, most practical cases are among these simplifiable ones.

The body of this chapter consists of four sections, each of which discusses the solution to this chapter's central question for one particular notion of simulation.

7.1 U-simulation in Hoare Logic

For U-simulation Figure 7.1 looks like Figure 7.2.

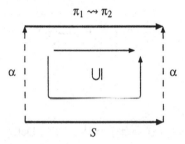

Fig. 7.2. What is the least refined S s.t. $S \subseteq_\alpha^U \pi_1 \leadsto \pi_2$?

Theorem 7.1 (U-simulation in Hoare logic)
Let $\pi_1, \pi_2 \in Pred^A$ and $\alpha \in Abs^{CA}$. The specification statement $\langle\alpha\rangle \pi_1 \leadsto [\alpha]\pi_2$ is the least refined program that U-simulates $\pi_1 \leadsto \pi_2$ w.r.t. α, i.e., for all $S \in Prog^C$

$$\{\langle\alpha\rangle \pi_1\} S \{[\alpha]\pi_2\} \quad \text{iff} \quad S \subseteq_\alpha^U \pi_1 \leadsto \pi_2 \ .$$

Proof:

$$\alpha^{-1} ; S ; \alpha \subseteq \pi_1 \leadsto \pi_2$$
$$\Leftrightarrow S ; \alpha \subseteq \alpha^{-1} \leadsto (\pi_1 \leadsto \pi_2) \qquad \text{Lemma 5.24.(i)}$$
$$\Leftrightarrow S ; \alpha \subseteq \pi_1 ; \alpha^{-1} \leadsto \pi_2 \qquad \text{Lemma 5.24.(vi)}$$
$$\Leftrightarrow S ; \alpha \subseteq \langle\alpha\rangle \pi_1 \leadsto \pi_2 \qquad \text{Lemma 5.26.(iii)}$$
$$\Leftrightarrow S \subseteq [\alpha] (\langle\alpha\rangle \pi_1 \leadsto \pi_2) \qquad \text{Lemma 5.25.(i)}$$
$$\Leftrightarrow S \subseteq \langle\alpha\rangle \pi_1 \leadsto [\alpha]\pi_2 \qquad \text{Lemma 5.25.(iv)} \qquad \square$$

7.2 L-simulation in Hoare Logic

For L-simulation Figure 7.1 looks like Figure 7.3. Recall that we already addressed this problem in Section 4.5, but on purely semantic grounds.

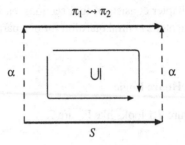

Fig. 7.3. What is the least refined S s.t. $S \subseteq^{\mathsf{L}}_{\alpha} \pi_1 \rightsquigarrow \pi_2$?

$$S \subseteq^{\mathsf{L}}_{\alpha} \pi_1 \rightsquigarrow \pi_2$$
$$\Leftrightarrow \alpha^{-1} ; S \subseteq (\pi_1 \rightsquigarrow \pi_2) ; \alpha^{-1} \qquad \text{Def. 4.1}$$
$$\Leftrightarrow S \subseteq \alpha^{-1} \rightsquigarrow ((\pi_1 \rightsquigarrow \pi_2) ; \alpha^{-1}) \qquad \text{Lemma 5.24.(i)}$$

Observe that the RHS of the last inclusion is not yet a specification statement since the arguments of the leads-to operator are not predicates. How can we express this relation by a specification statement? Expanding the meaning of this correctness formula according to the definitions given in Chapter 5 we arrive at the following semantic characterization of concrete level program S:

$$\mathcal{P}[\![S]\!]^{\mathrm{C}} \subseteq \left\{ (\sigma, \tau) \;\middle|\; \forall \zeta \left(\begin{array}{l} (\sigma, \zeta) \in \mathcal{A}[\![\alpha]\!]^{\mathrm{CA}} \\ \Rightarrow \exists \xi \left(\begin{array}{l} (\tau, \xi) \in \mathcal{A}[\![\alpha]\!]^{\mathrm{CA}} \\ \wedge (\zeta, \xi) \in \mathcal{P}[\![\pi_1 \rightsquigarrow \pi_2]\!]^{\mathrm{A}} \end{array} \right) \end{array} \right) \right\} \qquad (7.1)$$

To match the pattern of the semantics of a specification statement we have to replace the universally quantified abstract level state ζ by some new logical state δ coinciding with ζ. Therefore we introduce fresh logical variables $\vec{y}_0$ for normal variables $\vec{x}$ and fresh $\vec{b}_0$ for abstract level representation variables $\vec{a}$. Similarly we assume that $\vec{x}_0$ are the free logical variables of π_1 and π_2. Now define a concrete logical state space Γ^{C} by fixing the set of logical variables on the concrete level to the elements of $\vec{y}_0 \vec{b}_0$. The main task is to substitute all occurrences of $\vec{x}$ and $\vec{a}$ evaluated in ζ by $\vec{y}_0$ and $\vec{b}_0$ evaluated in δ.

Let $\zeta \in \Sigma^{\mathrm{A}}$ and choose $\delta \in \Gamma^{\mathrm{C}}$ such that $\zeta(\vec{x}) = \delta(\vec{y}_0)$ and $\zeta(\vec{a}) = \delta(\vec{b}_0)$, i.e., $\delta \stackrel{\mathrm{def}}{=} (\hbar : \vec{y}_0 \vec{b}_0 \mapsto \zeta(\vec{x}\vec{a}))$. This implies that $\zeta = (\hbar : \vec{x}\vec{a} \mapsto \delta(\vec{y}_0 \vec{b}_0))$, which we will exploit below in an application of Lemma 5.12. The two sides of the universally quantified implication inside the RHS of inclusion (7.1) are treated separately, starting with the LHS:

$$(\sigma,\zeta) \in \mathcal{A}[\![\alpha]\!]^{CA}$$

$$\Leftrightarrow (\sigma,\zeta) \in C[\![\alpha]\!]^{Var^C, Var^A} \wedge \sigma(\vec{x}) = \zeta(\vec{x}) \qquad \text{Cor. 5.16}$$

$$\Leftrightarrow (\delta,\sigma) \in C[\![\alpha[^{\vec{y}_0\vec{b}_0}/_{\vec{x}\vec{a}}]]\!]^C \wedge \sigma(\vec{x}) = \delta(\vec{y}_0) \qquad \text{Lemmas 5.12 and 5.13}$$

$$\Leftrightarrow (\delta,\sigma) \in C[\![\alpha[^{\vec{b}_0}/_{\vec{a}}]]\!]^C \wedge (\delta,\sigma) \in C[\![\vec{x} = \vec{y}_0]\!]^C \qquad \begin{array}{l}\vec{x} \cap fvar(\alpha) = \emptyset, \\ \text{Lemma 5.14}\end{array}$$

$$\Leftrightarrow (\delta,\sigma) \in C[\![\alpha[^{\vec{b}_0}/_{\vec{a}}] \wedge \vec{x} = \vec{y}_0]\!]^C \qquad \text{Lemma 5.14}$$

The predicate logic term in semantic brackets can be simplified further:

$$\alpha[^{\vec{b}_0}/_{\vec{a}}] \wedge \vec{x} = \vec{y}_0$$

$$\Leftrightarrow \exists\vec{a}\left(\alpha \wedge \vec{a} = \vec{b}_0\right) \wedge \vec{x} = \vec{y}_0 \qquad \text{pred. calc.}$$

$$\Leftrightarrow \exists\vec{a}\left(\alpha \wedge \vec{x}\vec{a} = \vec{y}_0\vec{b}_0\right) \qquad \vec{a} \cap fvar(\vec{x} = \vec{y}_0) = \emptyset$$

$$\Leftrightarrow \langle\alpha\rangle\,(\vec{x}\vec{a} = \vec{y}_0\vec{b}_0) \qquad \text{by (5.3)}$$

We proceed by applying Lemma 5.19 to the RHS, $(\zeta,\xi) \in \mathcal{P}[\![\pi_1 \leadsto \pi_2]\!]^A$, of the existentially quantified conjunction inside the RHS of inclusion (7.1) to obtain

$$(\delta,\xi) \in C\left[\!\left[\forall\vec{x}_0\left(\pi_1[^{\vec{y}_0\vec{b}_0}/_{\vec{x}\vec{a}}] \Rightarrow \pi_2\right)\right]\!\right]^{Lvar^C, Var^A}$$

In the last step we apply Lemma 5.17 to express the existential quantification over ξ syntactically using the diamond operator.

$$\exists\xi\left((\tau,\xi) \in \mathcal{A}[\![\alpha]\!]^{CA} \wedge (\delta,\xi) \in C\left[\!\left[\forall\vec{x}_0\left(\pi_1[^{\vec{y}_0\vec{b}_0}/_{\vec{x}\vec{a}}] \Rightarrow \pi_2\right)\right]\!\right]^{Lvar^C, Var^A}\right)$$

$$\Leftrightarrow (\delta,\tau) \in C\left[\!\left[\langle\alpha\rangle\forall\vec{x}_0\left(\pi_1[^{\vec{y}_0\vec{b}_0}/_{\vec{x}\vec{a}}] \Rightarrow \pi_2\right)\right]\!\right]^C$$

The following theorem summarizes the lengthy calculation above.

Theorem 7.2 (L-simulation in Hoare logic)
Let $\vec{x}$ denote the list of normal variables at abstraction level A, $\vec{a}$ the list of representation variables at that level, $\vec{x}_0$ the list of free logical variables of assertions π_1 and π_2 at that level, $\vec{y}_0$ a list of fresh logical variables of the same length as $\vec{x}$, $\vec{b}_0$ a list of fresh logical variables of the same length as $\vec{a}$, and α an abstraction relation from level C to level A. Then $\langle\alpha\rangle\,(\vec{x}\vec{a} = \vec{y}_0\vec{b}_0) \leadsto$ $\langle\alpha\rangle\,\forall\vec{x}_0\left(\pi_1[^{\vec{y}_0\vec{b}_0}/_{\vec{x}\vec{a}}] \Rightarrow \pi_2\right)$ specifies the least refined program that L-simulates

$\pi_1 \leadsto \pi_2$ w.r.t. α, i.e., for all $S \in Prog^C$:

$$\left\{ \langle\alpha\rangle\, (\vec{x}\vec{a} = \vec{y}_0\vec{b}_0) \right\} S \left\{ \langle\alpha\rangle\, \forall \vec{x}_0 \left(\pi_1[^{\vec{y}_0\vec{b}_0}/_{\vec{x}\vec{a}}] \Rightarrow \pi_2 \right) \right\} \quad \text{iff} \quad S \subseteq_\alpha^L \pi_1 \leadsto \pi_2 \ .$$

♠

Example 7.3 (cf. Example 2.5) Recall the bag example from Chapter 2, in which we represent a bag b of reals by two variables: the real-valued *sum* storing the sum of elements of b and the integer-valued *num* keeping track of the number of elements in b. Formally, the abstraction relation is given by the predicate $\Sigma_b b = sum \wedge \#b = num$. (For the sake of brevity we disregard the normal variable av for the moment.)

The operation $b := b \oplus x$ adding a real value stored in normal variable x to the bag is implemented by adding x to *sum* and incrementing *num* by 1. The abstract operation is specified exactly by $(b, x = b_0, x_0) \leadsto (b \oplus x_0, x = b_0, x_0)$. According to Theorem 7.2 the following Hoare triple has to be valid to ensure the correctness of the suggested implementation:

$$\{ \langle \Sigma_b b = sum \wedge \#b = num \rangle\, (x, b = y_0, c_0) \}$$
$$sum, num := sum + x, num + 1$$
$$\left\{ \langle \Sigma_b b = sum \wedge \#b = num \rangle\, \forall x_0, b_0 \left(\begin{array}{c} (x, b = x_0, b_0)[^{y_0,c_0}/_{x,b}] \\ \Rightarrow x, b = x_0, b_0 \oplus x_0 \end{array} \right) \right\}$$

This is certainly too complex, considering how simple the two assignments under consideration are. It will be improved upon in Example 7.8.   ♡

Next we investigate under which conditions the rather complicated solution suggested by Theorem 7.2 can be simplified. By Theorems 4.5 and 4.7 all four notions of simulation coincide if α is total and functional. The next corollary combines this fact with Lemma 3.14 and Theorem 7.1.

Corollary 7.4 If α is total and functional then $\langle\alpha\rangle\pi_1 \leadsto \langle\alpha\rangle\pi_2$ specifies the least refined program that L-simulates $\pi_1 \leadsto \pi_2$ w.r.t. α, i.e., for all $S \in Prog^C$

$$\{ \langle\alpha\rangle\pi_1 \} S \{ \langle\alpha\rangle\pi_2 \} \quad \text{iff} \quad S \subseteq_\alpha^L \pi_1 \leadsto \pi_2 \ .$$

Here, any $\langle\alpha\rangle$ may be replaced by $[\alpha]$ and any of our four notions of simulation can be substituted for L-simulation.   [PVS]

This corollary does not help in the bag example since there the abstraction relation is neither functional nor total. The next example shows why totality of the abstraction relation is in general indispensable in Cor. 7.4; the need for functionality is illustrated by Example 7.6.

Example 7.5 Suppose the operation "the value of the variable x storing natural numbers is incremented by 1 if it is even" specified as $x = 2 * x_0 \rightsquigarrow x = 2 * x_0 + 1$ is to be implemented by an operation on an integer variable y. The abstraction relation α is $x = y$. Hence (the relational semantics $\mathcal{A}[\![\alpha]\!]^{CA}$ of) α is functional but not total; only non-negative values of y are related to a value of x. Formally, we consider the following state spaces.

$$\Sigma^A = [\{x\} \longrightarrow \mathbb{N}]$$
$$\Gamma = [\{x_0\} \longrightarrow \mathbb{N}]$$
$$\Sigma^C = [\{y\} \longrightarrow \mathbb{Z}]$$

First, we calculate the abstract level semantics of the specification statement. (We use the shorthand 2N for the even natural numbers.)

$$\mathcal{P}[\![(x = 2 * x_0) \rightsquigarrow (x = 2 * x_0 + 1)]\!]^A$$

$$= \bigcap_{\gamma \in \Gamma} \left\{ (\zeta, \xi) \in (\Sigma^A)^2 \; \middle| \; \begin{array}{l} (\gamma, \zeta) \in C[\![x = 2 * x_0]\!]^A \\ \Rightarrow (\gamma, \xi) \in C[\![x = 2 * x_0 + 1]\!]^A \end{array} \right\}$$

$$= \bigcap_{n \in \mathbb{N}} \left\{ (\zeta, \xi) \in (\Sigma^A)^2 \mid \zeta(x) = 2 * n \Rightarrow \xi(x) = 2 * n + 1 \right\}$$

$$= \bigcap_{n \in 2\mathbb{N}} \left\{ (\zeta, \xi) \in (\Sigma^A)^2 \mid \zeta(x) = n \Rightarrow \xi(x) = n + 1 \right\}$$

$$= \left\{ (\zeta, \xi) \in (\Sigma^A)^2 \mid \zeta(x) \in 2\mathbb{N} \Rightarrow \xi(x) = \zeta(x) + 1 \right\}$$

Next, we compute the relation suggested by the simple solution.

$$S_{simple} \stackrel{\text{def}}{=} \mathcal{P}[\![\langle \alpha \rangle (x = 2 * x_0) \rightsquigarrow \langle \alpha \rangle (x = 2 * x_0 + 1)]\!]^C$$

Let $\sigma, \tau \in \Sigma^C$.

$(\sigma, \tau) \in S_{simple}$

$\Leftrightarrow \forall \gamma \in \Gamma \left(\begin{array}{l} (\gamma, \sigma) \in C[\![\langle \alpha \rangle (x = 2 * x_0)]\!]^C \\ \Rightarrow (\gamma, \tau) \in C[\![\langle \alpha \rangle (x = 2 * x_0 + 1)]\!]^C \end{array} \right)$

$\Leftrightarrow \forall \gamma \in \Gamma \left(\begin{array}{l} \exists \zeta \left((\sigma, \zeta) \in \mathcal{A}[\![\alpha]\!]^{CA} \wedge (\gamma, \zeta) \in C[\![x = 2 * x_0]\!]^A \right) \\ \Rightarrow \exists \xi \left((\tau, \xi) \in \mathcal{A}[\![\alpha]\!]^{CA} \wedge (\gamma, \xi) \in C[\![x = 2 * x_0 + 1]\!]^A \right) \end{array} \right)$

$\Leftrightarrow \forall \gamma \in \Gamma \left(\begin{array}{l} \exists \zeta (\sigma(y) = \zeta(x) \wedge \zeta(x) = 2 * \gamma(x_0)) \\ \Rightarrow \exists \xi (\tau(y) = \xi(x) \wedge \xi(x) = 2 * \gamma(x_0) + 1) \end{array} \right)$

$\Leftrightarrow \forall \gamma \in \Gamma (\sigma(y) = 2 * \gamma(x_0) \Rightarrow \tau(y) = 2 * \gamma(x_0) + 1)$

$\Leftrightarrow \forall n \in 2\mathbb{N} (\sigma(y) = n \Rightarrow \tau(y) = n + 1)$

$\Leftrightarrow (\sigma(y) \in 2\mathbb{N} \Rightarrow \tau(y) = \sigma(y) + 1)$

Thus, state pair $(\{y \mapsto 3\}, \{y \mapsto -4\})$ is an element of S_{simple} and $(\{y \mapsto 3\}, \{x \mapsto 3\}) \in \mathcal{A}[\![\alpha]\!]^{CA}$, but $\{y \mapsto -4\}$ is not in the domain of $\mathcal{A}[\![\alpha]\!]^{CA}$. Hence, S_{simple} does not L-simulate $x = 2 * x_0 \leadsto x = 2 * x_0 + 1$ w.r.t. α (see Figure 7.4).

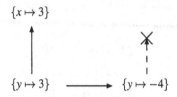

Fig. 7.4. Why S_{simple} is not a solution.

Note the subtle difference between S_{simple} and the proper solution according to Theorem 7.2.

$$\langle \alpha \rangle \, (x = x_0) \leadsto \langle \alpha \rangle \, (\forall y_0 \, ((even(x) \wedge x = y_0)[{}^{x_0}\!/_x] \Rightarrow x = y_0 + 1))$$

Its semantics is given by the following relation.

$$\{ \, ((\{y \mapsto 2n\}, \{y \mapsto 2n + 1\}) \mid n \in \mathbb{N} \, \}$$
$$\cup \{ \, ((\{y \mapsto n\}, \{y \mapsto m\}) \mid n \in \mathbb{N} \setminus \{ \, 2n \mid n \in \mathbb{N} \, \} \wedge m \in \mathbb{N} \, \}$$
$$\cup \{ \, ((\{y \mapsto n\}, \{y \mapsto m\}) \mid n \in \mathbb{Z} \setminus \mathbb{N} \wedge m \in \mathbb{Z} \, \}$$

Speaking in terms of values of y, this solution relates odd natural numbers only to all natural numbers while the simple solution relates them to all integers.

$\heartsuit$

Example 7.6 (cf. specification (5.8) on p. 118) Reconsider specification

$$\text{true} \leadsto x = x_0$$

in a particular semantic context where the domain of the values of both the only abstract program variable x and the only logical variable x_0 is given as $\mathbb{V}^A = \{1, 2\}$. This choice implies that there exist exactly two distinct abstract states $\{\sigma_1, \sigma_2\} = \Sigma^A$ and two distinct logical states $\{\gamma_1, \gamma_2\} = \Gamma^A$, giving values only to, respectively, x and x_0, say, $\sigma_i(x) = \gamma_i(x_0) = i$, for $i \in \{1, 2\}$. At the end of Section 5.5 (p. 119) we calculated $\mathcal{P}[\![\text{true} \leadsto x = x_0]\!] = \emptyset$.

We represent the abstract variable x by z on the concrete level. The domain of z is only the singleton set $\mathbb{V}^C = \{1\}$, so there exists only a single concrete state ρ. The abstraction relation α is maximal, i.e., $\mathcal{A}[\![\alpha]\!]^{CA} = \{(\rho, \sigma_1), (\rho, \sigma_2)\}$ (see Figure 7.5).

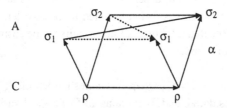

Fig. 7.5. Example 7.6: On the abstract level, dotted lines represent the γ_1 part of the intersection while plain lines stand for the γ_2 part. Clearly, their intersection is empty.

Next we calculate the semantics of the simple concrete level specification statement suggested by Cor. 7.4. The only pair of concrete states is (ρ, ρ).

$$(\rho, \rho) \in \mathcal{P}[\![\langle \alpha \rangle \, \text{true} \rightsquigarrow \langle \alpha \rangle \, (x = x_0)]\!]^C$$

$$\Leftrightarrow \forall \gamma \Big((\gamma, \rho) \in \mathcal{P}[\![\langle \alpha \rangle \, \text{true}]\!]^C \Rightarrow (\gamma, \rho) \in \mathcal{P}[\![\langle \alpha \rangle \, (x = x_0)]\!]^C \Big)$$

$$\Leftrightarrow \forall \gamma \left(\begin{array}{l} \exists \zeta \Big((\rho, \zeta) \in \mathcal{A}[\![\alpha]\!]^{CA} \wedge (\gamma, \zeta) \in \mathcal{P}[\![\text{true}]\!]^A \Big) \\ \Rightarrow \exists \xi \Big((\rho, \xi) \in \mathcal{A}[\![\alpha]\!]^{CA} \wedge (\gamma, \xi) \in C[\![x = x_0]\!]^A \Big) \end{array} \right)$$

$$\Leftrightarrow \forall \gamma (\exists \zeta \, (tt \wedge tt) \Rightarrow \exists \xi \, (tt \wedge \xi(x) = \gamma(x_0)))$$

$$\Leftrightarrow \forall \gamma (tt)$$

$$\Leftrightarrow tt$$

Relation $\{(\rho, \rho)\}$ violates the L-simulation condition for the given α and abstract operation. The proper solution is the empty relation.   ♡

The difference between the simple solution

$$\langle \alpha \rangle \, \pi_1 \rightsquigarrow \langle \alpha \rangle \, \pi_2$$

and the proper solution

$$\langle \alpha \rangle \, (\vec{x}\vec{a} = \vec{y_0}\vec{b_0}) \rightsquigarrow \langle \alpha \rangle \, \forall \vec{x_0} \left(\pi_1 [\vec{y_0}\vec{b_0} / \vec{x}\vec{a}] \Rightarrow \pi_2 \right)$$

shows up when one can encode either of the situations described in Examples 7.5 or 7.6 inside one's specification. However, when this is impossible, one can resort to the simpler solution $\langle \alpha \rangle \, \pi_1 \rightsquigarrow \langle \alpha \rangle \, \pi_2$, in order to specify the maximal concrete level program L-simulating the abstract specification $\pi_1 \rightsquigarrow \pi_2$.

This is the case, for instance, when one has freeze predicate $\vec{x} = \vec{x_0}$ as precondition, where $\vec{x}$ denotes the list of program variables, and $\vec{x_0}$ a corresponding list of logical variables. For then, given an initial value of $\vec{x}$, frozen in $\vec{x_0}$, the final values, if any, are described in terms of that one frozen value (and not more than one). This is formally stated in the next lemma and applied in Example 7.8. Note that totality and functionality of the abstraction relation are not required in this case.

Lemma 7.7 If π_1 is $\vec{x} = \vec{x}_0$, where $\vec{x}$ denotes the list of all program variables on the level considered, and $\vec{x}_0$ contains all free logical variables occurring in π_1 and π_2, then the maximal solution for S satisfying $S \subseteq_\alpha^L \pi_1 \rightsquigarrow \pi_2$ is $\langle \alpha \rangle \pi_1 \rightsquigarrow \langle \alpha \rangle \pi_2$.

Proof: We massage the postcondition of the general solution from Theorem 7.2 into the simple form. Let $\vec{y}_0$ be a list of fresh logical variables that has the same length as $\vec{x}$.

$$\langle \alpha \rangle \left(\forall \vec{x}_0 \left((\vec{x} = \vec{x}_0)[^{\vec{y}_0}/_{\vec{x}}] \Rightarrow \pi_2 \right) \right)$$

$$= \langle \alpha \rangle \left(\forall \vec{x}_0 \left((\vec{y}_0 = \vec{x}_0) \Rightarrow \pi_2 \right) \right) \qquad \text{Def. 5.7}$$

$$= \langle \alpha \rangle \left(\pi_2[^{\vec{y}_0}/_{\vec{x}_0}] \right) \qquad \text{pred. calc.}$$

$$= \left(\langle \alpha \rangle \pi_2 \right) [^{\vec{y}_0}/_{\vec{x}_0}] \qquad \text{Def. 5.7}$$

The last step is justified because logical variables do not occur freely in abstraction relations. Renaming the logical variables completes the proof. $\boxed{\text{PVS}}$

Example 7.8 (cf. Example 7.3) The task of checking whether the concrete level operation $sum, num := sum + x, num + 1$ correctly implements the abstract level operation $b := b \oplus x$ w.r.t. abstraction relation $\Sigma_b b = sum \wedge \#b = num$ can now be reduced to proving validity of a simpler Hoare triple.

$$\{ \langle \Sigma_b b = sum \wedge \#b = num \rangle \, (x, b = x_0, b_0) \}$$
$$sum, num := sum + x, num + 1$$
$$\{ \langle \Sigma_b b = sum \wedge \#b = num \rangle \, (x, b = x_0, b_0 \oplus x_0) \}$$

This condition is still not as simple as it could be, but is a step in the right direction when compared to what we achieved in Example 7.3. Next, we may either prove this directly, or try to massage both pre- and postcondition to simpler versions referring to logical variables that freeze initial values of concrete level program variables instead of abstract level ones. Let us try the first alternative.

By the assignment axiom and the consequence rule of Section 6.1, validity of this Hoare triple follows from validity of the implication

$$\langle \Sigma_b b = sum \wedge \#b = num \rangle \, (x, b = x_0, b_0)$$

$$\Rightarrow (\langle \Sigma_b b = sum \wedge \#b = num \rangle \, (x, b = x_0, b_0 \oplus x_0)) [^{sum+x, num+1}/_{sum, num}] \ .$$

By Def. 5.7 and (5.3) this amounts to proving

$$\exists b \, (\Sigma_b b = sum \wedge \#b = num \wedge x, b = x_0, b_0)$$
$$\Rightarrow \exists b \, (\Sigma_b b = sum + x \wedge \#b = num + 1 \wedge x, b = x_0, b_0 \oplus x_0) \ ,$$

which is equivalent to

$$\Sigma_b b_0 = sum \wedge \#b_0 = num \Rightarrow \Sigma_b (b_0 \oplus x_0) = sum + x_0 \wedge \#(b_0 \oplus x_0) = num + 1$$

This follows from the definitions of Σ_b and $\#$.

For the second alternative one could have guessed a specification of the concrete level operation, for instance:

$$x, sum, num = y_0, s_0, n_0 \rightsquigarrow x, sum, num = y_0, s_0 + x, n_0 + 1 \qquad (7.2)$$

If (7.2) refines the specification suggested by Lemma 7.7, that is,

$$\left(\begin{array}{c} \langle \Sigma_b b = sum \wedge \#b = num \rangle \, (x, b = x_0, b_0) \\ \rightsquigarrow \ \langle \Sigma_b b = sum \wedge \#b = num \rangle \, (x, b = x_0, b_0 \oplus x_0) \end{array} \right) , \qquad (7.3)$$

then our task is reduced to proving

$$\{x, sum, num = x_0, s_0, n_0\}$$
$$sum, num := sum + x, num + 1$$
$$\{x, sum, num = x_0, s_0 + x_0, n_0 + 1\}$$

which consists, like the derivation above, of an application of the consequence rule to an instance of the assignment axiom

$$\{x, sum + x, num + 1 = x_0, s_0 + x_0, n_0 + 1\}$$
$$sum, num := sum + x, num + 1$$
$$\{x, sum, num = x_0, s_0 + x_0, n_0 + 1\}$$

and the valid implication

$$x, sum, num = x_0, s_0, n_0 \Rightarrow x, sum + x, num + 1 = x_0, s_0 + x_0, n_0 + 1 \ .$$

Consequently it remains to prove that (7.2) indeed refines (7.3).

By the definitions of $\langle . \rangle$, Σ_b, and $\#$ the latter can be simplified:

$$x, sum, num = x_0, \Sigma_b b_0, \#b_0 \rightsquigarrow x, sum, num = x_0, \Sigma_b b_0 + x, \#b_0 + 1$$

By the adaptation axiom and the consequence rule one has to prove

$$\exists x', s', n' \left(\begin{array}{c} x', s', n' = x_0, \Sigma_b b_0, \#b_0 \\ \wedge \forall y_0, s_0, n_0 \left(\begin{array}{c} x', s', n' = y_0, s_0, n_0 \\ \Rightarrow x, sum, num = y_0, s_0 + x, n_0 + 1 \end{array} \right) \end{array} \right)$$

$$\Rightarrow x, sum, num = x_0, \Sigma_b b_0 + x, \#b_0 + 1$$

which is easy; the RHS is even equivalent to the LHS:

$$\exists x', s', n' \left(\begin{array}{l} x', s', n' = x_0, \Sigma_b b_0, \#b_0 \\ \wedge \forall y_0, s_0, n_0 \left(\begin{array}{l} x', s', n' = y_0, s_0, n_0 \\ \Rightarrow x, sum, num = y_0, s_0 + x, n_0 + 1 \end{array} \right) \end{array} \right)$$

$$\Leftrightarrow \forall y_0, s_0, n_0 \left(\begin{array}{l} x_0, \Sigma_b b_0, \#b_0 = y_0, s_0, n_0 \\ \Rightarrow x, sum, num = y_0, s_0 + x, n_0 + 1 \end{array} \right) \qquad \text{one-point rule}$$

$$\Leftrightarrow x, sum, num = x_0, \Sigma_b b_0 + x, \#b_0 + 1 \qquad \text{one-point rule}$$

$$\heartsuit$$

Conclusion of Examples 7.3 and 7.8 Applying the L-simulation theorem may result in inconveniently complicated specification statements because concrete level program variables are related to abstract level logical variables. This also holds to a slightly lesser extent for the solution suggested by Cor. 7.4 and Lemma 7.7. The clue to drastic simplification is to massage both pre- and postcondition to simpler versions referring to logical variables that freeze initial values of concrete level program variables instead of abstract level ones. By Lemma 5.30 and the expression of the strongest postcondition of a specification w.r.t. a precondition provided by the adaptation axiom, it is even possible to express the specification referring to abstract level logical variables exactly, but using the above-mentioned logical variables that freeze initial values of concrete level program variables only.

7.2.1 A Normal Form Theorem for Specifications

By considering the identity relation as abstraction relation, the L-simulation theorem suggests a normal form for specification statements.

Theorem 7.9 (Normal form)
Let $\vec{x}$ denote the list of program variables at the level under consideration, let $\vec{x}_0$ be the list of logical variables occurring freely in assertions π_1 and π_2 on that level, and let $\vec{y}_0$ be a list of fresh logical variables of the same length as $\vec{x}$. Then

$$\pi_1 \rightsquigarrow \pi_2 \quad = \quad (\vec{x} = \vec{y}_0) \rightsquigarrow \forall \vec{x}_0 \left(\pi_1 [\vec{y}_0/\vec{x}] \Rightarrow \pi_2 \right)$$

Proof: Regard all program variables as normal and take abstraction relation true $\in Pred^{0,0}$. The claim follows by Theorem 7.2 and Lemma 3.11.(iv). $\square$

7.3 L⁻¹-simulation in Hoare Logic

For L^{-1}-simulation Figure 7.1 looks like Figure 7.6.

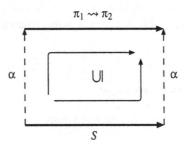

Fig. 7.6. What is the least refined S s.t. $S \subseteq_\alpha^{L^{-1}} \pi_1 \rightsquigarrow \pi_2$?

Now we have to solve

$$\{\rho_1\} S \{\rho_2\} \quad \text{iff} \quad S \subseteq_\alpha^{L^{-1}} \pi_1 \rightsquigarrow \pi_2$$

for ρ_1 and ρ_2. By reading Figure 7.6 from right to left we discover an instance of the L-simulation problem.

$$S \subseteq_\alpha^{L^{-1}} \pi_1 \rightsquigarrow \pi_2$$

$\Leftrightarrow$ (Def. 4.1)

$$S; \alpha \subseteq \alpha; \pi_1 \rightsquigarrow \pi_2$$

$\Leftrightarrow$ $((.)^{-1}$ is monotone and its own inverse)

$$(S; \alpha)^{-1} \subseteq (\alpha; \pi_1 \rightsquigarrow \pi_2)^{-1}$$

$\Leftrightarrow$ (Lemma 5.23)

$$\alpha^{-1}; S^{-1} \subseteq (\pi_1 \rightsquigarrow \pi_2)^{-1}; \alpha^{-1}$$

$\Leftrightarrow$ (Lemma 5.24)

$$\alpha^{-1}; S^{-1} \subseteq \neg\pi_2 \rightsquigarrow \neg\pi_1; \alpha^{-1}$$

$\Leftrightarrow$ (Theorem 7.2)

$$S^{-1} \subseteq \langle\alpha\rangle (\vec{x}\vec{a} = \vec{y}_0\vec{b}_0) \rightsquigarrow \langle\alpha\rangle \forall \vec{x}_0 \left(\neg\pi_2[\vec{y}_0\vec{b}_0/\vec{x}\vec{a}] \Rightarrow \neg\pi_1\right)$$

$\Leftrightarrow$ (Lemma 5.24)

$$S \subseteq \neg\langle\alpha\rangle \forall \vec{x}_0 \left(\neg\pi_2[\vec{y}_0\vec{b}_0/\vec{x}\vec{a}] \Rightarrow \neg\pi_1\right) \rightsquigarrow \neg\langle\alpha\rangle (\vec{x}\vec{a} = \vec{y}_0\vec{b}_0)$$

$\Leftrightarrow$ (Lemma 5.26)

$$S \subseteq [\alpha] \neg\forall \vec{x}_0 \left(\neg\pi_2[\vec{y}_0\vec{b}_0/\vec{x}\vec{a}] \Rightarrow \neg\pi_1\right) \rightsquigarrow [\alpha] (\vec{x}\vec{a} \neq \vec{y}_0\vec{b}_0)$$

$\Leftrightarrow$ (pred. calc.)

$$S \subseteq [\alpha]\, \exists \vec{x_0}\, \left(\neg \pi_2 [\vec{y_0}\vec{b_0}/\vec{x\vec{a}}] \wedge \pi_1\right) \rightsquigarrow [\alpha]\, (\vec{x\vec{a}} \neq \vec{y_0}\vec{b_0})$$

The complexity of the specification statement, especially the use of negations, strains one's capabilities of making up an intuition about the meaning of this solution.

7.4 U^{-1}-simulation in Hoare Logic

For U^{-1}-simulation Figure 7.1 looks like Figure 7.7.

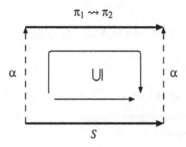

Fig. 7.7. What is the least refined S s.t. $S \subseteq_\alpha^{U^{-1}} \pi_1 \rightsquigarrow \pi_2$?

Now we have to find assertions ρ_1 and ρ_2 on the concrete level such that for all programs $S \in Prog^C$

$$\{\rho_1\}\, S\, \{\rho_2\} \quad \text{iff} \quad S \subseteq_\alpha^{U^{-1}} \pi_1 \rightsquigarrow \pi_2$$

holds. By Def. 4.1, $S \subseteq_\alpha^{U^{-1}} \pi_1 \rightsquigarrow \pi_2$ is equivalent to $S \subseteq \alpha ; \pi_1 \rightsquigarrow \pi_2 ; \alpha^{-1}$. Transforming the RHS relational term into a specification statement is straightforward, yet cumbersome. We leave this as an exercise to the conscientious readers. As we know from Theorems 4.10 and 4.5, whenever U^{-1}-simulation seems to be appropriate, L-simulation is even more appropriate.

7.5 Historical Background

A first version of our Theorem 7.1 appears in an unpublished memo of Zwiers [Z87]. The remaining results contained in this chapter are original, although we received advice from Ralph Back while working on a preliminary version of the proof of Theorem 7.2.

Exercises

7.1   (cf. Example 7.5) Construct a minimal (in the number of states/values) example showing that abstraction relation α has in general to be total for Cor. 7.4 to be applicable, i.e., for ensuring that $\langle\alpha\rangle\,\pi_1 \rightsquigarrow \langle\alpha\rangle\,\pi_2$ specifies the least refined program that L-simulates $\pi_1 \rightsquigarrow \pi_2$ w.r.t. α.

7.2   (U^{-1}-simulation theorem) Express $\alpha\,;\pi_1 \rightsquigarrow \pi_2\,;\alpha^{-1}$ as a specification statement.

8

An Extension to Total Correctness

In the state-based set-up, states are used to describe the initial/final state behavior of programs. In the partial correctness interpretation of this set-up, $(\sigma, \tau) \in \mathcal{P}[\![S]\!]$ means that there is a computation of program S starting in initial state σ and terminating in final state τ. Exactly the properly terminating computations of S are reflected by means of state pairs in $\mathcal{P}[\![S]\!]$ whereas blocking, diverging, and abnormally terminating (or aborting) computations are identified in that they are entirely ignored. For instance, the following programs all have the same partial correctness semantics, namely, the empty relation: the guard false $\rightarrow$, the loop **while** true **do skip od**, and the aborting program **abort**.

In the sequel the term *nontermination* stands for both divergent and abnormally terminating (or aborting) computations, that is, we continue to abstract from the difference between infinite loops and, for instance, division by zero.

The semantics employed in previous chapters is not capable of expressing termination of programs, for how would one express in the partial correctness interpretation that there is both a terminating computation for initial state σ and a nonterminating one? As a consequence every nonterminating program, denoted by the empty relation, is considered a correct implementation of every other program or specification; in other words, we have been concerned with development steps preserving partial correctness only. Clearly, this is an undesirable property of the theory developed so far in this monograph.

From the viewpoint of total correctness the nondeterministic possibility of nontermination is just as bad as guaranteed nontermination. This implies that these two cases should be identified in our model for total correctness, i.e., we need demonic nondeterminism (compare the discussion in Section 3.5.3). Moreover, from the total correctness point of view a terminating computation is considered better than a nonterminating one. Hence our new model should be such that a program guaranteed to terminate for initial state σ should satisfy more specifications than an otherwise equal program that may not terminate starting from σ.

In this chapter we improve upon the above-mentioned deficiency of the partial correctness model by adopting a different model of relations in which one can additionally express the nondeterministic possibility of nontermination (in the above sense). This possibility is characterized within our total correctness model in the same way as guaranteed nontermination. Consequently it forms an appropriate basis for reasoning about total correctness, since total correctness amounts to both partial correctness and guaranteed termination.

We shall redefine parts of our theory such that nontermination no longer refines termination but rather termination refines nontermination. This implies in the setting of total correctness refinement that every terminating program refines **abort**.

We introduce a special state $\bot$ called *bottom*, which is added as a new element to Σ to express nontermination on the semantic level. That termination indeed refines nontermination while keeping $\subseteq$ as refinement relation is ensured by adding all pairs (σ, τ) to a relation r once $(\sigma, \bot) \in r$. This corresponds to a pessimistic viewpoint in that there is no restriction whatever on the final state of a nonterminating computation; it may be any state at all (including bottom).

Although one can express nontermination by $\bot$ and therefore also the nondeterministic possibility of nontermination, this is not the case for deadlock (or blocking). Since deadlocking computations are not represented by state pairs within our model, we cannot express the nondeterministic possibility of deadlock in the presence of a terminating or nonterminating computation that starts in the same initial state. That a program is guaranteed to deadlock when started in initial state σ, however, is expressed in our model, namely by the absence of any state pair (σ, τ) in the semantics of that program. Therefore such programs, for instance guards, denote partial relations in our model.

Consequently the resulting model models termination in the usual operational sense only in case blocking situations are prevented from occurring. One way to achieve this is by imposing suitable syntactic restrictions. One version of these is discussed in Cor. 8.35.

As we shall explain in the rest of this chapter, certain technical difficulties arise from the complexity added to the semantic model when nontermination is incorporated:

- The semantic domain for relations is no longer closed under relational inversion.
- Intersection instead of union models recursion, with the added complexity that intersection does not distribute over sequential composition in general.

In Section 8.1 we present our semantic model for total correctness and a minimal amount of fixed point theory needed in later sections. In Section 8.2 we define the total correctness semantics of predicates, introducing a three-valued logic which we need later in Chapter 12 on VDM, define the semantics of abstraction relations, programs, relational terms, and correctness formulae in our total correctness set-up, and discuss the relationship between partial and total correctness.

8.1 Semantic Model and Basic Fixed Point Theory

The total correctness semantics $\mathcal{P}[\![S]\!]_\perp$ of program S will be defined such that $(\sigma, \perp) \notin \mathcal{P}[\![S]\!]_\perp$ means informally: S terminates when started in initial state σ, provided S does not deadlock.

For any set (or domain) of semantic objects O we let $O_\perp$ refer to the disjoint union of O with the singleton set $\{\perp_O\}$ and call the elements of O *proper* elements. This extra element is called *bottom* and is introduced in order to express and handle nontermination semantically. For instance, $\perp_\mathbb{V}$ denotes the meaning of division by zero, $\perp_\mathbb{B}$ denotes the result of comparing $\perp_\mathbb{V}$ with an element of $\mathbb{V}_\perp$ as in predicate $y \div (x - x) > z$, and $\perp_\Sigma$ is a final state of the semantics of both the infinite loop **while** true **do skip od** and the assignment $x := x \div 0$. Later on we shall abstract from the differences between these bottom elements $\perp_\mathbb{V}$, $\perp_\mathbb{B}$, $\perp_\Sigma$, etc. and use just $\perp$, whenever this causes no confusion.

Many of the functions involved in our semantic definitions for total correctness are *strict*, which means that they return bottom whenever an argument is bottom.

The total correctness versions of functions already introduced for partial correctness are syntactically distinguished from their partial correctness versions by appending subscript $\perp$. The partial and total correctness versions of a function usually agree on non-bottom arguments unless stated otherwise.

Binary relations on states that represent the meaning of abstraction relations or some piece of program text share a property described in the introduction to this chapter: the final state of a possibly nonterminating computation is completely undetermined. Technically the characterization of such relations is simplified by introducing the smallest such relation K first. For sets of variables V and W we define

$$K^{V,W} \overset{\text{def}}{=} \{\perp_{\Sigma^V}\} \times \Sigma_\perp^W \qquad\qquad K^V \overset{\text{def}}{=} K^{V,V} \qquad (8.1)$$

$$R_\perp^{V,W} \overset{\text{def}}{=} \{\, r \subseteq \Sigma_\perp^V \times \Sigma_\perp^W \mid K^{V,W} \subseteq r \supseteq r\,;K^{W,W} \,\} \qquad R_\perp^V \overset{\text{def}}{=} R_\perp^{V,V} \qquad (8.2)$$

For two abstraction levels C and A we define the following abbreviations:

$$K^{CA} \stackrel{\text{def}}{=} K^{Var^C, Var^A} \qquad\qquad R_\perp^{CA} \stackrel{\text{def}}{=} R_\perp^{Var^C, Var^A} \qquad (8.3)$$

$$K^C \stackrel{\text{def}}{=} K^{CC} \qquad\qquad R_\perp^C \stackrel{\text{def}}{=} R_\perp^{CC} \qquad (8.4)$$

We stipulate that — unless stated otherwise — in this chapter we only consider relations that are elements of a set $R_\perp^{V,W}$ for two finite variable sets V and W.

Definition 8.1 (Chains and cpo's) Let $(S, \sqsubseteq)$ be a poset (i.e., $\sqsubseteq$ is a reflexive, transitive, and antisymmetric binary relation on the set S) and let k be an I-indexed family of S-elements ($k \in S^I$) for a nonvoid index set I. We call k a *chain* if any two elements of k are comparable, that is,

$$\forall i, j \in I\, (k(i) \sqsubseteq k(j) \vee k(j) \sqsubseteq k(i)) \ .$$

By $Ch_I^\sqsubseteq(S)$ we refer to the set of such chains. Elements of $Ch_I^\sqsubseteq(S)$ are ordered by the pointwise extension of $\sqsubseteq$.

Usually we are interested in chains over arbitrary infinite index sets; these are collected in $Ch^\sqsubseteq(S)$.

We often use I as a dummy for the index set of a chain. That is, instead of verbosely stating "let I be a nonvoid index set and let $k \in Ch_I^\sqsubseteq(S)$", we just say "let $k \in Ch^\sqsubseteq(S)$".

$(S, \sqsubseteq)$ is a *complete partial order* (or *cpo*) if there exists a least element in S and all chains in $Ch^\sqsubseteq(S)$ possess a least upper bound (also called lub) in S. ♣

Observe that in the above definition we have not restricted the index set I, apart from being nonvoid. In practice, one often uses $\mathbb{N}$ as index set in the case of ω-chains (see Def. 3.19), and an ordinal in the case of transfinite chains (e.g. in Theorem 8.10). Since an ordinal α is identified with the chain of ordinals smaller than α, this does not lead to inconsistency (see Appendix B). Consequently one writes $(k(i))_{i<\alpha}$ instead of $(k(i))_{i\in\alpha}$.

Lemma 8.2 (Cpo of chains) Let $(A, \sqsubseteq)$ be a cpo; then $(Ch_I^\sqsubseteq(A), \sqsubseteq)$ is a cpo, too. The lub of $k \in Ch_I^\sqsubseteq(Ch_I^\sqsubseteq(A))$ is $\bigsqcup k \stackrel{\text{def}}{=} (\bigsqcup(k(i)(j))_{j\in J})_{i\in I}$. ♠

Notice that $(O_\perp, (\{\perp_O\} \times O_\perp) \cup id_O)$ is a — so-called *flat* — cpo. Flat cpo's have the property that each of their chains is made up at most two different elements. Either such a chain is constant $\langle o, o, \dots \rangle$ for some $o \in O_\perp$ or it can be split up into a constant prefix $\langle \perp_O, \perp_O, \dots \rangle$ followed by the constant sequence $\langle o, o, \dots \rangle$ for some $o \in O$.

We generalize the definition of ω-continuity (Def. 3.19) to functions between cpo's and to chains of arbitrary length. Recall from Def. 3.5 that a function between two partially ordered sets is monotone iff it is order-preserving, i.e., if two arguments are ordered in the domain of the function then the two results are ordered correspondingly in the range.

Definition 8.3 (Continuity) Let $(A, \leq)$ and $(B, \sqsubseteq)$ be two cpo's with lub functions $\bigvee$ and $\bigsqcup$, respectively. A monotone function $f : A \longrightarrow B$ is $\leq$-*continuous* (or just *continuous* in case the partial order $\leq$ is understood) iff it preserves lub's of $\leq$-chains, i.e., for all $k \in Ch_I^{\leq}(A)$, $f(\bigvee k) = \bigsqcup (f(k(i)))_{i \in I}$ holds. In case f only preserves lub's of ω-chains, f is called ω-*continuous*.   ♣

Observe that a continuous function is also ω-continuous, because $Ch_{\mathbb{N}}^{\sqsubseteq}(S)$ is contained in $Ch^{\sqsubseteq}(S)$; however, the converse is in general not true, as we show in the following example.

Example 8.4 Consider the set O consisting of all countable ordinals plus their union, i.e., the first uncountable ordinal $\aleph_1$. (See Appendix B for a primer on ordinals.) This set is a cpo w.r.t. $\in$ and its lub's are given by set union. Define $f : O \longrightarrow \mathbb{B}$ by $f(\kappa) \overset{\text{def}}{=} \kappa = \aleph_1$. Let $k \in Ch_{\mathbb{N}}^{\sqsubseteq}(O)$. Then, because the countable union of countable sets is again countable, $\bigcup k$ is $\aleph_1$ if, and only if, there exists an index $j \in \mathbb{N}$ with $k(j) = \aleph_1$. Otherwise $\bigcup k$ is still countable. Hence $f(\bigcup k) = \bigvee (f(k(j)))_{j \in \mathbb{N}}$. This means that f is ω-continuous.

On the other hand, $k \overset{\text{def}}{=} O \setminus \{\aleph_1\}$ is a chain not containing $\aleph_1$ but with lub $\aleph_1$. Consequently,

$$f(\bigcup k) = f(\aleph_1) = \textit{tt} \neq \textit{ff} = \bigvee(\textit{ff})_{j \in O \setminus \{\aleph_1\}} = \bigvee(k_0(j))_{j \in O \setminus \{\aleph_1\}} \; .$$

Hence f is not continuous according to Def. 8.3.   ♡

Lemma 8.5 A monotone function from a cpo to a finite cpo is continuous.

Proof: Let $(A, \leq)$ and $(B, \sqsubseteq)$ be two cpo's with lub functions $\bigvee$ and $\bigsqcup$, respectively. Let $f : A \longrightarrow B$ be monotone and let $k \in Ch^{\leq}(A)$. Then $(f(k(i)))_{i \in I}$ is a chain in B because f is monotone. Since B is finite this chain is eventually constant, i.e., there exists an index $j \in I$ such that $f(k(j))$ is maximal. Thus, $\bigsqcup (f(k(i)))_{i \in I} = f(k(j)) = f(\bigvee k)$.   □

Lemma 8.6 (Continuity of lub's) The lub function for chains in a cpo is continuous.

Proof: To clarify the exposition we take different symbols for the pointwise extension of an order in this proof: let $\bigsqcup$ and $\bigvee$ denote the lub functions of the cpo's $(A, \sqsubseteq)$ and $(Ch_I^{\sqsubseteq}(A), \leq)$, respectively. To show monotonicity of $\bigsqcup$, consider two chains $k, l \in Ch_I^{\sqsubseteq}(A)$ such that $k \leq l$. By the definition of $\leq$

this means that $\forall i \in I\,(k(i) \sqsubseteq l(i))$. Hence, $\forall i \in I\,(k(i) \sqsubseteq \bigsqcup l)$. Consequently, $\bigsqcup k \sqsubseteq \bigsqcup l$.

Let $k \in Ch_{\overline{f}}^{\leq}(Ch_{\overline{f}}^{\sqsubseteq}(A))$. Informally speaking, when seeking for the lub of all elements of elements of k ordered in rows and columns it does not matter whether one takes the lub of the column made up from the lub's of rows or vice versa.

$$
\begin{array}{c|cccc}
k(j_1): & k(j_1)(i_1), & k(j_1)(i_2), & \cdots & \bigsqcup(k(j_1)) \\
k(j_2): & k(j_2)(i_1), & k(j_2)(i_2), & \cdots & \bigsqcup(k(j_2)) \\
\vdots & \vdots & \vdots & \vdots & \vdots \\
\hline
\bigvee k: & \bigsqcup(k(j)(i_1))_{j\in J}, & \bigsqcup(k(j)(i_2))_{j\in J}, & \cdots & (8.5)
\end{array}
$$

Formally we have to show that

$$\bigsqcup \bigvee k = \bigsqcup \left(\bigsqcup k(j) \right)_{j\in J} \tag{8.5}$$

holds. By the definition of $\leq$, all $(k(j)(i))_{j\in J}$ are elements of $Ch_{\overline{f}}^{\sqsubseteq}(S)$. By monotonicity of $\bigsqcup$ the sequence of their limits also forms a chain belonging to $Ch_{\overline{f}}^{\sqsubseteq}(S)$. Thus, $\bigsqcup \left((\bigsqcup k(j))_{j\in J} \right)$ is well-defined. It is the lub of another set, i.e., $\{\, k(i)(j) \mid j \in J, i \in I \,\}$, which need not be a chain. By Lemma 8.2

$$\bigsqcup \bigvee k = \bigsqcup \left(\bigsqcup (k(i)(j))_{j\in J} \right)_{i\in I} ,$$

which is also the lub of $\{\, k(i)(j) \mid j \in J, i \in I \,\}$. Since the lub is unique, if it exists, (8.5) follows. □

Lemma 8.7 (Least fixed point of a continuous function) Let $(A, \sqsubseteq)$ be a cpo and let $f : A \longrightarrow A$ be continuous. Then f has a least fixed point μ_f, and μ_f equals $\bigsqcup(f^i(\perp_A))_{i\in\mathbb{N}}$.

Proof: The sequence $(f^i(\perp_a))_{i\in\mathbb{N}}$ is a chain by monotonicity of f. Moreover, $\bigsqcup(f^i(\perp_A))_{i\in\mathbb{N}}$ is a fixed point of f:

$$
\begin{aligned}
&f(\bigsqcup(f^i(\perp_A))_{i\in\mathbb{N}}) \\
&= \bigsqcup(f^{i+1}(\perp_A))_{i\in\mathbb{N}} && f \text{ is continuous} \\
&= \bigsqcup(f^i(\perp_A))_{i\in\mathbb{N}\setminus\{0\}} \\
&= \bigsqcup(f^i(\perp_A))_{i\in\mathbb{N}} && f^0(\perp_A) = \perp_A
\end{aligned}
$$

Now let $X \in A$ be any fixed point of f.

$$f(\perp_A) \sqsubseteq f(X) \qquad\qquad \perp_A \sqsubseteq X \text{ and } f \text{ is monotone}$$

$$\Rightarrow f(\bot_A) \sqsubseteq X \qquad\qquad f(X) = X \text{ since } X \text{ is a fixed point}$$
$$\Rightarrow \forall i \in \mathbb{N}\left(f^i(\bot_A) \sqsubseteq X\right) \qquad \text{induction on } i$$
$$\Rightarrow \bigsqcup (f^i(\bot_A))_{i \in \mathbb{N}} \sqsubseteq X \qquad \text{property of lub's}$$

Consequently, the least fixed point of f exists, and equals $\bigsqcup(f^i(\bot_A))_{i\in\mathbb{N}}$. $\quad\square$

This construction can be generalized to monotone functions, but this may require transfinite iteration, i.e., beyond $\mathbb{N}$. Now we have to introduce ordinals.

Definition 8.8 (Well-order, ordinal) $(A, <)$ is a *well-order* if $< \subseteq A^2$ is transitive and

- *well-founded*: Every nonvoid subset of A contains a $<$-least element.
- *irreflexive*: $a \not< a$, for $a \in A$.
- *semiconnex*: $a < b \lor b < a \lor a = b$, for $a, b \in A$.

Observe that well-foundedness excludes the existence of infinite descending chains in $(A, <)$.

By $(\mathbb{O}, <)$ we refer to the equivalence classes of well-orders under order isomorphisms. The elements of this class are called the *ordinals*. The equivalence class of $(\mathbb{N}_{<n}, <|_{\mathbb{N}_{<n}\times\mathbb{N}_{<n}})$ is also called n. An ordinal is a *limit ordinal* if it is neither 0 nor the successor of an ordinal. The first limit ordinal is ω; the natural numbers $\mathbb{N}$ ordered by $<$ belong to its equivalence class. $\quad\clubsuit$

For a short introduction to this topic and transfinite induction in particular, see Appendix B. Next we define what it means to iterate β times, for β an ordinal.

Definition 8.9 Let f be a monotone function on a cpo $(A, \sqsubseteq)$ and define

$$f^0 \overset{\text{def}}{=} id_A\ ,$$
$$f^{\beta+1} \overset{\text{def}}{=} f \circ f^\beta\ , \text{ and}$$
$$f^\beta \overset{\text{def}}{=} \bigsqcup (f^i)_{i<\beta} \text{ for } \beta \text{ a limit ordinal.} \qquad\qquad \clubsuit$$

Theorem 8.10 (Least fixed point of a monotone function)
If function f on the cpo $(A, \sqsubseteq)$ is monotone then the least fixed point of f exists, and there exists an ordinal κ such that $\bigsqcup(f^i(\bot_A))_{i<\kappa}$ is the least fixed point of f.

For a detailed proof and how the axiom of choice enters the scene, see, for instance, the corrigendum to [Nel87] or any of [HP72, Nel89, DP90].

Sketch of proof: Since f is monotone, on proves by transfinite induction that $f^\beta(\perp_A) \sqsubseteq f^\gamma(\perp_A)$ for ordinals β and γ such that $\beta < \gamma$. Let X be a fixed point of f. Another transfinite induction shows that $f^\beta(\perp_A) \sqsubseteq X$ for all ordinals β.

It follows that $\bigsqcup(f^i(\perp_A))_{i<\beta} \sqsubseteq X$ for any fixed point X of f and ordinal $\beta \neq 0$. As soon as $f^\beta(\perp_A) = f^{\beta+1}(\perp_A)$, we have immediately that $f^\beta(\perp_A)$ is a fixed point of f, since then $f^\beta(\perp_A) = f^{\beta+1}(\perp_A) = f(f^\beta(\perp_A))$.

Now let κ be the ordinal of $(A, \sqsubseteq)$, i.e., κ expresses the length of the longest possible strictly $\sqsubseteq$-increasing sequence in A. Then the sequence $(f^i(\perp_A))_{i<\kappa+1}$ cannot be strictly increasing. Thus $\bigsqcup(f^i(\perp_A))_{i<\kappa} = f(\bigsqcup(f^i(\perp_A))_{i<\kappa})$. Consequently, the least fixed point of f exists, and equals $\bigsqcup(f^i(\perp_A))_{i<\kappa}$. $\qquad\square$

For later reference we repeat one key observation that has occurred in the proofs of all fixed point lemmas so far.

Corollary 8.11 $\bigsqcup(f^i(\perp_A))_{i<\beta} \sqsubseteq \mu_f$ for any ordinal $\beta \neq 0$. $\qquad\spadesuit$

Lemma 8.12 $(R_\perp^{V,W}, \supseteq)$ is a cpo with least element $U_\perp^{V,W} \stackrel{\text{def}}{=} \Sigma_\perp^V \times \Sigma_\perp^W$ and intersection as least upper bound function. $(R_\perp^{V,V}, \supseteq)$ is closed under ";" and "$\cup$". On $R_\perp^{V,V}$ these two operators are monotone.

Proof: As a subset of $\mathfrak{P}(\Sigma_\perp^V \times \Sigma_\perp^W)$, $R_\perp^{V,W}$ is partially ordered by $\supseteq$. Now let $k \in Ch^\supseteq(R_\perp^{V,W})$. Its least upper bound exists in $\mathfrak{P}(\Sigma_\perp^V \times \Sigma_\perp^W)$ and is the intersection $\bigcap k \stackrel{\text{def}}{=} \bigcap\{ k(i) \mid i \in I \}$. It remains to prove that $\bigcap k \in R_\perp^{V,W}$. Since all chain elements $k(i)$ satisfy $K^{V,W} \subseteq k(i)$, this also holds for their intersection. Let $\sigma \in \Sigma_\perp^V$ such that, for all $i \in I$, $(\sigma, \perp_{\Sigma^W}) \in k(i)$. This implies that $\{\sigma\} \times \Sigma_\perp^W \subseteq k(i)$, for all $i \in \mathbb{N}$. Consequently, $\{\sigma\} \times \Sigma_\perp^W \subseteq \bigcap k$. Altogether, $\bigcap k \in R_\perp^{V,W}$.

The closure and monotonicity conditions are immediate. $\qquad\square$

It is an easy exercise to see that $R_\perp^{V,W}$ is also a cpo w.r.t. $\subseteq$ with least element $K^{V,W}$. In general $r \in R_\perp^{V,W}$ does not imply that $r^{-1} \in R_\perp^{W,V}$ because $K^{V,W} \subseteq r$ does not imply $K^{W,V} \subseteq r^{-1}$. In fact, only $U_\perp^{V,W}$ has an inverse in $R_\perp^{W,V}$, namely $U_\perp^{W,V}$.

The total correctness relational semantics of recursion is explained next. In Section 3.4 this was carried out from a partial correctness viewpoint. First we explain which elements the partial and total correctness semantics of recursion have in common by appealing to our operational understanding of recursion. When is a pair (σ, τ) of states contained in the semantics of recursion $\mu X.S(X)$? Operationally, its semantics is approximated by the infinite sequence of semantics of $S^i(\textbf{abort})$ for $i \in \mathbb{N}$. The semantics of such a term $S^i(\textbf{abort})$ correctly characterizes those pairs of initial/final states in the semantics of recursion

$\mu X.S(X)$ that require some recursion depth of less than i, e.g., calls with recursion depth 0 are modelled by $S(\textbf{abort})$. The semantics of $S^i(\textbf{abort})$ may very well differ from that of recursion $\mu X.S(X)$ in other pairs, since in $S^i(\textbf{abort})$ recursion at depth i or greater is modelled by nontermination. But here the similarity ends between the ways in which we have modelled recursion for partial and total correctness. This is because within the partial correctness world we have modelled nontermination differently from in the total correctness world, as analyzed below.

- For partial correctness nontermination means: there is no final state. Thus, no final state is produced by recursion at depths i or greater. Consequently, we have that $\mathcal{P}[\![S^i(\textbf{abort})]\!] \subseteq \mathcal{P}[\![\mu X.S(X)]\!]$, for all $i \in \mathbb{N}$, and hence the lub of the sequence $(\mathcal{P}[\![S^i(\textbf{abort})]\!])_{i\in\mathbb{N}}$ corresponds to the semantics of recursion as established in Cor. 3.23. This lub is a least fixed point since in the partial correctness semantic model the operations ";", "$\cup$", and "μX" are all (ω)-continuous. (See Section 3.4 and observe that the underlying partial order on sets of states is "$\subseteq$".)
- For total correctness the case is different, because nontermination is represented as follows: every final state is possible. Consider $\mathcal{P}[\![S^i(\textbf{abort})]\!]_\perp$, the total correctness semantics of the i-th approximation. Now for recursion depth i or greater, nontermination is modelled by the set of all states, i.e., in that case any state figures as a possible final state. Thus, $\mathcal{P}[\![S^i(\textbf{abort})]\!]_\perp \supseteq \mathcal{P}[\![\mu X.S(X)]\!]_\perp$ for all $i \in \mathbb{N}$, and hence $\bigcap_{i\in\mathbb{N}} \mathcal{P}[\![S^i(\textbf{abort})]\!]_\perp$, which is the lub (w.r.t. $(R_\perp, \supseteq)$) of the sequence $(\mathcal{P}[\![S^i(\textbf{abort})]\!]_\perp)_{i\in\mathbb{N}}$, is a first approximation of the semantics of recursion. However, taking lub's of such ω-chains in $(R_\perp, \supseteq)$ does not distribute over sequential composition (see Example 8.14 below), and hence the transformation induced by $S(X)$ need not be continuous. Therefore $\bigcap_{i\in\mathbb{N}} \mathcal{P}[\![S^i(\textbf{abort})]\!]_\perp$ is not necessarily a fixed point of that transformation.

The bottom state was introduced to characterize nonterminating computations within the initial/final state model. Is that intention already covered by the above definition of semantic domains like $R_\perp^C$? Not quite, since, for instance, relation K^C does not provide any final state to a computation started in a proper (read: non-bottom) state: $\forall \sigma \neq \perp \left(K^C(\{\sigma\}) = \emptyset\right)$. This behavior is sometimes called *miraculous* termination in the literature [MV94, BvW90]. The straightforward way to get rid of miracles is to restrict the semantics of programs to the total elements of $R_\perp^C$. Observe that such total relations are not suitable for modelling a guard that should deadlock for certain initial states, namely when this guard does not hold.

Another drawback of the set of total elements of $R_\perp^C$ is that it is not a cpo w.r.t. partial order $\supseteq$, since it does not necessarily have all lub's, as is demonstrated next.

Example 8.13 Consider the chain $(r_n)_{n \in \mathbb{N}} \in Ch_{\mathbb{N}}^{\supseteq}(R_{\perp}^C)$ where x is the only program variable on level C, $\mathbb{V}^C = \mathbb{N}$, and $r_n = K^C \cup \{ (\sigma, \tau) \in (\Sigma^C)^2 \mid \tau(x) \geq n \}$. Its only upper bound is K^C, which is not total, in contrast to all chain elements r_n. $\quad\heartsuit$

A convenient way to ensure totality of lub's of $\supseteq$-chains of total relations is to restrict the semantic domain even more: abandon infinite nondeterminism. For infinite nondeterminism is essential to the example above. But for our abstraction relations and specification statements, this restriction does not always make sense. The other language constructs do not introduce infinite nondeterminism.

The following example illustrates that sequential composition is not continuous in $(R_{\perp}, \supseteq)$.

Example 8.14 Let $Var^C = \{x, y\}$ and $\mathbb{V} = \mathbb{N}$. To simplify the exposition we identify each proper state $(\pitchfork : (x, y) \mapsto (n, m)) \in \Sigma^C$ with the pair (n, m) of natural numbers. Let $r \in R_{\perp}^C$ such that the non-K^C part of r is characterized as follows. For all $n, m \in \mathbb{N}$

$$r(\{(n,m)\}) = \begin{cases} \{1\} \times \mathbb{N} & \text{if } n = m = 0 \\ \{(n+1, m-1)\} & \text{if } m > 0 \wedge n > 0 \\ \emptyset & \text{otherwise} \end{cases} \quad (8.6)$$

(See Figure 8.1 for an illustration of the non-K^C part of r.) Observe that r is partial. For instance, $r(\{(0,5)\}) = \emptyset$. In Figure 8.1 the proper states without successor states form the first column and first row except for the intersection of these two, i.e., state $(0,0)$. Next we prove by induction on $i \in \mathbb{N}_{>0}$ that for all $n, m \in \mathbb{N}$

$$r^i(\{(n,m)\}) = \begin{cases} \{i\} \times \mathbb{N} & \text{if } n = m = 0 \\ \{(n+i, m-i)\} & \text{if } m \geq i \wedge n > 0 \\ \emptyset & \text{otherwise} \end{cases}$$

holds. For $i = 1$ the claim follows immediately from (8.6). In case $i = k + 1$ for some $k \in \mathbb{N}_{>0}$ (see Figure 8.2 for an illustration of $r^2 \setminus K^C$)

$$r^{k+1}(\{(n,m)\})$$

$$= \quad (\text{Def. 8.9})$$

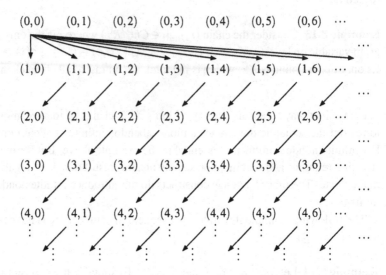

Fig. 8.1. A fragment of r: arrows from (n,m) indicate which state pairs are contained in $r(\{(n,m)\})$. If there is no arrow then $r(\{(n,m)\}) = \emptyset$.

$$r(r^k(\{(n,m)\}))$$
$$=\qquad \text{(induction hypothesis)}$$
$$\begin{cases} r(\{k\} \times \mathbb{N}) & \text{if } n = m = 0 \\ r(\{(n+k, m-k)\}) & \text{if } m \geq k \wedge n > 0 \\ r(\emptyset) & \text{otherwise} \end{cases}$$
$$=\qquad \text{(by (8.6))}$$
$$\begin{cases} \{k+1\} \times \mathbb{N} & \text{if } n = m = 0 \\ \{(n+(k+1), m-(k+1))\} & \text{if } m \geq k+1 \wedge n > 0 \\ \emptyset & \text{otherwise} \end{cases}$$

Consequently $r^i ; U_\perp^C = (\{(0,0),\perp\} \cup \{ (n,m) \mid m \geq i \wedge n > 0 \}) \times \Sigma_\perp^C$ for all $i \in \mathbb{N}_{>0}$. Thus, $\bigcap_{i \in \mathbb{N}} (r^i ; U_\perp^C) = \{(0,0),\perp\} \times \Sigma_\perp^C$ which we call f_ω. However, f_ω is not yet $\mu_{\lambda X . r;X}$ because $r ; f_\omega = K^C \subsetneqq f_\omega$. Not until one iteration later do we reach the least fixed point: $r ; K^C = K^C$.[1] Consequently, sequential

---

[1] The reason for reaching $\mu_{\lambda X . r;X}$ with $\bigcap_{i < \omega+1} (r^i ; U_\perp^C)$ is that the ordinal of $(\mathbb{N}^2, r)$ is $\omega + 1$. (See Theorem 8.10.)

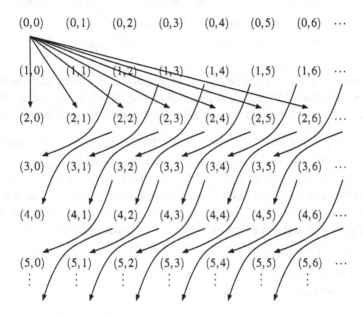

Fig. 8.2. A fragment of r^2. Observe that the elements of the second column also have no successor states.

composition is not continuous in $(R_\perp, \supseteq)$. Otherwise f_ω would have been the least fixed point of $\lambda X.r; X$ by Lemma 8.7.

After the presentation of our total correctness semantics of programs in Section 8.2 we shall see that r can be expressed by a specification statement. ♡

Definition 8.15 (Finitary sets and relations) Let S and T be sets. A set $s \subseteq S_\perp$ is *finitary* if either s is the whole of $S_\perp$ or s is a finite subset of S. Let $\mathcal{F}(S)$ denote the finitary subsets of $S_\perp$. Relation $r \subseteq T \times S_\perp$ is *finitary* iff $\forall t \in T\, (r(\{t\}) \in \mathcal{F}(S))$. Let $R_\mathcal{F}(T, S)$ denote all such finitary relations. ♣

Observe that the bottom element does not occur in finite finitary sets. Since the empty set is finitary we still have non-total relations which are finitary. However, lub's of chains of total finitary relations are now total.

Example 8.16 (cf. Example 8.14) Relation r from Example 8.14 is not finitary since $r(\{(0,0)\}) = \{\,(1,n) \mid n \in \mathbb{N}\,\}$, which is infinite but not the whole of $\Sigma_\perp^C$. ♡

For sets of variables $V, W \subseteq Var$ let $R_{\mathcal{F}}{}^{V,W}$ denote the finitary elements of $R_{\perp}^{V,W}$; let $U_{\perp}^{V,W}$ denote the common $\supseteq$-least element $\Sigma_{\perp}^{V} \times \Sigma_{\perp}^{W}$ of $R_{\perp}^{V,W}$ and $R_{\mathcal{F}}^{V,W}$.

For abstraction levels A and C we abbreviate $R_{\mathcal{F}}^{\Sigma^A, \Sigma^C}$ by $R_{\mathcal{F}}^{AC}$ and $U_{\perp}^{\Sigma^A, \Sigma^C}$ by $U_{\perp}^{AC}$. Similarly, $U_{\perp}^{C}$ and $R_{\mathcal{F}}^{C}$ abbreviate $U_{\perp}^{CC}$ and $R_{\mathcal{F}}^{CC}$, respectively.

Lemma 8.17 Let $k \in Ch^{\supseteq}(R_{\mathcal{F}}^{V,W})$. Then, for all $\sigma \in \Sigma_{\perp}^{V}$, there exists an index $i \in I$ such that $k(i)(\{\sigma\})$ is $\supseteq$-maximal among all relational images of the singleton set $\{\sigma\}$ through $k(j)$ for $j \in I$. Such chains are called *stationary*.[2]

Proof: Let $k \in Ch^{\supseteq}(R_{\mathcal{F}}^{V,W})$ and $\sigma \in \Sigma_{\perp}^{V}$. By monotonicity of the relational image operator in its first argument, the sequence $(k(i)(\{\sigma\}))_{i \in I}$ is a chain in the set of finitary subsets of $\Sigma_{\perp}^{W}$, which is a cpo w.r.t. $\supseteq$. In case all elements of this chain equal $\Sigma_{\perp}^{W}$, the index in question is arbitrary. Otherwise there exists an index $i \in I$ such that $k(i)(\{\sigma\})$ is finite. From i on there can be at most $|k(i)(\{\sigma\})|$ changes in the chain. Let j be the index of the last such change. Then the chain is constant from index j onwards. $\Box$

It follows immediately from this lemma that lub's of chains of total elements in $R_{\mathcal{F}}^{V,W}$ are total.

Lemma 8.18 $(R_{\mathcal{F}}^{V,W}, \supseteq)$ is a cpo, the so-called *Smyth cpo* [Smy78]. Its least element is $U_{\perp}^{V,W}$, and the lub of a chain $k \in Ch_{\bar{I}}^{\supseteq}(R_{\mathcal{F}}^{V,W})$ is $\bigcap k \overset{\text{def}}{=} \bigcap_{i \in I} k(i)$. The partial order $\supseteq$ is sometimes pronounced "refines to" or "is refined by".

Proof: The only interesting point to prove here is the existence of lub's of $\supseteq$-chains in $R_{\mathcal{F}}^{V,W}$. Let k be a $\supseteq$-chain in $R_{\mathcal{F}}^{V,W}$ and let $\sigma \in \Sigma_{\perp}^{V,W}$. We have to show that the relational image of $\{\sigma\}$ through the lub of k is finitary; this follows immediately from Lemma 8.17. $\Box$

Lemma 8.19 The cpo $(R_{\mathcal{F}}^{V,V}, \supseteq)$ has the following properties.

(i) $R_{\mathcal{F}}^{V,V}$ is closed under ";" and "$\cup$".

(ii) On $R_{\mathcal{F}}^{V,V}$ the operators ";" and "$\cup$" are continuous in both arguments.

Proof: We omit the superscripts ^{V} and ^{V,V} in this proof.

(i) Let $r, s \in R_{\mathcal{F}}$. The finite union of finitary sets is finitary. Thus, $r \cup s \in R_{\mathcal{F}}$. To show this for $r; s$, consider $\sigma \in \Sigma_{\perp}$. Since r is a finitary relation, the relational image of $\{\sigma\}$ through r is a finitary set.

---

[2] In the literature eventually constant chains are sometimes called *stationary*, but we reserve this term for the strictly weaker, pointwise notion introduced here.

In case $r(\{\sigma\})$ is finite, $(r;s)(\{\sigma\})$ is the finite union $\bigcup_{\tau \in r(\{\sigma\})} s(\{\tau\})$. Since s is a finitary relation, all $s(\{\tau\})$ for $\tau \in r(\{\sigma\})$ are finitary sets. Otherwise, i.e., in case $r(\{\sigma\})$ is $\Sigma_\perp$, we have that $(r;s)(\{\sigma\}) = s(\Sigma_\perp) = \Sigma_\perp$ since $K \subseteq s$. In both cases we have shown that $(r;s)(\{\sigma\})$ is a finitary set. Thus, $r;s \in R_{\mathcal{F}}$.

(ii) The monotonicity of ";" and "$\cup$" in both arguments has been proven in Lemma 3.8.

Let $k \in Ch^{\supseteq}(R_{\mathcal{F}})$ and $r \in R_{\mathcal{F}}$. By monotonicity of ";" and since $R_{\mathcal{F}}$ is closed under ";" the sequence $(k(i);r)_{i\in I}$ is a chain in $R_{\mathcal{F}}$, too. We prove

$$\left(\bigcap k\right);r = \bigcap(k(i);r)_{i\in I}$$

by showing that

$$\left(\left(\bigcap k\right);r\right)(\{\sigma\}) = \left(\bigcap(k(i);r)_{i\in I}\right)(\{\sigma\})$$

holds for all $\sigma \in \Sigma_\perp$.

By Lemma 8.17 k is stationary. Now let $\sigma \in \Sigma_\perp$. By stationarity there exists an index $n \in I$ such that $(\bigcap k)(\{\sigma\}) = k(n)(\{\sigma\})$. Thus $(\bigcap k;r)(\{\sigma\}) = (k(n);r)(\{\sigma\}) = (\bigcap(k(i);r)_{i\in I})(\{\sigma\})$. Observe that we have not exploited finitariness of r.

Similarly we prove that ";" is continuous in its second argument. This time, however, finitariness of r is necessary. Set $A \stackrel{\text{def}}{=} r(\{\sigma\})$. In case $A = \Sigma_\perp$, it follows that $(r;\bigcap k)(\{\sigma\}) = (\bigcap k)(A) = (\bigcap k)(\Sigma_\perp) = \Sigma_\perp = (\bigcap(r;k(i))_{i\in I})(\{\sigma\})$.

Otherwise, i.e., in case A is a finite subset of Σ, we have that $(r;\bigcap k)(\{\sigma\}) = (\bigcap k)(A) = \bigcup\{(\bigcap k)(\{\tau\}) \mid \tau \in A\}$. For each $\tau \in A$ there exists by stationarity an index $j_\tau \in I$ with $(\bigcap k)(\{\tau\}) = k(j_\tau)(\{\tau\})$. Thus, for the index j such that $k(j) = \max\{k(j_\tau) \mid \tau \in A\}$ this implies that $(\bigcap k)(A) = k(j)(A) = (r;k(j))(\{\sigma\}) = (\bigcap(r;k(i))_{i\in I})(\{\sigma\})$.

Continuity of "$\cup$" is straightforward. $\square$

As observed in the proof above, intersecting over a chain of finitary relations distributes over sequential composition on the right even in case the relation with which the intersection is composed is not finitary. For later use we stress this as a corollary.

Corollary 8.20 Let $k \in Ch^{\supseteq}(R_{\mathcal{F}})$ and $r \in R_\perp$. Then $\bigcap k;r = \bigcap(k(i);r)_{i\in\mathbb{N}}$. ♠

As observed before, $r \in R_{\mathcal{F}}^V$ does not imply that r is total, since $r(\{\sigma\}) = \emptyset$ can still occur for proper states σ, because $\emptyset$ is finitary. However, the total relations form a cpo closed under ";" and "$\cup$", which are also continuous.

Corollary 8.21 Let $R_{t,\mathcal{F}}^{V,W}$ denote the total elements of $R_{\mathcal{F}}^{V,W}$. $(R_{t,\mathcal{F}}^{V,W}, \supseteq)$ is a cpo with lub function $\bigcap$.

$R_{t,\mathcal{F}}^{V,V}$ is closed under ";" and "$\cup$"; these operators are continuous in both arguments.   ♠

The $R_{t,\mathcal{F}}^{V,W}$ are not the domains of relations we require, because they do not contain the semantics of Boolean guards (whereas they fit into $R_{\mathcal{F}}^{V,W}$), which are indispensable for our set-up. In Section 8.2 we use these facts to define the semantics of our programming language w.r.t. $R_\perp$. Then we consider a subset whose programs have semantics belonging to $R_{\mathcal{F}}$, and can later syntactically restrict that subset to programs such that the semantics of the remaining programs belongs to $R_{t,\mathcal{F}}$.

It is only for such programs S that $(\sigma, \perp) \notin \mathcal{P}[\![S]\!]_\perp$ means that S terminates for initial state σ in the usual sense, i.e., deadlock also is ruled out.

8.2 Interpretation Functions for Total Correctness

The evaluation of arithmetic expressions in a total correctness framework like ours depends on an interpretation $\mathfrak{I}_\perp = (\mathfrak{S}_\perp, \sigma)$, where $\mathfrak{S}_\perp = (\mathbb{V}_\perp, s_\perp)$, $\sigma \in \Sigma_\perp$, and $s_\perp$ is given by

- each constant $c \in Const$ is treated as by s, i.e., $c^{s_\perp} = c^s$,
- each n-ary arithmetic operator $op \in Op$ is mapped to a strict, n-ary function $op^{s_\perp} : \mathbb{V}_\perp^n \longrightarrow \mathbb{V}_\perp$, for instance, $\div^{s_\perp}(v, 0) = \perp_{\mathbb{V}}$.
- Each n-ary comparison operator $cop \in Cop$ is mapped to a strict, n-ary function $cop^{s_\perp} : \mathbb{V}_\perp^n \longrightarrow \mathbb{B}_\perp$.

The special rôle of $\perp_\Sigma$ is reflected in the definition of validity. A predicate p is valid in $\mathfrak{S}_\perp$, denoted by $\models_{\mathfrak{S}_\perp} p$, if $\models_{(\mathfrak{S}_\perp, \sigma)} p$ for all proper σ.

8.2.1 Predicates

For $V, W \subseteq Var$ and $\sigma \in \Sigma_\perp^V$ we define the strict extensions of state variation, composition, and projection.

$$(\perp_{\Sigma^V} : x \mapsto v) \stackrel{\text{def}}{=} \perp_{\Sigma^{V \cup \{x\}}}$$

$$(\sigma : x \mapsto \perp_{\mathbb{V}}) \stackrel{\text{def}}{=} \perp_{\Sigma^{V \cup \{x\}}}$$

$$\perp_{\Sigma^W} \dagger \sigma \stackrel{\text{def}}{=} \perp_{\Sigma^{V \cup W}} \quad (= \sigma \dagger \perp_{\Sigma^W})$$

$$\perp_{\Sigma^{V \cup W}} |_V \stackrel{\text{def}}{=} \perp_{\Sigma^V}$$

Definition 8.22 The total correctness semantics of expressions is given by the function

$$\mathcal{E}[\![.]\!]_{\perp} : Exp \longrightarrow (\Sigma_{\perp} \longrightarrow \mathbb{V}_{\perp})$$

which is strict in its second argument.

To define the value of expressions in a non-bottom state let $\sigma \in \Sigma$.

$$\mathcal{E}[\![c]\!]_{\perp} \sigma \stackrel{\text{def}}{=} c^{s\perp}$$

$$\mathcal{E}[\![x]\!]_{\perp} \sigma \stackrel{\text{def}}{=} \sigma(x)$$

$$\mathcal{E}[\![e_1 \ op \ e_2]\!]_{\perp} \sigma \stackrel{\text{def}}{=} op^{s\perp}(\mathcal{E}[\![e_1]\!]_{\perp} \sigma, \mathcal{E}[\![e_2]\!]_{\perp} \sigma) \qquad \clubsuit$$

We leave the common ground of classical, two-valued predicate logic and work within a three-valued logic based on $\mathbb{B}_{\perp} = \{ff, tt, \perp_{\mathbb{B}}\}$ instead. Several possible ways of defining the meaning of the logical connectives and quantifiers are given in the literature.

We opt for a definition which satisfies the following two conditions:[3]

(i) It defines "¬" as a monotone function on the flat cpo $\mathbb{B}_{\perp}$, and "⇒", "∨", and "∧" as monotone functions from $\mathbb{B}_{\perp} \times \mathbb{B}_{\perp}$ (ordered component-wise) to $\mathbb{B}_{\perp}$. Restricting these functions to $\mathbb{B}$ and $\mathbb{B} \times \mathbb{B}$, respectively, yields the classical logical connectives used in Chapter 5.

(ii) It defines $ff \wedge \perp = \perp \wedge ff = ff$, or equivalently, $tt \vee \perp = \perp \vee tt = tt$. When generalized to the universal and existential quantifiers this lets such reasonable predicates as $\exists x \left(\frac{1}{x} = 1 \right)$ denote tt and not $\perp$ as would be the case with a strict definition.

The first condition fixes our interpretation of "¬" completely:

¬	tt	ff	$\perp$
	ff	tt	$\perp$

Condition (i) does not completely determine our interpretations of the binary logical connectives; it leads to the following options:

⇒	tt	ff	$\perp$
tt	tt	ff	$\perp$
ff	tt	tt	$\{\perp, \boxed{tt}\}$
$\perp$	$\{\perp, \boxed{tt}\}$	$\perp$	$\perp$

---

[3] This coincides with the interpretation of the logical connectives given in LPF (Logic of Partial Functions) which is used by Jones in [J90] to formulate a proof theory for VDM. We shall return to this point in Chapter 12.

$\wedge$	tt	ff	$\perp$
tt	tt	ff	$\perp$
ff	ff	ff	$\{\perp, \boxed{ff}\}$
$\perp$	$\perp$	$\{\perp, \boxed{ff}\}$	$\perp$

$\vee$	tt	ff	$\perp$
tt	tt	tt	$\{\perp, \boxed{tt}\}$
ff	tt	ff	$\perp$
$\perp$	$\{\perp, \boxed{tt}\}$	$\perp$	$\perp$

Condition (ii) determines the one remaining interpretation for these connectives by imposing the boxed values in these tables.

Whereas the need for condition (ii) above is obvious, maybe condition (i) needs some additional motivation. $\mathbb{B}_\perp$ is a finite, flat cpo and therefore any monotone function over the cpo $\mathbb{B}_\perp \times \mathbb{B}_\perp$ (ordered component-wise) is continuous by Lemma 8.5; this applies in particular to "$\wedge$" and "$\vee$". Now continuity is of vital importance when reasoning about recursive procedures, because it links induction arguments on the recursion depth of a recursive procedure to the overall behavior of that procedure.[4]

Next we define $T[\![.]\!]_\perp$, since it cannot be derived from $C[\![.]\!]_\perp$ in the same way as $T[\![.]\!]$ was derived from $C[\![.]\!]$, namely by exploiting the equivalence between $\sigma \in C[\![p]\!]$ and $T[\![p]\!]\sigma = tt$. Now that we have three truth values, this correspondence allows only the derivation of $T[\![p]\!]_\perp \sigma \in \{ff, \perp_\mathbb{B}\}$ from $\sigma \notin C[\![p]\!]_\perp$.

Definition 8.23 The total correctness semantics of predicates is given by the function

$$T[\![.]\!]_\perp : Pred \longrightarrow (\Sigma_\perp \longrightarrow \mathbb{B}_\perp)$$

which is strict in its second argument. So we still have to define $T[\![.]\!]_\perp \sigma$ for $\sigma \in \Sigma$.

$$T[\![\text{false}]\!]_\perp \sigma \stackrel{\text{def}}{=} ff$$

$$T[\![e_1 \ cop \ e_2]\!]_\perp \sigma \stackrel{\text{def}}{=} cop^{s\perp}(\mathcal{E}[\![e_1]\!]_\perp \sigma, \mathcal{E}[\![e_2]\!]_\perp \sigma)$$

---

[4] For first one proves the property at hand by induction on recursion depth, i.e., one proves it for $\tau^i(\textbf{abort})$, for $i \in \mathbb{N}$, using a suitable induction step, and then continuity of τ allows one to generalize that property to $\mu X.\tau(X)$. E.g., proving a property of $\{ y \mid (y \in \mu X.\tau(X)) \wedge p(y) \}$, where $\mu X.\tau(X)$ is a set-valued recursive procedure, may be reduced by continuity of "$\{ y \mid . \}$", "$\wedge$", and "$y \in .$" to proving that property for $y \in \tau^i(\textbf{abort}) \wedge p(y)$, the former part of which can be proven by induction on recursion depth.

$$T[\![p_1 \Rightarrow p_2]\!]_\perp \sigma \stackrel{\text{def}}{=} \begin{cases} tt & \text{if } T[\![p_1]\!]_\perp \sigma = ff \text{ or } T[\![p_2]\!]_\perp \sigma = tt \\ ff & \text{if } T[\![p_1]\!]_\perp \sigma = tt \text{ and } T[\![p_2]\!]_\perp \sigma = ff \\ \perp_\mathbb{B} & \text{otherwise} \end{cases}$$

$$T[\![\forall x(p)]\!]_\perp \sigma \stackrel{\text{def}}{=} \begin{cases} tt & \text{if } T[\![p]\!]_\perp \sigma_x^v = tt, \text{ for all } v \in \mathbb{V} \\ ff & \text{if } T[\![p]\!]_\perp \sigma_x^v = ff, \text{ for some } v \in \mathbb{V} \\ \perp_\mathbb{B} & \text{otherwise} \end{cases}$$

And we define $C[\![p]\!]_\perp \stackrel{\text{def}}{=} \{ \sigma \in \Sigma_\perp \mid T[\![p]\!]_\perp \sigma = tt \}$. As in Defs 5.9 and 5.10, the semantics $T[\![.]\!]_\perp^V : Pred^V \longrightarrow (\Sigma_\perp^V \longrightarrow \mathbb{B}_\perp)$ and $T[\![.]\!]_\perp^{V,W} : Pred^{V,W} \longrightarrow ((\Sigma_\perp^V \times \Sigma_\perp^W) \longrightarrow \mathbb{B}_\perp)$ are derived from $T[\![.]\!]_\perp$. Let $V, W \subseteq Var$, $p \in Pred^V$, $q \in Pred^{V,W}$, $\sigma \in \Sigma_\perp^V$, $\tau \in \Sigma_\perp^W$, $\sigma' \in \Sigma$ and define

$$T[\![p]\!]_\perp^V \sigma \stackrel{\text{def}}{=} T[\![p]\!]_\perp (\sigma' \dagger \sigma)$$

$$C[\![p]\!]_\perp^V \stackrel{\text{def}}{=} \left\{ \sigma \in \Sigma_\perp^V \mid T[\![p]\!]_\perp^V \sigma = tt \right\}$$

$$T[\![q]\!]_\perp^{V,W} (\sigma, \tau) \stackrel{\text{def}}{=} T[\![q]\!]_\perp^{V \cup W} (\sigma \dagger \tau)$$

$$C[\![q]\!]_\perp^{V,W} \stackrel{\text{def}}{=} \left\{ (\sigma, \tau) \in \Sigma_\perp^V \times \Sigma_\perp^W \mid T[\![q]\!]_\perp^{V,W} (\sigma, \tau) = tt \right\} \qquad \clubsuit$$

The strictness of $T[\![.]\!]_\perp$ ensures that no predicate holds in bottom.

Corollary 8.24 Let $p \in Pred^V$, $q \in Pred^{V,W}$, $\sigma \in \Sigma_\perp^V$, and $\tau \in \Sigma_\perp^W$. Then the previous definition guarantees that

- $\perp_\Sigma \notin C[\![p]\!]_\perp$,
- $\perp_{\Sigma^V} \notin C[\![p]\!]_\perp^V$, and
- $(\sigma, \perp_{\Sigma^W}), (\perp_{\Sigma^V}, \tau) \notin C[\![q]\!]_\perp^{V,W}$. $\qquad \spadesuit$

8.2.2 Abstraction Relations

Although abstraction relations syntactically resemble certain predicates, their total correctness semantics is a mixture of predicate and program semantics. A strict semantics of abstraction relations would be unreasonable. For as we shall see in Section 9.1, abstraction relations from level C to level A should be assigned a meaning in $R_\perp^{CA}$, because this turns out to be the case for the relations occurring in the completeness proof; and we can prove soundness for such relations only, not for strict ones.

What if evaluation of the abstraction relation as a predicate in a pair (σ, ζ) of proper states delivers $\perp$? Such an abstraction relation should be semantically different from one that evaluates to ff in (σ, ζ). In the former case, such a σ is mapped to all abstract level states.

Definition 8.25 Let $\vec{x}$, $\vec{c}$, and $\vec{a}$ denote, as before, the lists of normal variables, representation variables on level C, and representation variables on level A, respectively. The total correctness semantics of abstraction relations from level C to level A

$$\mathcal{A}[\![.]\!]^{CA}_{\perp} : Abs^{CA} \longrightarrow R^{CA}_{\perp}$$

is defined as follows.

$$\mathcal{A}[\![\alpha]\!]^{CA}_{\perp} \stackrel{\text{def}}{=} \left\{ (\sigma, \zeta) \in \Sigma^C_{\perp} \times \Sigma^A_{\perp} \;\middle|\; \begin{array}{l} (\sigma|_{\vec{c}}, \zeta|_{\vec{a}}) \in C[\![\alpha]\!]^{\vec{c},\vec{a}}_{\perp} \wedge \sigma \equiv_{\vec{x}} \zeta \\ \vee \exists \xi \in \Sigma^{\vec{a}} \left(\mathcal{T}[\![\alpha]\!]^{\vec{c},\vec{a}}_{\perp}(\sigma|_{\vec{c}}, \xi) = \perp_{\mathbb{B}} \right) \end{array} \right\}$$

♣

Observe that the semantics of abstraction relations is well-defined. It is the condition $\exists \zeta \in \Sigma^{\vec{a}} \left(\mathcal{T}[\![\alpha]\!]^{\vec{c},\vec{a}}_{\perp}(\sigma|_{\vec{c}}, \zeta) = \perp_{\mathbb{B}} \right)$ in the definition above that guarantees that $K^{CA} \subseteq \mathcal{A}[\![\alpha]\!]^{CA}_{\perp}$ and $\mathcal{A}[\![\alpha]\!]^{CA}_{\perp} ; K^{CA} \subseteq \mathcal{A}[\![\alpha]\!]^{CA}_{\perp}$ are satisfied.

Definition 8.26 We say that relation $r \in R^{AC}_{\perp}$ *weakly terminates* when started *in state* $\sigma \in \Sigma^A_{\perp}$ if the state pair $(\sigma, \perp)$ does not occur in r. Then we say that σ belongs to the *domain of weak termination* $wt(r)$ of r.

$$wt(r) \stackrel{\text{def}}{=} \left\{ \sigma \in \Sigma^A_{\perp} \mid (\sigma, \perp) \notin r \right\} \tag{8.7}$$

We say that r *weakly terminates*, whenever r weakly terminates for each proper initial state $\sigma \in \Sigma^A$.

We shall also use wt to map each relational term to the domain of weak termination of its total correctness semantics.   ♣

Note that if $\sigma \in wt(r)$ it is still possible that $r(\{\sigma\}) = \emptyset$, which corresponds to guaranteed deadlock.

The above characterization of the semantics of abstraction relations seems over-complicated. In practical cases, i.e., when finalizations terminate weakly, L-simulation relations must terminate weakly, too. And if α terminates weakly, then $(\sigma, \zeta) \in \mathcal{A}[\![\alpha]\!]^{CA}_{\perp}$ holds simply iff $(\sigma|_{\vec{c}}, \zeta|_{\vec{a}}) \in C[\![\alpha]\!]^{\vec{c},\vec{a}}_{\perp} \wedge \sigma \equiv_{\vec{x}} \zeta \vee \sigma = \perp$. This corresponds only roughly with the union of K^{CA} and the partial correctness semantics of α.

Lemma 8.27 Weak termination of abstraction relation α is expressed by $\models_{\mathfrak{S}_{\perp}} \alpha \vee \neg\alpha$.

Proof:

$$\alpha \in Abs^{CA} \quad \text{weakly terminates}$$

$$\Leftrightarrow \forall \sigma \in \Sigma^C \left((\sigma, \perp) \notin \mathcal{A}[\![\alpha]\!]_\perp^{CA} \right) \qquad \text{Def. 8.26}$$

$$\Leftrightarrow \forall \sigma \in \Sigma^C, \zeta \in \Sigma^{\vec{a}} \left(T[\![\alpha]\!]_\perp^{\vec{c},\vec{a}}(\sigma|_{\vec{c}}, \zeta) \neq \perp_{\mathbb{B}} \right) \qquad \text{Def. 8.25}$$

$$\Leftrightarrow \forall \tau \in \Sigma^{\vec{c}\vec{a}} \left(T[\![\alpha]\!]_\perp^{\vec{c}\vec{a}}\tau \in \mathbb{B} \right) \qquad \text{Def. 8.23}$$

$$\Leftrightarrow \forall \tau \in \Sigma^{\vec{c}\vec{a}} \left(T[\![\alpha]\!]_\perp^{\vec{c}\vec{a}}\tau = tt \vee T[\![\neg\alpha]\!]_\perp^{\vec{c}\vec{a}}\tau = tt \right) \qquad \text{Def. 8.23}$$

$$\Leftrightarrow \forall \tau \in \Sigma^{\vec{c}\vec{a}} \left(T[\![\alpha \vee \neg\alpha]\!]_\perp^{\vec{c}\vec{a}}\tau = tt \right) \qquad \text{Def. 8.23}$$

$$\Leftrightarrow C[\![\alpha \vee \neg\alpha]\!]_\perp^{\vec{c}\vec{a}} = \Sigma^{\vec{c}\vec{a}} \qquad \text{Def. 8.23}$$

$$\Leftrightarrow \models_{\mathfrak{S}_\perp} \alpha \vee \neg\alpha \qquad \qquad \Box$$

Totality of abstraction relation $\alpha \in Abs^{CA}$ is ensured by (and, in case α weakly terminates, even equivalent to) $\forall \vec{c}(\exists \vec{a}(\alpha))$.

Lemma 8.28 $\mathcal{A}[\![\alpha]\!]_\perp^{CA}$ is total if $\forall \vec{c}(\exists \vec{a}(\alpha))$ is valid in $\mathfrak{S}_\perp$. If α terminates weakly, then the reverse implication also holds.

Proof:

$$\models_{\mathfrak{S}_\perp} \forall \vec{c}(\exists \vec{a}(\alpha))$$

$$\Leftrightarrow \forall \sigma \in \Sigma^0 \left(\sigma \in C[\![\forall \vec{c}(\exists \vec{a}(\alpha))]\!]_\perp^0 \right) \qquad \text{no free variables}$$

$$\Leftrightarrow T[\![\forall \vec{c}(\exists \vec{a}(\alpha))]\!]_\perp^0 \text{\usebox\mh} = tt \qquad \text{Def. 8.23}$$

$$\Leftrightarrow \forall \vec{v} \left(T[\![\exists \vec{a}(\alpha)]\!]_\perp^{\vec{c}} (\text{\usebox\mh} : \vec{c} \mapsto \vec{v}) = tt \right) \qquad \text{Def. 8.23}$$

$$\Leftrightarrow \forall \vec{v} \left(\exists \vec{w} \left(T[\![\alpha]\!]_\perp^{\vec{c}\vec{a}} (\text{\usebox\mh} : \vec{c}\vec{a} \mapsto \vec{v}\vec{w}) = tt \right) \right) \qquad \text{Def. 8.23}$$

$$\Leftrightarrow \forall \sigma \in \Sigma^{\vec{c}} \left(\exists \zeta \in \Sigma^{\vec{a}} \left(T[\![\alpha]\!]_\perp^{\vec{c},\vec{a}}(\sigma, \zeta) = tt \right) \right) \qquad \text{introduce states for } \vec{v} \text{ and } \vec{w}$$

$$\Rightarrow \forall \sigma \in \Sigma^C \left(\exists \zeta \in \Sigma^A \left((\sigma, \zeta) \in \mathcal{A}[\![\alpha]\!]_\perp^{CA} \right) \right) \qquad \text{Def. 8.25}$$

$$\Leftrightarrow \forall \sigma \in \Sigma_\perp^C \left(\exists \zeta \in \Sigma_\perp^A \left((\sigma, \zeta) \in \mathcal{A}[\![\alpha]\!]_\perp^{CA} \right) \right) \qquad \mathcal{A}[\![\alpha]\!]_\perp^{CA} \in R_\perp^{CA}$$

The only one-way implication in the derivation above can be reversed if there is no $\sigma \in \Sigma^{\vec{c}}$ such that there exists a state $\zeta \in \Sigma^{\vec{a}}$ with $T[\![\alpha]\!]_\perp^{\vec{c},\vec{a}}(\sigma, \zeta) = \perp_{\mathbb{B}}$. This is exactly the case if α is weakly terminating. $\qquad \Box$

Finitariness of (the total correctness semantics of) abstraction relations cannot be expressed syntactically in our first order logic, because to do so requires essential second order logic features [Sho67]. Therefore we have to check finitariness semantically for every L^{-1}-simulation relation.

8.2.3 Programs

In Def. 9.3 we shall define the set $T_\perp(A)$ of total correctness terms over an indexed family $A = (A_i)_{i \in I}$ of operations of a $\perp$-data type $\mathcal{A}$ just as we did for partial correctness in Def. 3.15. The total correctness semantics of a superset of $T_\perp(A)$ is given below, but no A_i occur in the syntax considered. The reason is as follows. By a result from recursive function theory [Sho67], every recursively enumerable relation can be expressed by a first order predicate over the natural numbers. This argument has been used in [Z89, Chapter 6] to prove that every such relation can be expressed by a specification statement. Since it is reasonable to assume that the operations of a data type are recursively enumerable, it follows that these can be expressed by specification statements. Consequently there is no need for additionally introducing A_i into our programming language. In concrete cases, for instance in examples presented in Part II of this monograph, the operations of a data type are given either as specifications or as concrete programs like assignments and loops.

In contrast to the approach followed in Def. 5.18, where a partial correctness semantics is given to *Prog*, in the definition of a total correctness semantics free occurrences of recursion variables inside programs are allowed. Consequently, one needs to introduce recursion variable environments to give meaning to those free occurrences. As remarked after Def. 5.18, the partial correctness semantics could have been given equally well in the way we pursue now; we just opted for the more convenient and simpler alternative. Why opt for the other alternative now? The answer is that, as we have seen in Example 8.14, sequential composition is no longer continuous in the cpo $(R_\perp, \supseteq)$ but merely monotone. Consequently, the meaning of $\mu X.S$ is not necessarily expressed by the lub of the ω-chain of finite approximations $S^i(\textbf{abort})$, but may require even further iteration (see Theorem 8.10). Describing such an additional iteration syntactically by $S^\kappa(\textbf{abort})$ for some transfinite ordinal κ results in general in an infinite syntactic object not belonging to *Prog*. Hence such a definition would fail for systematic reasons. We solve this problem by defining the meaning of $\mu X.S$ as the least fixed point of an associated transformation on the semantic level involving only the meaning of S and an recursion variable environment.

Definition 8.29 By $\Delta_\perp^C = [Rvar \longrightarrow R_\perp^C]$ we refer to the set of *recursion variable environments* on abstraction level C. The total correctness semantics of programs (not necessarily adhering to the syntactic restriction concerning the absence of free occurrences of recursion variables) on that level is given by the function

$$\mathcal{P}[\![.]\!]_\perp^C : Prog^C \longrightarrow (\Delta_\perp^C \longrightarrow R_\perp^C) \ ,$$

which is defined as follows. Let $(\sigma, \tau) \in \Sigma_{\perp}^{C} \times \Sigma_{\perp}^{C}$ and $\rho \in \Delta_{\perp}^{C}$.

$$(\sigma, \tau) \in \mathcal{P}[\![\mathbf{abort}]\!]_{\perp}^{C}(\rho) \stackrel{\text{def}}{=} tt$$

$$(\sigma, \tau) \in \mathcal{P}[\![\mathbf{skip}]\!]_{\perp}^{C}(\rho) \stackrel{\text{def}}{=} \sigma \in \{\perp, \tau\}$$

$$(\sigma, \tau) \in \mathcal{P}[\![x := e]\!]_{\perp}^{C}(\rho) \stackrel{\text{def}}{=} (\sigma : x \mapsto \mathcal{E}[\![e]\!]_{\perp}^{C}\sigma) \in \{\perp, \tau\}$$

$$(\sigma, \tau) \in \mathcal{P}[\![b \rightarrow]\!]_{\perp}^{C}(\rho) \stackrel{\text{def}}{=} T[\![b]\!]_{\perp}^{Var^{C}}\sigma = tt \wedge \sigma = \tau \vee T[\![b]\!]_{\perp}^{Var^{C}}\sigma = \perp_{\mathbb{B}}$$

$$(\sigma, \tau) \in \mathcal{P}[\![\phi \rightsquigarrow \psi]\!]_{\perp}^{C}(\rho) \stackrel{\text{def}}{=} \forall \gamma \in \Gamma^{C} \left((\gamma, \sigma) \in C[\![\phi]\!]_{\perp}^{C} \Rightarrow (\gamma, \tau) \in C[\![\psi]\!]_{\perp}^{C} \right)$$

$$\mathcal{P}[\![X]\!]_{\perp}^{C}(\rho) \stackrel{\text{def}}{=} \rho(X)$$

$$\mathcal{P}[\![S_1 ; S_2]\!]_{\perp}^{C}(\rho) \stackrel{\text{def}}{=} \mathcal{P}[\![S_1]\!]_{\perp}^{C}(\rho) ; \mathcal{P}[\![S_2]\!]_{\perp}^{C}(\rho)$$

$$\mathcal{P}[\![S_1 \ [\!] \ S_2]\!]_{\perp}^{C}(\rho) \stackrel{\text{def}}{=} \mathcal{P}[\![S_1]\!]_{\perp}^{C}(\rho) \cup \mathcal{P}[\![S_2]\!]_{\perp}^{C}(\rho)$$

$$\mathcal{P}[\![\mu X . S_1]\!]_{\perp}^{C}(\rho) \stackrel{\text{def}}{=} \mu_{\lambda r. \mathcal{P}[\![S_1]\!]_{\perp}^{C}(\rho : X \mapsto r)}$$

For programs S not containing free occurrences of recursion variables, we usually omit the recursion variable environment when referring to the semantics, i.e., we write $\mathcal{P}[\![S]\!]_{\perp}^{C}$ instead of $\mathcal{P}[\![S]\!]_{\perp}^{C}(\rho)$. ♣

This definition needs some explanation. Firstly, we observe that $\mathcal{P}[\![.]\!]_{\perp}^{C}$ is well-defined:

Lemma 8.30 For all $S \in Prog^{C}$ and $\rho \in \Delta_{\perp}^{C}$, $\mathcal{P}[\![S]\!]_{\perp}^{C}(\rho)$ is a member of $R_{\perp}^{C}$.

Proof: This is proven by induction on the structure of S. The base cases **abort** and **skip** are immediate since $U_{\perp}^{C}$ and $id_{\perp}^{C} \stackrel{\text{def}}{=} id^{C} \cup K^{C}$ are total, finitary elements of $R_{\perp}^{C}$. The meaning of $x := e$ is also an element of $R_{t,\mathcal{F}}^{C}$. If e is denoting in state σ (that means $\mathcal{E}[\![e]\!]_{\perp}\sigma \neq \perp_{V}$) then $(\sigma : x \mapsto \mathcal{E}[\![e]\!]_{\perp}^{C}\sigma)$ is a proper state, thus τ in the definition above is unique. Otherwise, τ is not restricted at all, i.e., it could be any element of $\Sigma_{\perp}^{C}$. This models our intention that it is observable whether the evaluation of an expression fails to terminate properly.

The meaning assigned to guard $b \rightarrow$ belongs to $R_{\mathcal{F}}^{C}$, i.e., it need not be total. Consider the three cases of $g \stackrel{\text{def}}{=} T[\![b]\!]_{\perp}^{Var^{C}}\sigma$.

$g = \perp_{\mathbb{B}}$: i.e., either σ is already $\perp_{\Sigma^{C}}$ or the evaluation of b in σ does not terminate properly. This is observable and the final state is any element of $\Sigma_{\perp}^{C}$.

$g = f\!f$: i.e., guard b does not hold. Then the computation is blocked at this point, i.e., $\mathcal{P}[\![b \rightarrow]\!]_{\perp}^{C}(\{\sigma\}) = \emptyset$.

$g = tt$: The guard holds in σ, hence $b \rightarrow$ behaves like **skip**.

The semantics of $\phi \rightsquigarrow \psi$ need neither be finitary nor total (see Example 8.31 below). But, at least, $\mathcal{P}[\![\phi \rightsquigarrow \psi]\!]_{\perp}^{C}$ belongs to $R_{\perp}^{C}$. Let $\sigma, \tau \in \Sigma_{\perp}^{C}$ such that $(\sigma, \perp) \in \mathcal{P}[\![\phi \rightsquigarrow \psi]\!]_{\perp}^{C}$. (For instance, $\perp$ is such a σ.) Then also $(\sigma, \tau) \in \mathcal{P}[\![\phi \rightsquigarrow \psi]\!]_{\perp}^{C}$:

$$(\sigma, \perp) \in \mathcal{P}[\![\phi \rightsquigarrow \psi]\!]_{\perp}^{C}$$

$$\Leftrightarrow \forall \gamma \in \Gamma^{C} \left((\gamma, \sigma) \in C[\![\phi]\!]_{\perp}^{C} \Rightarrow (\gamma, \perp) \in C[\![\psi]\!]_{\perp}^{C} \right) \qquad \text{Def. 8.29}$$

$$\Leftrightarrow \forall \gamma \in \Gamma^{C} \left((\gamma, \sigma) \in C[\![\phi]\!]_{\perp}^{C} \Rightarrow \perp \in C[\![\psi]\!]_{\perp} \right) \qquad \text{Def. 8.23}$$

$$\Leftrightarrow \forall \gamma \in \Gamma^{C} \left((\gamma, \sigma) \in C[\![\phi]\!]_{\perp}^{C} \Rightarrow \mathit{ff} \right) \qquad \text{Cor. 8.24}$$

$$\Rightarrow \forall \gamma \in \Gamma^{C} \left((\gamma, \sigma) \in C[\![\phi]\!]_{\perp}^{C} \Rightarrow (\gamma, \tau) \in C[\![\psi]\!]_{\perp}^{C} \right) \qquad \text{pred. calc.}$$

$$\Leftrightarrow (\sigma, \tau) \in \mathcal{P}[\![\phi \rightsquigarrow \psi]\!]_{\perp}^{C} \qquad \text{Def. 8.29}$$

Hence $K^{C} \subseteq \mathcal{P}[\![\phi \rightsquigarrow \psi]\!]_{\perp}^{C}$ and $\mathcal{P}[\![\phi \rightsquigarrow \psi]\!]_{\perp}^{C} ; K^{C} \subseteq \mathcal{P}[\![\phi \rightsquigarrow \psi]\!]_{\perp}^{C}$.

The induction steps for ";" and "$[\!]$" follow from Lemma 8.12. For μ-terms this follows from Theorem 8.10 by monotonicity of the operators involved. $\qquad\Box$

Secondly, we observe that the program constructs in $Prog_{\perp}^{C}$ are not necessarily continuous. This is illustrated in Example 8.31 below, which continues Examples 8.14 and 8.16. However, the program constructs are still monotone, and this suffices to guarantee the existence of least fixed points of the transformations induced by procedure bodies of recursive procedures.

Example 8.31 (cf. Example 8.16) Consider specification statement

$$S \stackrel{\text{det}}{=} (x, y) = (x_0, y_0) \rightsquigarrow \begin{pmatrix} (x_0 = 0 \Rightarrow y_0 = 0 \wedge x = 1) \\ \wedge (x_0 > 0 \Rightarrow (x, y) = (x_0 + 1, y_0 - 1)) \end{pmatrix}$$

in the context $Var^{C} = \{x, y\}$, $\mathbb{V} = \mathbb{N}$. Its semantics is exactly the non-finitary, partial relation r subject to Examples 8.14 and 8.16.

Hence, $\mathcal{P}[\![\mu X.S ; X]\!]_{\perp}^{C} = K^{C} \subsetneqq \{(0, 0), \perp\} \times \Sigma_{\perp}^{C} = \bigcap (\mathcal{P}[\![S^{i} ; \mathbf{abort}]\!]_{\perp}^{C})_{i \in \mathbb{N}}$. $\qquad\heartsuit$

The only source of non-finitary relations in our language is specification statements. As for abstraction relations, finitariness of specification statements cannot be expressed syntactically in our predicate logic since it is a first order logic. Therefore, in our set-up we have to check finitariness semantically.

Lemma 8.32 If S does not contain specification statements with non-finitary meaning and $\rho \in \Delta_{\mathcal{F}} \stackrel{\text{def}}{=} [Rvar \longrightarrow R_{\mathcal{F}}^{C}]$, then $\mathcal{P}[\![S]\!]_{\perp}^{C}(\rho) \in R_{\mathcal{F}}^{C}$ holds.

Proof: The only source of discontinuity is the specification statement. All other basic statements are finitary and finitariness is preserved by the program constructs, because the syntactic program constructs are modelled by the semantic operators ";", "$\cup$", and "μ.", which are continuous on $R_{\mathcal{F}}^C$ by Lemmas 8.19 and 8.18. Thus, by excluding specification statements with non-finitary semantics from $Prog^C$ one gains that $\mathcal{P}[\![S]\!]_{\perp}^C(\rho) \in R_{\mathcal{F}}^C$ for $\rho \in \Delta_{\mathcal{F}}^C$. Furthermore $\mathcal{P}[\![\mu X.S_1(X)]\!]_{\perp}^C = \bigcap(\mathcal{P}[\![S_1^i(\textbf{abort})]\!]_{\perp}^C)_{i \in \mathbb{N}}$ by Lemma 8.7. $\quad\square$

Thirdly, recall from the introduction to this chapter that we expect the semantics of a non-trivial guard to be a partial relation. This is indeed the case for the definition above: for instance, $\mathcal{P}[\![\textbf{false} \to]\!]_{\perp}^C = K^C$. However, $\mathcal{P}[\![S]\!]_{\perp}^C \in R_{t,\mathcal{F}}^C$ is ensured for programs $S \in Prog^C$ satisfying certain syntactic restrictions, e.g., those given in Cor. 8.35 below. The main reason for this is that, although $C[\![b]\!]_{\perp}^C \cup C[\![\neg b]\!]_{\perp}^C$ need not be the whole of Σ^C since b (as well as $\neg b$) might evaluate to $\perp$ in proper states, the definition of the semantics of guards ensures that $\mathcal{P}[\![b \to [\!] \neg b \to]\!]_{\perp}^C$ is total.

A sufficient condition for totality of a specification statement (more precisely, of its total correctness semantics) is presented in the next lemma. Observe that deciding totality of specification statements is just a special case of deciding the set of initial states for which a specification provides at least one final state instead of none. Because specifications are syntactic representatives of relations in our model, and relations in our model can only model guaranteed deadlock and not nondeterministic deadlock, absence of deadlock coincides for specification statements with totality of their total correctness semantics.

Lemma 8.33 On abstraction level C let $\vec{x}$ and $\vec{x}_0$ be lists of the program and logical variables respectively, and let $\phi, \psi \in Pred^C$. Then, for $\vec{y}_0$ a vector of fresh logical variables of the same length as $\vec{x}$ and $\sigma \in \Sigma^C$,

$$\sigma \models_{\Theta_{\perp}} \exists \vec{y}_0 \left(\forall \vec{x}_0 \left(\phi \Rightarrow \psi[\vec{y}_0/\vec{x}] \right) \right)$$

ensures that $\mathcal{P}[\![\phi \rightsquigarrow \psi]\!]_{\perp}^C$ does not deadlock in initial state σ.

This implies that $\mathcal{P}[\![\phi \rightsquigarrow \psi]\!]_{\perp}$ is total if it does not deadlock for any $\sigma \in \Sigma^C$, which follows from validity of (8.8):

$$\exists \vec{y}_0 \left(\forall \vec{x}_0 \left(\phi \Rightarrow \psi[\vec{y}_0/\vec{x}] \right) \right) \tag{8.8}$$

Proof: We prove that if (8.8) holds in proper state σ then $\mathcal{P}[\![\phi \rightsquigarrow \psi]\!]_{\perp}^C(\{\sigma\}) \neq \emptyset$, i.e., $\phi \rightsquigarrow \psi$ does not deadlock for initial state σ.

$$\sigma \models_{\Theta_{\perp}} \exists \vec{y}_0 \left(\forall \vec{x}_0 \left(\phi \Rightarrow \psi[\vec{y}_0/\vec{x}] \right) \right)$$

$\Leftrightarrow$ (def. of $\models_{\mathfrak{S}_\perp}$)

$$\sigma \in C[\![\exists \vec{y_0}\left(\forall \vec{x_0}\left(\phi \Rightarrow \psi[\vec{y_0}/\vec{x}]\right)\right)]\!]_\perp^C$$

$\Rightarrow$ (Def. 8.23, Lemmas 5.12 and 5.13)

$$\exists \tau \in \Sigma^C\left(\forall \gamma \in \Gamma^C\left((\gamma,\sigma) \in C[\![\phi]\!]_\perp^C \Rightarrow (\gamma,\tau) \in C[\![\psi]\!]_\perp^C\right)\right)$$

$\Rightarrow$ (predicate logic)

$$\exists \tau \in \Sigma_\perp^C\left(\forall \gamma \in \Gamma^C\left((\gamma,\sigma) \in C[\![\phi]\!]_\perp^C \Rightarrow (\gamma,\tau) \in C[\![\psi]\!]_\perp^C\right)\right) \qquad \Box$$

Example 8.34 Recall specification statement $x = x_0^2 \rightsquigarrow x = x_0$, i.e., (5.7) treated in Exercise 5.16. It fails on condition (8.8):

$$\exists v\left(\forall x_0\left(x = x_0^2 \Rightarrow (x = x_0)[^v/_x]\right)\right) \qquad (8.8)$$

$\Rightarrow \exists v\left(\forall x_0\left(1 = x_0^2 \Rightarrow v = x_0\right)\right) \qquad$ instance $x = 1$

$\Rightarrow \exists v\left(\begin{matrix}(1 = (-1)^2 \Rightarrow v = -1) \\ \wedge(1 = 1^2 \Rightarrow v = 1)\end{matrix}\right) \qquad$ instances $x_0 \in \{-1,1\}$

$\Rightarrow \exists v(v = -1 \wedge v = 1) \qquad$ pred. calc.

$\Leftrightarrow$ false

However, condition (8.8) is sufficient but not necessary. It could still be the case that $x = x_0^2 \rightsquigarrow x = x_0$ is implementable. Therefore, we calculate its total correctness semantics. Let $\sigma, \tau \in \Sigma_\perp$.

$(\sigma,\tau) \in \mathcal{P}[\![x = x_0^2 \rightsquigarrow x = x_0]\!]_\perp$

$\Leftrightarrow \forall \gamma \in \Gamma\left((\gamma,\sigma) \in C[\![x = x_0^2]\!]_\perp \Rightarrow (\gamma,\tau) \in C[\![x = x_0]\!]_\perp\right) \qquad$ Def. 8.29

$\Leftrightarrow \forall v \in \mathbb{Z}\left(\begin{matrix}((\pitchfork:x_0 \mapsto v),\sigma) \in C[\![x = x_0^2]\!]_\perp \\ \Rightarrow ((\pitchfork:x_0 \mapsto v),\tau) \in C[\![x = x_0]\!]_\perp\end{matrix}\right) \qquad Lvar = \{x_0\}$

$\Leftrightarrow \forall v \in \mathbb{Z}\left(\sigma(x) = v^2 \Rightarrow \tau(x) = v\right) \qquad$ Def. 8.23

$\Leftrightarrow \sigma(x) = \tau(x) = 0 \vee \neg\exists v \in \mathbb{Z}\left(\sigma(x) = v^2\right) \vee \sigma = \perp \qquad$ Exercise 8.12

Thus, $x = x_0^2 \rightsquigarrow x = x_0$ does indeed denote a partial relation, because there are no final states associated with initial states in which x is a square number. $\heartsuit$

Corollary 8.35 $\mathcal{P}[\![S]\!]_\perp^C \in R_{r,\mathcal{F}}^C$ holds for $S \in Prog^C$ if S does not contain non-finitary specification statements or free recursion variables and satisfies the following conditions:

- Guards occur only in groups whose members guard the alternatives of the constituent choice operators in one choice statement (e.g., $b_1 \rightarrow S_1 \,[\!]\, b_2 \rightarrow$

$S_2 \, [] \, b_3 \to S_3)$ such that the disjunction $(b_1 \lor b_2 \lor b_3)$ over this group yields true.

- Partial specification statements $\phi \rightsquigarrow \psi$ only occur

  - either suitably guarded such that their partiality does not matter
  - or in place of guards themselves.

  As a condition describing the domain of guaranteed freedom of deadlock of such a specification we use $\exists \vec{y_0} \left(\forall \vec{x_0} \left(\phi \Rightarrow \psi[\vec{y_0}/\vec{x}] \right) \right)$. ♠

For structured and safety-critical programs such a syntactic restriction is reasonable. Notice that in certain situations such a syntactic restriction represents an overkill. Considering for instance the choice statement above, it might very well be the case that $b_1 \lor b_2 \lor b_3$ holds prior to executing that statement, although $b_1 \lor b_2 \lor b_3 \not\Leftrightarrow$ true. If one wants to take such considerations into account one should use a theory for proving absence of deadlock, as presented, e.g., in [AO91, MP95].

In the next section we need the following characterization of a specification statement's domain of weak termination.

Lemma 8.36 $wt(\phi \rightsquigarrow \psi)$ is expressed by predicate $\exists \vec{x_0}(\phi)$.

Proof:

$$
\begin{aligned}
&wt(\phi \rightsquigarrow \psi) \\
&= \left\{ \sigma \in \Sigma_\perp^C \;\middle|\; (\sigma, \perp) \notin \mathcal{P}[\![\phi \rightsquigarrow \psi]\!]_\perp^C \right\} && \text{Def. 8.26} \\
&= \left\{ \sigma \in \Sigma_\perp^C \;\middle|\; \neg \forall \gamma \left((\gamma, \sigma) \in C[\![\phi]\!]_\perp^C \Rightarrow (\gamma, \perp) \in C[\![\psi]\!]_\perp^C \right) \right\} && \text{Def. 8.29} \\
&= \left\{ \sigma \in \Sigma_\perp^C \;\middle|\; \exists \gamma \left((\gamma, \sigma) \in C[\![\phi]\!]_\perp^C \right) \right\} && \text{Def. 8.23} \\
&= C[\![\exists \vec{x_0}(\phi)]\!]_\perp^{Var^C} && \text{Def. 8.23}
\end{aligned}
$$
□

8.2.4 Relational Terms and Correctness Formulae

The semantics of relational terms and correctness formulae for total correctness is similar to that for partial correctness, the difference being that now we work with total correctness semantics of assertions, abstraction relations, and programs. All this works because the semantics of relational terms and correctness formulae is defined modulo the semantics of programs, abstraction relations, and assertions.

Convention We do not define an extra total correctness semantics of relational terms and correctness formulae, but refer to the definitions from Section 5.4 instead. For applications of those definitions in this chapter, all semantic brackets $[\![.]\!]$ have to be replaced by $[\![.]\!]_\perp$, of course.

Using this convention we can apply Lemmas 5.24–5.26 in this chapter. These lemmas translate directly to the total correctness semantics because their semantic versions, Lemmas 3.11–3.13, hold for arbitrary relations.

For instance, we can prove that the total correctness semantics of a Hoare triple $\{\phi\} S \{\text{true}\}$ is *tt* iff S terminates weakly whenever the precondition ϕ holds.

Lemma 8.37 Let $S \in Prog^A$ and let $\vec{x}_0$ be the list of free logical variables of $\phi \in Pred^A$. Then $\mathcal{F}[\![\{\phi\} S \{\text{true}\}]\!]_\perp$ and $C[\![\exists \vec{x}_0 (\phi)]\!]_\perp \subseteq wt(S)$ are equivalent.

Proof:

$\qquad \mathcal{F}[\![\{\phi\} S \{\text{true}\}]\!]_\perp$

$\Leftrightarrow \mathcal{F}[\![\phi; S \subseteq \text{true}]\!]_\perp$ $\qquad\qquad\qquad\qquad$ Def. 5.27 on p. 116

$\Leftrightarrow \mathcal{F}[\![S \subseteq \phi \leadsto \text{true}]\!]_\perp$ $\qquad\qquad\qquad$ Cor. 5.29 on p. 117

$\Leftrightarrow \mathcal{R}[\![S]\!]_\perp \subseteq \mathcal{R}[\![\phi \leadsto \text{true}]\!]_\perp$ $\qquad\qquad$ Def. 5.27 on p. 115

$\Leftrightarrow \mathcal{P}[\![S]\!]_\perp^A \subseteq \mathcal{P}[\![\phi \leadsto \text{true}]\!]_\perp^A$ $\qquad\qquad$ Def. 5.22 on p. 113

$\Leftrightarrow \mathcal{P}[\![S]\!]_\perp^A \subseteq U^A \cup \overline{wt(\phi \leadsto \text{true})} \times \{\perp\}$ $\quad$ Defs 8.29 and 8.26

$\Leftrightarrow wt(S) \supseteq C[\![\exists \vec{x}_0 (\phi)]\!]_\perp^{Var^A}$ $\qquad\qquad\qquad$ Lemma 8.36, set theory $\qquad \square$

8.2.5 Partial vs. Total Correctness

There is a fundamental connection between partial correctness and termination on the one hand and total correctness on the other. As a rule of thumb

$$\text{partial correctness} + \text{termination} = \text{total correctness} \qquad (8.9)$$

However, due to the refined semantics given to assertions, this does not hold for some pathological examples, simply because, e.g., we did not care to give a meaning to terms like $\forall x \left(\frac{1}{x} = 1 \Rightarrow x = 1\right)$. The main result of this section is the separation theorem, which formalizes (8.9).

In this section we omit superscripts like ^{A} since we do not talk about different levels.

Theorem 8.38 (Separation)

Let $S \in Prog$ and $\phi, \psi \in Pred$ such that $C[\![.]\!]$ and $C[\![.]\!]_\perp$ coincide for ϕ, ψ, and all predicates occurring as guards or in specification statements within S. Furthermore we assume that each expression e on the RHS of an assignment in S evaluates independently of the semantics, i.e., $\mathcal{E}[\![e]\!] = \mathcal{E}[\![e]\!]_\perp$. Under these assumptions we may divide the task of proving total correctness into two subtasks, namely, proving termination and partial correctness:

$$\mathcal{F}[\![\{\phi\}\,S\,\{\psi\}]\!]_\perp \Leftrightarrow \mathcal{F}[\![\{\phi\}\,S\,\{\psi\}]\!] \wedge \mathcal{F}[\![\{\phi\}\,S\,\{\text{true}\}]\!]_\perp$$

The proof requires some more prerequisites, which we shall provide next.

Definition 8.39 The *nontermination part* $nt_\rho(S)$ of a program $S \in Prog$ in a recursion variable environment $\rho \in \Delta_\perp$ is defined by

$$nt_\rho(S) \stackrel{\text{def}}{=} \{\, (\sigma, \tau) \in \Sigma_\perp^2 \mid (\sigma, \perp) \in \mathcal{P}[\![S]\!]_\perp(\rho) \,\} \qquad \clubsuit$$

Lemma 8.40 $nt_\rho(S)$ has the following easily verified properties:

(i) $nt_\rho(.)$ is a monotone function; if S_1 refines S_2 in the total correctness interpretation, then S_1 terminates at least as much as S_2, i.e., $nt_\rho(S_1) \subseteq nt_\rho(S_2)$.

(ii) $nt_\rho(S) = \overline{wt_\rho(S)} \times \Sigma_\perp$ (for a straightforward adaptation of the *wt* function to programs with free occurrences of recursion variables.)

(iii) $nt_\rho(S) = \bigcup \{\, r \in R_\perp \mid r \subseteq \mathcal{P}[\![S]\!]_\perp(\rho) \wedge r; K = r \,\}$

(iv) $nt_\rho(S)\,;r = nt_\rho(S)$, for $r \in R_\perp$

(v) The nontermination part of particular programs is expressed as follows.

$$nt_\rho(\textbf{abort}) = U_\perp \tag{8.10}$$

$$nt_\rho(\textbf{skip}) = K \tag{8.11}$$

$$nt_\rho(x := e) = \{\, \sigma \in \Sigma_\perp \mid \mathcal{E}[\![e]\!]_\perp \sigma = \perp \,\} \times \Sigma_\perp \tag{8.12}$$

$$nt_\rho(b \to) = \{\, \sigma \in \Sigma_\perp \mid \mathcal{T}[\![b]\!]_\perp \sigma = \perp \,\} \times \Sigma_\perp \tag{8.13}$$

$$nt_\rho(\phi \rightsquigarrow \psi) = \overline{C[\![\exists \vec{x_0}\,(\phi)]\!]_\perp} \times \Sigma_\perp \tag{8.14}$$

$$nt_\rho(X) = \{\, \sigma \mid (\sigma, \perp) \in \rho(X) \,\} \times \Sigma_\perp \tag{8.15}$$

$$nt_\rho(S_1 \,[\!]\, S_2) = nt_\rho(S_1) \cup nt_\rho(S_2) \tag{8.16}$$

$$nt_\rho(S_1\,;S_2) = nt_\rho(S_1) \cup \mathcal{P}[\![S_1]\!]_\perp(\rho)\,;nt_\rho(S_2) \tag{8.17}$$

$$= \mathcal{P}[\![S_1]\!]_\perp(\rho)\,;nt_\rho(S_2)$$

$$nt_\rho(\mu X.T) = \mu_{\lambda r.nt_{(\rho:X \mapsto r)}(T)} \tag{8.18}$$

Proof: We only prove the most interesting case, namely recursion.

$$nt_\rho(\mu X.T)$$

$$= \{\, (\sigma, \tau) \in \Sigma_\perp^2 \mid (\sigma, \perp) \in \mathcal{P}[\![\mu X.T]\!]_\perp(\rho) \,\} \qquad \text{Def. 8.39}$$

$$= \left\{ (\sigma,\tau) \in \Sigma_\perp^2 \ \middle|\ (\sigma,\perp) \in \mu_{\lambda r. \mathcal{P}[\![T]\!]_\perp (\rho: X \mapsto r)} \right\} \qquad \text{Def. 8.29}$$

$$= \left\{ (\sigma,\tau) \in \Sigma_\perp^2 \ \middle|\ (\sigma,\perp) \in \bigcap_{i<\kappa} (f^i(U_\perp)) \right\} \qquad f(r) \stackrel{\text{def}}{=} \mathcal{P}[\![T]\!]_\perp (\rho_X^r),$$
$$\text{Th. 8.10}$$

$$= \bigcap_{i<\kappa} \left\{ (\sigma,\tau) \in \Sigma_\perp^2 \ \middle|\ (\sigma,\perp) \in f^i(U_\perp) \right\}$$

$$= \mu_{\lambda r. \{ (\sigma,\tau) \mid (\sigma,\perp) \in f(r) \}} \qquad\qquad\qquad \text{Th. 8.10}$$

$$= \mu_{\lambda r. nt_{(\rho: X \mapsto r)}(T)} \qquad\qquad\qquad\qquad \text{Def. 8.39} \qquad\qquad \square$$

Next we turn to the partial correctness semantics of programs. A minor problem results from our choice, in Def. 5.18, of a simpler definition of $\mathcal{P}[\![\mu X.T]\!]$ that circumvented recursion variable environments. However, as noted in the subsequent remark on page 109, we could have given an equivalent definition closer to the one for total correctness such that, for instance, within the cpo $(\mathfrak{P}(\Sigma^2), \subseteq)$:

$$\mathcal{P}[\![\mu X.T]\!](\rho) = \mu_{\lambda r \subseteq \Sigma^2. \mathcal{P}[\![T]\!]((\rho: X \mapsto r))}$$

and $\mathcal{P}[\![X]\!](\rho) = \rho(X)$ for $\rho \in \Delta = [Rvar \longrightarrow \mathfrak{P}(\Sigma^2)]$ a partial correctness recursion variable environment. To relate total to partial correctness recursion variable environments we define the function $._{\text{pc}} : \Delta_\perp \longrightarrow \Delta$ by $\rho_{\text{pc}} \stackrel{\text{def}}{=} \lambda X. (\rho(X) \setminus nt_\rho(X))$, for $\rho \in \Delta_\perp$.

Proof of the separation theorem: By induction on the structure of $S \in Prog$ we prove (8.19):

$$\mathcal{P}[\![S]\!]_\perp (\rho) = \mathcal{P}[\![S]\!](\rho_{\text{pc}}) \cup nt_\rho(S) \qquad\qquad\qquad (8.19)$$

Once this is proven, we conclude as follows. For assertions ϕ and ψ, and for program S without free occurrences of recursion variables:

$$\mathcal{F}[\![\{\phi\} S \{\psi\}]\!]_\perp$$
$$\Leftrightarrow C[\![\phi]\!]_\perp ; \mathcal{P}[\![S]\!]_\perp \subseteq C[\![\psi]\!]_\perp \qquad\qquad\qquad \text{Def. 5.27}$$
$$\Leftrightarrow C[\![\phi]\!]_\perp ; (\mathcal{P}[\![S]\!] \cup nt_{\text{fh}}(S)) \subseteq C[\![\psi]\!]_\perp \qquad\qquad (8.19)$$
$$\Leftrightarrow (C[\![\phi]\!]_\perp ; \mathcal{P}[\![S]\!] \subseteq C[\![\psi]\!]_\perp) \wedge (C[\![\phi]\!]_\perp ; nt_{\text{fh}}(S) \subseteq C[\![\psi]\!]_\perp) \qquad \text{rel. calc.}$$

We proceed with the two conjuncts separately, starting with the LHS.

$$C[\![\phi]\!]_\perp ; \mathcal{P}[\![S]\!] \subseteq C[\![\psi]\!]_\perp$$
$$\Leftrightarrow C[\![\phi]\!] ; \mathcal{P}[\![S]\!] \subseteq C[\![\psi]\!] \qquad\qquad\qquad \text{assumption for } \phi \text{ and } \psi$$
$$\Leftrightarrow \mathcal{F}[\![\{\phi\} S \{\psi\}]\!] \qquad\qquad\qquad\qquad \text{Def. 5.27}$$

Now for the RHS:

$$C[\![\phi]\!]_\perp \; ; nt_{\text{th}}(S) \subseteq C[\![\psi]\!]_\perp$$
$$\Leftrightarrow C[\![\phi]\!]_\perp \; ; nt_{\text{th}}(S) = \emptyset \qquad\qquad (\sigma, \perp) \notin C[\![\psi]\!]_\perp$$
$$\Leftrightarrow C[\![\phi]\!]_\perp \; ; \mathcal{P}[\![S]\!]_\perp \subseteq C[\![\text{true}]\!]_\perp \qquad \text{Def. 8.39, } C[\![\text{true}]\!]_\perp = \Gamma \times \Sigma$$
$$\Leftrightarrow \mathcal{F}[\![\{\phi\}\, S\, \{\text{true}\}]\!]_\perp \qquad\qquad \text{Def. 5.27}$$

Consequently, only (8.19) remains to prove. It is immediate for the base cases **abort** and **skip**:

$$\mathcal{P}[\![\mathbf{abort}]\!]_\perp(\rho) = U_\perp = \emptyset \cup \Sigma_\perp \times \Sigma_\perp = \mathcal{P}[\![\mathbf{abort}]\!](\rho_{\text{pc}}) \cup nt_\rho(\mathbf{abort})$$

$$\mathcal{P}[\![\mathbf{skip}]\!]_\perp(\rho) = id_\Sigma \cup K = \mathcal{P}[\![\mathbf{skip}]\!](\rho_{\text{pc}}) \cup nt_\rho(\mathbf{skip})$$

For guards, assignments, and specification statements, the proof of (8.19) depends on the assumptions made above, but is still easy.

$$\mathcal{P}[\![b \to]\!]_\perp(\rho) = id_{C[\![b]\!]} \cup K = \mathcal{P}[\![b \to]\!](\rho_{\text{pc}}) \cup nt_\rho(b \to)$$

(We need the assumption for predicate b to justify both equalities above.)

$$\mathcal{P}[\![x := e]\!]_\perp(\rho)$$
$$= \{ (\sigma, \tau) \in \Sigma_\perp^2 \mid (\sigma : x \mapsto \mathcal{E}[\![e]\!]_\perp \sigma) \in \{\perp, \tau\} \} \qquad \text{Def. 8.29}$$
$$= \{ (\sigma, \tau) \in \Sigma_\perp^2 \mid \tau = (\sigma : x \mapsto \mathcal{E}[\![e]\!]\sigma) \} \cup K \qquad \text{assumption}$$
$$= \mathcal{P}[\![x := e]\!](\rho_{\text{pc}}) \cup nt_\rho(x := e) \qquad \text{Def. 5.18, ass.}$$

$$\mathcal{P}[\![\phi \rightsquigarrow \psi]\!]_\perp(\rho)$$
$$= \{ (\sigma, \tau) \in \Sigma_\perp^2 \mid \forall \gamma((\gamma, \sigma) \in C[\![\phi]\!]_\perp \Rightarrow (\gamma, \tau) \in C[\![\psi]\!]_\perp) \} \qquad \text{Def. 8.29}$$
$$= \{ (\sigma, \tau) \in \Sigma_\perp^2 \mid \forall \gamma((\gamma, \sigma) \in C[\![\phi]\!] \Rightarrow (\gamma, \tau) \in C[\![\psi]\!]) \} \qquad \text{ass.}$$
$$= \left(\begin{array}{l} \{ (\sigma, \tau) \in \Sigma^2 \mid \forall \gamma((\gamma, \sigma) \in C[\![\phi]\!] \Rightarrow (\gamma, \tau) \in C[\![\psi]\!]) \} \\ \cup \{ (\sigma, \tau) \in \Sigma_\perp^2 \mid \forall \gamma((\gamma, \sigma) \notin C[\![\phi]\!]) \} \end{array} \right) \qquad \text{pred. calc.}$$
$$= \mathcal{P}[\![\phi \rightsquigarrow \psi]\!](\rho_{\text{pc}}) \cup nt_\rho(\phi \rightsquigarrow \psi) \qquad \text{Def. 5.18}$$

By our definition of ρ_{pc} we can also prove (8.19) for program X:

$$\mathcal{P}[\![X]\!]_\perp(\rho) = \rho(X) = \rho_{\text{pc}}(X) \cup nt_\rho(X) = \mathcal{P}[\![X]\!](\rho_{\text{pc}}) \cup nt_\rho(X)$$

Next come the induction steps, beginning with the choice construct:

$$\mathcal{P}[\![S_1 \,[\!]\, S_2]\!]_\perp(\rho)$$
$$= \mathcal{P}[\![S_1]\!]_\perp(\rho) \cup \mathcal{P}[\![S_2]\!]_\perp(\rho) \qquad \text{Def. 8.29}$$
$$= \mathcal{P}[\![S_1]\!](\rho_{\text{pc}}) \cup nt_\rho(S_1) \cup \mathcal{P}[\![S_2]\!](\rho_{\text{pc}}) \cup nt_\rho(S_2) \qquad \text{ind. hyp.}$$

$$= \mathcal{P}[\![S_1 \,[\!]\, S_2]\!](\rho_{\text{pc}}) \cup nt_\rho(S_1 \,[\!]\, S_2) \qquad\qquad \text{Def. 5.18, (8.16)}$$

As to sequential composition:

$$
\begin{aligned}
&\mathcal{P}[\![S_1 \,;S_2]\!]_\perp(\rho)\\
&= \mathcal{P}[\![S_1]\!]_\perp(\rho)\,;\mathcal{P}[\![S_2]\!]_\perp(\rho) &&\text{Def. 8.29}\\
&= (\mathcal{P}[\![S_1]\!](\rho_{\text{pc}}) \cup nt_\rho(S_1))\,;(\mathcal{P}[\![S_2]\!](\rho_{\text{pc}}) \cup nt_\rho(S_2)) &&\text{ind. hyp.}\\
&= \left(\begin{array}{l}\mathcal{P}[\![S_1]\!](\rho_{\text{pc}})\,;\mathcal{P}[\![S_2]\!](\rho_{\text{pc}}) \cup nt_\rho(S_1)\,;\mathcal{P}[\![S_2]\!](\rho_{\text{pc}})\\ \cup\,\mathcal{P}[\![S_1]\!](\rho_{\text{pc}})\,;nt_\rho(S_2) \cup nt_\rho(S_1)\,;nt_\rho(S_2)\end{array}\right) &&\text{Lemma 3.7.(iii)}\\
&= \mathcal{P}[\![S_1 \,;S_2]\!](\rho_{\text{pc}}) \cup nt_\rho(S_1)\,;\mathcal{P}[\![S_2]\!](\rho_{\text{pc}}) &&\text{Def. 5.18}\\
&\quad \cup\, \mathcal{P}[\![S_1]\!](\rho_{\text{pc}})\,;nt_\rho(S_2) \cup nt_\rho(S_1) &&\text{Lemma 8.40.(iv)}\\
&= \mathcal{P}[\![S_1 \,;S_2]\!](\rho_{\text{pc}}) \cup \mathcal{P}[\![S_1]\!](\rho_{\text{pc}})\,;nt_\rho(S_2) \cup nt_\rho(S_1) &&\text{Lemma 8.40.(iv)}\\
&= \mathcal{P}[\![S_1 \,;S_2]\!](\rho_{\text{pc}}) \cup nt_\rho(S_1 \,;S_2) &&\text{(8.17)}
\end{aligned}
$$

Before embarking on the induction step for recursion, we collect a few prerequisites. To simplify the exposition, let us agree on the following abbreviations:

$$f \stackrel{\text{def}}{=} \lambda r.\mathcal{P}[\![T]\!]_\perp((\rho:X \mapsto r)) \qquad\qquad f^{(i)} \stackrel{\text{def}}{=} f^i(U_\perp)$$

$$f_{\text{pc}} \stackrel{\text{def}}{=} \lambda r.\mathcal{P}[\![T]\!](\rho:X \mapsto r)_{\text{pc}} \qquad\qquad f_{\text{pc}}^{(i)} \stackrel{\text{def}}{=} f_{\text{pc}}^i(U_\perp)$$

$$g \stackrel{\text{def}}{=} \lambda r.nt_{(\rho:X \mapsto r)}(T) \qquad\qquad g^{(i)} \stackrel{\text{def}}{=} g^i(U_\perp)$$

Thus, $(f_{\text{pc}}^{(i)})_{i<\kappa}$ denotes the chain (in $(\mathfrak{P}(\Sigma^2), \subseteq)$) of approximations of the partial correctness semantics of $\mu X.T$, and $(g^{(i)})_{i<\kappa}$ denotes the chain (in $(R_\perp, \supseteq)$) of approximations of $nt_\rho(\mu X.T)$. A first key observation for the final induction step is that

$$f^{(\kappa)} = f_{\text{pc}}^{(\kappa)} \cup g^{(\kappa)} \qquad\qquad (8.20)$$

holds for all ordinals κ. We prove this next using transfinite induction. The base case for $\kappa = 0$ is easy:

$$f^{(0)} = f^0(U_\perp) = U_\perp = \emptyset \cup U_\perp = f_{\text{pc}}^0(U_\perp) \cup g^0(U_\perp) = f_{\text{pc}}^{(0)} \cup g^{(0)}$$

Next assume that (8.20) holds for some ordinal κ. Then we have to show that it also holds for $\kappa + 1$.

$$
\begin{aligned}
&f^{(\kappa+1)}\\
&= f(f^{(\kappa)}) &&\text{Def. 8.9}\\
&= \mathcal{P}[\![T]\!]_\perp(\rho:X \mapsto f^{(\kappa)}) &&\text{def. of } f\\
&= \mathcal{P}[\![T]\!](\rho:X \mapsto f^{(\kappa)})_{\text{pc}} \cup nt_{(\rho:X \mapsto f^{(\kappa)})}(T) &&\text{ind. hyp. (8.19)}
\end{aligned}
$$

$$= \mathcal{P}[\![T]\!](\rho_{pc} : X \mapsto f_{pc}^{(\kappa)} \cup g^{(\kappa)}) \cup nt_{(\rho:X\mapsto f_{pc}^{(\kappa)}\cup g^{(\kappa)})}(T) \quad \text{ind. hyp. (8.20)}$$

$$= \mathcal{P}[\![T]\!](\rho_{pc} : X \mapsto f_{pc}^{(\kappa)}) \cup nt_{(\rho:X\mapsto g^{(\kappa)})}(T) \quad \text{def. of } \cdot_{pc} \text{ and } nt_{\rho}(.)$$

$$= f_{pc}(f_{pc}^{(\kappa)}) \cup g(g^{(\kappa)}) \quad \text{def. of } f_{pc} \text{ and } g$$

$$= f_{pc}^{(\kappa+1)} \cup g^{(\kappa+1)} \quad \text{Def. 8.9}$$

Next let κ be a limit ordinal and assume (8.20) for all $i < \kappa$. We prove (8.20) for κ.

$$f^{(\kappa)}$$

$$= \bigcap_{i<\kappa} f^{(i)} \qquad \text{Def. 8.9}$$

$$= \bigcap_{i<\kappa} (f_{pc}^{(i)} \cup g^{(i)}) \qquad \text{ind. hyp. (8.20)}$$

$$= \bigcup_{i<\kappa} f_{pc}^{(i)} \cup \bigcap_{i<\kappa} g^{(i)} \qquad \text{Lemma 8.41 below}$$

$$= f_{pc}^{(\kappa)} \cup g^{(\kappa)} \qquad \text{Def. 8.9}$$

This proves (8.20). We finally turn to the induction step for recursion.

$$\mathcal{P}[\![\mu X.T]\!]_{\perp}(\rho)$$

$$= \mu_{\lambda r.\mathcal{P}[\![T]\!]_{\perp}(\rho:X\mapsto r)} \qquad \text{Def. 8.29}$$

$$= \bigcap_{i<\kappa} f^{(i)} \qquad \text{Th. 8.10}$$

$$= \bigcap_{i<\kappa} (f_{pc}^{(i)} \cup g^{(i)}) \qquad \text{(8.20)}$$

$$= \bigcup_{i<\kappa} (f_{pc}^{(i)}) \cup \bigcap_{i<\kappa} (g^{(i)}) \qquad \text{Lemma 8.41 below}$$

$$= \mu_{\lambda r.\mathcal{P}[\![T]\!](\rho:X\mapsto r)_{pc}} \cup \mu_{\lambda r.nt_{(\rho:X\mapsto r)}(T)} \qquad \text{Th. 8.10}$$

$$= \mu_{\lambda r \subseteq \Sigma^2.\mathcal{P}[\![T]\!](\rho_{pc}:X\mapsto r)} \cup \mu_{\lambda r.nt_{(\rho:X\mapsto r)}(T)} \qquad \text{def. of } \cdot_{pc}$$

$$= \mathcal{P}[\![\mu X.T]\!](\rho_{pc}) \cup nt_{\rho}(\mu X.T) \qquad \text{Def. 5.18, (8.18)} \qquad \Box$$

Lemma 8.41 Let $R, R' \subseteq \mathfrak{P}(D)$ for some set D such that $(R, \supseteq)$ and $(R', \subseteq)$ are cpo's with lub's $\bigcap$ and $\bigcup$, respectively. Let κ be an ordinal, let $(a_i)_{i<\kappa}$ be a chain in $(R', \subseteq)$ and let $(b_i)_{i<\kappa}$ be a chain in $(R, \supseteq)$ such that $(a_i \cup b_i)_{i<\kappa}$ is a chain in $(R, \supseteq)$. Then $\bigcap_{i<\kappa}(a_i \cup b_i) = \bigcup_{i<\kappa} a_i \cup \bigcap_{i<\kappa} b_i$ holds.

Proof: By mutual inclusion.

"$\subseteq$": Let $x \in \bigcap_{i<\kappa}(a_i \cup b_i)$. Then $\forall i < \kappa(x \in a_i \cup b_i)$. In case $x \notin b_i$ for some $i < \kappa$, then $x \in a_i$. Consequently, in that case one has that $x \in \bigcup_{i<\kappa} a_i$. Otherwise $\forall i < \kappa (x \in b_i)$, which implies $x \in \bigcap_{i<\kappa} b_i$. Thus, in both cases, $x \in \bigcup_{i<\kappa} a_i \cup \bigcap_{i<\kappa} b_i$.

"$\supseteq$": Let $x \in \bigcup_{i<\kappa} a_i \cup \bigcap_{i<\kappa} b_i$. Case $x \in \bigcap_{i<\kappa} b_i$ is immediate. Otherwise $x \in \bigcup_{i<\kappa} a_i$, that is, $x \in a_j$ for some $j < \kappa$. By the chain property of $(a_i)_{i<\kappa}$ it follows that $\forall j \leq i < \kappa (x \in a_i)$. On the other hand, since $(a_i \cup b_i)_{i<\kappa}$ is a chain w.r.t. $\supseteq$, also $\forall i < j (x \in a_i \cup b_i)$. Altogether, $x \in \bigcap_{i<\kappa} (a_i \cup b_i)$ holds. $\square$

As explained in Section 3.5, the traditional meaning of $\{\phi\} S \{\psi\}$ includes absence of deadlock for all computations of S starting in a state satisfying ϕ [Apt81]. That is, one has the following stronger requirement:

$$\forall \gamma, \sigma \left((\gamma, \sigma) \in C[\![\phi]\!]_\perp \Rightarrow \begin{pmatrix} \exists \tau ((\sigma, \tau) \in \mathcal{P}[\![S]\!]_\perp) \\ \wedge \forall \tau ((\sigma, \tau) \in \mathcal{P}[\![S]\!]_\perp \Rightarrow (\gamma, \tau) \in C[\![\psi]\!]_\perp) \end{pmatrix} \right)$$

The difference shows up only for some S violating the restrictions stated in Cor. 8.35; otherwise there is no difference from our total correctness interpretation of $\{\phi\} S \{\psi\}$, and this covers the cases considered in [Apt81].

8.3 Historical Background

The least fixed point theory of recursion originates in work by Bekić, Park, de Bakker, Mazurkiewicz, and Scott, cited in Section 3.6. Further early references include de Bakker's [dB71, dB80], Scott's [Sco70, Sco72a, Sco72b, Sco76, Sco77], and Strachey's [Str66, SW74]. An authoritative reference to the development of fixed point theory is Chapter 12, "Semantic Domains", by Gunther and Scott in [vL90].

In the context of binary relations, total correctness was syntactically characterized for the first time in Hitchcock and Park's [HP72], and semantically in Egli's [Egl75] and Smyth's [Smy78]. In the latter article, the so-called Smyth cpo is defined; this cpo constitutes "half" of the so-called Egli–Milner cpo, attributed independently to Egli and by Plotkin in [Plo76] to unpublished work of Milner's.

The first reference to proof rules for total correctness of while-programs within the framework of Hoare logic is [MP74] by Manna and Pnueli.

Exercises

8.1   Let A be a countably infinite set and define

$$F \stackrel{\text{def}}{=} \{ r \subseteq A^2 \mid \forall a \in A (r(a) \text{ is finite or } A) \} \ .$$

Prove (or disprove) the following claims:

    (a) $(F, \supseteq)$ is a cpo with least upper bound function $\bigcap$.
    (b) F is closed under ";" and "$\cup$".
    (c) Operators ";" and "$\cup$" on F are continuous in both arguments.

8.2 Let A be a set and let $(B, \sqsubseteq)$ be a cpo. Prove that $[A \longrightarrow B]$ ordered by the pointwise extension of $\sqsubseteq$ is a cpo.

8.3 Let $(A, \leq)$ be a poset and let $(B, \sqsubseteq)$ be a cpo. Prove that the monotone functions $[A \xrightarrow{\text{mon}} B]$ from $(A, \leq)$ to $(B, \sqsubseteq)$ ordered by the pointwise extension of $\sqsubseteq$ form a cpo.

8.4 (Finitary Egli–Milner order) Let A be a countably infinite set containing $\perp$ and define

$$\mathfrak{P}_{\text{E-M}}(A) \stackrel{\text{def}}{=} \{ s \in \mathfrak{P}(A) \setminus \{\emptyset\} \mid |s| < \omega \vee \perp \in s \} \ ,$$

and, for $s, t \in \mathfrak{P}_{\text{F-M}}(A)$,

$$s \sqsubseteq_{\text{E-M}} t \stackrel{\text{def}}{=} (\perp \in s \wedge s \setminus \{\perp\} \subseteq t) \vee (\perp \notin s \wedge s = t) \ .$$

Prove that $(\mathfrak{P}_{\text{E-M}}(A), \sqsubseteq_{\text{E-M}})$ is a cpo.

8.5 (Finitary Egli–Milner order, cf. Exercise 8.4) Consider the set

$$F \stackrel{\text{def}}{=} \{ f : A \longrightarrow \mathfrak{P}_{\text{E-M}}(A) \mid f(\perp) = A \}$$

ordered by the pointwise extension $\sqsubseteq$ of $\sqsubseteq_{\text{E-M}}$. Prove that $(F, \sqsubseteq)$ is a cpo.

Define sequential composition on F by

$$(f; g)(a) \stackrel{\text{def}}{=} \bigcup \{ g(b) \mid b \in f(a) \}$$

and the union on F by

$$(f \cup g)(a) \stackrel{\text{def}}{=} f(a) \cup g(a)$$

(for all $f, g \in F$ and $a \in A$). Prove that

    (a) F is closed under ";" and "$\cup$", and
    (b) ";" and "$\cup$" on F are continuous in both arguments.

8.6 Show that $(R_{\perp}^{\text{C}}, \subseteq)$ is a cpo which is closed under union and sequential composition.

8.7 Prove Cor. 8.21.

8.8 For $k \in \mathbb{N}$ modify Example 8.14 such that $\omega + k$ and, respectively, $\omega + \omega + k$ iterations are required to reach the least fixed point of $\lambda X. r; X$.

8.9 Prove Cor. 8.24.

8.10 Prove Cor. 8.35.

8.11   Calculate the total correctness semantics of

$$\{y = y_0\} \textbf{ while } x = 5 \textbf{ do } y := y + 1 \textbf{ od } \{y = y_0 \wedge x \neq 5\} \ .$$

8.12   Justify the last step of Example 8.34.

9

Simulation and Total Correctness

Simulation, our main technique for proving data refinement, also works for proving refinement of total correctness between data types based on the semantic model introduced in the previous chapter. However, certain complications arise; for instance, L^{-1}-simulation is unsound in case abstract operations expose infinite nondeterminism, which severely restricts the use of specification statements.

Section 9.1 extends the soundness and completeness results for simulation from Chapter 4 to total correctness. As the main result, we present in Section 9.2 a total correctness version of our L-simulation theorem from Chapter 7.

9.1 Simulation

The semantics-based notions of data type, data refinement, and simulation need not be defined anew. The only notion changed is that of observation since, through our total correctness program semantics, nonterminating behaviors have also become observable. It is essential to the understanding of total correctness simulation between data types to realize that, semantically speaking, abstraction relations are directed. In particular, the relational inverse of an abstraction relation from level C to level A is not an abstraction relation in the opposite direction, as is the case for partial correctness. Now it becomes clear why several authors prefer the name *downward simulation* for L-simulation and *upward simulation* for L^{-1}-simulation [HHS87]: the direction of an L-simulation relation is downwards, from the abstract to the concrete level, whence a more descriptive name for it would be *representation relation* or *downward simulation relation*. For this reason we redefine the meaning of $\subseteq_\beta^L$ such that β itself (and not its inverse) is used in the inclusions characterizing L-simulation.

Definition 9.1 ($\perp$-data type (cf. Def. 1.7)) Let J be an index set. Let N and Var^A denote finite sets of program variables such that $N \subseteq Var^A \subseteq Var$. Let $AI \in R_\perp^{N,Var^A}$, $AF \in R_\perp^{Var^A,N}$, and $A_j \in R_\perp^A$, for $j \in J$. Then

$$\mathcal{A} = (AI,(A_j)_{j \in J},AF)$$

is called a *total correctness data type* (or $\perp$-*data type*). Two $\perp$-data types are *compatible* if they agree on both the set of normal variables N and the index set J.

$\mathcal{A}$ is a *finitary data type* if all relations involved are finitary.   ♣

Definition 9.2 (Simulation of $\perp$-data types (cf. Def. 2.1)) Let $\mathcal{A}$ and C be compatible $\perp$-data types, $\mathcal{A} = (AI,(A_j)_{j \in J},AF)$ and $C = (CI,(C_j)_{j \in J},CF)$, and let $\alpha \in R_\perp^{CA}$ and $\beta \in R_\perp^{AC}$.

(i) C L-*simulates* $\mathcal{A}$ w.r.t. β (denoted $C \subseteq_\beta^L \mathcal{A}$) iff $CI \subseteq AI;\beta$, $\beta;CF \subseteq AF$, and $\beta;C_j \subseteq A_j;\beta$, for all $j \in J$.

(ii) C L^{-1}-*simulates* $\mathcal{A}$ w.r.t. α (denoted $C \subseteq_\alpha^{L^{-1}} \mathcal{A}$) iff $CI;\alpha \subseteq AI$, $CF \subseteq \alpha;AF$, and $C_j;\alpha \subseteq \alpha;A_j$, for all $j \in J$.

As in Def. 4.1 we overload the symbols $\subseteq_\beta^L$ and $\subseteq_\alpha^{L^{-1}}$ such that they also apply to pairs of operations $(C,A) \in R_\perp^C \times R_\perp^A$.   ♣

Definition 9.3 (Terms and programs over a $\perp$-data type) Let $Rvar$ be a set of recursion variables ranging over $R_\perp^A$ and an I-indexed family $A = (A_i)_{i \in I}$ of names of operations of some $\perp$-data type $\mathcal{A}$.

The set of *total correctness terms* over A is the smallest set $T_\perp(A)$ containing

(i) name $id_\perp^A$ for the relation $id^A \cup K^A$
(ii) name $U_\perp^A$ for the universal relation
(iii) members A_i of the family A
(iv) recursion variables X ranging over $R_\perp^A$
(v) $P;Q$ with $P,Q \in T_\perp(A)$
(vi) $P \cup Q$ with $P,Q \in T_\perp(A)$
(vii) $\mu X.P(X)$ with $P(X) \in T_\perp(A)$

μ serves as a binding operator for recursion variables.

Next we define the set $\mathcal{P}_\perp(A)$ of *total correctness programs over* A as those terms in $T_\perp(A)$ which do not contain free occurrences of recursion variables.

In case $\mathcal{A}$ is a finitary data type and recursion variables are restricted to range over $R_{\mathcal{F}}^A$ only in the characterization of $T_\perp(A)$ above, we say that $T_{\mathcal{F}}(A)$ is the set of *finitary terms over* A. Similarly, the set $\mathcal{P}_{\mathcal{F}}(A)$ of *finitary programs over*

A consists of the finitary terms over A without free occurrences of recursion variables. ♣

As in Chapters 1 and 3 we face here the distinction between syntax and semantics, since recursion variable X is necessarily a term. Consequently, as the next step one should define $\mathcal{P}[\![P]\!]_{\perp}^{A}$ for $P \in \mathcal{P}_{\perp}(A)$. Since this significantly reduces readability of the soundness and completeness proofs presented below, we identify within this section syntax with semantics as done in Section 3.4, following [SdB69]. $id_{\perp}^{A}$, $U_{\perp}^{A}$, A_i, and X stand within the remainder of this section for the relations they are intended to denote and, e.g., $\mu X.P(X)$ for the least fixed point of the transformation that maps the relation denoted by X to the relation denoted by $P(X)$. (Unless stated otherwise we always assume the order $\supseteq$ on total correctness relations.)

Lemma 9.4 $\mathcal{P}_{\perp}(A) \subseteq R_{\perp}^{A}$ and the program constructs of $T_{\perp}(A)$ are monotone. Moreover, in the finitary case, $\mathcal{P}_{\mathcal{F}}(A) \subseteq R_{\mathcal{F}}^{A}$ and the program constructs of $T_{\mathcal{F}}(A)$ are continuous.

Proof: The first claim is immediate. The second follows by induction on the structure of $P \in \mathcal{P}_{\mathcal{F}}(A)$. All base cases $id_{\perp}^{A}$, $U_{\perp}^{A}$, and the elements of A are finitary. By Lemma 8.19 the set $R_{\mathcal{F}}^{A}$ is closed under the operators ";" and "$\cup$", and these operators are continuous. By a second induction on the nesting depth of μ operators one shows that μ-terms are also continuous: since the least fixed point of a continuous function coincides with the lub of the chain of its finite approximations (Lemma 8.7), and since lub operators on chains are continuous (Lemma 8.6), $\mu X.S(X,Y)$ is continuous in Y for $S(X,Y) \in T_{\mathcal{F}}(A)$. □

9.1.1 Soundness

Proving soundness of simulation as a tool for proving refinement between $\perp$-data types is slightly more intricate than in the partial correctness world. This is due to the different semantics given to recursion, i.e., the presence of infinite intersection over $\supseteq$-chains of relations instead of infinite union over $\subseteq$-chains.

Theorem 9.5 (Soundness)
Both L- and L^{-1}-simulation are sound methods for proving termination-preserving data refinement between concrete level $\perp$-data types and abstract level finitary data types. In the case of L^{-1}-simulation this holds in general for finitary abstraction relations only.

Proof: The proof has the same structure as the one for partial correctness (see Theorem 4.10). Let $C = (CI, (C_j)_{j \in J}, CF)$ and $\mathcal{A} = (AI, (A_j)_{j \in J}, AF)$ be two compatible $\bot$-data types. Let $P(A) \in \mathcal{P}_\bot(A)$ and $P(C) \in \mathcal{P}_\bot(C)$, where program $P(C)$ is obtained from $P(A)$ by replacing each occurrence of an abstract operation A_j by the corresponding concrete operation C_j.

(i) First we treat L-simulation. Assume $C \subseteq^L_\beta \mathcal{A}$, where β is a representation relation from level A to level C, i.e., $\beta \in R^{AC}_\bot$.

First we show by induction over the structure of $P(A)$ that $P(C) \subseteq^L_\beta P(A)$.

The base case $id^A_\bot$ is trivial and for A_j the required property is assumed above. For $U^A_\bot$ we derive the following.

$$\beta ; U^C_\bot$$
$$\subseteq U^{AC}_\bot \qquad \text{set theory}$$
$$= U^A_\bot ; \beta \qquad \beta \text{ is surjective since } K^{AC} \subseteq \beta$$

We reconsider only the induction step for recursion since the proofs for sequential composition and nondeterministic choice work exactly as in the partial correctness version of this theorem. So consider the case that $P(A)$ is $\mu X . Q(A)(X)$. The induction hypothesis in this case is $(Q(C))^i (U^C_\bot) \subseteq^L_\beta (Q(A))^i (U^A_\bot)$, for all $i \in \mathbb{N}$.

$$\beta ; \mu X . Q(C)(X)$$
$$\subseteq \beta ; \bigcap ((Q(C))^i (U^C_\bot))_{i \in \mathbb{N}} \qquad \text{Lemma 9.4 for ``;'', Cor. 8.11}$$
$$\subseteq \bigcap (\beta ; (Q(C))^i (U^C_\bot))_{i \in \mathbb{N}} \qquad \text{set theory}$$
$$\subseteq \bigcap ((Q(A))^i (U^A_\bot) ; \beta)_{i \in \mathbb{N}} \qquad \text{induction hypothesis}$$
$$= \bigcap ((Q(A))^i (U^A_\bot))_{i \in \mathbb{N}} ; \beta \qquad \text{Cor. 8.20}$$
$$= \mu X . Q(A)(X) ; \beta \qquad \text{Lemmas 9.4 and 8.7}$$

As in the proof of Theorem 4.10 we conclude that $CI ; P(C) ; CF \subseteq AI ; P(A) ; AF$ using the induction argument above:

$$CI ; P(C) ; CF$$
$$\subseteq AI ; \beta ; P(C) ; CF \qquad \text{Def. 9.2: } CI \subseteq AI ; \beta$$
$$\subseteq AI ; P(A) ; \beta ; CF \qquad \text{induction}$$
$$\subseteq AI ; P(A) ; AF \qquad \text{Def. 9.2: } \beta ; CF \subseteq AF$$

(ii) Soundness of L^{-1}-simulation follows analogously. Assume that $C \subseteq^{L^{-1}}_\alpha \mathcal{A}$. This time proving the induction step for recursion requires that $\mathcal{A}$

is a finitary data type and α is finitary, i.e., $\alpha \in R_{\mathcal{F}}^{CA}$. The induction hypotheses are $(Q(C))^i(U_\perp^C) \sqsubseteq_\alpha^{L^{-1}} (Q(A))^i(U_\perp^A)$, for all $i \in \mathbb{N}$.

$$\mu X.Q(C)(X);\alpha$$

$\subseteq \bigcap((Q(C))^i(U_\perp^C))_{i\in\mathbb{N}};\alpha$ Lemma 9.4, Cor. 8.11

$\subseteq \bigcap((Q(C))^i(U_\perp^C);\alpha)_{i\in\mathbb{N}}$ set theory

$\subseteq \bigcap(\alpha;(Q(A))^i(U_\perp^A))_{i\in\mathbb{N}}$ induction hypotheses

$\subseteq \alpha;\bigcap((Q(A))^i(U_\perp^A))_{i\in\mathbb{N}}$ Lemma 8.19, α finitary

$= \alpha;\mu X.Q(A)(X)$ Lemmas 9.4 and 8.7 $\square$

The combination of recursion with non-finitary abstraction relations and operations on the abstract level may invalidate the soundness of L^{-1}-simulation as a method for proving termination-preserving refinement. A typical example of this comes next.

Example 9.6 There is no normal variable involved in this example. Concrete level program S^C:

begin var $b : \mathbb{B};$ **while** b **do** $(b := \text{true} \, [] \, b := \text{false})$ **od end**

does not refine the abstract level program S^A:

begin var $n : \mathbb{N};$ **while** $n > 0$ **do** $n := n - 1$ **od end**

such that termination is preserved. When started in a proper state, termination of S^C is not guaranteed since b might be initialized to true and each execution of the specification in the loop body might assign true to b, over and over again. On the other hand, whatever value $v \in \mathbb{N}$ the abstract level representation variable n assumes initially, the loop terminates after executing its body v times. However, the initial value of n is not restricted. We conclude that S^C does not refine S^A such that termination is preserved.

Next we present two $\perp$-data types C and $\mathcal{A}$ corresponding to S^C and S^A, respectively, and an abstraction relation α. Recalling that $\Sigma_\perp^0 = \{\perp, \text{ń}\}$, one has that $\mathcal{P}[\![S^A]\!]_\perp$ is $\{(\text{ń},\text{ń}),(\perp,\text{ń}),(\perp,\perp)\}$ whereas $\mathcal{P}[\![S^C]\!]_\perp$ additionally contains $(\text{ń},\perp)$, hence $\mathcal{P}[\![S^C]\!]_\perp \not\subseteq \mathcal{P}[\![S^A]\!]_\perp$.

$AI = \{ (\sigma,\tau) \in \Sigma_\perp^0 \times \Sigma_\perp^A \mid \tau = \perp \Rightarrow \sigma = \perp \}$

$A_1 = \{ (\sigma,\tau) \in \Sigma_\perp^A \times \Sigma_\perp^A \mid \sigma(n) \leq 0 \wedge \sigma = \tau \vee \sigma = \perp \}$

$\qquad (= \mathcal{P}[\![\neg n > 0 \rightarrow]\!]_\perp^A)$

$A_2 = \{ (\sigma,\tau) \in \Sigma_\perp^A \times \Sigma_\perp^A \mid \sigma(n) > 0 \wedge \tau(n) = \sigma(n) - 1 \vee \sigma = \perp \}$

$$(= \mathcal{P}[\![n > 0 \to n := n - 1]\!]_\perp^{A})$$

$$AF = \{\ (\sigma,\tau) \in \Sigma_\perp^A \times \Sigma_\perp^0 \mid \tau = \perp \Rightarrow \sigma = \perp\ \}$$

Observe that S^A denotes the same relation as $AI\,;\mu X.((A_2\,;X)\cup A_1)\,;AF$ and that AI is not finitary since $AI(\text{ᛗ}) = \Sigma^A = \{\ (\text{ᛗ}:n \mapsto v) \mid v \in \mathbb{N}\ \}$. The other constituents of $\mathcal{A}$ are finitary.

$$CI = \{\ (\sigma,\tau) \in \Sigma_\perp^0 \times \Sigma_\perp^C \mid \tau = \perp \Rightarrow \sigma = \perp\ \}$$

$$C_1 = \{\ (\sigma,\tau) \in \Sigma_\perp^C \times \Sigma_\perp^C \mid \neg\sigma(b) \wedge \sigma = \tau \vee \sigma = \perp\ \}\quad (= \mathcal{P}[\![\neg b \to]\!]_\perp^C)$$

$$C_2 = \{\ (\sigma,\tau) \in \Sigma_\perp^C \times \Sigma_\perp^C \mid \sigma(b) \wedge \tau \neq \perp \vee \sigma = \perp\ \}$$

$$(= \mathcal{P}[\![b \to (b := \text{true} [\!] b := \text{false})]\!]_\perp^C)$$

$$CF = \{\ (\sigma,\tau) \in \Sigma_\perp^C \times \Sigma_\perp^0 \mid \tau = \perp \Rightarrow \sigma = \perp\ \}$$

Similarly, S^C denotes the same relation as $CI\,;\mu X.((C_2\,;X)\cup C_1)\,;CF$. Furthermore, the constituents of C are finitary (Σ^C is finite). Next we construct an L^{-1}-simulation relation $\alpha \in R_\perp^{CA}$. It has to satisfy the simulation conditions:

   (i) $CI\,;\alpha \subseteq AI$

  (ii) $C_1\,;\alpha \subseteq \alpha\,;A_1$

 (iii) $C_2\,;\alpha \subseteq \alpha\,;A_2$

 (iv) $CF \subseteq \alpha\,;AF$

Since there is only one variable at each level of abstraction we abstract from their names, n and b, and just reason about their values instead of states, i.e., we treat $\Sigma_\perp^A$ as $\mathbb{N}_\perp$ and $\Sigma_\perp^C$ as $\mathbb{B}_\perp$.

- Point (iv) holds iff $(\perp,\perp) \in \alpha$ and $\exists v,w \in \mathbb{N}((tt,v),(ff,w) \in \alpha)$.
- Point (i) is satisfied iff neither of $(tt,\perp)$ and $(ff,\perp)$ is in α.
- Thus, point (ii) implies that $w = 0$.
- Altogether, and with point (iii), $\{\ (tt,n) \mid n > 0\ \} \subseteq \alpha$ and $(tt,0) \notin \alpha$.

Thus, $\{(\perp,\perp)\}\cup\{\ (b,n) \in \mathbb{B} \times \mathbb{N} \mid b \Leftrightarrow n > 0\ \}$ is a lower bound (w.r.t. $\subseteq$) for α and $K \cup \{\ (b,n) \in \mathbb{B} \times \mathbb{N} \mid b \Leftrightarrow n > 0\ \}$ is an upper bound. The simulation conditions and non-finitariness of α are guaranteed, regardless of our choice for α within these bounds. To satisfy $\alpha \in R_\perp^{CA}$ (and to be able to provide a syntactic representation) we choose the upper bound.

$$\alpha = \{\ (\sigma,\zeta) \in \Sigma_\perp^C \times \Sigma_\perp^A \mid (\sigma(b) \Leftrightarrow \zeta(n) > 0) \vee \sigma = \perp\ \}$$

(Observe that $\alpha = \mathcal{A}[\![b \Leftrightarrow n > 0]\!]_\perp^{CA}$.) We have managed to find an α such that $C \sqsubseteq_\alpha^{L^{-1}} \mathcal{A}$. But, as we have observed above, C does not refine $\mathcal{A}$ such that termination is preserved. Thus, L^{-1}-simulation is in general not a sound method for proving data refinement between $\perp$-data types in case α and AI (or any other abstract operation) are non-finitary. $\heartsuit$

Two remarks concerning this example are in order.

- Program S^C refines S^A in the partial correctness setting, and the corresponding data types are an example of L^{-1}-simulation in that setting.
- Program S^A refines S^C in the total correctness setting, and the corresponding $\perp$-data types are an example of L-simulation.

9.1.2 Completeness

The completeness result given in Theorem 4.17 also translates to our total correctness formalism. What remains to be checked is that the soundness theorem for simulation between finitary data types (Theorem 9.5) applies to the two relations occurring in the proof of Theorem 4.17. Recall the structure of that proof depicted in Figure 9.1.

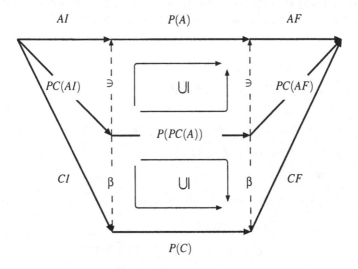

Fig. 9.1. Structure of the completeness proof.

Upward simulation $\ni$ has to be finitary, which is achieved by the following construction. We restrict $\ni$ such that its domain is $\mathcal{F}(\Sigma^A)$, i.e., the finite subsets of Σ^A and the whole of $\Sigma^A_\perp$. This $\ni$ is finitary, i.e., $\ni \in R_{\mathcal{F}}(\mathcal{F}(\Sigma^A), \Sigma^A)$, because $\ni(\{s\}) = s$, which is finitary for all $s \in \mathcal{F}(\Sigma^A)$. This restriction is possible only because all relations encountered on the abstract level are finitary. For the downward simulation relation

$$\beta \stackrel{\text{def}}{=} \bigcap_{P(A)\in\mathcal{P}_\perp(A)} ([(P(C);CF)](P(A);AF))$$

defined in Theorem 4.16 we have to show that it is an element of $R^{AC}_\perp$.

Recall from Def. 8.26 that a relation weakly terminates if it does not relate any proper state to bottom. By definition of β and $id^A_\perp \in \mathcal{P}_\perp(A)$ we have that β weakly terminates under the assumption that AF weakly terminates:

$$(\sigma,\perp) \in \beta$$

$$\Rightarrow (\sigma,\perp) \in [id^C_\perp;CF](id^A_\perp;AF) \qquad \text{def. of } \beta$$

$$\Leftrightarrow (\sigma,\perp) \in [CF]AF$$

$$\Leftrightarrow \forall\zeta \in \Sigma^{Var^A\cap Var^C}_\perp ((\perp,\zeta) \in CF \Rightarrow (\sigma,\zeta) \in AF) \qquad \text{Def. 3.10}$$

$$\Leftrightarrow \forall\zeta \in \Sigma^{Var^A\cap Var^C}_\perp ((\sigma,\zeta) \in AF) \qquad K \subseteq CF$$

$$\Leftrightarrow \sigma = \perp \qquad AF \text{ term. weakly}$$

This implies by contraposition that $\sigma \neq \perp \Rightarrow (\sigma,\perp) \notin \beta$, i.e., weak termination of AF implies that β terminates weakly. Next we prove that $K^C \subseteq \beta$:

$$(\perp,\sigma) \in \beta$$

$$\Leftrightarrow \quad \text{(definition of } \beta)$$

$$\forall P(A) \in \mathcal{P}_\perp(A)((\perp,\sigma) \in [P(C);CF](P(A);AF))$$

$$\Leftrightarrow \quad \text{(Def. 3.10)}$$

$$\forall P(A) \in \mathcal{P}_\perp(A), \zeta((\sigma,\zeta) \in P(C);CF \Rightarrow (\perp,\zeta) \in P(A);AF)$$

$$\Leftrightarrow \quad \text{(Lemma 9.4, } K \subseteq AF)$$

$$tt$$

Weak termination of β implies that $\beta;K^C \subseteq \beta$:

$$(\sigma,\tau) \in \beta;K^C$$

$$\Rightarrow (\sigma,\perp) \in \beta \qquad \text{def. of } K^C \text{ and ";"}$$

$$\Rightarrow \sigma = \perp \qquad \beta \text{ terminates weakly}$$

Altogether, $\beta \in R^{AC}_\perp$. Thus we establish the following theorem.

Theorem 9.7 (Completeness)

Let C and $\mathcal{A}$ be two compatible $\perp$-data types such that $\mathcal{A}$ is finitary. If the abstract finalization terminates weakly then L- and L^{-1}-simulation together are sufficient to prove that C refines $\mathcal{A}$ whenever this is the case.   ♠

9.2 An L-Simulation Theorem for Total Correctness

Recast for total correctness the main problem discussed in Chapter 7: Given an abstract level specification $\phi \rightsquigarrow \psi \in Prog^A$ and an representation relation $\beta \in Abs^{AC}$, how can one express the most general concrete level program $S \in Prog^C$ that is a total correctness L-simulation of $\phi \rightsquigarrow \psi$ with respect to β?

$$\beta; S \subseteq \phi \rightsquigarrow \psi; \beta \tag{9.1}$$

From Lemma 5.24 it follows (with our convention concerning the semantics of relational terms and correctness formulae from Section 8.2.4) that (9.1) is equivalent to the following semantic characterization of S.

$$S \subseteq \beta \rightsquigarrow (\phi \rightsquigarrow \psi; \beta) \tag{9.2}$$

As in Chapter 7 the remaining, bigger part of the problem is to express the RHS of (9.2) as a specification statement.

The clue to this part of the problem is the observation that the partial correctness solution is almost the total correctness solution, too. Modulo possible differences in the evaluation of the predicates ϕ, ψ, and β, only state pairs $(\sigma, \perp)$ must be added to the total correctness solution exactly for those σ for which nontermination is possible. Therefore it makes sense to compute the domain of termination of the RHS of (9.2), that is, we are looking for a predicate $\pi \in Pred^{Var^C}$ such that

$$wt(\beta \rightsquigarrow (\phi \rightsquigarrow \psi; \beta)) = C[\![\pi]\!]_{\perp}^{Var^A} \tag{9.3}$$

holds. To develop the solution formally, let $\vec{x}_0$ be the free logical variables of ϕ and ψ, let $\vec{x}$ be the normal variables, and let $\vec{a}$ and $\vec{c}$ be the abstract and concrete level representation variables, respectively.

$wt(\phi \rightsquigarrow \psi)$ is expressed by $\exists \vec{x}_0 (\phi)$ by Lemma 8.36. Furthermore, we may assume that β is weakly terminating $(wt(\beta) = \Sigma^A)$. This assumption is justified since finalizations terminate weakly and the finalization condition of L-simulation has to hold:

$$(\sigma, \perp) \in \mathcal{A}[\![\beta]\!]_{\perp}^{AC}$$
$$\Rightarrow \perp \in (\mathcal{A}[\![\beta]\!]_{\perp}^{AC}; CF)(\{\sigma\}) \qquad K \subseteq CF$$
$$\Rightarrow \perp \in (AF)(\{\sigma\}) \qquad \text{finalization condition}$$
$$\Rightarrow \sigma = \perp \qquad AF \text{ terminates weakly}$$

Thus, $\exists \vec{x}_0 (\phi)$ is also a syntactic characterization of $wt(\phi \rightsquigarrow \psi; \beta)$. Next we compute the domain of weak termination of the RHS of (9.2). Let $\sigma \in \Sigma_{\perp}^C$.

$$\sigma \in wt(\beta \rightsquigarrow (\phi \rightsquigarrow \psi; \beta))$$

$$\Leftrightarrow \neg\forall\zeta\left((\zeta,\sigma) \in \mathcal{A}[\![\beta]\!]_\bot^{AC} \Rightarrow (\zeta,\bot) \in \mathcal{R}[\![\phi \rightsquigarrow \psi;\beta]\!]_\bot\right) \qquad \text{Def. 8.26}$$

$$\Leftrightarrow \exists\zeta\left((\zeta,\sigma) \in \mathcal{A}[\![\beta]\!]_\bot^{AC} \wedge \zeta \in wt(\phi \rightsquigarrow \psi;\beta)\right) \qquad \text{Def. 8.26}$$

$$\Leftrightarrow \sigma \in C[\![\exists\vec{a}\,(\beta \wedge \exists\vec{x}_0\,(\phi))]\!]_\bot^{Var^C} \qquad\qquad\qquad\quad \text{Def. 8.23}$$

The following lemma explains how to fuse an extra condition into the precondition of a specification statement to narrow down the domain of termination.

Lemma 9.8 Let $\phi,\psi \in Pred^A$ and let $\pi \in Pred^{Var^A}$. For all $\sigma,\tau \in \Sigma_\bot^A$

$$(\sigma,\tau) \in \mathcal{P}[\![(\pi \wedge \phi) \rightsquigarrow \psi]\!]_\bot^A \Leftrightarrow \left(\sigma \in C[\![\pi]\!]_\bot^{Var^A} \Rightarrow (\sigma,\tau) \in \mathcal{P}[\![\phi \rightsquigarrow \psi]\!]_\bot^A\right)$$

Proof: Exercise.   □

The central result of this section can be understood as follows: the total correctness interpretation of the partial correctness solution is almost the total correctness solution. Almost, because its domain of weak termination is too big since it does not take ϕ into account. For the partial correctness solution, this is negligible by our normal form theorem (Theorem 7.9). This theorem depends on the fact that one cannot observe nontermination in the partial correctness semantics. For that very reason this normal form theorem does not hold for total correctness. The domain of weak termination of the total correctness solution is expressed by $\exists\vec{a}\,(\beta \wedge \exists\vec{x}_0\,(\phi))$. Adding this as a conjunct to the precondition of the the partial correctness solution yields the total correctness solution. (See Exercise 9.2.)

Although the resulting specification statement turns out to be even more complex than the partial correctness solution, we shall see in Example 11.5 that this extra conjunct in the precondition is essential in justifying the reduction of Reynolds' condition for data refinement to total correctness L-simulation.

Unfortunately, the development above, that is, the derivation of the solution's domain of weak termination and the last lemma, allow us to prove a simulation theorem only for total β. This is for technical reasons only, however; the direct proof of the following theorem reveals that this severe restriction on β can be discarded. This is by far the hardest proof in this chapter and can be skipped upon first reading.

Theorem 9.9

Let $\beta \in Abs^{AC}$ be weakly terminating. Let $\phi,\psi \in Pred^A$, let $\vec{x}_0$ be the (list of) free logical variables of ϕ and ψ, let $\vec{x}$ be the normal variables, and let $\vec{a}$ and $\vec{c}$ be the abstract and concrete level representation variables, respectively. Let $\vec{y}_0$

be a list of fresh logical variables matching $\vec{x}\vec{a}$. Specification statement

$$\exists \vec{a}\,(\beta \wedge \vec{x}\vec{a} = \vec{y}_0 \wedge \exists \vec{x}_0\,(\phi)) \rightsquigarrow \exists \vec{a}\left(\beta \wedge \forall \vec{x}_0\left(\phi[\vec{y}_0/\vec{x}\vec{a}] \Rightarrow \psi\right)\right)$$

expresses the maximal solution of $\beta\,;S \subseteq \phi \rightsquigarrow \psi\,;\beta$ in S.

Proof: Let $\sigma, \tau \in \Sigma_\perp^C$.

$(\sigma, \tau) \in S$

$\Leftrightarrow$ (by (9.2))

$\mathcal{A}[\![\beta]\!]_\perp^{AC}\,;\{(\sigma,\tau)\} \subseteq C[\![\phi \rightsquigarrow \psi]\!]_\perp^A\,;\mathcal{A}[\![\beta]\!]_\perp^{AC}$

$\Leftrightarrow$ (Def. 3.6)

$\forall \zeta \in \Sigma_\perp^A \left(\begin{array}{l} (\zeta, \sigma) \in \mathcal{A}[\![\beta]\!]_\perp^{AC} \\ \Rightarrow \exists \xi \in \Sigma_\perp^A \left((\zeta, \xi) \in C[\![\phi \rightsquigarrow \psi]\!]_\perp^A \wedge (\xi, \tau) \in \mathcal{A}[\![\beta]\!]_\perp^{AC}\right) \end{array} \right)$

$\Leftrightarrow$ (mutual impl., "$\Rightarrow$": immediate, "$\Leftarrow$": case $\zeta = \perp$: choose $\xi = \perp$)

$\forall \zeta \in \Sigma^A \left(\begin{array}{l} (\zeta, \sigma) \in \mathcal{A}[\![\beta]\!]_\perp^{AC} \\ \Rightarrow \exists \xi \in \Sigma_\perp^A \left((\zeta, \xi) \in C[\![\phi \rightsquigarrow \psi]\!]_\perp^A \wedge (\xi, \tau) \in \mathcal{A}[\![\beta]\!]_\perp^{AC}\right) \end{array} \right)$

$\Leftrightarrow$ (Def. 8.29)

$\forall \zeta \in \Sigma^A \left(\begin{array}{l} (\zeta, \sigma) \in \mathcal{A}[\![\beta]\!]_\perp^{AC} \\ \Rightarrow \exists \xi \in \Sigma_\perp^A \left(\forall \delta \left(\begin{array}{l} (\delta, \zeta) \in C[\![\phi]\!]_\perp^A \\ \Rightarrow (\delta, \xi) \in C[\![\psi]\!]_\perp^A \end{array} \right) \wedge (\xi, \tau) \in \mathcal{A}[\![\beta]\!]_\perp^{AC} \right) \end{array} \right)$

$\Leftrightarrow$ (mutual impl., "$\Leftarrow$": immediate, "$\Rightarrow$": Lemma 9.10.(i) below)

$\forall \zeta \in \Sigma^A \left(\begin{array}{l} (\zeta, \sigma) \in \mathcal{A}[\![\beta]\!]_\perp^{AC} \wedge \left(\begin{array}{l} \exists \delta \left((\delta, \zeta) \in C[\![\phi]\!]_\perp^A\right) \\ \vee \exists \xi \in \Sigma^A \left((\xi, \tau) \in \mathcal{A}[\![\beta]\!]_\perp^{AC}\right) \end{array} \right) \\ \Rightarrow \exists \xi \in \Sigma^A \left(\forall \delta \left(\begin{array}{l} (\delta, \zeta) \in C[\![\phi]\!]_\perp^A \\ \Rightarrow (\delta, \xi) \in C[\![\psi]\!]_\perp^A \end{array} \right) \wedge (\xi, \tau) \in \mathcal{A}[\![\beta]\!]_\perp^{AC} \right) \end{array} \right)$

$\Leftrightarrow$ (Lemma 5.12, β terminates)

$\forall \gamma \in \Gamma^C \left(\begin{array}{l} (\gamma, \sigma) \in C[\![\exists \vec{a}\,(\beta \wedge \vec{x}\vec{a} = \vec{y}_0)]\!]_\perp^C \\ \wedge \left(\begin{array}{l} \exists \delta \in \Gamma^A \left((\delta, \gamma) \in C[\![\phi[\vec{y}_0/\vec{x}\vec{a}]]\!]_\perp^{\vec{x}_0, \vec{y}_0}\right) \\ \vee \exists \xi \in \Sigma^A \left((\xi, \tau) \in \mathcal{A}[\![\beta]\!]_\perp^{AC}\right) \end{array} \right) \\ \Rightarrow \exists \xi \in \Sigma^A \left(\forall \delta \in \Gamma^A \left(\begin{array}{l} (\delta, \gamma) \in C[\![\phi[\vec{y}_0/\vec{x}\vec{a}]]\!]_\perp^{\vec{x}_0, \vec{y}_0} \\ \Rightarrow (\delta, \xi) \in C[\![\psi]\!]_\perp^A \end{array} \right) \right. \\ \left. \wedge (\xi, \tau) \in \mathcal{A}[\![\beta]\!]_\perp^{AC} \right) \end{array} \right)$

$\Leftrightarrow$ (Def. 8.23, β terminates)

$$\forall \gamma \in \Gamma^C \left(\begin{array}{l} (\gamma,\sigma) \in C[\![\exists \vec{a}\,(\beta \wedge \vec{x}\vec{a} = \vec{y}_0)]\!]_{\perp}^C \wedge \left(\begin{array}{l} \gamma \in C[\![\exists \vec{x}_0\,(\phi[^{\vec{y}_0}/_{\vec{x}\vec{a}}])]\!]_{\perp}^{\vec{y}_0} \\ \vee \tau \in C[\![\exists \vec{a}\,(\beta)]\!]_{\perp}^{\vec{x}\vec{c}} \end{array} \right) \\ \Rightarrow (\gamma,\tau) \in C[\![\exists \vec{a}\,(\beta \wedge \forall \vec{x}_0\,(\phi[^{\vec{y}_0}/_{\vec{x}\vec{a}}] \Rightarrow \psi))]\!]_{\perp}^C \end{array} \right)$$

$\Leftrightarrow$ ("$\Rightarrow$": pred. calc., "$\Leftarrow$": Lemma 9.10.(ii) below)

$$\forall \gamma \in \Gamma^C \left(\begin{array}{l} (\gamma,\sigma) \in C[\![\exists \vec{a}\,(\beta \wedge \vec{x}\vec{a} = \vec{y}_0)]\!]_{\perp}^C \wedge \gamma \in C[\![\exists \vec{x}_0\,(\phi[^{\vec{y}_0}/_{\vec{x}\vec{a}}])]\!]_{\perp}^{\vec{y}_0} \\ \Rightarrow (\gamma,\tau) \in C[\![\exists \vec{a}\,(\beta \wedge \forall \vec{x}_0\,(\phi[^{\vec{y}_0}/_{\vec{x}\vec{a}}] \Rightarrow \psi))]\!]_{\perp}^C \end{array} \right)$$

$\Leftrightarrow$ (Def. 8.23, Lemma 5.13)

$$\forall \gamma \in \Gamma^C \left(\begin{array}{l} (\gamma,\sigma) \in C[\![\exists \vec{a}\,(\beta \wedge \vec{x}\vec{a} = \vec{y}_0) \wedge \exists \vec{x}_0\,(\phi[^{\vec{y}_0}/_{\vec{x}\vec{a}}])]\!]_{\perp}^C \\ \Rightarrow (\gamma,\tau) \in C[\![\exists \vec{a}\,(\beta \wedge \forall \vec{x}_0\,(\phi[^{\vec{y}_0}/_{\vec{x}\vec{a}}] \Rightarrow \psi))]\!]_{\perp}^C \end{array} \right)$$

$\Leftrightarrow$ (pred. calc.)

$$\forall \gamma \in \Gamma^C \left(\begin{array}{l} (\gamma,\sigma) \in C[\![\exists \vec{a}\,(\beta \wedge \vec{x}\vec{a} = \vec{y}_0 \wedge \exists \vec{x}_0\,(\phi))]\!]_{\perp}^C \\ \Rightarrow (\gamma,\tau) \in C[\![\exists \vec{a}\,(\beta \wedge \forall \vec{x}_0\,(\phi[^{\vec{y}_0}/_{\vec{x}\vec{a}}] \Rightarrow \psi))]\!]_{\perp}^C \end{array} \right)$$

$\Leftrightarrow$ (Def. 8.29)

$$(\sigma,\tau) \in \mathcal{P}[\![\exists \vec{a}\,(\beta \wedge \vec{x}\vec{a} = \vec{y}_0 \wedge \exists \vec{x}_0\,(\phi)) \rightsquigarrow \exists \vec{a}\,\Big(\beta \wedge \forall \vec{x}_0\,\Big(\phi[^{\vec{y}_0}/_{\vec{x}\vec{a}}] \Rightarrow \psi\Big)\Big)]\!]_{\perp}^C$$

$\square$

The following rather technical lemma justifies two particular steps in the above proof.

Lemma 9.10

(i)

$$\left(\begin{array}{l} \forall \delta \left(\begin{array}{l} (\delta,\zeta) \in C[\![\phi]\!]_{\perp}^A \\ \Rightarrow (\delta,\perp) \in C[\![\psi]\!]_{\perp}^A \end{array} \right) \wedge (\perp,\tau) \in \mathcal{A}[\![\beta]\!]_{\perp}^{AC} \\ \wedge \neg \exists \xi \in \Sigma^A \left(\forall \delta \left(\begin{array}{l} (\delta,\zeta) \in C[\![\phi]\!]_{\perp}^A \\ \Rightarrow (\delta,\xi) \in C[\![\psi]\!]_{\perp}^A \end{array} \right) \wedge (\xi,\tau) \in \mathcal{A}[\![\beta]\!]_{\perp}^{AC} \right) \end{array} \right)$$

$$\Leftrightarrow \forall \delta \Big((\delta,\zeta) \notin C[\![\phi]\!]_{\perp}^A\Big) \wedge \forall \xi \in \Sigma^A \Big((\xi,\tau) \notin \mathcal{A}[\![\beta]\!]_{\perp}^{AC}\Big)$$

(ii) Proposition

$$(A \wedge (B \vee C) \Rightarrow D) \Leftarrow (A \wedge B \Rightarrow D) \tag{9.4}$$

is valid if

$$A \Leftrightarrow (\gamma,\sigma) \in C[\![\exists \vec{a}\,(\beta \wedge \vec{x}\vec{a} = \vec{y}_0)]\!]_{\perp}^C$$
$$B \Leftrightarrow \gamma \in C[\![\exists \vec{x}_0\,\Big(\phi[^{\vec{y}_0}/_{\vec{x}\vec{a}}]\Big)]\!]_{\perp}^{\vec{y}_0}$$

$$C \Leftrightarrow \tau \in C[\![\exists \vec{a}\,(\beta)]\!]_\perp^{\vec{x}\vec{c}}$$

$$D \Leftrightarrow (\gamma,\tau) \in C[\![\exists \vec{a}\,\Big(\beta \wedge \forall \vec{x_0}\,\big(\phi[^{\vec{r_0}}\!/\vec{x_a}] \Rightarrow \psi\big)\Big)]\!]_\perp^C$$

Proof: As to (i): By strictness $(\delta,\perp) \in C[\![\psi]\!]_\perp^A$ never holds. $(\perp,\tau) \in \mathcal{A}[\![\beta]\!]_\perp^{AC}$ follows by definition of $C[\![.]\!]_\perp^{AC}$ since $K^{AC} \subseteq \mathcal{A}[\![\beta]\!]_\perp^{AC}$. Consequently the LHS of the claimed equivalence is equivalent to

$$\forall \delta\Big((\delta,\zeta) \notin C[\![\phi]\!]_\perp^A\Big)$$

$$\wedge \neg \exists \xi \in \Sigma^A \left(\forall \delta\begin{pmatrix}(\delta,\zeta) \in C[\![\phi]\!]_\perp^A \\ \Rightarrow (\delta,\xi) \in C[\![\psi]\!]_\perp^A\end{pmatrix} \wedge (\xi,\tau) \in \mathcal{A}[\![\beta]\!]_\perp^{AC}\right)$$

The first part of this implies that $(\delta,\zeta) \in C[\![\phi]\!]_\perp^A \Rightarrow (\delta,\xi) \in C[\![\psi]\!]_\perp^A$ holds for all ξ in the second part. Consequently this LHS is true iff the RHS is.

As to (ii): To justify this proof step of the theorem above, we have to explain why in this particular case (9.4) holds, although, in general, only the reverse implication, $(A \wedge (B \vee C) \Rightarrow D) \Rightarrow (A \wedge B \Rightarrow D)$ is valid. Implication (9.4) fails only when γ,σ,τ can be found such that $A \wedge \neg B \wedge C$ holds whereas D does not. In the case above this is not possible because $\neg B \wedge C$ already implies D by definition of $C[\![.]\!]_\perp$. $\qquad\square$

9.3 Historical Background

Our soundness and completeness proofs in Section 9.1 have been inspired once again by [HHS87]. The material in Section 9.2 is original [EdR96].

Exercises

9.1   (cf. Example 9.6) Is it possible to construct in the total correctness setting an example of unsound L^{-1}-simulation such that only the abstraction relation is non-finitary?

9.2   Prove Lemma 9.8.

9.3*   (cf. Theorem 9.9) Formulate and prove a total correctness simulation theorem for L^{-1}-simulation.

10

Refinement Calculus

Binary relations on states are not the only semantic domain for representing sequential, nondeterministic programs. Since Dijkstra published his first paper on weakest preconditions in 1975 ([Dij75]), a rich theory based on monotone functions mapping sets of states to sets of states has emerged. Such functions are called *predicate transformers*. For instance, one models programs as functions mapping each postcondition to the corresponding weakest precondition. One branch of this theory concentrates on our primary subject, namely, the stepwise refinement of programs, possibly using data refinement techniques [B80, MV94, Mor89a, vW90]. The major drawback of predicate transformer as models of programs is that they are more complicated than binary relations because the domain of predicate transformers is richer than what we intend to model, i.e., not every predicate transformer represents one of our programs. But the predicate transformer approach also has its advantages. Several main results achieved in previous chapters, especially the completeness theorems (Chapters 4 and 9) and the calculation of maximal simulators (Chapters 7 and 9), require rather complicated proofs. The aim of this chapter is to demonstrate that more elegant and succinct proofs for these and also some new results exist, such as, for instance, isomorphism theorems between the relational and predicate transformer world for various forms of correctness and the use of Galois connections.

One of the first questions to be answered is: Why is the domain of predicate transformers richer than that of binary relations?

(i) Every relation can be mapped one-to-one to a predicate transformer, e.g., the partial correctness semantics relation r is mapped to predicate transformer $\lambda s. [r] s$.

(ii) Every predicate transformer generated this way distributes over intersections, that is, $[r] (s \cap s') = [r] s \cap [r] s'$.

(iii) There exist predicate transformers that do not distribute over conjunctions. For instance, let $r_1 \stackrel{\text{def}}{=} \mathcal{P}[\![x := 5]\!]$, $r_2 \stackrel{\text{def}}{=} \mathcal{P}[\![x := 7]\!]$, let P be the predicate transformer $\lambda s.([r_1]\, s \cup [r_2]\, s)$, and consider $s_1 \stackrel{\text{def}}{=} C[\![x = 5]\!]$ and $s_2 \stackrel{\text{def}}{=} C[\![x = 7]\!]$. Then $P(s_1 \cap s_2) = P(\emptyset) = \emptyset \neq \Sigma = P(s_1) = P(s_2) = P(s_1) \cap P(s_2)$.

(iv) Since P does not distribute over intersections, by point (ii) it cannot be expressed as $\lambda s.[r]\, s$ for any choice of r. Consequently, P does not correspond in this manner to any relation.

Moreover, in the world of predicate transformers a more general notion of inverses exists than for relations. Inverses in the sense of group theory (r; $r^{-1} = id$, r^{-1}; $r = id$) only exist for bijective relations. This has led to the development of an approximate notion of inverses in the relational calculus. This notion is an essential ingredient of the completeness proof of [HHS87] and characterizes the maximal relation a such that a; $b \subseteq c$ for given relations b and c. It is called weakest prespecification and occurs in our theory of binary relations as $[b]\, c$ in Chapter 3. All this is discussed in Section 10.3.

Because a stronger notion of inverses (although still not in the group-theoretical sense) exists in the predicate transformer world, simpler proofs of, e.g., the above-mentioned completeness theorem transposed to that world can be given. As it turns out, within this richer domain L- and L^{-1}-simulation become special cases of a single, more general notion of simulation.

Section 10.1 presents a brief account of basic lattice theory and Galois connections, which is then applied to predicate transformers and relations in order to derive our first isomorphism between the lattices of total correctness relations and conjunctive predicate transformers. After defining the weakest precondition semantics wp of our programming language in Section 10.2 this isomorphism is shown to be respected by the relational total correctness semantics $\mathcal{P}[\![.]\!]_\perp$ and the predicate transformer semantics wp; also implementability of predicate transformers is investigated.

Section 10.3 deals with data refinement and simulation between data types based on predicate transformers instead of relations. As one might expect from Chapter 9, infinite nondeterminism and total correctness do not fit together. The main results of this section are its soundness and completeness theorems for powersimulation. Powersimulation represents a unification of L- and L^{-1}-simulation within the setting of predicate transformers.

In Section 10.4 we return to partial correctness but in the predicate transformer setting. The so-called weakest liberal precondition semantics wlp of our programming language is given and a corresponding isomorphism result with the ordinary relational semantics $\mathcal{P}[\![.]\!]$ of Chapter 5 is established. After presenting the promised simplifications which predicate transformer theory offers, the chapter closes by putting these results into the proper perspective: if one wishes to implement specification $\phi \rightsquigarrow \psi$, the predicate transformer theory yields exactly the same maximal simulator as calculated in Theorem 7.9.

10.1 Lattice-theoretical Framework

The dominant rôle that binary relations on states play as our basic semantic domain in the previous chapters is taken over in this chapter by total, monotone set-to-set functions which are called predicate transformers.

Various possibilities exist for introducing the domain of predicate transformers mathematically: among others, as a lattice [BvW90, vW90] or an order-enriched category [GMdM92].

In this monograph we pursue the lattice-theoretical alternative since category theory is considered harder to start with than lattice theory and we use only very basic concepts. (On the other hand, category theory offers additional insight into the underlying canonical construction by which predicate transformers emerge from binary relations and binary relations emerge from total functions.)

We give below a modest introduction to the required concepts of lattice theory, based on Grätzer [Grä78] and von Wright [vW90].

10.1.1 Basic Lattice Theory

Recall from Chapter 3 the standard definitions of partially ordered sets and monotone/antitone functions: $(L, \leq)$ is a partially ordered set (or poset) iff binary relation $\leq \subseteq L^2$ is reflexive, transitive, and antisymmetric. A function f from poset $(L, \leq)$ to poset $(M, \preceq)$ is monotone (antitone) if it is order-preserving (order-reversing).

Definition 10.1 A poset $(L, \leq)$ is a *lattice* if each finite nonempty subset $K \subseteq L$ has a least upper bound $\bigvee K$ called *join* and a greatest lower bound $\bigwedge K$ called *meet* in L. The join of the two-element set $\{a, b\} \subseteq L$ is denoted $a \vee b$, its meet $a \wedge b$.

A lattice $(L, \leq)$ is *complete* if join and meet exist for every subset of L. A lattice is called *bounded* if it contains a least and a greatest element, which we denote by $\bot$ and $\top$, respectively. In a bounded lattice L, $\bar{a}$ is a *complement* of a iff $\bar{a} \wedge a = \bot$ and $\bar{a} \vee a = \top$; if $\bar{a}$ exists for all $a \in L$, L is *complemented*. A lattice L is called *distributive* if $a \wedge (b \vee c) = (a \wedge b) \vee (a \wedge c)$ holds for all $a, b, c \in L$. It is said to be *meet infinite distributive (MID)* if $a \vee \bigwedge_{i \in I} a_i = \bigwedge_{i \in I} (a \vee a_i)$;

dually, L is *join infinite distributive (JID)* if $a \wedge \bigvee_{i \in I} a_i = \bigvee_{i \in I} (a \wedge a_i)$, for all $a, a_i \in L$. A *Boolean lattice* is a complemented distributive lattice. ♣

Example 10.2 Recall the two-element set of truth values $\mathbb{B} = \{ff, tt\}$ and the binary relation $\Rightarrow$ on $\mathbb{B}$, propositional implication. The structure $(\mathbb{B}, \Rightarrow)$ is a partial order; moreover, it is a complete Boolean lattice. Meet and join are just $\wedge$ and $\vee$ from propositional logic. The least element of $\mathbb{B}$ is ff, and the greatest element is tt; they are mutual complements.

If S is a set, then the structure $(\mathfrak{P}(S), \subseteq)$ is a complete Boolean lattice with meet $\cap$, join $\cup$, $\bot = \emptyset$, and $\top = S$. It is called the *powerset lattice* of S.

For lattice $(L, \leq)$ and functions $f_1, f_2 \in [S \longrightarrow L]$, define a partial order on the function space $[S \longrightarrow L]$, called *pointwise extension* of $\leq$, by $f_1 \leq f_2 \stackrel{\text{def}}{=} \forall s \in S (f_1(s) \leq f_2(s))$.

$([S \longrightarrow L], \leq)$ is a lattice with, for finite nonempty $F \subseteq [S \longrightarrow L]$, join $\bigvee F = \lambda s. \bigvee \{ f(s) \mid f \in F \}$, and meet $\bigwedge F = \lambda s. \bigwedge \{ f(s) \mid f \in F \}$. Lattice $([S \longrightarrow L], \leq)$ is complete/bounded/distributive/complemented/Boolean whenever $(L, \leq)$ is. ♡

Lemma 10.3 (J. von Neumann [vN37]) Complete Boolean lattices are MID and JID.

Proof: (From [Grä78].) Let $(L, \leq)$ be a complete Boolean lattice. We only prove JID; MID follows by duality.

If $a, a_i \in L$, for $i \in I$, then $a \wedge a_i \leq a$ and $a \wedge a_i \leq \bigvee_{i \in I} a_i$ for any $i \in I$; therefore, $a \wedge \bigvee_{i \in I} a_i$ is an upper bound for $\{ a \wedge a_i \mid i \in I \}$. Now let u be any upper bound, that is, $a \wedge a_i \leq u$ for all $i \in I$. Then

$$a_i = a_i \wedge (a \vee \bar{a}) = (a_i \wedge a) \vee (a_i \wedge \bar{a}) \leq u \vee \bar{a} .$$

Thus

$$a \wedge \bigvee_{i \in I} a_i \leq a \wedge (u \vee \bar{a}) = (a \wedge u) \vee (a \wedge \bar{a}) = a \wedge u \leq u ,$$

showing that $a \wedge \bigvee_{i \in I} a_i$ is the least upper bound for $\{ a \wedge a_i \mid i \in I \}$. Since L is complete, this least upper bound is $\bigvee_{i \in I} (a \wedge a_i)$. □

Definition 10.4 Two lattices $(A, \leq)$ and $(B, \preceq)$ are *isomorphic* if there exists a bijection $\beta : A \longrightarrow B$ such that β and β^{-1} are monotone. We denote this by $(A, \leq) \simeq (B, \preceq)$ and call β an *isomorphism*. ♣

Example 10.5 $\beta : [A \longrightarrow \mathbb{B}] \longrightarrow \mathfrak{P}(A)$ defined by $\beta(f) \stackrel{\text{def}}{=} \{\, a \in A \mid f(a) = tt \,\}$ is an isomorphism between $([A \longrightarrow \mathbb{B}], \leq)$ and $(\mathfrak{P}(A), \subseteq)$. Consequently, $([A \longrightarrow \mathbb{B}], \leq) \simeq (\mathfrak{P}(A), \subseteq)$.

$\beta' : \mathfrak{P}(A \times B) \longrightarrow [A \longrightarrow \mathfrak{P}(B)]$ defined by $\beta'(r)(a) \stackrel{\text{def}}{=} r(\{a\})$ is an iso-morphism between $(\mathfrak{P}(A \times B), \subseteq)$ and $([A \longrightarrow \mathfrak{P}(B)], \subseteq_p)$, where $\subseteq_p$ is the pointwise extension of $\subseteq$. Thus, $(\mathfrak{P}(A \times B), \subseteq) \simeq ([A \longrightarrow \mathfrak{P}(B)], \subseteq_p)$.

For $(A, \leq)$ a complemented lattice, the complement function is an isomor-phism between $(A, \leq)$ and its dual, $(A, \geq)$. $\heartsuit$

Definition 10.6 Let $(L, \leq)$ be a lattice and $K \subseteq L$. Then $(K, \leq)$ is called a *sublattice* of L if K is nonvoid and closed under meet and join, such that these operations are restrictions of L's meet and join to K. In case L is complete, K is a *complete sublattice* of L iff the above condition holds for arbitrary meets and joins.   ♣

Observe that the top and bottom elements of a complete sublattice are neces-sarily those of the super-lattice because they can be expressed as the meet and join of the empty set.

The classical counterpart for complete lattices of our fixed point lemmas for cpo's in Chapter 8 is presented next.

Theorem 10.7 (Tarski)
The fixed points of any monotone function on a complete lattice form a com-plete lattice.   ♠

We do not present the proof here, since we use at most that least and great-est fixed points exist — and this follows already from the fact that complete lattices and their duals are cpo's and from Theorem 8.10.

Note The complete lattice of fixed points of a monotone function on a com-plete lattice S is in general not a (complete) sublattice of S. For instance, any constant function on a complete lattice has exactly one fixed point, which is both top and bottom in the complete lattice of fixed points of this particular function.   ◇

10.1.2 Lattices of Predicate Transformers

A predicate ϕ on a set of variables $V \subseteq Var$ can either be regarded as a total function from states Σ^V to $\mathbb{B}$, namely as is its semantics $\mathcal{T}[\![\phi]\!]^V$, or we can view ϕ as denoting a set of states, i.e., $C[\![\phi]\!]^V$. By Examples 10.2 and 10.5, $([\Sigma^V \longrightarrow \mathbb{B}], \leq)$, where $\leq$ is the pointwise extension of $\Rightarrow$, is a complete

Boolean lattice isomorphic to $(\mathfrak{P}(\Sigma^V), \subseteq)$. In the latter structure each element is a set containing exactly those states on which the predicate yields *tt* in the former structure. The two semantics, $\mathcal{T}[\![.]\!]$ and $\mathcal{C}[\![.]\!]$, respect this isomorphism; in other words, the diagram in Figure 10.1 commutes strongly. Meet $\cap$ and join $\cup$ from the powerset lattice are therefore used interchangeably with $\wedge$ and $\vee$ from propositional logic. In the sequel we often ignore the distinction between these isomorphic lattices.

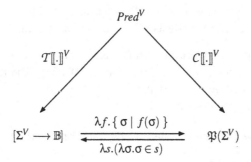

Fig. 10.1. The isomorphism between $([\Sigma^V \longrightarrow \mathbb{B}], \leq)$ and $(\mathfrak{P}(\Sigma^V), \subseteq)$ is respected by the pair of semantics $(\mathcal{T}[\![.]\!], \mathcal{C}[\![.]\!])$.

Definition 10.8 (Predicate transformers) By P^V we refer to the set of *semantic predicates* over V, ignoring the difference between $[\Sigma^V \longrightarrow \mathbb{B}]$ and $\mathfrak{P}(\Sigma^V)$. The top element $\Sigma^V \simeq \lambda\sigma.tt$ of P^V is denoted by $\top_\mathsf{P}$. Similarly we use $\bot_\mathsf{P}$ to refer to the bottom element $\emptyset \simeq \lambda\sigma.ff$.

The elements of $\mathsf{PT}_{W \leftarrow V} \stackrel{\text{def}}{=} [\mathsf{P}^V \stackrel{\text{mon}}{\longrightarrow} \mathsf{P}^W]$, the total, monotone functions from P^V to P^W, are called *predicate transformers*. The reversal of order in the subscript $\mathsf{PT}_{W \leftarrow V}$ is motivated by our aim to model programs as functions from postconditions to preconditions, opposite to the direction of computation. We denote the pointwise extension of $\leq$ on P to PT by the symbol $\preceq$.

For the same reason, the functional composition $P \circ Q$ of two predicate transformers $P \in \mathsf{PT}_{W \leftarrow V'}$ and $Q \in \mathsf{PT}_{V' \leftarrow V}$ is often written as $P ; Q$, resembling sequential composition. ♣

$\mathsf{PT}_{V \leftarrow V}$ forms a complete sublattice of $[\mathsf{P}^V \longrightarrow \mathsf{P}^V]$ closed under functional composition. This sublattice is bounded but not complemented since the complement of a monotone function is antitone but not necessarily monotone. We explain this below by way of a canonical example. It illustrates a property of all our predicate transformer lattices.

Example 10.9 Consider $V = \emptyset$. Then the state space is a singleton, $\Sigma^{\emptyset} = \{\text{m}\}$, $\top_P$ and $\bot_P$ are the only predicates, $P^{\emptyset} = \{\bot_P, \top_P\}$, and there are exactly four different total functions on $P^{\emptyset}$, only three of which are monotone:

$$\bot = \lambda\pi.\bot_P \quad \text{, which is both monotone and antitone}$$

$$1 = \lambda\pi.\pi \quad \text{, which is monotone but not antitone}$$

$$\overline{1} = \lambda\pi.\overline{\pi} \quad \text{, which is not monotone but antitone}$$

$$\top = \lambda\pi.\top_P \quad \text{, which is both monotone and antitone}$$

PT is $[P^{\emptyset} \longrightarrow P^{\emptyset}]$ without $\overline{1}$. Since PT is a sublattice of $[P^{\emptyset} \longrightarrow P^{\emptyset}]$ there is no complement for 1 in PT. Hence PT is not complemented. $\heartsuit$

Dijkstra has formulated several *healthiness conditions* which help to classify useful subclasses of predicate transformers [Dij76]. The following four conditions proposed by several authors [BvW90, GM93] differ slightly from Dijkstra's original classification.

Definition 10.10 Let S be an arbitrary predicate transformer. S is called

- *strict* iff $S(\bot_P) = \bot_P$,
- *disjunctive* iff it distributes over all nonempty disjunctions (joins),
- *total* iff $S(\top_P) = \top_P$,
- *conjunctive* iff it distributes over all nonempty conjunctions (meets).

There are sixteen combinations of these properties, each denoted by PT plus appropriate decorations introduced next. We denote strictness by superscript $\bot$, disjunctivity by subscript $_\vee$, totality by superscript $^\top$, conjunctivity by subscript $_\wedge$. For instance, the class of total, strict, conjunctive predicate transformers is denoted $PT_{\wedge}^{\top\bot}$.

Sometimes disjunctivity is too strong, but continuity is sufficient. Here continuity amounts to distributivity of joins of arbitrary chains.   ♣

The next lemma states that the subclasses of PT that we are interested in are complete lattices (used in order to obtain fixed points and because we need infinite meets).

Lemma 10.11 $(PT, \leq)$ and $(PT_\wedge, \leq)$ are complete lattices.

Proof: Exercise.   □

Remark $PT_\wedge$ is not a sublattice of PT because joins of conjunctive predicate transformers (in PT) are not necessarily conjunctive. An example of this phenomenon is given in the introduction to this chapter. However, meets in $PT_\wedge$ are the same as in PT. $\Diamond$

Lemma 10.12 The following (in)equalities hold for predicate transformers S and S_i, $i \in I$.

(i) MID: $S \vee \bigwedge_{i \in I} S_i = \bigwedge_{i \in I}(S \vee S_i)$

(ii) JID: $S \wedge \bigvee_{i \in I} S_i = \bigvee_{i \in I}(S \wedge S_i)$

(iii) $(\bigwedge_{i \in I} S_i) \mathbin{;} S = \bigwedge_{i \in I}(S_i \mathbin{;} S)$

(iv) $(\bigvee_{i \in I} S_i) \mathbin{;} S = \bigvee_{i \in I}(S_i \mathbin{;} S)$

(v) $S \mathbin{;} \bigwedge_{i \in I} S_i \leq \bigwedge_{i \in I}(S \mathbin{;} S_i)$. In case S is conjunctive this can be strengthened to an equality if I is nonvoid or S is also total.

(vi) $S \mathbin{;} \bigvee_{i \in I} S_i \geq \bigvee_{i \in I}(S \mathbin{;} S_i)$. If

- $(S_i)_{i \in I}$ is a chain and S is continuous, or
- S is disjunctive and, additionally, I is nonvoid or S is strict,

then this inequality can be strengthened to an equality.

Proof: Since the predicate transformers, $(\mathsf{PT}, \leq)$, are a complete sublattice of the complete Boolean lattice of predicate-to-predicate functions, MID and JID follow easily from Lemma 10.3. Claims (iii) and (iv) follow immediately from the definitions. We demonstrate only claim (vi). By monotonicity of sequential composition, that is, monotonicity of each predicate transformer, it follows that, for all $i \in I$, $(S \mathbin{;} \bigvee_{i \in I} S_i)\pi = S(\bigvee_{i \in I} S_i \pi) \geq S(S_i \pi) = (S \mathbin{;} S_i)\pi$, whence $S \mathbin{;} \bigvee_{i \in I} S_i \geq \bigvee_{i \in I}(S \mathbin{;} S_i)$. The strengthening follows directly from the definitions of either chains and continuity, or disjunctivity and strictness. $\square$

10.1.3 Galois Connections

In this section we briefly introduce a fundamental notion called *Galois connection* due to Birkhoff [Bir40] and Ore. We cite Ore:

… a general type of correspondence between structures which I have called Galois connexions. These correspondences occur in a great variety of mathematical theories and in several instances in the theory of relations.   [Ore44, p. 493]

It is this concept that allows us to propagate lemmas and theorems from one partial order to another, given that a certain relationship between these partial orders has been established. For readers familiar with category theory, Galois connections are just adjoints between partial orders; for the rest of us, we proceed with the following definition which (in its general form for classes instead of sets) is attributed in [HH85] to [Ore44] and [Sch53].

Definition 10.13 (Galois connection) Let $G : A \longrightarrow B$ and $F : B \longrightarrow A$ be monotone functions between posets $(A, \leq)$ and $(B, \preceq)$. Then (F, G) is called a *Galois connection* iff, for all $a \in A$ and $b \in B$, $F(b) \leq a \Leftrightarrow b \preceq G(a)$.   ♣

We recommend that readers unacquainted with this concept prove the following lemma to gain some insight into the variety of properties of Galois connections.

Lemma 10.14 (O. Ore [Ore44] and J. Schmidt [Sch53]) Let $G : A \longrightarrow B$ and $F : B \longrightarrow A$ be monotone functions between posets $(A, \leq)$ and $(B, \preceq)$. Then the following conditions (i) and (ii) are equivalent and imply the remaining ones, where $F^{\blacktriangleright} = FB$ and $G^{\blacktriangleright} = GA$ denote the ranges of the two functions:

- (i) (F, G) is a Galois connection.
- (ii) $FGa \leq a$ and $b \preceq GFb$ for all $a \in A$ and $b \in B$.
- (iii) G preserves meets and F preserves joins.
- (iv) $GFG = G$ and $FGF = F$.
- (v) $(GF)^2 = GF$ and $(FG)^2 = FG$.
- (vi) $F^{\blacktriangleright} = FG^{\blacktriangleright} = \{\, a \in A \mid FGa = a \,\}$ and
  $G^{\blacktriangleright} = GF^{\blacktriangleright} = \{\, b \in B \mid GFb = b \,\}$.
- (vii) When G and F are restricted to domains $F^{\blacktriangleright}$ and $G^{\blacktriangleright}$ then the resulting functions $\widetilde{G} : F^{\blacktriangleright} \longrightarrow G^{\blacktriangleright}$ and $\widetilde{F} : G^{\blacktriangleright} \longrightarrow F^{\blacktriangleright}$ are inverse to each other and order isomorphisms.

Proof: Exercise.   □

10.1.4 Relations and Predicate Transformers

Recall that $R_{\perp} = \{\, r \subseteq \Sigma_{\perp}^2 \mid K \subseteq r \wedge r; K \subseteq r \,\}$ denotes the set relations expressing our total correctness semantics, where $K = \{\perp\} \times \Sigma_{\perp}$. $R_{\perp}$ is a poset with the partial order relation $\supseteq$ pronounced "is refined by". Furthermore $(R_{\perp}, \supseteq)$ is a complete, distributive lattice which is closed under sequential composition but not complemented. Its top element is K and its bottom element is $U_{\perp} = \Sigma_{\perp}^2$.

Next we establish an isomorphism between $R_{\perp}$ and the conjunctive predicate transformers $\mathsf{PT}_{\wedge}$ that distributes over sequential composition.

To do so, let us first introduce a Galois connection $(\bigstar, [.])$ between PT and $R_{\perp}$ such that we can apply Lemma 10.14.(vii). Then, to prove the promised isomorphism, it only remains to show that $\bigstar$ is onto and the range of $[.]$ is $\mathsf{PT}_{\wedge}$, i.e., $\bigstar^{\blacktriangleright} = R_{\perp}$ and $[.]^{\blacktriangleright} = \mathsf{PT}_{\wedge}$.

$$[.] : R_{\perp} \longrightarrow \mathsf{PT}$$

$$[r] \stackrel{\text{def}}{=} \lambda s \subseteq \Sigma. \{\, \sigma \in \Sigma_{\perp} \mid \forall \tau \in \Sigma_{\perp} ((\sigma, \tau) \in r \Rightarrow \tau \in s) \,\} \qquad (10.1)$$

$$\bigstar : \mathsf{PT} \longrightarrow R_{\perp}$$

$$\bigstar P \stackrel{\text{def}}{=} \{ (\sigma,\tau) \in \Sigma_\perp \times \Sigma_\perp \mid \forall s \subseteq \Sigma(\sigma \in P(s) \Rightarrow \tau \in s) \} \qquad (10.2)$$

Well-definedness of [.] means that $[r]$ is monotone and that $\perp \notin [r]s$, for $r \in R_\perp$ and $s \subseteq \Sigma$. The latter follows from $K \subseteq r$ and $\perp \notin s$. Monotonicity of these functions is immediate. $\bigstar P \in R_\perp$ is proven in Lemma 10.16.

Lemma 10.15 $(\bigstar, [.])$ is a Galois connection.

Proof: We check the defining property of Galois connections, Def. 10.13.

$$\bigstar P \supseteq r$$

$\Leftrightarrow$ (by (10.2))

$$\forall \sigma,\tau \in \Sigma_\perp ((\sigma,\tau) \in r \Rightarrow \forall s \subseteq \Sigma(\sigma \in P(s) \Rightarrow \tau \in s))$$

$\Leftrightarrow$ (pred. calc.)

$$\forall s \subseteq \Sigma(\forall \sigma \in \Sigma_\perp (\sigma \in P(s) \Rightarrow \forall \tau \in \Sigma_\perp ((\sigma,\tau) \in r \Rightarrow \tau \in s)))$$

$\Leftrightarrow$ (set theory)

$$\forall s \subseteq \Sigma(P(s) \subseteq \{ \sigma \in \Sigma_\perp \mid \forall \tau \in \Sigma_\perp ((\sigma,\tau) \in r \Rightarrow \tau \in s) \})$$

$\Leftrightarrow$ (by (10.1))

$$P \leq [r] \qquad\qquad \square$$

Lemma 10.16 The range of $\bigstar$ is $R_\perp$ and the range of [.] is $\mathsf{PT}_\wedge$.

Proof: Let $P \in \mathsf{PT}$. To prove $\bigstar P \in R_\perp$ we have to show that $K \subseteq \bigstar P$ and $\bigstar P; K \subseteq \bigstar P$. Let $\sigma,\tau \in \Sigma_\perp$.

$$
\begin{aligned}
(\perp,\tau) \in \bigstar P &\Leftrightarrow \forall s \subseteq \Sigma(\perp \in P(s) \Rightarrow \tau \in s) &&(10.2)\\
&\Leftrightarrow \forall s \subseteq \Sigma(\mathit{ff} \Rightarrow \tau \in s) &&P(s) \subseteq \Sigma\\
&\Leftrightarrow \mathit{tt} &&\text{pred. calc.}
\end{aligned}
$$

Hence, $K \subseteq \bigstar P$.

$$
\begin{aligned}
(\sigma,\tau) \in \bigstar P; K &\Leftrightarrow (\sigma,\perp) \in \bigstar P &&\text{def. of } K\\
&\Leftrightarrow \forall s \subseteq \Sigma(\sigma \in P(s) \Rightarrow \perp \in s) &&(10.2)\\
&\Leftrightarrow \forall s \subseteq \Sigma(\sigma \in P(s) \Rightarrow \mathit{ff}) &&s \subseteq \Sigma\\
&\Rightarrow \forall s \subseteq \Sigma(\sigma \in P(s) \Rightarrow \tau \in s) &&\text{pred. calc.}\\
&\Leftrightarrow (\sigma,\tau) \in \bigstar P &&(10.2)
\end{aligned}
$$

Thus, $\bigstar P; K \subseteq \bigstar P$.

Next we show that $\bigstar[.] = id_{R_\perp}$, which proves that $\bigstar$ is onto. Let $r \in R_\perp$. Then, by Lemma 10.14.(ii), $\bigstar[r] \supseteq r$. Hence it suffices to show $\bigstar[r] \subseteq r$.

$$(\sigma,\tau) \in \bigstar[r]$$

$$\Leftrightarrow \forall s \subseteq \Sigma(\sigma \in [r]s \Rightarrow \tau \in s) \qquad\qquad (10.2)$$

$$\Leftrightarrow \forall s \subseteq \Sigma(\forall \rho \in \Sigma_\perp((\sigma,\rho) \in r \Rightarrow \rho \in s) \Rightarrow \tau \in s) \qquad (10.1)$$

$$\Rightarrow \forall \rho \in \Sigma_\perp((\sigma,\rho) \in r \Rightarrow \rho \in \Sigma\setminus\{\tau\}) \Rightarrow \tau \in \Sigma\setminus\{\tau\} \qquad \text{inst. } s = \Sigma\setminus\{\tau\}$$

$$\Leftrightarrow \exists \rho \in \Sigma_\perp((\sigma,\rho) \in r \wedge \rho \in \{\tau,\perp\}) \qquad\qquad \text{pred. calc.}$$

$$\Leftrightarrow (\sigma,\tau) \in r \vee (\sigma,\perp) \in r \qquad\qquad \text{pred. calc.}$$

$$\Rightarrow (\sigma,\tau) \in r \qquad\qquad \text{since } r; K \subseteq r$$

Monotonicity and conjunctivity of $[r]$ follow immediately from the definitions. Furthermore, $[.]$ maps onto $\mathsf{PT}_\wedge$, i.e., $\forall P \in \mathsf{PT}_\wedge (\exists r \in R_\perp ([r] = P))$. It is sufficient to show $\forall P \in \mathsf{PT}_\wedge ([\bigstar P] = P)$. Now let $P \in \mathsf{PT}_\wedge$ and $s \subseteq \Sigma$.

Any such s can be expressed as an intersection, in other words, the meet, of sets having at most one element less than Σ. Independently of s, Σ is such a set; thus this meet is always nonvoid.

$$s = \bigwedge \{ \Sigma\setminus\{\tau\} \mid \tau \in \Sigma_\perp \setminus s \} \qquad\qquad (10.3)$$

Let $\sigma \in \Sigma_\perp$.

$$\sigma \in [\bigstar P]s$$

$$\Leftrightarrow \forall \tau((\sigma,\tau) \in \bigstar P \Rightarrow \tau \in s) \qquad\qquad (10.1)$$

$$\Leftrightarrow \forall \tau(\forall t(\sigma \in P(t) \Rightarrow \tau \in t) \Rightarrow \tau \in s) \qquad (10.2)$$

$$\Leftrightarrow \forall \tau(\forall t(\tau \notin t \Rightarrow \sigma \notin P(t)) \Rightarrow \tau \in s) \qquad \text{pred. calc.}$$

$$\Leftrightarrow \forall \tau(\forall t \subseteq \Sigma\setminus\{\tau\}(\sigma \notin P(t)) \Rightarrow \tau \in s) \qquad \text{pred. calc.}$$

$$\Leftrightarrow \forall \tau(\sigma \notin P(\Sigma\setminus\{\tau\}) \Rightarrow \tau \in s) \qquad \begin{array}{l}\text{``}\Leftarrow\text{'': instance } t = \Sigma\setminus\{\tau\}, \\ \text{``}\Rightarrow\text{'': } P \text{ monotone}\end{array}$$

$$\Leftrightarrow \sigma \in \bigwedge \{ P(\Sigma\setminus\{\tau\}) \mid \tau \in \Sigma_\perp \setminus s \} \qquad \text{pred. calc., set theory}$$

$$\Leftrightarrow \sigma \in P\left(\bigwedge \{ \Sigma\setminus\{\tau\} \mid \tau \in \Sigma_\perp \setminus s \}\right) \qquad P \text{ conjunctive}$$

$$\Leftrightarrow \sigma \in P(s) \qquad\qquad (10.3) \qquad \Box$$

Theorem 10.17

$(R_\perp, \supseteq) \simeq (\mathsf{PT}_\wedge, \leq)$.

Proof: Lemmas 10.15 and 10.16 provide the prerequisites for an application of Lemma 10.14.(vii), which then ensures that $[.]$ is an order isomorphism between $R_\perp$ and $\mathsf{PT}_\wedge$. $\qquad \Box$

Lemma 10.18 Let $r_1, r_2, r_i \in R_\perp$ and $P_1, P_2, P_i \in \mathsf{PT}$, for $i \in I$.

  (i) $[r_1 ; r_2] = [r_1] ; [r_2]$.
  (ii) $\bigstar P_1 ; \bigstar P_2 \subseteq \bigstar(P_1 ; P_2)$.
  (iii) $[\bigcup_{i \in I} r_i] = \bigwedge_{i \in I} [r_i]$.
  (iv) $\bigcup_{i \in I}(\bigstar P_i) \subseteq (\bigwedge_{i \in I} P_i)$.

The two inclusions can be strengthened to equalities in case the predicate transformers involved are conjunctive.

Proof: Let $s \subseteq \Sigma$ and $\sigma \in \Sigma_\perp$.

$$\sigma \in ([r_1] ; [r_2])s$$
$$\Leftrightarrow \sigma \in [r_1]([r_2]s) \qquad\qquad \text{Def. 10.8}$$
$$\Leftrightarrow \sigma \in [r_1](\{ \sigma \in \Sigma_\perp \mid \forall \tau \in \Sigma_\perp ((\sigma, \tau) \in r_2 \Rightarrow \tau \in s) \}) \qquad (10.1)$$
$$\Leftrightarrow \forall \tau' \in \Sigma_\perp ((\sigma, \tau') \in r_1 \Rightarrow \forall \tau ((\tau', \tau) \in r_2 \Rightarrow \tau \in s)) \qquad (10.1)$$
$$\Leftrightarrow \forall \tau \in \Sigma_\perp (\exists \tau' ((\sigma, \tau') \in r_1 \wedge (\tau', \tau) \in r_2) \Rightarrow \tau \in s) \qquad \text{pred. calc.}$$
$$\Leftrightarrow \sigma \in [r_1 ; r_2]s \qquad\qquad (10.1)$$

By monotonicity of $;$ and Lemma 10.14.(ii) $P_1 ; P_2 \leq [\bigstar P_1] ; [\bigstar P_2]$, which, by the first part of this lemma, is equal to $[\bigstar P_1 ; \bigstar P_2]$. By monotonicity of $\bigstar$ this implies that $\bigstar(P_1 ; P_2) \supseteq \bigstar[\bigstar P_1 ; \bigstar P_2]$. The latter equals $\bigstar P_1 ; \bigstar P_2$ since $\bigstar[.] = id_{R_\perp}$, as proved in Lemma 10.16. This proves the second claim.

$$\left[\bigcup_{i \in I} r_i\right] s = \left\{ \sigma \;\middle|\; \forall \tau \left((\sigma, \tau) \in \bigcup_{i \in I} r_i \Rightarrow \tau \in s\right) \right\} \qquad (10.1)$$
$$= \bigcap_{i \in I} \{ \sigma \mid \forall \tau ((\sigma, \tau) \in r_i \Rightarrow \tau \in s) \} \qquad\qquad \text{set theory}$$
$$= \bigcap_{i \in I} ([r_i] s) \qquad\qquad (10.1)$$
$$= \left(\bigwedge_{i \in I} [r_i]\right) s$$

The last claim follows along the same lines as the second one. $\qquad\square$

Plotkin [Plo79] and Smyth [Smy83] prove various isomorphisms, for instance, between total, finitary relations and strict, continuous, conjunctive predicate transformers. These and related isomorphisms are the topic of [BK93].

As a consequence of the lemmas above, the least conjunctive refinement of a predicate transformer is easily expressed.

Lemma 10.19 $[\bigstar P]$ is the least conjunctive refinement of $P \in \mathsf{PT}$.

Proof: Let $P \in$ PT. Then $[\bigstar P]$ is conjunctive by Lemma 10.16 and refines P by Lemma 10.14.(ii). We finally prove that $[\bigstar P]$ is the least refined such predicate transformer. Every conjunctive predicate transformer can be expressed as $[r]$ for some $r \in R_\perp$ by Lemma 10.16.

$$P \leq [r] \Rightarrow [\bigstar P] \leq [\bigstar [r]] \qquad \bigstar \text{ and } [.] \text{ monotone}$$

$$\Leftrightarrow [\bigstar P] \leq [r] \qquad\qquad \text{Lemma } 10.14.\text{(iv)} \qquad\qquad \Box$$

This relationship is the subject of [Mor94] and will be exploited when defining implementability of programs in Section 10.2.3.

10.2 Predicate Transformer Semantics

Although the general concept behind predicate transformers is older (it appears, e.g., in [dBdR72, HP72, dBM75, dR76]), the name "predicate transformers" was first suggested by Dijkstra [Dij75, Dij76] for a mechanism which he used to give meaning to the formulae of a program verification calculus for total correctness that he developed. In this calculus, one uses expressions which read "Execution of the program S is guaranteed to terminate in a state satisfying the predicate ϕ" (written $wp(S)\phi$). Moreover, such expressions are used freely as though they themselves were predicates. For example one might write

$$x > 1 \Rightarrow wp(x := x + 1)(x > 2)$$

to express that if x is greater than 1 then execution of $x := x + 1$ is guaranteed to terminate and afterwards x is greater than 2.

Note that the predicate transformers that arise in this way map predicates in a direction opposite to the flow of computation: they map each possible postcondition onto a precondition sufficient to guarantee attainment of the postcondition.

At first it might seem that there is some freedom in the choice of this precondition (always choosing false for example), but this is not so, because, in writing $wp(S)\phi$, the intention is to assert no more than S establishes ϕ; hence the weakest such precondition is intended (i.e., the one which is most often true).

10.2.1 Weakest Precondition Semantics

Definition 10.20 (*wp*-semantics) By $\Delta_{PT} = [Rvar \longrightarrow$ PT] we refer to the set of *recursion variable environments*. If $s \subseteq \Sigma$ and $\rho \in \Delta_{\mathsf{PT}}$, then we define semantic function $wp : Prog \longrightarrow (\Delta_{\mathsf{PT}} \longrightarrow \mathsf{PT})$ as follows:

$$wp(\textbf{abort})(\rho)s \stackrel{\mathrm{def}}{=} \emptyset$$

$$wp(\textbf{skip})(\rho)s \stackrel{\mathrm{def}}{=} s$$

$$wp(x := e)(\rho)s \stackrel{\mathrm{def}}{=} \{\, \sigma \in \Sigma \mid (\sigma : x \mapsto \mathcal{E}[\![e]\!]_{\perp}\sigma) \in s \,\}$$

$$wp(b \rightarrow)(\rho)s \stackrel{\mathrm{def}}{=} C[\![\neg b]\!]_{\perp} \cup (C[\![b]\!]_{\perp} \cap s)$$

$$wp(\phi \rightsquigarrow \psi)(\rho)s \stackrel{\mathrm{def}}{=} \{\, \sigma \mid \exists \gamma ((\gamma, \sigma) \in C[\![\phi]\!]_{\perp} \wedge C[\![\psi]\!]_{\perp}(\{\gamma\}) \subseteq s) \,\}$$

$$wp(X)(\rho) \stackrel{\mathrm{def}}{=} \rho(X)$$

$$wp(S_1 ; S_2)(\rho) \stackrel{\mathrm{def}}{=} wp(S_1)(\rho) \,\dot{;}\, wp(S_2)(\rho)$$

$$wp(S_1 \,[\!]\, S_2)(\rho) \stackrel{\mathrm{def}}{=} wp(S_1)(\rho) \wedge wp(S_2)(\rho)$$

$$wp(\mu X . S)(\rho) \stackrel{\mathrm{def}}{=} \mu_{\lambda P . wp(S)(\rho : X \mapsto P)}$$

(Recall that $C[\![\psi]\!]_{\perp}(\{\gamma\})$ denotes the relational image of set $\{\gamma\}$ under relation $C[\![\psi]\!]_{\perp}$, thus $C[\![\psi]\!]_{\perp}(\{\gamma\}) \subseteq s$ abbreviates $\forall \sigma ((\gamma, \sigma) \in C[\![\psi]\!]_{\perp} \Rightarrow \sigma \in s)$.)

As usual, we tend to suppress the recursion variable environment since we concentrate on programs without free occurrences of recursion variables. ♣

Lemma 10.21 Function wp is well-defined.

Proof: Monotonicity of $wp(S)(\rho)s$ in s for atomic statements S follows since argument s occurs neither complemented nor on the LHS of a $\subseteq$ symbol in the definition above. Furthermore, sequential composition, meet, and forming least fixed points of predicate transformers preserve monotonicity. For the least fixed point of $\lambda P . wp(S)(\rho : X \mapsto P)$ to exist it is sufficient to prove monotonicity of $wp(S)(\rho : X \mapsto P)$ in P. This follows by a straightforward induction on the structure of S. □

Note We define the function wp in a semantic fashion, i.e., it maps a program (the only syntactic argument) via an environment to a function from sets of states to sets of states. A purely syntactic definition would have mapped programs and syntactic environments to a function from predicates to predicates. Such a function is harder to define for two reasons.

- First order predicates *Pred* are not strong enough to express the weakest precondition of recursion.
- In the presence of infinite nondeterminism, program constructors are still monotone but not necessarily continuous.

Consequently one needs a formalism for reasoning about partial correctness and termination for recursion over monotone program constructors, which additionally incorporates the predicate transformers induced by the resulting constructs. The theory required for defining such a formalism involves some deep fundamental research in logic and the theory of programs developed since the 1940s, leading up to the development of the monotone μ-calculus by David Park and colleagues, and the propositional μ-calculus by Dexter Kozen and colleagues, and is discussed in Section 3.5. In a different direction, Ralph Back uses the infinitary logic L_{ω_1,ω_1} to reason about the infinite nondeterminism inherent in specification statements [B81b]. L_{ω_1,ω_1} is a predicate logic with countably infinite disjunctions and conjunctions (that is what the first ω_1 stands for) and countably infinite quantification (indicated by the second ω_1). Well-foundedness can be expressed in this logic (for the monotone μ-calculus this is shown in Section 3.5), and also finiteness of domains (which can be done neither in *Pred* nor in the monotone μ-calculus). When specification statements are omitted from *Prog*, infinite nondeterminism vanishes, and finite quantification is sufficient to express weakest preconditions although infinite disjunction and conjunction are still required to cope with recursion.   ◇

10.2.2 Properties of wp

Before we present an example illustrating the weakest precondition of a simple specification statement we show how to express $wp(\phi \leadsto \psi)(C[\![\pi]\!]_\perp)$. This simplifies the exposition of later examples.

Lemma 10.22 Let $\vec{x}$ denote the program variables and $\vec{x}_0$ the logical variables on the level under consideration. Let $\phi, \psi \in Pred^{\vec{x}_0,\vec{x}}$ and $\pi \in Pred^{\vec{x}}$. If $T[\![\phi]\!]_\perp^{\vec{x}_0,\vec{x}}(\gamma,\sigma) = tt$ implies that $T[\![\psi]\!]_\perp^{\vec{x}_0,\vec{x}}(\gamma,\tau)$ does not evaluate to $\perp$ in any proper state $\tau \in \Sigma^{\vec{x}}$, then

$$wp(\phi \leadsto \psi)(C[\![\pi]\!]_\perp^{\vec{x}}) = C[\![\exists \vec{x}_0\,(\phi \wedge \forall \vec{x}(\psi \Rightarrow \pi))]\!]_\perp^{\vec{x}} \ .$$

Proof:

$$\sigma \in wp(\phi \leadsto \psi)(C[\![\pi]\!]_\perp^{\vec{x}})$$

$\Leftrightarrow$ (Def. 10.20)

$$\exists \gamma\Big((\gamma,\sigma) \in C[\![\phi]\!]_\perp^{\vec{x}_0,\vec{x}} \wedge C[\![\psi]\!]_\perp^{\vec{x}_0,\vec{x}}(\{\gamma\}) \subseteq C[\![\pi]\!]_\perp^{\vec{x}}\Big)$$

$\Leftrightarrow$ (Def. 3.6)

$$\exists \gamma\Big((\gamma,\sigma) \in C[\![\phi]\!]_\perp^{\vec{x}_0,\vec{x}} \wedge \forall \tau\Big((\gamma,\tau) \in C[\![\psi]\!]_\perp^{\vec{x}_0,\vec{x}} \Rightarrow \tau \in C[\![\pi]\!]_\perp^{\vec{x}}\Big)\Big)$$

⟺   (assumption)

$$\exists \gamma \left((\gamma, \sigma) \in C[\![\phi]\!]_{\perp}^{\vec{x_0}, \vec{x}} \wedge \forall \tau \left((\gamma, \tau) \in C[\![\psi \Rightarrow \pi]\!]_{\perp}^{\vec{x_0}, \vec{x}} \right) \right)$$

⟺   (Def. 8.23)

$$\sigma \in C[\![\exists \vec{x_0} (\phi \wedge \forall \vec{x} (\psi \Rightarrow \pi))]\!]_{\perp}^{\vec{x}} \qquad\qquad \Box$$

Example 10.23 We calculate the weakest precondition of the specification statement $x = x_0 \rightsquigarrow x = x_0 + 1$ w.r.t. postcondition $3 < x < 9$.

$$wp(x = x_0 \rightsquigarrow x = x_0 + 1)(C[\![3 < x < 9]\!]_{\perp})$$

$= C[\![\exists x_0 (x = x_0 \wedge \forall x (x = x_0 + 1 \Rightarrow 3 < x < 9))]\!]_{\perp}$ Lemma 10.22

$= C[\![\exists x_0 (x = x_0 \wedge 3 < x_0 + 1 < 9)]\!]_{\perp}$ one-point rule

$= C[\![3 < x + 1 < 9]\!]_{\perp}$ one-point rule

$= C[\![2 < x < 8]\!]_{\perp}$ arithmetic   ♡

Since they provide a useful abstraction for the rest of this chapter we define *assert statements*, $\{b\}$ for $b \in Bexp$, as an abbreviation for $b \rightarrow [\,] (\neg b \rightarrow$ **abort**). Recall the operational interpretation of guard $b \rightarrow$: when executed in a state satisfying b it behaves like **skip**, if b evaluates to $\perp$ the guard does not terminate, and otherwise it blocks. The assert statement $\{b\}$ behaves in the same way except that it does not terminate in case $b \rightarrow$ deadlocks. In contrast to nontrivial guards, assert statements are implementable because they correspond to total relations.

Lemma 10.24 The assert statement enjoys the following properties.

* $wp(\{b\})s = C[\![b]\!]_{\perp} \cap s$
* $wp(\{b\}) = wp((\vec{x} = \vec{x_0} \wedge b) \rightsquigarrow (\vec{x} = \vec{x_0}))$.
* $wp(\{b_1\} ; \{b_2\}) = wp(\{b_1 \wedge b_2\})$.
* $b_1 \Rightarrow b_2$ iff $wp(\{b_1\}) \leq wp(\{b_2\})$.

Proof: Exercise. $\Box$

Returning to the discussion of the correspondence between *wp* and our relational total correctness semantics above, we address the question whether *wp* has its intended meaning, i.e., whether condition $\mathcal{F}[\![\{\phi\} S \{\psi\}]\!]_{\perp}$ and $C[\![\phi]\!]_{\perp} \subseteq wp(S)(C[\![\psi]\!]_{\perp})$ are indeed equivalent. In other words, does the diagram in Figure 10.2 commute strongly? The answer is: No. If that had been true, we could have saved the trouble of defining *wp* above and resorted to $[\mathcal{P}[\![.]\!]_{\perp}]$ in place of *wp*. The crucial stumbling block concerns specification statements.

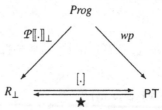

Fig. 10.2. Coincidence of $\mathcal{P}[\![.]\!]_\perp$ and *wp*.

Function *wp* is defined such that it respects the Galois connection between the two semantic domains in the sense that the diagram in Figure 10.2 commutes weakly. Here weak commutativity means that, for all S in *Prog*,

$$\bigstar wp(S) \supseteq \mathcal{P}[\![S]\!]_\perp \quad \text{and} \quad wp(S) \leq [\mathcal{P}[\![S]\!]_\perp] \qquad (10.4)$$

We shall see below that the LHS "$\supseteq$" can always be replaced by an equality sign. For programs constructed without using specification statements this also holds for the RHS "$\leq$", i.e., in that case the diagram even commutes strongly. Next we explain why this diagram does not commute strongly for certain programs involving $\phi \rightsquigarrow \psi$. Before doing so, we first give a motivation for the definition of $wp(\phi \rightsquigarrow \psi)$.

As usual with *wp* semantics the formula on the RHS of Def. 10.20 is the property required of programming variables so that execution of the conceptual program $\phi \rightsquigarrow \psi$ will achieve s. This formula is most intuitively read from the inside out.

- Formula $C[\![\psi]\!]_\perp(\{\gamma\}) \subseteq s$ takes account of the freedom enjoyed by $\phi \rightsquigarrow \psi$ when choosing a final state: it may pick any state satisfying ψ, and so if one wishes to terminate in a member of s then all states satisfying ψ better belong to s.
- This subformula is conjoined with ϕ. This is necessary because, unless ϕ holds, $\phi \rightsquigarrow \psi$ is completely unconstrained (it may even fail to terminate). Hence if one wishes to terminate in s then one must ensure that ϕ holds.
- Lastly, there is the existential quantification over the logical variables. This is best understood by thinking of ϕ and ψ as a family of predicate-pair specifications, indexed by the values of logical constants. Since $\phi \rightsquigarrow \psi$ is constrained by every such predicate pair, there need only be one predicate pair that ensures termination in s for $\phi \rightsquigarrow \psi$ to be adequately constrained.

Example 10.25 Recall Example 8.34, a more intricate example of a specification statement which we considered unimplementable in Chapter 8. We calculate the weakest precondition of the specification statement $S \stackrel{\text{def}}{=} x = x_0^2 \rightsquigarrow x = x_0$ w.r.t. postcondition $C[\![x = 2]\!]_\perp$.

$$
\begin{aligned}
& wp(S)(C[\![x = 2]\!]) \\
&= C[\![\exists x_0 \left(x = x_0^2 \wedge \forall x (x = x_0 \Rightarrow x = 2)\right)]\!]_\perp \qquad \text{Lemma 10.22} \\
&= C[\![\exists x_0 \left(x = x_0^2 \wedge x_0 = 2\right)]\!]_\perp \qquad\qquad\qquad \text{one-point rule} \\
&= C[\![x = 4]\!]_\perp \qquad\qquad\qquad\qquad\qquad\qquad \text{one-point rule}
\end{aligned}
$$

This is not just $C[\![\text{false}]\!]_\perp$, as one might have expected, because $wp(S)$ is not conjunctive but so-called *angelic* [B78, vW90].[1] To see that $wp(S)$ is not conjunctive, simply repeat the above calculation with postcondition $x = -2$. This also yields $x = 4$ as weakest precondition. Now $wp(S)(C[\![x = 2]\!]_\perp) \cap wp(S)(C[\![x = -2]\!]_\perp) = C[\![x = 4]\!]_\perp$ whereas $wp(S)(C[\![x = 2 \wedge x = -2]\!]_\perp) = wp(S)\emptyset = \emptyset$.

Observe that $[\mathcal{P}[\![S]\!]_\perp] \in \mathsf{PT}_\wedge$ is different from $wp(S)$. By Lemma 10.19, $[\mathcal{P}[\![S]\!]_\perp] = [\bigstar wp(S)]$ is the least conjunctive predicate transformer refining $wp(S)$. $\qquad\qquad\qquad\qquad\qquad\qquad\qquad\qquad\qquad\qquad\qquad\qquad\quad \heartsuit$

Theorem 10.26
If S does not contain specification statements, $wp(S)$ is conjunctive.

Proof: Structural induction. The base cases and the induction steps for sequential composition and choice are immediate. Consider the case $S = \mu X.T$. The function $f \stackrel{\text{def}}{=} \lambda P.wp(T)(\rho : X \mapsto P)$ on PT has a least fixed point μ_f by Theorem 10.7 because PT is a complete lattice and f is monotone. By Theorem 8.10 $\mu_f = \bigwedge_{i<\kappa}(f^i(\perp_{\mathsf{PT}}))$. Now observe that $\perp_{\mathsf{PT}} = \lambda s.\perp_\mathsf{P} \in \mathsf{PT}_\wedge$ and that f preserves conjunctivity. Since $\mathsf{PT}_\wedge$ and PT agree on meets and μ_f is expressible as a meet of elements of $\mathsf{PT}_\wedge$, also $\mu_f \in \mathsf{PT}_\wedge$. $\qquad\qquad \square$

On the other hand, $\bigstar(wp(S)) = \mathcal{P}[\![S]\!]_\perp$, as one easily verifies, holds for all programs $S \in Prog$, including those constructed using specification statements.

Theorem 10.27
For all programs S of our language *Prog*, $\bigstar wp(S) = \mathcal{P}[\![S]\!]_\perp$ and $wp(S) \leq [\mathcal{P}[\![S]\!]_\perp]$. The latter can be strengthened to an equality if S does not contain specification statements.

Proof: We prove $\bigstar wp(S) = \mathcal{P}[\![S]\!]_\perp$ by induction on the structure of $S \in Prog$. The cases **abort**, **skip**, $x := e$, and $b \rightarrow$ are easy. We demonstrate this for the

---

[1] In the predicate transformer world the adjective *angelic* is used to describe the semantic counterpart of programs that may adapt their behavior to the postconditions they are supposed to satisfy. Operationally, such programs employ some sort of backtracking.

guard $b \rightarrow$.

$$(\sigma, \tau) \in \bigstar wp(b \rightarrow)$$

$\Leftrightarrow$ (by (10.2), Def. 10.20)

$$\forall s \subseteq \Sigma (\sigma \in (C[\![\neg b]\!]_\perp \cup (C[\![b]\!]_\perp \cap s)) \Rightarrow \tau \in s)$$

$\Leftrightarrow$ (mutual implication, "$\Rightarrow$": instance $s = \Sigma \setminus \{\tau\}$)

$$\sigma \notin C[\![\neg b]\!]_\perp \wedge (\sigma \in C[\![b]\!]_\perp \Rightarrow \sigma = \tau)$$

$\Leftrightarrow$ (Def. 8.29)

$$(\sigma, \tau) \in P[\![b \rightarrow]\!]_\perp$$

Case S is a specification statement $\phi \rightsquigarrow \psi$:

$$(\sigma, \tau) \in \bigstar wp(\phi \rightsquigarrow \psi)$$

$\Leftrightarrow$ (by (10.2), Def. 10.20)

$$\forall s \subseteq \Sigma (\exists \gamma ((\gamma, \sigma) \in C[\![\phi]\!]_\perp \wedge C[\![\psi]\!]_\perp (\{\gamma\}) \subseteq s) \Rightarrow \tau \in s)$$

$\Leftrightarrow$ (pred. calc.)

$$\forall s \subseteq \Sigma, \gamma ((\gamma, \sigma) \in C[\![\phi]\!]_\perp \wedge C[\![\psi]\!]_\perp (\{\gamma\}) \subseteq s \Rightarrow \tau \in s)$$

$\Leftrightarrow$ ("$\Rightarrow$": instance $s = C[\![\psi]\!]_\perp (\{\gamma\})$)

$$\forall \gamma ((\gamma, \sigma) \in C[\![\phi]\!]_\perp \Rightarrow \tau \in C[\![\psi]\!]_\perp (\{\gamma\}))$$

$\Leftrightarrow$ (Def. 3.6)

$$\forall \gamma ((\gamma, \sigma) \in C[\![\phi]\!]_\perp \Rightarrow (\gamma, \tau) \in C[\![\psi]\!]_\perp)$$

$\Leftrightarrow$ (Def. 8.29)

$$(\sigma, \tau) \in P[\![\phi \rightsquigarrow \psi]\!]_\perp$$

A refined analysis of the claim we want to prove reveals that we overlooked recursion variables. Let $\rho \in \Delta_{PT}$ and define $\rho_\bigstar \stackrel{\text{def}}{=} \lambda X. \bigstar \rho(X)$. Then it is immediate that $\bigstar wp(X)(\rho) = \bigstar \rho(X) = \rho_\bigstar (X) = P[\![X]\!]_\perp (\rho_\bigstar)$.

The induction steps for sequential composition and choice are immediate. Case S is $\mu X.T$:

$$\begin{aligned}
\bigstar wp(\mu X.T)(\rho) &= \bigstar \mu_{\lambda P. wp(T)(\rho : X \mapsto P)} & \text{Def. 10.20} \\
&= \bigstar \bigvee_{i < \kappa} wp(T)^i (\rho : X \mapsto \perp_{PT}) & \text{Th. 8.10} \\
&= \bigcap_{i < \kappa} \bigstar wp(T)^i (\rho : X \mapsto \perp_{PT}) & \text{Lemma 10.14.(iii)} \\
&= \bigcap_{i < \kappa} P[\![T]\!]^i_\perp (\rho_\bigstar : X \mapsto \perp_{R_\perp}) & \text{ind. hyp.} \\
&= \mu_{\lambda r. P[\![T]\!]_\perp (\rho_\bigstar : X \mapsto r)} & \text{Th. 8.10}
\end{aligned}$$

$$= \mathcal{P}[\![\mu X.T]\!]_{\perp}(\rho_{\bigstar}) \qquad \text{Def. 8.29}$$

This implies that $[\bigstar wp(S)] = [\mathcal{P}[\![S]\!]_{\perp}]$ holds. By Lemma 10.14.(ii) it follows that $wp(S) \leq [\mathcal{P}[\![S]\!]_{\perp}]$. Programs without specification statements are conjunctive by Theorem 10.26. Conjunctive predicate transformers are the fixed points of $\bigstar[.]$. Thus, for such programs S, even $wp(S) = [\mathcal{P}[\![S]\!]_{\perp}]$ holds. $\qquad \square$

The lesson learned from Example 10.25 and Theorem 10.27 is that specification statements disturb an otherwise perfect correspondence between $C[\![\psi]\!]_{\perp} \subseteq wp(S)C[\![\phi]\!]_{\perp}$ and $\mathcal{F}[\![\{\psi\}S\{\phi\}]\!]_{\perp}$.

Theorem 10.28
For all programs S of our language *Prog* without specification statements, $wp(S)$ is continuous.

Proof: By Theorem 10.27 and Lemma 8.32 it only remains to prove that $[r]$ is continuous for finitary r. Let $r \in R_{\mathcal{F}}$, $k \in Ch^{\leq}(P)$, and $\sigma \in \Sigma_{\perp}$. Case $r(\{\sigma\}) = \Sigma_{\perp}$:

$$\sigma \in [r]\bigvee k \Leftrightarrow \forall \tau \in \Sigma_{\perp}\left((\sigma,\tau) \in r \Rightarrow \tau \in \bigvee k\right) \qquad (10.1)$$

$$\Leftrightarrow \forall \tau \in \Sigma_{\perp}\,(\exists i \in I\,(\tau \in k(i))) \qquad r(\{\sigma\}) = \Sigma_{\perp}$$

$$\Leftrightarrow \text{false} \qquad \text{inst. } \tau = \perp$$

$$\Leftrightarrow \exists i \in I\,(\forall \tau \in \Sigma_{\perp}\,(\tau \in k(i))) \qquad \text{inst. } \tau = \perp$$

$$\Leftrightarrow \exists i \in I\,(\forall \tau \in \Sigma_{\perp}\,((\sigma,\tau) \in r \Rightarrow \tau \in k(i))) \qquad r(\{\sigma\}) = \Sigma_{\perp}$$

$$\Leftrightarrow \sigma \in \bigvee([r]\,(k(i)))_{i \in I} \qquad (10.1)$$

Case $r(\sigma)$ does not contain $\perp$ and is finite: As before we derive that $\sigma \in [r]\bigvee k$ is equivalent to $\forall \tau \in \Sigma_{\perp}\,(\exists i \in I\,((\sigma,\tau) \in r \Rightarrow \tau \in k(i)))$. But this time there are only finitely many τ with $(\sigma,\tau) \in r$. For each of them there exists an index $i_{\tau} \in I$ such that $\tau \in k(i_{\tau})$. Since k is a chain, there exists an index j among those indices i_{τ} such that $\forall \tau \in r(\sigma)\,(\tau \in k(j))$. Thus, $\sigma \in \bigvee([r]\,(k(i)))_{i \in I}$ holds. $\qquad \square$

10.2.3 Implementability

Example 10.29 Reconsider the specification statement $\text{true} \rightsquigarrow (x = x_0)$ from Example 7.6. In the relational set-up for partial correctness it can only be implemented by non-terminating programs, e.g., **abort** (see Example 7.6), whereas it is not implementable for total correctness, i.e., there does not exist a program in our language implementing $\text{true} \rightsquigarrow (x = x_0)$ without specification statements while preserving termination.

What is the case in the predicate transformer set-up? The weakest precondition semantics of $\text{true} \rightsquigarrow (x = x_0)$ is definitely different from $\lambda \pi . \perp_\text{P}$, the *wp*-semantics of **abort**.

$$wp(\text{true} \rightsquigarrow (x = x_0))(C[\![\phi]\!]_\perp)$$
$$= C[\![\exists x_0 (\text{true} \wedge \forall x ((x = x_0) \Rightarrow \phi))]\!]_\perp \qquad \text{Lemma 10.22}$$
$$= C[\![\exists x_0 (\forall x ((x = x_0) \Rightarrow \phi))]\!]_\perp \qquad \text{pred. calc.}$$
$$= C[\![\exists x (\phi)]\!]_\perp \qquad \text{pred. calc.}$$

This predicate transformer is the top element of $\text{PT}_\vee^{\perp \top}$ but not conjunctive. Thus it differs from the *wp* semantics of all programs without specification statements, since those are all conjunctive. $wp(\textbf{abort})$ is the only conjunctive refinement of $wp(\text{true} \rightsquigarrow (x = x_0))$ but termination is not preserved. We conclude that $\text{true} \rightsquigarrow (x = x_0)$ is not implementable when refining total correctness, i.e., using *wp*.   ♡

Recall from Chapter 8 that the implementable part R_t of $R_\perp$ is the set of total relations in $R_\perp$. The structure $(R_t, \supseteq)$ is a not a complete lattice since it is not a cpo. (See Example 8.13 on page 155.)

Now one may conclude that $\{ [r] \mid r \in R_t \} = \text{PT}_\wedge^\perp$ is a set of implementable predicate transformers. Alas, there are implementable predicate transformers apart from $\text{PT}_\wedge^\perp$.

Example 10.30 Consider the specification statement

$$S = (x = 0 \wedge x_0 \in \{\{0,1\}, \{0,2\}\}) \rightsquigarrow (x \in x_0)$$

Predicate $\exists x_0 (x = 0 \wedge x_0 \in \{\{0,1\}, \{0,2\}\} \wedge \forall x (x \in x_0 \Rightarrow \phi))$ expresses the weakest precondition of S w.r.t. $C[\![\phi]\!]_\perp$ by Lemma 10.22. For $w \subseteq \{0,1,2\}$ define $\phi_w \stackrel{\text{def}}{=} C[\![x \in w]\!]_\perp$; then $S\phi_{\{0,1\}} = S\phi_{\{0,2\}} = C[\![x = 0]\!]_\perp$ but $S(\phi_{\{0,1\}} \cap \phi_{\{0,2\}}) = S\phi_{\{0\}} = \emptyset$. Consequently S is not conjunctive. On the other hand,

$$S' \stackrel{\text{def}}{=} \textbf{if } x = 0 \textbf{ then skip else abort fi}$$

satisfies $S \leq S'$, that is, S' is an implementation of S. Moreover, $[\bigstar wp(S)] = \mathcal{P}[\![S']\!]_\perp \in \text{PT}_\wedge^\perp$.   ♡

Any implementation of $P \in \text{PT}$ has to be conjunctive and strict. The $\leq$-least conjunctive predicate transformer refining P is $[\bigstar P]$. Implementability of P can be decided by checking strictness of $[\bigstar P]$.

Why is this a correct characterization? At first sight it is not clear that it captures the intended property, namely, there exists a strict, conjunctive predicate transformer refining P. Since $[\bigstar P]$ is the $\leq$-weakest conjunctive refinement of P, it is refined by any implementation of P. Furthermore, no refinement of a non-strict predicate transformer can be strict. We conclude: P has an implementation if, and only if, $[\bigstar P]$ is such an implementation.

Lemma 10.31 Program $S \in Prog$ is implementable in the predicate transformer world iff it is implementable in the relational total correctness world.

Proof: We show that strictness of $[\bigstar wp(S)]$ is equivalent to totality of the relational version $\mathcal{P}[\![S]\!]_\perp$ of S.

$$[\bigstar wp(S)] \in \mathsf{PT}^\perp$$
$$\Leftrightarrow [\bigstar wp(S)] \perp_\mathsf{P} = \perp_\mathsf{P} \qquad\qquad \text{Def. 10.10}$$
$$\Leftrightarrow \{ \sigma \mid \forall \tau ((\sigma, \tau) \in \bigstar wp(S) \Rightarrow \tau \in \emptyset) \} = \emptyset \qquad \text{(10.1) and Def. 10.8}$$
$$\Leftrightarrow \forall \sigma (\exists \tau ((\sigma, \tau) \in \bigstar wp(S))) \qquad\qquad \text{pred. calc.}$$
$$\Leftrightarrow \bigstar wp(S) \text{ is total} \qquad\qquad \text{Def. 3.6}$$
$$\Leftrightarrow \mathcal{P}[\![S]\!]_\perp \text{ is total} \qquad\qquad \text{Th. 10.27}$$

This is exactly the criterion for implementability of programs imposed in Chapter 8. □

Why do we check strictness of $[\bigstar wp(S)]$ instead of just $wp(S)$? Because strictness can be lost while constructing the least conjunctive refinement, as illustrated in Example 10.29.

10.3 Predicate Transformers and Data Refinement

The interpretation of $\leq$ as "is refined by" is sound with respect to our conception of total correctness refinement. Let S and S' be programs of our language. For total correctness we express that S is refined by S' relationally as follows.

$$\mathcal{P}[\![S]\!]_\perp \supseteq \mathcal{P}[\![S']\!]_\perp$$

This follows by monotonicity of $\bigstar$ from $wp(S) \leq wp(S')$. Theorem 10.27 and Example 10.25 suggest that the reverse implication generally does not hold. Only provided S' is free of specification statements may we continue reasoning:

$$\Rightarrow [\mathcal{P}[\![S]\!]_\perp] \leq [\mathcal{P}[\![S']\!]_\perp] \qquad [.] \text{ monotone}$$
$$\Leftrightarrow wp(S) \leq [\mathcal{P}[\![S']\!]_\perp] \qquad \text{Th. 10.27}$$
$$\Rightarrow wp(S) \leq wp(S') \qquad \text{assumption about } S', \text{ Th. 10.27}$$

This lack of equivalence forces us to extend our semantic definition of data refinement to deal with data types based on predicate transformers. We quickly review the essential definitions.

Definition 10.32 (Data type (cf. Def. 1.7)) Given that the constraints

- $AI \in PT_{\vec{x} \leftarrow \vec{x}\vec{a}}$
- $A_j \in PT_{\vec{x}\vec{a} \leftarrow \vec{x}\vec{a}}$, for $j \in J$,
- $AF \in PT_{\vec{x}\vec{a} \leftarrow \vec{x}}$, and

are met, $\mathcal{A} \stackrel{\text{def}}{=} (AI, (A_j)_{j \in J}, AF)$ defines a *data type* in the predicate transformer setting (also called PT-data type). ♣

Recall that two data types are compatible if they share the sets of normal variables and operation indices.

Definition 10.33 Let $\mathcal{A}$ and C be two compatible PT-data types with families A and C of operations. Data type C is a *data refinement* of $\mathcal{A}$ (denoted $\mathcal{A} \leq C$) if, for all suitable P, $AI \,\hat{;}\, P(A) \,\hat{;}\, AF \leq CI \,\hat{;}\, P(C) \,\hat{;}\, CF$. ♣

10.3.1 Simulation with Predicate Transformers

General convention In this section, let us identify

- programs of our language with their *wp*-semantics,
- predicates with their total correctness semantics, and
- pre- and postconditions with their total correctness relational semantics

unless stated otherwise.

Using this convention, we prove some additional properties of assert statements.

Lemma 10.34 Let $P \in PT$ and $s, \phi \subseteq \Sigma$.

(i) $\{s\}\phi = s \cap \phi$.
(ii) $P \,\hat{;}\, \{s\} \leq \{P(s)\} \,\hat{;}\, P$ (equality holds in case $P \in PT_\wedge$).
(iii) $P = \{P(\top_P)\} \,\hat{;}\, P$.

Proof: The first part follows immediately from the definition of assert statements and the general convention. We prove the remaining two parts pointwise.

$$(P \,\hat{;}\, \{s\})t = P(s \cap t) \qquad \text{first part}$$

$$\subseteq P(s) \cap P(t) \qquad P \text{ monotone}$$
$$= (\{P(s)\} \mathbin{;} P)t \qquad \text{first part}$$

For conjunctive P, "$\subseteq$" above can be replaced by "$=$".

$$(\{P(\top_P)\} \mathbin{;} P)t = P(\top_P) \cap P(t) \qquad \text{first part}$$
$$= P(t) \qquad P \text{ monotone} \qquad \square$$

Definition 10.35 (Powersimulation) Consider two compatible data types $\mathcal{A}$ and C. A predicate transformer $\alpha \in \mathsf{PT}_{Var^C \leftarrow Var^A}$ is called a *powersimulation* between $\mathcal{A}$ and C — this is expressed by $\mathcal{A} \leq_\alpha C$ — if the following conditions are met:

$$AI \leq CI \mathbin{;} \alpha \qquad \text{(init)}$$
$$\text{for all } j \in J: \quad \alpha \mathbin{;} A_j \leq C_j \mathbin{;} \alpha \qquad \text{(op}_j\text{)}$$
$$\alpha \mathbin{;} AF \leq CF \qquad \text{(fina)}$$

10.3.2 Soundness
Theorem 10.36 (Soundness of powersimulation)
Let $\mathcal{A}$ and C be compatible PT-data types and let $\alpha \in \mathsf{PT}_{Var^C \leftarrow Var^A}$ be strict and continuous. If $\mathcal{A} \leq_\alpha C$, then C is a data refinement of $\mathcal{A}$.

Proof: Let A and C denote the families of operations of two compatible PT-data types $\mathcal{A}$ and C. Let $\alpha \in \mathsf{PT}_{Var^C \leftarrow Var^A}$ be a strict and continuous power-simulation between $\mathcal{A}$ and C. We have to show that, for all pairs of programs $(P(A), P(C))$,

$$AI \mathbin{;} P(A) \mathbin{;} AF \leq CI \mathbin{;} P(C) \mathbin{;} CF \ .$$

Therefore, we first prove by induction on the structure of P that

$$\alpha \mathbin{;} P(A) \leq P(C) \mathbin{;} \alpha$$

holds for all pairs of programs $(P(A), P(C))$. This is immediate for the empty program (**skip**); for the aborting program it follows from strictness of α and the fact that **abort** is the zero of "$;$" in $\mathsf{PT}^\perp$. The remaining induction bases are covered by the assumptions (op$_j$) in Def. 10.35. Induction steps are sequential composition, choice, and recursion.

$$\alpha \mathbin{;} P_1(A) \mathbin{;} P_2(A) \leq P_1(C) \mathbin{;} \alpha \mathbin{;} P_2(A) \qquad \text{ind. hyp.}$$
$$\leq P_1(C) \mathbin{;} P_2(C) \mathbin{;} \alpha \qquad \text{ind. hyp.}$$

Next comes the choice operator.

$$\alpha \mathbin{;} (P_1(A) \mathbin{\square} P_2(A)) = \alpha \mathbin{;} \bigwedge_{i \in \{1,2\}} (P_i(A)) \qquad \text{Def. 10.20}$$

$$\le \bigwedge_{i \in \{1,2\}} (\alpha \mathbin{;} P_i(A)) \qquad \text{Lemma 10.12.(v)}$$

$$\le \bigwedge_{i \in \{1,2\}} (P_i(C) \mathbin{;} \alpha) \qquad \text{ind. hyp.}$$

$$= (\bigwedge_{i \in \{1,2\}} P_i(C)) \mathbin{;} \alpha \qquad \text{Lemma 10.12.(iii)}$$

$$= (P_1(C) \mathbin{\square} P_2(C)) \mathbin{;} \alpha \qquad \text{Def. 10.20}$$

Finally the least fixed point operator:

$$\alpha \mathbin{;} \mu X . Q(A)(X) \le \alpha \mathbin{;} \bigvee_{i < \kappa} ((Q(A))^i (\bot)) \qquad \text{Th. 8.10}$$

$$= \bigvee_{i < \kappa} (\alpha \mathbin{;} (Q(A))^i (\bot)) \qquad \text{Lemma 10.12.(vi)}$$

$$\le \bigvee_{i < \kappa} ((Q(C))^i (\bot) \mathbin{;} \alpha) \qquad \text{ind. hyp.}$$

$$= \bigvee_{i < \kappa} ((Q(C))^i (\bot)) \mathbin{;} \alpha \qquad \text{Lemma 10.12.(iv)}$$

$$= \mu X . Q(C)(X) \mathbin{;} \alpha \qquad \text{Cor. 8.11} \qquad \square$$

Note Observe that strictness and continuity of α are not required if recursion as a program constructor is dropped. $\qquad \diamondsuit$

10.3.3 Completeness

The main result of this section is a completeness theorem due to Paul Gardiner and Carroll Morgan [GM93, MV94] stating that (under certain restrictions) refinement can be proven using powersimulation. The proof of this result is based on the construction of a suitable powersimulation. Gardiner and Morgan motivate the operational aspect of the predicate transformer version of the [HHS87]-construction of the required abstraction relation as follows:

Consider a program that may use either the abstract datatype or the concrete, and imagine stopping this program during its execution: if it were using the abstract datatype then some sequence of operations $(AI \mathbin{;} P(A)$ say, where $P(A)$ is a sequence of operations drawn from $(A_j)_{j \in J}$ would have been applied; if it were using the concrete then a corresponding sequence of operations $(CI \mathbin{;} P(C))$ would have been applied. One can calculate concrete predicates from abstract ones by first using weakest precondition to look backwards through $AI \mathbin{;} P(A)$, and then using strongest postcondition to look forward through $CI \mathbin{;} P(C)$. Lastly, to obtain a concrete predicate whose truth is independent of the stopping point, the disjunction over all sequences is taken.

[GM93, pp. 373f]

Apparently, this construction requires some kind of inverse of weakest precondition predicate transformers, that is, strongest postcondition predicate transformers.

Definition 10.37 (Weak inverse [vW90]) Predicate transformer $\widetilde{P} \in \mathsf{PT}$ is a *weak inverse* of predicate transformer $P \in \mathsf{PT}$ if $\{P(\top_\mathsf{P})\} \leq P \mathbin{;} \widetilde{P}$ and $\widetilde{P} \mathbin{;} P \leq id$. Denote the least weak inverse of P by P^- if such a weak inverse exists. ♣

Observe that weak inverses are not unique: for instance, it is immediate that any strict disjunctive predicate transformer is a weak inverse of **abort**.

Lemma 10.38 Any conjunctive predicate transformer has a least weak inverse. That inverse is strict and disjunctive.

Proof: ([vW90, pp. 70f]) Let $P \in \mathsf{PT}_\wedge$. Define $P^- \overset{\text{def}}{=} \lambda s. \bigwedge \{\, t \mid s \subseteq P(t) \,\}$.

To see that P^- is strict and disjunctive, let $(s_i)_{i \in I}$ be an I-indexed family of predicates. (I might be empty, i.e., $\bigvee_i s_i = \bot_\mathsf{P}$.)

$$P^- \left(\bigvee_i s_i \right) = \bigwedge \left\{\, t \;\middle|\; \bigvee_i s_i \subseteq P(t) \,\right\}$$
$$= \bigwedge_i \bigwedge \{\, t \mid s_i \subseteq P(t) \,\}$$
$$= \bigwedge_i P^-(s_i)$$

Next, we check the two characteristic properties of inverses pointwise. The first property amounts by Lemma 10.34.(i) to proving $(P \mathbin{;} P^-)s \supseteq P(\top_\mathsf{P}) \cap s$ for all s.

$$(P \mathbin{;} P^-)s = P(P^-(s)) = P(\bigwedge \{\, t \mid s \subseteq P(t) \,\})$$

Case $s \subseteq P\top_\mathsf{P}$:

$$P(\bigwedge \{\, t \mid s \subseteq P(t) \,\}) = \bigwedge \{\, P(t) \mid s \subseteq P(t) \,\} \qquad P \in \mathsf{PT}_\wedge$$
$$\supseteq \bigwedge \{\, s' \mid s \subseteq s' \,\} \qquad\qquad P \text{ monotone}$$
$$= s$$
$$= P(\top_\mathsf{P}) \cap s \qquad\qquad s \subseteq P\top_\mathsf{P}$$

Case $s \not\subseteq PT_P$:

$$P(\bigwedge \{ t \mid s \subseteq P(t) \}) = P(\bigwedge \emptyset) \qquad\qquad P \text{ monotone}$$
$$= PT_P$$
$$\supseteq P(T_P) \cap s$$

For the second characteristic property of inverses observe that, for all s, $(P^- \,\dot{;}\,$
$P)s = \bigwedge \{ t \mid P(s) \subseteq P(t) \} \subseteq s$.

Next observe that $P^- \leq P^- \,\dot{;}\, \{PT_P\}$. To prove that P^- is the least inverse,
let Q be another inverse of P. Then $P^- \leq P^- \,\dot{;}\, \{PT_P\} \leq P^- \,\dot{;}\, P \,\dot{;}\, Q \leq id \,\dot{;}\, Q = Q$.
□

Corollary 10.39 Let P_1, P_2, and P_i for $i \in I$ be elements of $PT_\wedge$.

  (i) $id^- = id$.
  (ii) $P_2^- \,\dot{;}\, P_1^-$ is a weak inverse of $P_1 \,\dot{;}\, P_2$.
  (iii) $\bigvee_{i \in I} P_i^-$ is a weak inverse of $\bigwedge_{i \in I} P_i$.   ♠

The next two little lemmas simplify reasoning with weak inverses in the completeness proof.

Lemma 10.40 For any $P \in PT$ and $Q \in PT_\wedge$, if $P(T_P) \subseteq Q(T_P)$ then $P \leq Q \,\dot{;}\, Q^- \,\dot{;}\, P$.

Proof:

$$\begin{aligned}
P &= \{P(T_P)\} \,\dot{;}\, P && \text{Lemma 10.34} \\
&\leq \{Q(T_P)\} \,\dot{;}\, P && \text{assumption, Lemma 10.34} \\
&\leq Q \,\dot{;}\, Q^- \,\dot{;}\, P && \text{Def. 10.37}
\end{aligned}$$
□

Lemma 10.41 Let $\widetilde{P}$ be any weak inverse of $P \in PT_\wedge$. Then $\widetilde{P} \,\dot{;}\, \{P(T_P)\} \leq P^-$.

Proof:

$$\begin{aligned}
\widetilde{P} \,\dot{;}\, \{P(T_P)\} &\leq \widetilde{P} \,\dot{;}\, P \,\dot{;}\, P^- && \text{Def. 10.37} \\
&\leq P^- && \text{Def. 10.37}
\end{aligned}$$
□

Theorem 10.42 (Completeness [GM93])
Let $\mathcal{A}$ and $\mathcal{C}$ be two compatible PT-data types with families of operations
$A = (A_j)_{j \in J}$ and $C = (C_j)_{j \in J}$ such that

  A1 $\mathcal{A} \leq \mathcal{C}$,

A2 $CI, C_j \in \mathsf{PT}_\wedge$,

A3 $CF \in \mathsf{PT}^\perp$,

A4 AI, A_j are continuous, and

A5 $AF \in \mathsf{PT}^{\perp\top}$.

Then there exists a continuous, strict predicate transformer α such that $\mathcal{A} \leq_\alpha C$.

Proof: Define

$$\alpha \stackrel{\text{def}}{=} \bigvee_{l \in J^*} \left((CI \mathbin{;} P_l(C))^- \mathbin{;} (AI \mathbin{;} P_l(A)) \right) , \tag{10.5}$$

where J^* is the set of all finite sequences over J and $P_l(X)$ is defined recursively by $P_{\langle\rangle}(X) \stackrel{\text{def}}{=} id$ and $P_{l ^\frown \langle j\rangle}(X) \stackrel{\text{def}}{=} P_l(X) \mathbin{;} X_j$, for $j \in J$ and X a J-indexed family of operations.

First we show that α is indeed a powersimulation between $\mathcal{A}$ and C, then we prove its strictness and continuity.

We have to check (init), (op_j) for $j \in J$, and (fina) from Def. 10.35. For (init) we establish an instance of the assumption of Lemma 10.40:

$$
\begin{aligned}
AI(\top_\mathsf{P}) &= (AI \mathbin{;} AF)(\top_\mathsf{P}) && \text{A5: } AF \text{ total} \\
&\leq (CI \mathbin{;} CF)(\top_\mathsf{P}) && \text{A1: } \mathcal{A} \leq C \\
&\leq CI(\top_\mathsf{P}) && CI \text{ monotone}
\end{aligned}
$$

Hence the following application of Lemma 10.40 to prove (init) is justified. We use that (*) $P_{\langle\rangle}(X)$ is the unit element 1 of ";" in PT.

$$
\begin{aligned}
AI &\leq CI \mathbin{;} CI^- \mathbin{;} AI && \text{Lemma 10.40} \\
&= CI \mathbin{;} (CI \mathbin{;} P_{\langle\rangle}(C))^- \mathbin{;} (AI \mathbin{;} P_{\langle\rangle}(A)) && (*) \\
&\leq CI \mathbin{;} \alpha && \langle\rangle \in J^*, \text{ def. of } \alpha
\end{aligned}
$$

The proof of (op_j) will use the following property:

$$\{(AI \mathbin{;} P_l(A) \mathbin{;} A_j)(\top_\mathsf{P})\} \leq \{(CI \mathbin{;} P_l(C) \mathbin{;} C_j)(\top_\mathsf{P})\} , \tag{10.6}$$

proved by

$$
\begin{aligned}
&(AI \mathbin{;} P_l(A) \mathbin{;} A_j)(\top_\mathsf{P}) \\
&= (AI \mathbin{;} P_l(A) \mathbin{;} A_j \mathbin{;} AF)(\top_\mathsf{P}) && \text{A5: } AF \text{ total} \\
&\leq (CI \mathbin{;} P_l(C) \mathbin{;} C_j \mathbin{;} CF)(\top_\mathsf{P}) && \text{A1: } \mathcal{A} \leq C \\
&\leq (CI \mathbin{;} P_l(C) \mathbin{;} C_j)(\top_\mathsf{P}) && \text{A2: } CI, C_j \text{ monotone}
\end{aligned}
$$

Lemma 10.24 then ensures (10.6). For Lemma 10.40 we show

$$(((CI \mathbin{;} P_l(C))^- \mathbin{;} AI \mathbin{;} P_l(A)) \mathbin{;} A_j)(\top_\mathsf{P})$$

$$= ((CI \mathbin{\underline{;}} P_l(C))^- \mathbin{\underline{;}} AI \mathbin{\underline{;}} P_l(A) \mathbin{\underline{;}} A_j \mathbin{\underline{;}} AF)(\mathsf{T_P}) \qquad A5 : AF \text{ total}$$
$$\leq ((CI \mathbin{\underline{;}} P_l(C))^- \mathbin{\underline{;}} CI \mathbin{\underline{;}} P_l(C) \mathbin{\underline{;}} C_j \mathbin{\underline{;}} CF)(\mathsf{T_P}) \qquad A1 : \mathcal{A} \leq C$$
$$\leq (C_j \mathbin{\underline{;}} CF)(\mathsf{T_P}) \qquad\qquad\qquad\qquad \text{Def. } 10.37$$
$$\leq C_j(\mathsf{T_P}) \qquad\qquad\qquad\qquad\qquad C_j \text{ monotone}$$

Again, this justifies the application of Lemma 10.40 in the proof of (op$_j$) below.

$$\alpha \mathbin{\underline{;}} A_j$$
$$= \bigvee_{l \in J^*} \left((CI \mathbin{\underline{;}} P_l(C))^- \mathbin{\underline{;}} (AI \mathbin{\underline{;}} P_l(A)) \right) \mathbin{\underline{;}} A_j \qquad (10.5)$$
$$= \bigvee_{l \in J^*} \left((CI \mathbin{\underline{;}} P_l(C))^- \mathbin{\underline{;}} (AI \mathbin{\underline{;}} P_l(A)) \mathbin{\underline{;}} A_j \right) \qquad \text{Lemma } 10.12.\text{(iv)}$$
$$\leq \bigvee_{l \in J^*} \left(C_j \mathbin{\underline{;}} C_j^- \mathbin{\underline{;}} (CI \mathbin{\underline{;}} P_l(C))^- \mathbin{\underline{;}} (AI \mathbin{\underline{;}} P_l(A)) \mathbin{\underline{;}} A_j \right) \qquad \text{Lemma } 10.40$$
$$\leq C_j \mathbin{\underline{;}} \bigvee_{l \in J^*} \left(C_j^- \mathbin{\underline{;}} (CI \mathbin{\underline{;}} P_l(C))^- \mathbin{\underline{;}} AI \mathbin{\underline{;}} P_l(A) \mathbin{\underline{;}} A_j \right) \qquad \text{Lemma } 10.12.\text{(vi)}$$
$$= C_j \mathbin{\underline{;}} \bigvee_{l \in J^*} \begin{pmatrix} C_j^- \mathbin{\underline{;}} (CI \mathbin{\underline{;}} P_l(C))^- \mathbin{\underline{;}} \\ \{(AI \mathbin{\underline{;}} P_l(A) \mathbin{\underline{;}} A_j)(\mathsf{T_P})\} \mathbin{\underline{;}} AI \mathbin{\underline{;}} P_l(A) \mathbin{\underline{;}} A_j \end{pmatrix} \qquad \text{Lemma } 10.34.\text{(iii)}$$
$$\leq C_j \mathbin{\underline{;}} \bigvee_{l \in J^*} \begin{pmatrix} C_j^- \mathbin{\underline{;}} (CI \mathbin{\underline{;}} P_l(C))^- \mathbin{\underline{;}} \\ \{(CI \mathbin{\underline{;}} P_l(C) \mathbin{\underline{;}} C_j)(\mathsf{T_P})\} \mathbin{\underline{;}} AI \mathbin{\underline{;}} P_l(A) \mathbin{\underline{;}} A_j \end{pmatrix} \qquad (10.6)$$
$$\leq C_j \mathbin{\underline{;}} \bigvee_{l \in J^*} \left((CI \mathbin{\underline{;}} P_l(C) \mathbin{\underline{;}} C_j)^- \mathbin{\underline{;}} AI \mathbin{\underline{;}} P_l(A) \mathbin{\underline{;}} A_j \right) \qquad \text{Lemma } 10.41$$
$$= C_j \mathbin{\underline{;}} \bigvee_{\{l^\frown \langle j \rangle \,|\, l \in J^*\}} \left((CI \mathbin{\underline{;}} P_l(C))^- \mathbin{\underline{;}} AI \mathbin{\underline{;}} P_l(A) \right) \qquad \text{def. of } P_{l^\frown \langle j \rangle}$$
$$\leq C_j \mathbin{\underline{;}} \alpha \qquad (10.5)$$

The proof obligation (fina) for finalization is proven next.

$$\alpha \mathbin{\underline{;}} AF$$
$$= \bigvee_{l \in J^*} \left((CI \mathbin{\underline{;}} P_l(C))^- \mathbin{\underline{;}} (AI \mathbin{\underline{;}} P_l(A)) \right) \mathbin{\underline{;}} AF \qquad (10.5)$$
$$= \bigvee_{l \in J^*} \left((CI \mathbin{\underline{;}} P_l(C))^- \mathbin{\underline{;}} AI \mathbin{\underline{;}} P_l(A) \mathbin{\underline{;}} AF \right) \qquad \text{Lemma } 10.12.\text{(iv)}$$
$$\leq \bigvee_{l \in J^*} \left((CI \mathbin{\underline{;}} P_l(C))^- \mathbin{\underline{;}} CI \mathbin{\underline{;}} P_l(C) \mathbin{\underline{;}} CF \right) \qquad A1 : \mathcal{A} \leq C$$
$$\leq \bigvee_{l \in J^*} (CF) \qquad \text{Def. } 10.37$$

$$= CF \qquad\qquad\qquad\qquad\qquad J^* \neq \emptyset$$

For strictness of α we prove strictness of each constituent of α in (10.5).

$$((CI \mathbin{\underset{\cdot}{;}} P_l(C))^- \mathbin{\underset{\cdot}{;}} AI \mathbin{\underset{\cdot}{;}} P_l(A))(\bot_P)$$
$$= ((CI \mathbin{\underset{\cdot}{;}} P_l(C))^- \mathbin{\underset{\cdot}{;}} AI \mathbin{\underset{\cdot}{;}} P_l(A) \mathbin{\underset{\cdot}{;}} AF)(\bot_P) \qquad\qquad \text{A5: } AF \text{ strict}$$
$$\leq ((CI \mathbin{\underset{\cdot}{;}} P_l(C))^- \mathbin{\underset{\cdot}{;}} CI \mathbin{\underset{\cdot}{;}} P_l(C) \mathbin{\underset{\cdot}{;}} CF)(\bot_P) \qquad\qquad \text{A1: } \mathcal{A} \leq C$$
$$\leq CF(\bot_P) \qquad\qquad\qquad\qquad\qquad\qquad \text{Def. 10.37}$$
$$= \bot_P \qquad\qquad\qquad\qquad\qquad\qquad\qquad \text{A3: } CF \text{ strict}$$

Hence $\alpha(\bot_P) = \bot_P$.

Continuity of α follows from the continuity of AI and A_j for $j \in J$, since the weak inverse of $CI \mathbin{\underset{\cdot}{;}} P_l(C)$ is disjunctive and continuity is preserved by join. $\qquad\square$

Next we discuss to what extent the prerequisites of Theorem 10.42 restrict its applicability.

- Concrete initialization and operations should be conjunctive (A2). Note that this property does not necessarily hold for specification statements (see, e.g., Example 10.25), but, by Theorem 10.26, is true for all other programs.
- Both finalizations should be strict and the abstract one should additionally be total (A3, A5). Since this is, e.g., the case for the commonplace projection onto normal variables at block exit we do not consider this too severe a restriction.
- Abstract initialization and operations should be continuous (A4). This excludes some specification statements introducing infinite nondeterminism. The remainder of our language (its so-called *finitary* part) is continuous by Theorem 10.28, and hence is a suitable language for abstract level operations.

These drawbacks explain why infinite nondeterminism and total correctness do not really fit together. Since we prefer to keep our specification statements as general as they are, we sacrifice total correctness and step back to partial correctness. As in the relational world, partial correctness is easier. We achieve simpler yet stronger results.

10.4 Predicate Transformers and Partial Correctness

The theory presented so far can be recast for partial correctness. This allows some simplifications, e.g., since unique inverses exist. In particular we show

how to derive our main result of Chapter 7, that one can express maximal simulators using the $\rightsquigarrow$-operator, within the predicate transformer framework.

Most results presented so far in this chapter carry over to partial correctness. We state only the most important ones anew. When we appear to refer to a total correctness result in this section, we usually mean its partial correctness counterpart.

Lemma 10.43 $(\mathsf{PT}_\wedge^\top, \leq)$ is a complete lattice closed under sequential composition. It is a sublattice of $\mathsf{PT}_\wedge$.   ♠

Let $\mathcal{R}$ denote the set of binary relations on states. With respect to partial order $\supseteq$ it is a complete Boolean lattice, the dual of the powerset lattice of Σ^2 introduced in Example 10.2.

Theorem 10.44

$(\mathcal{R}, \supseteq) \simeq (\mathsf{PT}_\wedge^\top, \leq)$.

Proof: Observe first that $(\bigstar, [.])$ is a Galois connection when restricted to the state space without bottom involved here. $[r]$ is total and conjunctive for $r \in \mathcal{R}$. The rest of the proof proceeds as for Theorem 10.17.   □

10.4.1 Weakest Liberal Precondition Semantics

As there is a partial correctness version $\mathcal{P}[\![.]\!]$ of $\mathcal{P}[\![.]\!]_\perp$, there exists a well-behaved partial correctness analogue to the weakest precondition semantics presented in Section 10.2.1.

Definition 10.45 (*wlp-semantics*) Let $s \subseteq \Sigma$, let $\rho \in \Delta_{\mathsf{PT}}$, and define semantic function $wlp : Prog \longrightarrow (\Delta_{\mathsf{PT}} \longrightarrow \mathsf{PT})$ as follows:

$$wlp(\textbf{abort})(\rho)s \stackrel{\text{def}}{=} \top_\mathsf{P}$$

$$wlp(\textbf{skip})(\rho)s \stackrel{\text{def}}{=} s$$

$$wlp(x := e)(\rho) \stackrel{\text{def}}{=} \{\, \sigma \mid (\sigma : x \mapsto \mathcal{E}[\![e]\!]\sigma) \in s \,\}$$

$$wlp(b \rightarrow)(\rho)s \stackrel{\text{def}}{=} C[\![\neg b]\!] \cup s$$

$$wlp(\phi \rightsquigarrow \psi)(\rho)s \stackrel{\text{def}}{=} \{\, \sigma \mid \exists \gamma ((\gamma, \sigma) \in C[\![\phi]\!] \wedge C[\![\psi]\!](\{\gamma\}) \subseteq s) \,\}$$

$$wlp(X)(\rho) \stackrel{\text{def}}{=} \rho(X)$$

$$wlp(S_1 ; S_2)(\rho) \stackrel{\text{def}}{=} wlp(S_1)(\rho) \, ; wlp(S_2)(\rho)$$

$$wlp(S_1 \,[\!]\, S_2)(\rho) \stackrel{\text{def}}{=} wlp(S_1)(\rho) \wedge wlp(S_2)(\rho)$$

$$wlp(\mu X . S)(\rho) \stackrel{\text{def}}{=} \mu_{\lambda P. wlp(S)(\rho : X \mapsto P)}$$ ♣

This definition of *wlp* makes the diagram in Figure 10.3 (weakly) commutative.

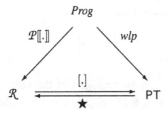

Fig. 10.3. Coincidence of $\mathcal{P}[\![.]\!]$ and *wlp*.

Alas, Example 10.25 applies equally to *wlp* instead of *wp* since in that example termination is not the issue. The similarity culminates in a *wlp* version of Theorem 10.27.

Theorem 10.46
For all programs $S \in Prog$ of our language, $\star wlp(S) = \mathcal{P}[\![S]\!]$ and $wlp(S) \leq [\mathcal{P}[\![S]\!]]$. The latter can be strengthened to an equality if S does not contain specification statements.

Proof: As usual, this is proven by structural induction. We demonstrate only one base case, the specification statement, and leave the rest of the proof as an exercise. First we show that $wlp(\phi \rightsquigarrow \psi) \leq [\mathcal{P}[\![\phi \rightsquigarrow \psi]\!]]$:

$$\sigma \in wlp(\phi \rightsquigarrow \psi)s$$
$$\Leftrightarrow \exists\gamma((\gamma,\sigma) \in C[\![\phi]\!] \wedge \forall\tau((\gamma,\tau) \in C[\![\psi]\!] \Rightarrow \tau \in s)) \qquad \text{Def. 10.45}$$
$$\Rightarrow \forall\tau(\exists\gamma((\gamma,\sigma) \in C[\![\phi]\!] \wedge ((\gamma,\tau) \in C[\![\psi]\!] \Rightarrow \tau \in s))) \qquad \text{pred. calc.}$$
$$\Rightarrow \forall\tau(\exists\gamma(((\gamma,\sigma) \in C[\![\phi]\!] \Rightarrow (\gamma,\tau) \in C[\![\psi]\!]) \Rightarrow \tau \in s)) \qquad \text{pred. calc.}$$
$$\Leftrightarrow \forall\tau(\forall\gamma((\gamma,\sigma) \in C[\![\phi]\!] \Rightarrow (\gamma,\tau) \in C[\![\psi]\!]) \Rightarrow \tau \in s) \qquad \text{pred. calc.}$$
$$\Leftrightarrow \forall\tau((\sigma,\tau) \in \mathcal{P}[\![\phi \rightsquigarrow \psi]\!] \Rightarrow \tau \in s) \qquad \text{Def. 5.18}$$
$$\Leftrightarrow \sigma \in [\mathcal{P}[\![\phi \rightsquigarrow \psi]\!]]s \qquad (10.1)$$

The Galois connection, Theorem 10.44, allows us to deduce

$$\star wlp(\phi \rightsquigarrow \psi) \supseteq \mathcal{P}[\![\phi \rightsquigarrow \psi]\!] \ .$$

It remains to prove that $\mathcal{P}[\![\phi \rightsquigarrow \psi]\!] \supseteq \star wlp(\phi \rightsquigarrow \psi)$:

$$(\sigma,\tau) \in \star wlp(\phi \rightsquigarrow \psi)$$
$$\Leftrightarrow \forall s(\sigma \in wlp(\phi \rightsquigarrow \psi)s \Rightarrow \tau \in s) \qquad (10.2)$$

$$\Rightarrow \sigma \in wlp(\phi \leadsto \psi)(\Sigma \setminus \{\tau\}) \Rightarrow \tau \in (\Sigma \setminus \{\tau\}) \qquad \text{inst. } s = \Sigma \setminus \{\tau\}$$
$$\Leftrightarrow \sigma \notin wlp(\phi \leadsto \psi)(\Sigma \setminus \{\tau\}) \qquad \text{pred. calc.}$$
$$\Leftrightarrow \neg \exists \gamma \big(T[\![\phi]\!](\gamma, \sigma) \wedge \forall \tau' \, (T[\![\psi]\!](\gamma, \tau') \Rightarrow \tau' \neq \tau)\big) \qquad \text{Def. 10.45}$$
$$\Leftrightarrow \forall \gamma ((\gamma, \sigma) \in C[\![\phi]\!] \Rightarrow (\gamma, \tau) \in C[\![\psi]\!]) \qquad \text{pred. calc.}$$
$$\Leftrightarrow (\sigma, \tau) \in \mathcal{P}[\![\phi \leadsto \psi]\!] \qquad \text{Def. 5.18} \qquad \square$$

We close this section with an analogue of the separation theorem for relational semantics, Theorem 8.38. Dijkstra and Scholten, for example, define $wp(S)\phi = wlp(S)\phi \wedge wp(S)\text{true}$ after introducing $wlp(S)\phi$ and $wp(S)\text{true}$.

Theorem 10.47 (Separation)
Let $S \in Prog$ and $\phi, \psi \in Pred$ such that $C[\![\pi]\!] = C[\![\pi]\!]_\perp$ for ϕ, ψ, and all predicates occurring as guards or in specification statements within S. Furthermore we assume that each expression e on the RHS of an assignment in S evaluates independently of the semantics, i.e., $\mathcal{E}[\![e]\!] = \mathcal{E}[\![e]\!]_\perp$. Under these assumptions we may divide the task of proving total correctness into two subtasks, namely, proving termination and partial correctness:

$$C[\![\phi]\!]_\perp \subseteq wp(S)C[\![\psi]\!]_\perp$$
$$\Leftrightarrow (C[\![\phi]\!] \subseteq wlp(S)C[\![\psi]\!]) \wedge (C[\![\phi]\!]_\perp \subseteq wp(S)C[\![\text{true}]\!]_\perp)$$

Proof: By induction on the structure of S. Case $S = \pi \leadsto \rho$: It suffices to show that $wp(S) = wlp(S)$. Let $s \in \mathrm{P}$.

$$wp(\pi \leadsto \rho)s$$
$$= \{ \, \sigma \mid \exists \gamma ((\gamma, \sigma) \in C[\![\pi]\!]_\perp \wedge C[\![\rho]\!]_\perp (\{\gamma\}) \subseteq s) \, \} \qquad \text{Def. 10.20}$$
$$= \{ \, \sigma \mid \exists \gamma ((\gamma, \sigma) \in C[\![\pi]\!] \wedge C[\![\rho]\!](\{\gamma\}) \subseteq s) \, \} \qquad \text{ass. for } \pi \text{ and } \rho$$
$$= wlp(\pi \leadsto \rho)s \qquad \text{Def. 10.45}$$

All other cases of S are proven with the Galois connections between predicate transformers and relations.

$$C[\![\phi]\!]_\perp \subseteq wp(S)C[\![\psi]\!]_\perp$$
$$\Leftrightarrow C[\![\phi]\!]_\perp \subseteq [\mathcal{P}[\![S]\!]_\perp] C[\![\psi]\!]_\perp \qquad \text{Th. 10.27}$$
$$\Leftrightarrow \mathcal{F}[\![\{\phi\} S \{\psi\}]\!]_\perp \qquad \text{Cor. 5.29}$$
$$\Leftrightarrow \mathcal{F}[\![\{\phi\} S \{\psi\}]\!] \wedge \mathcal{F}[\![\{\phi\} S \{\text{true}\}]\!]_\perp \qquad \text{Th. 8.38}$$
$$\Leftrightarrow C[\![\phi]\!] \subseteq [\mathcal{P}[\![S]\!]] C[\![\psi]\!] \wedge C[\![\phi]\!]_\perp \subseteq [\mathcal{P}[\![S]\!]_\perp] C[\![\text{true}]\!]_\perp \qquad \text{Cor. 5.29}$$
$$\Leftrightarrow C[\![\phi]\!] \subseteq wlp(S)C[\![\psi]\!] \wedge C[\![\phi]\!]_\perp \subseteq wp(S)C[\![\text{true}]\!]_\perp \qquad \begin{array}{l}\text{Ths 10.46}\\\text{and 10.27}\end{array}$$

$$\square$$

10.4.2 Simulation

Inverses

Definition 10.48 (Inverse [B78, vW90]) Predicate transformer $P^{-1} \in \mathsf{PT}$ is an *inverse* of predicate transformer $P \in \mathsf{PT}$ if $id \leq P \mathbin{;} P^{-1}$ and $P^{-1} \mathbin{;} P \leq id$.

♣

By Lemma 10.14.(ii) we conclude that (P^{-1}, P) is a Galois connection within P if P^{-1} exists.

Lemma 10.49 $P \in \mathsf{PT}$ has an inverse iff $P \in \mathsf{PT}_\wedge^\top$. If it exists, $P^{-1} \in \mathsf{PT}_\vee^\perp$ and $P^{-1} = P^-$.

Proof: Let $P \in \mathsf{PT}_\wedge^\top$. Define $P^{-1} \stackrel{\mathrm{def}}{=} \lambda\phi . \bigwedge\{\,\psi \mid \phi \subseteq P\psi\,\}$. We check the defining properties pointwise.

$$P^{-1} \mathbin{;} P\phi$$

$$\begin{aligned}
&= P^{-1}(P\phi) && \text{Def. 10.8} \\
&= \bigwedge\{\,\psi \mid P\phi \subseteq P\psi\,\} && \text{Def. 10.48} \\
&\subseteq \bigwedge\{\,\psi \mid \phi \subseteq \psi\,\} && P \in \mathsf{PT} \\
&= \phi \\
&= \bigwedge\{\,\phi' \mid \phi \subseteq \phi'\,\} \\
&\subseteq \bigwedge\{\,P\psi \mid \phi \subseteq P\psi\,\} && \text{set theory, property of lub's} \\
&= P\left(\bigwedge\{\,\psi \mid \phi \subseteq P\psi\,\}\right) && P \in \mathsf{PT}_\wedge^\top \\
&= P \mathbin{;} P^{-1}\phi
\end{aligned}$$

Assume P' is another inverse of P, then $P^{-1} \leq P'$.

$$P^{-1} = P^{-1} \mathbin{;} id \leq P^{-1} \mathbin{;} P \mathbin{;} P' \leq id \mathbin{;} P' = P'$$

$P' \leq P^{-1}$ follows similarly, hence P^{-1} is unique, because $\leq$ as a partial order is antisymmetric. Lemma 10.14.(iii) ensures that P^{-1} distributes over joins. Moreover, $P^{-1}\perp_\mathsf{P} = \bigwedge\{\,\psi \mid \perp_\mathsf{P} \subseteq P\psi\,\} = \perp_\mathsf{P}$. Thus, $P^{-1} \in \mathsf{PT}_\vee^\perp$. The constructions of inverse and weak inverse are identical; hence they coincide on the intersection $\mathsf{PT}_\wedge^\top = \mathsf{PT}_\wedge^\top \cap \mathsf{PT}_\wedge$ of their domains. □

Inverses have several interesting properties, some of which are collected in the next corollary, which follows from the uniqueness of inverses and Cor. 10.39.

Corollary 10.50 Let P_1, P_2, and P_i, for $i \in I$, be elements of $\mathsf{PT}_\wedge^\top$.

(i) Inversion is antitone: $P_1 \leq P_2 \Leftrightarrow P_2^{-1} \leq P_1^{-1}$

(ii) Inversion reverses the order of sequential composition: $(P_1 \, ; P_2)^{-1} = P_2^{-1} \, ; P_1^{-1}$

(iii) $(\bigwedge_{i \in I} P_i)^{-1} = \bigvee_{i \in I} P_i^{-1}$ ♠

Two more aspects of the Galois connection (P^{-1}, P) prove to be useful.

Lemma 10.51

(i) $S \leq T \, ; [r]^{-1} \quad \Leftrightarrow \quad S \, ; [r] \leq T$

(ii) $S \leq [r] \, ; T \quad \Leftrightarrow \quad [r]^{-1} \, ; S \leq T$

Proof:

$$S \leq T \, ; [r]^{-1} \Rightarrow S \, ; [r] \leq T \, ; [r]^{-1} \, ; [r] \qquad \text{monotonicity}$$
$$\Rightarrow S \, ; [r] \leq T \qquad \text{Def. 10.48}$$
$$\Rightarrow S \, ; [r] \, ; [r]^{-1} \leq T \, ; [r]^{-1} \qquad \text{monotonicity}$$
$$\Rightarrow S \leq T \, ; [r]^{-1} \qquad \text{Def. 10.48}$$

The second claim follows similarly:

$$S \leq [r] \, ; T \Rightarrow [r]^{-1} \, ; S \leq [r]^{-1} \, ; [r] \, ; T \qquad \text{monotonicity}$$
$$\Rightarrow [r]^{-1} \, ; S \leq T \qquad \text{Def. 10.48}$$
$$\Rightarrow [r] \, ; [r]^{-1} \, ; S \leq [r] \, ; T \qquad \text{monotonicity}$$
$$\Rightarrow S \leq [r] \, ; T \qquad \text{Def. 10.48} \qquad \square$$

Next, we show how to express the relational image by means of an inverse.

Lemma 10.52 If $r \subseteq \Sigma^2$ and $s \subseteq \Sigma$, then $r(s) = [r]^{-1} s$.

Proof:

$$r(s)$$
$$= \{ \, \tau \mid \exists \sigma ((\sigma, \tau) \in r \wedge \sigma \in s) \, \} \qquad \text{Def. 3.6}$$
$$= \bigwedge \{ \, t \subseteq \Sigma \mid \forall \tau (\exists \sigma ((\sigma, \tau) \in r \wedge \sigma \in s) \Rightarrow \tau \in t) \, \}$$
$$= \bigwedge \{ \, t \subseteq \Sigma \mid \forall \sigma (\sigma \in s \Rightarrow \forall \tau ((\sigma, \tau) \in r \Rightarrow \tau \in t)) \, \}$$
$$= \bigwedge \{ \, t \subseteq \Sigma \mid s \leq [r]t \, \} \qquad (10.1)$$
$$= [r]^{-1} s \qquad \text{Lemma 10.38} \square$$

Another application of the inverse concerns expression of the specification statement.

Lemma 10.53 $wlp(\phi \leadsto \psi)$ is expressed by $[C[\![\phi]\!]]^{-1} \, {}_\circ^\circ \, [C[\![\psi]\!]]$.

Proof: We use the above expression of relational image to derive an alternative expression for specification statements.

$$\sigma \in wlp(\phi \leadsto \psi)s$$
$$\Leftrightarrow \exists \gamma ((\gamma, \sigma) \in C[\![\phi]\!] \wedge \forall \tau ((\gamma, \tau) \in C[\![\psi]\!] \Rightarrow \tau \in s)) \qquad \text{Def. 10.45}$$
$$\Leftrightarrow \exists \gamma ((\gamma, \sigma) \in C[\![\phi]\!] \wedge \gamma \in [C[\![\psi]\!]]s) \qquad (10.1)$$
$$\Leftrightarrow \sigma \in [C[\![\phi]\!]]^{-1} ([C[\![\psi]\!]]s) \qquad \text{Lemma 10.52}$$
$$\Leftrightarrow \sigma \in ([C[\![\phi]\!]]^{-1} \, {}_\circ^\circ \, [C[\![\psi]\!]])s \qquad \text{Def. 10.8} \qquad \square$$

Normalization

The $\leq$-weakest conjunctive and total refinement of a predicate transformer P is $[\bigstar P]$. For by Lemma 10.19 $[\bigstar P]$ is the least conjunctive refinement of $P \in \mathsf{PT}$ and totality follows by Theorem 10.44. We show that $[\bigstar P]$ can be expressed using the normalization theorem 7.9. And, since all predicate transformers can be written as $wlp(\phi \leadsto \psi)$, this expression is a calculator for $\bigstar$.

Theorem 10.54 (Normalization)
Let $\vec{x}$ denote the finite list of program variables, let $\vec{y}_0$ be a list of fresh logical variables of the same length, and let $\vec{x}_0$ be the list of all free logical variables in ϕ and ψ. Then $wlp(\vec{x} = \vec{y}_0 \leadsto \forall \vec{x}_0 \, (\phi[\vec{y}_0/\vec{x}] \Rightarrow \psi))$ is the least conjunctive and total refinement of $wlp(\phi \leadsto \psi)$.

Proof: First observe that $[C[\![\vec{x} = \vec{y}_0]\!]]^{-1} \in \mathsf{PT}_{\vec{x} \leftarrow \vec{y}_0}$ is not only disjunctive and strict, like every inverse, but also conjunctive and total (*). This follows from the similarity between $[C[\![\vec{x} = \vec{y}_0]\!]]$ and the unit element of PT. Relation $C[\![\vec{x} = \vec{y}_0]\!]^{\vec{y}_0, \vec{x}} = \{ (\gamma, \sigma) \mid \gamma(\vec{y}_0) = \sigma(\vec{x}) \}$ is only a renaming of variables $\vec{y}_0$ to $\vec{x}$. Similarly, predicate transformer $[C[\![\vec{x} = \vec{y}_0]\!]]$ renames variables $\vec{x}$ to $\vec{y}_0$ because it relates postconditions to preconditions. In particular, $[C[\![\vec{x} = \vec{y}_0]\!]] (C[\![\pi]\!]^{\vec{x}}) = C[\![\pi[\vec{y}_0/\vec{x}]]\!]^{\vec{y}_0}$. Its inverse then amounts to the reverse substitution.

We start with the $\leq$-weakest conjunctive and total refinement of $wlp(\phi \leadsto \psi)$ expressed using the Galois connection of Theorem 10.44:

$$[\bigstar wlp(\phi \leadsto \psi)]$$
$$= [\mathcal{P}[\![\phi \leadsto \psi]\!]] \qquad \text{Th. 10.46}$$
$$= \left[\mathcal{P}[\![(\vec{x} = \vec{y}_0) \leadsto \forall \vec{x}_0 \left(\phi[\vec{y}_0/\vec{x}] \Rightarrow \psi\right)]\!]\right] \qquad \text{Th. 7.9}$$
$$= \left[\bigstar wlp\left((\vec{x} = \vec{y}_0) \leadsto \forall \vec{x}_0 \left(\phi[\vec{y}_0/\vec{x}] \Rightarrow \psi\right)\right)\right] \qquad \text{Th. 10.46}$$
$$= \left[\bigstar \left([C[\![\vec{x} = \vec{y}_0]\!]]^{-1} \, {}_\circ^\circ \, \left[C[\![\forall \vec{x}_0 \left(\phi[\vec{y}_0/\vec{x}] \Rightarrow \psi\right)]\!]\right]\right)\right] \qquad \text{Lemma 10.53}$$

$$= [C[\![\vec{x} = \vec{y}_0]\!]]^{-1} \mathbin{\raisebox{0.2ex}{\scriptsize$\stackrel{}{,}$}} \left[C[\![\forall \vec{x}_0 \left(\phi[\vec{y}_0/\vec{x}] \Rightarrow \psi \right)]\!] \right] \qquad\qquad (*)$$

$$= wlp \left(\vec{x} = \vec{y}_0 \rightsquigarrow \forall \vec{x}_0 \left(\phi[\vec{y}_0/\vec{x}] \Rightarrow \psi \right) \right) \qquad\qquad \text{Lemma 10.53} \ \ \square$$

As observed by Hesselink [Hes90], any predicate transformer can be expressed as the sequential composition of a strict disjunctive and a total conjunctive predicate transformer.

Lemma 10.55 (Predicate transformer factorization) Let $P \in \mathsf{PT}_{V \leftarrow W}$. Define relations a and b as follows:

$$a \stackrel{\text{def}}{=} \left\{ (\sigma, \tau) \in \mathfrak{P}(\Sigma^V) \times \Sigma^V \mid \tau \in \sigma \right\}$$

$$b \stackrel{\text{def}}{=} \left\{ (\sigma, \tau) \in \mathfrak{P}(\Sigma^V) \times \Sigma^W \mid \forall s \subseteq \Sigma^W \, (\sigma \subseteq P(s) \Rightarrow \tau \in s) \right\}$$

Then $P = [a]^{-1} \mathbin{\raisebox{0.2ex}{\scriptsize$\stackrel{}{,}$}} [b]$.

Proof: A simple calculation reveals that $[a]^{-1} = \lambda X : \mathfrak{P}(\mathfrak{P}(\Sigma^V)). \bigcup X$ and $[b] = \lambda s. \mathfrak{P}(P(s))$. By monotonicity of P the sequential composition of $[a]^{-1}$ and $[b]$ is equal to P. $\qquad\qquad\qquad\qquad\qquad\qquad\qquad\qquad\qquad\qquad\qquad\qquad\qquad\square$

The construction underlying this proof can also be applied to relations instead of predicate transformers. Then one obtains that each relation can be expressed as the sequential composition of (the graph of) a total function and an inverse of (the graph of) a total function. This common construction becomes particularly clear when presented using category theory [GMdM92].

In the next section we shall apply the previous lemma to a powersimulation to display the connection between the completeness result for predicate transformers and the one for partial correctness relations.

Simulation and powersimulation

There is a close interplay between partial correctness relational simulation and powersimulation. L- and L^{-1}-simulation are special cases of powersimulation, as we shall see next. Assume, for instance, that relation $\beta \subseteq \Sigma^A \times \Sigma^C$ is an L-simulation relation between concrete relation $C \subseteq \Sigma^C \times \Sigma^C$ and abstract relation $A \subseteq \Sigma^A \times \Sigma^A$:

$$
\begin{array}{ll}
A \mathbin{;} \beta \supseteq \beta \mathbin{;} C & \text{Def. 2.1} \\[4pt]
\Leftrightarrow [A \mathbin{;} \beta] \leq [\beta \mathbin{;} C] & \text{Th. 10.44} \\[4pt]
\Leftrightarrow [A] \mathbin{\raisebox{0.2ex}{\scriptsize$\stackrel{}{,}$}} [\beta] \leq [\beta] \mathbin{\raisebox{0.2ex}{\scriptsize$\stackrel{}{,}$}} [C] & \text{Lemma 10.18} \\[4pt]
\Leftrightarrow [\beta]^{-1} \mathbin{\raisebox{0.2ex}{\scriptsize$\stackrel{}{,}$}} [A] \leq [C] \mathbin{\raisebox{0.2ex}{\scriptsize$\stackrel{}{,}$}} [\beta]^{-1} & \text{Lemma 10.51}
\end{array}
$$

This last line is exactly the condition required for $[\beta]^{-1}$ to be a powersimulation for the pair of operations $([C],[A])$. Note that this is a special powersimulation, namely one that is strict and disjunctive. Similarly, L^{-1}-simulations correspond to total, conjunctive powersimulations. Let $\alpha \subseteq \Sigma^C \times \Sigma^A$ be an L^{-1}-simulation between C and A from above:

$$\alpha\,;A \supseteq C\,;\alpha \qquad\qquad \text{Def. 2.1}$$
$$\Leftrightarrow [\alpha\,;A] \leq [C\,;\alpha] \qquad\qquad \text{Th. 10.44}$$
$$\Leftrightarrow [\alpha]\,\hat{;}\,[A] \leq [C]\,\hat{;}\,[\alpha] \qquad\qquad \text{Lemma 10.18}$$

These two correspondences allow us to sketch a link between the completeness result of this chapter and the one of Chapter 4. Let $\mathcal{A}$ and $\mathcal{C}$ be two compatible data types, $\mathcal{A} = (AI,(A_i)_{i\in I},AF)$ and $\mathcal{C} = (CI,(C_i)_{i\in I},CF)$, such that $\mathcal{C}$ refines $\mathcal{A}$, that is, for all program skeletons P:

$$AI\,;P((A_i)_{i\in I})\,;AF \supseteq CI\,;P((C_i)_{i\in I})\,;CF$$

Since $[.]$ is an isomorphism preserving sequential composition, choice, and recursion, this implies, for all P, that

$$[AI]\,;P(([A_i])_{i\in I})\,;[AF] \supseteq [CI]\,;P(([C_i])_{i\in I})\,;[CF] \quad,$$

i.e., $[\mathcal{A}] \stackrel{\text{def}}{=} ([AI],([A_i])_{i\in I},[AF])$ is refined by $[\mathcal{C}] \stackrel{\text{def}}{=} ([CI],([C_i])_{i\in I},[CF])$ in the predicate transformer setting for partial correctness. Thus, there exists a powersimulation β such that $\mathcal{A} \leq_\beta \mathcal{C}$, by Theorem 10.42. Next we split this powersimulation into two parts. Observe that applying Lemma 10.55 to powersimulation $\beta \in \mathrm{PT}_{Var^C \leftarrow Var^A}$ yields a sequence of two powersimulations, $[a]^{-1}\,;[b]$, one of them corresponding to an L-simulation relation and the other corresponding to an L^{-1}-simulation relation (both with respect to an intermediate data type, the one obtained by the powerset construction).

Maximal simulators

Another example of the simplifying effect of predicate transformers can be seen when considering the calculation of maximal simulators. Next, a predicate tranformer analogue of the L-simulation calculator $L_{\beta^{-1}} = \lambda X.\beta \rightsquigarrow (X\,;\beta)$ from Def. 4.11 is given.

Lemma 10.56 Let $\beta \subseteq \Sigma^A \times \Sigma^C$ and let $A \in \mathrm{PT}_{Var^A \leftarrow Var^A}$. Then $[\beta]^{-1}\,\hat{;}\,A\,\hat{;}\,[\beta]$ is the least refined predicate transformer that powersimulates A w.r.t. $[\beta]^{-1}$. Furthermore, the function $\lambda X.[\beta]^{-1}\,\hat{;}\,X\,\hat{;}\,[\beta]$ is monotone.

Proof: By Lemma 10.51 and Def. 10.35. $\qquad\qquad\qquad\qquad\qquad\Box$

In Chapter 7 we saw that the calculation of L-simulations required difficult arguments and resulted in a nontrivial calculated expression, when working in the relational framework for partial correctness. Here we see that this particular calculation is simplified by the use of predicate transformers.

Lemma 10.57 Let $\phi, \psi \in Pred^A$ and $\beta \in Abs^{AC}$. Then $wlp(\langle\beta\rangle\,\phi \rightsquigarrow \langle\beta\rangle\,\psi)$ is the least refined predicate transformer that powersimulates $wlp(\phi \rightsquigarrow \psi)$ w.r.t. powersimulation $[\beta]^{-1}$.

Proof:

$$\left[\mathcal{A}[\![\beta]\!]^{AC}\right]^{-1} \underset{\sim}{;} wlp(\phi \rightsquigarrow \psi) \leq X \underset{\sim}{;} \left[\mathcal{A}[\![\beta]\!]^{AC}\right]^{-1}$$

$\Leftrightarrow$ (Lemma 10.53)

$$\left[\mathcal{A}[\![\beta]\!]^{AC}\right]^{-1} \underset{\sim}{;} \left[C[\![\phi]\!]^{A}\right]^{-1} \underset{\sim}{;} \left[C[\![\psi]\!]^{A}\right] \leq X \underset{\sim}{;} \left[\mathcal{A}[\![\beta]\!]^{AC}\right]^{-1}$$

$\Leftrightarrow$ (Cor. 10.50)

$$\left[C[\![\phi]\!]^{A} ; \mathcal{A}[\![\beta]\!]^{AC}\right]^{-1} \underset{\sim}{;} \left[C[\![\psi]\!]^{A}\right] \leq X \underset{\sim}{;} \left[\mathcal{A}[\![\beta]\!]^{AC}\right]^{-1}$$

$\Leftrightarrow$ (Lemma 10.51)

$$\left[C[\![\phi]\!]^{A} ; \mathcal{A}[\![\beta]\!]^{AC}\right]^{-1} \underset{\sim}{;} \left[C[\![\psi]\!]^{A}\right] \underset{\sim}{;} \left[\mathcal{A}[\![\beta]\!]^{AC}\right] \leq X$$

$\Leftrightarrow$ (Lemma 10.18)

$$\left[C[\![\phi]\!]^{A} ; \mathcal{A}[\![\beta]\!]^{AC}\right]^{-1} \underset{\sim}{;} \left[C[\![\psi]\!]^{A} ; \mathcal{A}[\![\beta]\!]^{AC}\right] \leq X$$

$\Leftrightarrow$ (Cor. 5.16)

$$\left[C[\![\phi]\!]^{A} ; (\mathcal{A}[\![\beta]\!]^{CA})^{-1}\right]^{-1} \underset{\sim}{;} \left[C[\![\psi]\!]^{A} ; (\mathcal{A}[\![\beta]\!]^{CA})^{-1}\right] \leq X$$

$\Leftrightarrow$ (Lemma 5.26)

$$\left[\left\langle \mathcal{A}[\![\beta]\!]^{CA}\right\rangle C[\![\phi]\!]^{A}\right]^{-1} \underset{\sim}{;} \left[\left\langle \mathcal{A}[\![\beta]\!]^{CA}\right\rangle C[\![\psi]\!]^{A}\right] \leq X$$

$\Leftrightarrow$ (Lemma 5.17)

$$\left[C[\![\langle\beta\rangle\,\phi]\!]^{Lvar^A, Var^C}\right]^{-1} \underset{\sim}{;} \left[C[\![\langle\beta\rangle\,\psi]\!]^{Lvar^A, Var^C}\right] \leq X$$

$\Leftrightarrow$ (Lemma 10.53)

$$wlp(\langle\beta\rangle\,\phi \rightsquigarrow \langle\beta\rangle\,\psi) \leq X \qquad\qquad \square$$

Why is the proof of Lemma 10.57 so much simpler than the one for the L-simulation theorem in Chapter 7? And how does this result relate to the completeness theorem of this chapter and the simulation theorems of Chapter 7?

First of all, $wlp(\phi \rightsquigarrow \psi)$ need be neither conjunctive nor continuous. Thus it is not necessarily an abstract level operation specification of a data type to which the completeness theorem applies. However, if Lemma 10.57 is applied to the least conjunctive and total refinement of $\phi \rightsquigarrow \psi$ characterized in Theorem 10.54 one ends up exactly with the specification statement calculated in Theorem 7.9. In this context six specifications are interesting. These are listed below. As usual, let $\beta \in Abs^{AC}$ and let $\vec{x}$, $\vec{a}$, and $\vec{c}$ denote the lists of normal variables and representation variables on the abstract and concrete level respectively. Let $\vec{x}_0$ denote the list of logical variables occurring freely in assertions $\phi, \psi \in Pred^A$.

- The starting point of our analysis is

$$wlp(\phi \rightsquigarrow \psi) \tag{10.7}$$

- By Theorem 10.54 its least total and conjunctive refinement is

$$wlp\left((\vec{x}\vec{a} = \vec{y}_0\vec{a}_0) \rightsquigarrow \forall \vec{x}_0 \left(\phi[^{\vec{y}_0\vec{a}_0}/_{\vec{x}\vec{a}}] \Rightarrow \psi\right)\right) \tag{10.8}$$

(for suitable lists of fresh logical variables $\vec{y}_0$ and $\vec{a}_0$).

- By Lemma 10.57 the result of applying the L-simulation calculator to (10.7) is

$$wlp(\langle\beta\rangle\,\phi \rightsquigarrow \langle\beta\rangle\,\psi) \tag{10.9}$$

- Its least total and conjunctive refinement is, again by Theorem 10.54,

$$wlp\left((\vec{x}\vec{c} = \vec{y}_0\vec{c}_0) \rightsquigarrow \forall \vec{x}_0 \left((\langle\beta\rangle\,\phi)[^{\vec{y}_0\vec{c}_0}/_{\vec{x}\vec{c}}] \Rightarrow \langle\beta\rangle\,\psi\right)\right) \tag{10.10}$$

(for a suitable list of fresh logical variables $\vec{c}_0$).

- The result of applying the L-simulation calculator to (10.8) is, again by Lemma 10.57,

$$wlp\left(\langle\beta\rangle\,(\vec{x}\vec{a} = \vec{y}_0\vec{a}_0) \rightsquigarrow \langle\beta\rangle\,\forall \vec{x}_0 \left(\phi[^{\vec{y}_0\vec{a}_0}/_{\vec{x}\vec{a}}] \Rightarrow \psi\right)\right) \tag{10.11}$$

- Once more by Theorem 10.54, the least total and conjunctive refinement of (10.11) is

$$wlp\left((\vec{x}\vec{c} = \vec{z}_0\vec{d}_0) \rightsquigarrow \forall \vec{y}_0\vec{a}_0 \left(\begin{array}{l}(\langle\beta\rangle\,(\vec{x}\vec{a} = \vec{y}_0\vec{a}_0))[^{\vec{z}_0\vec{d}_0}/_{\vec{x}\vec{c}}] \\ \Rightarrow \langle\beta\rangle\,\forall \vec{x}_0 \left(\phi[^{\vec{y}_0\vec{a}_0}/_{\vec{x}\vec{a}}] \Rightarrow \psi\right)\end{array}\right)\right) \tag{10.12}$$

(for suitable lists of fresh logical variables $\vec{z}_0$ and $\vec{d}_0$).

As explained below, these predicate transformers are related as follows.

$$(10.7) \quad \leq_{[\mathcal{A}[\![\beta]\!]^{AC}]^{-1}} \quad (10.9) \quad \leq \quad (10.10)$$

$$\leq \qquad\qquad \leq \qquad\qquad \leq$$

$$(10.8) \quad \leq_{[\mathcal{A}[\![\beta]\!]^{AC}]^{-1}} \quad (10.11) \quad \leq \quad (10.12)$$

Most relationships are clear by construction of the predicate transformers in question. Only two vertical ones, $(10.9) \leq (10.11)$ and $(10.10) \leq (10.12)$, need further explanation. The first can be understood as follows. By Lemma 10.56 the L-simulation calculator is monotone; thus (10.9) is refined by (10.11) because (10.7) is refined by (10.8). Next we explain why (10.9) and (10.11) are different in general. The former is expressed by

$$\left[\mathcal{A}[\![\beta]\!]^{AC}\right]^{-1} \,\overset{.}{;}\, \left[C[\![\phi]\!]^{A}\right]^{-1} \,\overset{.}{;}\, \left[C[\![\psi]\!]^{A} \,;\, \mathcal{A}[\![\beta]\!]^{AC}\right] \qquad (10.13)$$

whereas the latter can be written as

$$\left[\mathcal{A}[\![\beta]\!]^{AC}\right]^{-1} \,\overset{.}{;}\, \left[C[\![\vec{x}\vec{a} = \vec{y}_0\vec{a}_0]\!]^{A}\right]^{-1} \,\overset{.}{;}\, \left[C[\![\forall \vec{x}_0 \left(\phi[^{\vec{y}_0\vec{a}_0}/_{\vec{x}\vec{a}}] \Rightarrow \psi\right)]\!]^{A} \,;\, \mathcal{A}[\![\beta]\!]^{AC}\right]$$
$$(10.14)$$

Next observe that, by Lemma 10.49, in case $\left[\mathcal{A}[\![\beta]\!]^{AC}\right]$ is strict and disjunctive but $\left[C[\![\phi]\!]^{A}\right]$ is not, (10.14) is total and conjunctive because $\left[C[\![\vec{x}\vec{a} = \vec{y}_0\vec{a}_0]\!]^{A}\right]$ is strict and disjunctive. On the other hand, (10.14) need not be total and conjunctive. Consequently (10.9) and (10.11) are different in general.

Finally, what about (10.10) and (10.12)? By monotonicity of $\lambda X.[\bigstar X]$, (10.10) is refined by (10.12) since (10.9) is refined by (10.11). How about the other direction? That is an open problem.

10.5 Historical Background

The refinement calculus unifies several independently developed strands.

One of these is an approach to characterizing the semantics of programming language constructs using functions mapping predicates to predicates, called predicate transformers after Dijkstra's [Dij75], rather than by means of functions mapping states to states, called state transformers.

Other early references to concepts which were later called predicate transformers are contained in [dBdR72, HP72, dBM75, dR76, Dij76, Pra76]. Pratt's work [Pra76] led to a separate strand, called dynamic logic, of results culminating, e.g., in Harel's dissertation [Har79]; the emphasis in dynamic logic is on decidability, complete axiomatizations, and total correctness.

A separate development leading to the so-called refinement calculus goes back to [B78] published as [B80], in which program derivation through algebraic manipulation of predicate transformers is stressed, leading to an impressive sequence of papers, e.g., [B81b, B81a, B88b, BvW90] and culminating in, for instance, von Wright's [vW90, vW92b, vW92a].

This development influenced another strand, partly originating from the Programming Research Group at Oxford University, e.g., Morris's [Mor87, Mor89a, Mor89b], Morgan's [Mor88, Mor90, Mor94], Gardiner and Morgan's [GM91, GM93], and [GMdM92] by Gardiner *et al.*

In the relatively short history of computer science the study of isomorphisms between relations (also called state transformers) and predicate transformers has a long tradition, possibly starting with Wand [Wan77a] and ending (to date) with Bonsangue's work [BK93, Bon96] and Rewitzky and Brink's work, e.g., [RB95]. An independent study of isomorphisms between state transformers and predicate transformers in the context of domain theory started out with Plotkin's [Plo79] and Smyth's [Smy83].

Exercises

10.1   Prove Theorem 10.7.

10.2   Prove Lemma 10.11.

10.3   Prove Lemma 10.14.

10.4   Give an alternative proof of Lemma 10.3 using the Galois connection stated by $a \wedge b \leq c \Leftrightarrow b \leq \bar{a} \vee c$.

10.5* Give a detailed proof of Theorem 10.26. *Hint:* Show that conjunctive functions are monotone.

10.6   (Weak inverse)

    (a) Complete the proof of Lemma 10.38.

    (b) Prove Cor. 10.39.

10.7   Prove Lemma 10.43.

10.8   Show that $[.]^{-1}$ is an isomorphism between $\mathcal{R}$ and $\mathsf{PT}_\vee^\perp$.

10.9   Complete the proof of Theorem 10.46.

10.10 Complete the proof Lemma 10.49: show that P has an inverse only if $P \in \mathsf{PT}_\wedge^\top$.

10.11* Formulate and prove a partial correctness version of the completeness theorem (Theorem 10.42).

Picture Gallery

In this monograph we compare many methods for proving data refinement, and explain the theory behind these methods, as well. But who are the researchers behind these methods and this theory? What do they look like? And what do they themselves consider as their main contributions? Some of these researchers, or, in the case of Hans Bekić and David Park, their wives, were willing to help us with our attempt to answer these questions. This resulted in the following collection of photographs and nutshell captions.

Martín Abadi

Martín Abadi coauthored a number of fundamental papers on the verification of concurrent systems together with Leslie Lamport, amongst others, [AL91]. He further became known for his work on the analysis of security protocols [BAN90], and for his monograph on the foundations of object-oriented languages [AC96], which he wrote together with Luca Cardelli.

Ralph J. R. Back

Ralph Back is the founding father of the refinement calculus. In his thesis [B78] he extended Dijkstra's predicate transformer approach to program
construction with a specification statement and an explicit relation of refinement between programs. A revision of the thesis appeared as a Mathematical
Centre Tract [B80]. Besides algorithmic refinement, the thesis also showed
how to do data refinement in a systematic manner, by piecewise changing the
data representation in program fragments. In [B88a] he starts to use fixed
points of monotone transformations — in his work always predicate transformers — when reasoning about recursion in the refinement calculus. Continuous
transformers would have been too restrictive because of the presence of specification statements, which need not be continuous. By 1990 he had developed,
together with Joakim von Wright, a full-fledged calculational approach to program refinement, in particular with respect to data refinement. This calculus
allows for both angelic and demonic nondeterminism in program statements,
and is formulated in higher order logic; its theorems are proven mechanically
using the Cambridge HOL system. In another line of his research, carried
out in cooperation with Kaisa Sere since 1988, he generalizes the refinement
calculus approach to parallel and distributed systems, using action systems developed in the early 1980s together with Reino Kurki-Suonio.

Hans Bekić

Hans Bekić (1936–1982) [J84], is shown here in front of the San Marco cathedral in Venice. Hans, an early pioneer, is known for his work on VDL, the predecessor of VDM, and belongs to the select group of discoverers of the least fixed point characterization of recursion. In particular, he discovered how to express the simultaneous least fixed point solution of systems of equations (corresponding to mutually recursive procedures) by iterating their single least fixed point solutions. Hans Bekić was the first to develop a truly mathematical theory of processes in which the important combinators, such as parallel composition, were modelled as functions of higher type [Bek71] (see also [Mil89, page 247]).

Jaco W. de Bakker

This picture of Jaco de Bakker dates from the time when he coauthored what is considered one of the most influential unpublished papers in computer science, entitled "A Theory of Programs — An outline of joint work by J. W. de Bakker and Dana Scott", which contains the first formulation of the μ-calculus (least fixed point) approach to recursion. He is known as one of the originators of the relational calculus in programming theory (jointly with Willem-Paul de Roever [dBdR72]), for his early foundational work on program verification, e.g., [dB71, dB80], and for his lifelong interest in the semantics of programming languages [dBdV96].

Paul H. B. Gardiner, Carroll C. Morgan, C. A. R. Hoare, He Jifeng, and Jeff W. Sanders

This picture shows, from left to right, Paul Gardiner, Carroll Morgan, Tony Hoare, He Jifeng, and Jeff Sanders, the five collaborators of the Oxford Computing Laboratory who contributed most to the subject of this monograph. He Jifeng, Tony Hoare and Jeff Sanders wrote one of its keystones [HHS87]. Carroll Morgan was, together with Paul Gardiner, one of the first to publish on the Oxford approach to the refinement calculus.

Susan L. Gerhart

Susan Gerhart is a pioneer in the areas of correctness-preserving program transformations [Ger75, Ger78, LdRG79] and of electronic tool support for program verification [G+80, LEG81]. She was the first to formulate the four-point recipe quoted in Section 11.2.4, and referred to by us as Reynolds' method (consult Section 11.4 for the reason why). Let us explain the importance of her techniques. In 1978, Stanley Lee and the senior author were trying to find correctness proofs for some complicated list copying algorithms, and came to the conclusion that "first generation principles, with which one can easily verify a three-line greatest common divisor algorithm, do not directly enable one to verify a 10,000 line operating system (or even a 50 line list-processing algorithm). To verify complex programs, additional techniques of organization, analysis and manipulation are required" [LdRG79]. Her program transformation technique enabled us to generate these correctness proofs, because its structuring capabilities allowed an order-of-magnitude increase in the size and complexity of programs which could be verified.

Eric C. R. Hehner

Rick Hehner is an expert on the simple formulation of program verification methods; his syntactic characterization of L-simulation is the most elegant one we encountered. It is interesting to observe that the specification statement has been discovered independently by several people. For instance, in Rick Hehner's first paper on formal methods [Heh79], which had appeared as a technical report in 1976, he introduced a refinement methodology in which an early form of specification statement plays an essential rôle, and in which recursion is integrated in a particularly natural way. In [Heh84a] Rick decided to use predicates instead of predicate transformers, and in [Heh89] he dropped the use of least fixed points, realizing that he did not need them once a time variable was available. He is currently working on unified algebra, which seeks to unify Booleans with numbers, values with types, and logic with algebra. If he continues at this rate, there will soon be nothing left!

C. A. R. Hoare

Tony Hoare is shown in this picture while lecturing at the Marktoberdorf Sum-
merschool in 1988. Tony has contributed more than anyone else to the subject of this monograph by his pioneering work on Hoare logic, on simulation methods, and on calculi for concurrency and program development. His
publications on Communicating Sequential Processes [Hoa78, Hoa85] have
influenced the design and the semantics of, and the way of reasoning about,
many programming languages for distributed computation. From him originates Hoare's Law of Large Programs: "Inside every large program is a small
program struggling to get out", expressing his lifelong pursuit of simplicity.

Cliff B. Jones

Cliff Jones founded the VDM approach together with Dines Bjørner [BJ78], and has been relentlessly promoting formal techniques for program development within industry. He started his career at Heinz Zemanek's IBM Development Laboratory in Vienna, and, after spending many years as a professor at Manchester University, has now returned to industry at Harlequin, a company specializing in formal methods. He documented the rich history of VDM, which originates in VDL, in [J92]. Cliff is one of the first to have recognized the importance of compositional reasoning for the development of concurrent systems, and developed this insight in his dissertation on the rely/guarantee formalism for shared variable concurrency [J81]. He was accepted as a doctoral student at Oxford, although he had never obtained an undergraduate degree.

Bengt Jonsson

Bengt Jonsson established the equivalence between simulation methods based on refinement mappings, history and prophecy variables on the one hand, and L- and L^{-1}-simulation on the other hand. His dissertation on a methodology for the verification of distributed systems by proving refinement provides an elegant synthesis of temporal logic and simulation-based methods. He is known for his work on the semantics of asynchronous concurrent systems, and on decidability and undecidability results for systems communicating via FIFO channels. But there is more to his life than mere formal methods. In earlier days, he developed mastery of the keyboard by playing classical piano, but Chopin scores are now replaced by LATEX documents, although he still accompanies his sons (6 and 8 years old) when they play the violin.

Leslie Lamport

Leslie Lamport made some of the truly seminal contributions to the theory of distributed and concurrent systems, and their formal verification. Together with Martín Abadi he wrote one of the most influential papers on the refinement of reactive systems [AL91]. His current approach to the specification and verification of such systems is based on his temporal logic of actions TLA [Lam94] [Lam94]. As if this were not enough, he is also the author of LATEX, the most extensively used system for typesetting scientific documents (which has of course been used for preparing this manuscript). Leslie is frequently asked to speak at scientific meetings, partly because of his independent opinions and controversial remarks, which often force one to reevaluate old beliefs in a new light.

Nancy A. Lynch

Nancy Lynch has contributed to the subject of this monograph by her work on possibilities mappings [Lyn83], and her paper on forward and backward simulation for timing based systems [LV91]. She is known for her research on I/O automata, carried out together with Mark Tuttle, and for her comprehensive textbook on distributed algorithms [Lyn96], in which she both presents a classification of a representative collection of such algorithms and gives a convincing explanation of the intuition behind them, backed up by rigorous arguments for their correctness.

Antoni Mazurkiewicz
Antoni Mazurkiewicz is one of the founding fathers of the Polish school of programming theory. He is especially known for his work on the partial order theory of truly concurrent systems, and is the inventor of the concept of Mazurkiewicz traces. Antoni belongs to the group of five discoverers of the least fixed point characterization of recursion (the others are Hans Bekić, Jaco de Bakker, David Park, and Dana Scott). These discoveries were but a passage in his multifaceted career, which also includes active participation in the anti-Communist movement during Poland's transition to the present republic.

Robin Milner

An animated and involved Robin Milner sat in front of a blackboard covered with formulae describing the world which he has helped to create. Robin was the first to formulate an (algebraic) notion of simulation between programs, which he subsequently extended to a proper notion of bisimulation in close collaboration with David Park. He was also the first to develop a process algebraic approach to concurrency (by his work on CCS, SCCS, and the π-calculus), LCF (probably the first theoretically based yet practical tool for machine-assisted proof construction), and ML (the first language to include polymorphic type inference and a type-safe exception handling mechanism). It is a testimony to the flexibility and perception of quality inside the English university system that neither Robin Milner nor Tony Hoare ever wrote a doctoral dissertation, and yet they occupy the highest academic positions attainable in their field.

 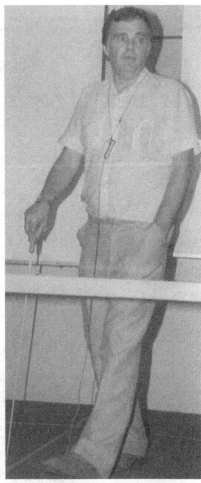

David M. R. Park

David Park (1935–1990) [PdBM$^+$94], one of the founding fathers of the μ-calculus, is particularly known for his studies of its monotone variant. For instance, he expressed termination of recursive programs over recursively defined data structures inside the monotone μ-calculus together with Peter Hitchcock, proved the inexpressibility of finiteness of sets in this calculus, and indicated several ways how to formulate fairness in it. He also established how to express the proper notion of bisimulation by means of greatest fixed points. After more and more people published their discoveries of the use of fixed points within their domains of expertise, he suggested the following more transparent way of titling such papers: " ... discovered least fixed points, too."

John C. Reynolds

John Reynolds, known for his pioneering work in formal semantics, programming languages, type theory, and the application of category theory to computer science, has contributed to this book by his textbook on program verification and program development in the setting of Algol-like languages [Rey81]. John's word is regarded by many as final in matters of formalization.

Dana S. Scott

This picture of Dana Scott was taken by Ben Spiegel. Dana's name will be familiar to most serious students of Computer Science. Together with Christopher Strachey he developed the first fully adequate mathematical models for the semantics of programming languages, which the two of them called denotational semantics, and for which they used models of the λ-calculus. Until 1969 only so-called term models were known for this calculus; these were in Dana's opinion not satisfactory, being syntactically based. Thus motivated, he discovered how to obtain truly semantic models, and subsequently applied these in his work on denotational semantics. Years before that, he worked together with Michael Rabin on the theory of finite automata; this resulted in [RS59], referenced in every textbook on the subject. In 1997 he was awarded the Swedish Rolf Schock Prize for Logic and Philosophy.

Eugene W. Stark

At one fell swoop Eugene Stark formulated in his 1984 thesis [Sta84] a notion of simulation between specifications for concurrent programs, and proved this notion to be sound, complete (provided the specifications involved satisfy certain well-formedness conditions), and equivalent to the possibilities mapping technique of Nancy Lynch and her student John Goree [Gor83, Lyn83]. He also integrated his simulation theory with a compositional rely-guarantee-based style of specification in the sense of Jones [J81] for proving safety and liveness properties of concurrent programs. To our knowledge he is therefore the first one to have proved a notion of simulation between programs both sound and complete.

He describes his experiences while obtaining these results as follows:

Pursuing a Ph.D. in Computer Science at M.I.T. is not an experience for the faint of heart. My own eventual escape from the clutches of the 'Tute was facilitated by a number of tricks that I used in order to maintain my motivation (and sanity!) during especially difficult periods. One of my favorites was the following: each morning I would arise early, so as to arrive at the office at about 7 am, a full three hours before the daily chatter of the other inhabitants was in full swing. After scribbling furiously on a notepad for several hours, by about 2 pm my thoughts had become disjointed enough that I could have some really interesting ideas. By about 3 pm I could often convince myself that I had made a most amazing discovery. The key was to postpone until the next morning the working out of the details, so that the next day's work would be well underway before I discovered that it had all been merely a hallucination.

[personal communication]

Part II
Applications

This part presents an overview of some existing formalisms for proving data refinement. We analyze for each of the selected formalisms how it relates to simulation in its various shapes (partial vs. total correctness, relational vs. predicate transformer semantics). This allows us to compare the power of these formalisms when it comes to data refinement. The reader should be warned, however, that this does not at all imply a ranking that should be used as a guideline for selecting a particular method for a development project.

In Chapters 11 and 12, Reynolds' method and VDM are described and related to the results of Part I, and in Chapter 13 this is done for Z, Hehner's method, and Back's refinement calculus. In Section 13.1 we not only introduce the Z-notation and state Z's method for proving data refinement, but also explain why the latter is equivalent, modulo notation, with the VDM method for proving data refinement as stated in Chapter 12. Consequently, Z does not introduce anything new from the point of view of data refinement, although it constitutes a considerable improvement w.r.t. the important topic of structuring specifications.

The main result of these chapters is that these methods can be considered as applications of the L-simulation principle. Back's refinement calculus is similar to the one presented in Chapter 10 in that it is based on weakest precondition predicate transformer semantics and in that its notion of simulation is a kind of powersimulation. However, Ralph Back has gone one step further by relaxing his programming language to incorporate arbitrary meets and joins of programs.

Finally we introduce in Chapter 14 two methods that were originally developed for proving refinement between specifications of concurrent systems:

- Abadi and Lamport's method, which is based on total and functional simulation relations called *refinement mappings*. Two auxiliary variable constructions, called *history variables* and *prophecy variables*, are added to overcome the limitations of this restricted class of simulations. In combination with refinement mappings, history variables allow one to mimic L-simulation, while in combination with prophecy variables they mimic L^{-1}-simulations. Consequently Abadi and Lamport's method is complete.
- In retrospect, Lynch's method can be regarded as a blend between Abadi and Lamport's method and the combination of L- and L^{-1}-simulation. Lynch's *possibilities mappings* are L-simulation relations and she combines them with prophecy variables. Hence, her method is also complete.

11
Reynolds' Method

11.1 Introduction

This chapter is based on the fifth chapter of John Reynolds' book "The craft of programming" [Rey81]. The material in Section 11.2 is taken verbatim from his book.

In contrast to Part I, Reynolds is mainly concerned with top-down development of programs rather than proving refinement between data types. His method of deriving programs is called *stepwise refinement* and was introduced in [Wir71] and [DDH72]. One of his development techniques, however, is related to data refinement. In this chapter we shall present and analyze this technique and show that it amounts to L-simulation.

In a given program Reynolds inspects each particular variable of some abstract data type separately, and shows how the choice of a way to implement that variable is guided by the number and relative frequency of the operations performed on it. This allows differentiation between the implementation of different variables of the same data type.

Reynolds uses Hoare-style partial correctness specifications. However, none of his program transformation steps increases the domain of possible nontermination. Therefore his examples of refinement are also refinements in a total correctness interpretation.

In Section 11.3 we relate Reynolds' method to L-simulation. At the last stage of our analysis of Reynolds' method we shall see that we have to interpret some of his operations in a total correctness setting to bridge a gap between his requirements and those for partial correctness L-simulation. Formally, this is supported by the L-simulation theorem for total correctness, Theorem 9.9.

We close this chapter with some remarks on the history of this method.

We discuss Reynolds' method using one of his larger examples. In this example Reynolds shows in passing that at the most abstract levels one is not necessarily interested in total correctness. Only after a number of refinement steps is total correctness obtained, and then the termination argument is separated from the partial correctness proof.

The programming language Reynolds uses in his book is richer than ours. It has arrays, local variables, procedures, and even jumps. This is also reflected in his version of Hoare logic. Fortunately, only arrays are indispensable for the chosen examples, and then they are used in the simplest possible way (e.g., indexed expressions are not used as array indices). So no complication arises from their use. For the details of Hoare logic rules about array handling we refer to [dB80, Rey81]. The cosmetic changes we have applied to Reynolds' examples only involve moving local variable declarations to the outermost block and the use of non-recursive procedures.

Within the following section from Reynolds' book we distinguish our remarks by setting them apart

---

like this

---

and our (rare) footnotes from Reynolds' own text by using a sans-serif type face.

11.2 Running Example: Finding Paths in Directed Graphs

11.2.1 Directed Graphs

A *directed graph* consists of a set **node** whose members are called *nodes*, and a set **edge** whose members are called *edges* (or sometimes *arcs*). Each edge is an ordered pair $\langle x, y \rangle$ of nodes which is said to *go from x to y*. We will only consider finite directed graphs. More specifically, we will assume that the sizes of **node** and **edge** are bounded by integers N and E respectively.

A node y is said to be an *immediate successor of x* if and only if there is an edge from x to y. We write Λ for the function from nodes to sets of nodes such that $\Lambda(x)$ is the set of immediate successors of x.

For our purposes it will be convenient to regard function Λ, rather than the set **edge**, as the fundamental description of the edge structure of a directed graph. It will also be convenient to extend this function to accept sets of nodes. When S is a set of nodes we write $\Lambda(S)$ for the set of nodes that are immediate successors of some member of S. Thus, $y \in \Lambda(S)$ if and only if $y \in \Lambda(x)$ for some $x \in S$.

A nonempty sequence $\langle x_0, x_1, \ldots, x_n \rangle$ of nodes is said to be a *path* of n steps from x_0 to x_n if and only if each pair of adjacent nodes is an edge, i.e., if

$x_i \in \Lambda(x_{i-1})$ for each $i \in [1..n]$.[1] Notice that the step number is the number of edges in the path, which is one less than the number of nodes, that the minimum step number is zero, and that a path of one step is just an edge.

A node y is said to be *reachable* from a node x if and only if there is a path (of any number of steps) from x to y. Just as the edge structure can be represented by the function Λ, so reachability can be represented by the function Λ^*, from nodes to sets of nodes, such that $\Lambda^*(x)$ is the set of nodes that are reachable from x. Thus $y \in \Lambda^*(x)$ if and only if there is a path from x to y.

As with Λ, we will extend Λ^* to act on sets of nodes by defining $\Lambda^*(S)$ to be the set of nodes that are reachable from some member of S.

11.2.2 An Abstract Program for Reachability

As a first example of a program dealing with a directed graph, we consider computing, for a given node x, the set $\Lambda^*(x)$ of nodes that can be reached from x.

In the abstract version of our program, we will use two new data types: **node**, whose values are nodes of the graph, and **set**, whose values are sets of nodes. The relevant primitive operations will be conventional mathematical operations on sets and their members. The input will be the node x and the function Λ that describes the edge structure of the graph. The output will be a set variable T whose final value will be $\Lambda^*(x)$.

The basic idea of the algorithm is to "grow" the set T by starting with the set $\{x\}$ and repeatedly adding nodes that can be reached from x. Thus T will always satisfy the invariant

$$I \stackrel{\text{def}}{=} T \subseteq \Lambda^*(x) \wedge x \in T$$

The growth will be carried out by repeatedly adding to T nodes that can be reached in a single step from some node that is already in T, and the algorithm will stop when such growth is no longer possible. This will occur when $\Lambda(T) \subseteq T$, i.e., when every node that can be reached in one step from a member of T is already a member of T.

Thus an initial version of the abstract algorithm is

```
var x : node ; T : set;
function Λ(X : set) : set;
    ⋮
{true}
```

---

[1] An interval $[a..b]$ of integers abbreviates the set $\{ i \in \mathbb{Z} \mid a \leq i \leq b \}$.

    begin var y : **node**;
      $T := \{x\}$;
      $\{\textbf{geninv } I : T \subseteq \Lambda^*(x) \wedge x \in T\}$
      while $\neg\Lambda(T) \subseteq T$ **do**
        $y := a \ member \ of \ T$;
        $\{\textbf{geninv } II : y \in \Lambda^*(x)\}$
        $T := T \cup \Lambda(y)$
      od
    end
    $\{T = \Lambda^*(x)\}$.

Since they describe input and output, the identifiers x, Λ and T are not bound in this program. We adopt the convention of specifying the types of such identifiers in a preface to the program.

The symbol **geninv** indicates that I and II are *general invariants*. This means that each of these assertions holds continuously (at the present level of abstraction) from its point of occurrence to the end of the immediately enclosing block.

The outer invariant I ensures that the statement $y := a \ member \ of \ T$ will achieve the inner invariant II. In turn, II ensures that $T := T \cup \Lambda(y)$ will preserve I, since $y \in \Lambda^*(x)$ implies $\Lambda(y) \subseteq \Lambda^*(x)$.

Notice that $y := a \ member \ of \ T$ is an indeterminate operation, since it does not specify which member of T is to become the value of y. This indeterminacy will turn out to be useful when we transform our program into concrete form, since it will provide a degree of freedom that will permit us to construct a faster program.

When the program terminates, the invariant I will ensure $x \in T$ and the falsity of the **while** statement test will ensure $\Lambda(T) \subseteq T$. It follows that $\Lambda^*(x) \subseteq T$, i.e., that T contains every node that can be reached from x. The proof is by induction on the number of steps. The only node that can be reached in zero steps is x itself, whose presence in T is ensured by $x \in T$. If a node w can be reached in $n + 1$ steps, then it can be reached in one step from some node z that can be reached in n steps. By the induction hypothesis z belongs to T, so that w belongs to $\Lambda(T)$, and the halting condition $\Lambda(T) \subseteq T$ implies that w belongs to T.

On the other hand, the invariant I ensures $T \subseteq \Lambda^*(\{x\})$, i.e., that every node in T can be reached from x. In conjunction with $\Lambda^*(x) \subseteq T$, this implies the desired consequent of the program.

The next step in developing an abstract algorithm is to express the statement $T := T \cup \Lambda(y)$ in terms of more elementary operations. For this purpose, we introduce a **for** statement that describes iteration over the members of a finite set. In general, we write **for** $K \in S$ **do** B **od** to indicate that B is to be performed once for each member of the set S, with K denoting each member in turn. The order in which the members of S are iterated over is left indeterminate.

This construct can be used to express the addition of $\Lambda(y)$ to T as an iteration over $\Lambda(y)$ of a statement that adds individual nodes to T. Thus we replace $T := T \cup \Lambda(y)$ by

$$\textbf{for } z \in \Lambda(y) \textbf{ do } T := T \cup \{z\} \textbf{ od } .$$

The virtue of this replacement is that it decouples the representations of T and Λ. If we left $T := T \cup \Lambda(y)$ in the abstract program, then in the transformation to a concrete program the realization of the union operation would depend upon both the representation of T and the representation of $\Lambda(y)$. Thus the choice of these representations would have to be made jointly to ensure that the union could be performed efficiently. But in transforming **for** $z \in \Lambda(y)$ **do** $T := T \cup \{z\}$ **od**, one can deal separately with the transformation of $T := T \cup \{z\}$, which only involves the representation of T, and the transformation of the iterative control mechanism **for** $z \in \Lambda(y)$ **do** ... **od**, which only involves the representation of $\Lambda(y)$.

This decoupling is particularly advantageous since Λ is an input and T is an output of our program. Although we will not consider the matter explicitly when we choose representations, in the "real world" the representation of Λ has to be suitable for some program segment that computes Λ, and the representation of T has to be suitable for some other program segment that uses T. In this situation, anything which couples the choice of these representations could complicate the programming task disastrously.

On the other hand, by replacing $T := T \cup \Lambda(y)$ by a **for** statement, we are excluding certain ways of implementing the union operation. Although it will turn out that these implementations are not desirable, this is not evident from the abstract algorithm. Our arguments for the replacement are merely heuristic, and do not guarantee that it is a step in the right direction. More generally, while data representation structuring is a systematic way of constructing programs, it is not a magic tool that ensures optimal design choices.

At this point we must admit that, although the initial version of our abstract algorithm is partially correct, it is possible that it may never terminate. The difficulty is that $y := a$ *member of* T may repeatedly set y to the same member of T. But once **for** $z \in \Lambda(y)$ **do** $T := T \cup \{z\}$ **od** has been performed for a particular y, it is a waste of time to repeat this operation for the same y. Indeed if y is chosen to be the same node ad infinitum, the program will never terminate.

To overcome this difficulty we will partition T into a set P of processed nodes that have already been chosen as y, and a set U of unprocessed nodes that have not yet been chosen. Then, by always choosing y to be an unprocessed node, we can guarantee that each execution of the **while** statement body will increase the number of processed nodes, so that termination must occur within N steps.

The first step is to modify the abstract program by introducing P and U as local set variables, along with appropriate statements for maintaining their values:

> **var** x : **node** ; T : **set**;
> **function** $\Lambda(X$: **set**) : **set**;
> $\vdots$
> $\{\text{true}\}$
> **begin var** y : **node** ; P, U : **set**;
> $\quad T := \{x\} ; P := \emptyset ; U := \{x\}$;
> $\quad \{\textbf{geninv}\; I : T \subseteq \Lambda^*(x) \wedge x \in T \wedge P \cup U = T \wedge P \cap U = \emptyset\}$
> $\quad \{\textbf{whileinv} : \Lambda(P) \subseteq T\}$
> $\quad \textbf{while}\; \neg \Lambda(T) \subseteq T\; \textbf{do}$
> $\qquad y := a\; member\; of\; T$;
> $\qquad \langle P := P \cup \{y\} ; U := U \setminus \{y\} \rangle_I$;
> $\qquad \{\textbf{geninv}\; II : y \in \Lambda^*(x) \wedge y \in P \wedge \Lambda(P \setminus \{y\}) \subseteq T\}$
> $\qquad \textbf{for}\; z \in \Lambda(y)\; \textbf{do}$
> $\qquad\quad \textbf{if}\; z \notin T\; \textbf{then}$
> $\qquad\qquad \langle T := T \cup \{z\} ; U := U \cup \{z\} \rangle_I$
> $\qquad\quad \textbf{fi}$
> $\qquad \textbf{od}$
> $\qquad \{\Lambda(y) \subseteq T\}$
> $\quad \textbf{od}$
> **end**
> $\{T = \Lambda^*(x)\}$.

Since only the new variables P and U are affected by this modification, the assertions in the original abstract program remain valid.

The symbol **whileinv** indicates that $\Lambda(P) \subseteq T$ holds at its point of occurrence and after each execution of the **while** statement body.

Initially x, which is the only member of T, is unprocessed. Each time a member of T is chosen as y, it becomes processed. Each time a new node z is added to T, it is unprocessed. (Note the necessity of the qualification "new", which is reflected in the test $z \notin T$ in the body of the **for** statement. If z already belongs to T, it may be a processed node). It is easy to see that P and U will always form a partition of T, so that $P \cup U = T$ and $P \cap U = \emptyset$ can be added to the general invariant I. However, this invariant is only continuously true if the two sections enclosed in angled brackets subscripted with I are regarded as indivisible actions. We will subscript such a program fragment in *atomic brackets* with the name of a general invariant whenever that invariant may be temporarily falsified within the fragment.

Just prior to the **for** statement, y is placed in P, and neither y nor P are changed by the **for** statement body. Thus $y \in P$ can be added to the general invariant II.

Initially $\Lambda(P) \subseteq T$ holds since P is empty. Assume that this condition holds at the beginning of the **while** statement body. Then $\Lambda(P \setminus \{y\}) \subseteq T$ will hold after y is added to P, and will continue to hold throughout the **for** statement since y and P are never changed and T is only enlarged. Thus $\Lambda(P \setminus \{y\}) \subseteq T$ can be added to II. Then since this condition still holds upon completion of the **for** statement, and the **for** statement achieves $\Lambda(y) \subseteq T$, the condition $\Lambda(P) \subseteq T$ will again hold upon completion of the **while** statement body. Thus $\Lambda(P) \subseteq T$ is an invariant of the **while** statement (but not a general invariant).

If U is empty then the partition condition implies $P = T$, and the invariant $\Lambda(P) \subseteq T$ implies $\Lambda(T) \subseteq T$, which is a sufficient condition for terminating the **while** statement. Thus we may replace

$$\textbf{while } \neg\Lambda(T) \subseteq T \textbf{ do} \ldots \textbf{od}$$

by

$$\textbf{while } U \neq \emptyset \textbf{ do} \ldots \textbf{od} \ .$$

Of course, the old test $\neg\Lambda(T) \subseteq T$ may become false while U is still nonempty, but this only means that our program may continue to loop unnecessarily. Correctness is not affected, since we never used the assumption that $\neg\Lambda(T) \subseteq T$ held at the beginning of the **while** statement body.

At this stage, it is clear that U will be a nonempty subset of T when a member of T is chosen as y. Thus we may replace

$$y := a \ member \ of \ T$$

by

$$y := a \ member \ of \ U \ .$$

By restricting the choice of y to U, we ensure that each execution of the

while statement body will add a new node to P. Thus the number of such executions cannot exceed the bound N on the number of nodes in the graph.

Each execution of the **for** statement body iterates over the immediate successors of y or, equally well, over the edges that emanate from y. Thus, since the **for** statement is executed for distinct nodes y, the total number of executions of its body cannot exceed the bound E on the number of edges in the graph.

The body of the conditional statement within the **for** statement always adds a new node to T, which initially contains the single member x. Thus the total number of executions of this body cannot exceed $N - 1$.

These bounds on the number of executions of various parts of our program are as close as we can come to understanding efficiency on the abstract level, since time and space requirements, even to an order of magnitude, will depend upon the choice of representations and the realization of primitive operations. In fact, since they determine the relative frequency with which various primitive operations will be performed, the bounds on number of executions will be crucial for deciding which representations should be used to obtain an efficient concrete program.

The intermediate assertions have served their purpose in demonstrating the correctness of our abstract program, and can now be discarded. Actually there is a small but significant exception. Since $P \cup U = T$ and $z \notin T$ will hold just prior to $T := T \cup \{z\}$, the assertion $z \notin U$ will hold afterwards, so that the following statement $U := U \cup \{z\}$ will insert a *new* member into U. This fact will turn out to be significant for the choice of the representation of U.

At this stage the abstract program illustrates a concept that will reappear later and play a central rôle in the development of data representation structuring. Consider a variable that is local to a program (or at least whose final value is not used outside of the program). Such a variable is said to be *auxiliary* if all of its occurrences lie within statements whose only effect is to assign to the variable. More generally, a set of variables is said to be *auxiliary* if all of their occurrences lie within statements whose only effect is to assign to members of the set.

The importance of this concept is that the value of an auxiliary variable cannot affect the flow of control or the values of any nonauxiliary variable. As a consequence, one can eliminate auxiliary variables, by deleting their declarations and the statements that assign to them, without affecting the behavior of the program.

The set variable P is easily seen to be auxiliary in our abstract program, and can therefore be eliminated. Thus, stripped of the scaffolding used to construct it, the abstract program is

```
var x : node ; T : set;
function Λ(X : set) : set;
```

$\vdots$

```
{true}
begin var y : node ; U : set;
  T := {x} ; U := {x};
  while U ≠ ∅ do
    y := a member of U;
    U := U \ {y};
    for z ∈ Λ(y) do
      if z ∉ T then
        T := T ∪ {z};
        {z ∉ U}
        U := U ∪ {z}
      fi
    od
  od
end
{T = Λ*(x)}.
```

11.2.3 The Representation of Finite Sets

We have purposely chosen an algorithm involving finite sets since there is no universally "best" way of representing such sets. Inevitably, choosing a representation to make one primitive operation as efficient as possible will force other primitive operations to be less efficient than in some other representation. Thus a wise choice of a representation can only be made in light of the particular needs of the abstract program, i.e., which primitive operations are used and with what relative frequencies. Moreover, it is often advantageous to choose distinct representations for different set variables.

The following are four fairly obvious ways of representing a set S:

(1) One can enumerate S with an array. Thus S might be the image of the segment of an array W over the interval $[a..b]$.

$$S = \{ W(i) \mid i \in [a..b] \}$$

This representation has the advantage that one can insert an element into S in constant time, i.e., in a time independent of the size of S, by simply appending the element to the array segment at one end or the other. One can also test whether S is empty in constant time by simply testing $a > b$.

However, unless there is some control over the number of times a set member may occur in the array segment, the size of the segment can grow far larger than the size of S. This is a sufficiently serious defect to make this representation unsuitable for our purposes.

(2) One can enumerate S by an array segment without duplicate elements:

$$S = \{ W(i) \mid i \in [a..b] \} \wedge \forall a \leq i < j \leq b (W(i) \neq W(j))$$

Prohibiting duplication ensures that the number $card(S)$ of elements in S satisfies $card(S) = b - a + 1$, so that any bound on the size of S provides a bound on storage requirements. Not only can the emptiness of S be tested in constant time, as in (1), but more generally the size of S can be determined in constant time. On the other hand, to test whether a particular element belongs to S one must perform a linear search, in time of order $card(S)$.

The price of avoiding duplication is the time required to insert an element into S. In general, one must perform a linear search, in time of order $card(S)$, to see if the element is already present. However, this search can be avoided if it is known that the element being inserted does not belong to S, so that a new element can be inserted in constant time. This is one of several cases where a fine distinction in the nature of a primitive operation can have a major effect on its efficiency.

Another case is deletion. To delete a *specified* element from S one must perform a linear search to locate the element, in time of order $card(S)$. However to delete an *unspecified member*, i.e., to choose an arbitrary member of S and delete it, one can simply remove an element from one end of the array segment, in constant time.

Finally, consider iterating over the set S, i.e., executing **for** $K \in S$ **do** B **od**. Excluding the time required to execute B repeatedly $card(S)$ times, the control of this iteration will require an array scan taking time of order $card(S)$.

(3) If an ordering relation can be defined for the type of elements in S, then one can enumerate S by a strictly ordered array segment:

$$S = \{ W(i) \mid i \in [a..b] \} \wedge \forall a \leq i < j \leq b (W(i) < W(j)) \ .$$

Now binary search can be used in place of linear search, so that an element can be tested for membership in time of order $\log(card(S))$. On the other hand, when an element is inserted or a specified element is deleted, it may be necessary to move a sizable subsegment of the array to preserve the ordering. Thus the time required to insert an element, even when it is known to be new, is of order $card(S)$ in the worst case. The order of magnitude times for the other operations discussed in (2) remain unchanged.

(4) Suppose S is known always to be a subset of some fixed, finite universe $\mathcal{U}$ (which would be **node** in the case of a set of nodes). Then S can be represented by a Boolean array C with domain $\mathcal{U}$ such that $C(x)$ records whether x belongs to S:

$$\forall x \in \mathcal{U}(C(x) = (x \in S)) \ .$$

The number of elements in C is $card(\mathcal{U})$, which may be much larger than the maximum size of S. In many cases, however, this is compensated by the fact that an individual Boolean array element is much smaller than an array element that must represent a member of S.

In general this kind of representation, called a *characteristic vector*, is complementary to enumeration by an array. Testing membership, or inserting or deleting a specified element can be done in constant time by testing or setting a single array element. However, testing emptiness or deleting an unspecified member requires searching C up to the first true element, which needs time of order $card(\mathcal{U}) - card(S)$ in the worst case and $card(\mathcal{U})/card(S)$ on the average. (Note that the situation deteriorates as S becomes smaller). Even worse, determining size or iterating over all members of S requires a scan of the entire array, using time of order $card(\mathcal{U})$, regardless of the size of S.

There are many other useful representations of sets, often involving tree or list structures.

11.2.4 Representation of the Set Variables T and U

Having discussed the general properties of several representations of sets, we return to the specific problem of determining reachability in a directed graph. We have established the (partial) correctness of the abstract program at the end of Section 11.2.2. Now we must choose representations for the abstract variables in this program and use these representations to transform the program into concrete form.

Fortunately, this kind of problem is not monolithic. In many cases, the representations of different data types, or even of different variables of the same type, can be considered in isolation from one another. In this case, we will separately consider the representations of the set variables T and U, the set function Λ, and finally the representation of nodes themselves.[2]

Consider T. In the abstract program it is subject to three operations: the initialization $T := \{x\}$, which is only performed once, the membership test $z \notin T$, which is performed at most E times, and the insertion $T := T \cup \{z\}$, which is performed at most $N - 1$ times. It is obviously more important to optimize the membership test and insertion than the initialization. For this purpose, the best of the four representations discussed is clearly the characteristic vector (4), which permits both a membership test and an insertion to be performed in constant time.

Actually, this conclusion is premature. Since T is an output variable, its representation must be suitable, not only to the program we are writing to produce its value, but also to some other program that will use this value. In a real application, this might cause us to choose a different representation for T, or to simultaneously compute T in more than one representation, or to convert T to another representation after it has been computed. But to keep our example tractable we will assume that a characteristic vector is suitable for the program that will use the value of T.

Now we must transform our program to replace the abstract variable by a concrete variable representing its value. To do this, we will use the following general method:

R1 One or more concrete variables are introduced to store the representation of one or more abstract variables.

R2 A general invariant called the *representation invariant* is introduced, which describes the relationship between the abstract and concrete variables.

R3 Each assignment to an abstract variable (or more generally, each assignment that affects the representation invariant) is augmented with assignments to the concrete variables that reestablish the representation invariant (or achieve it, in case of an initialization).

R4 Each expression that contains an abstract variable but occurs outside of an assignment to an abstract variable is replaced by an expression that does not contain abstract variables but is guaranteed by the representation invariant to have the same value.

The last step will render the abstract variables auxiliary, so that their declarations and assignments can be eliminated.

---

[2] In this excerpt, we omit Reynolds' discussion of the representation of the set function Λ and the nodes.

In the present case, the concrete variable will be a characteristic vector whose domain is **node**:

$$C : \textbf{array}[\textbf{node}] \textbf{ of } \mathsf{Bool};$$

This array must be specified globally since it represents the output of our program. The representation invariant is

$$\alpha \stackrel{\text{def}}{=} \forall z \in \textbf{node}\,(C(z) = (z \in T))\ .$$

To achieve α the initialization $T := \{x\}$ can be augmented with

$$\textbf{for } z \in \textbf{node do } C(z) := (z = x) \textbf{ od}\ .$$

The only other assignment to T is $T := T \cup \{z\}$. To reestablish α after this assignment, we add $C(z) := \mathsf{true}$.

The only occurrence of T in an expression outside of an assignment to T is in the test $z \notin T$. According to α this test is equivalent to, and can therefore be replaced by, $\neg C(z)$.

The result of this transformation is

```
var x : node ; T : set ; C : array[node] of Bool;
function Λ(X : set) : set;
 ⋮
{true}
begin var y : node ; U : set;
  T := {x} ; for z ∈ node do C(z) := (z = x) od;
  {geninv α : ∀z ∈ node (C(z) = (z ∈ T))}
  U := {x};
  while U ≠ ∅ do
    y := a member of U;
    U := U \ {y};
    for z ∈ Λ(y) do
      if ¬C(z) then
        ⟨T := T ∪ {z} ; C(z) := true⟩α;
        {z ∉ U}
        U := U ∪ {z}
      fi
    od
  od
end
{T = Λ*(x) ∧ ∀z ∈ node (C(z) = (z ∈ Λ*(x)))}.
```

We have extended the consequent of the program to express the result $\Lambda^*(x)$ in terms of the concrete variable C.

At this stage T is an auxiliary variable and can be eliminated from the program. The representation invariant α can also be dropped, since it has served its purpose in demonstrating the correctness of the program transformation.

Next we consider the set variable U. Besides the initialization $U := \{x\}$, it is subject to three operations, each of which will be performed no more than N times: the emptiness test $U \neq \emptyset$, the choice and deletion of an unspecified member $y := a$ *member of* U ; $U := U \setminus \{y\}$, and the insertion $U := U \cup \{z\}$, in which z is guaranteed to be a new member by the preceding assertion $\{z \notin U\}$.

Because of the emptiness test and the choice of an unspecified member, a characteristic vector would be an unsuitable representation for U. In fact, of the representation methods discussed in Section 11.2.3, only enumeration by an array without duplicate elements (2) permits all three of the frequent operations to be performed in constant time. (Since U is a local variable, we do not need to consider the requirements of an external program).

To implement this representation we introduce, at the same block level as U, the concrete variables

$$W : \mathbf{array}[1..N] \ \mathbf{of\ node} ; a,b : \mathsf{Integer}$$

and the representation invariant

$$\beta \overset{\mathrm{def}}{=} 1 \leq a \leq b+1 \wedge U = \{ W(i) \mid a \leq i \leq b \}$$
$$\wedge \forall a \leq i < j \leq b (W(i) \neq W(j)) .$$

(Here the first conjunct ensures that 1 is a suitable lower bound for the domain of W. The fact that N is a suitable upper bound will be established later.) To achieve this invariant, the initialization $U := \{x\}$ is augmented with $a := 1 ; b := 1 ; W(1) := x$.

The transformation of the abstract operation of choosing and deleting an unspecified member of U is somewhat complicated, since it involves both replacing an expression containing U and augmenting an assignment to U, and since indeterminacy must be resolved. The representation invariant implies that the indeterminate expression a *member of* U can be replaced by $W(k)$ for any value of k in $[a..b]$ (which must be a nonempty interval since U is nonempty). Then after the next operation $U := U \setminus \{y\}$, the representation invariant can be regained by deleting the kth element from the segment of W over $[a..b]$.

Clearly this deletion can be done more easily if $W(k)$ is located at one end or the other of the array segment. Thus we may either (1) replace a *member of* U by $W(a)$ and add $a := a+1$ after $U := U \setminus \{y\}$, or (2) replace a *member of*

U by $W(b)$ and add $b := b - 1$ after $U := U \setminus \{y\}$. Notice that the freedom to make these especially efficient choices is a consequence of leaving *a member of U* indeterminate at the abstract level.

The only other assignment to U is $U := U \cup \{z\}$. Here, since the precedent $z \notin U$ ensures that duplication will be avoided, β can be regained by appending z to the upper end of the array segment, i.e., by adding the statements $b := b + 1 ; W(b) := z$. (Note that appending z to the lower end of the array segment might violate $1 \leq a \leq b + 1$.)

Finally, β implies that the test $U \neq \emptyset$ can be replaced by $a \leq b$. Thus we have

var x : **node** ; C : **array**[**node**] **of** Bool;
function $\Lambda(X : $ **set**$)$: **set**;
$\vdots$

{true}
begin var y : **node** ; U : **set** ; W : **array**$[1..N]$ **of node** ; a, b : Integer;
  for $z \in$ **node do** $C(z) := (z = x)$ **od**;
  $U := \{x\} ; a := 1 ; b := 1 ; W(1) := x$;
  {**geninv** $\beta : 1 \leq a \leq b + 1 \wedge U = \{ W(i) \mid i \in [a..b] \}$
    $\wedge \forall i \in [a..b] (W(i) \neq W(j))$}
  while $a \leq b$ **do**

$$y := \left(\begin{array}{cc} W(a) & (1) \\ W(b) & (2) \end{array} \right) ;$$

$$\left\langle U := U \setminus \{y\} ; \left(\begin{array}{cc} a := a + 1 & (1) \\ b := b - 1 & (2) \end{array} \right) \right\rangle_\beta ;$$

    for $z \in \Lambda(y)$ **do**
      if $\neg C(z)$ **then**
        $C(z) :=$ true;
        $\{z \notin U\}$
        $\langle U := U \cup \{z\} ; b := b + 1 ; W(b) := z \rangle_\beta$
      fi
    od
  od
end
$\{\forall z \in$ **node** $(C(z) = (z \in \Lambda^*(x)))\}$.

The variable b is initialized to one and is only increased by the statement $b := b + 1$, which can be performed at most $N - 1$ times. Thus $b \leq N$ will hold throughout the program. This implies $[1..b] \subseteq [1..N]$, which in conjunction with $1 \leq a \leq b + 1$ implies $[a..b] \subseteq [1..N]$, so that the declared bounds of W are adequate to avoid subscript errors.

The numbers in parentheses label alternate ways of implementing the choose-and-delete operation. When option (1) is used, nodes are added to one end of $W[a..b]$ and removed from the other. As a consequence, W behaves as a *queue*, i.e., its element values are removed in the same order as they are entered. When option (2) is used, nodes are added and removed from the same end of $W[a..b]$. As a consequence, W behaves as a *stack*, i.e., when a node is removed it is always the most recently entered node remaining in the stack.

The difference between (1) and (2) has a profound effect upon the order in which the members of $\Lambda^*(x)$ are processed by our algorithm. When (1) is used, the nodes in $\Lambda^*(x)$ enter T in a *breadth-first* order, i.e., in increasing order of the minimum number of steps from x. When (2) is used, these nodes enter T in a *depth-first* order, i.e., after a node y has entered T, all nodes that can be reached from y (via a path which does not go through a member of T) will enter T before any other nodes.

At this stage, U is an auxiliary variable that can be eliminated, along with the intermediate assertions.

11.3 Analysis of Data Refinement à la Reynolds

In the previous section we presented several examples of data refinement à la Reynolds. We have encountered his four-point recipe (R1–R4) for constructing a concrete program implementing a given abstract one. In this section we analyze the relationship between Reynolds' data refinement examples, his recipe, and the theory developed in Part I.

This analysis takes place in three steps. Section 11.3.1 provides a rather naïve formalization of Reynolds' recipe. In Section 11.3.2 part of this analysis has to be reformulated since it fails to capture exactly what Reynolds has done in his example in Section 11.2. We shall find out that the correspondence between partial correctness L-simulation and Reynolds' method may disappear in the case of partial abstraction relations.

Finally, in Section 11.3.3, we shall see that these problems vanish when we adopt our total correctness interpretation of Reynolds' operations. As observed before, all the refinement steps in his book preserve total correctness, i.e., during any of his refinement steps the domain of nontermination of an operation at most shrinks. The total correctness interpretation of an L-simulation relation $\alpha \in Abs^{AC}$ is by Def. 8.25 always total when viewed from level C upwards since $\perp$ on the abstract level is related to each concrete state in $\Sigma_{\perp}^{C}$.

11.3.1 Reynolds' Recipe

Consider an abstract program A with normal variables $\vec{x}$ and representation variables $\vec{a}$. To unify the treatment of assignment statements below, each assignment $a := e_A$ to an abstract representation variable a is extended to a simultaneous assignment $\vec{a} := \vec{e_A}$ with the same meaning, i.e., $\vec{e_A} = \vec{a}[e_A/a]$. Similarly each assignment $x := e_A$ to a normal variable x is extended to a simultaneous assignment $\vec{x} := \vec{e_A}$ to all normal variables. When introducing assignments to concrete representation variables we shall assume that these also come in the form of simultaneous assignments to all of them.

In a first approximation, an implementation C is obtained from program A by following Reynolds' recipe reformulated using our notation:

(i) Concrete variables $\vec{c}$ are introduced to store the representation of $\vec{a}$.

(ii) A representation invariant $\alpha \in Pred^{\vec{c},\vec{a}}$ is introduced.

(iii) Each assignment $\vec{a} := \vec{e_A}$ to abstract representation variables is augmented with an assignment $\vec{c} := \vec{e_C}$ to the concrete variables that reestablishes α (or achieves it, in the case of initialization).

(iv) Each expression $e_A \in Exp^{\vec{x}\vec{a}}$ that contains an abstract variable but occurs outside of an assignment to an abstract variable is replaced by an expression $e_C \in Exp^{\vec{x}\vec{c}}$ that does not contain abstract variables but is guaranteed by α to have the same value.

Finally the concrete program C results from eliminating the declarations of and assignments to $\vec{a}$.

To apply our theory of data refinement from Part I we interpret certain parts of A and C as constituents of two data types, $\mathcal{A}$ and $\mathcal{C}$, and show that C L-simulates $\mathcal{A}$ w.r.t. α. Soundness and incompleteness of this recipe as a data refinement method then follow immediately from Chapters 1 and 4.

Initialization and finalization

From the third point of the recipe we deduce the following condition for the initialization operations.

$$\{\text{true}\}\, \vec{a} := \vec{e_A}\, ; \vec{c} := \vec{e_C}\, \{\alpha\}$$

All assignments encountered in Section 11.2 terminate if the preceding assertion (here true) holds. Thus, although it is a partial correctness Hoare triple, the line above holds if and only if

$$\alpha[\vec{e_C}/\vec{c}][\vec{e_A}/\vec{a}]$$

is valid, that is, because the abstract and concrete representation variables are disjoint,

$$\alpha[^{\vec{e}_A \vec{e}_C}/_{\vec{a}\vec{c}}] \tag{11.1}$$

is valid.[3]

Our L-simulation condition for initialization (init^L from Def. 2.1 on page 21) informally means that for each state produced by the concrete initialization there exists a state produced by the abstract one such that these two states satisfy α. In our framework, initialization operations include the introduction of the representation variables. If we had chosen to deal with local variable introduction on the syntactic level, init^L would have been represented syntactically as follows.

begin var $\vec{c} : C$; $\vec{c} := \vec{e}_C \subseteq$ **begin var** $\vec{a} : \mathcal{A}$; $\vec{a} := \vec{e}_A$; α^{-1}

Semantically, the intended condition is expressed by the following inclusion.

$$\left\{ (\sigma, \tau) \in \Sigma^{\vec{x}} \times \Sigma^C \mid \sigma \equiv_{\vec{x}} \tau \right\} ; \left\{ (\tau, (\tau : \vec{c} \mapsto \mathcal{E}[\![\vec{e}_C]\!]^{\vec{x}\vec{c}}\tau)) \mid \tau \in \Sigma^C \right\}$$
$$\subseteq \left\{ (\sigma, \tau) \in \Sigma^{\vec{x}} \times \Sigma^A \mid \sigma \equiv_{\vec{x}} \tau \right\}$$
$$; \left\{ (\tau, (\tau : \vec{a} \mapsto \mathcal{E}[\![\vec{e}_A]\!]^{\vec{x}\vec{a}}\tau)) \mid \tau \in \Sigma^A \right\} ; (\mathcal{A}[\![\alpha]\!]^{CA})^{-1}$$

(Recall that $\sigma \equiv_{\vec{x}} \tau$ expresses that $\sigma(y) = \tau(y)$ for y in $\vec{x}$.) Observe that $\vec{e}_C, \vec{e}_A \in Exp^{\vec{x}}$ since the values of representation variables are undefined before. This inclusion can be reduced to

$$\left\{ (\sigma, \tau) \in \Sigma^{\vec{x}} \times \Sigma^C \mid \tau = (\sigma : \vec{c} \mapsto \mathcal{E}[\![\vec{e}_C]\!]^{\vec{x}}\sigma) \right\}$$
$$\subseteq \left\{ (\sigma, \tau) \in \Sigma^{\vec{x}} \times \Sigma^A \mid \tau = (\sigma : \vec{a} \mapsto \mathcal{E}[\![\vec{e}_A]\!]^{\vec{x}}\sigma) \right\} ; (\mathcal{A}[\![\alpha]\!]^{CA})^{-1} \ ,$$

which is equivalent to

$$\forall \sigma \in \Sigma^{\vec{x}} \left(((\sigma : \vec{c} \mapsto \mathcal{E}[\![\vec{e}_C]\!]^{\vec{x}}\sigma), (\sigma : \vec{a} \mapsto \mathcal{E}[\![\vec{e}_A]\!]^{\vec{x}}\sigma)) \in \mathcal{A}[\![\alpha]\!]^{CA} \right) \ .$$

By Cor. 5.16 and the substitution lemma (Lemma 5.12) this is equivalent to validity of Reynolds' condition (11.1).

Reynolds neglects finalizations in his recipe because his finalizations do not impose a non-trivial extra condition. In a slightly extended syntax one would describe this condition by

$$\alpha^{-1} ; \textbf{end} \subseteq \textbf{end} \ ,$$

---

[3] Definedness of the expressions e_A and e_C justifies the use of an ordinary two-valued predicate logic rather than the three-valued one developed in Chapter 8.

where the LHS and RHS **end** symbols belong to the concrete and abstract level, respectively. The intention formulated in this inclusion is captured semantically by

$$(\mathcal{A}[\![\alpha]\!]^{CA})^{-1} ; \{\, (\sigma, \sigma|_{\vec{x}}) \mid \sigma \in \Sigma^C \,\} \subseteq \{\, (\sigma, \sigma|_{\vec{x}}) \mid \sigma \in \Sigma^A \,\} \ .$$

This follows immediately by our definition of $\mathcal{A}[\![\alpha]\!]^{CA}$, reflecting the discussion in Section 2.3.2.

Assignments to representation variables

According to the third step of Reynolds' method, an assignment $a := e_A$ of an expression $e_A \in Exp^{\vec{a}}$ to an abstract representation variable is augmented with assignments to concrete representation variables $c := e_C \,; c' := e'_C \,; \ldots$ to reestablish the abstraction relation. To unify the presentation of these assignments as specification statements below, the abstract level assignment is extended to a simultaneous assignment $\vec{a} := \vec{e}_A$ to all abstract representation variables $\vec{a}$ at level A without changing the overall meaning, that is, $\vec{e}_A = \vec{a}[^{e_A}/_a]$. For the same reason, the assignments to concrete representation variables are extended to $\vec{c} := \vec{e}_C$, contracting them into a single simultaneous assignment. Thus, one has to prove that

$$\{\alpha\} \, \vec{a} := \vec{e}_A \,; \vec{c} := \vec{e}_C \, \{\alpha\}$$

holds, where α denotes the representation invariant. According to the assignment axiom, the sequential composition rule, the consequence rule, and since $\vec{a}$ and $\vec{c}$ are disjoint, this is equivalent to proving

$$\alpha \Rightarrow \alpha[^{\vec{e}_C \vec{e}_A}/_{\vec{c}\vec{a}}] \ , \tag{11.2}$$

since Reynolds assumes that assignments terminate whenever their precondition (in this case α) holds.

If one specifies the isolated abstract assignment within our framework exactly[4] by

$$\vec{a}\vec{x} = \vec{a}_0\vec{x}_0 \rightsquigarrow \vec{a}\vec{x} = \vec{e}_A[^{\vec{a}_0\vec{x}_0}/_{\vec{a}\vec{x}}]\vec{x}_0$$

one can use Lemma 7.7 (for preconditions of this form) to obtain a condition for assignment $\vec{c} := \vec{e}_C$ to concrete variables that holds iff it L-simulates $\vec{a} := \vec{e}_A$ w.r.t. α:

$$\left\{\exists \vec{a} \,(\alpha \wedge \vec{a}\vec{x} = \vec{a}_0\vec{x}_0)\right\} \vec{c} := \vec{e}_C \left\{\exists \vec{a} \left(\alpha \wedge \vec{a}\vec{x} = \vec{e}_A[^{\vec{a}_0\vec{x}_0}/_{\vec{a}\vec{x}}]\vec{x}_0\right)\right\}$$

---

[4] To specify exactly means that specification and operation are semantically the same.

By the assignment axiom and the consequence rule this holds if

$$\exists \vec{a}\,(\alpha \wedge \vec{a}\vec{x} = \vec{a}_0 \vec{x}_0) \Rightarrow \left(\exists \vec{a}\left(\alpha \wedge \vec{a}\vec{x} = \vec{e}_A[^{\vec{a}_0 \vec{x}_0}/_{\vec{a}\vec{x}}]\vec{x}_0\right)\right)[^{\vec{e}_C}/_{\vec{c}}]$$

is true. By the definition of substitution and some predicate logic reasoning this is equivalent to

$$\alpha[^{\vec{a}_0}/_{\vec{a}}] \Rightarrow \alpha[^{\vec{e}_C}/_{\vec{c}}][^{\vec{e}_A[^{\vec{a}_0}/_{\vec{a}}]}/_{\vec{a}}] \ ,$$

which in turn is equivalent to our interpretation (11.2) of Reynolds' condition.

Tests and assignments to normal variables

Step four of Reynolds' recipe concerns tests and assignments to normal variables.

Consider an expression e_A that contains an abstract variable but occurs outside of an assignment to an abstract variable. It is replaced by an expression e_C that does not contain abstract variables but is guaranteed by α to have the same value.

$$\alpha \Rightarrow e_A = e_C \tag{11.3}$$

In case e_A is a Boolean test in $Pred^{\vec{x}\vec{a}}$ (occurring in conditionals or loops) then e_C is also a Boolean test and an element of $Pred^{\vec{x}\vec{c}}$. The L-simulation conditions we have to check are

$$\alpha^{-1}\,; e_C \to\ \subseteq e_A \to\,; \alpha^{-1}$$

and also

$$\alpha^{-1}\,; \neg e_C \to\ \subseteq \neg e_A \to\,; \alpha^{-1}$$

in case the translation to the nucleus of our programming language (namely, the constructs defined before Def. 5.18 on page 109, not the abbreviations from Section 5.3.1) reveals that the negation of the test is also involved. Both conditions follow immediately from (11.3) and our definitions of semantics of abstraction relations and Boolean tests. (The formal derivation within our Hoare logic and predicate calculus is rather complicated — although feasible.)

In case $e_A \in Exp^{\vec{x}\vec{a}}$ occurs within the RHS of an assignment $\vec{x} := \vec{e}[^{e_A}/_t]$ to normal variables we have to prove that

$$\alpha^{-1}\,; \vec{x} := \vec{e}[^{e_C}/_t] \subseteq \vec{x} := \vec{e}[^{e_A}/_t]\,; \alpha^{-1} \ .$$

(Here t denotes a fresh variable whose sole purpose is to serve as a target for substitution inside expression $e \in Exp^{\{t\}\cup\vec{x}}$.) The proof is easy and therefore omitted.

Not yet discussed are the so-called normal operations in programs A and C. Consult Section 2.3.2 for a discussion of this topic. By Lemma 2.8 our choice of semantics for abstraction relations ensures that the L-simulation condition holds for normal operations, too.

Altogether we obtain that the pair (C, A) is an instance of a data refinement step between two data types that is provable using L-simulation.

When looking at Reynolds' examples, however, we shall see in the next section that our interpretation of Reynolds' recipe has been too naïve.

11.3.2 Reynolds' Example Revisited

Next we compare Reynolds' recipe as interpreted above with the facts provided by his example. As we shall see, we observe a discrepancy; the given interpretation of Reynolds' verification conditions for operations and expressions does not cover all cases. This is demonstrated by way of examples drawn from Section 11.2. We are forced to adapt his conditions in a suitable manner — fortunately without sacrificing the correspondence to L-simulation, except in one case.

The rôle of intermediate assertions

One of the flaws in the argument above is that we ignore the assertions in front of abstract operations when checking whether a concrete operation reestablishes the representation invariant.

Example 11.1 Let us see how Reynolds implements $U := U \cup \{z\}$ in the version of his program on page 271 by $b := b + 1 ; W(b) := z$. Our naïve interpretation (11.2) of the third point of Reynolds' recipe for this step is

$$\{\beta\}\, U := U \cup \{z\} ; b := b + 1 ; W(b) := z\, \{\beta\} \ ,$$

with β as defined on page 270. This Hoare triple is certainly not valid. The data invariant part of β, i.e., the conjunct $\forall a \leq i < j \leq b\,(W(i) \neq W(j))$, is not valid after executing these assignments starting in a state in which $\beta \wedge z \in U$ holds. Adding $z \notin U$ to the precondition yields a valid Hoare triple. This is formalized next. ♡

A simultaneous assignment $\vec{a} := \vec{e}_A$ is augmented with assignments $\vec{c} := \vec{e}_C$ to concrete representation variables to reestablish the abstraction relation α whenever assertion ϕ holds right in front of the abstract assignment. Thus, one has to prove that

$$\{\phi \wedge \alpha\}\, \vec{a} := \vec{e}_A ; \vec{c} := \vec{e}_C\, \{\alpha\}$$

holds. This is also expressed by $(\phi \wedge \alpha)^{-1}; \vec{c} := \vec{e}_C \subseteq \vec{a} := \vec{e}_A; \alpha^{-1}$ as depicted in Figure 11.1. In the same manner as in the naïve formalization, validity of the Hoare triple above boils down to proving

$$\models \phi \wedge \alpha \Rightarrow \alpha[^{\vec{e}_C \vec{e}_A}/_{\vec{c}\vec{a}}] \ . \tag{11.4}$$

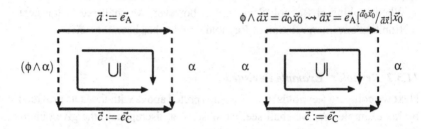

Fig. 11.1. Reynolds' condition in the presence of an intermediate assertion ϕ.

Fig. 11.2. L-simulation condition in the presence of an intermediate assertion ϕ.

An exact specification of the abstract assignment that takes assertion ϕ into account is

$$\phi \wedge \vec{a}\vec{x} = \vec{a}_0\vec{x}_0 \rightsquigarrow \vec{a}\vec{x} = \vec{e}_A[^{\vec{a}_0\vec{x}_0}/_{\vec{a}\vec{x}}]\vec{x}_0 \ . \tag{11.5}$$

Next we compare L-simulation of this specification w.r.t. α with satisfaction of (our formulation of) Reynolds' condition (11.4). (See Figure 11.2.) Theorem 7.2 provides the least refined specification L-simulating the abstract operation (11.5) as specified w.r.t. α:

$$\exists \vec{a} \left(\alpha \wedge \vec{a}\vec{x} = \vec{b}_0\vec{y}_0 \right)$$
$$\rightsquigarrow^* \exists \vec{a} \left(\alpha \wedge \forall \vec{a}_0\vec{x}_0 \left((\phi \wedge \vec{a}\vec{x} = \vec{a}_0\vec{x}_0)[^{\vec{b}_0\vec{y}_0}/_{\vec{a}\vec{x}}] \Rightarrow \vec{a}\vec{x} = \vec{e}_A[^{\vec{a}_0\vec{x}_0}/_{\vec{a}\vec{x}}]\vec{x}_0 \right) \right)$$

By the assignment axiom and the consequence rule this means that one has to prove for assignment $\vec{c} := \vec{e}_C$:

$$\exists \vec{a} \left(\alpha \wedge \vec{a}\vec{x} = \vec{b}_0\vec{y}_0 \right)$$
$$\Rightarrow \left(\exists \vec{a} \left(\alpha \wedge \forall \vec{a}_0\vec{x}_0 \left(\begin{matrix} (\phi \wedge \vec{a}\vec{x} = \vec{a}_0\vec{x}_0)[^{\vec{b}_0\vec{y}_0}/_{\vec{a}\vec{x}}] \\ \Rightarrow \vec{a}\vec{x} = \vec{e}_A[^{\vec{a}_0\vec{x}_0}/_{\vec{a}\vec{x}}]\vec{x}_0 \end{matrix} \right) \right) \right) [^{\vec{e}_C}/_{\vec{c}}] \ .$$

By the definition of substitution and some predicate logic simplification this is equivalent to validity of

$$\alpha[^{\vec{b}_0}/_{\vec{a}}] \wedge \vec{x} = \vec{y}_0$$
$$\Rightarrow \exists \vec{a} \left(\alpha[^{\vec{e}_C}/_{\vec{c}}][^{\vec{a}}/_{\vec{a}}] \wedge (\phi[^{\vec{b}_0\vec{y}_0}/_{\vec{a}\vec{x}}] \Rightarrow \vec{a}\vec{x} = \vec{e}_A[^{\vec{b}_0\vec{y}_0}/_{\vec{a}\vec{x}}]\vec{y}_0) \right) \ ,$$

which can be simplified to validity of

$$\alpha \Rightarrow \exists \vec{d} \left(\alpha[^{\vec{e}_C \vec{d}}/_{\vec{c}\vec{d}}] \wedge (\phi \Rightarrow \vec{d} = \vec{e}_A) \right) .$$

This condition follows from our interpretation (11.4) of Reynolds condition iff α satisfies $\alpha \Rightarrow \exists \vec{d} \left(\alpha[^{\vec{e}_C}/_{\vec{c}}] \right)$. Does the latter condition hold in all of Reynolds' examples? No: for instance, it does not hold for Example 11.1 above, as shown below.

Example 11.2 (Example 11.1 continued) In the previous example we encountered the representation invariant

$$\beta = 1 \le a \le b + 1 \wedge U = \{ W(i) \mid a \le i \le b \}$$
$$\wedge \forall a \le i < j \le b \, (W(i) \ne W(j)) ,$$

operations $U := U \cup \{z\}$ and $b := b + 1$; $W(b) := z$ on the abstract and concrete level respectively, and intermediate assertion $\phi = z \notin U$.

Let us check the condition ensuring equivalence between Reynolds' condition and the L-simulation requirement in this particular case: Is[5]

$$\beta \Rightarrow \exists U \left(\beta[^{b+1,(W:b+1 \mapsto z)}/_{b,W}] \right)$$

valid? Validity of this predicate implies that it holds, for instance, in a state σ mapping U to $\{5\}$, z to 5, a and b to 1, and W to a function in $[\{1,2\} \longrightarrow \mathbb{Z}]$ that maps 1 to 5. This is the case iff

$$\exists U \left(\begin{array}{l} U = \{(\sigma(W) : 1 + 1 \mapsto 5)(1), (\sigma(W) : 1 + 1 \mapsto 5)(2)\} \\ \wedge (\sigma(W) : 1 + 1 \mapsto 5)(1) \ne (\sigma(W) : 1 + 1 \mapsto 5)(2) \end{array} \right) ,$$

which simplifies to $\exists U \, (U = \{5\} \wedge 5 \ne 5)$, i.e., *ff*. ♡

Consequently, within a partial correctness setting, we cannot always reduce Reynolds' method to L-simulation. However, we shall prove in Section 11.3.3 that in a total correctness setting Example 11.1 still provides an instance of L-simulation.

Indeterminate expressions

There is another flaw in our naïve formalization of point four of Reynolds' recipe. In his example Reynolds uses indeterminate expressions like *a member of U* in an assignment to normal variable *y* on the abstract level. He replaces

---

[5] Observe that we treated a single assignment to an array cell as an assignment to the whole array. This is a standard technique to deal with arrays in Hoare logic. To express this assignment, we use the state variant notation from Def. 5.1 on the syntactic level to denote the variant of an array and on the semantic level to denote the variant of a function.

this expression, for instance, by $W(a)$ on the concrete level as described on page 270. The condition we have derived above looks rather awkward in this case,

$$\beta \wedge U \neq \emptyset \Rightarrow W(a) = a \; member \; of \; U \;,$$

and does not make much sense since we do not know how to compare an indeterminate expression with a value.

On the other hand L-simulation holds between the concrete and abstract assignments to y. Ignoring variables not involved in this operation, we may specify the abstract operation exactly by $U = U_0 \wedge U \neq \emptyset \rightsquigarrow U = U_0 \wedge y \in U$. By Theorem 7.2, the assignment axiom, and the consequence rule the L-simulation criterion

$$\beta^{-1} ; y := W(a) \subseteq (U = U_0 \wedge U \neq \emptyset \rightsquigarrow U = U_0 \wedge y \in U) ; \beta^{-1}$$

follows from validity of

$$\langle \beta \rangle (U = V_0) \Rightarrow \left(\langle \beta \rangle \forall U_0 \left(\begin{matrix} (U = U_0 \wedge U \neq \emptyset)[^{V_0}/_U] \\ \Rightarrow U = U_0 \wedge y \in U \end{matrix} \right) \right) [^{W(a)}/_y] \qquad (11.6)$$

which we prove next. By the definition of substitution and some predicate logic reasoning it can be reformulated as follows:

(11.6)

$\Leftrightarrow \langle \beta \rangle (U = V_0) \Rightarrow \langle \beta \rangle (V_0 \neq \emptyset \Rightarrow U = V_0 \wedge W(a) \in V_0)$

$\Leftrightarrow \models \beta[^{V_0}/_U] \Rightarrow (\beta[^{V_0}/_U] \wedge V_0 \neq \emptyset \Rightarrow W(a) \in V_0)$

$\Leftrightarrow \models \beta \wedge U \neq \emptyset \Rightarrow W(a) \in U$

$\Leftarrow \models 1 \leq a \leq b+1 \wedge U = \{ W(i) \mid a \leq i \leq b \} \wedge U \neq \emptyset \Rightarrow W(a) \in U$

Validity of the last line is immediate.

Reynolds treats this operation less formally. (See the two paragraphs starting on page 270: "The transformation ... indeterminate at the abstract level.") We interpret his reduction of indeterminacy at the abstract level as the existence of an output at that level, i.e., by an existential quantification, because this happens to be the only sound interpretation we can think of. In case the expression at the concrete level is also indeterminate the condition has to hold for all possible values.

To formalize assigning indeterminate expressions to variables we introduce *random assignments* to our programming language. They combine the nondeterministic aspect of specification statements with the operational appeal of ordinary assignments. Reynolds' $y := a$ *member of* U, for instance, is expressed by $y := y'.y' \in U$.

In general, whenever predicate π occurs in a random assignment $x := x'.\pi$ it denotes a predicate over program variables and variable x', where x' is a fresh variable of the same type as normal variable x. Execution of this statement assigns a value v to x such that $\pi[{}^v/_{x'}]$ holds if such a value exists, and aborts otherwise. If x is the only program variable we let $x := x'.\pi$ abbreviate $x = x_0 \rightsquigarrow \pi[{}^{x_0}/_x][{}^x/_{x'}]$. Otherwise freeze predicate $\vec{y} = \vec{y_0}$ for the remaining program variables $\vec{y}$ must be added as a conjunct to both operands of the leads-to operator. As before, in order to specify such an operation whenever assertion ϕ precedes the statement we want to specify, one has to add ϕ as a conjunct to the precondition.

$$\{\phi\}x := x'.\pi \quad \overset{\text{def}}{=} \quad x = x_0 \wedge \vec{y} = \vec{y_0} \wedge \phi \rightsquigarrow \pi[{}^{x_0}/_x][{}^x/_{x'}] \wedge \vec{y} = \vec{y_0} \quad (11.7)$$

The (partial correctness) Hoare logic axiom for random assignment

$$\vdash \left\{ \forall x' \left(\pi \Rightarrow \psi[{}^{x'}/_x] \right) \right\} x := x'.\pi \left\{ \psi \right\}$$

is an immediate consequence of the *wlp*-adaptation axiom from page 124 for specification (11.7) with $\phi = \text{true}$.

Lemma 11.3 The (partial correctness) Hoare logic axiom for random assignment is sound.

Proof: Consider the precondition according to the *wlp*-adaptation axiom:

$$\forall d_0, \vec{z_0} \left(\begin{matrix} \forall x_0, \vec{y_0} \left(x, \vec{y} = x_0, \vec{y_0} \Rightarrow (\pi[{}^{x_0}/_x][{}^x/_{x'}] \wedge \vec{y} = \vec{y_0})[{}^{d_0, \vec{z_0}}/_{x, \vec{y}}] \right) \\ \Rightarrow \psi[{}^{d_0, \vec{z_0}}/_{x, \vec{y}}] \end{matrix} \right)$$

By the one-point rule this is simplified twice:

$$\Leftrightarrow \forall d_0, \vec{z_0} \left(\pi[{}^{d_0}/_{x'}] \wedge \vec{z_0} = \vec{y} \Rightarrow \psi[{}^{d_0, \vec{z_0}}/_{x, \vec{y}}] \right)$$

$$\Leftrightarrow \forall x' \left(\pi \Rightarrow \psi[{}^{x'}/_x] \right) \qquad \qquad \square$$

W.l.o.g. we assume that there is only a single program variable of each kind, i.e., a normal variable x, an abstract representation variable a, and a concrete one, c. Let $\pi^A \in Pred^{\{x,a,x'\}}$ and $\pi^C \in Pred^{\{x,c,x'\}}$ be two predicates that correspond to Reynolds' possibly indeterminate expressions e_A and e_C. Let $\phi \in Pred^{\{x,a\}}$ be the assertion that Reynolds has placed in front of abstract indeterminate assignment $x := e_A$. To justify that e_A may be replaced by e_C we reinterpret condition R4 of Reynolds' recipe by requiring that if representation invariant α and intermediate assertion ϕ hold then — modulo decrease of nondeterminism — e_A and e_C have the same value.

$$\alpha \wedge \phi \Rightarrow \forall x' \left(\pi^C \Rightarrow \pi^A \right) \tag{11.8}$$

How does this relate to L-simulation? When preceded by assertion ϕ, Reynolds' abstract level operation $x := e_A$ is specified by

$$x = x_0 \wedge a = a_0 \wedge \phi \rightsquigarrow a = a_0 \wedge \pi^A [^{x_0, a_0}/_{x,a}][^x/_{x'}] \ .$$

By our general L-simulation theorem (Theorem 7.2), the abstract operation just specified is L-simulated by $x := x'.\pi^C$ w.r.t. α iff this concrete operation refines

$$\exists a \left(\alpha \wedge x = y_0 \wedge a = b_0 \right)$$
$$\rightsquigarrow \exists a \left(\alpha \wedge \forall x_0, a_0 \left(\begin{array}{l} (x = x_0 \wedge a = a_0 \wedge \phi)[^{y_0, b_0}/_{x,a}] \\ \Rightarrow a = a_0 \wedge \pi^A [^{x_0, a_0}/_{x,a}][^x/_{x'}] \end{array} \right) \right) \ .$$

By the consequence rule and the axiom for random assignment this refinement is equivalent to validity of

$$\exists a \left(\alpha \wedge x = y_0 \wedge a = b_0 \right)$$
$$\Rightarrow \forall x' \left(\pi^C \Rightarrow \exists a \left(\alpha \wedge \left(\phi[^{y_0, b_0}/_{x,a}] \Rightarrow a = b_0 \wedge \pi^A [^{y_0, b_0}/_{x,a}] \right) \right) \right) \ ,$$

which simplifies to

$$\forall x' \left(\begin{array}{l} \alpha[^{b_0}/_a] \wedge x = y_0 \wedge \pi^C \\ \Rightarrow \exists a' \left(\alpha[^{a'}/_a] \wedge \left(\phi[^{y_0, b_0}/_{x,a}] \Rightarrow a' = b_0 \wedge \pi^A [^{y_0, b_0}/_{x,a}] \right) \right) \end{array} \right) \ .$$

Renaming y_0 and b_0 to x and a, respectively, reduces this to validity of

$$\forall x' \left(\alpha \wedge \pi^C \Rightarrow \exists a' \left(\alpha[^{a'}/_a] \wedge \left(\phi \Rightarrow a' = a \wedge \pi^A \right) \right) \right) \ ,$$

which follows immediately from requirement (11.8). In this derivation totality of α is not required since representation variables are not assigned to.

11.3.3 Problem with Partial Abstraction Relations

How can we solve the problem encountered in Examples 11.1 and 11.2? Let us look at the difference between Reynolds' condition and our L-simulation criterion in case the abstract operation is preceded by an assertion ϕ which Reynolds exploits in his refinement step. In general we interpret Reynolds' conditions for an abstract operation specified by $\pi_1 \rightsquigarrow \pi_2$, concrete operation C, representation invariant β, and intermediate assertion ϕ on the abstract level by (see Figure 11.3)

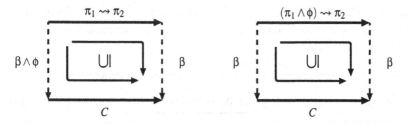

Fig. 11.3. Reynolds' condition.

Fig. 11.4. L-simulation condition from Section 11.3.2.

$$(\phi \wedge \beta) ; C \subseteq \pi_1 \leadsto \pi_2 ; \beta \qquad (11.9)$$

whereas the best approximation by an L-simulation condition is (see Figure 11.4 and compare with Section 11.3.2)

$$\beta ; C \subseteq (\phi \wedge \pi_1) \leadsto \pi_2 ; \beta . \qquad (11.10)$$

What is a typical pair of states (σ, τ) contained in (the meaning of) C and witnessing the difference between (11.10) and (11.9)?

(i) τ is not in the range of β, and
(ii) σ is in the range of β but none of the abstract states ζ related by β to σ satisfies ϕ.

If C consists just of this single pair (σ, τ) then (11.9) holds since $(\phi \wedge \beta) ; C$ is empty, but (11.10) does not hold since $\beta ; C$ contains (ζ, τ) for some ζ. (See Figure 11.5.)

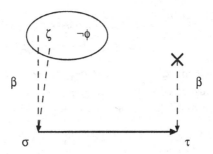

Fig. 11.5. Reynolds' condition is satisfied but the L-simulation requirement is violated.

Lemma 11.4 In general, $(11.10) \Rightarrow (11.9)$, and, iff β denotes a surjective relation from abstract to concrete states or its domain is contained in the meaning of ϕ, the converse also holds.

Proof: Using Lemma 5.24, (11.9) and (11.10) can be massaged into

$$C \subseteq \underbrace{(\phi \wedge \beta) \rightsquigarrow (\pi_1 \rightsquigarrow \pi_2 ; \beta)}_{R \stackrel{\text{def}}{=}} \tag{11.11}$$

and

$$C \subseteq \underbrace{\beta \rightsquigarrow ((\phi \wedge \pi_1) \rightsquigarrow \pi_2 ; \beta)}_{L \stackrel{\text{def}}{=}} , \tag{11.12}$$

respectively. Next we prove that $L \subseteq R$, and, under the restriction mentioned above, also $R \subseteq L$. To simplify the exposition of the proof we shall use the following abbreviations:

- $b_{\zeta,\sigma} \stackrel{\text{def}}{=} (\zeta,\sigma) \in \mathcal{A}[\![\beta]\!]^{AC}$,
- $i_\zeta \stackrel{\text{def}}{=} \zeta \in C[\![\phi]\!]^{Var^A}$,
- $p_{\gamma,\zeta} \stackrel{\text{def}}{=} (\gamma,\zeta) \in C[\![\pi_1]\!]^A$,
- $q_{\gamma,\xi} \stackrel{\text{def}}{=} (\gamma,\xi) \in C[\![\pi_2]\!]^A$, and
- $l_{\zeta,\xi} \stackrel{\text{def}}{=} \forall \gamma (p_{\gamma,\zeta} \Rightarrow q_{\gamma,\xi})$.

Let $\sigma, \tau \in \Sigma^C$. We calculate a characteristic predicate for L in terms of these abbreviations.

$$(\sigma,\tau) \in \mathcal{R}[\![L]\!]^{Var^C, Var^C} \Leftrightarrow \forall \zeta \left(b_{\zeta,\sigma} \Rightarrow \exists \xi \left(\forall \gamma (i_\zeta \wedge p_{\gamma,\zeta} \Rightarrow q_{\gamma,\xi}) \wedge b_{\xi,\tau} \right) \right)$$
$$\Leftrightarrow \forall \zeta \left(b_{\zeta,\sigma} \Rightarrow \exists \xi \left((i_\zeta \Rightarrow l_{\zeta,\xi}) \wedge b_{\xi,\tau} \right) \right)$$

Similarly, we proceed with R.

$$(\sigma,\tau) \in \mathcal{R}[\![R]\!]^{Var^C, Var^C} \Leftrightarrow \forall \zeta \left(b_{\zeta,\sigma} \wedge i_\zeta \Rightarrow \exists \xi \left(l_{\zeta,\xi} \wedge b_{\xi,\tau} \right) \right)$$
$$\Leftrightarrow \forall \zeta \left(b_{\zeta,\sigma} \Rightarrow \left(i_\zeta \Rightarrow \exists \xi \left(l_{\zeta,\xi} \wedge b_{\xi,\tau} \right) \right) \right)$$

Thus $L \subseteq R$ follows from $\exists \xi \left((i_\zeta \Rightarrow l_{\zeta,\xi}) \wedge b_{\xi,\tau} \right) \Rightarrow \left(i_\zeta \Rightarrow \exists \xi \left(l_{\zeta,\xi} \wedge b_{\xi,\tau} \right) \right)$, which obviously holds. (Just consider the cases of i_ζ.)

The inverse inclusion, $R \subseteq L$, holds if, and only if,

$$\forall \sigma, \tau \in \Sigma^C, \zeta \in \Sigma^A \left(b_{\zeta,\sigma} \wedge \neg i_\zeta \Rightarrow \exists \xi \left(b_{\xi,\tau} \right) \right)$$

holds. This is the case iff $\mathcal{A}[\![\beta]\!]^{AC}(\Sigma^A) = \Sigma^C$ or $(\mathcal{A}[\![\beta]\!]^{AC})^{-1}(\Sigma^C) \subseteq C[\![\phi]\!]^{Var^A}$, in other words, iff β denotes a surjective relation or the domain of that relation is contained in the meaning of ϕ. ∎ PVS

Our reasoning above is still correct when we switch from partial to total correctness semantics as defined in Chapter 8. Is surjectivity of $\mathcal{A}[\![\beta]\!]^{AC}_\perp$ still a restriction then? No, this relation is by definition surjective since we defined $\mathcal{A}[\![\beta]\!]^{AC}_\perp$ such that it contains K^{AC}, i.e., $\perp_{\Sigma^A}$ is related to each element of $\Sigma^C_\perp$ by $\mathcal{A}[\![\beta]\!]^{AC}_\perp$. Consequently, within our setting of total correctness, Reynolds' method implies L-simulation.

In the following example we illustrate this correspondence between the total correctness L-simulation solution and Reynolds' solution.

Example 11.5 (cf. Example 11.1) The relational interpretation of Reynolds' condition for the concrete operation $b := b + 1 \, ; W(b) := z$ to implement the abstract operation $U := U \cup \{z\}$ w.r.t. representation invariant β,

$$(z \notin U \wedge \beta) \, ; b := b + 1 \, ; W(b) := z \subseteq U := U \cup \{z\} \, ; \beta \, ,$$

is certainly valid. This is also true in our total correctness interpretation. Next we shall see that the corresponding condition based on L-simulation is valid in the total correctness interpretation. In contrast, we have concluded in Example 11.2 that this is not the case for the partial correctness interpretation.

As before we ignore all program variables not involved in this step, to simplify the exposition. We specify the abstract assignment $U := U \cup \{z\}$ exactly by $z \notin U \wedge U, z = U_0, z_0 \rightsquigarrow U, z = U_0 \cup \{z_0\}, z_0$.

Now we can use the total correctness L-simulation theorem (Theorem 9.9) to specify the least refined concrete program implementing this abstract specification w.r.t. β while preserving termination by

$$\exists U \, (\beta \wedge \exists U_0, z_0 \, (z \notin U \wedge U, z = U_0, z_0)) \wedge \exists U \, (\beta \wedge U, z = V_0, y_0)$$

$$\rightsquigarrow \exists U \left(\beta \wedge \forall U_0, z_0 \left(\begin{array}{l} (z \notin U \wedge U, z = U_0, z_0)[^{V_0, y_0}\!/_{U, z}] \\ \Rightarrow U, z = U_0 \cup \{z_0\}, z_0 \end{array} \right) \right)$$

By writing β as a function $b(U, W, a, b)$ of its free variables this specification can be simplified to

$$b(V_0, W, a, b) \wedge z = y_0 \wedge z \notin V_0$$

$$\rightsquigarrow \exists U \, (b(U, W, a, b)) \wedge (y_0 \notin V_0 \Rightarrow z = y_0 \wedge b(V_0 \cup \{y_0\}, W, a, b))$$

The concrete level program $b := b + 1 \, ; W(b) := z$ implements this specification since

(i) this sequence of assignments is guaranteed to terminate when started in a state satisfying the precondition and

(ii) when it does so, it terminates in a state satisfying the postcondition.

The first point is obvious. We use Hoare's assignment axiom to express the second point.

$$b(V_0, W, a, b) \wedge z = y_0 \wedge z \notin V_0$$

$$\Rightarrow \exists U \, (b(U, (W : b + 1 \mapsto z), a, b + 1))$$

$$\wedge \, (y_0 \notin V_0 \Rightarrow z = y_0 \wedge b(V_0 \cup \{y_0\}, (W : b + 1 \mapsto z), a, b + 1))$$

This is valid iff

$$b(V_0, W, a, b) \wedge y_0 \notin V_0 \Rightarrow b(V_0 \cup \{y_0\}, (W : b + 1 \mapsto y_0), a, b + 1)$$

is valid, which follows directly from the definition of (b and) β. $\heartsuit$

11.3.4 Summary

In the above sections we have demonstrated that the applications of Reynolds' method considered there are instances of L-simulation (possibly only for total correctness), and therefore, his method is sound but still incomplete. We neither have sufficient space nor intend to prove that such is the case for all examples in Chapter 5 of his book. Suffice to say that we have analyzed these other examples and come to the conclusion that they are covered by the cases listed above and are therefore also instances of L-simulation.

Theorem 11.6

Whenever Reynolds' data refinement method is applied to transform an abstract program A into a concrete one C using a representation invariant α, there exist

- a program skeleton P and
- two total correctness data types $\mathcal{A}$ and C

such that

- A denotes $P(\mathcal{A})$,
- C denotes $P(C)$, and
- C L-simulates $\mathcal{A}$ w.r.t. α in our total correctness framework.

In case $\mathcal{A}[\![\alpha]\!]^{CA}$ is total the above holds in the partial correctness interpretation.

$\spadesuit$

Remark We call Theorem 11.6 a theorem to stress its importance. However, its claim is not proven as rigorously as the theorems in Part I because its evidence depends on our necessarily subjective interpretation of Reynolds' method. $\Diamond$

In the more advanced parts of the fifth chapter, "Data Representation Structuring", of his book Reynolds applies his recipe successfully to a series of increasingly difficult examples. In one of these examples he demonstrates the benefits of an *incomplete* representation, that is, the use of a non-surjective abstraction relation. The unrepresented abstract states, however, are unreachable. Another example introduces an *ambiguous* representation; this corresponds to a non-functional abstraction relation.

Observe that our analysis of Reynolds' method is unaffected by these two properties — ambiguity and incompleteness of representation.

11.4 Historical Background

The four-point recipe quoted in Section 11.2.4 called there by us Reynolds' method has an interesting history, going back to the pioneer years of formal methods. To the best of our knowledge, Reynolds' method was first formulated as an independent technique for proving program correctness in Susan Gerhart's [Ger78], and later by John Reynolds in [Rey81]. The first record of its application in a refereed medium appears to be [LdRG79], where it was applied to prove correctness of three list-copying algorithms.

However, its first application seems to appear in Peter Lucas's [Luc68], i.e., in 1968! Ten years later, the technique reappears in two reports: [Bli78] by Andrzej Blikle and [B78] by Ralph Back, in the revised version of which it is applied on [B80, p. 80]. The fact that the method was known as a folk-theorem, although it had not been formulated before (only applied), seems to have been the reason why [Ger78] was not accepted by *Acta Informatica*. In this respect it shares the fate of another illustrious publication on refinement, Robin Milner's [Mil71], which was rejected by the *Journal of the Association of Computing Machinery*. At the time, refinement techniques were apparently not considered worth publishing in an academic journal!

One of the most impressive applications of John Reynolds' method to date is contained in Chapter 5 of his book [Rey81] and consists of a derivation of Robert Tarjan's strongest component algorithm, which was Reynolds' answer to a challenge by Donald Knuth that such really important algorithms could not be proven correct due to the unwieldiness of the proof procedure. That Reynolds' method is still alive and kicking is testified by the fact that it has been used as the basis for formulating a technique for proving refinement in the setting of temporal logic in volume III of Zohar Manna and Amir Pnueli's magnum opus *The Temporal Logic of Reactive and Concurrent Systems* [MP92, MP95, MP00]. (Volume III is devoted to proving progress properties.)

Exercises

11.1   (Taken from [Rey81]) Write an abstract program to solve the "single-source-single-sink" reachability problem, i.e., write a program in the style of Reynolds that accepts two nodes x and v and the function Λ, and sets the Boolean variable *reachable* to true if and only if $v \in \Lambda^*(x)$. The simplest approach is to modify the program developed in Section 11.2 to terminate when and if v is added to T.

A more complex but efficient approach is possible if the input also includes an "immediate predecessor function" *Pred* such that $y \in Pred(x)$ if and only if $x \in \Lambda(y)$. Then one can alternate between generating the set of nodes that can be reached from x and generating the set of nodes that can be reached backwards from v. Termination occurs when these sets intersect or when either set is complete.

Introduce invariants for your program and prove its correctness using these.

11.2   (Taken from [Rey81]) Transform the abstract program from Exercise 11.1 to introduce representations for the set variables in the refinement style of Reynolds as presented above. In the version that searches both forward from x and backwards from v, you should be able to fit two enumerating array segments within a single array with domain $[1..N]$.

11.3   Let op^A and op^C be value-returning operations on level A and C, respectively, such that they do not affect normal variables, and let α be a representation invariant between these two levels. Show that validity of

$$\{\alpha\}\, y^A := op^A\, ; y^C := op^C\, \{\alpha \wedge y^A = y^C\}$$

implies L-simulation between op^C and op^A w.r.t. α.

11.4   Show that $y := W(a)$ L-simulates $U = U_0 \wedge U \neq \emptyset \rightsquigarrow U = U_0 \wedge y \in U$ w.r.t. β as defined on page 270.

11.5   Give an analysis, similar to the analyses presented in Section 11.3.2, of indeterminate expressions occurring on the RHS of assignments to representation variables.

12
VDM

12.1 Introduction

In the glossary of terms in his book [J90] Cliff Jones explains the origin of the name **Vienna Development Method**.

> VDM is the name given to a collection of notation and concepts which grew out of the work of the IBM Laboratory, Vienna. The original application was the denotational description of programming languages. The same specification technique has been applied to many other systems. Design rules which show how to prove that a design satisfies its specification have been developed. [J90, p. 294]

Of the techniques mentioned above, Bicarregui *et al.* [BFL⁺94] stress three as the main ones: the specification language VDM-SL, data refinement techniques, and operation decomposition techniques, where the latter term refers to refinement as opposed to data refinement, for instance, the implementation of a specification statement by a loop.

One keyword in the quote above is 'rule'. Nowadays the first impression a student might get when learning and practising VDM is that of a huge collection of rules to guide writing specifications. Indeed, specifying with VDM mostly comprises two activities carried out together:

- writing specifications of, e.g., types, functions, and operations in the specification language and

- discarding proof obligations — preferably by formal proof — that ensure, for instance, that a type[1] is nonempty, a function specification is well-formed, a specification of an operation is satisfiable, or a specification is implemented by an operation.

---

[1] The denotation of a type is in VDM identified with a set and often expressed by invariants.

Of course, we focus in this monograph on the proof obligations that arise in the process of data refinement.[2]

The reasons behind this large palette of rules are twofold:

(i) VDM is one of the first specification formalisms aimed at wide-scale industrial use. As remarked earlier, this requires a fixed syntactic format, because this makes a formalism easier to learn, specifications easier to debug, and offers the possibility of machine-checking proofs. But first and foremost, to be successful within industry such a formalism should facilitate and support practical use. Consequently one finds in VDM many different characterizations [J90], called laws, to pin down the meaning of such simple functions over underlying data domains as, e.g., elems q, returning the elements of a finite sequence q. As examples of such laws one finds, e.g., elems $q = \{\, q(i) \mid i \in \text{dom } q \,\}$, elems $(append(s,q)) = \{s\} \cup$ elems q, elems $\langle\,\rangle = \emptyset$, etc., which are not independent. This will be illustrated in the footnotes accompanying Section 12.2.

(ii) VDM provides a framework for reasoning syntactically about data types in a setting of total correctness. Consequently, its logic is three-valued; indeed, its underlying interpretation has already been defined in Section 8.2 by $\mathcal{T}[\![.]\!]_\perp$.

Specifications and proof obligations in VDM are all given in terms of predicates, or, in the latter case, also in terms of sequents with predicates in both positions: antecedent and succedent. To indicate the particular three-valued logic underlying the VDM sequent calculus we denote such a sequent by $p \vdash_3 q$ instead of just $p \vdash q$. More precisely, VDM syntax is interpreted in a framework based on a non-strict, three-valued predicate logic [Che86, JM94], called LPF (acronym of **L**ogic of **P**artial **F**unctions), where the third value represents the undefined or non-denoting terms just as in Section 8.2. In this logic some axioms and rules from standard first order predicate logic are simply unsound: for instance, the law of the excluded middle (tertium non datur) $\vdash p \vee \neg p$ and the deduction theorem ($\vdash p \Rightarrow q$ iff $p \vdash q$) are unsound in LPF. A (relatively) complete proof system for LPF is presented in [JM94]. It is more complex than corresponding proof systems for classical, two-valued predicate logic, which explains why so much of the palette of rules is dedicated to predicates. Because of the seman-

---

[2] Data refinement is called *data reification* in the VDM community. *Webster's Dictionary* defines the verb 'reify' as 'to treat (an abstraction) as the real thing'. We tend to stick to the more common term.

tic similarity between VDM and our notion of validity of a predicate in the total correctness interpretation, we could have used that proof system to deal with predicates in Chapter 8. However, our interest in predicates is somewhat limited (when compared to VDM) since our correctness formulae are inclusions between relational terms, and not predicates.

We introduce part of the VDM notation by way of an example borrowed from Jones's book [J90]. Except for a minor relaxation of some proof obligations and a few explanatory remarks concerning the meaning of VDM nomenclature, Section 12.2 is taken from that book.

Throughout Section 12.2 paragraphs appearing

---

like this

---

and footnotes appearing in a sans-serif typeface stem from us, not from Jones.

A data refinement step in VDM concerns two data types rather than two programs as was the case with Reynolds' method in the previous chapter. Section 12.3 analyzes VDM's data refinement proof obligations. It is demonstrated that VDM data refinement implies total correctness L-simulation.

12.2 Example: Dictionary

12.2.1 A Spell-Checker Specification

Consider the task of checking a large text file against a dictionary of known words. There are, of course, many representation details about the text file to be resolved. But the crucial design decisions undoubtedly concern the representation of the dictionary. If this is to store tens of thousands of words in a way which facilitates efficient searching, some ingenuity is required in design — this issue is returned to below as an example of data refinement. Applying the dictum of abstraction, the representation issue can — and should — be postponed. For a specification the only concern is with a finite, unordered collection of distinct words — the state of this system can be presented as

$$\text{type } Dict = Word\text{-}set \ ,$$

indicating that $Dict$ is the type of finite sets of type $Word$. Even $Word$ need not be further defined at this point. There is a positive advantage in postponing this implementation-specific information: the specification is thereby made more abstract. The operation which must be invoked once per word in the text should return true if, and only if, its argument is a member of the state; its specification is

$$CHECKWORD\,(w : Word)\,b : \mathbb{B}$$
$$\text{ext rd } dict : Dict$$
$$\text{post } b \Leftrightarrow w \in dict$$

---

which introduces some new notation. This chunk of VDM specification language means that the operation specified takes a *Word* as argument upon invocation and returns a Boolean value. It has read-only access to an external state component of type *Dict* (as indicated by "ext rd") to which it refers using the local name *dict*. The postcondition is introduced via the keyword "post" which will be referred to in the verification conditions concerning *CHECKWORD* as *post- CHECKWORD*. Notice that $w \in dict$ yields a truth value and thus the equality with the Boolean result, b, is defined using the equivalence operator. The concept of precondition is introduced with the next operation. The precondition is omitted in the *CHECKWORD* specification because this operation is always applicable. If we had to denote its precondition it would be "true".

The initial state for the system might be the empty set of words:[3]

$$\text{init } dict_0 \triangleq \emptyset$$

An operation to add one word to a dictionary can be specified:

$$ADDWORD\,(w : Word)$$
$$\text{ext wr } dict : Dict$$
$$\text{pre } w \notin dict$$
$$\text{post } dict = \overleftarrow{dict} \cup \{w\}$$

This time the external state component may also be written by the operation specified, as indicated by the two keywords "ext wr". The precondition restricts the situations in which the operation is required to work properly. Only if the value of type *Word* that is passed as parameter upon invocation is not yet contained in the set of words which the external state component represents is it ensured that this operation terminates and that after termination the postcondition holds. The hooked occurrence of the external state variable *dict* in the postcondition refers to the value of *dict* immediately before invocation of *ADDWORD* (which is also the value referred to by the undecorated occurrence of *dict* in the precondition). In the postcondition the undecorated occurrence refers to the final value, i.e., the one established by the operation. This convention is used in VDM to avoid logical variables.

This specification appears simple precisely because an apposite[4] data type is used in defining its state. Of course, representation details have to be faced

---

[3] The VDM symbol $\triangleq$ is a syntactic counterpart of our $\overset{\text{def}}{=}$.

[4] *Webster's Dictionary* defines the adjective 'apposite' as 'neatly appropriate'.

in the design process but a concise specification is achieved by postponing implementation details.

It is interesting to note that the precondition of *ADDWORD* is not necessary at the level of description. It might, however, be important for the development and this justified its being recorded. It can be a mistake to become so involved in the abstraction that the needs of the implementation are entirely ignored. In fact, the crucial decision here is whether or not the user accepts this limitation.

Assuming that the dictionary is large, the designer is faced with the problem of choosing a representation which makes efficient searching possible. The choice must reflect not only algorithms but also storage usage — wasted store could cause excessive paging and subvert the performance of a representation which was chosen to support some particular algorithm. The designer has to consider many facets of efficiency. Here, some alternative representations are considered. The first is chosen for pedagogic, rather than realistic, reasons. Suppose the dictionary is represented by a sequence without duplicates. This gives

$$\text{type } Dicta = Word^* \text{ ,}$$

---

indicating finite sequences of type *Word*. Sequences are shorthands for special maps[5] in VDM, namely, maps whose domains are finite prefixes of the positive integers, e.g., the sequence notation for $\{1 \mapsto a, 2 \mapsto n, 3 \mapsto t\}$ is $\langle a,n,t \rangle$. In the case of a dictionary *Dicta*, we have a sequence of words.

A *data invariant* restricts the elements of type *Dicta* to sequences without duplicates. (Recall the discussion of set representations in Section 11.2.3.)

$$inv\text{-}Dicta(ws) \triangleq \text{card elems } ws = \text{len } ws$$

Operator card returns the cardinality of a finite set, elems and len return the set of elements, respectively, the length of a finite sequence.

The (functional) relationship between the representation and the abstraction is easily expressed:

$$retr\text{-}Dict : Dicta \longrightarrow Dict$$
$$retr\text{-}Dict(ws) \triangleq \text{elems } ws$$

Here, *retr-Dict* can be said to be retrieving the abstract set from among the irrelevant ordering information of the sequence values.

[5] A *map* in VDM is a function with finite domain.

One straightforward property which is required of retrieve functions is that they be *total*. In this case there is no doubt about *retr-Dict* since the elems operator is total on sequences.[6] In some cases, however, it is necessary to tighten an invariant on the representation in order to ensure that the retrieve function is defined for all values which can arise.

12.2.2 Adequacy

It is intuitively clear that there should be at least one representation for any abstract value. This property is embodied in the *adequacy* proof obligation which, for the case of *Dicta*, is shown next.

There must be at least one sequence (without duplicates) which can be retrieved onto any possible set value:

$$d \in Dict \vdash_3 \exists da : Dicta \bullet retr\text{-}Dict(da) = d$$

The result here is obvious[7] and the formal proof is skipped.

Formally speaking, an LPF-sequent $p \vdash_3 q$ is valid iff whenever p holds in an interpretation q also holds in that interpretation. Observe that this corresponds in the setting of classical logic with two truth values to, for all σ, $\sigma \in C[\![p]\!]_\perp \Rightarrow \sigma \in C[\![q]\!]_\perp$ but not necessarily to $\sigma \in C[\![p \Rightarrow q]\!]_\perp$; this correspondence holds only if $T[\![p]\!]_\perp \sigma \neq \perp$.

Observe the different notation for quantification in VDM. Our $\forall x \in X \, (x \neq y)$ is denoted $\forall x : X \bullet x \neq y$ in VDM. The scope of a quantifier extends to the end of line unless there are brackets delimiting the scope. Indentation of continuation lines is used to indicate that these lines also belong to the scope. The scope never ranges over the turnstile symbol ($\vdash_3$). In all cases occurring in this chapter the scope should be obvious. Recall that we decorate the turnstile with subscript 3 to distinguish it from the ordinary turnstile indicating provability for two-valued predicate logic because premises (the formulae on the LHS of the turnstile) and conclusions (the formula on its RHS) are evaluated in LPF instead of classical first order logic.

12.2.3 More Dictionary Representations

One way to provide for efficient searching is to split the dictionary into sections by word length. Each such section is then stored in alphabetical order. As words are scanned from the text to be checked, their length is computed. The relevant dictionary section can then be located via a table and the word to be

---

[6] Therefore, in the setting of Section 8.2, a retrieve function would correspond to an abstraction relation $\alpha \in Abs^{CA}$ whose semantics (minus K^{CA}) is a total function from concrete level proper states to abstract level proper states.

[7] One applies, for instance, the rule elems $\langle \rangle = \emptyset$ to show that the empty list $\langle \rangle$ is a suitable initial value for *da*.

tested sought in the selected section. The search can use a technique known as 'binary search', which is efficient because it relies on the order.

A series of distinct design decisions are embodied in this description. A record of the first design decision can be given in terms of the following objects:

$$\text{type } \textit{Dictb} = \textit{Section}^*$$

$$\text{inv } \textit{Dictb}(sl) \triangleq \forall i : \text{dom } sl \bullet (\forall w : sl(i) \bullet \text{len } w = i) \land \textit{is\_ordered}(sl(i))$$

$$\text{type } \textit{Section} = \textit{Word}^*$$

$$\text{type } \textit{Word} = \textit{Letter}^+$$

Notice that, in order to describe the invariant, it has been necessary to say more about *Word* than on the abstract level. Here, we define *Word* to be the set of finite, nonempty sequences of letters. The retrieve function required here is

$$\textit{retr-Dict}_b : \textit{Dictb} \longrightarrow \textit{Dict}$$
$$\textit{retr-Dict}_b(sl) \triangleq \bigcup \text{elems } sl$$

Here again there is no difficulty with totality, since both distributed union "$\bigcup$" and elems are total; adequacy can be established by a simple induction argument.

The preceding representation required that a whole word be scanned before any searching could be done. A student project on this example proposed a way of using each letter as it is scanned. The initial proposal was to use Pascal arrays indexed by letters; the value stored in such arrays were to be pointers to other arrays; all of the arrays were allocated on the heap; nil pointers were to be used to mark where words ended. Using the VDM map notation, it is possible to represent this by nesting maps as follows:

$$\text{type } \textit{Dicte} = \textit{Letter} \xrightarrow{m} \textit{Dicte} \ ,$$

---

with *Letter* $\xrightarrow{m}$ *Dicte* indicating the set of maps from *Letter* to *Dicte* itself.

The word-set

$$\{\langle a,n,d \rangle, \langle a,n,t \rangle\}$$

can then be represented by

$$\{a \mapsto \{n \mapsto \{d \mapsto \{\}, t \mapsto \{\}\}\}\}$$

Note how maps are used to define *Dicte* recursively. By this use of recursion one has in principle the capacity to represent infinite words. Since these do not occur on the abstract level *Dict* of the dictionary, only finite use of recursion is intended, ending in an element $\langle\,\rangle \in Dicte$ which maps no letters, representing the empty dictionary $\emptyset$. This restriction can be expressed by a data type invariant *inv-Dicte* which states that the recursion depth in the definition of *Dicte* is finite, as worked out below.

Notice how the lack, for example, of any word beginning with *b* is shown by the absence of this letter from the domain of the outer map.

But one must also notice that this representation is not adequate (with respect to any retrieve function)! There is, for example, no way of adding a word in *Dicte* which is a prefix of an existing word (consider $\langle a, n \rangle$). On realizing this, the students had to add an indicator to each array (in Pascal, a record is used with a Boolean value and the array of pointers as its fields) to mark additionally the end of a prefix — here:

$$Dictc :: eow : \mathbb{B}$$
$$map : Letter \xrightarrow{m} Dictc,$$

---

together with a data type invariant[8] that ensures the finiteness of recursion depth:

$inv\text{-}Dictc(d) \triangleq \exists n : \mathbb{N} \bullet maps\_in\_depth(n,d) = \{\langle\,\rangle\}$, and
$maps\_in\_depth(n, mk\text{-}Dictc(e,m)) \triangleq$
  if $n = 0$ then $\{m\}$ else $\bigcup\{ maps\_in\_depth(n-1, m(x)) \mid x \in \text{dom } m \}$

To construct a value of a composite type[9] like *Dictc* VDM employs a so-called *make-function*, $mk\text{-}Dictc : \mathbb{B} \times (Letter \xrightarrow{m} Dictc) \longrightarrow Dictc$, which is specific to that type. (Such make-functions exist for each composite type in VDM.)

For a pictorial insight into the structure of a variable of type *Dictc* look at Figure 12.1, which shows a value of type *Dictc* representing a dictionary that contains only four words, namely the elements of the set $\{a, an, and, ant\}$.

The retrieve function required is defined by recursion:

$retr\text{-}Dict_c : Dictc \longrightarrow Dict$
$retr\text{-}Dict_c(mk\text{-}Dictc(e,m)) \triangleq$
  $\bigcup\{ \{ append(l,w) \mid w \in retr\text{-}Dict_c(m(l)) \} \mid l \in \text{dom } m \} \cup \{ \langle\,\rangle \mid e \}$

---

[8] Recall from Chapters 1 and 4 the rôle of data invariants. A data (type) invariant is introduced whenever one wants to restrict the state space of one's model.
[9] Composite types in VDM are like records in Pascal.

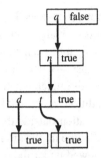

Fig. 12.1. A value of type *Dictc*.

12.2.4 Proof Obligations for Operation Modelling

The abstract specification consists of a set of states, the initial states, and operations. The design task is to respecify the operations on the chosen state representation.

The proof obligations needed for operations have to cope with two complications. Firstly, operations themselves are partial (cf. their precondition[10]) and nondeterministic (cf. their postcondition);[11] secondly, retrieve functions are normally many-to-one and thus their inverses are not functions. One way of comprehending the resulting proof rules is to view the operations on the representation via the retrieve function. The basic proof obligations for *operation modelling* are the *domain rule* and the *result rule*.[12]

Domain rule

$$c : C, \; pre\text{-}A(retr\text{-}A(c)) \vdash_3 pre\text{-}C(c)$$

Result rule

$$\overleftarrow{c}, c : C, \; pre\text{-}A(retr\text{-}A(\overleftarrow{c})) \wedge post\text{-}C(\overleftarrow{c}, c) \vdash_3 post\text{-}A(retr\text{-}A(\overleftarrow{c}), retr\text{-}A(c))$$

These rules can be extended in an obvious way[13] to cope with inputs and results

---

[10] By *pre-A* we refer to the precondition of operation *A*, analogous to *post-A* for its postcondition.

[11] In this chapter we yet have to encounter a nondeterministic operation. However, it should already be clear at this point that, since postconditions are just predicates, nondeterminism is easily introduced, e.g., via a postcondition $x > \overleftarrow{x}$ to describe that variable x is increased by an unspecified amount.

[12] The validity of the proof rules here relies on the adequacy of the representation. The concept of viewing under the retrieve function can be formalized by requiring that representation operations respect the equivalence relation induced on the representation states by the retrieve function.

[13] The obvious way here is the following: add inputs as parameters to both pre- and postconditions. Results occur as parameters in postconditions only.

of operations since these do not get changed by refinement: it is the behavior — as seen via the inputs/outputs — which is preserved by refinement.

The second of these proof obligations can be seen as requiring that any pair of states in the *post-C* relation must — when viewed under the retrieve function — satisfy the *post-A* relation. An implementation should not be rejected for an unnecessarily wide precondition, nor should it be forced to perform any particular (e.g., *post-C*) computation outside the required domain. Thus the first conjunct of the antecedent of the implication limits the proof obligation to those states which — when viewed under the retrieve function — satisfy the abstract preconditions.

The explanation of the result rule argues against requiring too much of the operations on the concrete level. It must, however, be remembered that the specification of the operations on the concrete level consist of two parts. The result rule ensures that the postcondition is not too wide; the domain rule requires that the precondition of the operation on the representation is not too narrow.

The *CHECKWORD* operation would be respecified on *Dicta* by

$$CHECKWORDa\,(w:Word)\,b:\mathbb{B}$$
$$\text{ext rd } ws:Dicta$$
$$\text{post } b \Leftrightarrow \exists i:\text{dom } ws \bullet ws(i) = w$$

Remember that elements *ws* of type *Dicta* are sequences without duplicates. This implies that there is a non-trivial data invariant which induces a proof obligation for every operation on *Dicta*, namely, one has to show that the data type invariant is preserved by the operation. But since *CHECKWORDa* has only read access to the global variable *ws* this is obvious.

Recall that the retrieve function is:

$$retr\text{-}Dict(ws) \triangleq \text{elems } ws$$

For the *CHECKWORD* operations, the domain rule

$$ws:Dicta,\ w:Word,\ pre\text{-}CHECKWORD(w,retr\text{-}Dict(ws))$$
$$\vdash_3 pre\text{-}CHECKWORDa(w,ws)$$

is vacuously true because the operation on the concrete level is total. Noting that the precondition of the abstract operation is also true, the result rule becomes:

$$ws:Dicta,\ w:Word,\ b:\mathbb{B},\ post\text{-}CHECKWORDa(w,ws,b)$$
$$\vdash_3 post\text{-}CHECKWORD(w,retr\text{-}Dict(ws),b)$$

which follows from[14]

$$ws : Word^*, w : Word, b : \mathbb{B}, b \Leftrightarrow \exists i : \text{dom } ws \bullet ws(i) = w$$
$$\vdash_3 b \Leftrightarrow w \in \text{elems } ws \ .$$

Thus, *CHECKWORDa* can be said to model *CHECKWORD*.

The *ADDWORD* operation changes the state and can be modelled by

> $ADDWORDa\,(w : Word)$
> ext wr $ws : Dicta$
> pre $\neg\exists i : \text{dom } ws \bullet ws(i) = w$
> post $ws = append(w, \overleftarrow{ws})$

Remember that one has to check that *ADDWORDa* preserves *inv-Dicta*. The domain rule becomes

$$ws : Dicta, w : Word, pre\text{-}ADDWORD(w, retr\text{-}Dict(ws))$$
$$\vdash_3 pre\text{-}ADDWORDa(w, ws)$$

which is easily proven. The result rule becomes

$$\overleftarrow{ws}, ws : Dicta, w : Word,$$
$$pre\text{-}ADDWORD(w, retr\text{-}Dict(\overleftarrow{ws})), post\text{-}ADDWORDa(w, \overleftarrow{ws}, ws)$$
$$\vdash_3 post\text{-}ADDWORD(w, retr\text{-}Dict(\overleftarrow{ws}), retr\text{-}Dict(ws))$$

which is again straightforward. Thus *ADDWORDa* models *ADDWORD*. If these are the only operations, the data refinement step has been justified and attention can be turned to the next step of development.

It is also necessary to show that the initial states correspond — with respect to the retrieve function. The proof is straightforward in this case and is shown explicitly only on examples where the initial states are less obvious.

The third dictionary representation above is more interesting. In this case the initial state is worth special consideration. The proof obligation for initial states is (with $retr\text{-}Dict_c : Dictc \longrightarrow Dict$):

$$dictc_0 : Dictc \vdash_3 retr\text{-}Dict_c(dictc_0) = dict_0$$

This can be satisfied with

$$dictc_0 = mk\text{-}Dictc(false, \langle \, \rangle)$$

---

[14] Formal proofs of obligations involving basic functions like elems depend on rules about these functions, for instance, $ws : Word^* \vdash_3 \text{elems } ws = \{ ws(i) \mid i \in \text{dom } ws \}$ and $ws : Word^* \vdash_3 \text{dom } (append(w, ws)) = \text{dom } ws \cup \{\text{len } ws + 1\}$.

12.2.5 Generalizations and Further Proof Obligations

It has been made clear that the behavior of a data type is what is to be specified
and verified. But there are steps of refinement which cannot be proved correct
by the rules given above even though the putative implementation manifests
the same behavior as the specification.[15] Thus, it is clear that the given rules
are too weak in the sense that they are sufficient but not necessary. Although
they cover a very large percentage of the development steps which one is likely
to meet, it is useful to know the more general rule.

The key to the more general rule is to realize that the retrieve function can
revert to a relation. The proof rules above capitalized on the one-to-many situation brought about by the lack of bias.[16] If this restriction no longer applies,
the many-to-many situation can be represented by the abstraction relation:

$$rel : A \times C \longrightarrow \mathbb{B}$$

What can we say in case there is a non-functional abstraction relation? We
extract the following general proof rules from [J90, p. 221f]. With these more
general rules, there is no adequacy proof obligation. The domain rule is similar
to the one above:

$$c : C, \ a : A, \ rel(a,c), \ pre\text{-}A(a) \vdash_3 pre\text{-}C(c)$$

The result rule is

$$\overleftarrow{c}, c : C, \ \overleftarrow{a} : A, \ rel(\overleftarrow{a}, \overleftarrow{c}), \ pre\text{-}A(\overleftarrow{a}), \ post\text{-}C(\overleftarrow{c}, c)$$
$$\vdash_3 \exists a : A \bullet post\text{-}A(\overleftarrow{a}, a) \wedge rel(a, c)$$

Proofs using these results are left as exercises. In general, they become more
difficult than proofs using the rules of Section 12.2.4, if for no other reason
than the appearance of the existential quantifier.

It is also necessary to handle initial states. The general form of specifying initial states
in VDM is by means of an *initialization predicate* instead of a fixed, single initial state.
VDM has special notation for expressing state relevant information. Recall the concrete
level of the bag example (see Examples 2.5 and 2.11). In VDM the representation
variables, the data invariant, and the initial state are recorded as follows:

$$
\begin{aligned}
&\text{state } C \text{ of} \\
&\quad sum : \mathbb{R} \\
&\quad num : \mathbb{Z} \\
&\quad \text{inv } mk\text{-}C(s,n) \triangleq n = 0 \Rightarrow s = 0 \\
&\quad \text{init } mk\text{-}C(s,n) \triangleq n = 0 \wedge s = 0
\end{aligned}
$$

---

[15] For instance our bag example from Chapter 1 is not covered by those rules.
[16] Recall from Chapter 1 that a data type is *biased* if its underlying model contains
information which cannot be extracted using the operations of that data type.

Proof obligations for well-formedness and satisfiability of both the invariant and the initialization predicate arise.

- The invariant is Boolean-valued over the cross-product of the field types:

$$s : \mathbb{R},\ n : \mathbb{Z} \vdash_3 inv\text{-}C(mk\text{-}C(s,n)) : \mathbb{B}$$

- Type C is inhabited:

$$\vdash_3 \exists s : \mathbb{R}, n : \mathbb{Z} \bullet inv\text{-}C(mk\text{-}C(s,n))$$

- The initialization is Boolean-valued over the state type:

$$c : C \vdash_3 init\text{-}C(c) : \mathbb{B}$$

Recall that $c : C$ means that c is a proper value of type C, i.e., $inv\text{-}C(c)$ holds.
- There exists a state for which the initialization predicate holds:

$$\vdash_3 \exists c : C \bullet init\text{-}C(c)$$

12.3 Analysis of Data Refinement in VDM

Disregarding the syntactic sugar established by VDM, the specifications resemble Hoare-style specifications because they mainly consist of pre- and post-conditions. Some differences remain:

- Neither pre- nor postconditions refer to logical variables. Instead, postconditions may refer directly to the value a variable had before execution of the operation under consideration using the hooked version of the variable's name.

- Operations are named and may have parameters and a result. Read-only and read–write accessible variables are distinguished. From the data refinement point of view, these features are negligible. Therefore, we do not handle parameters and results in this section. For the moment, we restrict ourselves to VDM operations not using these features. At the end of this chapter, in Section 12.3.3, we will sketch how to model these features within our theory.

Section 12.3.1 investigates the meaning of VDM specifications and proof obligations to bridge the gap between VDM syntax and our framework. These preparations enable us to prove in Section 12.3.2 the main result of this chapter, that VDM reification implies total correctness L-simulation.

12.3.1 Implicit Specifications

Next we analyze the constituents of a typical implicit specification of a VDM operation (under the restriction just mentioned).

$$OP\,()$$
$$\text{ext wr } x : X$$
$$\text{pre } p(x)$$
$$\text{post } q(\overleftarrow{x},x)$$

It has

- a *name OP*,
- (read and) write access to an *external variable x* of type X,
- a *precondition $p(x)$*, and
- a *postcondition $q(\overleftarrow{x},x)$*.

External variables are called external because they are the variables an operation has access to that are not local to the operation concerned (they may be normal or representation variables). Recall that this specification also introduces the name *pre-OP* for p and *post-OP* for q. As usual in VDM, dependence of predicates on variables is expressed by adding these variables as parameters such as x in the definition of the precondition. This convention is used in VDM in place of explicit substitution. For instance, one simply uses $p(\overleftarrow{x})$ where we would write $p[\overleftarrow{x}/x]$.

Syntax and Semantics of Pre- and Post-Conditions

Pre- and postconditions are predicates. For our purpose it suffices to ignore the notational differences between our predicates and the ones in VDM. Thus we describe the syntactic class of VDM preconditions on level A as a subclass of Hoare-style assertions on that level, namely all those which do not contain free occurrences of logical variables. Only program variables from level A are admitted. This restriction is ensured by setting $Lvar^A$ to $\emptyset$, for the moment.

$$Jpre^A \stackrel{\text{def}}{=} Pred^{Var^A}$$

Their semantics is determined by a function $\mathcal{T}[\![.]\!]^A_\perp : Jpre^A \longrightarrow (\Sigma^A_\perp \longrightarrow \mathbb{B}_\perp)$ similar to the one given for total correctness Hoare-style assertion except for the omission of logical states. In the sequel we do not distinguish these two semantic functions any longer.

The syntactic class of VDM postconditions on level A is a superclass of the VDM preconditions. In addition to program variables from level A their hooked versions may also occur in postconditions.

$$Jpost^{A} \stackrel{\text{def}}{=} Pred^{\overleftarrow{Var^{A}},Var^{A}}$$

Their semantics is determined by a function $\mathcal{T}[\![.]\!]_{\perp}^{A} : Jpost^{A} \longrightarrow (\Sigma_{\perp}^{A} \times \Sigma_{\perp}^{A} \longrightarrow \mathbb{B}_{\perp})$ that relies on an interpretation function $\mathcal{E}[\![.]\!]_{\perp} : Exp \longrightarrow (\Sigma_{\perp} \times \Sigma_{\perp} \longrightarrow \mathbb{V}_{\perp})$ such that, e.g., $\mathcal{E}[\![x]\!]_{\perp}(\sigma,\tau) = \tau(x)$, and $\mathcal{E}[\![\overleftarrow{x}]\!]_{\perp}(\sigma,\tau) = \sigma(x)$. The definition of such semantics is exactly that of Def. 8.23 except for this difference, hence we omit it. The same connection between truth-valued semantics $\mathcal{T}[\![.]\!]_{\perp}^{A}$ and set-valued semantics $C[\![.]\!]_{\perp}^{A}$ as in Chapter 8 applies.

$$\sigma \in C[\![p(x)]\!]_{\perp}^{A} \Leftrightarrow \mathcal{T}[\![p(x)]\!]_{\perp}^{A}\sigma = tt \qquad \text{(for } p(x) \in Jpre^{A})$$

$$(\sigma,\tau) \in C[\![q(\overleftarrow{x},x)]\!]_{\perp}^{A} \Leftrightarrow \mathcal{T}[\![q(\overleftarrow{x},x)]\!]_{\perp}^{A}(\sigma,\tau) = tt \quad \text{(for } q(\overleftarrow{x},x) \in Jpost^{A})$$

$$(12.1)$$

Proof Obligations Introduced by Specifications

In VDM a number of obligations arise with a specification of a VDM operation *OP* like the one introduced at the beginning of Section 12.3.1. They serve as check points for the specifier to increase his confidence in the quality of his specification. To simplify the presentation we assume that the data invariant of type X is trivial, i.e., true.

Remark Even if that data invariant is non-trivial, no extra proof obligation arises. All values of read–write accessible external variables stay by definition within the bounds of the data invariant even if the postcondition of an operation does not explicitly say so. This is because in VDM $c : C$ means that c is a proper value of type C, i.e., *inv-C(c)* holds. Consequently, in our analysis of the proof obligations of VDM below, no invariant is mentioned explicitly anymore since they are part of the declarations such as, e.g., $\overleftarrow{c},c : C$ in the result rule in Section 12.2.4. ◊

- The name *OP* is fresh.
- The type X is already declared.
- Both pre- and postconditions are *well-formed*:

  – The precondition $p(x)$ is defined for all values of x in X.

  $$x : X \vdash_{3} p(x) : \mathbb{B}$$

  On the semantic level this is expressed by[17]

  $$\forall \sigma \in \Sigma^{x} (\mathcal{T}[\![p(x)]\!]_{\perp}\sigma \neq \perp) \qquad (12.2)$$

---

[17] If the data invariant had been some non-trivial predicate *inv-X(x)* we would have written $\forall \sigma \in \Sigma_{\perp}^{x} (\sigma \in C[\![inv\text{-}X(x)]\!]_{\perp} \Rightarrow \mathcal{T}[\![p(x)]\!]_{\perp}\sigma \neq \perp)$.

- The postcondition is defined for all values of $\overleftarrow{x}$ and x in X such that the precondition evaluates to true in $\overleftarrow{x}$.

$$\overleftarrow{x}, x : X, \ p(\overleftarrow{x}) \vdash_3 q(\overleftarrow{x},x) : \mathbb{B}$$

This holds iff

$$\forall \sigma, \tau \in \Sigma^x \left(\sigma \in C[\![p(x)]\!]_\perp \Rightarrow T[\![q(\overleftarrow{x},x)]\!]_\perp(\sigma,\tau) \neq \perp \right) \qquad (12.3)$$

As explained in the next section, the restriction to well-formedness is an essential prerequisite for maintaining consistency between the proof obligations for refinement in their original formulation of [J90] and the version presented here, which is due to [BFL+94].

- The specification is *satisfiable*, that is, whenever the precondition is true in $\overleftarrow{x}$, there exists x in X such that the postcondition holds. Observe that satisfiability of a specification ensures absence of deadlock for that specification, i.e., it denotes a total relation.[18] Hence our semantic basis is isomorphic to the one assumed by VDM.

$$\overleftarrow{x} : X, \ p(\overleftarrow{x}) \vdash_3 \exists x : X \bullet q(\overleftarrow{x},x)$$

Or, expressed semantically

$$\forall \sigma \in \Sigma^x_\perp \left(\sigma \in C[\![p(x)]\!]_\perp \Rightarrow \exists \tau \in \Sigma^x_\perp \left((\sigma,\tau) \in C[\![q(\overleftarrow{x},x)]\!]_\perp \right) \right) \qquad (12.4)$$

Proof Obligation for Refinement

VDM has a more programming-language-like notation for describing functions explicitly, which we shall not investigate further. Just assume that there is some operation *IMP* that has read–write access to x. In proof obligations such an operation can be treated as a binary relation on values of x in VDM; for instance, there is a notion $(\overleftarrow{x},x) \in IMP$ associated with it, denoting that *IMP* has the ability to transform $\overleftarrow{x}$ to x. One has to prove the following sequent in order to ensure that *IMP* refines *OP*.

$$\overleftarrow{x} : X, \ p(\overleftarrow{x}) \vdash_3 (\exists x : X \bullet (\overleftarrow{x},x) \in IMP)$$
$$\wedge (\forall x : X \bullet (\overleftarrow{x},x) \in IMP \Rightarrow q(\overleftarrow{x},x)) \qquad (12.5)$$

---

[18] As explained in Chapter 8, within our total correctness semantics one cannot express the nondeterministic possibility of deadlock. The concept of nondeterministic deadlock is an operational one — it cannot be specified within this semantics. When one considers the meaning of a specification, there is no associated concept of computation, and therefore no nondeterministic deadlock is specified. Note that this does not imply that a program implementing a specification does not have the possibility of deadlock. However, the only source of nondeterminism in VDM is (implicit) specifications, which do not contain our choice operator "$[\!]$". Hence the nondeterministic possibility of deadlock is even not expressible. All VDM operations are required to terminate whenever the precondition of their specification is satisfied. Hence there is no deadlock in VDM specifications.

Hence, *IMP* refines the operation specified if, and only if,

- *IMP* generates a final state whenever the precondition is satisfied, and
- all final states generated by *IMP* from initial states that satisfy the precondition satisfy the postcondition.

Observe the difference between proof obligation (12.5) and the — in a subtle way more restrictive — original version of Jones in [J90]:

$$\vdash_3 \overleftarrow{x} : X, \; pre\text{-}OP(\overleftarrow{x}) \Rightarrow (\exists x : X \bullet (\overleftarrow{x}, x) \in IMP)$$
$$\wedge \, (\forall x : X \bullet (\overleftarrow{x}, x) \in IMP \Rightarrow post\text{-}OP(\overleftarrow{x}, x))$$

$$(12.6)$$

Note that, if we require pre- and postconditions to be well-formed, then (12.5) and (12.6) are equivalent. To illustrate the difference that may arise otherwise, consider the following two specifications, in which the precondition of *OP1* is not well-formed.

OP1 ()	*OP2* ()
ext wr $x : \mathbb{Z}$	ext wr $x : \mathbb{Z}$
pre $\frac{1}{x} = 1$	pre $x = 1$
post $x = 5$	post $x = 5$

Here, $(\overleftarrow{x}, x) \in OP2$ is equivalent to $\overleftarrow{x} = 1 \Rightarrow x = 5$. Then, according to (12.6), *OP2* does not refine specification *OP1*. Consider initial state $x = 0$. Substituting *OP2* for *IMP*, it is for example required that

$$\vdash_3 \frac{1}{0} = 1 \Rightarrow \forall x : X \bullet (0, x) \in OP2 \Rightarrow x = 5$$

holds. This is not the case, because

- $\frac{1}{0} = 1$ is undefined (its value is $\bot$ by Def. 8.22),
- $(0, 6) \in OP2$ is true, but
- $6 = 5$ is false, thus,
- $\forall x : X \bullet (0, x) \in OP2 \Rightarrow x = 5$ is false by Def. 8.23, hence
- $\frac{1}{0} = 1 \Rightarrow \forall x : X \bullet (0, x) \in OP2 \Rightarrow x = 5$ evaluates to $\bot$, cf. the table for "$\Rightarrow$" on page 161.

On the other hand, it is easy to see that *OP2* satisfies specification *OP1* according to (12.5). Since we want this to be the case — for which refinement of *OP1* would be more natural than *OP2* — we opt for characterization (12.5) of refinement.

The same difference applies to many of the proof obligations presented here, for example, domain and result rules, and explains why we prefer the versions of these rules given in [BFL$^+$94] over those given in [J90].

A Specification Statement for VDM

The term $\phi \rightsquigarrow \psi$ is defined in Chapter 5 such that it denotes the maximal solution of $\{\phi\} S \{\psi\}$ in S. Next we define $p \overset{\jmath}{\rightsquigarrow} q$ in an analogous fashion such that it denotes the maximal solution to *IMP* in (12.5).

$$\mathcal{P}[\![p \overset{\jmath}{\rightsquigarrow} q]\!]_\perp \overset{\text{def}}{=} \left\{ (\sigma,\tau) \in (\Sigma_\perp^x)^2 \;\middle|\; \sigma \in C[\![p(x)]\!]_\perp \Rightarrow (\sigma,\tau) \in C[\![q(\overleftarrow{x},x)]\!]_\perp \right\}$$

$$(12.7)$$

Given this semantic characterization one has to prove that this is indeed the maximal solution to *IMP* in the proof obligation for satisfaction of *OP*.

Before doing so, we explain why proof obligation (12.5) is semantically expressed by

$$\forall \sigma \in \Sigma_\perp^x \left(\sigma \in C[\![p]\!]_\perp \Rightarrow \left(\begin{array}{l} \exists \tau \in \Sigma_\perp^x ((\sigma,\tau) \in \mathcal{P}[\![IMP]\!]_\perp) \\ \wedge \forall \tau \in \Sigma_\perp^x \left(\begin{array}{l} (\sigma,\tau) \in \mathcal{P}[\![IMP]\!]_\perp \\ \Rightarrow (\sigma,\tau) \in C[\![q]\!]_\perp \end{array} \right) \end{array} \right) \right) \quad (12.8)$$

Observe that we have included $\perp$-states in the range of all quantifications above. For $\forall \sigma \in \Sigma_\perp^x (\ldots)$ and $\exists \tau \in \Sigma_\perp^x (\ldots)$ this does not matter; the $\perp$-subscript could have been omitted. However, it is essential to include $\perp$ in the range of the $\forall \tau \in \Sigma_\perp^x (\ldots)$ quantification. For imagine that $(\sigma, \perp) \in \mathcal{P}[\![IMP]\!]_\perp$. Then this implies, since $(\sigma, \perp) \notin C[\![q]\!]_\perp$, that the inner implication is false, and therefore, provided $C[\![p]\!]_\perp$ is nonempty, that (12.8) is false. If we had not considered this case, nondeterminism could have been refined by nontermination of *IMP*. For instance, (12.8) would have been satisfied by choosing $p = q = \text{true}$ and *IMP* = **abort**. But this refinement step should not be regarded as preserving total correctness, because true $\overset{\jmath}{\rightsquigarrow}$ true always terminates when started in a proper state and this is not the case for **abort**.

Lemma 12.1 $p \overset{\jmath}{\rightsquigarrow} q$ is the maximal solution for *IMP* in (12.5).

Proof: Assume $\mathcal{P}[\![.]\!]_\perp$ has been suitably extended to cover *IMP* as well. Then the proof obligation for satisfaction (12.5) is semantically expressed by (12.8). First we prove that $p \overset{\jmath}{\rightsquigarrow} q$ is a solution for *IMP*, i.e., that substituting the RHS of (12.7) for $\mathcal{P}[\![IMP]\!]_\perp$ in (12.8) leads to a valid formula. Let $\sigma \in \Sigma_\perp^x$ such that $\sigma \in C[\![p]\!]_\perp$. By the satisfiability condition (12.4) for the postcondition there exists $\tau \in \Sigma^x$ with $(\sigma,\tau) \in C[\![q]\!]_\perp$. Thus, the existentially quantified conjunct in the RHS of (12.8) holds.

Next let $\tau \in \Sigma_\perp^x$ such that $(\sigma,\tau) \in \mathcal{P}[\![p \overset{\jmath}{\rightsquigarrow} q]\!]_\perp$. Then, by (12.7), $(\sigma,\tau) \in C[\![q]\!]_\perp$ is true. Hence, the universally quantified conjunct of the RHS of (12.8) holds, too.

Second we prove that if *IMP* satisfies specification *OP*, then $\mathcal{P}[\![IMP]\!]_\perp \subseteq \mathcal{P}[\![p \overset{\mathcal{J}}{\leadsto} q]\!]_\perp$. Let $\sigma, \tau \in \Sigma_\perp^x$ with $(\sigma, \tau) \in \mathcal{P}[\![IMP]\!]_\perp$. In case $\sigma \in C[\![p]\!]_\perp$ the universally quantified conjunct of the RHS of (12.8) implies $(\sigma, \tau) \in C[\![q]\!]_\perp$. By (12.7), $(\sigma, \tau) \in \mathcal{P}[\![p \overset{\mathcal{J}}{\leadsto} q]\!]_\perp$. In case $\sigma \notin C[\![p]\!]_\perp$ this is even more obvious. $\square$

Another conclusion drawn from this proof is that, mathematically speaking, conditions (12.2) and (12.3) are superfluous. (These conditions are introduced in [BFL+94] but do not occur in [J90].)

The Original Model of VDM

The semantic model which we have used so far to analyze VDM arose from our own interpretation of this method. However, Cliff Jones suggested another semantic model in [J87]. In that paper, VDM pre/post specifications are interpreted as pairs. The first component of such a pair is a set of proper states and the second a binary relation on proper states. These two components happen to coincide with the semantics $C[\![.]\!]_\perp$ given to VDM pre- and postconditions in this chapter. That is, Jones' interpretation of an implicit specification with precondition $p \in Jpre^A$ and postcondition $q \in Jpost^A$ is given by the pair $(C[\![p]\!]_\perp^A, C[\![q]\!]_\perp^A)$. He defines a refinement relation *sat* between two of such pairs as follows. If $d, d' \subseteq \Sigma$ and $r, r' \subseteq \Sigma^2$, then (d, r) *sat* $(d', r') \Leftrightarrow d' \subseteq d \wedge d' \triangleleft r \subseteq r'$, where the so-called *domain restriction* operator $\triangleleft$ is defined by $d \triangleleft r \overset{\text{def}}{=} \{ (\sigma, \tau) \in r \mid \sigma \in d \}$. Next we analyze the two conjuncts in this definition in detail.

$d' \subseteq d$: Operation (d, r) should be applicable whenever (d', r') is.

$d' \triangleleft r \subseteq r'$: If (d', r') is applicable and (d, r) is applied instead, then only results that could have been produced by (d', r') are generated.

That the *sat* relation and our notion of refinement are equivalent is the subject of the following theorem, which we have proven using PVS.

Theorem 12.2
If $p, p' \in Jpre^A$ and $q, q' \in Jpost^A$, then

$$((C[\![p]\!]_\perp^A, C[\![q]\!]_\perp^A) \, sat \, (C[\![p']\!]_\perp^A, C[\![q']\!]_\perp^A)) \Leftrightarrow (\mathcal{P}[\![p \overset{\mathcal{J}}{\leadsto} q]\!]_\perp^A \subseteq \mathcal{P}[\![p' \overset{\mathcal{J}}{\leadsto} q']\!]_\perp^A)$$

Proof: Let $d \overset{\text{def}}{=} C[\![p]\!]_\perp^A$, $d' \overset{\text{def}}{=} C[\![p']\!]_\perp^A$, $r \overset{\text{def}}{=} C[\![q]\!]_\perp^A$, and $r' \overset{\text{def}}{=} C[\![q]\!]_\perp^A$. Then, e.g., $\mathcal{P}[\![p \overset{\mathcal{J}}{\leadsto} q]\!]_\perp^A = d \triangleleft r \cup \overline{d} \triangleleft U_\perp^A$, where the complement $\overline{d}$ of d is taken in $\Sigma_\perp^A$.

$(d, r) \, sat \, (d', r')$

$\Leftrightarrow (d' \subseteq d) \wedge (d' \triangleleft r \subseteq r')$ def. of *sat*

$$\Leftrightarrow (\overline{d} \subseteq \overline{d'}) \wedge (d' \triangleleft r \subseteq d' \triangleleft r') \qquad\qquad \text{property of } \triangleleft$$

$$\Leftrightarrow (\overline{d} \triangleleft U_\perp^A \subseteq \overline{d'} \triangleleft U_\perp^A) \wedge (d \triangleleft r \subseteq d' \triangleleft r' \cup \overline{d'} \triangleleft U_\perp^A) \qquad d \setminus d' \subseteq \overline{d'}$$

$$\Leftrightarrow \overline{d} \triangleleft U_\perp^A \cup d \triangleleft r \subseteq \overline{d'} \triangleleft U_\perp^A d' \triangleleft r' \cup \overline{d'} \triangleleft U_\perp^A \qquad\quad \text{"}\Leftarrow\text{"}: d \cap \overline{d} = \emptyset$$

$$\boxed{\text{PVS}}$$

The price we paid for keeping inclusion as the refinement relation was a more involved definition of $\mathcal{P}[\![p \overset{\mathcal{J}}{\leadsto} q]\!]_\perp$, whereas Jones had to compensate for a simpler definition of an interpretation of VDM specifications by a more complex refinement relation.

Translation Theorem

Given the apparent similarity between Hoare-style specification statements and their VDM counterparts, we may ask whether and how we should translate one into the other. The translation from VDM to Hoare-style is straightforward but the opposite direction requires the use of a non-strict equality operator. For this purpose only we will add this non-strict operator to the comparison operators admitted in $Jpre^A$ and $Jpost^A$. For proper states σ its meaning is defined as follows.

$$\mathcal{T}[\![t_1 == t_2]\!]_\perp \sigma \overset{\text{def}}{=} \mathcal{T}[\![t_1]\!]_\perp \sigma = \mathcal{T}[\![t_2]\!]_\perp \sigma$$

Observe the difference between strict and non-strict equality: $\frac{1}{0} = 0$ evaluates to $\perp$ while $\frac{1}{0} == 0$ reduces to ff in proper states. As a consequence, we obtain a useful connection between the truth-valued semantics of $\pi ==$ true and the set-valued semantics of π for predicates π. For proper states σ,

$$\mathcal{T}[\![\pi == \text{true}]\!]_\perp \sigma \in \mathbb{B} \quad \text{and} \quad \mathcal{T}[\![\pi == \text{true}]\!]_\perp \sigma \Leftrightarrow \sigma \in C[\![\pi]\!]_\perp \qquad (12.9)$$

Alternatively, one can introduce a *definedness* operator Δ that yields true whenever its argument is defined and false otherwise.

Theorem 12.3

Let $\phi, \psi \in Pred^{x_0, x}$. In the total correctness interpretation the following equalities hold.

$$p \overset{\mathcal{J}}{\leadsto} q = (p \wedge x = x_0) \leadsto q[^{x_0}/_{\overline{x}}]$$

$$\phi \leadsto \psi = (\exists x_0 : X \bullet \phi) \overset{\mathcal{J}}{\leadsto} (\forall x_0 : X \bullet (\phi[^{\overline{x}}/_x] == \text{true}) \Rightarrow (\psi == \text{true}))$$

Proof: Let $\sigma, \tau \in \Sigma_\perp^x$. For proving the first equation we start with the RHS.

$$(\sigma, \tau) \in \mathcal{P}[\![p \wedge x = x_0 \leadsto q[^{x_0}/_{\overline{x}}]]\!]_\perp$$

$$\Leftrightarrow \qquad \text{(Def. 8.29)}$$

$$\forall \gamma \in \Gamma \left((\gamma, \sigma) \in C[\![p \wedge x = x_0]\!]_\perp \Rightarrow (\gamma, \tau) \in C[\![q[^{x_0}/_{\overleftarrow{x}}]]\!]_\perp \right)$$

$\Leftrightarrow$ (Def. 8.23, Lemma 5.12)

$$\forall \gamma \in \Gamma \left(\sigma \in C[\![p]\!]_\perp \wedge \gamma(x_0) = \sigma(x) \Rightarrow ((\gamma : \overleftarrow{x} \mapsto \gamma(x_0))|_{\overleftarrow{x}}, \tau) \in C[\![q]\!]_\perp \right)$$

$\Leftrightarrow$ (pred. calc., (12.1))

$$\sigma \in C[\![p]\!]_\perp \Rightarrow (\sigma, \tau) \in C[\![q]\!]_\perp$$

$\Leftrightarrow$ (by (12.7))

$$(\sigma, \tau) \in \mathcal{P}[\![p \overset{\mathcal{J}}{\leadsto} q]\!]_\perp$$

Within the proof of the second equation, let $\overleftarrow{\sigma}$ abbreviate $(\sigma : \overleftarrow{x} \mapsto \sigma(x))|_{\overleftarrow{x}}$.

$$(\sigma, \tau) \in \mathcal{P}[\![(\exists x_0 : X \bullet \phi) \overset{\mathcal{J}}{\leadsto} (\forall x_0 : X \bullet (\phi[\overleftarrow{x}/_x] == \text{true}) \Rightarrow (\psi == \text{true}))]\!]_\perp$$

$\Leftrightarrow$ (def. of $\mathcal{P}[\![p \overset{\mathcal{J}}{\leadsto} q]\!]_\perp$ in (12.7))

$$\sigma \in C[\![\exists x_0 : X \bullet \phi]\!]_\perp$$
$$\Rightarrow (\sigma, \tau) \in C[\![\forall x_0 : X \bullet (\phi[\overleftarrow{x}/_x] == \text{true}) \Rightarrow (\psi == \text{true})]\!]_\perp$$

$\Leftrightarrow$ (def. of $C[\![q(\overleftarrow{x}, x)]\!]_\perp$ in (12.1))

$$\sigma \in C[\![\exists x_0 : X \bullet \phi]\!]_\perp$$
$$\Rightarrow T[\![\forall x_0 : X \bullet (\phi[\overleftarrow{x}/_x] == \text{true}) \Rightarrow (\psi == \text{true})]\!]_\perp (\sigma, \tau) = tt$$

$\Leftrightarrow$ (Def. 8.23)

$$\exists \delta \in \Gamma((\delta, \sigma) \in C[\![\phi]\!]_\perp)$$
$$\Rightarrow \forall \gamma \in \Gamma \left(T[\![\phi[\overleftarrow{x}/_x] == \text{true} \Rightarrow \psi == \text{true}]\!]_\perp (\gamma, \overleftarrow{\sigma} \dagger \tau) \right)$$

$\Leftrightarrow$ (Def. 8.23, Lemmas 5.13 and 5.12)

$$\exists \delta \in \Gamma((\delta, \sigma) \in C[\![\phi]\!]_\perp)$$
$$\Rightarrow \forall \gamma \in \Gamma(T[\![\phi == \text{true}]\!]_\perp (\gamma, \sigma) \Rightarrow T[\![\psi == \text{true}]\!]_\perp (\gamma, \tau))$$

$\Leftrightarrow$ (pred. calc., (12.9))

$$\forall \delta \in \Gamma((\delta, \sigma) \in C[\![\phi]\!]_\perp \Rightarrow \forall \gamma \in \Gamma((\gamma, \sigma) \in C[\![\phi]\!]_\perp \Rightarrow (\gamma, \tau) \in C[\![\psi]\!]_\perp))$$

$\Leftrightarrow$ (pred. calc.)

$$\forall \gamma \in \Gamma((\gamma, \sigma) \in C[\![\phi]\!]_\perp \Rightarrow (\gamma, \tau) \in C[\![\psi]\!]_\perp)$$

$\Leftrightarrow$ (Def. 8.29)

$$(\sigma, \tau) \in \mathcal{P}[\![\phi \leadsto \psi]\!]_\perp \qquad \qquad \square$$

Notice that in this proof we used (12.9) in an essential way. Even if we drop the well-formedness conditions for VDM pre- and postconditions, our specifications are more general (or worse) than VDM specifications. For instance, spec-

ification true $\leadsto x = x_0$ translates to $(\exists x_0 : X \bullet \text{true}) \overset{\jmath}{\leadsto} (\forall x_0 : X \bullet (\text{true}[\overleftarrow{x}/x] ==$
true$) \Rightarrow ((x = x_0) == \text{true}))$, which simplifies to true $\overset{\jmath}{\leadsto}$ false. This violates
the satisfiability condition (12.4) that expresses totality of the specified relation.

12.3.2 Data Refinement in VDM

To analyze the proof obligations of VDM we consider the following entities throughout this section:

- An abstract level type declaration

$$\text{type } A = T^A$$

together with a data invariant expressed by predicate P^A

$$\text{inv } a \triangleq P^A$$

and an initialization predicate

$$\text{init } a \triangleq Q^A$$

none of which is further specified here. Recall that the lines above also introduce aliases *inv-A* for P^A and *init-A* for Q^A as well as some well-formedness proof obligations.

- An implicitly specified abstract level operation *OPA* with precondition $p^A(a)$ and postcondition $q^A(\overleftarrow{a}, a)$. It has read and write access to the external variable a of type A.

$$
\begin{aligned}
&OPA\,() \\
&\text{ext wr } a : A \\
&\text{pre } p^A \\
&\text{post } q^A
\end{aligned}
$$

An analogous set of entities is assumed on the concrete level.

$$
\begin{aligned}
&\text{type } C = T^C \\
&\text{inv } c \triangleq P^C \\
&\text{init } c \triangleq Q^C \\
&OPC\,() \\
&\text{ext wr } c : C \\
&\text{pre } p^C \\
&\text{post } q^C
\end{aligned}
$$

Retrieve Relations

The connection between the state spaces of the two levels under consideration is provided by the retrieve relation r. In VDM syntax,

$$r : A \times C \longrightarrow \mathbb{B}$$

In our set-up this corresponds to $r \in Abs^{AC}$. As we argued in Chapter 8, the semantics of a retrieve relation is different from that of the predicate it is expressed by. The well-formedness condition for r means that the representation relation predicate is defined for all pairs of abstract and concrete states. This precludes cases covered by the complicated second disjunct in Def. 8.25 of $\mathcal{A}[\![.]\!]_\perp^{AC}$ on page 164.

$$a : A,\ c : C \vdash_3 r(a,c) : \mathbb{B}$$

This means that the predicate semantics of r does not evaluate to bottom in a pair of proper states.

$$\forall \zeta \in C[\![P^A]\!]_\perp, \sigma \in C[\![P^C]\!]_\perp \left(\mathcal{T}[\![r]\!]_\perp^{Var^A, Var^C}(\zeta, \sigma) \neq \perp \right)$$

For the same technical reasons as in Chapter 8 we require the semantics of retrieve relations to contain — in addition to the state pairs suggested by the predicate semantics — all state pairs $(\perp, \sigma)$, namely, relation K^{AC} from Chapter 8 is always contained in $\mathcal{A}[\![r]\!]_\perp^{AC}$.

Adequacy of Initialization

All concrete initial states must be related to some abstract initial state.

$$c : C,\ init\text{-}C(c) \vdash_3 \exists a : A \bullet r(a,c) \wedge init\text{-}A(a)$$

Semantically, this requirement is captured by:

$$\forall \sigma \in C[\![P^C]\!]_\perp$$
$$\left(\sigma \in C[\![Q^C]\!]_\perp \Rightarrow \exists \zeta \in C[\![P^A]\!]_\perp \left((\zeta, \sigma) \in \mathcal{A}[\![r]\!]_\perp^{AC} \wedge \zeta \in C[\![Q^A]\!]_\perp \right) \right)$$
$$(12.10)$$

This can be simplified to $C[\![Q^C]\!]_\perp \subseteq \mathcal{A}[\![r]\!]_\perp^{AC}(C[\![Q^A]\!]_\perp)$.

Domain Rule

The domain rule requires the concrete operation to be applicable in all concrete states that are related to abstract states in which the abstract operation is applicable.

$$a : A,\ c : C,\ r(a,c),\ pre\text{-}OPA(a) \vdash_3 pre\text{-}OPC(c)$$

The semantics of this instance of the domain rule follows.

$$\forall \zeta \in C[\![P^A]\!]_\perp, \sigma \in C[\![P^C]\!]_\perp$$
$$\left((\zeta,\sigma) \in \mathcal{A}[\![r]\!]_\perp^{AC} \wedge \zeta \in C[\![p^A]\!]_\perp \Rightarrow \sigma \in C[\![p^C]\!]_\perp \right)$$

Result Rule

Whenever the concrete operation produces a final state and the abstract operation is applicable, then it can produce a related abstract final state.

$$\overleftarrow{a} : A, \; \overleftarrow{c}, c : C, \; r(\overleftarrow{a}, \overleftarrow{c}), \; pre\text{-}OPA(\overleftarrow{a}), \; post\text{-}OPC(\overleftarrow{c}, c)$$
$$\vdash_3 \exists a : A \bullet post\text{-}OPA(\overleftarrow{a}, a) \wedge r(a, c)$$

The semantics of this instance of the result rule is

$$\forall \zeta \in C[\![P^A]\!]_\perp, \sigma, \tau \in C[\![P^C]\!]_\perp$$
$$\left(\begin{array}{l} (\zeta,\sigma) \in \mathcal{A}[\![r]\!]_\perp^{AC} \wedge \zeta \in C[\![p^A]\!]_\perp \wedge (\sigma,\tau) \in C[\![q^C]\!]_\perp \\ \Rightarrow \exists \xi \in C[\![P^A]\!]_\perp \left((\zeta,\xi) \in C[\![q^A]\!]_\perp \wedge (\xi,\tau) \in \mathcal{A}[\![r]\!]_\perp^{AC} \right) \end{array} \right)$$

Except for the restriction to states in which the abstract level precondition holds, this resembles the L-simulation requirement for operations.

Data Reification Implies L-Simulation

Now assume that all the proof obligations listed above are satisfied; does L-simulation then also hold? The central result of this chapter answers this question positively.

The concepts in VDM that correspond to our normal variables are parameters, results, and external variables not subject to the current refinement step. (See Section 12.3.3.) However, the gist of the proof of the implication between VDM proof obligations and those for L-simulation is already clear when we assume the set of normal variables to be empty. (The general case is left to the reader to check in Exercise 12.8.)

Theorem 12.4

For data types whose operations do not involve parameters or results, VDM data reification implies total correctness L-simulation.

Proof: We assume that the types and operations introduced in Section 12.3.2 fulfill all obligations VDM requires. We show that these proof obligations imply the L-simulation conditions for the corresponding semantic objects. The L-simulation condition for initialization is

$$init^C \subseteq init^A ; r \; . \tag{12.11}$$

There is, however, no initialization operation in VDM, but there are initialization predicates. Since there are no normal variables, an initialization operation would start in either of the two states constituting $\Sigma_\perp^0 = \{\hat{m}, \perp\}$. We prove these two cases separately. We assume as usual that starting in $\perp$ may result in any final state. Therefore, (12.11) follows for the $\perp$ case from $K^{AC} \subseteq \mathcal{A}[\![r]\!]_\perp^{AC}$.

$$\{\perp\} \times \Sigma_\perp^C \subseteq \{\perp\} \times \Sigma_\perp^A ; K^{AC}$$

Starting in the only proper state in $\Sigma_\perp^0$, i.e., $\hat{m}$, leads to a member of the semantics of the initialization predicates on that level. By adequacy of the initialization (12.10), each concrete initial state is related to at least one abstract initial state.

$$\{\hat{m}\} \times C[\![Q^C]\!]_\perp \subseteq \{\hat{m}\} \times C[\![Q^A]\!]_\perp ; \mathcal{A}[\![r]\!]_\perp^{AC}$$

This establishes (12.11) for the non-$\perp$ case.

The L-simulation condition for the pairs of operations is

$$r ; (p^C \overset{\mathcal{I}}{\leadsto} q^C) \subseteq (p^A \overset{\mathcal{I}}{\leadsto} q^A) ; r$$

Let $\zeta \in \Sigma_\perp^A$ and $\tau \in \Sigma_\perp^C$ such that $(\zeta, \tau) \in \mathcal{R}[\![r ; p^C \overset{\mathcal{I}}{\leadsto} q^C]\!]_\perp$. Then there exists $\sigma \in \Sigma_\perp^C$ such that $(\zeta, \sigma) \in \mathcal{A}[\![r]\!]_\perp^{AC}$ and $(\sigma, \tau) \in \mathcal{P}[\![p^C \overset{\mathcal{I}}{\leadsto} q^C]\!]_\perp$.

The interesting case is $\zeta \in C[\![p^A]\!]_\perp$. From strictness of $C[\![p^A]\!]_\perp$ and well-formedness of r it follows that neither ζ nor σ is $\perp$. By the domain rule, $\sigma \in C[\![p^C]\!]_\perp$. By the semantics of the VDM specification $(\sigma, \tau) \in C[\![q^C]\!]_\perp$ and by strictness of $C[\![.]\!]_\perp$ also $\tau \neq \perp$. All premises of the result rule are fulfilled and we conclude that there exists $\xi \in \Sigma^A$ with $(\zeta, \xi) \in C[\![q^A]\!]_\perp$ and $(\xi, \tau) \in \mathcal{A}[\![r]\!]_\perp^{AC}$. Altogether, $(\zeta, \tau) \in \mathcal{R}[\![p^A \overset{\mathcal{I}}{\leadsto} q^A ; r]\!]_\perp$.

In case $\zeta \notin C[\![p^A]\!]_\perp$ we have that $(\zeta, \perp) \in \mathcal{P}[\![p^A \overset{\mathcal{I}}{\leadsto} q^A]\!]_\perp$. Since furthermore $K^{AC} \subseteq \mathcal{A}[\![r]\!]_\perp^{AC}$, it follows that $(\zeta, \tau) \in \mathcal{R}[\![p^A \overset{\mathcal{I}}{\leadsto} q^A ; r]\!]_\perp$.

Finalizations, fin^A and fin^C, are not mentioned explicitly in VDM. They coincide with projections on the set of normal variables (which is empty at this point of our analysis), i.e., finalizations relate proper states to $\hat{m}$ only and $\perp$ to $\Sigma_\perp^0$. In particular, finalizations are weakly terminating, which implies

$$(\zeta, \perp) \in \mathcal{A}[\![r]\!]_\perp^{AC} \Rightarrow \zeta = \perp .$$

Thus, the finalization condition $r ; fin^C \subseteq fin^A$ is trivially satisfied. $\square$

Easy consequences of this theorem are soundness and incompleteness of the VDM proof obligations for data refinement.

Because of the lack of well-formedness and satisfiability conditions in our theory the reduction of L-simulation to VDM data refinement in general fails.

12.3.3 Extensions

To ease the exposition above, we have considered only operations that

- have no local variables and one external variable (which is read–write accessible),
- have no return value, and
- have no parameters.

The following sections informally explain how to extend our analysis above such that read-only accessible external variables, parameters, and results are also handled properly.

Read-only Accessible External Variables

VDM read-only accessible external variables enter the picture easily. They can be seen as shorthands for read–write accessible ones that the operation is not allowed to change. Thus, we may replace any declaration and use of a read-only variable v in the specification of an operation

$$\vdots$$

$$\text{ext rd } v : V$$

$$\vdots$$

$$\text{post } q(v, \dots)$$

by a read–write accessible variable plus a freeze predicate in the postcondition.

$$\vdots$$

$$\text{ext wr } v : V$$

$$\vdots$$

$$\text{post } q(v, \dots) \wedge v = \overleftarrow{v}$$

Parameters and Results

Parameters and results are slightly more difficult to deal with. We would have omitted their treatment, were it not that they are essential to VDM.

A VDM specification describes the external behaviour of a system through the set of operations which act upon some internal state. All that can be observed is the outcome of a sequence of operation invocations involving values passed as parameters and returned as results.

[BFL$^+$94, p. 190]

Our relational language does not allow for parameters or results as the VDM formalism does, but these can be modelled using normal variables. Since all parameters in VDM are passed by value, parameters can be seen as read-only variables. Their values are not allowed to change between the initial and final states of an operation. The value of a normal variable representing the result of a VDM operation is unspecified in the initial state and determined by the postcondition in the final state.

Theorem 12.5
VDM data reification implies total correctness L-simulation.

Proof: Similar to that for Theorem 12.4. The details are left as an exercise.

□

12.4 Historical Background

For an account of the roots of VDM we refer to [J92]. The first book on VDM is [BJ78] by Dines Bjørner and Cliff B. Jones. In [J90] two sets of rules are developed, one based on retrieve functions, and the other on retrieve relations. The relationship between these two sets from the perspective of implementation bias is studied in [Hay90]. Further developments on VDM can be found in [BFL⁺94].

Exercises

12.1   Specify operations *ADDBAG* and *MEANBAG* in VDM that match the operations used on the abstract level in Example 2.5, i.e., *ADDBAG* adds an element to an external variable representing a bag and *MEAN-BAG* returns the average of the bag elements. Show that your specifications are well-formed and satisfiable.
         Hint: Usually bags are modelled in VDM as maps from their base type (e.g., T) to positive integers (i.e., $T \overset{m}{\to} N_1$ in the example chosen).

12.2   (cf. Exercise 12.1) Specify two operations *ADDBAGa* and *MEAN-BAGa* in VDM that match the operations used on the concrete level in Example 2.5. Show that your specifications are well-formed and satisfiable.

12.3   (cf. Exercises 12.1 and 12.2) Specify a retrieve relation between the state spaces of the previous two exercises and prove its well-formedness. Specify initial states and show their correspondence. Prove that the operations specified in Exercise 12.2 model the ones from Exercise 12.1 with respect to your retrieve relation.

12.4   (Dictionaries) Specify operations *CHECKWORDb* and *ADDWORDb*
        that access an external variable of type *Dictb*, show that they are well-
        formed, and prove that they model their respective counterparts on the
        Dict level.

12.5   (cf. Exercise 12.4) Specify operations *CHECKWORDc* and *ADD-
        WORDc* accessing an external variable of type *Dictc*, show that they
        are well-formed, and prove that they model their respective counter-
        parts on the *Dictb* level.
        Hint: This requires the invention of a suitable retrieve relation.

12.6   Formulate and prove a simulation theorem for VDM.
        Hint: Exploit the translation theorem and the L-simulation theorem
        for total correctness.

12.7*   Invent proof obligations for data refinement based on L^{-1}-simulation
        instead of L-simulation. Prove their soundness.

12.8   Adapt the proof of Theorem 12.4 to Theorem 12.5.

13

Z, Hehner's Method, and Back's Refinement Calculus

In this chapter we briefly introduce and discuss three more methods. These are Z, Hehner's method, and Back's Refinement Calculus. We do not intend to describe them in as much detail as Reynolds' method and VDM in the previous two chapters. We concentrate just on the data refinement aspects of these methods and analyze quickly how they compare to the methods already discussed.

All three methods discussed in this chapter turn out to be quite different members of the L-simulation community.

Originally Z was invented as another notation for Zermelo–Fränkel set theory. However, it evolved to a development style (or method) for specifications. Although invented by academics, Z is nowadays relatively popular in industry, especially in Europe. As will turn out at the end of our discussion of Z in Section 13.1, there is not much difference between Z and VDM from the data refinement point of view. The subtle differences between these two methods apart from the notational ones are analyzed elsewhere; see e.g. [HJN93].

Hehner arrives at a strikingly simple syntax-based development method by using first order predicate logic as the specification language [Heh93]. Whereas VDM uses two predicates, namely pre- and postconditions, Hehner needs only a single predicate. Moreover he interprets his predicates in a classical two-valued model similar to ours from Section 5.2 for two sets of variables: input and output variables. As we shall see in Section 13.2, Hehner's notion of *data transformer* corresponds to a total L-simulation relation combined with the solution to the L-simulation problem given in Section 7.2.

Ralph Back and Joakim von Wright, on the other hand, developed a calculus of comparable elegance, but based on a lattice-theoretical framework for weakest precondition predicate transformer semantics [BvW90, vW90]. As we shall prove in Section 13.3, Back's notion of data refinement when restricted to conjunctive operations is equivalent to total correctness relational L-simulation.

Powersimulation as introduced in Section 10.3.1 is in some sense more general because we proved soundness of strict and continuous powersimulations whereas Back restricts himself to strict and disjunctive powersimulations.

13.1 Z

The Z notation is a formal specification language developed at Oxford University's Programming Research Group in the late 1970s and early 1980s by Abrial, Sufrin, and Sørensen. It is based on a typed set theory. Besides being a formal language, Z also incorporates notions of operation refinement and data refinement that are closely related to those of VDM.

Recently, several comparisons of Z and VDM have been published. These do not deal with data refinement, however, but rather with expressiveness aspects [Hay92, HJN93] or with internal reasoning about specifications, such as consistency checks and discharging of proof obligations. See e.g. [Lin93, LvK94, Lin94] for an overview. [Gil90] describes a translator from Z to VDM-SL.

In this section, we will only sketch such features of Z as are needed for discussing its approach to data refinement. For a detailed introduction, see [Wor92] or [Dil90]. A full account of Z can be found in the reference manual [Spi92b].[1]

13.1.1 Basic Features of Z

Z's approach to specification is state-based. It contains a graphical notation (called *schema*) for describing state information. Schemas can be used in two ways:

- either to specify states
- or to specify state transitions (relations in general).

In a Z specification, the first step is to introduce the "given sets" that are needed but whose internal structure is irrelevant for the problem. In our example, we have *Real* as a given set, and in Z this is written as

[*Real*]

Next, we define the state space. For the implementation, we have a record type with a data invariant. In schema notation, this is written as

---

[1] The parts of Z presented here do not always conform to the standard syntax as checkable with Mike Spivey's *f*UZZ specification checker ([Spi92a]). In several places, the syntax has been modified to ease the exposition.

$$
\begin{array}{|l}
\hline
\_BagC \underline{\hspace{8cm}} \\
\quad sum : Real \\
\quad n : \mathrm{N} \\
\hline
\quad (n = 0) \Rightarrow (sum = 0) \\
\hline
\end{array}
$$

The headline of this schema includes the *schema name* (here *BagC*). The upper part of the box is the *signature part*, which contains the collection of variables together with their types that constitutes the state. The lower part of the box is the *property part* of the schema. It contains a predicate that must hold for all valid states (i.e. the data invariant). The set N of natural numbers is predefined in Z.

There is also a "flat" form of notation for schemas:

$$BagC \,\hat{=}\, [\,sum : Real; n : \mathrm{N} \mid (n = 0) \Rightarrow (sum = 0)\,]$$

The abstract state space consists of bags of real numbers. As in VDM, bags are modelled by finite maps:

$$\mathrm{bag}\, X == X \nrightarrow \mathrm{N}_1$$

where X is some set and $\nrightarrow$ denotes finite partial functions. The data invariant for this type is *true*. This is depicted by an empty (non-existent) property part of the corresponding schema:

$$
\begin{array}{|l}
\hline
\_BagA \underline{\hspace{8cm}} \\
\quad b : \mathrm{bag}\ Real \\
\hline
\end{array}
$$

Now we want to describe state transitions like *ADD*. For this purpose, we first need the concept of *systematic decoration*: if S is a schema, then S' is the schema that is derived from S by suffixing every variable name with a prime and leaving the rest unchanged. E.g. *BagC′* is equivalent to the (anonymous) schema

$$
\begin{array}{|l}
\hline
\quad sum' : Real \\
\quad n' : \mathrm{N} \\
\hline
\quad (n' = 0) \Rightarrow (sum' = 0) \\
\hline
\end{array}
$$

Other possible decoration symbols are "?" and "!"; in general, a decoration consists of a string of these symbols, e.g. "?′ !".

An important feature for modularization of specifications is the possibility of *including a schema S* in another schema S_1. This is done by including the name S in the signature part of S_1; it means that the signature of S is part of that of S_1 and that the property part of S is added to that of S_1 (via conjunction). So we have that e.g.

```
┌─ NonEmptyBagC ─────────────────────────────────────
│ BagC
│ elements : N
├────────────────────────────────────────────────────
│ n < elements ∧ n ≠ 0
└────────────────────────────────────────────────────
```

is equivalent to

```
┌─ NonEmptyBagC ─────────────────────────────────────
│ sum : Real
│ n : N
│ elements : N
├────────────────────────────────────────────────────
│ (n = 0) ⇒ (sum = 0)
│ n < elements ∧ n ≠ 0
└────────────────────────────────────────────────────
```

If the predicate part of a schema contains more than one predicate, these are to be understood as connected by conjunction.

Now we have everything at hand to *specify operations*. As in VDM, such specifications refer to the state before the operation (in this chapter called the *before state*) and the state afterwards (the *after state*). By convention, the after state variables are decorated with a prime, and both states together are described by the delta (Δ) schema:[2]

```
┌─ Δstate ───────────────────────────────────────────
│ state
│ state'
└────────────────────────────────────────────────────
```

For the special case of operations that do not change the state, there is the special Ξ schema:

```
┌─ Ξstate ───────────────────────────────────────────
│ Δstate
├────────────────────────────────────────────────────
│ "all state components remain unchanged"
└────────────────────────────────────────────────────
```

---

[2] Note that this schema does not have any "computational content"; its sole purpose is to combine the two signatures and to provide a concise way of using them together (by schema inclusion).

Another convention is that input variables are decorated with "?" and output variables with "!".

As an example, we specify the *ADD* operation:

```
┌─ ADDA ─────────────────────────────────────────
│ ΔBagA
│ x? : Real
├───────────────────────────────────────────────
│ b' = b ⊕ x
└───────────────────────────────────────────────
```

This schema describes those pairs of states (b, b') that fulfill the predicate in the property part with respect to an input number $x?$, i.e. where $x?$ is added to the bag. ⊎ denotes bag union, and $\{x_1, \dots, x_n\}_b$ denotes the bag containing $x_1, \dots, x_n$ (for $n \geq 0$).

The operation *MEAN* does not change the state, but has a precondition:

```
┌─ MEANA ────────────────────────────────────────
│ ΞBagA
│ av! : Real
├───────────────────────────────────────────────
│ b ≠ ∅_b
│ av! = mean(b)
└───────────────────────────────────────────────
```

As in the VDM example, the function $mean : BagA \setminus \{\emptyset_b\} \to Real$ is left unspecified.

Unlike in VDM, the precondition of an operation is not expressed independently of the postcondition; there is only one condition in the operation's property part. But if a schema defining a state-changing operation (e.g. including a delta schema) is given, the precondition can be extracted. It can be stated by means of a schema whose signature is that of the original one restricted to the before state and the input variables, as explained below.

For the exact definition, we first have to define what it means to *hide variables* that are part of a schema signature. If S is a schema and $\{x_1, \dots, x_n\}$ is a subset of the variables declared in S, then $S \setminus (x_1, \dots, x_n)$ is a schema. Its signature is that of S with $x_1, \dots, x_n$ removed, and the property is true exactly in those states that are a restriction of a state of S that satisfies the property of S. In general, this can be expressed by taking the original property, existentially quantified over $x_1, \dots, x_n$. E.g. if S is of the form

$$\begin{array}{|l}\hline \_S \\ \hline x : T_1 \\ y : T_2 \\ \hline P(x,y) \\ \hline \end{array}$$

then $S \setminus (x)$ is the schema

$$\begin{array}{|l}\hline y : T_2 \\ \hline \exists x : T_1 \bullet P(x,y) \\ \hline \end{array}$$

The *precondition of a schema* S defining a state transformation is the schema
pre S derived from S by hiding all output variables $x!$ and all variables y' referring to the after state. In our example, we have

pre $MEANA = MEANA \setminus (b', av!)$

which is the schema

$$\begin{array}{|l}\hline b : \text{bag} : Real \\ \hline \exists b' : \text{bag } Real;\ av! : Real \bullet b' = b \land b \neq \emptyset_b \land av! = mean(b) \\ \hline \end{array}$$

Since the precondition requires the existence of a suitable after state, we can
see that Z is a *total correctness formalism* (as is VDM): if the precondition
is satisfied, the operation is guaranteed to terminate in a state satisfying the
postcondition (i.e. the schema's full property).

In many cases, the existential quantification can be eliminated by transforming the property into an equivalent one. In our example, we can derive

$$\begin{array}{|l}\hline \_\text{pre } MEANA \\ \hline b : \text{bag } Real \\ \hline b \neq \emptyset_b \\ \hline \end{array}$$

since *mean* is a total function from nonempty bags to real numbers, and thus
the quantifier vanishes. This means that the precondition only requires a reasonable before state in order to guarantee the existence of a result and an after
state (and hence termination).

A last point we have to mention is the use of *schema names in predicates*.
If a schema name is directly preceded by a quantifier, this is equivalent to a
quantification over all the schema's variables, e.g.

$\forall NonEmptyBagC \bullet P \Leftrightarrow \forall sum : Real; n : \mathbb{N}; elements : \mathbb{N} \bullet P$

If the schema name occurs in a formula, it stands for the predicate in the property part:

$\forall sum : Real; n : \mathbb{N} \bullet \exists elements : \mathbb{N} \bullet NonEmptyBagC$

is equivalent to

$\forall sum : Real; n : \mathbb{N} \bullet \exists elements : \mathbb{N} \bullet n < elements \wedge n \neq 0$

For the sake of completeness, we define the implementations of the operations *ADD* and *MEAN*:

ADDC
$\Delta BagC$
$x? : Real$

$sum' = sum + x?$
$n' = n + 1$

MEANC
$\Xi BagC$
$av! : Real$

$n \neq 0$
$av! = sum/n$

13.1.2 Data Refinement Proof Obligations in Z

Assume an abstract state space *AState* and a concrete state space *CState* with initial states *InitA'* and *InitC'*, respectively. (By convention, initial states are always "after states", and therefore they are decorated with a prime.) Consider an abstract operation *AOp* on *AState* with additional input $x? : X$ and output $y! : Y$.[3] Then the schema for *AOp* is of the following form:

---

[3] This setting can easily be extended: non-existent additional parameters can simply be ignored and several additional variables of the same kind, e.g. several input variables, can be comprised in one record-typed variable.

```
┌─AOp─────────────────────────────────────────────────────
│ ΔAState
│ x? : X
│ y! : Y
│──────────
│
│ ...
└─────────────────────────────────────────────────────────
```

If we want to implement *AOp* by a concrete operation *COp* on *CState* (defined by a similar schema), we first have to set up the connection between the two kinds of states. In Z, this is done with an *abstraction schema Abs*. Its signature is that of *AState* joined with that of *CState*, and the property part contains the characteristic predicate of the desired relation. Note that since *Abs* does not necessarily define a function (in either direction), any kind of relation can be expressed.

In our bag example, we have

```
┌─AbsBagC────────────────────────────────────────────────
│ b : bag Real
│ sum : Real
│ n : ℕ
│──────────
│ sum = Σ_{x∈dom b} x * b(x) ∧ n = Σ_{x∈dom b} b(x)
└─────────────────────────────────────────────────────────
```

Adequacy

The first proof obligation that we encounter is *adequacy*: every abstract state must have at least one concrete counterpart, i.e. *Abs* must define a relation that is total on its range:

$$\forall AState \bullet \exists CState \bullet Abs$$

This proof obligation can be relaxed a little: not every abstract state need be represented; it is sufficient to represent only those that are reachable using *AOp* when starting in an initial state satisfying *InitA'*. This reachability condition should be included in the data invariant (property part) of *AState*.

In our example, we have to prove

$$\forall BagA \bullet \exists BagC \bullet AbsBagC$$

which is equivalent to

$$\forall b : \text{bag } Real \bullet \exists sum : Real; n : \mathbb{N} \bullet$$
$$sum = \sum_{x\in\text{dom} b} x * b(x) \wedge n = \sum_{x\in\text{dom} b} b(x)$$

Correspondence of initial states

The next proof obligation requires that every concrete initial state must represent an abstract initial state:

$$\forall\, CState' \bullet InitC' \Rightarrow (\exists\, AState' \bullet InitA' \wedge Abs')$$

(note the decoration of *Abs*). In our example, we have

$$InitBagA' \;\hat{=}\; [\,b' : \text{bag } Real \mid b' = \emptyset_b\,]$$

$$InitBagC' \;\hat{=}\; [\,sum' : Real;\, n' : \mathbb{N} \mid sum' = 0 \wedge n' = 0\,]$$

and the correspondence is obvious.

Applicability

The third proof obligation corresponds to the *domain rule* of VDM. It concerns the *applicability of the concrete operation*:

$$\forall\, AState;\, CState;\, x? : X \bullet \text{pre } AOp \wedge Abs \Rightarrow \text{pre } COp$$

This says that whenever we are in a concrete state that represents an abstract state satisfying the abstract precondition, then the concrete precondition also holds. The only difference between this rule and the domain rule is the slight difference in the concept of preconditions in VDM and Z.

Similarly to the abstract case, we can derive for the *MEANC* operation

```
┌─ pre MEANC ──────────────────────────────────────────
│  BagC
│  ───────────────
│  n ≠ 0
└──────────────────────────────────────────────────────
```

and the proof is evident.

Correctness

The last proof obligation corresponds to VDM's *result rule* in its general form (cf. Section 12.2.5 starting on page 300). It concerns the *correctness of the concrete operation*:

$$\forall\, AState;\, CState;\, CState';\, x? : X;\, y! : Y \bullet$$
$$\text{pre } AOp \wedge Abs \wedge COp \Rightarrow (\exists\, AState' \bullet Abs' \wedge AOp)$$

In words: Assume that the concrete operation starts in a state that represents an abstract state for which the abstract precondition holds (i.e. termination of the abstract operation is guaranteed). Then every final concrete state must represent a possible final abstract state. Again, the only difference from VDM's rule is the concept of preconditions. Therefore, the kind of simulation that is proven using this rule is the same as in VDM. Hence both are equivalent to L-simulation, provided the abstraction relation is total.

In our *ADD* example, we have no output variable. Therefore, the proof obligation reduces to

$$\forall BagA; BagC; BagC'; x? : \mathbb{N} \bullet$$
$$\text{pre } ADDA \wedge AbsBagC \wedge ADDC \Rightarrow$$
$$(\exists BagA' \bullet AbsBagC' \wedge ADDA)$$

or, in completely expanded form,

$$\forall b : \text{bag } Real; sum, sum' : Real; n, n' : \mathbb{N}; x? : Real \bullet$$
$$sum = \Sigma_{x \in \text{dom} b} x * b(x) \wedge n = \Sigma_{x \in \text{dom} b} b(x) \wedge$$
$$sum' = sum + x? \wedge n' = n + 1 \Rightarrow$$
$$(\exists b' : \text{bag } Real \bullet sum' = \Sigma_{x \in \text{dom} b'} x * b'(x) \wedge n' = \Sigma_{x \in \text{dom} b'} b'(x) \wedge$$
$$b' = b \uplus \{x?\}_b)$$

which again is straightforward to prove.

Functional abstraction relation

In the case of a total and functional abstraction relation, i.e., where we have ($\exists_1$ denoting the unique existential quantifier)

$$\forall CState \bullet \exists_1 AState \bullet Abs$$

the adequacy and applicability conditions remain the same, but the other two conditions become simpler (the existential quantifiers disappear).

Correspondence of initial states is expressed by

$$\forall AState'; CState' \bullet InitC' \wedge Abs \Rightarrow InitA'$$

and correctness of *COp* by

$$\forall AState; AState'; CState; CState'; x? : X; y! : Y \bullet$$
$$\text{pre } AOp \wedge Abs \wedge COp \wedge Abs' \Rightarrow AOp$$

These conditions correspond to the simpler versions of the VDM rules for the case of a functional abstraction relation (cf. Section 12.2.4 beginning on page 297). Consequently, Z does not introduce anything new from the point of view of data refinement when compared with VDM. This explains why we do not consider Z anymore.

13.2 Hehner's Method for Data Refinement

In the preface to his book *A Practical Theory of Programming*, Eric Hehner compares his theory with, amongst others, several methods introduced earlier in this book, namely, Hoare logic, refinement calculus, and VDM.

> The theory in this book is simpler than any of those just mentioned. In it, a specification is just a boolean expression. Refinement is just ordinary implication. This theory is also more general than those just mentioned, applying to both terminating and nonterminating computation, to both sequential and parallel computation, to both stand-alone and interactive computation. [Heh93, p. 1]

As indicated above, Eric Hehner uses predicates to describe specifications, programs, and abstraction relations. To overcome the common problem with specifications and programs of referring to and relating two different states of the same variable in a predicate he sticks to the convention that unprimed/primed variables denote values before/after execution of an operation. For instance, the predicate $x' = x + 1$ expresses the operation $x := x + 1$ (in case x is the only state variable). As in VDM and Z, the decoration convention extends to expressions and predicates. For later reference let $Pred^V_{\mathcal{H}} \stackrel{\text{def}}{=} Pred^{V,V'}$ denote the syntactic class of *Hehner-style predicates* over primed and unprimed versions of variables drawn from some set V.

In Hehner's theory a data type $\mathcal{A}$ can be characterized by defining the following entities (in brackets we name the corresponding notion in our nomenclature):

- the *user's variables* x of type X (normal variables)
- the *implementor's variables* a of type A (representation variables)
- a family $(A_i)_{i \in I} \in (Pred^{xa}_{\mathcal{H}})$ of predicates over primed and unprimed versions of variables x and a (specifications of operations)

Observe that instead of making initialization and finalization operations explicit, Hehner assumes that local variables have arbitrary initial values (of the proper type, however), and that their final values are simply ignored. Formally he realizes this by defining **var** $a : A ; S$ by $\exists a, a' : A (S)$ for $S \in Pred^{xa}_{\mathcal{H}}$. That is, local variables are hidden through an existential quantification over their initial and final values. Observe that, officially, $\exists a, a' : A (S)$ is not an element of $Pred^{x,x'}$ because our quantification is not constrained by a type like A. However, $\exists a, a' : A (S)$ is just an abbreviation for $\exists a, a' (A(a) \wedge A(a') \wedge S)$, where type constant A is interpreted as a function from $\mathbb{V}$ to $\mathbb{B}$ yielding *tt* exactly for those values belonging to the model of type A. As in Part I of this monograph, we ignore such typing in the rest of our treatment of Hehner's method, to simplify the exposition.

By $\mathcal{H}[\![.]\!]^V$ we refer to the relation-valued semantics $C[\![.]\!]^{V,V'}$ of predicates that evaluates unprimed (primed) variables using the first (second) element of a state pair. We abbreviate $\mathcal{H}[\![.]\!]^{x,a}$ to $\mathcal{H}[\![.]\!]^A$ etc.

For $W \subseteq V \subseteq Var$ let Π_W^V denote the graph $\{\ (\sigma,\sigma|_W)\ |\ \sigma \in \Sigma^V\ \}$ of the projection function from Σ^V to Σ^W. Then the meaning of Hehner's implicit initialization and finalization is given by $(\Pi_x^{x,a})^{-1}$ and $\Pi_x^{x,a}$, respectively. This can be seen as follows.

$$(\zeta,\xi) \in \mathcal{H}[\![\exists a, a'\,(S)]\!]^x$$

$$\Leftrightarrow \exists v, w\left(\left(\zeta_{\flat a}^v, \xi_{a'}^w\right) \in \mathcal{H}[\![S]\!]^A\right)$$

$$\Leftrightarrow (\zeta,\xi) \in (\Pi_x^{x,a})^{-1} ; \mathcal{H}[\![S]\!]^A ; \Pi_x^{x,a}$$

Next consider another set of implementor's variables c of type C. To transpose $\mathcal{A}$ such that it uses c in place of a, Hehner suggests [Heh93, p. 116] introducing a *data transformer*, which is a predicate α over a and c such that

$$\forall c\,(\exists a\,(\alpha)) \tag{13.1}$$

In our terminology, $\alpha \in Abs^{AC}$ denotes an abstraction relation which is total on the concrete state space. For the given interpretation of local variable declarations this is equivalent to the initialization condition for L-simulation, $CI \subseteq AI ; \beta$, where, in this case, $CI = (\Pi_x^{x,c})^{-1}$, $AI = (\Pi_x^{x,a})^{-1}$, and $\beta = \mathcal{A}[\![\alpha]\!]^{AC}$:

$$\mathcal{T}[\![\forall c\,(\exists a\,(\alpha))]\!]\text{ᆧ}$$

$\Leftrightarrow$ (definitions from Section 5.2)

$$\forall \sigma \in \Sigma^C \left(\exists \xi \in \Sigma^A \left(\mathcal{T}[\![\alpha]\!]^{Var^A, Var^C}(\xi,\sigma)\right)\right)$$

$\Leftrightarrow$ (mutual implication, "$\Rightarrow$": $x \notin fvar(\alpha)$, Lemma 5.13)

$$\forall \sigma \in \Sigma^C \left(\exists \xi \in \Sigma^A \left((\xi,\sigma) \in \mathcal{A}[\![\alpha]\!]^{AC}\right)\right)$$

$\Leftrightarrow$ (def. of Π)

$$(\Pi_x^{x,c})^{-1} \subseteq (\Pi_x^{x,a})^{-1} ; \mathcal{A}[\![\alpha]\!]^{AC}$$

Hehner's interpretation of block ends implies the L-simulation finalization condition $\beta ; CF \subseteq AF$, where, in this case, $CF = \Pi_x^{x,c}$ and $AF = \Pi_x^{x,a}$:

$$\mathcal{A}[\![\alpha]\!]^{AC} ; \Pi_x^{x,c} \subseteq \Pi_x^{x,a}$$

Regardless of α, this is satisfied as long as its interpretation projected on normal variables is at most the identity relation, which holds by definition of $\mathcal{A}[\![.]\!]^{AC}$ (see Def. 5.15).

How about operations A_i? Hehner suggests transforming each specification predicate A_i to a predicate C_i over x and c, defined by

$$C_i \stackrel{\text{def}}{=} \forall a \left(\alpha \Rightarrow \exists a' \left(\alpha' \wedge A_i \right) \right) \tag{13.2}$$

Next we prove that (13.2) formalizes that C_i expresses the maximal solution to the L-simulation problem from Chapter 7 for abstract operation A_i and abstraction relation α. Let $Y \in Pred^C_{\mathcal{H}}$. We prove that Y refines C_i iff Y L-simulates A_i w.r.t. α:

$$\mathcal{H}[\![Y]\!]^C \subseteq \mathcal{H}[\![C_i]\!]^C$$

$$\Leftrightarrow \mathcal{H}[\![Y]\!]^C \subseteq \mathcal{H}[\![\forall a \left(\alpha \Rightarrow \exists a' \left(\alpha' \wedge A_i \right) \right)]\!]^C \tag{13.2}$$

$$\Leftrightarrow T[\![\forall x, c, x', c' \left(Y \Rightarrow \forall a \left(\alpha \Rightarrow \exists a' \left(\alpha' \wedge A_i \right) \right) \right)]\!]\text{rh} \quad \text{def. of } \mathcal{H}[\![.]\!]$$

$$\Leftrightarrow T[\![\forall x, a, x', c' \left(\exists a \left(\alpha \wedge Y \right) \Rightarrow \exists a' \left(\alpha' \wedge A_i \right) \right)]\!]\text{rh} \quad \text{pred. calc.}$$

$$\Leftrightarrow \mathcal{A}[\![\alpha]\!]^{AC} ; \mathcal{H}[\![Y]\!]^C \subseteq \mathcal{H}[\![A_i]\!]^A ; \mathcal{A}[\![\alpha]\!]^{AC} \quad \text{def. of } \mathcal{H}[\![.]\!]$$

(In steps justified by the definition of $\mathcal{H}[\![.]\!]$ we also used our basic definitions from Section 5.2.) Observe that we did not exploit totality of α in the last proof. The only reason for introducing (13.1) is that Hehner does not use an explicit initialization operation. However, as observed in Section 4.3, one may solve this problem by using data invariants to restrict the concrete state space to some reasonable subspace of Σ^C.

We summarize the analysis in a theorem.

Theorem 13.1 (Hehner's data transformer enforces L-simulation)
If the family $(C_i)_{i \in I}$ of specifications is obtained by applying one of Hehner's data transformers to each of the specifications $(A_i)_{i \in I}$ then this is also a case of L-simulation. ♠

Our basic notion to express specifications is the specification statement; how do Hehner's predicates relate to these leads-to terms? Specifications $\phi \leadsto \psi$ using logical variables x_0 can be easily translated into predicates $S \in Pred^A_{\mathcal{H}}$ using the decoration convention. For the opposite translation we assume fresh logical variables x_0 and a_0. These translations are semantics-preserving maps between two sets of syntactic entities representing binary relations on states, as proved below.

$$t_{\mathcal{H}}(\phi \leadsto \psi) \stackrel{\text{def}}{=} \forall x_0 \left(\phi \Rightarrow \psi[^{x', a'}/_{x,a}] \right) \tag{13.3}$$

$$t^{\mathcal{H}}(S) \stackrel{\text{def}}{=} (x, a = x_0, a_0) \leadsto S[^{x_0, a_0}/_{x,a}][^{x, a}/_{x', a'}] \tag{13.4}$$

Lemma 13.2 $\mathcal{H}[\![t_{\mathcal{H}}(\phi \leadsto \psi)]\!]^A = \mathcal{P}[\![\phi \leadsto \psi]\!]^A$ and $\mathcal{P}[\![t^{\mathcal{H}}(S)]\!]^A = \mathcal{H}[\![S]\!]^A$.

Proof: The first equality is easy. For let $\zeta, \xi \in \Sigma^A$, then

$$(\zeta, \xi) \in \mathcal{H}[\![t_{\mathcal{H}}(\phi \rightsquigarrow \psi)]\!]^A$$

$$\Leftrightarrow (\zeta, \xi) \in \mathcal{H}\left[\!\left[\forall x_0 \left(\phi \Rightarrow \psi[^{x',a'}/_{x,a}]\right)\right]\!\right]^A \qquad (13.3)$$

$$\Leftrightarrow \forall \gamma \left((\gamma, \zeta) \in C[\![\phi]\!]^A \Rightarrow (\gamma, \xi) \in C[\![\psi]\!]^A\right) \qquad \text{def. of } \mathcal{H}[\![.]\!]^A$$

$$\Leftrightarrow (\zeta, \xi) \in \mathcal{P}[\![\phi \rightsquigarrow \psi]\!]^A \qquad \text{Def. 5.18}$$

To prove the second equality we start with its LHS:

$$(\zeta, \xi) \in \mathcal{P}[\![(x, a = x_0, a_0) \rightsquigarrow S[^{x_0,a_0}/_{x,a}][^{x,a}/_{x',a'}]]\!]^A$$

By Def. 5.18:

$$\Leftrightarrow \forall \gamma \left((\gamma, \zeta) \in C[\![x, a = x_0, a_0]\!]^A \Rightarrow (\gamma, \xi) \in C[\![S[^{x_0,a_0}/_{x,a}][^{x,a}/_{x',a'}]]\!]^A\right)$$

Let $\xi' \stackrel{\text{def}}{=} (\xi : x', a' \mapsto \xi(x,a))|_{x',a'}$. Then, by Def. 5.10 and Lemma 5.12,

$$\Leftrightarrow \forall \gamma \left(\begin{array}{l} \gamma(x_0, a_0) = \zeta(x, a) \\ \Rightarrow ((\gamma : x, a \mapsto \gamma(x_0, a_0))|_{x,a}, \xi') \in C[\![S]\!]^{\{x,a\},\{x',a'\}} \end{array}\right)$$

$$\Leftrightarrow (\zeta, \xi') \in C[\![S]\!]^{\{x,a\},\{x',a'\}} \qquad \text{one-point rule}$$

$$\Leftrightarrow (\zeta, \xi) \in \mathcal{H}[\![S]\!]^A \qquad \text{def. of } \mathcal{H}[\![.]\!]^A \qquad \square$$

Hehner's predicate-based set-up together with our translation functions allows a much simpler proof of our L-simulation theorem (Theorem 7.2), which states that $\langle \alpha \rangle (x, a = y_0, b_0) \rightsquigarrow \langle \alpha \rangle \forall x_0 (\phi[^{y_0,b_0}/_{x,a}] \Rightarrow \psi)$ is the least refined program that L-simulates $\pi_1 \rightsquigarrow \pi_2 \in \text{Prog}^A$ w.r.t. $\alpha \in \text{Abs}^{AC}$. (As before, we assume that x are the normal variables for levels A and C, a are the abstract level representation variables, x_0 are the logical variables occurring freely in ϕ or ψ, and y_0 and b_0 are (lists of) fresh logical variables serving to freeze the values of x and a, respectively.)

Alternative proof of Theorem 7.2: We first apply (13.3) to obtain a predicate with the same meaning as $\phi \rightsquigarrow \psi$, and second (13.2) to arrive at the following predicate denoting the maximal relation that is an L-simulation of $\phi \rightsquigarrow \psi$ w.r.t. α.

$$\forall a \left(\alpha \Rightarrow \exists a' \left(\alpha' \wedge \forall x_0 \left(\phi \Rightarrow \psi[^{x',a'}/_{x,a}]\right)\right)\right) \qquad (13.3), (13.2)$$

$$= \forall y_0, b_0 \left(\begin{array}{l} \exists a (\alpha \wedge x, a = y_0, b_0) \\ \Rightarrow \exists a' \left(\alpha' \wedge \forall x_0 \left(\phi[^{y_0,b_0}/_{x,a}] \Rightarrow \psi[^{x',a'}/_{x,a}]\right)\right) \end{array}\right) \qquad \text{pred. calc.}$$

$$= \langle \alpha \rangle (x, a = y_0, b_0) \rightsquigarrow \langle \alpha \rangle \forall x_0 \left(\phi[^{y_0, b_0}/_{x, a}] \Rightarrow \psi \right) \tag{13.3}$$

The last line above corresponds to the leads-to term derived in Theorem 7.2.

□

13.2.1 L^{-1}-simulation in Hehner's set-up

Now that we have seen how simply L-simulation is expressed in Hehner's set-up, we derive an analogue of L^{-1}-simulation in this framework. First we list the L^{-1}-simulation conditions adapted to Hehner's theory.

$$(\Pi_x^{x,c})^{-1} ; \mathcal{A}[\![\alpha]\!]^{CA} \subseteq (\Pi_x^{x,a})^{-1} \tag{init$^{L^{-1}}$}$$

$$\mathcal{H}[\![C_i]\!]^C ; \mathcal{A}[\![\alpha]\!]^{CA} \subseteq \mathcal{A}[\![\alpha]\!]^{CA} ; \mathcal{H}[\![A_i]\!]^A \tag{op$_i^{L^{-1}}$}$$

$$\Pi_x^{x,c} \subseteq \mathcal{A}[\![\alpha]\!]^{CA} ; \Pi_x^{x,a} \tag{fina$^{L^{-1}}$}$$

By $\mathcal{A}[\![\alpha]\!]^{AC} = (\mathcal{A}[\![\alpha]\!]^{CA})^{-1}$ and Lemma 3.9.(ii) ("$^{-1}$" reverses the order of arguments of ";") the initialization condition (init$^{L^{-1}}$) is equivalent to the finalization condition for L-simulation above, $\Pi_x^{x,c} ; \mathcal{A}[\![\alpha]\!]^{CA} \subseteq \Pi_x^{x,a}$, which is a tautology for our definition of $\mathcal{A}[\![.]\!]^{AC}$. Thus (init$^{L^{-1}}$) holds.

Similarly, the finalization condition (fina$^{L^{-1}}$) is equivalent to the initialization condition for L-simulation (init^L) above. Consequently it is equivalent to totality of α. It remains to derive a Hehner-style predicate expression for the least refined concrete operation C_i implementing abstract operation A_i w.r.t. α.

$$Y \subseteq_\alpha^{L^{-1}} A_i$$
$$\Leftrightarrow \forall c, a' \left(\exists c' (\alpha' \wedge Y) \Rightarrow \exists a (\alpha \wedge A_i) \right)$$
$$\Leftrightarrow \forall c, c' \left(Y \Rightarrow \forall a' (\alpha' \Rightarrow \exists a (\alpha \wedge A_i)) \right)$$

Consequently, C_i should be defined as follows.

$$C_i \overset{\text{def}}{=} \forall a' \left(\alpha' \Rightarrow \exists a (\alpha \wedge A_i) \right)$$

Using Lemma 13.2, we generate a new expression for the solution to our L^{-1}-simulation problem from Section 7.3.

We start our derivation with an abstract level specification statement $\phi \rightsquigarrow \psi \in Prog^A$ and an abstraction relation $\alpha \in Abs^{CA}$. The corresponding least L^{-1}-simulation is then expressed by

$$t^{\mathcal{H}} \left(\forall a' (\alpha' \Rightarrow \exists a (\alpha \wedge t_{\mathcal{H}} (\phi \rightsquigarrow \psi))) \right)$$

This is equal to

$$(x, c = y_0, c_0) \rightsquigarrow \left(\forall a' (\alpha' \Rightarrow \exists a (\alpha \wedge t_{\mathcal{H}} (\phi \rightsquigarrow \psi))) \right) [^{y_0, c_0}/_{x,c}][^{x,c}/_{x',c'}]$$

by (13.4). Let us concentrate on the postcondition, which, by Lemma 5.13 and the definition of substitution is the same as

$$\forall a' \left(\alpha[^{a'}/_a] \Rightarrow \exists a \,(\alpha[^{c_0}/_c] \wedge (t_{\mathcal{H}}(\phi \rightsquigarrow \psi))[^{y_0}/_x][^x/_{x'}]) \right) \;.$$

By (13.3) this equals

$$\forall a' \left(\alpha[^{a'}/_a] \Rightarrow \exists a \left(\alpha[^{c_0}/_c] \wedge (\forall x_0 \left(\phi \Rightarrow \psi[^{x',a'}/_{x,a}] \right))[^{y_0}/_x][^x/_{x'}] \right) \right) \;.$$

Hence the final expression for the solution is

$$(x,c = y_0,c_0) \rightsquigarrow \forall a' \left(\alpha[^{a'}/_a] \Rightarrow \exists a \left(\alpha[^{c_0}/_c] \wedge \forall x_0 \left(\phi[^{y_0}/_x] \Rightarrow \psi[^{a'}/_a] \right) \right) \right)$$

This may still be considered an improvement over the expression achieved in Section 7.3, that is,

$$[\alpha] \,\exists x_0 \,(\neg\psi[^{y_0,a_0}/_{x,a}] \wedge \phi) \rightsquigarrow [\alpha] \,(x,a \neq y_0,a_0) \;,$$

because one can argue that the use of negation in the latter is more distracting than the length of the former (especially because the conciseness is mostly due to the use of the box operator).

We close this section with the remark that Hehner's approach to (data) refinement is, as shown above, easily extendible to cover L^{-1}-simulation as well. The introduction of data invariants and/or initialization predicates then yields a stunningly simple and elegant method for data refinement, which is complete.

13.3 Back's Refinement Calculus

In the late 1970s Ralph Back was one of the first to advocate a calculational approach to program and data refinement based on weakest precondition predicate transformer semantics [B78]. To considerable extent his (and his former Ph.D. student Joakim von Wright's) work has determined the content of Chapter 10. So what are the differences between Back and von Wright's and our refinement calculus that are relevant to data refinement?

13.3.1 The Language

In Back's set-up programs are identified with their weakest precondition semantics. The distinction between syntax and semantics is almost suppressed by choosing a syntax that directly reflects the semantic objects in mind, i.e., elements of the complete lattice of predicate transformers (see Chapter 10). In the early years, Back used a language closer to while-programs with non-deterministic assignments [B80, B81b]. He then made the above-mentioned distinction more clearly. Nowadays [BvW90], his basic command language hardly resembles an imperative programming language anymore. On the other hand, a language like our *Prog* can be easily embedded into Back's command language using abbreviations, just as we did in Section 5.3.1 for conditionals and loops. One advantage of choosing such an abstract language is that its weakest precondition semantics is obvious because, e.g., recursion is not explicit in this language but arbitrary meets and joins are. Reasoning about properties of programs written in this language also benefits from its simplicity and power.

It is complete in the sense that any predicate transformer can be expressed in it in a more constructive way than using our version of the powerset construction for predicate transformers (see Lemma 10.55).

For a list v of distinct variables let $\mathsf{P}_v \stackrel{\text{def}}{=} [\Sigma^v \longrightarrow \mathbb{B}]$ denote the set of *semantic predicates* over v. These predicates are ordered by the pointwise extension $\leq$ of the implication order on $\mathbb{B}$. We adapt the semantic notion of a state variant to semantic predicate $P \in \mathsf{P}_v$ such that $P[d/x](\sigma) \stackrel{\text{def}}{=} P(\sigma_x^d)$ for all states $\sigma \in \Sigma^v$, variables $x \in v$, and values d.

Back's command language contains analogues of our guards and assert statements, denoted $\langle u \approx d \rangle$ and $\langle u = d \rangle$, respectively. Each of these tests for equality of the list u of program variable values with one fixed list d of values only. Furthermore there is a local variable declaration and deterministic initialization command $\langle +u := d \rangle$, and a corresponding block ending command $\langle -u \rangle$. These are the basic commands. They can be combined to form more complex commands using sequential composition, as usual, and arbitrary meets and joins of commands. For instance, our guard $x > 0 \rightarrow$ is expressed by $\bigwedge_{v > 0} \langle x \approx v \rangle$.

The following definitions are taken almost verbatim from [BvW90].

Definition 13.3 (Command language) The syntactic category of *commands* with typical element S is defined by:

$$
\begin{aligned}
S ::= \ & \langle u = d \rangle && \textit{(strict test)} \\
| \ & \langle u \approx d \rangle && \textit{(miraculous test)} \\
| \ & \langle +u := d \rangle && \textit{(variable introduction)} \\
| \ & \langle -u \rangle && \textit{(variable elimination)} \\
| \ & S_1 ; S_2 && \textit{(sequential composition)} \\
| \ & \bigwedge_{i \in I} S_i && \textit{(demonic choice)}
\end{aligned}
$$

$$\bigvee_{i \in I} S_i \qquad \text{(angelic choice)}$$

In the above u denotes a list of variables and d a list of values of the same length as u. (Values and constants denoting them are identified here.) I denotes an arbitrary, nonvoid index set.   ♣

Each command can be interpreted as a predicate transformer, depending on the sets of program variables considered as input and output. These sets have to be determined before defining the interpretation of commands.

Definition 13.4 (Arity of commands) The *arity* of commands is given as follows. $S : v \to w$ for a command S and lists of variables v and w means that S has arity $v \to w$.

$$
\begin{aligned}
&\langle u = d \rangle : v \to v &&\text{if } u \subseteq v \\
&\langle u \approx d \rangle : v \to v &&\text{if } u \subseteq v \\
&\langle +u := d \rangle : v \to uv \\
&\langle -u \rangle : uv \to v \\
&S_1 \,;S_2 : v \to w &&\text{if } S_1 : v \to v' \text{ and } S_2 : v' \to w \text{ for some } v' \\
&\bigwedge_{i \in I} S_i : v \to w &&\text{if } S_i : v \to w \text{ for each } i \in I \\
&\bigvee_{i \in I} S_i : v \to w &&\text{if } S_i : v \to w \text{ for each } i \in I
\end{aligned}
$$

By $C_{v \to w}$ we refer to the set of all commands that have arity $v \to w$.   ♣

Observe that if $S : v \to w$ for some command S and two lists of variables v and w, and if v' and w' are lists containing the elements of v and w, respectively, then also $S : v' \to w'$. Hence the arity of a command is not uniquely determined, although the minimal such arity is.

Definition 13.5 (Meaning of commands) The *meaning* of a command $S : v \to w$ is an element of $\text{PT}_{v \leftarrow w}$. Let $\pi \in Pred_w$.

$$
\begin{aligned}
\langle u = d \rangle (\pi) &\overset{\text{def}}{=} (u = d) \wedge \pi \\
\langle u \approx d \rangle (\pi) &\overset{\text{def}}{=} (u = d) \Rightarrow \pi \\
\langle +u := d \rangle (\pi) &\overset{\text{def}}{=} \pi[d/u] \\
\langle -u \rangle (\pi) &\overset{\text{def}}{=} \pi \\
S_1 \,;S_2 (\pi) &\overset{\text{def}}{=} S_1 (S_2(\pi))
\end{aligned}
$$

$$\left(\bigwedge_{i \in I} S_i \right)(\pi) \stackrel{\text{def}}{=} \bigwedge_{i \in I}(S_i(\pi))$$

$$\left(\bigvee_{i \in I} S_i \right)(\pi) \stackrel{\text{def}}{=} \bigvee_{i \in I}(S_i(\pi)) \qquad \clubsuit$$

It is important to realize that not all constructs of this language preserve or satisfy Dijkstra's healthiness conditions for weakest preconditions as listed in Def. 10.10 on page 200.

Corollary 13.6 Commands have the following easily verified properties. (The negative results depend on the reasonable assumption of at least two distinct values in the carrier set.)

(i)   Strict tests are conjunctive and strict but neither disjunctive nor total.
(ii) Miraculous tests are disjunctive and total but neither conjunctive nor strict.
(iii) Variable introduction is strict, total, disjunctive, and conjunctive.
(iv) Variable elimination is strict, total, disjunctive, and conjunctive.
(v)   Sequential composition preserves each of the four properties, provided both arguments satisfy it.
(vi) Demonic choice preserves strictness, conjunctivity, and totality but not necessarily disjunctivity.
(vii) Angelic choice preserves totality, disjunctivity, and strictness but not necessarily conjunctivity. $\qquad \spadesuit$

The core of Back's command language defined above is hardly appropriate for writing programs, but the elements of our language *Prog* are definable in terms of commands (see, e.g., [BvW90]). Since we focus on the data refinement aspects of Back's calculus the details of this definition are omitted here.

13.3.2 Refinement

Back's refinement relation between commands is similar to the one introduced in Chapter 10, that is, for two commands of the same arity $S, T \in C_{v \to w}$ we say that S *is refined by* T (or $S \leq T$) iff

$$\forall \pi \in \mathsf{P}_w \left(S(\pi) \leq T(\pi) \right)$$

holds. That S may be replaced by T in any command context whenever $S \leq T$ holds, follows from monotonicity of the compound constructs of the command language. Back and von Wright call this the *subcommand replacement property*. It is proven by structural induction and generalizes to command contexts for multiple subcommands:

$$\bigwedge_{i=1}^{n}(S_1 \leq T_1) \quad \Rightarrow \quad S(S_1,\dots,S_n) \leq S(T_1,\dots,T_n)$$

Owing to the generality of the command language, refinement is no longer correctly characterized as possibly increasing the domain of termination or decreasing the amount of nondeterminism. Now there are four possible aspects of S that T may improve upon:

- increase the domain of termination ($S(\mathsf{T_P})$)
- decrease the amount of demonic nondeterminism
- increase the domain of miracles ($S(\perp_{\mathsf{P}})$)
- increase the amount of angelic nondeterminism

Note that these four possibilities are not completely independent; for instance, decreasing the amount of demonic nondeterminism to 0 possibilities increases the domain of miracles (or miraculous termination, as we called it in Chapter 8).

The Galois connection from Chapter 10 also applies here.

Theorem 13.7 (Galois connection)

$(\bigstar, [.])$, defined by

$$[.] : R_{\perp}^{v,w} \longrightarrow \mathsf{PT}_{v \leftarrow w}$$

$$[r] \stackrel{\text{def}}{=} \lambda\pi \in \mathsf{P}_w.(\lambda\sigma \in \Sigma^v.\forall\tau \in \Sigma_{\perp}^w ((\sigma,\tau) \in r \Rightarrow \pi(\tau)))$$

$$\bigstar : \mathsf{PT}_{v \leftarrow w} \longrightarrow R_{\perp}^{v,w}$$

$$\bigstar P \stackrel{\text{def}}{=} \{ (\sigma,\tau) \in \Sigma_{\perp}^v \times \Sigma_{\perp}^w \mid \forall\pi \in \mathsf{P}_w (P(\pi)(\sigma) \Rightarrow \pi(\tau)) \}$$

is a Galois connection between $(\mathsf{PT}_{v \leftarrow w}, \leq)$ and $(R_{\perp}^{v,w}, \supseteq)$. Hence, $\bigstar$ and $[.]$ are isomorphisms when restricting $\bigstar$'s domain and $[.]$'s range to the set of conjunctive elements of $\mathsf{PT}_{v \leftarrow w}$. Moreover, $[r]$ is total iff r is weakly terminating, that is, $\forall\sigma \in \Sigma_{\perp}^v ((\sigma, \perp) \in r \Rightarrow \sigma = \perp)$.   ♠

13.3.3 Data Refinement

Recall from Def. 10.48 on page 227 the definition of an inverse of a predicate transformer: Q is an inverse of P iff $id \leq P \,\dot{;}\, Q$ and $Q \,\dot{;}\, P \leq id$. The inverse of a predicate transformer P exists iff P is total and conjunctive; it is denoted by P^{-1}.

The meaning of the inverse of a total and conjunctive command is defined to be the inverse of the command's meaning.

Like Reynolds' method, Back's notion of data refinement focuses on programs, not data types. The starting point is a pair of commands, $A : ax \to ax$ and $C : cx \to cx$, and the question whether C is obtained from A by replacing abstract representation variables, a, by concrete ones, c. To replace A by C as such is not in general useful because of the arity clash. The task is to find *encoding* commands $\alpha : ax \to cx$ and $\beta : ax \to cx$ which are both total and conjunctive such that $A \leq \alpha \,\dot{;}\, C \,\dot{;}\, \beta^{-1}$. We call the strict and disjunctive command β^{-1} a *decoding*. In the sequel we shall study the case $\alpha = \beta$. This case is abbreviated to $A \leq_\alpha C$.

Next observe that Lemma 10.51 applies to commands S and T, and total and conjunctive commands P, that is

$$S \leq T \,\dot{;}\, P^{-1} \quad \Leftrightarrow \quad S \,\dot{;}\, P \leq T \quad \text{and} \quad S \leq P \,\dot{;}\, T \quad \Leftrightarrow \quad P^{-1} \,\dot{;}\, S \leq T$$

Consequently, $A \leq_\alpha C$ is equivalent to $\alpha^{-1} \,\dot{;}\, A \leq C \,\dot{;}\, \alpha^{-1}$. Back's data refinement is thus a case of powersimulation. To be precise, α^{-1} is a special powersimulation, namely, a strict and disjunctive one. As in our discussion of the relationship between simulation and powersimulation following Lemma 10.55 on pp. 230f, it follows that, in case A and C are conjunctive, Back's data refinement condition is equivalent to the L-simulation condition for total correctness applied to the isomorphic images of A, C, and α (in the corresponding domains of total correctness relations).

Theorem 13.8 (Back's data refinement vs. total correctness L-simulation)
Let $A : ax \to ax$ and $C : cx \to cx$ be conjunctive and let $\alpha : ax \to cx$ be total and conjunctive. Then the following equivalence holds.

$$A \leq_\alpha C \quad \Leftrightarrow \quad \star C \subseteq^{\mathsf{L}}_{\star \alpha} \star A$$

Proof:

$A \leq_\alpha C$	
$\Leftrightarrow A \,\dot{;}\, \alpha \leq \alpha \,\dot{;}\, C$	Lemma 10.51
$\Leftrightarrow \star(A \,\dot{;}\, \alpha) \supseteq \star(\alpha \,\dot{;}\, C)$	Th. 13.7, Cor. 13.6.(v)
$\Leftrightarrow \star A \,;\, \star\alpha \supseteq \star\alpha \,;\, \star C$	Lemma 10.18, A, C, and α are conjunctive
$\Leftrightarrow \star C \subseteq^{\mathsf{L}}_{\star\alpha} \star A$	Def. 9.2 $\qquad\qquad \square$

Similarly, we can bridge the gap in the opposite direction.

Theorem 13.9 (Total correctness L-simulation vs. Back's data refinement)
Let $A \in R_\perp^A$ and $C \in R_\perp^C$. Let $\alpha \in R_\perp^{AC}$ be weakly terminating. Then the following equivalence holds.

$$[A] \leq_{[\alpha]} [C] \quad \Leftrightarrow \quad C \subseteq_\alpha^L A$$

Proof:

$$[A] \leq_{[\alpha]} [C]$$

$\Leftrightarrow \star [C] \subseteq_{\star[\alpha]}^L \star [A] \qquad$ Th. 13.8

$\Leftrightarrow C \subseteq_\alpha^L A \qquad\qquad \star[.] = id_{R_\perp}$ by Th. 13.7 and Lemma 10.14.(vii)

$\qquad\qquad\qquad\qquad\qquad\qquad\qquad\qquad\qquad\qquad\qquad\qquad\qquad$ □

As we have seen in Section 10.3.3, the powersimulation constructed in the completeness proof is continuous but not necessarily disjunctive.[4] As a consequence, Back's notion of data refinement is slightly more restrictive than that of provability with powersimulations from Chapter 10. This leads us to the discussion of simulation.

13.3.4 Simulation

In the above, we have apparently confused data refinement as such with simulation as a method for proving data refinement. This is a consequence of the program-centered view of data refinement in Back and von Wright's setup. Thanks to the subcommand replacement property stated above, $T(A) \leq T(\alpha; C; \alpha^{-1})$ holds for arbitrary command contexts T whenever $A \leq_\alpha C$. This generalizes to J-indexed families of commands A and C such that $A_j \leq_\alpha C_j$, for $j \in J$, and a command context T mapping each such family to a command.

As Back and von Wright point out, one is hardly interested in an implementation $T(C)$ of $T(A)$ which is plastered with encodings and decodings. Fortunately, many of them can be removed. Back and von Wright present the following lemma, which is an immediate consequence of the properties of inverses.

Lemma 13.10 ([BvW90])

$$A_1 \leq_\alpha C_1 \wedge A_2 \leq_\alpha C_2 \Rightarrow A_1; A_2 \leq_\alpha C_1; C_2$$

$$\forall i \in I (A_i \leq_\alpha C_i) \Rightarrow \bigwedge_{i \in I} A_i \leq_\alpha \bigwedge_{i \in I} C_i$$

---

[4] Recall that disjunctivity of a predicate transformer P means that P distributes arbitrary nonempty disjunctions, whereas for continuity of P distributing disjunctions of chains is sufficient.

$$\forall i \in I \, (A_i \leq_\alpha C_i) \Rightarrow \bigvee_{i \in I} A_i \leq_\alpha \bigvee_{i \in I} C_i \qquad \spadesuit$$

Our normal operations are called *indifferent commands*. Back and von Wright define them with respect to the encoding command α as those which do not refer to variables referred to by α. This implies that $S \leq_\alpha S$ for S indifferent w.r.t. α. Together with the previous lemma this notion allows one to reduce the amount of encoding and decoding by pushing them to the outside of compound commands.

Exercises

13.1   Redo Example 1.4 in Z.
13.2   Redo the dictionary example from Chapter 12 in Z.

14

Refinement Methods due to
Abadi and Lamport and to Lynch

In Chapter 1 we saw that abstraction relations, rather than abstraction functions, are the natural concept to formulate proof principles for establishing data refinement, i.e., simulation. This impression was reinforced in Chapter 4 by establishing completeness of the combination of L- and L^{-1}-simulation for proving data refinement. How then is it possible that such an apparently practical method as VDM promotes the use of total abstraction functions instead? Notice that in our set-up such functions are the most restrictive version of abstraction relations, because for them the four versions of simulation are all equivalent. Should this not lead to a serious degree of incompleteness, in that it offers a much weaker proof method than L-simulation, which is already incomplete on its own? As we shall see in this chapter this is not necessarily the case. Combining total abstraction functions with so-called auxiliary variables allows the formulation of proof principles which are equal in power to L- and L^{-1}-simulation. Auxiliary variables are program variables to which assignments are added inside a program not for influencing the flow of control but for achieving greater expressiveness in the formulation of abstraction functions and assertions. Following [AL91] such total abstraction functions are called *refinement mappings*. The chances for an abstraction relation (from a concrete data type to an abstract data type) to be functional can be increased by artificially inflating the concrete level state space via the introduction of auxiliary variables on that level.

By recording part of the history of a computation in an auxiliary variable, called a *history variable*, and combining this with refinement mappings, a proof method equivalent to L-simulation is obtained. Analogously, by predicting part of the possible future choices in an auxiliary variable, called a *prophecy variable*, in combination with refinement mappings, a proof method equivalent to L^{-1}-simulation can be formulated. These equivalences were originally established by Bengt Jonsson [Jon91]. Carroll Morgan [Mor88] proved that auxiliary-variable techniques are special cases of powersimulation as introduced in Chapter 10. Because the works of Martín Abadi and Leslie Lamport have been influential in establishing the claim that refinement mappings are well suited for proving refinement between concurrent programs, we shall partly follow their approach in Section 14.1, but adapted to a setting of nondeterministic sequential programs. However, our proof that, whenever data type C refines data type $\mathcal{A}$, this fact can also be proven using the combination of refinement mappings and the auxiliary-variable techniques mentioned above is based on the completeness result of Chapter 4, where we exploit the equivalence between these techniques and L-, respectively, L^{-1}-simulation.[1]

There is also room for an alternative approach, which can be seen as a mixture of simulation and auxiliary-variable techniques. In Section 14.2 we shall see how completeness can be obtained for a method based on L-simulation and prophecy variables. This method is due to Nancy Lynch. She originally used it in [Lyn90] to formulate a theory of refinement for I/O automata, a model for distributed systems introduced by Mark Tuttle in his master's thesis. A minor technical difference between Nancy Lynch's *possibilities mappings* and L-simulation is that she uses functions from concrete states to sets of abstract states whereas we use relations between these state spaces. The two spaces $[\Sigma^C \longrightarrow \mathfrak{P}(\Sigma^A)]$ and $\mathfrak{P}(\Sigma^C \times \Sigma^A)$ are isomorphic, however. (See Example 10.5 on page 197.)

14.1 Auxiliary Variables and Refinement Mappings

In this section we investigate the completeness of simulation with total functions as abstraction relations. A total function that is a simulation relation between a data types C and $\mathcal{A}$ is called a *refinement mapping* from C to $\mathcal{A}$. This definition agrees with the definition given by Abadi and Lamport in [AL91], where refinement mappings are used to prove refinement between state transition systems.

As observed above, merely using refinement mappings does not lead to a complete method; but combined with auxiliary variables they provide a complete proof method for data refinement, as we shall prove in this section. Auxiliary variables are variables used to strengthen the expressive power of assertion languages recording (or prophesying) state changes. No method for proving correctness of concurrent (or distributed) programs is (relatively) complete without them (see e.g. [Owi75, Apt81, Apt83]). The significance of this re-

---

[1] The original completeness proof of Abadi and Lamport is more complex because their method addresses the problem of proving refinement between specifications of concurrent programs, and hence takes fairness into account. This is not necessary within our purely sequential setting.

sult is that the same holds for proving data refinement in a sequential setting, at least when abstraction relations are restricted to (the quite natural notion of) refinement mappings. To this end we use two different types of auxiliary variables, namely *history* and *prophecy variables* [AL91]. In [Jon91] Bengt Jonsson clarified the connection between L- and L^{-1}-simulation on the one hand and auxiliary variables on the other within the framework of fair labelled transition systems.[2] We reformulate this connection in our setting of data types, and prove that refinement mappings when combined with history variables are as powerful as L-simulation and when combined with prophecy variables as powerful as L^{-1}-simulation. An immediate consequence of these results and the ones in Chapter 4, i.e., soundness and completeness of L- and L^{-1}-simulation, is that the combination of refinement mappings with history variables and prophecy variables is sound and complete for proving data refinement.

14.1.1 Refinement Mappings

A refinement mapping is another name for a VDM retrieve function: both express total and functional simulation relations.

Definition 14.1 (Refinement mapping) Let $\mathcal{A}$ and C be two compatible data types; $\mathcal{A} = (AI, (A_j)_{j \in J}, AF)$ and $C = (CI, (C_j)_{j \in J}, CF)$. Abadi and Lamport call our normal and representation variables *external* and *internal*, respectively. A total function f from Σ^C to Σ^A preserving values of external variables $\vec{x}$ is called a *refinement mapping* from C to $\mathcal{A}$ iff the following conditions are satisfied.

$$(\zeta, \sigma) \in CI \Rightarrow (\zeta, f(\sigma)) \in AI \qquad \text{R1}$$

$$(\sigma, \tau) \in C_j \Rightarrow (f(\sigma), f(\tau)) \in A_j \qquad \text{R2}$$

$$(\tau, \xi) \in CF \Rightarrow (f(\tau), \xi) \in AF \qquad \text{R3}$$

♣

Next we prove that refinement mappings are special cases of simulation relations.

Lemma 14.2 If $f : \Sigma^C \longrightarrow \Sigma^A$ is a refinement mapping from C to $\mathcal{A}$ then the graph $\{ (\sigma, f(\sigma)) \mid \sigma \in \Sigma^C \}$ of f is a total and functional U^{-1}-simulation

---

[2] Although he uses the terms forward and backward simulation for L-, respectively, L^{-1}-simulation.

relation, and therefore also an L-, L^{-1}-, and U-simulation relation, between C and $\mathcal{A}$.

Proof: If we identify function f with its graph

- R1 can be reformulated as $CI \subseteq AI ; f^{-1}$,
- for $j \in J$, R2 implies $C_j \subseteq f ; A_j ; f^{-1}$, and
- R3 ensures $CF \subseteq f ; AF$.

Thus, (the graph of) f is a U^{-1}-simulation relation between C and $\mathcal{A}$. Since f is a function, its graph is also an L-, L^{-1}-, and U-simulation relation by Theorem 4.5. To avoid the use of inverses we sometimes resort to the L^{-1}-simulation version of the relational conditions above:

- $CI ; f \subseteq AI$
- $C_j ; f \subseteq f ; A_j$
- $CF \subseteq f ; AF$ □

As an immediate consequence of this lemma and the soundness theorem (Theorem 4.10) we achieve that existence of a refinement mapping proves data refinement.

Corollary 14.3 If there exists a refinement mapping from C to $\mathcal{A}$ then C is a data refinement of $\mathcal{A}$.   ♠

We illustrate the (restricted) power of refinement mappings by variations on Example 2.3.

Example 14.4 Exchange the rôles of abstract and concrete level in Example 2.3, i.e., consider the same two compatible data types $\mathcal{A}$ and C but this time $\mathcal{A}$ is the data type on the concrete level.

$\mathcal{A}$	$=$	$(AI,(A_j)_{j\in\{1,2\}},AF)$	C	$=$	$(CI,(C_j)_{j\in\{1,2\}},CF)$
AI	$=$	$\{(\sigma,a_0)\}$	CI	$=$	$\{(\sigma,c_0)\}$
A_1	$=$	$\{(a_0,a_1),(a_0,a_2)\}$	C_1	$=$	$\{(c_0,c_1)\}$
A_2	$=$	$\{(a_1,a_3),(a_2,a_4)\}$	C_2	$=$	$\{(c_1,c_3),(c_1,c_4)\}$
AF	$=$	$\{(a_3,\tau),(a_4,\rho)\}$	CF	$=$	$\{(c_3,\tau),(c_4,\rho)\}$

We omit the details of normal and representation variables. Just assume that if two states have the same index, for instance, a_3 and c_3, then they agree on the values of normal variables. In addition, a_1 and a_2 agree on normal but differ on representation variables. With Abadi and Lamport's notion of external vs. internal this fact can be described as: the two states are *externally* equal but *internally* different. Define the total function f from the concrete

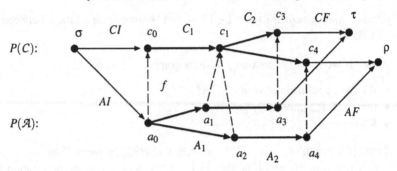

Fig. 14.1. A refinement mapping.

state space $\{a_0, a_1, a_2, a_3, a_4\}$ to the abstract one $\{c_0, c_1, c_3, c_4\}$ by enumeration of its graph.

$$f \stackrel{\text{def}}{=} \{(a_0, c_0), (a_1, c_1), (a_2, c_1), (a_3, c_3), (a_4, c_4)\}$$

R1–R3 obviously hold; thus f is a refinement mapping from $\mathcal{A}$ to C. See Figure 14.1 for a state transition diagram of a typical pair of programs, namely, $CI; C_1; C_2; CF$ and $AI; A_1; A_2; AF$.   ♡

Refinement mappings on their own are too weak to prove every data refinement correct. Example 2.3 differs from Example 14.4 in that the rôles of $\mathcal{A}$ and C are interchanged, and that we proved that no L-simulation relation exists in that case. In particular, there does not exist such a relation which is in addition total and functional. Hence, refinement mappings also fail to prove Example 2.3 correct.

We give another example to demonstrate incompleteness of refinement mappings. In this case no L^{-1}-simulation relation exists between C and $\mathcal{A}$ although an L-simulation exists, whereas in Example 2.3 no L-simulation exists although an L^{-1}-simulation exists. Since refinement mappings are both L- and L^{-1}-simulation relations, non-existence of a refinement mapping follows from non-existence of either kind of simulation relation.

Example 14.5 As another variation on Example 2.3, read the two data types (repeated in Example 14.4) from right to left, i.e., consider the following two compatible data types based on those defined in Example 2.3. (See Figure 14.2.)

$$\begin{array}{rcl|rcl}
\mathcal{B} & = & (BI, (B_j)_{j\in\{1,2\}}, BF) & \mathcal{D} & = & (DI, (D_j)_{j\in\{1,2\}}, DF) \\
\hline
BI & = & AF^{-1} & DI & = & CF^{-1} \\
B_1 & = & A_1^{-1} & D_1 & = & C_1^{-1} \\
B_2 & = & A_2^{-1} & D_2 & = & C_2^{-1} \\
BF & = & AI^{-1} & DF & = & CI^{-1}
\end{array}$$

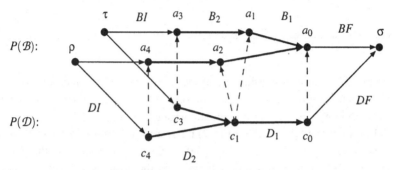

Fig. 14.2. No refinement mapping possible in c_1.

The symmetry between L- and L^{-1}-simulation explains why there does not exist an L^{-1}-simulation relation that proves data refinement between $\mathcal{D}$ and $\mathcal{B}$. Again, refinement mappings fail to prove that $\mathcal{D}$ is a data refinement of $\mathcal{B}$ because refinement mappings are also special cases of L^{-1}-simulation relations. ♡

In both examples, 2.3 and 14.5, the reason for non-existence of a refinement mapping is that two externally equal but internally different abstract states are represented by a single concrete state. Therefore, the intended relation between concrete and abstract state space is non-functional. The difference between these two examples lies in the direction in which one has to look to find the cause for the non-functionality.

In Example 2.3 (see Figure 14.3) one has to look to the right of the current position in the computation graphs to find out that the abstract level has revealed the internal difference — it is now externally visible, i.e., reflected in the normal variables — and the concrete level offers a similar nondeterministic choice. Looking to the right of the current position in the computation depicted in Figure 14.3 coincides with predicting the future of the computation.

One might say that in Figure 14.3 the nondeterministic choice at the abstract level has been postponed for some step at the concrete level, but this choice is still made. Consequently, a refinement mapping would have to guess the value

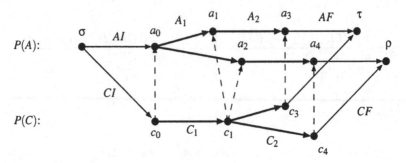

Fig. 14.3. No refinement mapping possible in c_1.

returned by the nondeterministic abstract operation. But since the concrete level nondeterminism is resolved later (by further operations) any guess made by a refinement mapping is potentially wrong.

In Example 14.5 (see Figure 14.2) the reason for non-existence of a refinement mapping is to be sought to the left of the current position in the abstract and concrete level computation graphs. At the abstract level two branches starting in two different states, a_1 and a_2, end in the same state, a_0, while at the concrete level these two branches are represented by a single branch. Consequently, a refinement mapping would have to separate these branches, which cannot be done by a refinement mapping. Looking to the left from a position in the computation graph depicted in Figure 14.2 can be interpreted as recalling the past, i.e., the history, of the computation.

Abadi and Lamport's solution to these problems is to artificially inflate the concrete level state space by introducing auxiliary representation variables such that a refinement mapping can be found. Auxiliary variables do not influence the flow of control; they are allowed only in programs occurring as intermediate levels of refinement proofs. They are not intended to occur within real implementations since that would waste computational resources.

The problem illustrated in Example 2.3 is solved by introducing *prophecy variables*, the one of Example 14.5 by *history variables*. These two classes of auxiliary variables are introduced in the following two sections.

14.1.2 History Variables

Intuitively, history variables are added to a data type in order to duplicate concrete states that represent different abstract states, on the basis of different computation histories. Using this technique of duplication of states, joined branches are separated.

In Example 14.5 state c_1 has two different occurrences. One is due to application of D_2 to c_3, and the other to application of D_2 to c_4. If we add a second component to c_1 to distinguish these occurrences on the basis of different computation histories, the previously joined branches (c_3, c_1) and (c_4, c_1) become separated.

In the following we give a formal definition of adding a history variable to a data type and prove that the resulting data type is equivalent to the original one.

Definition 14.6 (History variable) The data type $C^h = (CI^h, (C_j^h)_{j \in J}, CF^h)$ is obtained from $C = (CI, (C_j)_{j \in J}, CF)$ by adding a *history variable* iff the following conditions are satisfied:

$$\Sigma^h \subseteq \Sigma^C \times \Sigma_h \qquad \text{(for some state space } \Sigma_h) \qquad\qquad \text{H1}$$

$$CI^h ; \Pi_1 = CI \qquad \text{(where } \Pi_1 \text{ denotes the projection from } \Sigma^h \text{ to } \Sigma^C) \qquad \text{H2}$$

$$((s,h),(s',h')) \in C_j^h \Rightarrow (s,s') \in C_j \qquad\qquad \text{H3}$$

$$(s,s') \in C_j \wedge (s,h) \in \Sigma^h \Rightarrow \exists h' \left((s',h') \in \Sigma^h \wedge ((s,h),(s',h')) \in C_j^h \right) \qquad \text{H4}$$

$$\Pi_1 ; CF = CF^h \qquad\qquad \text{H5}$$

♣

The first condition says that we add an extra state component. Condition H2 expresses that the initialization should coincide after projection on the original component with the original initialization on the Σ^C-components. Condition H3 is equivalent to $\Pi_1^{-1} ; C_j^h ; \Pi_1 \subseteq C_j$, i.e., C_j^h U-simulates C_j w.r.t. Π_1, which is by Theorems 4.5 and 4.7 equivalent to C_j^h L^{-1}-simulates C_j w.r.t. Π_1, since Π_1 is total and functional. Condition H4 is equivalent to $\Pi_1 ; C_j \subseteq C_j^h ; \Pi_1$, i.e., C_j L-simulates C_j^h w.r.t. Π_1^{-1}. Condition H5 states that finalization of the resulting data type is essentially the finalization of the original one.

Intuitively, a companion component is added to Σ^C, which is properly initialized (H1 and H2), records (to a certain extent) the history of the computation as "time" moves forward (H4), does not influence the flow of control (H3), and disappears at the end of the computation by a projection (H5). The word "forward" in this account helps one to remember that adding history variables at the concrete level is, as we shall see, equivalent to L-simulation, which is also called forward simulation. (This equivalence is established in Theorem 14.12.)

In the following lemmas we prove that C L-simulates C^h w.r.t. Π_1^{-1} and C^h L^{-1}-simulates C w.r.t. Π_1, implying that C refines C^h, and C^h refines C, i.e., C and C^h are equivalent.

Lemma 14.7 If C^h is obtained from C by adding a history variable then C L-simulates C^h w.r.t. Π_1^{-1}.

Proof: The only interesting point to prove is $\Pi_1 ; C_j \subseteq A_j^h ; \Pi_1$, for $j \in J$. Let $((s,h),s') \in \Pi_1 ; C_j$. Then $(s,h) \in \Sigma^h$ and $(s,s') \in C_j$. Thus, by H4, there exists h' such that $(s',h') \in \Sigma^h$ and $((s,h),(s',h')) \in C_j^h$. Thus, $((s,h),s') \in C_j^h ; \Pi_1$.

□

Lemma 14.8 If C^h is obtained from C by adding a history variable then C^h L^{-1}-simulates C w.r.t. Π_1.

Proof: The only interesting point is to prove $C_j^h ; \Pi_1 \subseteq \Pi_1 ; C_j$, for $j \in J$. Let $((s,h),s') \in C_j^h ; \Pi_1$. Then there exists $h' \in \Sigma_h$ such that $((s,h),(s',h')) \in C_j^h$. Thus, by condition H3, $(s,s') \in C_j$. Consequently $((s,h),s') \in \Pi_1 ; C_j$.   □

Example 14.9 Let us reconsider Example 14.5. We add a history variable to $\mathcal{D}$ to achieve a new data type $\mathcal{D}^h = (DI^h, (D_j^h)_{j \in \{1,2\}}, DF^h)$ and give a refinement mapping from $\mathcal{D}^h$ to $\mathcal{B}$.

We define the extra component as an element of Σ^C.

$$\Sigma^h \stackrel{\text{def}}{=} \{(c_3,c_3),(c_4,c_4),(c_1,c_3),(c_1,c_4),(c_0,c_0)\}$$

Then $\Sigma^h \subseteq \Sigma^C \times \Sigma^C$, i.e., condition H1 is satisfied. Define the initialization by

$$DI^h \stackrel{\text{def}}{=} \{(\tau,(c_3,c_3)),(\rho,(c_4,c_4))\} \ .$$

Then $DI^h ; \Pi_1 = \{(\tau,c_3),(\rho,c_4)\} = DI$. Thus condition H2 is satisfied. The operations of $\mathcal{D}^h$ are defined as follows.

$$D_2^h \stackrel{\text{def}}{=} \{((c_4,c_4),(c_1,c_4)),((c_3,c_3),(c_1,c_3))\}$$
$$D_1^h \stackrel{\text{def}}{=} \{((c_1,c_4),(c_0,c_0)),((c_1,c_3),(c_0,c_0))\}$$

Since $(c_4,c_1) \in D_2$ and $(c_3,c_1) \in D_2$, condition H3 is satisfied for $j = 2$. It is easy to see that condition H3 for $j = 1$ and condition H4 for both operations are satisfied, too. Finalization DF^h of $\mathcal{D}^h$ is defined next such that condition H5 is satisfied.

$$DF^h \stackrel{\text{def}}{=} \{((c_0,c_0),\sigma)\}$$

Thus, $\mathcal{D}^h$ is obtained from $\mathcal{D}$ by adding a history variable. Now it is easy to see that the mapping $f : \Sigma^h \longrightarrow \Sigma^A$

$$f = \{((c_3,c_3),a_3),((c_4,c_4),a_4),((c_1,c_3),a_1),((c_1,c_4),a_2),((c_0,c_0),a_0)\}$$

is a refinement mapping from $\mathcal{D}^h$ to $\mathcal{B}$ since conditions R1–R3 are satisfied. (See Figure 14.4.)   ♡

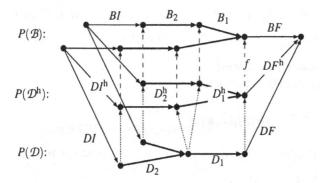

Fig. 14.4. After adding a history variable to $\mathcal{D}$ there exists a refinement mapping to $\mathcal{B}$.

In the next lemma we prove that, if *"C* refines $\mathcal{A}$*"* can be proven by

(i) adding a history variable to C, leading to C^h, and

(ii) proving the existence of a refinement mapping from C^h to $\mathcal{A}$,

then it can be proven using L-simulation.

Lemma 14.10 *If* C^h *is obtained from* C *by adding a history variable and* f *is a refinement mapping from* C^h *to* $\mathcal{A}$ *then* C *L-simulates* $\mathcal{A}$ *w.r.t.* $\Pi_1^{-1}; f$.

Proof: C L-simulates C^h w.r.t. Π_1^{-1} by Lemma 14.7. C^h L-simulates $\mathcal{A}$ w.r.t. f by Lemma 14.2. Hence, by Cor. 4.4, C L-simulates $\mathcal{A}$ w.r.t. $\Pi_1^{-1}; f$. $\qquad\square$

In the next lemma we prove that if *"C* refines $\mathcal{A}$*"* can be proven using L-simulation then it can be proven by adding a history variable to C and giving a refinement mapping from C^h to $\mathcal{A}$.

Lemma 14.11 *If* C *L-simulates* $\mathcal{A}$ *w.r.t.* $\alpha \subseteq \Sigma^C \times \Sigma^A$ *then there exist a data type* C^h *obtained from* C *by adding a history variable, and a refinement mapping from* C^h *to* $\mathcal{A}$.

Proof: We first define a data type C^h, prove that C^h is obtained from C by adding a history variable, and then define a refinement mapping from C^h to $\mathcal{A}$.

The data type C^h has abstract states added as an extra component to C's concrete states. The state space of C^h is defined by $\Sigma^h \stackrel{\text{def}}{=} \alpha$. Obviously, condition H1 is satisfied. The initialization of C^h is defined by

$$CI^h \stackrel{\text{def}}{=} \left\{ \left(s, (s', h')\right) \mid (s, s') \in CI \wedge (s', h') \in \alpha \wedge (s, h') \in AI \right\} \ .$$

Obviously, $CI^h ; \Pi_1 \subseteq CI$. On the other hand, since $CI \subseteq AI ; \alpha^{-1}$, we have

$$CI \subseteq \{ (s,s') \mid \exists h' ((s,h') \in AI \land (s',h') \in \alpha) \land (s,s') \in CI \} = CI^h ; \Pi_1 \ .$$

Thus, condition H2 is satisfied.

For $j \in J$, we define operation C_j^h by

$$C_j^h \stackrel{\text{def}}{=} \left\{ ((s,h),(s',h')) \; \middle| \; \begin{array}{l} (s,s') \in C_j \land (h,h') \in A_j \\ \land (s,h) \in \alpha \land (s',h') \in \alpha \end{array} \right\} \ .$$

Obviously, condition H3 is satisfied. We now prove condition H4.

$$\begin{aligned}
& (s,s') \in C_j \land (s,h) \in \Sigma^h \\
\Leftrightarrow \ & (s,s') \in C_j \land (s,h) \in \alpha \\
\Rightarrow \ & (h,s') \in A_j ; \alpha^{-1} \land (s,s') \in C_j \land (s,h) \in \alpha \ , \text{ since } \alpha^{-1} ; C_j \subseteq A_j ; \alpha^{-1} \\
\Rightarrow \ & \exists h' ((h,h') \in A_j \land (s',h') \in \alpha \land (s,s') \in C_j \land (s,h) \in \alpha) \\
\Leftrightarrow \ & \exists h' \left((s',h') \in \Sigma^h \land ((s,h),(s',h')) \in C_j^h \right)
\end{aligned}$$

The finalization of C^h is defined by

$$CF^h \stackrel{\text{def}}{=} \{ ((s,h),s') \mid (s,s') \in CF \land (s,h) \in \alpha \} \ .$$

Then $\Pi_1 ; CF = CF^h$ holds. It remains to define a refinement mapping from C^h to $\mathcal{A}$. Our candidate is the projection function $\Pi_2 : \Sigma^h \longrightarrow \Sigma^A$ that maps (s,h) to h. Obviously, Π_2 is a total function. We now check conditions R1–R3.

R1 follows from

$$\begin{aligned}
CI^h ; \Pi_2 &= \left\{ (s,h') \; \middle| \; \exists s' \left((s,(s',h')) \in CI^h \land (s',h') \in \alpha \right) \right\} \\
&= \{ (s,h') \mid \exists s' \, ((s,s') \in CI \land (s',h') \in \alpha \land (s,h') \in AI) \} \\
&\subseteq AI
\end{aligned}$$

Condition R2 follows from the definition of C_j^h. Condition R3 follows from

$$\begin{aligned}
CF^h &= \{ ((s,h),s') \mid (s,h) \in \alpha \land (s,s') \in CF \} \\
&\subseteq \{ ((s,h),s') \mid \exists s'' \, ((s'',h) \in \alpha \land (s'',s') \in CF \land (s,h) \in \alpha) \} \\
&= \{ ((s,h),s') \mid (h,s') \in \alpha^{-1} ; CF \land (s,h) \in \alpha \} \\
&\subseteq \{ ((s,h),s') \mid (h,s') \in AF \land (s,h) \in \alpha \} \ , \text{ by } \alpha^{-1} ; CF \subseteq AF \\
&= \Pi_2 ; AF \hspace{6cm} \square
\end{aligned}$$

Combining Lemmas 14.10 and 14.11 leads to:

Theorem 14.12

Let C and $\mathcal{A}$ be compatible data types. "C refines $\mathcal{A}$" can be proven using

L-simulation iff there exist a data type C^h obtained from C by adding a history variable and a refinement mapping from C^h to $\mathcal{A}$. ♠

14.1.3 Prophecy Variables

Intuitively, prophecy variables are added at the concrete level in order to guess now which values will be returned at the abstract level in the future by a non-deterministic operation.

In the following we give a formal definition of adding a prophecy variable to a data type and prove that the resulting data type is equivalent to the original one.

Definition 14.13 (Prophecy variable) Data type $C^p = (CI^p, (C_j^p)_{j \in J}, CF^p)$ is obtained from data type $C = (CI, (C_j)_{j \in J}, CF)$ by adding a *prophecy variable* iff the following conditions are satisfied:

$$\Sigma^p \subseteq \Sigma^C \times \Sigma_p \quad \text{(for some state space } \Sigma_p) \tag{P1}$$

$$CI^p = CI ; \Pi_1^{-1} \quad \text{(where } \Pi_1 \text{ denotes the projection from } \Sigma^p \text{ to } \Sigma^C) \tag{P2}$$

$$((s,p),(s',p')) \in C_j^p \Rightarrow (s,s') \in C_j \tag{P3}$$

$$(s,s') \in C_j \wedge (s',p') \in \Sigma^p \Rightarrow \exists p \left((s,p) \in \Sigma^p \wedge ((s,p),(s',p')) \in C_j^p \right) \tag{P4}$$

$$CF = \Pi_1^{-1} ; CF^p \tag{P5}$$

♣

The main difference between the definitions of history and prophecy variable is that, since P4 is equivalent to $C_j ; \Pi_1^{-1} \subseteq \Pi_1^{-1} ; C_j^p$, condition P4 expresses that C_j L^{-1}-simulates C_j^p, whereas condition H4 in the definition of history variables is equivalent to C_j L-simulates C_j^h.

Again, a companion component is added to Σ^C. However, the difference between this component and a history variable is that this component records changes which will be made in the future, since, for a given computation, condition P4 stipulates that it provides at present (i.e., the stage connected with s) in p the information about what will happen in the future (stage s' where information p' is already available). I.e., the Σ_p component follows the computation in a backward direction. Condition P3 states, as we have seen before, that the prophecy component does not influence the flow of control (i.e., is an auxiliary variable).

Conditions P2 and P5 reflect the intuition that prophecy variables can be thought of as history variables for which the direction of computation has been reversed, i.e., flows from the future towards the past. Consequently, P2 should look like H5, and P5 like H2. This can be seen as follows. Reversing the flow of computation for a given data type $C = (CI, (C_j)_{j \in J}, CF)$ yields another data type, $C^{-1} \stackrel{\text{def}}{=} (CF^{-1}, (C_j^{-1})_{j \in J}, CI^{-1})$; in particular, this reversal turns (the relational inverse of) an initialization into a finalization and vice versa. Now condition P2 for C and C^p is equivalent to condition H5 for C^{-1} and $(C^p)^{-1}$:

$$CI^p = CI ; \Pi_1^{-1} \qquad\qquad \text{P2}$$
$$\Leftrightarrow (CI^p)^{-1} = (CI ; \Pi_1^{-1})^{-1}$$
$$\Leftrightarrow (CI^p)^{-1} = \Pi_1 ; CI^{-1} \qquad \text{— this is H5 for } C^{-1} \text{ and } (C^p)^{-1}$$

A similar argument shows the correspondence between P5 and H2. The word "backward" in this account helps one to remember that adding a prophecy variable at the concrete level is, as we shall see in Theorem 14.19, equivalent to L^{-1}-simulation, which is also called backward simulation in the literature.

In the following lemmas we prove that C L^{-1}-simulates C^p w.r.t. Π_1^{-1} and that C^p L-simulates C w.r.t. Π_1. This implies that C and C^p are equivalent.

Lemma 14.14 If C^p is obtained from C by adding a prophecy variable then C L^{-1}-simulates C^p w.r.t. Π_1^{-1}.

Proof: The only interesting point is to prove $C_j ; \Pi_1^{-1} \subseteq \Pi_1^{-1} ; C_j^p$, for $j \in J$.

Let $(s, (s', p')) \in C_j ; \Pi_1^{-1}$. Then $(s', p') \in \Sigma^p$ and $(s, s') \in C_j$. Thus, by condition P4, there exists $p \in \Sigma_p$ such that $(s, p) \in \Sigma^p$ and $((s, p), (s', p')) \in C_j^p$. Thus $(s, (s', p')) \in \Pi_1^{-1} ; C_j^p$. $\qquad\qquad\square$

Lemma 14.15 If C^p is obtained from C by adding a prophecy variable then C^p L-simulates C w.r.t. Π_1.

Proof: The only interesting point is to prove $\Pi_1^{-1} ; C_j^p \subseteq C_j ; \Pi_1^{-1}$, for $j \in J$.

Let $(s, (s', p')) \in \Pi_1^{-1} ; C_j^p$. Then there exists $p \in \Sigma^p$ s.t. $((s, p), (s', p')) \in C_j^p$. Thus, by condition P3, $(s, s') \in C_j$. This implies $(s, (s', p')) \in C_j ; \Pi_1^{-1}$. $\qquad\square$

Example 14.16 Let C and $\mathcal{A}$ be defined as in Example 14.4. (See Figure 14.3.) We demonstrate how one can use a prophecy variable and a refinement mapping to prove that C refines $\mathcal{A}$. We define the extra component added to Σ^C to be Σ^A, and define $\Sigma^p \subseteq \Sigma^C \times \Sigma^A$ by

$$\Sigma^p \stackrel{\text{def}}{=} \{(c_0, c_0), (c_1, c_3), (c_1, c_4), (c_3, c_3), (c_4, c_4)\}$$

such that condition P1 is trivially satisfied. The constituents of C^p are defined as the relational inverses of the corresponding operations of $\mathcal{D}^h$ in Example 14.9, just as the constituents of $\mathcal{D}$ are inverses of components of C.

$$CI^p \overset{\text{def}}{=} \{(\sigma,(c_0,c_0))\} \qquad\qquad (= (DF^h)^{-1})$$

$$C_1^p \overset{\text{def}}{=} \{((c_0,c_0),(c_1,c_3)),((c_0,c_0),(c_1,c_4))\} \quad (= (D_1^h)^{-1})$$

$$C_2^p \overset{\text{def}}{=} \{((c_1,c_3),(c_3,c_3)),((c_1,c_4),(c_4,c_4)),\} \quad (= (D_2^h)^{-1})$$

$$CF^p \overset{\text{def}}{=} \{((c_3,c_3),\tau),((c_4,c_4),\rho)\} \qquad (= (DI^h)^{-1})$$

One can easily check that conditions P1–P5 are satisfied. One notes that if we forget about the Σ^C-components in Σ^p, C_j^p and A_j are identical, for $j \in \{1,2\}$. This suggests that we take the projection on Σ^A as refinement mapping.

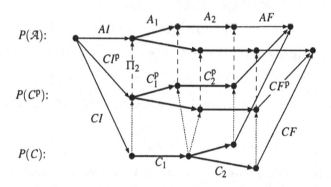

Fig. 14.5. After adding a prophecy variable to C there exists a refinement mapping to $\mathcal{A}$.

The reader can easily check that the projection function $\Pi_2 : \Sigma^p \longrightarrow \Sigma^A$ (defined by $\Pi_2(s,p) = p$) is a refinement mapping from C^p to $\mathcal{A}$. Thus, we proved "C refines $\mathcal{A}$" by adding a prophecy variable to C, obtaining C^p, and giving a refinement mapping from C^p to $\mathcal{A}$. (See Figure 14.5.)   ♡

In the next lemma we prove that L^{-1}-simulation is at least as powerful as the combination consisting of prophecy variables and refinement mappings.

Lemma 14.17 If C^p is obtained from C by adding a prophecy variable and f is a refinement mapping from C^p to $\mathcal{A}$ then $C\ L^{-1}$-simulates $\mathcal{A}$ w.r.t. $\Pi_1^{-1};f$.

Proof: $C\ L^{-1}$-simulates C^p w.r.t. Π_1^{-1} by Lemma 14.14. $C^p\ L^{-1}$-simulates $\mathcal{A}$ w.r.t. f by Lemma 14.2. Hence, by Cor. 4.4, $C\ L^{-1}$-simulates $\mathcal{A}$ w.r.t. $\Pi_1^{-1};f$.

□

Next we prove that the combination of prophecy variables with refinement mappings is at least as powerful as L^{-1}-simulation, i.e., whenever "C refines $\mathcal{A}$" can be proven with L^{-1}-simulation, it can be proven by adding a prophecy variable to C and proving the existence of a refinement mapping from C^p to $\mathcal{A}$.

Lemma 14.18 If C L^{-1}-simulates $\mathcal{A}$ w.r.t. α then there exist a data type C^p obtained from C by adding a prophecy variable, and a refinement mapping from C^p to $\mathcal{A}$.

Proof: We first define a data type C^p, prove that C^p is obtained from C by adding a prophecy variable, and then give a refinement mapping from C^p to $\mathcal{A}$. The data type C^p is defined as follows.

$$\Sigma^p \overset{\text{def}}{=} \left\{ (s,p) \mid s \in \Sigma^C \wedge p \in \Sigma^A \wedge (s,p) \in \alpha \right\}$$

$$CI^p \overset{\text{def}}{=} \left\{ (s,(s',p')) \mid (s,s') \in CI \wedge (s',p') \in \alpha \wedge (s,p') \in AI \right\}$$

$$C_j^p \overset{\text{def}}{=} \left\{ ((s,p),(s',p')) \mid (s,s') \in C_j \wedge (p,p') \in A_j \wedge \{(s,p),(s',p')\} \subseteq \alpha \right\}$$

$$CF^p \overset{\text{def}}{=} \left\{ ((s,p),s') \mid (s,s') \in CF \wedge (s,p) \in \alpha \wedge (p,s') \in AF \right\}$$

Obviously, condition P1 is satisfied. Let us check condition P2. From $CI ; \alpha \subseteq AI$ it follows that

$$CI ; \Pi_1^{-1} = \left\{ (s,(s',p')) \mid (s,s') \in CI \wedge (s',p') \in \alpha \right\} = CI^p \ ,$$

so that condition P2 is satisfied. Condition P3 is trivially fulfilled, and condition P4 follows by $C_j ; \alpha \subseteq \alpha ; A_j$. Finally consider condition P5.

$$\begin{aligned}
\Pi_1^{-1} ; CF^p &= \left\{ (s,s') \mid \exists p\, ((s,p) \in \alpha \wedge ((s,p),s') \in CF^p) \right\} \\
&= \left\{ (s,s') \mid \exists p\, ((s,p) \in \alpha \wedge (s,s') \in CF \wedge (p,s') \in AF) \right\} \\
&= CF \ , \text{ since } CF \subseteq \alpha ; AF
\end{aligned}$$

The projection $\Pi_2 : \Sigma^p \longrightarrow \Sigma^A$ onto the second component of Σ^p is taken as the refinement mapping. This is a total function and conditions R1–R3 are checked easily.   □

Combining Lemmas 14.17 and 14.18 leads to the following result:

Theorem 14.19
Let C and $\mathcal{A}$ be compatible data types. "C refines $\mathcal{A}$" can be proven using L^{-1}-simulation iff there exist a data type C^p obtained from C by adding a prophecy variable and a refinement mapping from C^p to $\mathcal{A}$.   ♠

Example 14.20 ([AL91, GM93]) Consider two compatible data types $\mathcal{A}$ and C with just a single operation (apart from initialization and finalization, of course). There is just a single normal variable, i, ranging over $N_{<10}$, i.e., the natural numbers less than 10. On the abstract level there is a representation variable j of the same type as i, whereas on the concrete level only a Boolean-valued representation variable b is present. As usual in examples, we simplify the exposition by identifying states with tuples of values such that values of normal variables come first. For instance, $\zeta \in \Sigma^A$ is identified with $(\zeta(i), \zeta(j))$ and so forth.

$$\mathcal{A} = (AI, A_1, AF) \text{ , where:}$$
$$AI = \{ (0, (0, m)) \mid m \in N_{<10} \}$$
$$A_1 = \{ ((n, m+1), (n+1, m)) \mid n, m \in N_{<9} \}$$
$$\cup \{ ((n, 0), (n, 0)) \mid n \in N_{<10} \}$$
$$AF = \{ ((n, m), n) \mid n, m \in N_{<10} \}$$

Thus, if the initial value of j is $m \in N_{<10}$, then the first m calls of operation A_1 will increment i but further calls will have no effect. The nondeterministic initialization of j determines in advance how many increments can occur. (See Figure 14.6.)

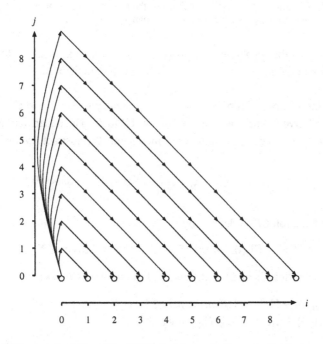

Fig. 14.6. The graph of AI and A_1. (AF is just the projection onto the first component.) All upward arrows belong to AI, and all downward arrows to A_1.

$$C = (CI, C_1, CF) \text{ , where:}$$
$$CI = \{ (0, (0, v)) \mid v \in \mathbb{B} \}$$
$$C_1 = \{ ((n, f\!f), (n+1, f\!f)) \mid n \in \mathbb{N}_{<9} \}$$
$$\cup \{ ((n, v), (n, t\!t)) \mid n \in \mathbb{N}_{<10} \wedge v \in \mathbb{B} \}$$
$$CF = \{ ((n, v), n) \mid n \in \mathbb{N}_{<10} \wedge v \in \mathbb{B} \}$$

If b is $f\!f$ and $0 \leq i < 9$ then C_1 might increment i and preserve the value of b, or might not increment i and set b to $t\!t$. But once b becomes $t\!t$, further calls have no effect. (See Figure 14.7.)

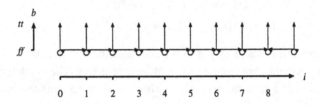

Fig. 14.7. The graph of CI and C_1. (CF is just the projection onto the first component.) Horizontal arrows increase i; vertical arrows change b from $f\!f$ to $t\!t$.

The observable behavior of a program $P(A)$ over $\mathcal{A}$ is identical to that of $P(C)$. Both increment i to some value less than 10 and then start behaving like **skip**.

In order to prove C refines $\mathcal{A}$ we add a prophecy variable p to C, resulting in C^p, and give a refinement mapping from C^p to $\mathcal{A}$. The added variable with values in $\mathbb{N}_{<10}$ predicts the number of increments the abstract level will carry out.

$$\Sigma^p = \left\{ (n, v, m) \in \mathbb{N}_{<10} \times \mathbb{B} \times \mathbb{N}_{<10} \;\middle|\; \begin{array}{l} (m \geq 0 \wedge n + m < 10 \wedge \neg v) \\ \vee (m = 0 \wedge v) \end{array} \right\}$$

The initialization CI^p is defined by

$$CI^p \stackrel{\text{def}}{=} \{ (0, (0, v, m)) \mid (0, v, m) \in \Sigma^p \wedge v \in \mathbb{B} \wedge m \in \mathbb{N}_{<10} \}$$

and the operation C_1^p of C^p is the union of the following two sets:

- $\{ ((n, f\!f, m+1), (n+1, f\!f, m)) \mid n, m \in \mathbb{N}_{<10} \}$
- $\{ ((n, v, 0), (n, t\!t, 0)) \mid n \in \mathbb{N}_{<10} \wedge v \in \mathbb{B} \}$

The finalization of C^p is again projection on the i-component, $CF^p \stackrel{\text{def}}{=} \Pi_1$.

We first prove that C^p is obtained from C by adding a prophecy variable.

P1 is immediate.

P2: $CI^P = CI$; Π_I^{-1} holds, since for all $v \in \mathbb{B}$ there exists $m \in \mathbb{N}_{<10}$ such that $(0, v, m) \in \Sigma^P$.

P3: Assume $((n, v, m), (n', v', m')) \in C_I^P$. Case $n' = n + 1 \wedge \neg v \wedge \neg v' \wedge m > 0 \wedge m' = m - 1$: Since $n + m < 10$, we have $n < 9$. Thus $((n, v), (n', v')) \in C_1$. Case $n' = n \wedge v' \wedge m' = m = 0$ is obvious, since $((n, v), (n', v')) \in C_1$.

P4: Assume $((n, v), (n', v')) \in C_1$ and $(n', v', m') \in \Sigma^P$. Case $\neg v \wedge n < 9 \wedge n' = n + 1 \wedge \neg v'$: $(n', v', m') \in \Sigma^P$ implies $n' + m' < 10$. Thus $n + 1 + m' < 10$. Let $m \stackrel{\text{def}}{=} m' + 1$. Then $n + m < 10 \wedge m > 0$. This implies $(n, v, m) \in \Sigma^P \wedge ((n, v, m), (n', v', m')) \in C_I^P$. Case $v' \wedge n' = n$: v' implies $m' = 0$. Let $m \stackrel{\text{def}}{=} 0$. Then $(n, v, m) \in \Sigma^P$ and $((n, v, m), (n', v', m')) \in C_I^P$.

P5 is satisfied, i.e., $CF = \Pi_I^{-1}$; CF^P, since for all $(n, v) \in \Sigma^C$ there exists m such that $(n, v, m) \in \Sigma^P$.

The reader should check that the function $f : \Sigma^P \longrightarrow \Sigma^A$ defined by $f(n, v, m) \stackrel{\text{def}}{=} (n, m)$ is a refinement mapping from C^P to $\mathcal{A}$. ♡

One final remark is due on the difference between history and prophecy variables as used in the proofs of [AL91]. History variables are used to record part of the history at the concrete level. By contrast, prophecy variables can be used to record decisions made both

(i) in the future at the concrete level and

(ii) in the present step at the abstract level.

This difference emerges from the completeness proof for Abadi and Lamport's method: there one uses the second alternative above, whereas in practical examples mostly the first alternative is used.

14.1.4 Completeness

The proposed technique for proving refinement between data types, consisting of the following steps:

- proving the existence of a refinement mapping
- adding a history variable
- adding a prophecy variable

is sound. This follows from Cor. 14.3, Lemma 14.7, and Lemma 14.14 by soundness of L- and L^{-1}-simulation. Consequently one has the following step-wise approach to proving refinement between compatible data types.

Corollary 14.21 Let C and $\mathcal{A}$ be compatible data types. If there exist intermediate data types $C_1, \ldots, C_n$ such that $C_1 = C$, $C_n = \mathcal{A}$ and for all i, $1 \le i \le n-1$, one of the following conditions holds:

- there exists a refinement mapping from C_i to C_{i+1},
- C_{i+1} is obtained from C_i adding a history variable,
- C_{i+1} is obtained from C_i adding a prophecy variable,

then C refines $\mathcal{A}$.

Proof: By Lemmas 14.7, 14.14, and Theorem 4.10 we obtain C_i refines C_{i+1}, for $i = 1, \ldots, n-1$. Since refinement is transitive, C refines $\mathcal{A}$. $\qquad\square$

We now use the completeness result of Section 4.6 to prove that whenever C refines $\mathcal{A}$ this can be proven using refinement mappings, history and prophecy variables.

Theorem 14.22

Let C and $\mathcal{A}$ be compatible data types such that C refines $\mathcal{A}$. Refinement mappings, history and prophecy variables are sufficient to prove that C is a data refinement of $\mathcal{A}$.

Proof: By Theorems 4.17, 14.12, 14.19, and Cor. 14.21. $\qquad\square$

14.2 Possibilities Mappings

Intuitively, a possibilities mapping is an L-simulation relation mimicking a refinement mapping. Possibilities mappings assign to every state at the concrete level a set of states at the abstract level (rather than just a single one, as refinement mappings). This adds power to refinement mappings because the set of such possibilities mappings $[\Sigma^C \longrightarrow \mathfrak{P}(\Sigma^A)]$ is isomorphic to the set $\mathfrak{P}(\Sigma^C \times \Sigma^A)$ of abstraction relations by Example 10.5 on page 197. As we shall see in this section, L-simulation relations and possibilities mappings are isomorphic images of each other, i.e., existence of a possibilities mapping is equivalent to existence of an L-simulation relation.

Possibilities mappings have been used extensively for proving refinements. They have been introduced in the context of I/O-automata by Lynch and Tuttle [LT87], and originate from [Gor83, Lyn83]. Lynch [Lyn90] argues the usefulness of possibilities mappings and gives several examples. Merritt [Mer90], and Lynch and Vaandrager [LV91] have addressed the questions of soundness and completeness.

We now study possibilities mappings in the set-up of this book, and prove similar soundness and completeness results to those in the previous section.

Let $F : \Sigma^C \longrightarrow \mathfrak{P}(\Sigma^A)$ be some function. We identify F with relation $\alpha(F) \subseteq \Sigma^C \times \Sigma^A$ defined by $(\sigma, \zeta) \in \alpha(F)$ iff $\zeta \in F(\sigma)$. In the sequel we also write F for relation $\alpha(F)$. Similarly, F^{-1} will be identified with $\alpha(F)^{-1}$.

Definition 14.23 (Possibilities mappings) A total function $F : \Sigma^C \longrightarrow \mathfrak{P}(\Sigma^A)$ is called a *possibilities mapping* from data type $C = (CI, (C_j)_{j \in J}, CF)$ to compatible data type $\mathcal{A} = (AI, (A_j)_{j \in J}, AF)$ if the following conditions are satisfied.

$$CI \subseteq AI ; F^{-1} \tag{M1}$$

$$(\sigma, \sigma') \in C_j \wedge \tau \in F(\sigma) \Rightarrow \exists \tau' \in \Sigma^A \left((\tau, \tau') \in A_j \wedge \tau' \in F(\sigma') \right) \tag{M2}$$

$$F^{-1} ; CF \subseteq AF \tag{M3}$$

♣

Conditions M1 and M3 relate initial states and final states, respectively. They are the same conditions as in the definition of L-simulation. Condition M2 states that if $\tau \in F(\sigma)$ and (σ, σ') is a transition at the concrete level, then there exists a transition (τ, τ') at the abstract level with $\tau' \in F(\sigma')$.

As a preparation for our soundness proof of the method of possibilities mappings we have the following lemma, which relates possibilities mappings to L-simulations:

Lemma 14.24 Let $\mathcal{A} = (AI, (A_j)_{j \in J}, AF)$ and $C = (CI, (C_j)_{j \in J}, CF)$ be two compatible data types and let $F : \Sigma^C \longrightarrow \mathfrak{P}(\Sigma^A)$ be a total function from the state space of C to that of $\mathcal{A}$. Then the following two conditions are equivalent.

  (i) F is a possibilities mapping from C to $\mathcal{A}$.
 (ii) C L-simulates $\mathcal{A}$ w.r.t. F.

Proof: Let $F : \Sigma^C \longrightarrow \mathfrak{P}(\Sigma^A)$ be a total function and let $j \in J$. To establish the lemma, it suffices to show that condition M2 and the L-simulation condition for the j-th operations

$$F^{-1} ; C_j \subseteq A_j ; F^{-1} \tag{14.1}$$

are equivalent.

M2 $\Rightarrow$ (14.1): Assume that M2 is true. Let $(\tau, \sigma') \in F^{-1} ; C_j$. Then, for some state $\sigma \in \Sigma^C$, $(\tau, \sigma) \in F^{-1}$ and $(\sigma, \sigma') \in C_j$ are satisfied. In other words, $\tau \in F(\sigma)$ and $(\sigma, \sigma') \in C_j$ are true. From M2 we obtain that there exists some state $\tau' \in \Sigma^A$ such that $(\tau, \tau') \in A_j$ and $\tau' \in F(\sigma')$. Consequently, $(\tau, \tau') \in A_j$ and $(\tau', \sigma') \in F^{-1}$. Therefore, $(\tau, \sigma') \in A_j ; F^{-1}$ holds. We conclude that $F^{-1} ; C_j \subseteq A_j ; F^{-1}$ is true.

(14.1) $\Rightarrow$ M2: Assume that (14.1) is true. Let σ, σ', τ be such that $(\sigma, \sigma') \in C_j$ and $\tau \in F(\sigma)$ hold. We then have that $(\tau, \sigma) \in F^{-1}$, and hence that $(\tau, \sigma') \in F^{-1}; C_j$ is true. Because of condition (14.1), $(\tau, \sigma') \in A_j; F^{-1}$. Thus, for some state τ' both $(\tau, \tau') \in A_j$ and $(\tau', \sigma') \in F^{-1}$ are satisfied. We conclude that $(\tau, \tau') \in A_j$ and $\tau' \in F(\sigma')$ hold. Consequently, M2 is true. $\square$

As an immediate consequence, we have the following soundness result:

Lemma 14.25 If F is a possibilities mapping from C to $\mathcal{A}$ then C refines $\mathcal{A}$.

Proof: According to the previous lemma, C *L*-simulates $\mathcal{A}$ w.r.t. F, if F is a possibilities mapping from C to $\mathcal{A}$. $\square$

Before addressing the question of completeness, note that we have the following corollary that follows immediately from Lemma 14.24 and Theorem 14.19.

Corollary 14.26 Let $F : \Sigma^C \longrightarrow \mathfrak{P}(\Sigma^A)$ be a total function. The three clauses below are equivalent:

  (i) F is a possibilities mapping from C to $\mathcal{A}$.
  (ii) C *L*-simulates $\mathcal{A}$ w.r.t. $\alpha(F)$.
  (iii) There exist a data type C^h obtained from C by adding a history variable, and a refinement mapping from C^h to $\mathcal{A}$.   ♠

As before, auxiliary variables will be used to obtain completeness. The proof of completeness of possibilities mappings given here uses the completeness result for refinement mappings. As a preparation for our proof, we formulate how a possibilities mapping from data type C to $\mathcal{A}$ can be obtained canonically from a refinement mapping from C to $\mathcal{A}$. Every refinement mapping induces a possibilities mapping in a natural way.

Lemma 14.27 If f is a refinement mapping from C to $\mathcal{A}$, then F defined by $F(\sigma) = \{f(\sigma)\}$ is a possibilities mapping from C to $\mathcal{A}$.

Proof: Clearly, F is a total function; and F maps every $\sigma \in \Sigma^C$ to a singleton. We now show that the clauses M1–M3 all hold:

Ad M1: Let $(\tau, \sigma) \in CI$. Consider state τ' with $\tau' = f(\sigma)$. (The existence of τ' follows from function f being total.) Condition R2 of refinement mappings implies that $(\sigma, \tau') \in AI$. Therefore, $(\tau, \sigma) \in AI; F^{-1}$ follows.

Ad M2: Let $j \in J$, and let $\sigma, \sigma' \in \Sigma^C$ and $\tau \in \Sigma^A$ such that $(\sigma, \sigma') \in C_j$ and $\tau \in F(\sigma)$ hold. Thus, $\tau = f(\sigma)$ is true. From condition R3 of refinement mappings, we obtain that $(f(\sigma), f(\sigma')) \in A_j$ is satisfied. Consequently, for $\tau' = f(\sigma')$, $(\tau, \tau') \in A_j$ and $\tau' \in F(\sigma')$ follow.

Ad M3: The proof is similar to those above, and therefore omitted.   □

As an immediate consequence of the above-mentioned relationship between refinement mappings and possibilities mappings, and the completeness result for refinement mappings, we have the following completeness theorem for possibilities mappings.

Theorem 14.28
Possibilities mappings and prophecy variables are sufficient to prove that C is a data refinement of $\mathcal{A}$ whenever this is the case.   ♠

Readers familiar with Nancy Lynch's book on distributed algorithms [Lyn96] will notice that on page 225 of her book the formulation of (L-)simulation is different from that given in Def. 14.23. Although this is partially due to her different setting, her definition when compared to Def. 14.23 also requires states considered at the concrete and abstract level to be reachable.

However, this does not make any substantial difference, because every possibilities mapping that has only the reachable states at the concrete level as domain can be extended to one on the full state space by simply mapping all unreachable states to the empty set of abstract states.

14.3 Historical Background

In this book we have discussed, or mentioned, several soundness and completeness results for proving refinement between data types [Nip86, HHS87, Mer90, AL91, Jon91, LV91]. Actually, the last four of these concern proving refinement between specifications for concurrent processes. The connection between the latter and the theory of data refinement is as follows:

- One can view a data type as a process whose communications correspond to invocations of that data type.
- The techniques discussed in this book can be used for proving preservation of invariance and termination properties during refinement, but not for proving preservation of fairness properties.

In the context of proving refinement between specifications for concurrent processes, there is an important predecessor, whom we have not mentioned as yet, namely Eugene Stark. He obtained his soundness and completeness results [Sta84, Sta88] in his thesis in 1984. He introduces the notion of conceptual state specification, which is a kind of temporal logic specification in which so-called conceptual state variables are introduced, a concept akin to Lamport's state functions [Lam83]. Conceptual state variables are auxiliary variables which record an abstract representation of the internal state of a process, and serve merely to increase the expressive power of his temporal logic. Then he develops a technique for proving refinement — he uses the term entailment — between two conceptual state specifications, and gives a completeness result for his technique, which states that refinement can always be proved once the specifications involved satisfy certain well-formedness conditions which can be independently checked; these conditions resemble some of those introduced later in [AL91]. Stark's proof technique makes use of the concept of simulation between machines, and is a generalization of the simulation techniques developed in this book. He also proves in his thesis that this concept is equivalent to the possibilities mapping technique of Nancy Lynch and her former student John Goree [Gor83, Lyn83]. In the context of I/O automata, Bengt Jonsson obtained a similar completeness result in his thesis [Jon87, Jon94].

Exercises

14.1   Show that Examples 2.3 and 14.5 are not minimal, i.e., construct smaller examples that show the incompleteness of L- and L^{-1}-simulation on their own.

14.2   Complete the proof of Lemma 14.18.

14.3   Finish Example 14.20: prove that function f defined in the example is indeed a refinement mapping.

14.4   (a) Give data types C and $\mathcal{A}$ such that C refines $\mathcal{A}$ but this cannot be proven using exclusively L- or L^{-1}-simulation.

         (b) Prove this refinement using refinement mappings, history variables, and prophecy variables.

Appendix A
An Introduction to Hoare Logic

Hoare logic is a formal system for reasoning about Hoare-style correctness formulae. It originates from C. A. R. Hoare's 1969 paper "An axiomatic basis for computer programming" [Hoa69], which introduces an axiomatic method for proving programs correct. Hoare logic can be viewed as the structural analysis of R. W. Floyd's semantically based inductive assertion method.

Hoare's approach has received a great deal of attention ever since its introduction, and has had a significant impact on methods both for designing and verifying programs. It owes its success to three factors:

(i) The first factor, which it shares with the inductive assertion method, is its *universality*: it is *state-based*, characterizes programming constructs as transformers of states, and therefore applies in principle to every such construct.

(ii) The second factor in its success is its *syntax directedness*: every rule for a composed programming construct reduces proving properties of that construct to proving properties of its constituent constructs. In case the latter are also formulated as Hoare style correctness formulae — when characterizing parallelism this is not always the case — Hoare logic is even compositional: proving Hoare style correctness formulae for composed constructs is reduced to proving Hoare style correctness formulae for their constituent constructs without any additional knowledge about the latter's implementation. Hoare's 1969 logic is compositional.

Compositional Hoare logics can also be regarded as design calculi. In such a design calculus a proof rule is interpreted as a design rule, in which a specific design goal, that of developing a program satisfying certain properties, is reduced to certain subgoals (and, in general, the satisfaction of certain verification conditions), obtained by reading that rule upside-down. This is illustrated by interpreting Hoare's rule for sequential composition

$$\frac{\{\pi\}\,S_1\,\{\kappa\},\{\kappa\}\,S_2\,\{\rho\}}{\{\pi\}\,S_1\,;S_2\,\{\rho\}}$$

as a design rule:

(a) Given the goal of developing a program S satisfying $\{\pi\}\,S\,\{\rho\}$, assume the designer's decision is to split S up as a sequential composition of two subprograms S_1 and S_2. What consequences does this decision have for the specifications of S_1 and S_2?

(b) The sequential composition rule answers this question by postulating the existence of an intermediate assertion κ, embodying the sequential interface between S_1 and S_2, such that $\{\pi\}\,S_1\,\{\kappa\}$ and $\{\kappa\}\,S_2\,\{\rho\}$ are satisfied. Since Hoare logic is sound, this is a sufficient condition for obtaining $\{\pi\}\,S_1\,;S_2\,\{\rho\}$, and since Hoare logic is complete (in a sense made precise later), finding such an assertion κ is also a necessary condition for obtaining $\{\pi\}\,S_1\,;S_2\,\{\rho\}$.

(c) Moreover, these are the only tasks which the designer has to solve, after his design decision in point (a). No matter how S_1 is implemented in the end, as long as $\{\pi\}\,S_1\,\{\kappa\}$ is satisfied this has no further influence on the development of a subprogram S_2 satisfying $\{\kappa\}\,S_2\,\{\rho\}$. I.e., all the possible interaction between S_1 and S_2 is already captured by $\{\pi\}\,S_1\,\{\kappa\}$ and $\{\kappa\}\,S_1\,\{\rho\}$. Consequently, the goal of developing a program S satisfying $\{\pi\}\,S\,\{\rho\}$, is, as a consequence of applying the design rule for sequential composition, split up into two subgoals $\{\pi\}\,S_1\,\{\kappa\}$ and $\{\kappa\}\,S_2\,\{\rho\}$ which can be dealt with separately. This is an immediate consequence of working within a compositional formalism.

This explains why Hoare logic can also be used for program design.

(iii) The third factor contributing to its success is the extraordinarily simple way in which Hoare logic characterizes sequential composition and iteration. E.g., in case the of iteration all that is required is the preservation of an invariant. So far, this simplicity has not been surpassed by any (more sophisticated) formalism developed later. Hoare logic has set the standard of how to deal with these constructs.

It is a testimony to the success of Hoare logic that it has been applied and generalized to almost every language construct in sequential and parallel programming alike, with applications ranging from pattern matching to graphical languages, and that it can be used for proving fault tolerance as well as real time and hardware properties [dRdBH+].

We present here a self-contained analysis of the basis of Hoare logic for some simple sequential programming constructs, in a version suitable for proving (data) refinement. For the reader interested in user-oriented texts on Hoare logic a number of excellent books are available [Dah92, DF88, Gri81, Kal90], of varying degrees of difficulty. As to mathematical rigor and depth, J. W. de Bakker's scholarly handbook [dB80] and K. R. Apt's 50-page survey [Apt81] remain the standard sources on the foundations of Hoare logic for sequential programming (especially regarding the procedure concept), sources from which we freely borrow.

The structure of these sections on Hoare logic is as follows. We first present this logic for while-programs, and then for the specification statement and recursive procedures.

A.1 Hoare Logic of While Programs

Recall that our sets of variables are of two disjoint kinds: program variables and logical variables. To express terms, Boolean expressions, and assertions we use a first order language $\mathcal{L}$ over these sets of variables with equality. We use the letters a, b, x, y, z for program variables, their subscripted versions x_0, y_0, z_0 etc. for logical variables, the letter e (for *expression*) for a term of $\mathcal{L}$ which does not contain any logical variables, the letter b (for *Boolean expression*) for a quantifier-free formula of $\mathcal{L}$ not containing any logical variables, and finally Greek letters π, ρ, κ for formulae (*assertions*) of $\mathcal{L}$.

The class of while-programs $\mathcal{W}$ is the least class of programs such that

 (i) for every program variable x and expression e, $x := e \in \mathcal{W}$,
 (ii) if $S_1, S_2 \in \mathcal{W}$ then $S_1 ; S_2 \in \mathcal{W}$, and, for every Boolean expression b,
   - **if** b **then** S_1 **else** S_2 **fi** $\in \mathcal{W}$ and
   - **while** b **do** S_1 **od** $\in \mathcal{W}$.

The basic formulae of Hoare logic are partial correctness formulae $\{\pi\} S \{\rho\}$, also called *triples*, where π and ρ denote assertions and (in this appendix) $S \in \mathcal{W}$. Given an interpretation $\mathfrak{I} = (S, \sigma)$ of $\mathcal{L}$, the meaning of $\{\pi\} S \{\rho\}$ is given after Def. 5.27 by $\mathcal{F}[\![\pi ; S \subseteq \rho]\!]_{\mathfrak{I}}$, also written as $\models_{\mathfrak{I}} \pi ; S \subseteq \rho$, and expresses the following intuition: whenever π holds before execution of S, and S terminates, then ρ holds after execution of S.

A triple $\{\pi\}S\{\rho\}$ is called *valid*, written $\models \{\pi\}S\{\rho\}$, if $\models_\mathfrak{I} \{\pi\}S\{\rho\}$ holds for every interpretation $\mathfrak{I}$. Obviously, $\{\pi\}S\{\text{true}\}$ is valid for all preconditions π, and, as we shall see, so is the assignment axiom below.

Hoare logic is a system for formal reasoning about such triples. Its axioms and proof rules are the following.

$$\text{assignment axiom} \quad \{\pi[^e/_x]\}\,x := e\,\{\pi\}$$

$$\text{composition rule} \quad \frac{\{\pi\}S_1\{\kappa\},\{\kappa\}S_2\{\rho\}}{\{\pi\}S_1\,;S_2\{\rho\}}$$

$$\text{if-then-else rule} \quad \frac{\{\pi\wedge b\}S_1\{\rho\},\{\pi\wedge \neg b\}S_2\{\rho\}}{\{\pi\}\,\textbf{if}\ b\ \textbf{then}\ S_1\ \textbf{else}\ S_2\ \textbf{fi}\{\rho\}}$$

$$\text{while rule} \quad \frac{\{\pi\wedge b\}S\{\pi\}}{\{\pi\}\,\textbf{while}\ b\ \textbf{do}\ S\ \textbf{od}\{\pi\wedge \neg b\}}$$

As usual, $\pi[^e/_x]$ stands for the result of substituting e for the free occurrences of x in π.

In fact this axiom and these rules are *schemes*. Consider, e.g., the assignment "axiom". Applying it to the assertion $x \geq 7$ and the assignment $x := 7$ results in the axiom (which is not a scheme) $\{(x \geq 7)[^7/_x]\}\,x := 7\,\{x \geq 7\}$. The same holds for our "rules". Consider, e.g., the composition "rule". Applying it to the assignments $y := 3$ and $x := y + 4$, and the assertions true, $y + 4 \geq 7$, and $x \geq 7$ yields the rule (which is not a scheme):

$$\frac{\{\text{true}\}y := 3\,\{y+4 \geq 7\},\{y+4 \geq 7\}x := y+4\,\{x \geq 7\}}{\{\text{true}\}y := 3\,;x := y+4\,\{x \geq 7\}}$$

Example A.1 As a typical example of a proof in this system, take for $\mathfrak{L}$ the language of Peano arithmetic $\mathfrak{L}_P$ augmented with the minus operator, and consider the program S_0 for computing the integer division of two natural numbers x and y:

$$S_0 \stackrel{\text{def}}{=} a := 0\,;b := x\,;\textbf{while}\ b \geq y\ \textbf{do}\ b := b-y\,;a := a+1\ \textbf{od}$$

We now prove that

$$\{x \geq 0 \wedge y \geq 0\}S_0\{a*y+b = x \wedge 0 \leq b < y\} \ , \qquad\qquad \text{(A.1)}$$

that is, if x and y are nonnegative integers and if S_0 terminates, then a is the integer quotient of x divided by y and b is the remainder.[1]

The proof runs as follows. By the assignment axiom,

$$\{0 * y + x = x \wedge x \geq 0\} \, a := 0 \, \{a * y + x = x \wedge x \geq 0\} \tag{A.2}$$

and

$$\{a * y + x = x \wedge x \geq 0\} \, b := x \, \{a * y + b = x \wedge b \geq 0\} \ . \tag{A.3}$$

So, by the composition rule,

$$\{0 * y + x = x \wedge x \geq 0\} \, a := 0; b := x \, \{a * y + b = x \wedge b \geq 0\} \ . \tag{A.4}$$

Now,

$$x \geq 0 \wedge y \geq 0 \Rightarrow 0 * y + x = x \wedge x \geq 0 \tag{A.5}$$

is true. So (A.5) and (A.4) imply

$$\{x \geq 0 \wedge y \geq 0\} \, a := 0; b := x \, \{a * y + b = x \wedge b \geq 0\} \ . \tag{A.6}$$

On the other hand, by the assignment axiom,

$$\left\{ \begin{aligned} &(a+1) * y + b - y = x \\ &\wedge b - y \geq 0 \end{aligned} \right\} b := b - y \left\{ \begin{aligned} &(a+1) * y + b = x \\ &\wedge b \geq 0 \end{aligned} \right\} \tag{A.7}$$

and

$$\{(a+1) * y + b = x \wedge b \geq 0\} \, a := a + 1 \, \{a * y + b = x \wedge b \geq 0\} \ . \tag{A.8}$$

So, by the composition rule,

$$\left\{ \begin{aligned} &(a+1) * y + b - y = x \\ &\wedge b - y \geq 0 \end{aligned} \right\} \begin{aligned} b := b - y; \\ a := a + 1 \end{aligned} \left\{ \begin{aligned} &a * y + b = x \\ &\wedge b \geq 0 \end{aligned} \right\} \ . \tag{A.9}$$

Now,

$$a * y + b = x \wedge b \geq 0 \wedge b \geq y \Rightarrow (a+1) * y + b - y = x \wedge b - y \geq 0 \tag{A.10}$$

is true, so (A.10) and (A.9) imply

$$\left\{ \begin{aligned} &a * y + b = x \\ &\wedge b \geq 0 \wedge b \geq y \end{aligned} \right\} \begin{aligned} b := b - y; \\ a := a + 1 \end{aligned} \left\{ \begin{aligned} &a * y + b = x \\ &\wedge b \geq 0 \end{aligned} \right\} \ . \tag{A.11}$$

And (A.11) implies, by the while rule,

$$\left\{ \begin{aligned} &a * y + b = x \\ &\wedge b \geq 0 \end{aligned} \right\} \begin{aligned} &\textbf{while } b \geq y \textbf{ do} \\ &\quad b := b - y; a := a + 1 \\ &\textbf{od} \end{aligned} \left\{ \begin{aligned} &a * y + b = x \\ &\wedge b \geq 0 \wedge b < y \end{aligned} \right\} \ . \tag{A.12}$$

---

[1] Observe that this natural language description is equivalent to (A.1) because the values of x and y are not changed inside S_0.

Finally, (A.6) and (A.12) imply (A.1) by the composition rule.   ♡

Several remarks are in order. First, to justify the above proof we have to explain
how we derived (A.6) from (A.4) and (A.5), and (A.11) from (A.10) and (A.9).
These steps, although intuitively clear, still lack a formal basis. The missing
proof rule which we used here is the following:

$$\text{consequence rule} \quad \frac{\pi \Rightarrow \pi_1, \{\pi_1\} S \{\rho_1\}, \rho_1 \Rightarrow \rho}{\{\pi\} S \{\rho\}}$$

In the example we used this rule for $\rho_1 = \rho$, but in general the above version is
required.

This rule forces us to include assertions among the formulae of Hoare logic.
Denote the resulting system by $\mathfrak{H}$.

Now, to get (A.5) and (A.10), we have to augment $\mathfrak{H}$ with a formal proof
system concerning assertions. In this particular case, any theory T in the underlying $\mathfrak{L}$ in which (A.5) and (A.10) can be proven will do. The proofs of
(A.5) and (A.10) in T, concatenated with the sequence (A.2)–(A.12), (A.1) of
correctness formulae and assertions, finally form a proof of (A.1) in $\mathfrak{H} \cup T$.

This interpretation is by no means satisfactory for our purposes. We do not
care whether (A.5) and (A.10) are theorems of a theory T. All we need to
know is that (A.5) and (A.10) are true in the domain of integers.

Finally we draw attention to the fact that $\models \{\pi\} S \{\rho\}$ does not imply that
whenever π holds S terminates. E.g., $\models \{\text{true}\}$ **while** true **do** $x := x$ **od** $\{\text{false}\}$
certainly holds (because **while** true **do** $x := x$ **od** nowhere terminates) and a
proof of this fact immediately follows from the while rule, taking true as the
invariant of $x := x$. This argument illustrates why $\models \{\pi\} S \{\text{false}\}$ implies that
S does not terminate in π.

A.2 Soundness and Relative Completeness of $\mathfrak{H}$

There are two basic questions that have to be answered for $\mathfrak{H}$ (in fact for any
alleged proof system):

- Is $\mathfrak{H}$ *sound*? That is, is every correctness formula that can be derived in $\mathfrak{H}$
  true?

- Is $\mathfrak{H}$ *adequate*? That is, is it possible to derive in $\mathfrak{H}$ every true correctness
  formula? (Adequacy is also called completeness.)

The following sections present the answers.

A.2.1 Soundness of $\mathfrak{H}$

Prior to proving soundness of $\mathfrak{H}$ we first need more notation. Distinguish in a proof rule its *premise*, the part above the horizontal bar, from its *conclusion*, which is the part below that bar. A proof rule is called *sound* if, for all interpretations $\mathfrak{I}$, whenever its premise is true under $\mathfrak{I}$, then so is its conclusion. As we shall see, the composition, if-then-else, while, and consequence rules are all sound.

Let us assume for the moment that validity of the axioms and soundness of the rules of $\mathfrak{H}$ have been proved. Then how does one prove that every deduction in $\mathfrak{H}$ leads to a true result, i.e., $\mathfrak{H}$ is sound? Let A be a set of assertions. Write $A \vdash_{\mathfrak{H}} \{\pi\} S \{\rho\}$ to express that there exists a proof of $\{\pi\} S \{\rho\}$ in $\mathfrak{H}$ which uses A as the set of assumptions for the consequence rule. We have thus shown above that (A.5), (A.10) $\vdash_{\mathfrak{H}}$ (A.1).

Then the fact that the axioms of $\mathfrak{H}$ are valid and the proof rules of $\mathfrak{H}$ are sound implies by induction on the length of proofs the following theorem, which states that the proof system $\mathfrak{H}$ is sound.

Theorem A.2

For every interpretation $\mathfrak{I}$, set of assertions A, and triple $\{\pi\} S \{\rho\}$ the following holds: if all assertions of A are true under $\mathfrak{I}$ and $A \vdash_{\mathfrak{H}} \{\pi\} S \{\rho\}$, then $\{\pi\} S \{\rho\}$ is true under $\mathfrak{I}$. ♠

Lemma A.3 The axioms of $\mathfrak{H}$ are valid and the rules of $\mathfrak{H}$ are sound.

Proof: We prove validity of the assignment axiom and soundness of the composition and while rules.

Validity of the assignment axiom is proven as follows:

$$\models_{\mathfrak{I}} \{\pi[{}^e/_x]\} x := e \{\pi\}$$

$\Leftrightarrow$ (Def. 5.27)

$$\forall \gamma, \sigma, \tau ((\gamma, \sigma) \in C[\![\pi[{}^e/_x]]\!] \wedge (\sigma, \tau) \in \mathcal{P}[\![x := e]\!] \Rightarrow (\gamma, \tau) \in C[\![\pi]\!])$$

$\Leftrightarrow$ (Lemma 5.8)

$$\forall \gamma, \sigma, \tau \left(\begin{array}{l} (\gamma, (\sigma : x \mapsto \mathcal{E}[\![e]\!]\sigma)) \in C[\![\pi]\!] \wedge \tau = (\sigma : x \mapsto \mathcal{E}[\![e]\!]\sigma) \\ \Rightarrow (\gamma, \tau) \in C[\![\pi]\!] \end{array} \right)$$

which is true, independently of interpretation $\mathfrak{I}$.

Soundness of the composition rule is proved by

$$\models_{\mathfrak{I}} \{\pi\} S_1 \{\kappa\} \wedge \{\kappa\} S_2 \{\rho\}$$

$\Leftrightarrow$ (Def. 5.27)

$$\forall \gamma, \sigma_1, \tau_1 ((\gamma, \sigma_1) \in C[\![\pi]\!] \wedge (\sigma_1, \tau_1) \in \mathcal{P}[\![S_1]\!] \Rightarrow (\gamma, \tau_1) \in C[\![\kappa]\!])$$
$$\wedge \forall \gamma, \sigma_2, \tau_2 ((\gamma, \sigma_2) \in C[\![\kappa]\!] \wedge (\sigma_2, \tau_2) \in \mathcal{P}[\![S_2]\!] \Rightarrow (\gamma, \tau_2) \in C[\![\rho]\!])$$

$\Rightarrow$ (Def. 5.18)

$$\forall \gamma, \sigma_1, \tau_2 ((\gamma, \sigma_1) \in C[\![\pi]\!] \wedge (\sigma_1, \tau_2) \in \mathcal{P}[\![S_1 ; S_2]\!] \Rightarrow (\gamma, \tau_2) \in C[\![\rho]\!])$$

$\Leftrightarrow$ (Def. 5.27)

$$\models_{\mathfrak{I}} \{\pi\} S_1 ; S_2 \{\rho\}$$

Finally, soundness of the while rule is proven:

(i) It follows from Def. 5.27 and the other definitions in Chapter 5 that

$$\models_{\mathfrak{I}} \{\pi\} \textbf{ while } b \textbf{ do } S \textbf{ od} \{\pi \wedge \neg b\} \tag{A.13}$$

$$\Leftrightarrow \forall \gamma, \sigma, \tau \left(\begin{array}{l} (\gamma, \sigma) \in C[\![\pi]\!] \wedge (\sigma, \tau) \in \mathcal{P}[\![\textbf{while } b \textbf{ do } S \textbf{ od}]\!] \\ \Rightarrow (\gamma, \tau) \in C[\![\pi \wedge \neg b]\!] \end{array} \right) \tag{A.14}$$

(ii) It can be proven (see Exercise A.4) that $(\sigma, \tau) \in \mathcal{P}[\![\textbf{while } b \textbf{ do } S \textbf{ od}]\!]$ iff for some $k \geq 0$ there exists a sequence of states $\sigma_0 \sigma_1 \ldots \sigma_k$ such that $\sigma_0 = \sigma$ and $\sigma_k = \tau$, $\sigma_i \in C[\![b]\!]$ and $(\sigma_i, \sigma_{i+1}) \in \mathcal{P}[\![S]\!]$ for $0 \leq i < k$, and $\sigma_k \in C[\![\neg b]\!]$.

(iii) Next, assume invariance of π under S provided b holds prior to the execution of S:

$$\models_{\mathfrak{I}} \{\pi \wedge b\} S \{\pi\}$$

$$\Leftrightarrow \forall \gamma, \sigma', \tau' \left(\begin{array}{l} (\gamma, \sigma') \in C[\![\pi \wedge b]\!] \wedge (\sigma', \tau') \in \mathcal{P}[\![S]\!] \\ \Rightarrow (\gamma, \tau') \in C[\![\pi]\!] \end{array} \right) \tag{A.15}$$

(iv) Consequently, by combining point (ii) with (A.15), one obtains by induction on i that $(\gamma, \sigma_0) \in C[\![\pi \wedge b]\!]$ implies that

- $(\gamma, \sigma_0) \in C[\![\pi \wedge b]\!]$ and $(\sigma_i, \sigma_{i+1}) \in \mathcal{P}[\![S]\!]$ for $0 \leq i < k$, and
- $(\gamma, \sigma_k) \in C[\![\pi \wedge \neg b]\!]$.

(v) Since by point (ii) $\sigma_0 = \sigma$, $\sigma_k = \tau$, and $(\sigma, \tau) \in \mathcal{P}[\![\textbf{while } b \textbf{ do } S \textbf{ od}]\!]$, by point (iv) $(\gamma, \sigma_0) \in C[\![\pi \wedge b]\!]$ implies that $(\gamma, \sigma_k) \in C[\![\pi \wedge \neg b]\!]$, and σ, τ have been chosen arbitrarily, we obtain (A.14) under assumption $\models_{\mathfrak{I}} \{\pi \wedge b\} S \{\pi\}$. Thus (A.13) holds by point (i). $\qquad \square$

An example of an invalid axiom can be obtained by extending our language with integer array c and characterizing an assignment to subscripted variable $c[i]$ in that array by Hoare's assignment axiom:

$$\{\pi [^e/_{c[i]}]\} c[i] := e \{\pi\} .$$

The reason why this formula is unsound is that in case, e.g., $1 = c[1]$, an assignment to $c(c[i])$ will in general also change the value of its alias $c[1]$, as a result of which execution of $c[c[1]] := 2$ need not result in $c[c[1]] = 2$ as the precondition, because $c[1]$ may have changed its value. This is worked out in Exercise A.5.

Finally we briefly mention Dijkstra's guarded command language [Dij76] and its associated Hoare logic.

Apart from **abort, skip,** and assignments, this language contains in our setup the following statements for $n \in \mathbb{N}_{>0}$:

- Guarded selection:

$$\left(\square_{1 \leq i \leq n} b_i \rightarrow S_i\right) \stackrel{\text{def}}{=} \begin{cases} b_1 \rightarrow S_1 & \text{if } n = 1 \\ \left(\square_{1 \leq i \leq n-1} b_i \rightarrow S_i\right) \square \, b_n \rightarrow S_n & \text{otherwise} \end{cases}$$

- Guarded loop:

$$* \left(\square_{1 \leq i \leq n} b_i \rightarrow S_i\right) \stackrel{\text{def}}{=} \mu X. \left(\left(\square_{1 \leq i \leq n} b_i \rightarrow S_i\right); X \cup \neg \bigvee_{1 \leq i \leq n} b_i \rightarrow\right)$$

Their associated proof rules closely resemble those for the if-then-else and while statements:

$$\text{guarded selection rule} \quad \frac{\{\pi \wedge b_i\} S_i \{\rho\}, 1 \leq i \leq n}{\{\pi\} \left(\square_{1 \leq i \leq n} b_i \rightarrow S_i\right) \{\rho\}}$$

$$\text{guarded loop rule} \quad \frac{\{\pi \wedge \bigvee_{1 \leq i \leq n} b_i\} \left(\square_{1 \leq i \leq n} b_i \rightarrow S_i\right) \{\pi\}}{\{\pi\} * \left(\square_{1 \leq i \leq n} b_i \rightarrow S_i\right) \{\pi \wedge \neg \bigvee_{1 \leq i \leq n} b_i\}}$$

For later use, we record the axiom for the **abort** statement, expressing that **abort** never terminates.

$$\text{abort axiom} \quad \{\text{true}\} \, \textbf{abort} \, \{\text{false}\}$$

A.3 Loop Invariants

Let us return to the combinatorics of $\mathfrak{H}$, look again at Example A.1, and see what is the crucial step in this deduction.

Like all formal proofs, the proof of (A.1) is tedious and difficult to follow. We are not accustomed to following a line of reasoning expressed in such small steps. However, it is easy to observe that the whole argument boils down to one crucial step: observing that (A.11) holds. Once we guess the assertion $r \stackrel{\text{def}}{=} a * y + b = x \wedge b \geq 0$, to find the proof is straightforward. Since (A.11) holds, r is called an *invariant* of the loop **while** $b \geq y$ **do** $b := b - y; a := a + 1$ **od**.

Since (A.6) holds, we say that the program $a := 0; b := x$ *establishes* r. Since (A.12) holds, we say that the program **while** $b \geq y$ **do** $b := b - y; a := a + 1$ **od** *preserves* r.

A concise way of embedding this information into the program S is simply to annotate it with the desired assertion(s). To illustrate this point, we now take a different example. It is easy to see that

$$\left\{ x \geq 0 \land y \geq 0 \right\} \begin{array}{l} a := x; b := y; z := 1; \\ \textbf{while } b \neq 0 \textbf{ do } b := b - 1; z := z * a \textbf{ od} \end{array} \left\{ z = x^y \right\}$$

is true in the standard model of the natural numbers once we write it as

$\{x \geq 0 \land y \geq 0\}$
  $a := x; b := y; z := 1;$
  while $b \neq 0$ **do**
    $\{z * a^b = x^y\}$
    $b := b - 1; z := z * a$
  od
$\{z = x^y\}$

Thinking in terms of establishing an invariant, and preserving it, has immediate implications for reasoning about programs and their design. For example, in the case of the above program, an observation that the loop

$$\textbf{while } even(b) \textbf{ do } b := \frac{b}{2}; a := a * a \textbf{ od}$$

preserves the invariant $z * a^b = x^y$ leads to the following improvement.

$\{x \geq 0 \land y \geq 0\}$
  $a := x; b := y; z := 1;$
  while $b \neq 0$ **do**
    $\{z * a^b = x^y\}$
    while $even(b)$ **do**
      $\{z * a^b = x^y\}$
      $b := \frac{b}{2}; a := a * a$
    od;
    $b := b - 1; z := z * a$
  od
$\{z = x^y\}$

In both cases it is Theorem A.2 which allows us to infer that the correctness formulae are true in the standard model of the natural numbers.

The fact that such a simple way of reasoning about loops is possible in Hoare logic, and in no essentially different formalism such as, e.g., temporal logic, justifies the third factor listed in the introduction to this chapter, which explains the success of Hoare logic.

A.4 The Issue of Completeness of $\mathfrak{H}$

This section is based on [Apt81].

Whereas the question of soundness of a method concerns its being correct, the question of its completeness concerns the scope of its applicability, i.e., the circumstances under which it can be successfully applied. Contrary to what is usually thought, this question is of practical interest. For it is the experience of the senior author that every formal system suggested or submitted to him which has neither been proven sound nor complete (in a sense to be made precise below) has been without exception either unsound or incomplete. That is, if one does not do one's homework — here, does not give those proofs — the formal systems delivered are either unreliable, because unsound, or clumsy, because incomplete. Independent evidence for this can be found in [Old83].

First of all, the system $\mathfrak{H}$ by itself is incomplete. For the correctness formula

$$\{\rho[^e/_x]\}\, x := e\, \{\text{true}\}$$

is obviously valid, yet it is unprovable in $\mathfrak{H}$, for the simple reason that there is no way to prove the assertion $\rho \Rightarrow \text{true}$ or $\rho[^e/_x] \Rightarrow \text{true}$.

This suggests extending $\mathfrak{H}$ with an axiom system dealing with such assertions. This is of no help either. For, given any interpretation $\mathfrak{I}$ and assertion $\rho, \models_\mathfrak{I} \{\text{true}\}\, x := x\, \{\rho\}$ iff $\models_\mathfrak{I} \rho$. So whenever there exists no axiom system for proving $\{\, \rho \mid \models_\mathfrak{I} \rho\, \}$, as is for instance the case with the standard interpretation $\mathfrak{I}_N$ of the natural numbers, there is no hope of obtaining a complete extension of $\mathfrak{H}$, either.

As a second attempt, one might think that the source of incompleteness in this argument comes from considering arbitrary assertions. However, this is not true either. For, given any interpretation $\mathfrak{I}$, program S fails to halt for all initial values of its variables iff $\models_\mathfrak{I} \{\text{true}\}\, S\, \{\text{false}\}$. Hence, for any class $\mathfrak{S}_0$ of programs, if $\mathfrak{L}$ and $\mathfrak{I}$ are such that the halting problem for $\mathfrak{S}_0$ is undecidable, then the set of programs S in $\mathfrak{S}_0$ for which $\models_\mathfrak{I} \{\text{true}\}S\{\text{false}\}$ holds is not recursively enumerable [Sho67, LP81].

So even if we restrict our assertion language to $\{\text{true}, \text{false}\}$ the fact that the halting problem for $\mathfrak{I}_N$ is undecidable prevents us from obtaining a complete extension of $\mathfrak{H}$, since such an extension can only generate a recursively enumerable set of formulae.

Of course, one may question here our preoccupation with $\mathfrak{I}_N$. This has the simple reason that only interpretations such as $\mathfrak{I}_N$ allow us to generate loop invariants for any given valid correctness formulae about a **while** statement, as will be shown later.

As a third attempt, consider the set $Tr_{\mathfrak{I}}$ of formulae true under $\mathfrak{I}$, and define $\mathfrak{H}$ to be complete relative to $Tr_{\mathfrak{I}}$, if the inverse of theorem A.2 holds: For all interpretations $\mathfrak{I}$ and all correctness formulae $\{\pi\}S\{\rho\}$, if $\models_{\mathfrak{I}} \{\pi\}S\{\rho\}$ then $Tr_{\mathfrak{I}} \vdash_{\mathfrak{H}} \{\pi\}S\{\rho\}$. Even this does not hold in general. Mitchell Wand exhibits in [Wan78] a particular language $\mathcal{L}$ with an interpretation $\mathfrak{I}$ and a correctness formula $\{\phi\}$ **while** b **do** S_1 **od** $\{\psi\}$ such that this formula holds in $\mathfrak{I}$ and yet $Tr_{\mathfrak{I}} \not\vdash_{\mathfrak{H}} \{\phi\}$ **while** b **do** S_1 **od** $\{\psi\}$, since its loop invariant is not first-order definable. Hence incompleteness arises because the necessary intermediate assertions cannot be expressed in $\mathcal{L}$ with this particular interpretation.

This leads to our fourth, and successful attempt, which is due to Stephen A. Cook. Consider relative completeness only for those languages, such as Peano arithmetic $\mathcal{L}_p$, for which these intermediate assertions are definable [Coo78].

This brings us back to the box operator introduced in Sections 5.2.2 and 5.4. Recall that

$$C[\![[r]\,\pi]\!]_{\mathfrak{I}} = \{\,(\gamma,\sigma) \mid \forall\zeta((\sigma,\zeta) \in C[\![r]\!]_{\mathfrak{I}} \Rightarrow (\gamma,\zeta) \in C[\![\pi]\!]_{\mathfrak{I}})\,\}\ .$$

Now let $\mathfrak{S}_0$ be a class of programs. Call the language $\mathcal{L}$ *expressive relative to* $\mathfrak{I}$ *and* $\mathfrak{S}_0$ if, for all assertions π and programs $S \in \mathfrak{S}_0$, there exists an assertion ρ which defines $C[\![[r]\,\pi]\!]_{\mathfrak{I}}$ in $\mathcal{L}$ (i.e., such that $\{\,(\gamma,\sigma) \mid (\gamma,\sigma) \models_{\mathfrak{I}} \rho\,\} = C[\![[r]\,\pi]\!]_{\mathfrak{I}}$).

Definition A.4 A proof system $\mathfrak{G}$ for $\mathfrak{S}_0$ is *complete (in the sense of Cook)*, if, for every interpretation $\mathfrak{I}$ such that $\mathcal{L}$ is expressive relative to $\mathfrak{I}$ and $\mathfrak{S}_0$, and for every correctness formula $\{\pi\}S\{\rho\}$ with $S \in \mathfrak{S}_0$ the following holds: if $\models_{\mathfrak{I}} \{\pi\}S\{\rho\}$ then $Tr_{\mathfrak{I}} \vdash_{\mathfrak{G}} \{\pi\}S\{\rho\}$.   ♣

Later on we prove that $\mathcal{L}_p$ is expressive relative to $\mathfrak{I}_N$ and $\mathcal{W}$. Hence languages having this property exist.

Theorem A.5

The proof system $\mathfrak{H}$ for while-programs in $\mathcal{W}$ is complete in the sense of Cook.

Proof: By induction on the structure of while-program $S \in \mathcal{W}$. Let $\mathcal{L}$ be expressive relative to $\mathfrak{I}$ and $\mathcal{W}$.
Case S is $x := e$:

$$\models_{\mathfrak{I}} \{\pi\}x := e\{\rho\}$$
$$\Leftrightarrow \forall\gamma,\sigma((\gamma,\sigma) \in C[\![\pi]\!] \Rightarrow (\gamma,(\sigma : x \mapsto \mathcal{E}[\![e]\!]\sigma)) \in C[\![\rho]\!])$$

$$\Leftrightarrow \models_{\mathfrak{I}} \pi \Rightarrow \rho[^{e}/_{x}] \ , \text{ by Lemma 5.8 (substitution).}$$

Therefore, by the assignment axiom and the consequence rule, $\vdash_{\mathfrak{H}} \{\pi\} x :=$ $e\{\rho\}$.

Case S is $S_1 ; S_2$:

$$\models \{\pi\} S_1 ; S_2 \{\rho\}$$

$$\Leftrightarrow \forall \gamma, \sigma, \sigma', \tau \left(\begin{array}{l} (\gamma, \sigma) \in C[\![\pi]\!]_{\mathfrak{I}} \wedge (\sigma, \sigma') \in \mathcal{P}[\![S_1]\!]_{\mathfrak{I}} \wedge (\sigma', \tau) \in \mathcal{P}[\![S_2]\!]_{\mathfrak{I}} \\ \Rightarrow (\gamma, \tau) \in C[\![\rho]\!]_{\mathfrak{I}} \end{array} \right)$$

$$\Leftrightarrow \forall \gamma, \sigma, \sigma' \left(\begin{array}{l} (\gamma, \sigma) \in C[\![\pi]\!]_{\mathfrak{I}} \wedge (\sigma, \sigma') \in \mathcal{P}[\![S_1]\!]_{\mathfrak{I}} \\ \Rightarrow \forall \tau ((\sigma', \tau) \in \mathcal{P}[\![S_2]\!]_{\mathfrak{I}} \Rightarrow (\gamma, \tau) \in C[\![\rho]\!]_{\mathfrak{I}}) \end{array} \right)$$

This is equivalent to $\models_{\mathfrak{I}} \{\pi\} S_1 \{\kappa\}$ and $\models_{\mathfrak{I}} \{\kappa\} S_2 \{\rho\}$, where κ expresses $[S_2]\rho$ in $\mathfrak{L}$. This implies $\vdash_{\mathfrak{H}} \{\pi\} S_1 \{\kappa\}$ and $\vdash_{\mathfrak{H}} \{\kappa\} S_2 \{\rho\}$ by the induction hypothesis. We use the composition rule to derive $\vdash_{\mathfrak{H}} \{\pi\} S_1 ; S_2 \{\rho\}$.

Case S is **if** b **then** S_1 **else** S_2 **fi** is proven similarly.

Case S is **while** b **do** S_1 **od**: to establish $\vdash_{\mathfrak{H}} \{\kappa\}$ **while** b **do** S_1 **od** $\{\rho\}$ we must find a loop invariant κ such that $\vdash_{\mathfrak{H}} \{\kappa \wedge b\} S_1 \{\kappa\}$, $\models_{\mathfrak{I}} \pi \Rightarrow \kappa$, and $\models_{\mathfrak{I}} \kappa \wedge \neg b \Rightarrow \rho$.

We take for κ the expression in $\mathfrak{L}$ for $[\mathbf{while}\ b\ \mathbf{do}\ S_1\ \mathbf{od}]\rho$; then $\models_{\mathfrak{I}} \pi \Rightarrow \kappa$ is satisfied by Lemma 5.25. Proving $\models_{\mathfrak{I}} \{\kappa \wedge b\} S_1 \{\kappa\}$ and $\models_{\mathfrak{I}} \kappa \wedge \neg b \Rightarrow \rho$ is equally simple.

Hence, by the induction hypothesis $\vdash_{\mathfrak{H}} \{\kappa \wedge b\} S_1 \{\kappa\}$, therefore by the while rule $\vdash_{\mathfrak{H}} \{\kappa\}$ **while** b **do** S_1 **od** $\{\kappa \wedge \neg b\}$, and finally by the consequence rule $\vdash_{\mathfrak{H}} \{\kappa\}$ **while** b **do** S_1 **od** $\{\rho\}$. □

Inspection of the proof above reveals that the essential problem with this kind of completeness is, in fact, how to define $[\mathbf{while}\ b\ \mathbf{do}\ S_1\ \mathbf{od}]\rho$. Taking for $\mathfrak{L}$ the language of Peano arithmetic $\mathfrak{L}_P$ and for $\mathfrak{I}$ the standard model $\mathfrak{I}_{\mathrm{N}}$ of the natural numbers, we sketch below how $[\mathbf{while}\ b\ \mathbf{do}\ S_1\ \mathbf{od}]\rho$ can be defined using a technique called *Gödel encoding*.

Lemma A.6 Consider **while** b **do** S_1 **od**. If, for every assertion π, $[S_1]\pi$ is expressible in $\mathfrak{L}_P$ then for every assertion ρ there exists an assertion κ such that

$$\models_{\mathfrak{I}_{\mathrm{N}}} [\mathbf{while}\ b\ \mathbf{do}\ S_1\ \mathbf{od}]\rho \Leftrightarrow \kappa \ . \tag{A.16}$$

Proof: Our aim is to define assertion $\kappa \in \mathfrak{L}_P$ such that $\sigma \models \kappa$ iff there exist $k \in \mathrm{N}$ and $\sigma_0, \ldots, \sigma_k$ such that $\sigma = \sigma_0$, $\sigma_k \models \rho$, $\sigma_k \models \neg b$, and for all $i \in \mathrm{N}_{<k}$, $\sigma_i \in C[\![b]\!]$ and $(\sigma_i, \sigma_{i+1}) \in \mathcal{P}[\![S_1]\!]$. Let $\vec{x}$ be the list $x_1, \ldots, x_n$ of variables occurring in b, S_1, and ρ. Then κ only restricts the variables in $\vec{x}$, and we can

represent the states σ_i by a finite list $\vec{x}_i$ of variables $x_{1i}, \ldots, x_{ni}$. Thus κ should be equivalent to

$$\exists k \in \mathbb{N} \, \exists \vec{x}_0, \ldots, \vec{x}_k \left(\begin{array}{l} \vec{x} = \vec{x}_0 \wedge (\rho \wedge \neg b)[\vec{x}_k/\vec{x}] \\ \wedge \, \forall i \in \mathbb{N}_{<k} \left(b[\vec{x}_i/\vec{x}] \wedge ([S_1] \, (\vec{x} = \vec{x}_{i+1}))[\vec{x}_i/\vec{x}] \right) \end{array} \right)$$

Note that by assumption $[S_1] \, (\vec{x} = \vec{x}_{i+1})$ is expressible in $\mathcal{L}_P$. Our main problem is that the existential quantification over $\vec{x}_0, \ldots, \vec{x}_k$ cannot be expressed in a first order language by writing out the list of variables $\vec{x}_0, \ldots, \vec{x}_k$ in full because we do not know the value of k. To solve this problem, we use $y_j \in \mathbb{N}$ to encode the list $x_{j1}, \ldots, x_{jk}$. In a picture:

$$
\begin{array}{ccccc}
\vec{x}_0 & \vec{x}_1 & \ldots & \vec{x}_k & \\
\wr & \wr & \cdots & \wr & \\
\overbrace{(x_{10}} & \overbrace{x_{11}} & \cdots & \overbrace{x_{1k})} & \sim \quad y_1 \\
\vdots \quad \vdots & \vdots & & \vdots \quad \vdots & \vdots \\
\underbrace{(x_{n0}} & \underbrace{x_{n1}} & \cdots & \underbrace{x_{nk})} & \sim \quad y_n
\end{array}
$$

This technique is called *Gödel encoding* and allows $len(y) = k$ and $\Pi_i(y) = x$ to be expressed as assertions in $\mathcal{L}_P$ such that

- $len(y) = k$ iff y encodes a sequence of length k, and
- $\Pi_i(y) = x$ iff y encodes a sequence of length at least i, and x is the i-th element of the sequence encoded by y.

Then we define κ to denote the assertion:

$$\exists k, y_1, \ldots, y_n \in \mathbb{N}$$
$$\left(\begin{array}{l} \forall i \in [1..n] \, (len(y_i) = k + 1 \wedge x_i = \Pi_0(y_i)) \\ \wedge \, (\rho \wedge \neg b) \left[\Pi_k(y_1), \ldots, \Pi_k(y_n) / x_1, \ldots, x_n \right] \\ \wedge \, \forall i \in [0..k-1] \\ \left((b \wedge [S_1] \, (\forall j \in [1..n] \, (x_j = \Pi_{i+1}(y_j)))) \right) \left[\Pi_i(y_1), \ldots, \Pi_i(y_n) / x_1, \ldots, x_n \right] \end{array} \right)$$

Hence κ can be expressed in $\mathcal{L}_P$ and, using the definition of κ above, we can now prove (A.16) as follows:

$$\sigma \models [\textbf{while } b \textbf{ do } S_1 \textbf{ od}] \rho$$
$$\Leftrightarrow \exists \sigma_k \, ((\sigma, \sigma_k) \in \mathcal{P}[\![\textbf{while } b \textbf{ do } S_1 \textbf{ od}]\!] \wedge \sigma_k \models \rho)$$
$$\Leftrightarrow \exists k \in \mathbb{N}, \sigma_0, \ldots, \sigma_k \left(\begin{array}{l} \sigma = \sigma_0 \wedge (\sigma_k \models \rho) \\ \wedge \, \forall i \in \mathbb{N}_{<k} \, (\sigma_i \in C[\![b]\!] \wedge (\sigma_i, \sigma_{i+1}) \in \mathcal{P}[\![S_1]\!]) \end{array} \right)$$
$$\Leftrightarrow \kappa \qquad\qquad\qquad\qquad\qquad\qquad\qquad\qquad\qquad\qquad\qquad\qquad \square$$

In order to prove that $\mathcal{L}_P$ is expressive relative to $\mathfrak{I}_N$ and $\mathcal{W}$, we still need the following lemma.

Lemma A.7

(i) $\models_{\mathfrak{I}_N} [x := e]\rho \Leftrightarrow \rho[^e/_x]$

(ii) $\models_{\mathfrak{I}_N} [S_1 ; S_2]\rho \Leftrightarrow [S_1]([S_2]\rho)$

(iii) $\models_{\mathfrak{I}_N} [\textbf{if } b \textbf{ then } S_1 \textbf{ else } S_2 \textbf{ fi}]\rho \Leftrightarrow b \wedge [S_1]\rho \vee \neg b \wedge [S_2]\rho$

Proof: Exercise. □

Theorem A.8
The language of Peano arithmetic is expressive relative to the standard model of the natural numbers and the class of while-programs.

Proof: Immediate from Lemmas A.6 and A.7. □

Two remarks should be made:

(i) In view of Lemma 5.25, expressiveness relative to $\mathfrak{I}$ and $\mathfrak{S}_0$ can be based on the strongest postcondition (i.e., the sequential composition of two relational terms: a Hoare-style assertion and a while-program), instead of on the box operator; see e.g. [Apt81].

(ii) The invariant κ in $\mathcal{L}_P$, which exists by Lemma A.6 and satisfies (A.16), is of interest only insofar as it establishes Hoare's 1969 axiomatization of while-programs as being theoretically adequate, i.e., complete in the sense of Cook. In general, invariants obtained by using Gödel encoding are of no help in designing correct programs, nor do they figure in any actual correctness proof for any given concrete program, for the simple reason that they are never in the back of the mind of any designer of some actual algorithm.

A.5 Characterizing the Specification Statement and the Adaptation Problem

To prepare for our formulation of the recursion rule, we first characterize the specification statement in Hoare logic:

$$\text{specification axiom} \quad \vdash \{\phi\}\, \phi \rightsquigarrow \psi \,\{\psi\}$$

This axiom is valid by Lemma 5.24.(i). Reasoning about the specification statement in Hoare logic is based on the equivalence

$$\models_{\mathfrak{I}} \{\pi\}\, \phi \rightsquigarrow \psi \,\{\rho\} \quad \Leftrightarrow \quad \models_{\mathfrak{I}} \pi \subseteq [\phi \rightsquigarrow \psi]\rho \ ,$$

which holds by Lemma 5.25.(i). Therefore, and to obtain completeness in the sense of Cook, one needs to express $[\phi \rightsquigarrow \psi]\rho$ within our assertion language.

Lemma A.9 Let $\vec{x}$ express the vector of free program variables inside assertions ϕ, ψ, and ρ, let $\vec{x_0}$ express the vector of free logical variables inside ϕ and ψ, and let $\vec{y_0}$ express a vector of fresh logical variables of the same length as $\vec{x}$.

$$\models [\phi \rightsquigarrow \psi]\rho \Leftrightarrow \forall \vec{y_0} \left(\forall \vec{x_0} \left(\phi \Rightarrow \psi[\vec{y_0}/\vec{x}] \right) \Rightarrow \rho[\vec{y_0}/\vec{x}] \right)$$

Proof: By definition of the semantics of relational terms (Def. 5.22) and the substitution and coincidence lemmas (Lemmas 5.8, 5.6, and 5.13). $\qquad \Box$

This expressibility result is integrated into Hoare logic by introducing the following adaptation rule for arbitrary statements S.

$$[\,]\text{-adaptation rule} \qquad \frac{\{\phi\}\,S\,\{\psi\}}{\left\{ \forall \vec{y_0} \left(\forall \vec{x_0} \left(\phi \Rightarrow \psi[\vec{y_0}/\vec{x}] \right) \Rightarrow \rho[\vec{y_0}/\vec{x}] \right) \right\} S\,\{\rho\}}$$

where $\vec{x}, \vec{x_0}$, and $\vec{y_0}$ are chosen as in Lemma A.9.

The idea behind this rule is the following. Suppose one wants to build up a library of (hardware or software) modules, where each of their specifications is given by a Hoare triple. The intention is that every property of such a module should be implied by that triple, or rather, by its pre- and postconditions only, without the need to read a manual about the functioning of S or to inspect its hardware structure or program text.

Properly speaking, this approach impels us to introduce correctness formulae $\{\pi\}\,X\,\{\rho\}$ for relational variables, in order to express our intention that inspection of the internal workings of S is forbidden. Correspondingly, a formula such as $\{\pi\}\,X\,\{\rho\}$ is called a *black-box specification*. To define the meaning of $\models_{\mathfrak{I}} \{\pi\}\,X\,\{\rho\}$ one has to extend the concept of interpretation $\mathfrak{I}$ to a triple $\langle \mathfrak{S}, \sigma, \delta \rangle$ with δ a relational variable environment, i.e., a mapping of relational variables to their meanings.

Such black-box formulae only make sense in the context of implications between correctness formulae of the form:

$$\text{For all } X_1, \ldots X_n, \bigwedge_{i=1}^{n} \{\pi_i\}\,X_i\,\{\rho_i\} \Rightarrow \{\pi\}\,S(X_1, \ldots, X_n)\,\{\rho\}, \qquad (A.17)$$

whose validity is defined by: for all interpretations $\mathfrak{I}$, whenever $\models_{\mathfrak{I}} \{\pi_i\}\,X_i\,\{\rho_i\}$ holds for $i = 1, \ldots, n$, then $\models_{\mathfrak{I}} \{\pi\}\,S(X_1, \ldots, X_n)\,\{\rho\}$ is satisfied.

Note that any dependency upon a particular choice of interpretation for X_i is eliminated by quantifying over all X_i.

This approach makes sense especially for reasoning about data types, where the formulae $\{\pi_i\}\, X_i\, \{\rho_i\}$ are used to characterize the primitive operations, here named X_i, of a data type, and formulae $\{\pi\}\, S(X_1, \ldots, X_n)\, \{\rho\}$ express properties of program constructs S using that data type.

Now that the meaning of such implications between black-box formulae and programs using black boxes, i.e., modules, is clarified, we turn to the question of how to prove implications of the form (A.17) within our Hoare logic, in particular whether their introduction calls for new rules.

By a theorem of Zwiers [Z89], compositional Hoare logics satisfy the following property: in order to prove (A.17) for arbitrary n it suffices to be able to prove such implications for $n = 1$, i.e., one should be able to prove

$$\forall X. \{\pi_0\}\, X\, \{\rho_0\} \Rightarrow \{\pi\}\, S(X)\, \{\rho\} \ldots \tag{A.18}$$

whenever this formula is valid.

And proving (A.18) inside Hoare logic obviously reduces to proving formulae of the form

$$\forall X. \{\pi_0\}\, X\, \{\rho_0\} \Rightarrow \{\pi\}\, X\, \{\rho\} \ldots \tag{A.19}$$

whenever they are valid. This latter property is called *adaptation completeness* [Old83, Z89].

Together with the consequence rule, our [ ]-adaptation rule is adaptation complete. For suppose (A.19) holds for all interpretations $\Im$. Then this applies in particular to choosing $\pi_0 \rightsquigarrow \rho_0$ for X:

$$\models \{\pi_0\}\, \pi_0 \rightsquigarrow \rho_0\, \{\rho_0\} \Rightarrow \{\pi\}\, \pi_0 \rightsquigarrow \rho_0\, \{\rho\} \ .$$

Hence $\models \pi \Rightarrow [\pi_0 \rightsquigarrow \rho_0]\rho$ follows, since we already established validity of correctness formula $\{\pi_0\}\, \pi_0 \rightsquigarrow \rho_0\, \{\rho_0\}$ above.

Since under assumption $\vdash \{\pi_0\}\, X\, \{\rho_0\}$ one proves $\vdash \{[\pi_0 \rightsquigarrow \rho_0]\rho\}\, X\, \{\rho\}$ using the [ ]-adaptation rule (where we assume $[\pi_0 \rightsquigarrow \rho_0]\rho$ to be expressed by an equivalent assertion), an application of the consequence rule leads to $\vdash \{\pi\}\, X\, \{\rho\}$.

For a systematic treatment of relational variables inside Hoare logic we refer to [Z89], since this is beyond the scope of this monograph. However, there exists a shortcut, as the above completeness result already indicates. For why not reason about terms $\pi \rightsquigarrow \rho$ instead of about variables X satisfying $\{\pi\}\, X\, \{\rho\}$? Then (A.18) reduces to

$$\{\pi\}\, S(\pi_0 \rightsquigarrow \rho_0)\, \{\rho\} \ldots \tag{A.20}$$

This can be understood as follows. Since $\models \{\pi_0\} X \{\rho_0\} \Leftrightarrow X \subseteq (\pi_0 \leadsto \rho_0)$, and terms $S(X)$ are by Lemmas 3.8 and 3.17 monotone in X, one has $\models X \subseteq (\pi_0 \leadsto \rho_0) \Rightarrow \pi \,; S(X) \subseteq \pi \,; S(\pi_0 \leadsto \rho_0)$. Also, (A.20) implies that $\pi \,; S(\pi_0 \leadsto \rho_0) \subseteq \rho$. Combining these two results yields that $\models \{\pi\} S(\pi_0 \leadsto \rho_0) \{\rho\}$ implies $\models_{\mathfrak{I}} \{\pi_0\} X \{\rho_0\} \Rightarrow \{\pi\} S(X) \{\rho\}$ for all $\mathfrak{I}$. Within Hoare logic, this argument requires introduction of the $\leadsto$-substitution rule:

$$\leadsto\text{-substitution rule} \quad \frac{\{\pi_0\} S_1 \{\rho_0\} \,, \{\pi\} S_2(\pi_0 \leadsto \rho_0) \{\rho\}}{\{\pi\} S_2(S_1) \{\rho\}} \quad ,$$

where $S_2(\pi_0 \leadsto \rho_0) \stackrel{\text{def}}{=} S_2[{}^{\pi_0 \leadsto \rho_0}/x]$, $S_2(S_1) \stackrel{\text{def}}{=} S_2[{}^{S_1}/x]$, and substitution of a term S for X is defined similarly as in Section 5.2, in that clashes between free variables Y of S, occurring when S is substituted for X within the scope of a μY-operator, are prevented by suitable renaming of the bound variable Y inside the scope of μY.

Observe that the $\leadsto$-substitution rule provides a tool for structuring our reasoning in a way which is analogous to that used in hierarchical program development. Rather than proving $\{\pi\} S_2(S_1) \{\rho\}$ from scratch on the basis of the structure of $S_2(S_1)$, one proves the more abstract property $\{\pi\} S_2(\pi_0 \leadsto \rho_0) \{\rho\}$ first, and then uses the fact that S_1 refines the specification $\pi_0 \leadsto \rho_0$ for deducing $\{\pi\} S_2(S_1) \{\rho\}$, thus modularizing our way of reasoning.

Lemma A.10 The [ ]-adaptation rule is sound.

Proof: Let $\mathfrak{I}$ be an interpretation.

   (i) $\models_{\mathfrak{I}} \{[S]\rho\} S \{\rho\}$ holds by Lemma 5.25.

  (ii) $\models_{\mathfrak{I}} \{\phi\} S \{\psi\}$ iff $\models_{\mathfrak{I}} S \subseteq \phi \leadsto \psi$ by Lemma 5.24.

 (iii) $\models \rho_1 \subseteq \rho_2$ implies $\models_{\mathfrak{I}} [\rho_2]\rho \Rightarrow [\rho_1]\rho$, as follows by definition of the box operator.

 (iv) Taking S for ρ_1 and $(\phi \leadsto \psi)$ for ρ_2 in point (iii), from point (ii) follows that $\models_{\mathfrak{I}} \{\phi\} S \{\psi\}$ implies $\models_{\mathfrak{I}} [\phi \leadsto \psi]\rho \Rightarrow \models_{\mathfrak{I}} [S]\rho$.

  (v) By (i), (iv), and soundness of the consequence rule $\models_{\mathfrak{I}} \{\phi\} S \{\psi\}$ implies $\models_{\mathfrak{I}} \{[\phi \leadsto \psi]\rho\} S \{\rho\}$.

 (vi) $\models [\phi \leadsto \psi]\rho \Leftrightarrow \forall \vec{y_0}(\forall \vec{x_0}(\phi \Rightarrow \psi[{}^{\vec{y_0}}/{}_{\vec{x_0}}]) \Rightarrow \rho[{}^{\vec{y_0}}/{}_{\vec{x_0}}])$, by Lemma A.9 with $\vec{x}, \vec{x_0}$ and $\vec{y_0}$ as in Lemma A.9.

(vii) Consequently, since $\mathfrak{I}$ is arbitrary, points (v) and (vi) imply soundness of the [ ]-adaptation rule. $\square$

Next assume again that $\models \{\pi\} (\phi \leadsto \psi) \{\rho\}$ holds. By the [ ]-adaptation rule and the specification axiom one obtains $\vdash \{[\phi \leadsto \psi]\rho\} (\phi \leadsto \psi) \{\rho\}$. Since

$\models \{\pi\}(\phi \rightsquigarrow \psi)\{\rho\}$ iff $\models \pi \Rightarrow [\phi \rightsquigarrow \psi]\rho$, this implies $\vdash \{\pi\}(\phi \rightsquigarrow \psi)\{\rho\}$, using the consequence rule.

Consequently the specification axiom and the [ ]-adaptation rule provide, together with the consequence rule, a sound and also complete, i.e. in the sense of Cook, way of reasoning about the specification statement.

An alternative way of reasoning about the specification statement is based on the following two observations concerning the *strongest postcondition* operator *sp*:

(i) $\models_\exists \{\pi\}(\phi \rightsquigarrow \psi)\{\rho\} \Leftrightarrow \models_\exists sp(\pi, \phi \rightsquigarrow \psi) \Rightarrow \rho$

(ii) $\models_\exists sp(\pi, \phi \rightsquigarrow \psi) \Leftrightarrow \exists \vec{y}_0(\forall \vec{x}_0(\phi[\vec{y}_0/\vec{x}] \Rightarrow \psi) \wedge \pi[\vec{y}_0/\vec{x}])$, with $\vec{x}$ expressing the vector of programming variables in ϕ, ψ and π, $\vec{x}_0$ the vector of free logical variables inside ϕ and ψ, and $\vec{y}_0$ a vector of fresh logical variables of the same length as $\vec{x}$

and the following rule:

$$sp\text{-adaptation rule} \quad \frac{\{\phi\}\,S\,\{\psi\}}{\{\pi\}\,S\,\{\exists \vec{y}_0(\forall \vec{x}_0(\phi[\vec{y}_0/\vec{x}] \Rightarrow \psi) \wedge \pi[\vec{y}_0/\vec{x}])\}}$$

with $\vec{x}$, $\vec{x}_0$, $\vec{y}_0$ as above. This is worked out in the exercises.

A.6 The Recursion Rule

To simplify the discussion we restrict our attention to the case of one recursive procedure only. All of our results can be straightforwardly generalized to an arbitrary number of recursive procedures; see [dB80].

Our Hoare style rule for recursion is based on Scott's induction rule [SdB69], though we use the specification statement in its formulation.

$$\text{recursion rule} \quad \frac{\{\pi\}\,S(\pi \rightsquigarrow \rho)\{\rho\}}{\{\pi\}\,\mu X.S(X)\{\rho\}}$$

The intuition behind this rule is that its premise, $\{\pi\}\,S(\pi \rightsquigarrow \rho)\{\rho\}$, expresses the proof of an induction step in an abstract formulation of an induction argument on the recursion depth of a call of $\mu X.S(X)$. In the original formulation of Scott's induction rule the proof of this step is formulated by

$$\{\pi\}\,X\,\{\rho\} \vdash \{\pi\}\,S(X)\{\rho\}, \dots \tag{A.21}$$

with X a free recursion variable, which expresses that $\{\pi\}\,S(X)\{\rho\}$ is to be proven under assumption $\{\pi\}\,X\,\{\rho\}$.

Since $\vdash \{\pi\}\,\mathbf{abort}\,\{\rho\}$ always holds by the abort axiom, and $\mathbf{abort}$ is a possible choice for X, by (A.21) $\vdash \{\pi\}\,S(\mathbf{abort})\{\rho\}$ follows. This argument can be generalized to $\vdash \{\pi\}\, S^i(\textbf{abort})\,\{\rho\}$, $i \in \mathbb{N}$. Since $S^i(\textbf{abort})$ expresses the behavior of $\mu X.S(X)$ restricted to recursion depth below i, this establishes the correspondence between the induction argument expressed by Scott's induction rule and an argument on recursion depth.

Now (A.21) can be reformulated within our framework by $\{\pi\}\, S(\pi \rightsquigarrow \rho)\,\{\rho\}$, since all that is required by (A.21) is to prove $\{\pi\}\, S(X)\,\{\rho\}$ using the assumption $X \subseteq \pi \rightsquigarrow \rho$ about X, and that is also expressed by $\{\pi\}\, S(\pi \rightsquigarrow \rho)\,\{\rho\}$.

Lemma A.11 The recursion rule is sound.

Proof: Recall that **abort** denotes the empty relation. Hence $\models \textbf{abort} \subseteq \pi \rightsquigarrow \rho$. Consequently $S(\textbf{abort}) \subseteq S(\pi \rightsquigarrow \rho)$, by monotonicity of our operators (see Lemmas 3.8 and 3.17). Since $\models S(\pi \rightsquigarrow \rho) \subseteq \pi \rightsquigarrow \rho$ holds by the premise of the recursion rule, one obtains also that $\models S(\textbf{abort}) \subseteq \pi \rightsquigarrow \rho$.

This argument can be easily extended by induction on i to $\models S^i(\textbf{abort}) \subseteq \pi \rightsquigarrow \rho$, for $i \in \mathbb{N}$. Consequently $\models \bigcup_{i \in \mathbb{N}} S^i(\textbf{abort}) \subseteq \pi \rightsquigarrow \rho$, and hence, by Lemma 3.20, $\models \mu X.S(X) \subseteq \pi \rightsquigarrow \rho$, which is equivalent to $\models \{\pi\}\, \mu X.S(X)\,\{\rho\}$.
$\square$

Completeness in the sense of Cook can also be established for the system $\mathfrak{H}$ + specification axiom + [ ]-adaptation rule + recursion rule; this follows from results of [Old83].

Example A.12 Let S_0 denote the following program:

if $x = 0$ **then** $y := 1$ **else** $x := x - 1\,;X\,;x := x + 1\,;y := y * x$ **fi** ,

i.e., calling $\mu X.S_0(X)$ results in calculating $x!$, the factorial of x, as the value of y. We prove

$$\{x \geq 0\}\,\mu X.S_0(X)\,\{y = x!\} \ .$$

By the recursion rule, we need to prove

$$\{x \geq 0\}\,S_0(x \geq 0 \rightsquigarrow y = x!)\,\{y = x!\} \ .$$

First of all, we have, by the specification axiom,

$$\{x \geq 0\}\,x \geq 0 \rightsquigarrow y = x!\,\{y = x!\} \tag{A.22}$$

By the assignment axiom,

$$\{y * x = x!\}\,y := y * x\,\{y = x!\} \tag{A.23}$$

and

$$\{y * (x+1) = (x+1)!\}\,x := x + 1\,\{y * x = x!\} \ . \tag{A.24}$$

So, by the composition rule

$$\{y*(x+1) = (x+1)!\}x := x+1; y := y*x\{y = x!\} \ . \tag{A.25}$$

Since the implication

$$y = x! \Rightarrow y*(x+1) = (x+1)! \tag{A.26}$$

is true, by the consequence rule and (A.22)

$$\{x \ge 0\}(x \ge 0 \rightsquigarrow y = x!)\{y*(x+1) = (x+1)!\} \ . \tag{A.27}$$

Formulae (A.25) and (A.27) imply, by the composition rule,

$$\{x \ge 0\}(x \ge 0 \rightsquigarrow y = x!); x := x+1; y := y*x\{y = x!\} \ . \tag{A.28}$$

On the other hand, since the implication

$$x \ge 0 \wedge x \ne 0 \Rightarrow x-1 \ge 0 \tag{A.29}$$

is true, and, by the assignment axiom,

$$\{x-1 \ge 0\}x := x-1\{x \ge 0\} \ , \tag{A.30}$$

we obtain by the consequence rule

$$\{x \ge 0 \wedge x \ne 0\}x := x-1\{x \ge 0\} \ . \tag{A.31}$$

By the composition rule we get from (A.28) and (A.31)

$$\left\{x \ge 0 \wedge x \ne 0\right\}\begin{matrix} x := x-1; (x \ge 0 \rightsquigarrow y = x!); \\ x := x+1; y := y*x \end{matrix}\left\{y = x!\right\} \ . \tag{A.32}$$

Since

$$x \ge 0 \wedge x = 0 \Rightarrow 1 = x! \tag{A.33}$$

is true, and, by the assignment axiom,

$$\{1 = x!\}y := 1\{y = x!\} \ , \tag{A.34}$$

the consequence rule implies

$$\{x \ge 0 \wedge x = 0\}y := 1\{y = x!\} \ . \tag{A.35}$$

Formulae (A.32) and (A.35) finally imply by the if-then-else rule

$$\{x \ge 0\}S_0(x \ge 0 \rightsquigarrow y = x!)\{y = x!\} \tag{A.36}$$

which was to be proven.

Of course, strictly speaking, we only proved that

$$(A.26), (A.29), (A.33) \vdash \{x \ge 0\}\mu X, S_0(X)\{y = x!\} \ . \qquad \heartsuit$$

In the next example we illustrate why the $[\,]$-adaptation rule is *necessary*, since it is proven in [Apt81] that without such a rule the property below cannot be established in our proof system.

Example A.13 We prove

$$\{x = z_0\}\,\mu X.S_0(X)\,\{x = z_0\} \tag{A.37}$$

with S_0 as above, i.e. the values of program variable x before and after calling the factorial procedure $\mu X.S_0(X)$ are the same. Observe that in order to express this property it is necessary to use a logical variable, in this case z_0 (cf. Example 5.32).

To prove (A.37), it is enough to establish the premise

$$\{x = z_0\}\,S_0(x = z_0 \rightsquigarrow x = z_0)\,\{x = z_0\} \tag{A.38}$$

of the recursion rule. For this, it is necessary to prove

$$\{x = z_0 - 1\}\,x = z_0 \rightsquigarrow x = z_0\,\{x = z_0 - 1\}\ , \tag{A.39}$$

for then (A.38) easily follows, by applying the assignment axiom and the composition and consequence rules to get from (A.39)

$$\left\{x = z_0\right\}\begin{array}{l} x := x - 1\,; (x = z_0 \rightsquigarrow x = z_0);\\ x := x + 1\,; y := y * x \end{array}\left\{x = z_0\right\}\ . \tag{A.40}$$

By the consequence rule one can conjoin the precondition with the assertion $x \neq 0$. Also

$$\{x = z_0 \wedge x = 0\}\,y := 1\,\{x = z_0\}\ . \tag{A.41}$$

By the if-then-else rule we now obtain (A.38). So, all that remains to prove is (A.39). Applying the $[\,]$-adaptation rule to $\{x = z_0\}\,x = z_0 \rightsquigarrow x = z_0\,\{x = z_0\}$ with respect to postcondition $x = z_0 - 1$ one gets

$$\begin{array}{l} \{\forall y_0\,(\forall z_0\,(x = z_0 \Rightarrow (x = z_0)[^{y_0}/_x]) \Rightarrow (x = z_0 - 1)[^{y_0}/_x])\}\\ \quad x = z_0 \rightsquigarrow x = z_0\\ \{x = z_0 - 1\}\ . \end{array} \tag{A.42}$$

We prove

$$\models \forall y_0\left(\begin{array}{l}\forall z_0\,(x = z_0 \Rightarrow (x = z_0)[^{y_0}/_x])\\ \Rightarrow (x = z_0 - 1)[^{y_0}/_x]\end{array}\right) \Leftrightarrow x = z_0 - 1\ , \tag{A.43}$$

i.e.,

$$\models \forall y_0\,(\forall z_0\,(x = z_0 \Rightarrow y_0 = z_0) \Rightarrow y_0 = z_0 - 1) \Leftrightarrow x = z_0 - 1\ , \tag{A.44}$$

which is obtained after carrying out the substitutions in (A.43). Firstly,

$$\models \forall z_0 \, (x = z_0 \Rightarrow y_0 = z_0) \Leftrightarrow x = y_0 \, , \qquad (A.45)$$

and secondly,

$$\models \forall y_0 \, (x = y_0 \Rightarrow y_0 = z_0 - 1) \Leftrightarrow x = z_0 - 1 \, . \qquad (A.46)$$

Consequently, (A.44) follows, and therefore (A.43). By applying the consequence rule to (A.42), we obtain (A.39). ♡

Exercises

A.1 Prove Theorem A.2.

A.2 Formulate an axiom scheme for **skip**, and prove its validity.

A.3 Prove soundness of the if-then-else and consequence rules.

A.4 Prove that $(\sigma, \tau) \in \mathcal{P}[\![\textbf{while } b \textbf{ do } S \textbf{ od}]\!]$ iff for some $k \in \mathbb{N}$ there exists a sequence of states $\sigma_0 \sigma_1 \dots \sigma_k$ such that $\sigma_0 = \sigma$ and $\sigma_k = \tau$, $\sigma_i \in C[\![b]\!]$ and $(\sigma_i, \sigma_{i+1}) \in \mathcal{P}[\![S]\!]$ for $0 \le i < k$, and $\sigma_k \in C[\![\neg b]\!]$.

A.5 (a) Show by means of an example that Hoare's assignment axiom is not valid when x is replaced by a subscripted variable $c[i]$.

    (b) How could a valid axiom for assignments $c[i] := e$ to subscripted variables be obtained?

    Hint: Since there is only one name for c available, namely "c" itself, rewrite $c[i] := e$ as an assignment to c (instead of to $c[i]$, for which more names, i.e., aliases, may be available).

A.6 Prove soundness of the guarded selection and guarded loop rules.

A.7 Let **repeat** S **until** b **od** denote the program S; **while** $\neg b$ **do** S **od**. Prove soundness of the following rule.

$$\text{repeat rule} \quad \frac{\{\rho\} S \{q\}, q \wedge \neg b \to \rho}{\{\rho\} \textbf{repeat } S \textbf{ until } b \, \{q \wedge b\}}$$

A.8 Let $\mathcal{L}$ be expressive relative to $\mathfrak{J}$ and $\mathcal{W}$. Prove that

$$\models_{\mathfrak{J}} \{\pi\} \textbf{if } b \textbf{ then } S_1 \textbf{ else } S_2 \textbf{ fi} \{\rho\}$$

implies

$$\vdash_{\mathfrak{H}} \{\pi\} \textbf{if } b \textbf{ then } S_1 \textbf{ else } S_2 \textbf{ fi} \{\rho\} \, ,$$

i.e., give the missing case in the proof of Theorem A.5.

A.9　　Let $\mathcal{L}$ be expressive relative to $\mathfrak{I}$ and $\mathcal{W}$, and let

$$\models_{\mathfrak{I}} \{\pi\} \textbf{ while } b \textbf{ do } S_1 \textbf{ od } \{\rho\}$$

hold. Furthermore, let κ be an expression for $[\textbf{while } b \textbf{ do } S_1 \textbf{ od}]\rho$ in $\mathcal{L}$. Prove $\models_{\mathfrak{I}} \{\kappa \wedge b\} S_1 \{\kappa\}$ and $\models_{\mathfrak{I}} \kappa \wedge \neg b \Rightarrow \rho$.

A.10　Prove Lemma A.7.

A.11　Indicate the changes to be made in the proof of Lemma A.6 to define the strongest postcondition $sp(\pi, \textbf{while } b \textbf{ do } S_1 \textbf{ od})$ in $\mathcal{L}_P$ under interpretation $\mathfrak{I}_{\mathbb{N}}$.

A.12　Give syntactic characterizations for

　　　(a) $sp(\pi, x := e)$,
　　　(b) $sp(\pi, S_1 ; S_2)$, and
　　　(c) $sp(\pi, \textbf{if } b \textbf{ then } S_1 \textbf{ else } S_2 \textbf{ fi})$

　　　in $\mathcal{L}_P$ in the vein of Lemma A.7 but for strongest postconditions, and prove equivalence between your characterizations and the corresponding strongest postconditions.

A.13　Prove $\models_{\mathfrak{I}} sp(\pi, \phi \rightsquigarrow \psi) \Leftrightarrow \exists \vec{y_0}(\forall \vec{x_0}(\phi[^{\vec{y_0}}\!/_{\vec{x}}] \Rightarrow \psi) \wedge \pi[^{\vec{y_0}}\!/_{\vec{x}}])$, with $\vec{x}$ the vector of program variables in ϕ, ψ, and π, $\vec{x_0}$ the vector of free logical variables in ϕ and ψ, and $\vec{y_0}$ a vector of new logical variables of the same length as $\vec{x}$.

A.14　Prove soundness of the sp-adaptation rule.

A.15　Prove that the sp-adaptation rule, the specification axiom, and the consequence rule together provide a way of reasoning about the specification statement which is complete in the sense of Cook.

A.16　Prove $\{x \geq 0\} \mu X . S_0(X) \{y \geq 1\}$ for S_0 as in Example A.12.

Appendix B

A Primer on Ordinals and Transfinite Induction

(A previous version was originally compiled in Dutch by Ron Koymans.)

B.1 Well-orders

Definition B.1 Let R denote a binary relation over the set X, i.e., $R \subseteq X^2$. Instead of writing $(x,y) \in R$, we shall write xRy. We call R a (*total* or *linear*) *order* of X when R is:

- (i) *irreflexive*, that is, $\neg xRx$ holds for every $x \in X$,
- (ii) *asymmetric*, that is, $xRy \Rightarrow \neg yRx$ holds for all $x, y \in X$,
- (iii) *transitive*, that is, $xRy \wedge yRz \Rightarrow xRz$ holds for all $x, y, z \in X$, and
- (iv) *semiconnex*, that is, $xRy \vee yRx \vee x = y$ holds for all $x, y, z \in X$. ♣

Remark Every transitive and irreflexive relation is asymmetric, i.e., condition (ii) above follows from conditions (i) and (iii). ◇

Definition B.2 Let X denote a set, R an order of X, and let $Y \subseteq X$. Then $x \in Y$ is called a *least element of* Y when xRy holds for all $y \in Y \setminus \{x\}$. ♣

Remark Least elements need not always exist, e.g., for $Y = X = \mathbb{Z}$ (the set of all integers) with order $<$ (less than). In case a least element exists, it is unique by asymmetry of orders. ◇

Definition B.3 An order R of set X is called a *well-order* of X when every nonvoid subset of X has a least element. ♣

Without proof, we mention that the following induction principle is sound:

Definition B.4 ($\in$-**induction**) Call

$$\forall a \, (\forall b \, (b \in a \Rightarrow P(b)) \Rightarrow P(a)) \Rightarrow \forall a \, (P(a)) \tag{B.1}$$

the *principle of ∈-induction*, in which quantification is over sets, and P expresses an arbitrary property of sets.   ♣

Theorem B.5
The ∈-induction principle is sound.   ♠

Definition B.6 A set a is called *transitive* when $b \in a \wedge c \in b \Rightarrow c \in a$ holds for all b and c.   ♣

(An equivalent formulation is: $b \in a \Rightarrow b \subseteq a$.)

Definition B.7 A *structure* is a pair (A, R) where A denotes a set and R a relation over A. Structure (A, R) is called a well-order when R is a well-order of A. A one-to-one and onto function $h : A \longrightarrow B$ between structures (A, R) and (B, S) is called an *isomorphism* if $S = \{ (h(a), h(b)) \mid aRb \}$.

The *epsilon relation* $\in_A$ over A is defined by: $\in_A \overset{\text{def}}{=} \{ (a, b) \in A^2 \mid a \in b \}$. An *epsilon structure* is a structure of the form $(A, \in_A)$; this structure is called transitive when A is transitive.   ♣

Without proof we mention the following important theorem:

Theorem B.8
Every well-order (A, R) is isomorphic to a transitive epsilon structure $(B, \in_B)$; the isomorphism and B are completely determined by (A, R).   ♠

This theorem leads to the following definition.

Definition B.9 The *order type* of a well-order (A, R) is the unique transitive set B such that (A, R) is isomorphic to $(B, \in_B)$.   ♣

B.2 Ordinals

The order type of a well-order is also called an *ordinal*. This is, therefore, a transitive set which is well-ordered by its epsilon relation. However, we shall base the theory of ordinals on a simpler characterization of this concept.

Definition B.10 An *ordinal* is a transitive set of transitive sets.   ♣

Lemma B.11 The elements of ordinals are ordinals.

Proof: Let α be an ordinal and $a \in \alpha$. Then a is transitive by Def. B.10. All elements $b \in a$ are also transitive because α is transitive.   □

Theorem B.12

For every pair of ordinals α and β one has that $\alpha \in \beta$ or $\beta \in \alpha$ or $\alpha = \beta$.

Proof: We use $\in$-induction over α to show that for every ordinal α

$$\forall \beta (\alpha \in \beta \vee \beta \in \alpha \vee \alpha = \beta) \tag{B.2}$$

holds. Hence the induction hypothesis is

$$\forall \gamma (\gamma \in \alpha \Rightarrow \forall \beta (\gamma \in \beta \vee \beta \in \gamma \vee \gamma = \beta)) \tag{B.3}$$

on the basis of which we need to prove (B.2). To do so we apply $\in$-induction for a second time, now over β. This results in a second induction hypothesis:

$$\forall \gamma (\gamma \in \beta \Rightarrow \alpha \in \gamma \vee \gamma \in \alpha \vee \alpha = \alpha) \tag{B.4}$$

and now we have to show that $\alpha \in \beta$ or $\beta \in \alpha$ or $\alpha = \beta$ holds. To do so, let us assume

$$\alpha \notin \beta \quad \wedge \quad \beta \notin \alpha \tag{B.5}$$

and prove $\alpha = \beta$.

(i) If $\gamma \in \alpha$ then $\beta \notin \gamma$ and $\gamma \neq \beta$ (otherwise $\beta \in \alpha$ would be implied by transitivity of α, contradicting our assumption (B.5)). Now (B.3) implies that $\gamma \in \beta$.

(ii) If $\gamma \in \beta$ then $\alpha \notin \gamma$ and $\gamma \neq \alpha$ (otherwise $\alpha \in \beta$ would be implied by transitivity of β, contradicting our assumption (B.5)). Now (B.4) implies that $\gamma \in \alpha$.

Altogether, $\gamma \in \alpha \Leftrightarrow \gamma \in \beta$, for all γ. Consequently $\alpha = \beta$. $\qquad \square$

Corollary B.13 Let α be an ordinal. Then $(\alpha, \in_\alpha)$ is a well-order.

Proof: It is easy to see that $\in_\alpha$ is a order of α using the fact that $x \notin x$ for every set x, the definition of transitivity of a set, and Theorem B.12. It therefore remains to prove that every nonempty subset of α has a least element. Let $X \subseteq \alpha$ such that $X \neq \emptyset$. We prove that $\bigcap X = \{ z \mid \forall y \in X (z \in y) \}$ is the least element of X.

- Elements of $\bigcap X$ are transitive, since if $z \in \bigcap X$ then $X \subseteq \alpha$ and α transitive imply $z \in \alpha$ because $X \neq \emptyset$ implies $\exists y \in X (z \in y)$. Hence z is transitive.
- $\bigcap X$ is also transitive. For if $z \in \bigcap X$ and $x \in z$ then $\forall y \in X (x \in Z \wedge z \in y)$ holds, and hence, since $y \in X (\subseteq \alpha)$ is transitive, $\forall y \in X (x \in y)$ holds, i.e., $x \in \bigcap X$.

Next we show that

$$\forall z \in X \left(z \neq \bigcap X \Rightarrow \bigcap X \in z \right) \tag{B.6}$$

Assume, to the contrary, that $z \in X \wedge z \neq \bigcap X \wedge \bigcap X \notin z$. By Lemma B.11 z is an ordinal. We just proved that $\bigcap X$ is also an ordinal. Consequently, Theorem B.12 implies that $z \in \bigcap X$, i.e., $\forall y \in X \, (z \in y)$ holds. By choosing $y = z$ one obtains $z \in z$, contradiction.

If we can also show that $\bigcap X \in X$ than the proof is finished, for together with (B.6) this implies that $\bigcap X$ is the least element of X. Since $\bigcap X \notin \bigcap X$ and by the definition of $\bigcap X$ one has that $\neg \forall y \in X \, (\bigcap X \in y)$, i.e., $\exists y \in X \, (\bigcap X \notin y)$. Using (B.6) this implies immediately $\bigcap X \in X$.   □

Remark One verifies easily that the order type of a well-order is an ordinal (according to Def. B.10, using Theorem B.8 and Def. B.9). Conversely every ordinal α is the order type of the well-order $(\alpha, \in_\alpha)$. The ordinals are therefore exactly the order types of well-orders.   ◇

Notation: One writes $\alpha < \beta$ or also $\beta > \alpha$ instead of $\alpha \in \beta$, and $\alpha \leq \beta$ or also $\beta \geq \alpha$ instead of $\alpha \subseteq \beta$ (for ordinals α and β).

Definition B.14 Let x denote a set. Define $x^+ \overset{\text{def}}{=} x \cup \{x\}$.   ♣

Using the operation just defined we now define sets $0, 1, 2, \dots$ which will play the rôle of natural numbers.

Definition B.15 Define recursively $0 \overset{\text{def}}{=} \emptyset$ and $n+1 \overset{\text{def}}{=} n^+$.   ♣

Definition B.16 a is called a *successor set* if $0 \in a$ and $\forall x \, (x \in a \Rightarrow x^+ \in a)$.   ♣

One can show that such successor sets exist, and that there exists a least successor set, called ω.

Definition B.17 $\omega \overset{\text{def}}{=} \{ y \mid \forall a \, (0 \in a \wedge \forall x \, (x \in a \Rightarrow x^+ \in a) \Rightarrow y \in a) \}$.   ♣

Theorem B.18 (Principle of complete induction)
Call

$$\Phi(0) \wedge \forall x \in \omega \left(\Phi(x) \Rightarrow \Phi(x^+) \right) \Rightarrow \forall x \in \omega (\Phi(x))$$

the principle of complete induction. Then this principle holds for all formulae Φ.

Proof: Assuming $\Phi(0) \wedge \forall x \in \omega(\Phi(x) \Rightarrow \Phi(x^+))$ holds, $\{ x \in \omega \mid \Phi(x) \}$ is a successor set. Because ω is the least successor set, necessarily $\omega \subseteq \{ x \mid \Phi(x) \}$, hence $\forall x \in \omega(\Phi(x))$ holds. $\qquad\square$

From now on let $\mathbb{O}$ denote the class[1] of all ordinals.

Theorem B.19

  (i) $0 \in \mathbb{O}$

  (ii) $\alpha \in \mathbb{O} \Rightarrow \alpha^+ \in \mathbb{O}$

  (iii) $a \subseteq \mathbb{O} \Rightarrow \bigcup a \in \mathbb{O}$

  (iv) $\omega \in \mathbb{O}$

Proof:

  (i) This follows directly from Def. B.10 and B.15.

  (ii) Because $\alpha^+ = \alpha \cup \{\alpha\}$, one has that $b \in \alpha^+$ is equivalent to $b \in \alpha \vee b = a$. Consequently α^+ and its elements are transitive.

  (iii) $b \in \bigcup a \Leftrightarrow \exists c \in a (b \in c)$; moreover, $c \in \mathbb{O}$. It is again easy to check that $\bigcup a$ itself and its elements are transitive.

  (iv) First we show that $\omega \subseteq \mathbb{O}$ using complete induction. This is a direct consequence of the first two parts of this theorem. Because ordinals are transitive and ω therefore is a set of transitive sets, we are finished with the proof once we show that ω itself is transitive, i.e., $\forall x \in \omega(x \subseteq \omega)$. This is again proven using complete induction: $0 \subseteq \omega$ and if $x \in \omega$ and $x \subseteq \omega$ then also $x \cup \{x\} = x^+ \in \omega$. $\qquad\square$

Corollary B.20 Any ordinal $\alpha \neq 0$ satisfies exactly one of the following two properties:

  (i) α has a largest element β (in the sense of $<$), and then $\alpha = \beta^+$, or

  (ii) α has no largest element, as expressed by $\alpha \subseteq \bigcup \alpha$. $\qquad\spadesuit$

Definition B.21 $\alpha \in \mathbb{O}$ is called *limit*, notation $\lim(\alpha)$, in case $\alpha \subseteq \bigcup \alpha$ and $\alpha \neq 0$. $\qquad\clubsuit$

In Theorem B.5, we stated soundness of the $\in$-induction principle. On account of Cor. B.20 we obtain soundness of a comparable induction principle.

Theorem B.22 (Principle of transfinite induction)
The following principle, called principle of transfinite induction, is sound: If

- $\alpha \in \mathbb{O} \vee \alpha = \mathbb{O}$,

[1] For technical reasons $\mathbb{O}$ cannot be a set. The more general concept of *class* is required here.

- $0 \in \alpha \Rightarrow P(0)$,
- $\forall \beta \, (\beta^+ \in \alpha \wedge P(\beta) \Rightarrow P(\beta^+))$, and
- $\forall \gamma \, (\lim(\gamma) \wedge \gamma \in \alpha \wedge \forall \beta \, (\beta \in \gamma \Rightarrow P(\beta)) \Rightarrow P(\gamma))$ hold,

then $\forall \beta \in \alpha \, (P(\beta))$.   ♠

Observe that in case $\alpha = \mathbb{O}$ the above principle allows one to prove P for all ordinals and can be simplified to:

$$\left(\begin{array}{l} P(0) \wedge \forall \alpha \, (P(\alpha) \Rightarrow P(\alpha^+)) \\ \wedge \forall \alpha \, (\lim(\alpha) \wedge \forall \beta \, (\beta < \alpha \Rightarrow P(\beta)) \Rightarrow P(\alpha)) \end{array} \right) \Rightarrow \forall \alpha \, (P(\alpha))$$

B.3 Ordinal Arithmetic

Definition B.23 Define the *sum* of two ordinals recursively as follows:

$$\alpha + 0 \stackrel{\text{def}}{=} \alpha \tag{B.7}$$

$$\alpha + \beta^+ \stackrel{\text{def}}{=} (\alpha + \beta)^+ \tag{B.8}$$

$$\alpha + \gamma \stackrel{\text{def}}{=} \bigcup_{\beta < \gamma} (\alpha + \beta) \text{ , for limit ordinals } \gamma \tag{B.9}$$

♣

Example B.24 • $\alpha + 1 = \alpha + 0^+ = (\alpha + 0)^+ = \alpha^+$.
- $0 + \alpha = \alpha$. We prove this using transfinite induction. The property $P : \mathbb{O} \longrightarrow \mathbb{B}$ in question is given by $P(\alpha) \stackrel{\text{def}}{=} 0 + \alpha = \alpha$.

  – $P(0)$ is equivalent to $0 + 0 = 0$, which follows by (B.7).
  – To prove $P(\alpha^+)$ we may assume $P(\alpha)$.

  $$\begin{aligned} 0 + \alpha^+ &= (0 + \alpha)^+ &&\text{by (B.8)} \\ &= \alpha^+ &&\text{induction hypothesis} \end{aligned}$$

  – To prove $P(\alpha)$ in case α is a limit ordinal we may assume $P(\beta)$ for all smaller ordinals.

  $$\begin{aligned} 0 + \alpha &= \bigcup_{\beta < \alpha} (0 + \beta) &&\text{by (B.9)} \\ &= \bigcup_{\beta < \alpha} \beta &&\text{induction hypotheses} \\ &= \alpha &&\text{by (B.9)} \end{aligned}$$

- $1 + \omega = \bigcup_{n < \omega} (1 + n) = \bigcup_{n < \omega} (n + 1) = \bigcup_{n < \omega} n^+ = \bigcup_{n < \omega} n = \omega$.

- $\omega + 1 = \omega^+ \neq \omega = 1 + \omega$, i.e., taking the sum operation on ordinals is not commutative in general. ♡

Without proof we state the following properties of the sum operation on ordinals.

Lemma B.25 Let $\alpha, \beta, \gamma \in \mathbb{O}$.

(i) $\alpha + (\beta + \gamma) = (\alpha + \beta) + \gamma$
(ii) $\alpha + \beta < \alpha + \gamma \Leftrightarrow \beta < \gamma$
(iii) $\alpha + \beta = \alpha + \gamma \Leftrightarrow \beta = \gamma$
(iv) $\alpha < \beta \Rightarrow \alpha + \gamma \leq \beta + \gamma$
(v) $\alpha + \gamma < \beta + \gamma \Rightarrow \alpha < \beta$ ♠

Similarly, one can define product and power operations on ordinals. This can be found, e.g., in [Sho67].

Appendix C
Notational Convention

To organize the text we adopt the standard techniques established by mathematicians, i.e., we introduce terms and names formally in *definitions*, immediate consequences of them in *corollaries*, helpful facts in *lemmas*, and main results in *theorems*, etc. We do so by starting a new paragraph with a boldface keyword and, for later reference, a pair of numbers, for instance, **Definition 6.12**. The first number indicates the chapter in which this item occurs while the second number counts these items within each chapter. To mark the end of such an item we employ the following symbols:

♣: definition

♠: lemma, corollary, or theorem, in case the proof is skipped

♡: example

◇: note or remark

[PVS]: proof checked with PVS

□: proof by hand (This symbol stands for "qed", which is a common shorthand for the traditional Latin phrase **q**uod **e**rat **d**emonstrandum.)

The symbol $\stackrel{\text{def}}{=}$ denotes "equals by definition", that is, the object on the left equals the object on the right by definition.

Glossary of Symbols

In this section we devote a line each to most of the symbols used in the book. Each of those lines comprises of three columns: the symbol itself appears in the left column, followed by a short description of its meaning in the middle, and on the right there is a number referring to the page on which this symbol is explained.

Chapter 1

A	abstract level	104
C	concrete level	105
$\mathcal{A}$	abstract level data type	14
C	concrete level data type	15
$\stackrel{\text{def}}{=}$	defining equality	394
$\emptyset$	empty set	9
id	identity relation	50
$\mathfrak{P}(A)$	powerset	50
$R\,;S$	sequential composition	51
R^{-1}	(relational) inverse	51
$\overline{R}$	complement	51
$R(A)$	relational image	51
$\langle\,\rangle$	empty linear list	9
append	linear list constructor	9
elts	elements	9
first	first	9
rest	rest	9
pick	pick an element	9
last	last	35

Chapter 2

$\{.\}_b$	bag	27
$\emptyset_b$	empty bag	27
$\oplus$	insertion into a bag	27
Σ_b	sum of a bag	27
$\#$	cardinality of a bag	27
$\mathbb{V}$	values	12
Pvar	program variables	12
Σ	states	12
$[.\longrightarrow.]$	function space	12
$\{.\mid.\}$	set comprehension	50
$\subseteq$	refinement relation	54
$\subseteq^L_\alpha$	L-simulation	21
$\subseteq^{L^{-1}}_\alpha$	L^{-1}-simulation	21
$\subseteq^U$	U-simulation	21
$\subseteq^{U^{-1}}$	U^{-1}-simulation	21

Chapter 3

$\downarrow(.)$	upper bounds	50

Appendix D
Precedences

We employ parentheses to indicate aggregation. To save parentheses we assign priorities to various operators of our languages. Operators with higher priority bind tighter than those with lower. Moreover, we order our languages such that operators belonging to one language all rank above those of another. The ranking among languages is as follows:

- (i) meta-language (lowest)
- (ii) correctness formulae *Cform*
- (iii) relational terms *Rel*
- (iv) programs *Prog*
- (v) predicates *Pred*
- (vi) expressions *Exp* (highest)

Within the languages, the priorities are as follows. (We mention only the operators used most often; the priorities of those used less frequently should become clear from the context.) In the predicate logic part of our meta-language we re-use the priorities listed for *Pred*.

We have only one operator ($\subseteq$) for correctness formulae; thus there is no need for introducing priority.

Relational terms

- (i) $\cup$ (lowest)
- (ii) $\cap$
- (iii) $\rightsquigarrow$
- (iv) ;
- (v) $\neg$
- (vi) $^{-1}$
- (vii) $\langle . \rangle$, $[.]$ (highest)

Programs

(i) μ (lowest)

(ii) ▯

(iii) ;

(iv) $\rightarrow$

(v) $\rightsquigarrow$

(vi) := (highest)

Predicates

(i) $\Leftrightarrow$ (lowest)

(ii) $\Rightarrow$, $\Leftarrow$

(iii) $\vee$

(iv) $\wedge$

(v) $\neg$

(vi) $=$, $<$, $\leq$, $\in$, ... (highest)

Expressions

(i) $+$, $-$ (lowest)

(ii) $*$

(iii) ^{i}

(iv) function application (highest)

Bibliography

[AC96] Martín Abadi and Luca Cardelli. *A Theory of Objects*. Monographs in Computer Science. Springer-Verlag, 1996.

[AdB94] Pierre H. M. America and Frank S. de Boer. Reasoning about dynamically evolving process structures. *Formal Aspects of Computing*, 6(3):269–317, 1994.

[AGM92] Samson Abramsky, Dov M. Gabbay, and Tom S. E. Maibaum, editors. *Handbook of Logic in Computer Science*, volume 2 Background: Computational Structures. Oxford University Press, 1992.

[AL91] Martín Abadi and Leslie Lamport. The existence of refinement mappings. *Theoretical Computer Science*, 82(2):253–284, May 1991.

[ALW89] Martín Abadi, Leslie Lamport, and Pierre Wolper. Realizable and unrealizable specifications. In *Proceedings ICALP'89*, volume 372 of *LNCS*, pages 1–7. Springer-Verlag, 1989.

[AO91] Krzysztof R. Apt and Ernst-Rüdiger Olderog. *Verification of Sequential and Concurrent Programs*. Springer-Verlag, 1991.

[Apt81] Krzysztof R. Apt. Ten years of Hoare's logic: A survey — part I. *ACM Transactions on Programming Languages and Systems*, 3(4):431–483, October 1981.

[Apt83] Krzysztof R. Apt. Formal justification of a proof system for Communicating Sequential Processes. *Journal of the ACM*, 30(1):197–216, January 1983.

[B78] Ralph J. R. Back. On the correctness of refinement steps in program development. Technical Report A-1978-4, Department of Computer Science, University of Helsinki, 1978.

[B80] Ralph J. R. Back. Correctness preserving program refinements: Proof theory and applications. Mathematical Centre Tracts 131, Mathematisch Centrum, Amsterdam, 1980.

[B81a] Ralph J. R. Back. On correct refinement of programs. *Journal of Computer and System Sciences*, 23(1):49–68, 1981.

[B81b] Ralph J. R. Back. Proving total correctness of nondeterministic programs in infinitary logic. *Acta Informatica*, 15:233–249, 1981.

[B88a] Ralph J. R. Back. A calculus of refinements for program derivations. *Acta Informatica*, 25:593–624, 1988.

[B88b] Ralph J. R. Back. Data refinement in the refinement calculus. Reports on Computer Science & Mathematics, Ser. A 68, Åbo Akademi University, Department of Computer Science, 1988.

[B90] Ralph J. R. Back. Refinement calculus, part II: Parallel and reactive programs. In de Bakker *et al.* [dBdRR90], pages 67–93.

[BAN90] Michael Burrows, Martín Abadi, and Roger M. Needham. A logic of authentication. *ACM Transactions on Computer Systems*, 8(1):18–36, February 1990. Also appeared in *Proceedings of the 12th ACM Symposium on Operating System Principles*, December 1989.

[Bek69] Hans Bekić. Definable operations in general algebra, and the theory of automata and flow charts. Unpublished notes, IBM Laboratory Vienna, 1969.

[Bek71] Hans Bekić. Towards a mathematical theory of processes. Technical Report TR 25.125, IBM Laboratory Vienna, 1971. Also published in: [J84, pages 168–206].

[Ber97] Rudolf Berghammer. Semantik von Programmiersprachen. Course Notes, Institut für Informatik und Praktische Mathematik, Christian-Albrechts-Universität zu Kiel, Wintersemester 1996/97. (In German).

[BFL⁺94] Juan C. Bicarregui, John S. Fitzgerald, Peter A. Lindsay, Richard Moore, and Brian Ritchie. *Proof in VDM: A Practitioner's Guide*. FACIT Series. Springer-Verlag, 1994.

[BHK89] Jan A. Bergstra, Jan Heering, and Paul Klint, editors. *Algebraic Specification*. ACM Press. Addison-Wesley, 1989.

[Bir40] Garrett Birkhoff. *Lattice Theory*. AMS Colloquium Publications. American Mathematical Society, Providence, 1st edition, 1940.

[BJ78] Dines Bjørner and Cliff B. Jones, editors. *The Vienna Development Method: The Meta-Language*, volume 61 of *LNCS*. Springer-Verlag, 1978.

[BK93] Marcello M. Bonsangue and Joost N. Kok. Isomorphisms between predicate and state transformers. In *Proceedings of the symposium MFCS '93*, volume 711 of *LNCS*, pages 301–310. Springer-Verlag, 1993.

[BK94] Marcello M. Bonsangue and Joost N. Kok. The weakest precondition calculus: Recursion and duality. *Formal Aspects of Computing*, 6:71–100, 1994.

[Bli78] Andrzej Blikle. Specified programming. ICS PAS 333, Institute of Computer Science of the Polish Academy of Sciences, Warsaw, Poland, 1978.

[BM87] Richard S. Bird and Lambert G. L. T. Meertens. Two exercises found in a book on algorithmics. In Lambert G. L. T. Meertens, editor, *Program Specification and Transformations*, pages 451–457. Elsevier Science Publishers B. V., North Holland, 1987.

[Bon96] Marcello M. Bonsangue. *Topological Dualities in Semantics*. PhD thesis, Vrije Universiteit Amsterdam, November 1996.

[BR83] Stephen D. Brooks and William C. Rounds. Behavioral equivalence relations induced by programming logics. In Josep Díaz, editor, *Proceedings 10th ICALP*, volume 154 of *LNCS*, pages 97–108. Springer-Verlag, 1983.

[BS82] Manfred Broy and Gunther Schmidt, editors. *Theoretical Foundations of Programming Methodology*. NATO Advanced Study Institutes Series. Reidel, Dordrecht, 1982.

[BvW90] Ralph J. R. Back and Joakim von Wright. Refinement calculus, part I: Sequential nondeterministic programs. In de Bakker *et al.* [dBdRR90], pages 43–66.

[BW82] Manfred Broy and Manfred Wirsing. Partial abstract data types. *Acta Informatica*, 18:47–64, 1982.

[CC77] Patrick Cousot and Radhia Cousot. Abstract interpretation: A unified lattice model for static analysis of programs by construction or approximation of fixpoints. In *4th POPL, Los Angeles, CA*, pages 238–252, January 1977.

[CC92a] Patrick Cousot and Radhia Cousot. Abstract interpretation and applications to logic programs. *Journal of Logic Programming*, 13(2-3):103–179, July 1992. A readable version is available at http://www.dmi.ens.fr/~cousot/COUSOTpapers/JLP92.shtml.

[CC92b] Patrick Cousot and Radhia Cousot. Abstract interpretation frameworks. *Journal of Logic and Computation*, 2(4):511–547, August 1992.

[CEW58] Irving M. Copi, Calvin C. Elgot, and Jesse B. Wright. Realization of events by logical nets. *Journal of the ACM*, 5(2):181–196, 1958.

[Che86] Jen Huan Cheng. A logic for partial functions. Technical Report UMCS-86-7-1, Department of Computer Science, University of Manchester, January 1986. PhD thesis.

[Cle86] J. Craig Cleaveland. *An Introduction to Data Types*. Addison Wesley, 1986.

[Cle94] Tim Clement. Comparing two approaches to data reification. In Naftalin *et al.* [NDB94], pages 118–133.

[Coo75] Stephen A. Cook. Axiomatic and interpretive semantics for an ALGOL fragment. Technical Report 79, Dept. of Computer Science, Univ. of Toronto, 1975.

[Coo78] Stephen A. Cook. Soundness and completeness of an axiom system for program verification. *SIAM Journal of Computing*, 7(1):70–90, February 1978.

[Cou81] Patrick Cousot. Semantic foundation of program analysis. In Steven S. Muchnick and Neil D. Jones, editors, *Program Flow Analysis: Theory and Applications*, Chapter 10, pages 303–342. Prentice-Hall, 1981.

[Cou90] Patrick Cousot. *Methods and Logics for Proving Programs*, Chapter 15, pages 841–993. Volume B of van Leeuwen [vL90], 1990.

[Cou96] Patrick Cousot. Abstract interpretation. *ACM Computing Surveys*, 28(2):324–328, June 1996.

[CT51] Louise H. Chin and Alfred Tarski. Distributive and modular laws in the arithmetic of relation algebras. *University of California Publications in Mathematics (New Series)*, 1:341–384, 1951.

[CU89] Wei Chen and Jan Tijmen Udding. Towards a calculus of data refinement. In Jan L. A. van de Snepscheut, editor, *Proceedings of the International Conference on Mathematics of Program Construction*, volume 375 of *LNCS*, pages 197–218, Berlin, June 1989. Springer-Verlag.

[CZdR91] Jos Coenen, Job Zwiers, and Willem-Paul de Roever. Assertional data reification proofs: Survey and perspective. In J. M. Morris and R. C. Shaw, editors, *Proceedings of the 4th Refinement Workshop*, Workshops in Computing, pages 91–114. Springer-Verlag, 1991.

[Dah92] Ole-Johan Dahl. *Verifiable Programming*. Prentice Hall, 1992.

[dB71] Jaco W. de Bakker. Recursive procedures. Mathematical Centre Tracts 24, Mathematisch Centrum, Amsterdam, 1971.

[dB76] Jaco W. de Bakker. Semantics and termination of nondeterministic recursive programs. In S. Michaelson and R. Milner, editors, *Proceedings 3rd ICALP*, pages 435–477. Edinburgh University Press, 1976.

[dB80] Jaco W. de Bakker. *Mathematical Theory of Program Correctness*. Prentice Hall, 1980.

[dBdR72] Jaco W. de Bakker and Willem-Paul de Roever. A calculus for recursive program schemes. In Maurice Nivat, editor, *Automata, Languages, and Programming, Proceedings of a Symposium Organized by IRIA*, pages 167–196. North-Holland/American Elsevier, July 1972.

[dBdRR90] Jaco W. de Bakker, Willem-Paul de Roever, and Grzegorz Rozenberg, editors. *Stepwise Refinement of Distributed Systems, REX Workshop, May 29–June 2, 1989, Mook, The Netherlands*, volume 430 of *LNCS*. Springer-Verlag, 1990.

[dBdV96] Jaco W. de Bakker and Erik de Vink. *Control Flow Semantics*. MIT Press, 1996.

[dBM75] Jaco W. de Bakker and Lambert G. L. T. Meertens. On the completeness of the inductive assertion method. *Journal of Computer and System Sciences*, 11:323–357, 1975.

[dBS89] Jaco W. de Bakker and Dana S. Scott. *A Theory of Programs*, pages 1–30. In Klop *et al.* [Klo89], 1989. Liber Amoricum.

[DDH72] Ole-Johan Dahl, Edsger W. Dijkstra, and C. A. R. Hoare. *Structured Programming*, volume 8 of *APIC Studies in Data Processing*. Academic Press, 1972.

[DF88] Edsger W. Dijkstra and Wim H. J. Feijen. *A Method of Programming*. Addison Wesley, 1988.

[Dij75] Edsger W. Dijkstra. Guarded commands, nondeterminacy and formal derivation of programs. *Communications of the ACM*, 18(8):453–457, 1975.

[Dij76] Edsger W. Dijkstra. *A Discipline of Programming*. Prentice Hall, 1976.

[Dil90] Anthony Diller. *Z — An Introduction to Formal Methods*. Wiley, 1990.

[dNH83] Rocco de Nicola and Matthew C. B. Hennessy. Testing equivalence for processes. In Josep Díaz, editor, *Proceedings 10th ICALP*, volume 154 of *LNCS*, pages 548–560. Springer-Verlag, 1983.

[DP90] Brian A. Davey and Hilary A. Priestley. *Introduction to Lattices and Order*. Cambridge Mathematical Textbooks. Cambridge University Press, 1990.

[dR76] Willem-Paul de Roever. Recursive program schemes: Semantics and proof theory. Mathematical Centre Tracts 70, Mathematisch Centrum, Amsterdam, 1976. Appeared first as PhD thesis, Vrije Universiteit Amsterdam, January 1975.

[dRdBH+] Willem-Paul de Roever, Frank de Boer, Ulrich Hannemann, Jozef Hooman, Yassine Lakhnech, Paritosh Pandya, and Xu Qiwen. State-based proof theory of concurrency: From noncompositional to compositional methods. To appear.

[DS90] Edsger W. Dijkstra and Carel S. Scholten. *Predicate Calculus and Program Semantics*. Texts and Monographs in Computer Science. Springer-Verlag, 1990.

[EdR96] Kai Engelhardt and Willem-Paul de Roever. Simulation of specification statements in Hoare logic. In Wojciech Penczek and Andrzej Szałas, editors, *Mathematical Foundations of Computer Science 1996, 21st International Symposium, MFCS '96, Cracow, Poland, Proceedings*, volume 1113 of *LNCS*, pages 324–335. Springer-Verlag, September 1996.

[Egl75] Herbert Egli. A mathematical model for nondeterministic computations. Technical report, ETH Zürich, 1975.

[Eme90] E. Allen Emerson. *Temporal and Modal Logic*, Chapter 16, pages 995–1072. Volume B of van Leeuwen [vL90], 1990.

[FHV96] Marcelo F. Frias, Armando M. Haeberer, and Paulo A. S. Veloso. A finite axiomatization for fork algebras. *Journal of the IGPL*, 1996.

[FM97] Marcelo F. Frias and Roger D. Maddux. Completeness of the relational calculus MU_2. In *Third International Seminar on the Use of Relational Methods in Computer Science*, pages 205–214, January 1997. A full version appears in *Proceedings LICS'98*.

[G+80] Susan L. Gerhart *et al.* An overview of AFFIRM: a specification and verification system. In S. H. Lavington, editor, *Proceedings of IFIP 80*, pages 343–348, Amsterdam, 1980. North-Holland.

[Gar90] Paul H. B. Gardiner. Data refinement of maps. Technical report, Oxford University Computing Laboratory PRG, August 1990.

[Gar95] Paul H. B. Gardiner. Algebraic proofs of consistency and completeness. *Theoretical Computer Science*, 150:161–191, 1995.

[GB96] Thomas F. Gritzner and Rudolf Berghammer. A relation algebraic model of robust correctness. *Theoretical Computer Science*, 159:245–270, 1996.

[Ger75] Susan L. Gerhart. Correctness preserving program transformations. In *Proceedings 2nd Symposium on Principles of Programming Languages*, pages 54–66, 1975.

[Ger78] Susan L. Gerhart. Two proof techniques for transferral of program correctness. Marina del Rey, CA, Information Science Institute, 1978.

[Ger90] Rob Gerth. Foundations of compositional program refinement. In de Bakker *et al.* [dBdRR90], pages 777–808.

[GH78] John V. Guttag and James J. Horning. The algebraic specification of abstract data types. *Acta Informatica*, 10(1):27–52, 1978.

[GHM78] John V. Guttag, Ellis Horowitz, and David R. Musser. Abstract data types and software validation. *Communications of the ACM*, 21(12):1048–1064, 1978.

[Gil90] Stephen Gilmore. *Correctness-Oriented Approaches to Software Development*. PhD thesis, Queen's University of Belfast, November 1990. Also available as Technical Report CST-76-91, Department of Computer Science, University of Edinburgh, April 1991.

[Gin68] A. Ginzburg. *Algebraic Theory of Automata*. Academic Press, 1968.

[GM91] Paul H. B. Gardiner and Carroll C. Morgan. Data refinement of predicate transformers. *Theoretical Computer Science*, 87:143–162, 1991.

[GM93] Paul H. B. Gardiner and Carroll C. Morgan. A single complete rule for data refinement. *Formal Aspects of Computing*, 5(4):367–382, 1993.

[GMdM92] Paul H. B. Gardiner, Clare Martin, and Oege de Moore. An algebraic construction of predicate transformers. In Richard S. Bird, Carroll C. Morgan, and Jim C. P. Woodcock, editors, *Mathematics of Program Construction, Second International Conference, Oxford, U. K., June/July 1992, Proceedings*, volume 669 of *LNCS*, pages 100–121. Springer-Verlag, 1992.

[Göd31] Kurt Gödel. Über formal unentscheidbare Sätze der Principia Mathematica und verwandter Systeme, I. *Monatshefte für Mathematik und Physik*, 38:173–198, 1931.

[Gor75] G. A. Gorelick. A complete axiomatic system for proving assertions about recursive and non-recursive programs. Technical Report 75, Department of Computer Science, University of Toronto, 1975.

[Gor83] John A. Goree, Jr. Internal consistency of a distributed transaction system with orphan detection. Technical Report MIT/LCS/TR-286, Massachusetts Institute of Technology, Laboratory for Computer Science, January 1983.

[GP85] David Gries and J. Prins. A new notion of encapsulation. In *Symposium on Language Issues in Programming Environments*. SIGPLAN, June 1985.

[Grä78] George Grätzer. *General Lattice Theory*, volume 52 of *Lehrbücher und Monographien aus dem Gebiete der exakten Wissenschaften: Mathematische Reihe*. Birkhäuser, 1978.

[Gri81] David Gries. *The Science of Programming*. Texts and Monographs in Computer Science. Springer-Verlag, 1981.

[GS93] David Gries and Fred B. Schneider. *A Logical Approach to Discrete Math*. Texts and Monographs in Computer Science. Springer-Verlag, 1993.

[Gut75] John V. Guttag. *The Specification and Application to Programming of Abstract Data Types*. Technical report CSRG-59, Computer System Research Group, Department of Computer Science, University of Toronto, 1975.

[Gut77] John V. Guttag. Abstract data types and the development of data structures. *Communications of the ACM*, 20(6):396–404, June 1977.

[Har79] David Harel. *First-Order Dynamic Logic*, volume 68 of *LNCS*. Springer-Verlag, 1979. (A revision of Logics of Programs: Axiomatics and Descriptive Power. Doctoral Thesis, Department of EECS, MIT. Cambridge, MA, May, 1978).

[Hay87] Ian J. Hayes, editor. *Specification Case Studies*. Prentice Hall, 1987.

[Hay90] Ian J. Hayes. Bias in VDM full abstraction and the functional retrieve rules for data refinement. Technical report 162, Department of Computer Science, University of Queensland, May 1990.

[Hay92] Ian J. Hayes. VDM and Z: A comparative case study. *Formal Aspects of Computing*, 4(1):76–99, 1992.

[He 89] He Jifeng. Process simulation and refinement. *Formal Aspects of Computing*, 1(3):229–241, 1989.

[Heh79] Eric C. R. Hehner. do considered od: A contribution to the programming calculus. *Acta Informatica*, 11:287–304, 1979. Appeared first as Technical Report CSRG-75 of the University of Toronto Computer Systems Research Group in November 1976.

[Heh84a] Eric C. R. Hehner. *The Logic of Programming*. Prentice Hall, 1984.

[Heh84b] Eric C. R. Hehner. Predicative programming part I. *Communications of the ACM*, 27:134–143, 1984.

[Heh84c] Eric C. R. Hehner. Predicative programming part II. *Communications of the ACM*, 27:144–151, 1984.

[Heh89] Eric C. R. Hehner. Termination is timing. In J. L. A. van de Snepscheut, editor, *Proceedings of the International Conference on Mathematics of Program Construction*, volume 375 of *LNCS*, pages 36–47. Springer-Verlag, June 1989.

[Heh93] Eric C. R. Hehner. *A Practical Theory of Programming*. Texts and Monographs in Computer Science. Springer-Verlag, 1993.

[Hes90] Wim H. Hesselink. Modalities of nondeterminacy. In *Beauty is our Business: A Birthday Salute to Edsger W. Dijkstra*, pages 182–193. Springer-Verlag, 1990.

[HH85] Horst Herrlich and Miroslav Hušek. Galois connections. In Austin Melton, editor, *Mathematical Foundations of Programming Semantics, International Conference, Manhattan, Kansas*, volume 239 of *LNCS*, pages 122–134. Springer-Verlag, April 1985.

[HH86a] C. A. R. Hoare and He Jifeng. The weakest prespecification, part I. *Fundamenta Informaticae*, 9:51–84, 1986.

[HH86b] C. A. R. Hoare and He Jifeng. The weakest prespecification, part II. *Fundamenta Informaticae*, 9:217–252, 1986.

[HH90] He Jifeng and C. A. R. Hoare. Data refinement in a categorical setting. Technical Report PRG-90, Oxford University Computing Laboratory PRG, November 1990.

[HHS86] He Jifeng, C. A. R. Hoare, and Jeff W. Sanders. Data refinement refined. In B. Robinet and R. Wilhelm, editors, *Proceedings of the European Symposium on Programming (ESOP 86)*, volume 213 of *LNCS*, pages 187–196, Saarbrücken, FRG, March 1986. Springer-Verlag.

[HHS87] C. A. R. Hoare, He Jifeng, and Jeff W. Sanders. Prespecification in data refinement. *Information Processing Letters*, 25:71–76, 1987.

[Hit74] Peter Hitchcock. *An approach to formal reasoning about programs*. PhD thesis, University of Warwick, 1974.

[HJN93] Ian J. Hayes, Cliff B. Jones, and John E. Nicholls. Understanding the differences between VDM and Z. *FACS Europe*, 1(1):7–30, Autumn 1993.

[Hoa69] C. A. R. Hoare. An axiomatic basis for computer programming. *Communications of the ACM*, 12(10):576–583, 1969.

[Hoa72] C. A. R. Hoare. Proofs of correctness of data representation. *Acta Informatica*, 1:271–281, 1972.

[Hoa78] C. A. R. Hoare. Communicating sequential processes. *Communications of the ACM*, 21(8):666–677, 1978.

[Hoa85] C. A. R. Hoare. *Communicating Sequential Processes*. Prentice Hall, 1985.

[HP72] Peter Hitchcock and David M. R. Park. Induction rules and termination proofs. In Maurice Nivat, editor, *Automata, Languages, and Programming, Proceedings of a Symposium Organized by IRIA*, pages 225–251. North-Holland/American Elsevier, 1972.

[HPS76] David Harel, Amir Pnueli, and J. Stavi. Completeness issues for inductive assertions and Hoare's method. Technical report, Department of Mathematical Sciences, Tel-Aviv University, 1976.

[HU79] John E. Hopcroft and Jeffrey D. Ullman. *Introduction to Automata Theory, Languages, and Computation*. Addison Wesley, 1979.

[J70] Cliff B. Jones. A technique for showing that two functions preserve a relation between their domains. Technical report LR 25.3.067, IBM Laboratory Vienna, April 1970.

[J80] Cliff B. Jones. *Software Development: a Rigorous Approach*. Prentice Hall, 1980.

[J81] Cliff B. Jones. Development methods for computer programs including a notion of inference. Technical Monograph 25, Oxford University Computing Laboratory PRG, 1981.

[J84] Cliff B. Jones, editor. *Programming Languages and their Definition, Selected Papers of H. Bekić*, volume 177 of *LNCS*. Springer-Verlag, 1984.

[J87] Cliff B. Jones. VDM proof obligations and their justification. In Dines Bjørner, Cliff B. Jones, Mícheál Mac an Airchinnigh, and Erich J. Neuhold, editors, *VDM '87 VDM — A Formal Method at Work*, volume 252 of *LNCS*, pages 260–286. VDM-Europe, Springer-Verlag, March 1987.

[J90] Cliff B. Jones. *Systematic Software Development using VDM*. Prentice Hall, 2nd edition, 1990. Out of print. Available via ftp at `ftp://ftp.cs.man.ac.uk/pub/`

cbj/ssdvdm.ps.gz.

[J92] Cliff B. Jones. The search for tractable ways of reasoning about programs. Technical Report UMCS-92-4-4, Department of Computer Science, University of Manchester, March 1992.

[JJLM91] Cliff B. Jones, Kevin D. Jones, Peter A. Lindsay, and Richard Moore. *mural — A Formal Development Support System*. Springer-Verlag, 1991.

[JM94] Cliff B. Jones and Cornelius A. Middelburg. A typed logic of partial functions reconstructed classically. *Acta Informatica*, 31(5):399–430, 1994.

[Jon87] Bengt Jonsson. *Compositional Verification of Distributed Systems*. PhD thesis, Uppsala University, 1987. The results of this thesis have been published in [Jon94].

[Jon90] Bengt Jonsson. On decomposing and refining specifications of distributed systems. In de Bakker *et al.* [dBdRR90], pages 361–385.

[Jon91] Bengt Jonsson. Simulations between specifications of distributed systems. In Jos C.M. Baeten and Jan Frisco Groote, editors, *Proceedings CONCUR '91, 2nd International Conference on Concurrency Theory, Amsterdam, The Netherlands*, volume 527 of *LNCS*, pages 346–360. Springer-Verlag, August 1991.

[Jon94] Bengt Jonsson. Compositional specification and verification of distributed systems. *ACM Transactions on Programming Languages and Systems*, 16(2):259–303, 1994.

[JZ92] Wil Janssen and Job Zwiers. From sequential layers to distributed processes, deriving a minimum weight spanning tree algorithm, (extended abstract). In *Proceedings 11th ACM Symposium on Principles of Distributed Computing*, pages 215–227. ACM, 1992.

[Kal90] Anne Kaldewaij. *Programming: The Derivation of Algorithms*. Prentice Hall, 1990.

[Klo89] J. W. de Bakker, 25 jaar semantiek. CWI, Amsterdam, 1989. Liber Amoricum.

[Kna28] B. Knaster. Un théorème sur les fonctions d'ensembles. *Ann. Société Polonaise de Mathématique*, 6:133–134, 1928.

[Kön32] D. König. Theorie der endlichen und unendlichen Graphen. Technical report, Leipzig, 1932.

[Koz83] Dexter Kozen. Results on the propositional μ-calculus. *Theoretical Computer Science*, 27:333–354, 1983.

[KP75] Assaf J. Kfoury and David M. R. Park. On the termination of program schemas. *Information and Control*, 29:243–251, 1975.

[Lam83] Leslie Lamport. Specifying concurrent program modules. *ACM Transactions on Programming Languages and Systems*, 2:190–220, 1983.

[Lam94] Leslie Lamport. The temporal logic of actions. *ACM Transactions on Programming Languages and Systems*, 16(3):872–923, May 1994. Also appeared as DEC SRC Research Report 79.

[LdRG79] Stanley Lee, Willem-Paul de Roever, and Susan L. Gerhart. The evolution of list-copying algorithms, and the need for structuring program verification. In *Proceedings of the 6th annual ACM symposium on the principles of programming languages (POPL 79)*, pages 53–67, New York, January 1979. ACM.

[LEG81] Stanley Lee, Roddy W. Erickson, and Susan L. Gerhart. Finding a design error in a distributed system: A case study. In *Proceedings of IEEE Computer Society's Symposium on Reliability in Distributed Software and Database Systems*, 1981.

[LF80] Nancy A. Lynch and Michael J. Fischer. A technique for decomposing algorithms that use a single shared variable. Technical Report GIT-ICS-80-14, Georgia Institute of Technology, School of Information and Computer Science, October 1980.

[LG86] Barbara Liskov and John V. Guttag. *Abstraction and specification in program development*. McGraw-Hill, 1986.

[Lin93] Peter A. Lindsay. Reasoning about Z specifications: a VDM perspective. Technical Report 93-20, Software Verification Research Centre, Department of Computer Science, University of Queensland, October 1993.

[Lin94] Peter A. Lindsay. On transferring VDM verification techniques to Z. In Naftalin *et al.* [NDB94], pages 190–213.

[LP81] Harry R. Lewis and Christos H. Papadimitriou. *Elements of the Theory of Computation*. Prentice Hall, 1981.

[LT87] Nancy A. Lynch and Mark R. Tuttle. Hierarchical correctness proofs for distributed algorithms. In *Proceedings 6th Annual ACM Symposium on Principles of Distributed Computing*, pages 137–151, 1987.

[Luc68] Peter Lucas. Two constructive realizations of the block concept and their equivalence. Technical Report TR 25.085, IBM Laboratory Vienna, January 1968.

[LV91] Nancy A. Lynch and Frits Vaandrager. Forward and backward simulation for timing-based systems. In Jaco W. de Bakker, Cees Huizing, Willem-Paul de Roever, and Grzegorz Rozenberg, editors, *Real Time: Theory in Practice, Proceedings*, volume 600 of *LNCS*, pages 397–446. Springer-Verlag, 1991.

[LvK94] Peter A. Lindsay and Erik van Keulen. Case studies in the verification of specifications in VDM and Z. Technical Report 94-3, Software Verification Research Centre, Department of Computer Science, University of Queensland, March 1994.

[Lyn50] Roger C. Lyndon. The representation of relational algebras. *Annals of Mathematics (2)*, 51:707–729, 1950.

[Lyn56] Roger C. Lyndon. The representation of relational algebras II. *Annals of Mathematics (2)*, 63:294–307, 1956.

[Lyn61] Roger C. Lyndon. Relation algebras and projective geometries. *Michigan Mathematical Journal*, 8:21–28, 1961.

[Lyn83] Nancy A. Lynch. Concurrency control for resilient nested transactions. In *Proceedings of the Second ACM SIGACT-SIGMOD Symposium on Principles of Database Systems*, pages 166–181, March 1983.

[Lyn90] Nancy A. Lynch. Multivalued possibility mappings. In de Bakker *et al.* [dBdRR90], pages 519–543.

[Lyn96] Nancy A. Lynch. *Distributed Algorithms*. Morgan Kaufmann, 1996.

[Mac71] Saunders Mac Lane. *Categories for the Working Mathematician*, volume 5 of *Graduate Texts in Mathematics*. Springer-Verlag, 1971.

[Mad96] Roger D. Maddux. Relation-algebraic semantics. *Theoretical Computer Science (Fundamental Study)*, 160:1–85, 1996.

[Maz71] Antoni Mazurkiewicz. Proving algorithms by tail functions. *Information and Control*, 18:220–226, 1971.

[MC80] Mila E. Majster-Cederbaum. A simple relation between relational and predicate transformer semantics for nondeterministic programs. *Information Processing Letters*, 11(4, 5):190–192, December 1980.

[Men87] Elliott Mendelson. *Introduction to Mathematical Logic.* Wadsworth and Brooks, Pacific Grove California, 3rd edition, 1987.

[Mer90] Michael Merritt. Completeness theorems for automata. In de Bakker *et al.* [dBdRR90], pages 544–560.

[Mil69] Robin Milner. The difficulty of verifying a program with unnatural data representation. Techical Report 3, Computation Services Department, University College of Swansea, January 1969.

[Mil70] Robin Milner. A formal notion of simulation between programs. Techical Report 14, Computation Services Department, University College of Swansea, October 1970.

[Mil71] Robin Milner. An algebraic definition of simulation between programs. In *Proceedings of 2nd Joint Conference on Artificial Intelligence*, pages 481–489. BCS, 1971.

[Mil80] Robin Milner. *A Calculus of Communicating Systems*, volume 92 of *LNCS*. Springer-Verlag, 1980.

[Mil89] Robin Milner. *Communication and Concurrency.* Prentice-Hall, 1989.

[Mor82] Joseph M. Morris. Assignment and linked data structures. In Manfred Broy and Gunther Schmidt, editors, *Theoretical Foundations of Programming Methodology*, pages 35–41. Reidel, 1982.

[Mor87] Joseph M. Morris. A theoretical basis for stepwise refinement and the programming calculus. *Science of Computer Programming*, 9(3):287–306, December 1987.

[Mor88] Carroll C. Morgan. Auxiliary variables in data refinement. *Information Processing Letters*, 29(6):293–296, December 1988.

[Mor89a] Joseph M. Morris. Laws of data refinement. *Acta Informatica*, 26:287–308, 1989.

[Mor89b] Joseph M. Morris. Programs from specifications. In Edsger W. Dijkstra, editor, *Formal Development of Programs and Proofs.* Addison-Wesley, 1989.

[Mor90] Carroll C. Morgan. *Programming from Specifications.* Prentice Hall, 1990.

[Mor94] Carroll C. Morgan. The cuppest capjunctive capping, and Galois. In A. W. Roscoe, editor, *A Classical Mind: Essays in Honour of C. A. R. Hoare*, pages 317–332. Prentice Hall, 1994.

[MP74] Zohar Manna and Amir Pnueli. Axiomatic approach to total correctness of programs. *Acta Informatica*, 3:253–263, 1974.

[MP92] Zohar Manna and Amir Pnueli. *The Temporal Logic of Reactive and Concurrent Systems: Specification.* Springer-Verlag, 1992.

[MP95] Zohar Manna and Amir Pnueli. *Temporal Verification of Reactive Systems: Safety.* Springer-Verlag, 1995.

[MP00] Zohar Manna and Amir Pnueli. *Temporal Verification of Reactive Systems: Liveness.* Springer-Verlag, 2000. Forthcoming.

[MRG88] Carroll C. Morgan, Ken Robinson, and Paul H. B. Gardiner. On the refinement calculus. Technical Monograph PRG-70, Oxford University Computing Laboratory PRG, 1988.

[Mül97] Markus Müller-Olm. *Modular Compiler Verfication: A Refinement-Algebraic Approach Advocating Stepwise Abstraction*, volume 1283 of *LNCS*. Springer-Verlag, 1997.

[MV94] Carroll C. Morgan and Trevor Vickers. *On the Refinement Calculus.* FACIT. Springer-Verlag, 1994.

[Myh57] John Myhill. Finite automata and representation of events. *Fundamental Concepts in the Theory of Systems* 57–64, Wright Air Development Center, 1957.

[NDB94] Maurice Naftalin, Tim Denvir, and Miquel Bertran, editors. *FME '94 - Industrial Benefit of Formal Methods. Proceedings of the Second International Symposium of Formal Methods Europe, Barcelona, Spain,* volume 873 of *LNCS.* Springer-Verlag, October 1994.

[Nel87] Greg Nelson. A generalization of Dijkstra's calculus. Technical Report 16, Digital Systems Research Center, April 1987.

[Nel89] Greg Nelson. A generalization of Dijkstra's calculus. *ACM Transactions on Programming Languages and Systems,* 11(4):517–561, October 1989.

[Nip86] Tobias Nipkow. Non-deterministic data types: Models and implementations. *Acta Informatica,* 22(16):629–661, March 1986.

[Old83] Ernst-Rüdiger Olderog. On the notion of expressiveness and the rule of adaptation. *Theoretical Computer Science,* 24:337–347, 1983.

[Old85] Ernst-Rüdiger Olderog. Specification-oriented programming in TCSP. *NATO ASI Series F: Computer and System Sciences,* 13, 1985.

[Old91] Ernst-Rüdiger Olderog. *Nets, Terms and Formulae.* Cambridge University Press, 1991.

[Ore44] Oystein Ore. Galois connexions. *Transaction of the AMS,* 55:493–513, 1944.

[ORS92] Sam Owre, John M. Rushby, and Natarajan Shankar. PVS: A prototype verification system. In Deepak Kapur, editor, *11th International Conference on Automated Deduction (CADE),* volume 607 of *Lecture Notes in Artificial Intelligence,* pages 748–752, Saratoga, NY, June 1992. Springer-Verlag.

[Owi75] Susan Owicki. *Axiomatic Proof Techniques for Parallel Programs.* Report tr 75-251, Cornell University, Ithaca, NY, Department of Computer Science, 1975.

[Par69] David M. R. Park. Fixpoint induction and proofs of program properties. *Machine Intelligence,* 5:59–78, 1969.

[Par76] David M. R. Park. Finiteness is μ-ineffable. *Theoretical Computer Science,* 3(2):173–181, November 1976.

[Par80] David M. R. Park. On the semantics of fair parallelism. In *Abstract Software Specification,* volume 86 of *LNCS,* pages 504–526. Springer-Verlag, 1980.

[Par81a] David M. R. Park. Concurrency and automata on infinite sequences. In Peter Deussen, editor, *Theoretical Computer Science: 5th GI-Conference, Karlsruhe,* volume 104 of *LNCS,* pages 167–183. Springer-Verlag, March 1981.

[Par81b] David M. R. Park. A predicate transformer for weak fair iteration. In *6th IBM Symposium on Mathematical Foundations of Computer Science, Hakone, Japan,* 1981.

[Par90] Helmut A. Partsch. *Specification and Transformation of Programs.* Texts and Monographs in Computer Science. Springer-Verlag, 1990.

[PdBM+94] Michael Paterson, Jaco W. de Bakker, Robin Milner, Maurice Nivat, Bill Wadge, Peter Welch, and Steve Matthews. Obituary: David Michael Ritchie Park (1935–1990), in memoriam. *Theoretical Computer Science,* 133:187–200, 1994.

[Pie91] Benjamin C. Pierce. *Basic Category Theory for Computer Scientists.* Foundations of Computing. The MIT Press, Cambridge, MA, 1991.

[PK93] Paritosh Pandya and Narayan Kumar. Private communication, 1993.

[Plo74] Gordon D. Plotkin. LCF considered as a programming language. Technical Report Memo SAI-RM-8, School of Artificial Intelligence, University of Edinburgh, 1974.

[Plo76] Gordon D. Plotkin. A powerdomain construction. *SIAM Journal on Computation*, 5(3):452–487, 1976.

[Plo79] Gordon D. Plotkin. Dijkstra's predicate transformer and Smyth's powerdomain. In Dines Bjørner, editor, *Proceedings of the Winter School on Abstract Software Specification*, volume 86 of *LNCS*, pages 527–553. Springer-Verlag, 1979.

[Plo83] Gordon D. Plotkin. Domains. Available, e.g., at URL http://w3-theory. di.unipi.it/~vladi/CATS/share/PLOTKIN/Domains.dvi.gz, 1983.

[Pra76] Vaughan R. Pratt. Semantical considerations on Floyd–Hoare logic. Technical Report MIT/LCS/TR-168, Massachusetts Institute of Technology, August 1976.

[Ram90] Sethu Ramesh. On the completeness of modular proof systems. *Information Processing Letters*, 36:195–201, 1990.

[RB95] Ingrid M. Rewitzky and Chris Brink. Predicate transformers as power operations. *Formal Aspects of Computing*, 7(2):169–182, 1995.

[Rey81] John C. Reynolds. *The Craft of Programming*. Prentice Hall, 1981. Out of print. Reproductions are available from the author at John_Reynolds@e.ergo. cs.cmu.edu.

[RS59] Michael O. Rabin and Dana S. Scott. Finite automata and their decision problems. *IBM Journal of Research and Development*, 3(2):114–125, 1959.

[Sch95] E. Schröder. *Algebra der Logik*, volume 3. Teubner, Leipzig, Germany, 1895.

[Sch53] J. Schmidt. Beiträge zur Filtertheorie II. *Mathematische Nachrichten*, 10:197–232, 1953.

[Sch77] Jerald Schwarz. Generic commands — a tool for partial correctness formalisms. *Computer Journal*, 20(2):151–155, 1977.

[Sch81] Oliver Schoett. Ein Modulkonzept in der Theorie abstrakter Datentypen. IfI-HH-B81 81, Universität Hamburg, Fachbereich Informatik, 1981.

[Sco70] Dana S. Scott. Outline of a mathematical theory of computation. In *Proceedings, 4th Annual Princeton Conference on Information Sciences and Systems*, pages 169–176, 1970.

[Sco72a] Dana S. Scott. Continuous lattices. In F. W. Lawvere, editor, *Toposes, Algebraic Geometry and Logic*, volume 274 of *Lecture Notes in Mathematics*, pages 97–136. Springer-Verlag, 1972.

[Sco72b] Dana S. Scott. Lattice theory, data types and semantics. In R. Rustin, editor, *Symp. Formal Semantics*, pages 64–106. Prentice-Hall, 1972.

[Sco76] Dana S. Scott. Data types as lattices. *SIAM Journal on Computing*, 5:522–587, 1976.

[Sco77] Dana S. Scott. Logic and programming language. *Communications of the ACM*, 20:634–641, 1977.

[SdB69] Dana S. Scott and Jaco W. de Bakker. A theory of programs. Seminar notes, IBM Seminar, Vienna, 1969.

[SdR87] Frank Stomp and Willem-Paul de Roever. A correctness proof of a minimum-weight spanning tree algorithm (extended abstract). In R. Popescu-Zeletin, G. Le Lann, and K. H. (Kane) Kim, editors, *Proceedings of the 7th International Conference on Distributed Computing Systems*, pages 440–447. Computer Society Press of the IEEE, 1987.

[Sho67] Joseph R. Shoenfield. *Mathematical Logic.* Addison-Wesley, 1967.

[Sie89] Dirk Siefkes, editor. *J. Richard Büchi: Finite Automata, Their Algebras and Grammars.* Springer-Verlag, 1989.

[Smy78] Michael B. Smyth. Powerdomains. *Journal of Computer and System Sciences,* pages 23–36, 1978.

[Smy83] Michael B. Smyth. Power domains and predicate transformers: A topological view. In Josep Díaz, editor, *Proceedings 10th ICALP,* volume 154 of *LNCS,* pages 662–675. Springer-Verlag, 1983.

[Spi88] J. Michael Spivey. *Understanding Z — A Specification Language and its Formal Semantics.* Cambridge Tracts in Computer Science. Cambridge University Press, 1988.

[Spi92a] J. Michael Spivey. *The ƒUZZ Manual.* Computing Science Consultancy, 2 Willow Close, Garsington, Oxford OX44 9AN, 2nd edition, July 1992.

[Spi92b] J. Michael Spivey. *The Z Notation: A Reference Manual.* Prentice Hall, 2nd edition, 1992.

[SS71] Dana S. Scott and Christopher Strachey. Toward a mathematical semantics for computer languages. In J. Fox, editor, *Proceedings Symposium on Computers and Automata,* pages 19–46. Polytechnic Institute of Brooklyn Press, 1971.

[SS93] Gunther Schmidt and Thomas Ströhlein. *Relations and Graphs.* EATCS Monographs on Theoretical Computer Science. Springer-Verlag, 1993.

[ST85] Don Sannella and Andrzej Tarlecki. On observational equivalence and algebraic specification. In Hartmut Ehrig, Christiane Floyd, Maurice Nivat, and James Thatcher, editors, *Mathematical Foundations of Software Development, Proceedings of the International Joint Conference on Theory and Practice of Software Development (TAPSOFT), Berlin. Volume 1: Colloquium on Trees in Algebra and Programming (CAAP '85),* volume 185 of *LNCS,* pages 308–322. Springer-Verlag, 1985.

[Sta84] Eugene W. Stark. *Foundations of a theory of specification for distributed systems.* PhD thesis, Massachusetts Institute of Technology, Laboratory for Computer Science, Cambridge, MA, 1984. Published as Technical Report MIT/LCS/TR-342.

[Sta88] Eugene W. Stark. Proving entailment between conceptual state specifications. *Theoretical Computer Science,* 56(1):135–154, January 1988.

[Sti92] Colin Stirling. *Modal and Temporal Logics,* Chapter 5, pages 477–563. Volume 2 Background: Computational Structures of Abramsky *et al.* [AGM92], 1992.

[Str66] Christopher Strachey. Towards a formal semantics. In T. B. Steel Jr., editor, *Formal Language Description Languages for Computer Programming,* pages 198–220. North-Holland, 1966.

[SW74] Christopher Strachey and Christopher P. Wadsworth. Continuations: a mathematical semantics for handling full jumps. Technical Monograph 11, Oxford University Computing Laboratory PRG, 1974.

[Tar41] Alfred Tarski. On the calculus of relations. *The Journal of Symbolic Logic,* 6(3):73–89, September 1941.

[Tar55] Alfred Tarski. A lattice-theoretical fixpoint theorem and its applications. *Pacific Journal of Mathematics,* 5:285–309, 1955.

[Ten94] Robert D. Tennent. Correctness of data representations in Algol-like languages. In A. W. Roscoe, editor, *A Classical Mind, Essays in Honour of C. A. R. Hoare,* Chapter 23, pages 405–417. Prentice-Hall International, 1994.

[TZ88] John V. Tucker and Jeffery I. Zucker. *Program Correctness over Abstract Data Types, with Error-Stat Sematics.* Number 6 in CWI Monographs. North-Holland, 1988.

[vD85] Nick W. P. van Diepen. Integer-square-root. Technical report, Centre for Mathematics and Computer Science, Amsterdam, 1985.

[vDdR86] Nick W. P. van Diepen and Willem-Paul de Roever. Program derivation through transformations: The evolution of list-copying algorithms. *Science of Computer Programming*, 6:213–272, 1986.

[vK95] Burghard von Karger. An algebraic approach to temporal logic. In Peter D. Mosses, Mogens Nielsen, and Michael I. Schwartzbach, editors, *Proceedings of the Sixth International Joint Conference on Theory and Practice of Software Development*, volume 915 of *LNCS*, pages 232–246. Springer-Verlag, 1995.

[vKH95] Burghard von Karger and C. A. R. Hoare. Sequential calculus. *Information Processing Letters*, 53(3):123–130, 1995.

[vL90] Jan van Leeuwen, editor. *Handbook of Theoretical Computer Science: Formal Models and Semantics*, volume B. Elsevier/MIT Press, 1990.

[vN37] John von Neumann. Lectures on continuous geometries, 1936/37. Institute of Advanced Studies, Princeton, NJ.

[vW90] Joakim von Wright. *A Lattice-theoretical Basis for Program Refinement.* PhD thesis, Åbo Akademi University, 1990.

[vW92a] Joakim von Wright. Data refinement and the simulation method. Reports on Computer Science & Mathematics, Ser. A 137, Åbo Akademi University, Department of Computer Science, July 1992.

[vW92b] Joakim von Wright. The lattice of data refinement. Reports on Computer Science & Mathematics, Ser. A 130, Åbo Akademi University, Department of Computer Science, February 1992.

[Wad76] William W. Wadge. A complete natural deduction system for the relational calculus. Theory of computation report, University of Warwick, 1976.

[Wal93] Igor Walukiewicz. On completeness of the μ-calculus. In *Proceedings, Eighth Annual IEEE Symposium on Logic in Computer Science*, pages 136–146, 1993.

[Wal95] Igor Walukiewicz. Completeness of Kozen's axiomatisation of the propositional μ-calculus. In *Proceedings, Tenth Annual IEEE Symposium on Logic in Computer Science*, pages 14–24, San Diego, CA, June 1995.

[Wal96] Igor Walukiewicz. A note on the completeness of Kozen's axiomatisation of the propositional μ-calculus. *Bulletin of Symbolic Logic*, 2(3):349–366, September 1996.

[Wan77a] Mitchell Wand. A characterization of weakest preconditions. *Journal of Computer and System Sciences*, 15(2):209–212, 1977.

[Wan77b] Mitchell Wand. Fixed-point constructions in order-enriched categories. Technical Report 23, Computer Science Department, Indiana University, Bloomington, IN 47401, USA, February 1977.

[Wan78] Mitchell Wand. A new incompleteness result for Hoare's system. *Journal of the ACM*, 25(1):168–175, 1978.

[Wir71] Niklaus Wirth. Program development by stepwise refinement. *Communications of the ACM*, 14:221–227, 1971.

[Wir90] Martin Wirsing. *Algebraic Specifications*, Chapter 13, pages 675–788. Volume B of van Leeuwen [vL90], 1990.

[Wor92] John B. Wordsworth. *Software Development with Z: a Practical Approach to Formal Methods in Software Engineering*. International Computer Science Series. Addison-Wesley, 1992.

[Z87] Job Zwiers. Untitled manuscript. Unpublished, 1987.

[Z89] Job Zwiers. *Compositionality, Concurrency and Partial Correctness: Proof Theories for Networks of Processes, and Their Relationship*, volume 321 of *LNCS*. Springer-Verlag, 1989.

[Z90] Job Zwiers. Predicates, predicate transformers and refinement. In de Bakker *et al.* [dBdRR90], pages 759–776.

[ZCdR92] Job Zwiers, Jos Coenen, and Willem-Paul de Roever. A note on compositional refinement. In *Proceedings of the 5th Refinement Workshop*, Workshops in Computing. Springer-Verlag, 1992.

[ZdR89] Job Zwiers and Willem-Paul de Roever. Predicates are predicate transformers: A unified compositional theory for concurrency. In *Proceedings of the 8th ACM Symposium on Principles of Distributed Computing (PODC)*. ACM Press, 1989.

Index

Page numbers in bold indicate places where entries are defined or introduced.

Printed in the United States
By Bookmasters